John,

With many thanks for your help
and encouragement to me and my subject

Adrian
October 1992

# Mental

# Handicap

# and the Law

AUSTRALIA
The Law Book Company
Brisbane · Sydney · Melbourne · Perth

CANADA
Carswell
Ottawa · Toronto · Calgary · Montreal · Vancouver

**Agents**

Steimatzky's Agency Ltd., Tel Aviv;
N.M. Tripathi (Private) Ltd., Bombay;
Eastern Law House (Private) Ltd., Calcutta;
M.P.P. House, Bangalore;
Universal Book Traders; Delhi;
Aditya Books, Delhi;
MacMillan Shuppan KK, Tokyo;
Pakistan Law House, Karachi, Lahore

# MENTAL HANDICAP AND THE LAW

BY

**Gordon R. Ashton**, LL.B.,
*Solicitor*

WITH SCOTS LAW CONTRIBUTED BY

**Adrian D. Ward**, M.B.E., LL.B.,
*Solicitor*

LONDON
SWEET & MAXWELL
1992

Published in 1992 by
Sweet & Maxwell Limited of
South Quay Plaza, 183 Marsh Wall
London, E14 9FT
Printed in Great Britain by
BPCC Hazells Ltd
Member of BPCC Ltd.

**A catalogue record for this book is available from the British Library**

ISBN 0-421-420006

**To my son PAUL**

without whom this book would not have been written

# FOREWORD

It is a mark of the change in social attitudes in recent decades that the rights of those who suffer from mental handicap have at last become increasingly recognised. It is indeed a paradox that in former times those who were often by reason of their handicap in most need of the law's protection were sometimes the last to receive it. Happily times change and both those who suffer from a disability and, as importantly, those who care for them are now more conscious that the law is available for their use and benefit. Their task, and that of those who advise them, will be made a great deal easier by the publication of this invaluable work which gathers together the increasing amount of statute law, case law and other materials which have appeared in recent years.

Any practitioner would do well to consult this book before advising in relation to this extensive and complex branch of the law. The authors are to be congratulated both in their perspicacity in identifying the need for such a book and in the manner in which they have discharged their task.

Moreover, coming from north of the River Tweed I also see a further reason for commending it. Not only does it deal with the law as it appears in England and Wales but also with that of Scotland, which of course is in some respects different. Where appropriate the authors have drawn comparisons between the two systems but, to which system's advantage, I must leave the reader to judge.

*The Right Honourable*
*the Lord Mackay of Clashfern,*
*The Lord Chancellor.*

July 1992

# Preface

This book has been written for the benefit of people with a mental handicap and their families, and I hope that its contents will assist all concerned with their welfare including lawyers, social workers and others called upon to advise on aspects of the law and procedure. I am not a writer of legal books, but a country solicitor who happens to have a mentally handicapped child and in consequence has had to consider areas of law which would otherwise have seemed of little significance. The average lawyer is ill-equipped to deal with the wide range of problems encountered by such people. Many fail to recognise the distinction between mental illness and mental handicap, and the law tends to group both topics together under the heading "mental health", but the distinction is important and should be treated so in practice.

There are many books for legal practitioners that clarify the rights and duties of the individual, but in England none concentrating upon those with a mental handicap. They and their families usually receive advice from special interest groups (social workers, charities and other rights organisations) but this may not be comprehensive and tends to mix policy with law. A lawyer who is consulted often finds that he needs access to the full range of his legal library - and beyond - to advise upon what the client sees as basic problems. There is a thirst for information by all concerned and this book is an attempt to fill the gap that undoubtedly exists. It cannot hope to do so completely in a first edition, but if the perceived need is a reality future editions may emerge or other legal writers develop the subject further. In regard to some topics, such as welfare benefits, the text will soon become out of date and should only be treated as a general guide, but other topics covered in this book may not have been written about elsewhere. I hope that the experiences and ideas that I have been able to draw upon from lawyers and parents with whom I am in contact may be of benefit to others.

We tend to view a situation according to our own experiences, which may or not be comprehensive. When I started to write this book my perspective was of parents living in an ordinary home seeking to bring up an ordinary family who find that they have a mentally handicapped child with all the problems, legal and otherwise, that this brings. This is a situation that I often come across and these are the people I set out to help. However, any legal book must cover the full range of personal circumstances and wherever possible I have tried to identify various different situations and point the reader in the right direction.

The book was not intended to be so long, but in more than four years that I have spent researching and writing it has simply grown as I have discovered just how much material there is that is relevant. At a late stage the opportunity arose to incorporate the law of Scotland by joining forces with Adrian Ward who had already published two books on the subject. I am indebted to him for reading all my text and fitting in his own material. We have endeavoured to state the law of both countries as at May 1, 1992, though we have taken account of some more recent developments.

I hope that this book will lead to more comprehensive knowledge of this field of law and provoke some much needed law reform. I would be pleased to hear from readers who have found this book useful (or otherwise), with suggestions or information as to areas of law and practice which could (or should) have been dealt with.

Gordon R. Ashton
England                                                              July 1992

Gordon Ashton's original concept was that I should write a single separate chapter on Scots law, but as early drafts of his chapters began to reach me one by one, I quickly realised that the attention of Scottish readers should not be focused away from the main bulk of Gordon's material, which contained so much by way of comment and insight which would be valid in Scotland. Moreover, time and again I recognised familiar fundamental issues and problems, albeit clothed in different detailed rules and somewhat foreign terminology. Thus two small-town general legal practitioners from Britain's two distinct legal traditions attempted instead an ambitious integrated approach. The result is that where possible (and where headings do not indicate otherwise) English and Scots law are dealt with simultaneously, but where the material demands we have written separate sections, parts or - on one topic only - chapters. This approach has entailed a year of reading, re-reading and editing each others material, and we have both commented frankly upon all aspects of it (yet have confounded bystanders by starting as strangers and ending as friends, rather than the reverse!). We hope that the result is a text equally satisfactory to readers from both jurisdictions, and that each set of readers will not find too distracting the juxtaposition of equivalent material from the other system, but rather will gain as much from the insights which this provides as have the authors.

In overall concept and content this remains Gordon Ashton's book. I have been happy to be towed along in the slipstream of his commitment, breadth of knowledge and prodigious work, which lasted from initial outline to producing the final pages on a home desk-top publishing system.

Adrian D. Ward
Scotland                                                             July 1992

# ACKNOWLEDGMENTS

In addition to my wife Marion and daughters Deborah and Clare, who accepted and perhaps even enjoyed the mental absence (if not incapacity) of a husband and father for more than four long years, and my partners who recognised (even if they did not agree) that this book was far more important to me than the office, the following people deserve specific mention for their support.

My introduction to this subject was through the Law Society's Group for the Welfare of People with a Mental Handicap of which I am a founder member. My eyes were opened when I first attended meetings of the group, and I determined then that this subject should not be restricted to a small number of lawyers most of whom, on enquiry, proved to be parents of a handicapped child. I always enjoy discussions in the Law Society's Mental Health and Disability Sub-Committee of which I am a member, and welcome the contact with other members from various backgrounds with different perspectives. They have all, perhaps unwittingly, been used by me from time to time to develop some aspect of this book, especially Ian Bynoe from MIND and Evelyn McEwen from Age Concern. I joined the committee to contribute on mental handicap, as distinct from mental illness with which it had largely been concerned, and Penny Letts as secretary has always shown genuine concern for my pre-occupation and given my items sufficient prominence on the agenda. I was glad to assist with her own book. Collaboration with Richard Oerton, a London solicitor, provided a new dimension to my writing on the topic of financial provision by parents and I am indebted to him for his painstaking tuition in the art of writing and his subsequent encouragement. The decision to write this book originated from my contact with him in 1988.

It has been rewarding to maintain contacts with the national charities concerned with different aspects of mental handicap, whether this be MENCAP, MIND, the National Autistic Society or Down's Syndrome Association, to mention just a few. My close association with Lydia Sinclair, solicitor and Director of Legal Services at MENCAP, has proved invaluable in giving me insight into problem areas and needs that I would not otherwise have encountered, and she has contributed material for parts of this book which I have acknowledged in footnotes.

Whenever I have approached those in authority I have received helpful responses and information, whether this be the Charity Commissioners, Inland Revenue, DSS, local authorities or government departments. Informal encouragement from Mrs A B Macfarlane, Master of the Court of Protection, and her willingness to make time for a chat, has been of more value than she perhaps realised in giving me the determination to complete this task. Chapter 10A has benefitted greatly from her careful comments.

After three years of work with no end in sight, my publishers suggested that Scottish law should be included, and as I was in contact with Adrian Ward who had already published material in Scotland, I put it to him. He rose to the bait, perhaps not realising how much work would be involved, and since then has studiously edited my output and added the Scottish dimension. This book may therefore be added to the short list of legal textbooks that are multi-national! Following two enjoyable lecture trips to Northern Ireland I would have liked to include that country in the text, but my task was already too great and readers over there will have to rely upon their own translation which I understand is a skill that they have already acquired.

I must also thank the many lawyers and other professionals who have taken the trouble to correspond with me. In regard to specific chapters the following deserve mention. Dr. William B. Spry, consultant psychiatrist (for Chapter 1), Paul Ridout, solicitor (for Chapter 7), District Judge Nasreen Pearce (for Chapter 9, Part IVA), and I M Davies in the legal department of the Charity Commission at Liverpool (for Chapter 11)

Finally, but most important of all, I thank all those individuals with a mental handicap, their parents and carers whom I have had the pleasure to meet. They have brought me down to earth so often and it is for them that this book has been written. I hope that it may help them.

Gordon R. Ashton.
July 1992

Yet again my family, and colleagues and staff, have uncomplainingly absorbed the consequences of research and authorship fitted in around the demands of a busy practice. The Scottish Society for the Mentally Handicapped have responded unstintingly to my various requests for information and help, and the office of the Accountant of Court, the Crown Office and the Scottish Office have also been generous in making material available and permitting me to use it. Colin McKay read the text in draft, and selected parts were read by Derek G.B. Addison, W.A. Gilchrist, Linda Kerr and Professor J. Alistair M. Inglis: although most of this help was given against short deadlines, the meticulous checking and helpful comments of all resulted in many improvements to the text. Evelyn Brookmire gave invaluable support in typing on word processor a host of separate pieces of text, cross-referring them to Gordon Ashton's drafts, formatting them on disk compatibly with his equipment, and keeping track of much further material similarly processed in subsequent rounds of input and editing.

Those who have assisted us both should not be regarded as having endorsed any of the content, and the authors remain responsible for the final text.

Adrian D. Ward
July 1992

# TERMINOLOGY

Words do not always have the same meaning to different people, and it is difficult to adopt a terminology which consistently conveys the intended meaning. The authors have not provided "translations" where this would be unnecessarily cumbersome or repetitious. The following clarification of key words used throughout the book is appropriate.

*England and Wales*

In some instances we correctly refer to both countries, but in most places (and in particular in headings) we merely refer to England for the sake of brevity. Unless stated otherwise, any such reference is intended to include Wales.

*Gender*

Throughout the text the expression "he" and "his" are intended to include "she" and "her" and, unless indicated to the contrary, male terminology includes female. The two authors, both being male, do not wish to give the impression of being sexist, but have sought to avoid the text becoming clumsy and the approach adopted in statutes did not seem inappropriate.

*Child*

In some situations "child" may mean a person who has not attained legal majority, but another common meaning is a son or daughter, in which event "child" may refer to an infant or an adult. Throughout the text we have tried to make it clear which meaning is intended.

*Infant*

This word is generally used in England and Wales to indicate a person who has not attained legal majority, which means the age of 18 years. In Scotland other ages may be significant and appropriate terminology is then used.

*Social services*

In Scotland the reference would be to *social work*.

*Chattel*

This term is not used in Scotland, but the equivalent is "corporeal moveable property".

# United Nations Declaration on the Rights of Mentally Retarded Persons

*Article I*

The mentally retarded person has, to the maximum degree of feasibility, the same basic rights as other human beings.

*Article II*

The mentally retarded person has a right to proper medical care and physical therapy and to such education, training, rehabilitation and guidance as will enable him to develop his ability and maximum potential.

*Article III*

The mentally retarded person has a right to economic security and to a decent standard of living. He has a right to perform productive work or to engage in any other meaningful occupation to the fullest possible extent of his capabilities.

*Article IV*

Whenever possible, the mentally retarded person should live with his own family or with foster parents and participate in different forms of community life. The family with which he lives should receive assistance. If care in an institution becomes necessary, it should be provided in surroundings and other circumstances as close as possible to those of normal life.

*Article V*

The mentally retarded person has a right to a qualified guardian when this is required to protect his personal wellbeing and interests.

*Article VI*

The mentally retarded person has a right to protection from exploitation, abuse and degrading treatment. If prosecuted for any offence, he shall have a right to due process of law with full recognition being given to his degree of mental responsibility.

*Article VII*

When mentally retarded persons are unable, because of the severity of their handicap, to exercise all their rights in a meaningful way or should it become necessary to restrict or deny some or all of these rights, the procedure used for that restriction or denial of rights must contain proper legal safeguards against every form of abuse. This procedure must be based on an evaluation of the social capability of the mentally retarded person by qualified experts and must be subject to periodic review and to the right of appeal to higher authorities.

# Contents

# TABLE OF CASES

# TABLE OF STATUTES

# TABLE OF STATUTORY INSTRUMENTS

xlvii

# TABLE OF TREATIES

# TABLE OF SOCIAL SECURITY COMMISSIONERS' DECISIONS

# CHAPTER 1    INTRODUCTORY

There is no universal definition of *mental handicap* and even this terminology may soon be replaced by *learning disability*. There is also no separate body of law dealing with persons with a mental handicap, so the law that concerns them and their families and carers must be extracted from the general law. In some areas the law is far from satisfactory, failing to deal with situations or dealing with them in a manner generally felt to be inappropriate, and not infrequently it is so difficult to interpret the law that the adviser cannot say with any degree of certainty what the position is. Dealing with such clients raises special challenges, and an understanding of the problems they face and their special needs is essential. In this chapter we set the scene, first by outlining some of these problems and needs, and then by seeking to define the client group.

## PART I - BACKGROUND

### Policies

It has been estimated that more than 1 per cent. of the population has some degree of mental handicap, but statistics give no indication of the degree of handicap. In recent years a greater awareness has developed of the problems, needs and rights of people with a mental handicap, and they are being moved out of institutional care, where they effectively had no rights other than those afforded by the rules of the institution, into the community. Two distinct rights are being promoted, namely:
- to self determination, and freedom from unnecessary constraints and interference; and
- to the provision of assistance and services in such a way as to facilitate freedom of choice and enable individuals to maximise their potential.

### Independence

The Jay Report[1] states that mentally handicapped adults who wish to leave the parental home should have the opportunity to do so, and set down three broad principles:
1. they have a right to enjoy normal patterns of life within the community;
2. they have a right to be treated as individuals;
3. they will require additional help from the communities in which they live and from professional services if they are to develop their maximum potential as individuals.

It concluded that the family should not continue to be regarded as the central agent in care and support until parents are old and

---

[1]    Committee of Enquiry into Mental Handicap Nursing and Care (1979).

infirm, and that the community and professional services must assume a greater responsibility. A wider range of accommodation should be available thus allowing the handicapped individual to make a choice, jointly with the family, of an independent life.[2]

*Discrimination*
A person with a mental handicap should have a right not to be discriminated against by reason of such handicap. Within the UK there is no legal protection for those with disabilities against unfair discrimination based upon prejudice, fear or ignorance, yet care in the community depends on the absence of discrimination. Some countries promote such protection and this gives more meaning to the integration aspect of community care.[3]

*Risk taking*
Any change of environment or new opportunity involves some risk and there are many arguments for and against encouraging people with a mental handicap to take risks. We all learn by our mistakes and need the opportunity to do so, but risks can involve moral, physical and emotional dangers for the individual and vulnerability to criticism for carers if things go wrong. Many parents provide a protective environment, keeping to well tried routines and avoiding risks, whereas professionals tend to adopt a more imaginative approach involving opportunities. There is also a tendency for parents to concentrate upon what their child cannot do thereby adopting a negative approach to questions of care planning, but instead of listing weaknesses and potential problems it is possible to identify strengths and build on these. A more positive approach gives greater potential for development by focusing upon what the individual enjoys doing and the skills that are possessed.

**Role of the law**

The law must play its part in fulfilling society's expectations as to the preservation of the rights of people with a mental handicap and other members of the community in their interaction with one another. It would be discriminatory to have a separate body of law dealing with such people, but all fields of law must contain modifications or enhancements to cater for the limitations of certain individuals. The role of the law in regard to vulnerable individuals should be to:
  - protect from abuse          (a negative role);
  - enhance the quality of life   (a positive role);
  - enforce duties to society     (a restrictive role).
Many laws have a dual function, and the objectives of some may be doubtful, but the modifications and enhancements that have been made appear to fall within these categories. Unfortunately the

---

2    It is now generally accepted that social life, autonomy and opportunities to develop self-help skills are limited at home.

3    Notably USA, Canada and parts of Australia, and see the Civil Rights (Disabled Persons) Bill 1992. .

approach of the legislature has been piecemeal, dealing only with specific problems when they have been identified and only then to the extent that parliamentary time was available. In consequence only problems that have proved more conspicuous or troublesome have been dealt with, and their underlying causes have not been addressed. The courts have been left to apply the law in this incomplete form and to expand the framework according to the perceptions and prejudices of individual judges. An underlying philosophy must be developed as a basis for future legislation and for development of the common law and interpretation of the statutory provisions that do exist.

*Underlying principles*
A consensus is emerging as to the fundamental principles which should guide the application and development of the law:
- all people are presumed to be competent and to have the same rights and status, except as specifically provided or determined;
- any modification or intervention should be the minimum necessary in the particular case;
- people should be enabled and encouraged to exercise and develop their own capacity and to participate in decisions to the maximum extent possible.

## Decision making

The law assumes the ability of the individual to make decisions, and this raises problems for those who are unable to do so. In some cases, although the individual can make decisions others are unwilling to recognise them, either because of inability to communicate or behavioural characteristics which create an impression of lack of mental ability.

*Tests of capacity*
The Law Commission[4] has identified three approaches to the question of capacity adopted in different circumstances:
- *Outcome*, whereby capacity is determined by the content of the individual's decision. Is a decision which is judged as foolish by definition incompetently made?
- *Status*, whereby it is judged according to physical or mental status such as age, place of residence or diagnosis without any further consideration of the actual competence of the individual.
- *Understanding*, whereby the personal ability of the individual to make the particular decision is assessed. Does he understand the nature and likely consequences of the decision and can he communicate his decision? Most individuals have some level of capacity which should be identified and respected.

---

4   (In England and Wales) Consultation Paper No.119: *Mentally Incapacitated Adults and Decision-Making: An Overview* - May 1991.

*Decision makers*

Where decisions need to be made which the handicapped person is incapable of making, these can only be taken by others and a procedure is needed to appoint decision makers and resolve disputes. In practice, routine decisions are taken and carried out on the basis of practicalities without reference to legal procedures, but problems arise if a decision is taken which someone concerned will not accept or a decision is needed that no-one can or will take. Parents who have brought up a seriously mentally handicapped child do not usually realise that they have no further legal status when their child attains 18 years (or 16 years for most purposes in Scotland).

There are two fields of decision-making:

(a) *Personal decisions* (*e.g.* where to live)

Although there may be an urgent need to make a personal decision, English law makes no provision for delegation except in the limited range of circumstances covered by the Mental Health Act whereas Scotland has also the recently revived but as yet little used tutor-dative procedure. In both countries, personal decisions are usually made by carers, but sometimes by others on grounds of necessity or expediency. Such decisions may simply not be made at all, or may be made by the wrong person or for the wrong reasons, or they may be challenged. The person taking responsibility for the decision may feel vulnerable. The biggest problem is often the uncertainty of those concerned with the welfare of the incapacitated individual as to their rights and duties, and the procedures to be followed.

(b) *Management decisions* (*e.g.* financial arrangements)

The law provides for delegation to an agent (*e.g.* an attorney, English receiver or Scottish curator) of the power to enter into a transaction and this may enable personal decisions to be carried into effect but the agent may be reluctant to make such decisions. If he is a professional person he should consult the carers who may make the personal decision leaving him to deal with the money. In some cases the agent is a relative willing to adopt both roles, but in others he makes personal decisions by default simply because there is no-one else to do so.

*Types of decision*

Seven types of decision have been identified[5]:

(a) *day-to-day living* (*e.g.* what to eat or wear, whether to have a bath or a haircut);

(b) *activities involving more risk* (*e.g.* going out alone, sports, holidays, making new friends);

(c) *major life decisions* (*e.g.* where to live, whether to enter residential care, getting married or having children);

(d) *minor routine medical treatment* (*e.g.* dentistry, cervical

---

5    The Law Commission (in England and Wales) - see above, n.4.

smear tests, vaccinations);

(e) *medical treatment with advantages and disadvantages* (*e.g.* replacement of teeth by dentures);

(f) *controversial medical treatment* (*e.g.* sterilisation, abortion, participation in medical research);

(g) *legal or financial matters* (*e.g.* claiming benefits, managing money, buying and selling property, making a will).

Some of these may be made by others, but the more personal decisions (such as getting married) are not capable of delegation so cannot be made at all if the individual does not have the personal capacity to decide. Options that the rest of us take for granted may thus be denied to those who lack the capacity to choose, and as this is a severe restriction on personal freedom it may be appropriate to assess capacity in the light of the risk to the individual inherent in the particular decision involved.

*Choice*
Making choices is a skill that may not come easily to a person with a mental handicap who has been used to having decisions made by others. There may be ability to choose from an offered range of options but not to identify the options, so the person who provides the options has effective control over freedom of choice. What appears to be an informed choice is then merely a selection from a limited range of options chosen by a carer, and the choice may even then be influenced as much by the desire of the individual to win the approval of the carer as to develop his own personality.

*Consent*
To what extent must the individual consent to, or acquiesce in, a decision made by another on his behalf? There may be no effective means for someone incapable of making decisions to object except perhaps by disruptive behaviour which will then be controlled in other ways. Are some of the behaviour problems that arise a consequence of deprivation of the right to make decisions? The experienced carer will encourage participation in decision-making and this may minimise behaviour problems, but there must inevitably be a compromise between the rights of the individual, the needs of others and the resources available. Others may recognise what is happening in a particular instance and intervene, whereupon the law is involved or found to be unavailable.

*Delegation*
If personal decisions are to be delegated, the law must provide for:
- the type of decisions involved and level of capacity required;
- those persons in respect of whom delegation is permitted;
- how the incapacity is determined and verified;
- how a finding of incapacity may be challenged or terminated;
- who is to have the delegated powers *e.g.* whether certain relatives have priority;
- how the delegation is to take place;
- how and on what basis the powers are to be exercised;

- whether and if so to what extent the powers are limited;
- what supervision there is to be;
- how and when the delegation may be withdrawn;
- any complaints procedure and how it will operate.

The law may either enable someone to be given powers, or participate in the manner in which those powers are exercised. It may adopt a passive role, only becoming involved if there is a dispute, or an active role, insisting that set procedures are always carried out.

*Basis of decisions*
The law must also specify on what basis delegated decisions are to be made. Should it be:

- the *best interests* approach - adopted by parents but rejected by their children when they reach maturity;   or
- the application of *substituted judgment* - that which the individual would have chosen if capable of making a choice?

There may be no real conflict between these approaches and indeed it will rarely be appropriate to concentrate on one to the exclusion of the other. If they are applied together rather than seen as alternatives, the question becomes: *What would he, if not suffering from the particular lack of capacity, consider to be in his own best interests?* Thus it is the perceived view of the incapacitated person as to best interests that is adopted, rather than that of the decision-maker. Unlike the elderly, persons with a mental handicap have no past pattern of decision-making that can be followed, but they should not be stereo typed and a different choice should be made for different persons even though there is little indication from the individual as to the type of person he or she is or would like to be.

*Best interests*
A too narrow approach to best interests should not be adopted. It may, for example, not be wise for a person with limited finances to spend money on a luxury, but this could prove a valuable tonic and enhance the quality of life. All implications of a decision should be weighed in the balance just as we do for ourselves, but it is the balance that the incapacitated person would have adopted (where this can be identified) that should be applied rather than that which the decision-maker would choose. It may be difficult to separate the best interests of the handicapped person from those of the carers and what is in the best interests of carers may also be in the best interests of the person cared for, but it should not be forgotten that the objective is to give the latter as much autonomy as possible within the constraints that of necessity apply. We all make decisions that we know are not in our best interests, but are entitled to be foolish at times and must then live with the consequences. Where decisions are made on behalf of persons who lack competence this "right to be foolish" cannot often be exercised, but if the individual is clearly making that choice of his own initiative then the situation may be different.

## Advocacy

An advocate in this context is a person who pleads the cause of another and generally takes such action on his behalf as may be necessary to secure the services that are required and to enable him to enjoy his legal rights to the full. This may involve speaking to others in person and by telephone, filling in forms, attending meetings and even providing representation at tribunals. It can be invaluable, because the true advocate seeks to ascertain and express what the individual wants whereas parents may state what they think the individual would (or should) want, which is usually what the parents think is most suitable. There are two main types:

### Citizen-advocacy

An ordinary member of the community is encouraged to enter into a relationship with the individual and then, based upon the knowledge learnt from that relationship, to speak on his behalf and represent his interests in circumstances and areas that affect them. This *lay advocate* has no legal status but should nevertheless stand up for the rights of the individual as he would for his own. It may be a relative, volunteer or occasionally staff member, who should be independent of those who provide direct services to the individual.

A recent development aimed at giving disabled persons more influence over their lives is the creation of advocacy schemes. These were initially introduced in some mental handicap hospitals but there is a growing awareness of the role of an advocate in the provision of care in the community.[6]

### Self-advocacy

Self-advocacy means encouraging people with a mental handicap to express their wishes and, of equal importance, taking notice of such wishes. Their ability to form and express views must never be overlooked, especially by lawyers who are concerned about the legal rights of individuals but may all too easily fall into the trap of talking about them rather than to them. Historically, people with mental handicaps have always had others speak for them but this is changing, and they are forming themselves into independent groups and learning to be self-advocates.[7]

## Complaints

On occasion the individual will wish to complain about poor treatment by the provider of some service, or of the inadequacy or lack of some service provision. In this respect he will be in the same position as anyone else and no special law or rules apply. However, by reason of the mental handicap there may be a

---

6 An independent national service is not yet available. In some jurisdictions advocacy schemes form an important part of provision for mentally disordered people.

7 Many groups call themselves *People First* indicating that they are human beings first and that their disabilities are second.

communication problem, or a lack of awareness that things are not as good as they should be, so in practice any complaint is likely to be pursued by a carer. When the cause for complaint is the conduct of the carer, or the body providing care, there may be no-one to take up the case unless the problem is identified by a concerned professional or onlooker, neither of whom may have the status or capacity to do anything about it.[8] A personal *advocate* has a particularly valuable role in these circumstances.

## Lawyer's role

A lawyer may take the role of legal adviser/litigator or a wider role of adviser/advocate. Whilst the wider role is encouraged, the narrower role is important because it may be necessary to clarify relevant rights and duties, negotiate on the basis of them and enforce them. Lawyers have developed considerable skills in negotiating on behalf of and promoting the rights of individuals who for one reason or another are at a disadvantage in looking after their own interests. Those same skills can be put to good use on behalf of mentally handicapped people and their carers.

As in the case of other professionals, lawyers need education and training. Although the legal profession is threatened with the loss through competition of work which has been its traditional preserve and is looking for new areas of work, little has been done to develop expertise in acting for those who lack mental capacity.[9] The individual with a mental handicap is entitled to an independent lawyer who must be prepared to listen to and communicate with the client however much patience this may require. Instructions will often be given by a parent or carer and the lawyer may be acting in the common interest, but conflict of interest situations do arise and the golden rule is to ask *Who is my client?* If this is the handicapped person then the lawyer must act in the best interests of that person, and not of the parent or carer on grounds of expediency. A balancing act will often be necessary, but the handicapped person is entitled to have his views respected even if they cannot be followed.

Despite facing considerable emotional and practical problems in caring for their mentally handicapped child, parents soon learn that they face a world that resembles at best a maze and at worst a jungle. They encounter many well-intentioned people, but also an administrative bureaucracy that varies from insensitive to obstructive. Stress and exhaustion caused by the continuous task of coping may produce an attitude of defeatism, yet persistence is required in obtaining the services that are needed and the financial benefits that are an entitlement. The adviser must exhibit patience and tolerance yet possess that degree of determination required to

---

8   In Scotland, they should in this situation report the matter to the Mental Welfare Commission for Scotland.

9   This includes the elderly who often have considerable wealth, yet few practices are active in promoting their needs.

achieve results. There are many pitfalls, some of which have yet to be explored, but the absence of information from a single source has been one of the principal problems.

## Conclusion

The problem posed by people with a mental handicap is that they cannot make any, or all, necessary decisions (*i.e.* receive and process information and make a conscious choice) so are incapable of living without some degree of supervision by or reliance upon others. They are in consequence vulnerable. The purpose of the law must be to protect them from exploitation, abuse or neglect whilst preventing them from causing disruption in a well ordered society. An equally important purpose is to assist them to achieve their own personal potential in a society that may not be as caring as its policy makers by giving them enforceable rights. In the process, the law must be capable of defining the people in need of this type of special treatment.

# PART II - DEFINITION OF MENTAL HANDICAP

## Introduction

It would be convenient if there was a precise definition of "mental handicap" so that we could readily identify those members of society to whom different rules apply or who are eligible for a special range of benefits, but this is not and could never be the case. The term is used loosely in society and although it conveys a fairly consistent impression to most people (and is used in this book for that reason) it does not have a precise meaning. It must be distinguished from mental illness which is a different condition although this is not always recognised by the public.

In practice there may be similarities between the needs and legal treatment of mentally ill and mentally handicapped people, but the medical diagnosis and treatment are quite different. In general terms, people *become* mentally ill when they suffer a disturbance affecting their emotional, social and cognitive functioning and behaviour, but people *are* mentally handicapped because they have a brain that will not develop or function normally. Mentally ill people need medical treatment which may result in partial or total cure, whereas those suffering from a mental handicap cannot be cured and instead need education and training so as to make them acceptable members of society able to fulfil their personal potential. The situation is further confused in that the consequences of brain damage to an adult by head injury may be regarded by care organisations and lawyers as being akin to mental handicap whereas the medical profession may treat this as mental illness. Care and supervision may also be needed for the protection and welfare of the individual or of others, and in some cases there is also physical disability which could result in regular medical treatment being necessary.

## DISABILITIES

Disability has two elements. The first is the limitation imposed upon the individual by reason of his or her physical, mental or sensory impairment, and the second is the disadvantage or handicap which this imposes on the individual in his or her environment. The commonly used terms impairment, disability and handicap are frequently treated as if they mean the same thing, but they do not. In 1982 the World Health Organisation (W.H.O.) provided the following definitions to distinguish the differing aspects of an illness or condition:

**Impairment:** a permanent or transitory psychological, physiological or anatomical loss or abnormality of structure or function.
**Disability:**   any restriction or prevention of the performance of an activity, resulting from an impairment, in the manner or within the range considered normal for a human being.
**Handicap:**   a disability that constitutes a disadvantage for a given individual in that it limits or prevents the fulfilment of a role that is normal depending on age, sex, social and cultural factors, for that individual.

### Mental handicap

We are only concerned with mental handicap, so seek to define this term and draw attention to specific legal definitions that apply for particular purposes. An early distinction between mental handicap and mental illness is found in a statute of 1886 which provided that "idiots or imbeciles do not include lunatics".[10]

*Causes*
The causes of mental handicap are varied and in many cases unknown, but fall into the following general categories:

**Genetic abnormalities:**
the largest single cause is Down's Syndrome but there are hundreds of others, and in some medical intervention at an early stage can arrest the process and lead to near normal development.[11]
**External factors;** these comprise:
  *disease*   e.g. german measles;
  *toxins*   substances taken during pregnancy or vaccine damage;
  *trauma*   birth injury or trauma in childhood.
**Non-specific abnormalities:**
the largest category, comprising all those conditions which have not yet been recognised. These are people who are at the lower end of the normal range of distribution of intelligence, but many are near the borderline and may not require any great amount of specialist services and some probably go unrecognised. The great majority of the population fall between IQ 90 and 110 with increasingly fewer numbers as the figure rises or falls, and an IQ of 70 or less has been chosen for this category purely on a statistical basis. Environmental and social factors may play a part. The medical name for this group is *idiopathic* being part of the normal distribution of the population.

---

10  Idiots Act 1886, s.27. It has been said judicially that "it is impossible to distinguish between unsoundness of mind and insanity" - Merriman P. in *Smith* v. *Smith (otherwise Hand)* [1940] P 179.

11  *e.g.* phenylketonuria and hypothyroidism. There is thus some medical treatment for handicap itself!

The traditional view that mentally handicapped children are born to people with a mental handicap is seldom true, though hereditary factors may be involved.

*Classification*

Until recently identification tended to be based upon level of intelligence as identified by the IQ score (intelligence quotient). Such assessment is of little use to care workers who prefer to classify people according to their degree of independence which involves consideration of levels of competence in performing skills such as eating, dressing, communication and social skills. The lawyer wishes to establish whether the individual is capable of making a reasoned and informed decision (the test of *capacity*), although when advising parents and carers may need to assess the degree of dependence (*e.g.* when considering what financial provision should be made). There can be no universally applied test because the capacity required will depend upon the nature of the decision to be made.

The following table brings together some of the classifications of degree of mental handicap[12]:

| Degree | IQ | W.H.O. definition | Terms |
|---|---|---|---|
| mild | 50-70 | Slow development but can be educated within limits; with training can take ordinary employment and live independently. | subnormal moron feeble minded mildly retarded |
| moderate | 36-49 | Backward but capable of caring for self; need work in sheltered employment. | severely subnormal imbecile |
| severe | 20-35 | Backward but not completely dependent on others. | mentally defective retarded |
| profound | below 20 | Need constant care and supervision; not capable of caring for self. | profoundly retarded idiot |

*Terminology*

Words used by society to describe mental ability have traditionally tended to convey a judgment as to whether the condition (or the person) is good or bad. For this reason terms such as moron, idiot and imbecile are no longer used by the caring professions. More recently there has been no consistency in the terminology adopted by professionals; in England and Wales the official term used to be "mental subnormality", whereas in Scotland it was "mental deficiency", in the U.S.A. it was "mental retardation" and only in Ireland was the term "mental handicap" adopted. In England the legal term adopted in 1983 was "mental impairment" whereas in the following year the Scottish legal system chose "mental

---

12  Based upon a Table in *Accident of Birth - Aspects of Mental Handicap* by Fred Heddell. Published by the BBC in 1980.

handicap".[13] "Learning disability" and "intellectual impairment"
are increasingly being used, but these do not yet adequately convey
the meaning in society so we use the expressions "person with a
mental handicap" and "mentally handicapped person". The former
is a more correct use of language, though the latter is used where
less cumbersome.

*Social terminology*
There are many voluntary groups that concentrate upon particular
types of mental handicap,[14] and it is convenient (and reassuring to
the parents) to identify a handicap by means of a name or label
which is immediately recognised by the public. It is therefore
helpful to be aware of the more common names although they may
not necessarily represent a precise medical classification and have
no legal significance. The largest single category is Down's
Syndrome (mongolism) but other identified conditions are
cerebral palsy (spasticity), autism, hydrocephalus, and the effects
of meningitis and encephalitis. Some children are referred to as
being hyper-active although this condition frequently subsides as
they grow up, and often reference is made to a person being
mentally retarded, which indicates the effect of the condition but
does not point to its cause. Each identified condition exhibits its
own features, whether these be in the form of behaviour or
physical manifestations - most of us can identify a Down's child or
a person who has cerebral palsy.

*Fundamentals*
There are certain criteria that are invariably present:
   - impaired or incomplete intellectual development;
   - a permanent disability;
   - does not develop as quickly or learn as readily as others;
   - the ability to learn and put learning to use is limited;
   - limited capacity in speech, reading, writing and arithmetic;
   - difficulty in acquiring social skills.

**Mental illness**

Mental illness can take many forms but may be distinguished from
mental handicap in that treatment is appropriate and a cure may be
possible. The term covers both neurosis[15] and psychosis[16] although
only the latter is meant when using old terms such as lunatic.
There is no statutory definition but there are medical criteria:
   (a) it is an acquired condition (*i.e.* the person has previously
       been normal);
   (b) the condition must satisfy the diagnostic criteria of one or

---

13  In Australia the term used is "intellectually disadvantaged citizens" and in
    New Zealand it is "people with intellectual handicaps".
14  See Appendix I.
15  A functional derangement due to disorders of the nervous system, *e.g.*
    hysteria, hypochondria, phobias, obsessive behaviour and depression.
16  A severe mental derangement involving the whole personality, *e.g.* paranoia,
    schizophrenia and manic depression.

more particular groups.
Nowadays we still have as high rates of psychotic disorder as ever but these cases are much more treatable. There are ever increasing levels of neurotic disorder, especially in the case of elderly senile people who in terms of needs, ability and capability have much in common with the handicapped though such term would not be applied to them. Medically they are classified as suffering from an acquired organic brain syndrome, usually due to vascular changes.

*Legal treatment*
Most of the provisions of the (English) Mental Health Act 1983, including those relating to the detention of patients and the appointment of guardians, relate to problems raised by mental illness although an individual with a mental handicap who exhibits "abnormally aggressive or seriously irresponsible conduct" will come within the statutory provisions as is explained in Chapter 4. In the Mental Health (Scotland) Act 1984 the term "mental disorder" is defined as covering both mental handicap and mental illness, and is used extensively, including in relation to matters such as detention and statutory guardianship. "Mental handicap" is also used (for example in the criteria for detention).

*Overlap with mental handicap*
Various studies have shown that mentally handicapped people have a higher incidence of mental illness than the normal population. Schizophrenia (though probably not manic depressive illness) is more common, as is neurotic illness due perhaps to the problem of communication and to stresses perceived by a handicapped person in situations that may not be found stressful to persons of normal ability. Such neurotic disturbances may be manifested by anxiety, insomnia, depression or behaviour disorder.

**Physical handicap**

There may be physical disabilities, sometimes severe, associated with mental handicap and this could include unusual appearance. But just as the absence of physical manifestations may disguise an underlying mental handicap, so may physical disabilities create an impression of mental handicap which is not justified.

*Effect on capacity*
The law is concerned with the *capacity* of the individual, whereas this may in practice depend upon *ability*. These distinct concepts may become confused with inappropriate consequences, *e.g:*
  - an individual who cannot communicate or has limited physical functions may not be permitted to open a bank account notwithstanding that his thought processes are unaffected;
  - an individual who can both talk coherently and sign his name may be allowed to open a bank account notwithstanding that he has a serious mental handicap which, if realised, would establish that he did not have the capacity to do so.
Lawyers should recognise the difference between *ability* and

*capacity* and ensure that the correct tests are applied. A basic understanding of the nature and extent of any disability is needed if the individual's true potential is to be recognised and achieved.

## Medical classification

In the medical world mental handicap is still regarded as a condition of the developmental years; once a person has acquired a normal ability and then subsequently loses it this is a different matter. Medically such people are classified as having *acquired organic brain syndrome* which constitutes a mental illness as recognised by the Mental Health Acts even though treatment may not be possible. Thus 18 years is normally regarded as the age after which the condition is acquired and prior to this it would be treated as developmental. The medical profession is not totally dogmatic about this age, though maturity is normally achieved at about this time, and the needs of the individual are paramount depending on the resources available.

### Brain damage

In the case of brain damage this distinction may be of little significance to social workers and others seeking to care for the individual and may be seen as illogical by lawyers. Is the motor-cyclist who suffers brain damage in an accident at 17 years to be treated in law as any different from a similarly affected person who had such accident at 19 years? Is the former to be treated for life as a case of mental handicap and the latter as mental illness?

### Dementia (senility)

Dementia is also an acquired organic brain syndrome, and whilst the circumstances and needs of a person who is senile are different to those of a person with a mental handicap, to a lawyer many of the same problems arise, in particular inability to make decisions.

### Medical distinction

From a medical point of view the problems presented by the different classifications of disability appear to differ. There may be real differences between mental handicap and the effects on a mature person of a head injury, meningitis or encephalitis. The method of care, education, training and assistance adopted for an individual with a mental handicap may be inappropriate for such person, and different services may be needed. Brain damage appears to fall rather uncomfortably between mental illness and mental handicap and adequate provision may not be available.

### A legal distinction?

This medical distinction appears to be recognised in law. While the Mental Health (Scotland) Act 1984 uses the term mental handicap, neither mental handicap nor sub-normality are mentioned in the Mental Health Act 1983 which only uses the term *mental impairment,* but this includes the phrase "arrested or incomplete development of mind" and if a person's mind has fully developed he will not subsequently come within this phrase.

From a legal point of view, similarity may be found between these medically different disabilities in the common inability to make all necessary decisions. However, the person with a mental handicap will never have had a greater degree of understanding than that now displayed, whereas those who have developed normally and then suffered an illness or accident causing the disability will have at an earlier stage enjoyed a greater level of ability. This may be relevant when it comes to making decisions for the individual.

## LEGAL DEFINITIONS

The White Paper *Better Services for the Mentally Handicapped*[17] defined a person who is mentally handicapped as a person who does not develop in childhood as quickly as other children nor attain the full mental capacities of a normal adult. This may not be an adequate definition for the law because it overlooks those who develop normally but subsequently develop a mental handicap by reason of accident or illness. More important than the cause of the handicap is the effect and we are considering, to a greater or lesser extent, persons who are incapable of making decisions and managing their affairs, who need special care or protection and for whom there is no cure.

### Historical

The condition has been recognised by the law from early times. Stroud's Judicial Dictionary reveals this definition[18]:

> "*Ideot* is that he is a foole naturall from his birth, and knoweth not how to account or number twenty pence, or cannot name his father or mother, nor of what age himselfe is, or such like easie and common matters; so that it appeareth hee hath no manner of understanding, of reason of government of himselfe, which is for his profit or disprofit etc."

Thus it is clear that the law has long recognised the problem of mental handicap even though its treatment may have been more concerned with the welfare of society than of the individual. The term *feeble minded* was adopted for a period and terms commonly now used as insults have been included in statutes until recently, such as the Mental Deficiency Act 1913 which defined *idiots* as "persons so defective in mind from birth or from an early age as to be unable to guard themselves against common physical dangers" and *imbeciles* as:

> "persons in whose case there existed from birth or from an early age mental defectiveness not amounting to idiocy, yet so pronounced that they were incapable of managing themselves or their affairs or, in the case of children, of being taught to do so."

The definitions in the Mental Deficiency & Lunacy (Scotland) Act, 1913 were similar, though idiots were defined as "deeply defective".

The Mental Health Act 1959 defined *severe subnormality* as:

---

17  DHSS (1971) - Cmnd. 4683 HMSO.
18  Termes de la Ley - see reference to "idiot".

"a state of arrested or incomplete development of the mind which includes
subnormality of intelligence, and is of such a nature or degree that the patient
is incapable of living an independent life or guarding himself against serious
exploitation, or will be so incapable when of an age to do so."

and the lesser classification of *subnormality* as being of a nature or
degree which requires or is susceptible to medical treatment or
other special care or training of the patient. The Mental Health
(Scotland) Act, 1960 defined mental disorder as "mental illness or
mental deficiency however caused or manifested". Mental
deficiency was not defined.

## Statutory

Legal definitions which cover mental handicap tend to be different
for different purposes and the means and severity of assessment
also vary. In practice the mode of assessment may be of more
significance than the test to be applied in deciding whether a
person is, or is not, mentally handicapped. In the absence of a
definition statutes often rely upon undefined phrases such as
unsoundness of mind which appear to beg the question, though this
particular phrase is defined in the Trustee Act 1925 as: incapable
from infirmity of mind of managing his own affairs. Such
definitions are intended to include other conditions.

### Specific terms

The most commonly relied upon definitions are to be found in the
Mental Health Acts. In England, the 1983 Act defines mental
disorder as:

"mental illness, arrested or incomplete development of mind, psychopathic
disorder and any other disorder or disability of mind."

A similar definition appeared in the Mental Health Act 1959. This
definition is intentionally very wide, but the more limited concept
of *mental impairment* is defined as:

"a state of arrested or incomplete development of mind (not amounting to
severe mental impairment) which includes significant impairment of
intelligence and social functioning and is associated with abnormally
aggressive or seriously irresponsible conduct on the part of the person
concerned."

The definition of *severe mental impairment* is the same save that
*severe* is used instead of *significant* in describing the degree of
impairment. The typical individual with a mental handicap will not
come within these definitions because the element of abnormally
aggressive or seriously irresponsible conduct will not be present.

A similar definition of mental disorder is found in the Registered
Homes Act 1984, and in the Residential Care Homes Regulations
1984 *mental handicap* is defined as:

"a state of arrested or incomplete development of mind which includes
impairment of intelligence and social functioning."

so in that context mental disorder can include mental handicap, but
it has been held that senility is not a mental handicap but can

amount to a mental disorder.[19] The Sexual Offences Act 1967 defines *severe mental handicap* in similar terms but with the addition of the word "severe",[20] and the Police and Criminal Evidence Act 1984 includes the word "significant" instead.[21] These definitions omit the final qualification of mental impairment in the Mental Health Act so are of more general application.

The Mental Health (Scotland) Act 1984 defines mental disorder as:

"mental illness or mental handicap however caused or manifested."

Except for the substitution of mental handicap for mental deficiency, this is the same as the definition in the Mental Health (Scotland) Act, 1960. The 1984 Act refers to two categories of mental handicap, mental impairment and severe mental impairment, for which the definitions are the same as in England (see above). However mental handicap clearly covers any mental handicap, not only those involving significant or severe impairment, therefore mental disorder also includes any mental handicap. Elsewhere in the 1984 Act, and in a range of other legislation, the Mental Health Act definition of mental disorder is inappropriately used as if it were a definition of mental incapacity, which it is not.[22]

*Conflict*

A recent definition of *severely mentally impaired* is found in the Local Government Finance Act 1988 in regard to the personal community charge (the poll tax)[23]:

"a state of arrested or incomplete development of mind, which involves severe impairment of intelligence and social functioning, or an injury to the brain causing severe impairment of intelligence and social functioning which appears to be permanent."

Here, for the first time in a statutory definition, is recognition that the mental impairment need not have arisen from childhood but may have been caused by a later injury. Earlier definitions based solely on arrested or incomplete development do not appear to cover brain damage cases.

This new definition was only intended to be valid for the purpose of claiming exemption from the community charge, and not to categorise the individual for any other purpose, but social workers became reluctant to register mentally handicapped individuals for poll tax exemption for fear that it may have knock-on effects (*e.g.* restriction on sexual relationships, or unnecessary detention under the Mental Health Acts) because of the similarity of the definitions. The following new definition was however introduced into the

---

19  Commissioners decision R(SB) 17/88.
20  *Mental defective* is used in the Sexual Offences Act 1956 and is defined in similar terms by Mental Health (Amendment) Act 1982, Sched.3.
21  s.77(3).
22  A person's mental handicap may result in legal incapacity for some purposes but not others.
23  Sched.1, para 4(3).

1988 Act before the tax took effect in England[24]:

> "A person is severely mentally impaired if he has a severe impairment of intelligence and social functioning (however caused) which appears to be permanent."

The Scottish author has argued that such definitions can only be meaningful (if at all) if interpreted in relation to capacity for a particular purpose, and limited to that purpose.[25]

## General

In a recent Report dealing with people with a mental handicap the Social Services Committee of the House of Commons needed to define the people with whom it was concerned and did so in this oblique way[26]:

> "Mental handicap is nearly always present from birth or early childhood, and is an irreversible condition where a person's brain does not develop as quickly or function as well as other people's. People with a mental handicap can develop their abilities with the right kind of education and support from the community in which they live. The term 'mental handicap' is a focus of debate and a number of alternatives have been preferred, namely, 'learning difficulty/disability', 'intellectual disability', or 'people with intellectual handicaps'. In this Report we use the term 'people with a mental handicap'."

## CONCLUSION

The problem remains of defining those persons loosely referred to as mentally handicapped. Perhaps this classification has no legal significance, though meaningful in a medical and social context. Usually the law is concerned with *capacity,* and incapacity arises through reasons other than mental handicap such as senility, mental illness or brain damage after maturity. It may be that an all-encompassing definition is neither necessary nor appropriate and that different tests should be applied for different purposes, as at present appears to be the case. There are great dangers in providing a definition in one statute and then adopting it for other purposes. An example is the definition of mental disorder in successive Mental Health Acts which does not involve any assessment of degree of impairment, yet is used in situations where it is the extent of the mental incapacity (rather than the fact of mental disorder) that is really in issue. It was intended to be restrictive because it dealt with situations where people could be compulsorily detained, yet a similar definition is found in legislation intended to convey rights or entitlements for mentally incapacitated people where a less restrictive definition would be

---

24  The Personal Community Charge (Exemption for the Severely Mentally Impaired) Order 1990, Art.2(2) which substitutes para. 4(3) in Sched.1.

25  So that, for example, "significant impairment of intelligence and social functioning" in the Mental Health (Scotland) Act 1984, s.106 (offences concerning sexual exploitation) should be interpreted as if it continued with "in relation to coping with and expressing her own sexuality, and guarding herself from sexual exploitation". See *The Power to Act*, pp.82-85.

26  *Community Care: Services for people with a mental handicap and people with a mental illness*, Eleventh Report - Session 1989-90.

more appropriate. Where, without any cross-reference, the same definition is used in two or more quite different contexts, there can be a similar danger that it may be assumed that everyone who falls within that definition for one purpose will also do so for the others, when in fact they may not.

It may be appropriate to enquire as to the circumstances in which the situation of a mentally handicapped person might be referred to law. Usually such persons are controlled by the rules, formal or informal, of their environment which may be the family or a residential care home. The individual may be almost by definition unable to assert any legal rights unless assisted by an advocate. The doctor, the social worker and the lawyer each have their own approaches to the significance of mental handicap and these may be different to that of the carers. It is only when there is conflict between such persons, perhaps by reason of their different perspectives, that reference is made to the law and ultimately to the courts, and then some fundamental questions must be asked. Some of these questions are addressed in this book.

*Terminology*

Within the Department of Health the phrase "people with learning disabilities" has now been adopted instead of mentally handicapped people.[27] This is likely to become, in a number of years time, the terminology to use but it has not been adopted for this book because it would not convey a meaning to the average lawyer.[28] It is interesting to note that a book published in 1982 stated[29]:

> "Mental handicap is a relatively new term, now in general use and preferred to mental deficiency or mental subnormality, which are legal terms. ...It may be argued that mental handicap is too wide a term to be helpful, but experience has shown that terminology is important in determining people's attitudes and expectations and in avoiding misconceptions."

Terminology may change but the fundamental problems continue, and there is a danger that all that will result is confusion in the minds of the public. The present terminology may have gone out of fashion in only 10 years but is still widely accepted and does in practice appear to convey a more specific meaning than learning disability. Only time will tell which phrase survives and how soon other expressions will be introduced.

---

[27] Press release from Department of Health, June 25, 1991.

[28] At a recent conference for lawyers a lecture using this title was widely thought to be about education.

[29] David Clarke, *Mentally Handicapped People - Living and Learning* (Bailliere Tindall).

# CHAPTER 2    SITUATION OF THE INDIVIDUAL

## INTRODUCTION

An individual in society enjoys a package of legal rights and is subject to a range of legal duties. Some of these come from the common law, but the majority are found in statutes which often modify common law rights and duties. A person with a mental handicap has the same rights and duties as the rest of society though in some instances these are modified or supplemented by reason of the handicap. In other instances such modification or supplement is badly needed.[1] The standard rights and duties do not always cope adequately with the special needs of particular groups, and just as these have grown up piecemeal so have the modifications and additions most of which have not been judicially interpreted. It can be difficult to identify the rights and duties of an ordinary individual, but in the case of a person with a mental handicap that difficulty is increased, and knowledge of the law may raise as many questions as it answers.

### Rights

We have neither a Bill of Rights nor a Constitution setting out fundamental and inalienable rights. The *Universal Declaration of Human Rights*[2] though not legally enforceable, provides that everyone has the right to a standard of living adequate for the health and well-being of himself and his family, including food, clothing, housing, medical care and necessary social services, and the right to security in the event of disability. The United Nations *Declaration on the Rights of Mentally Retarded Persons*[3] acknowledges that such people have the same basic rights as other human beings and calls for certain fundamental rights to be universally recognised. These are not legally binding but indicate the standards expected from each country 20 years ago. There have been considerable social advances since then.

### Capacity

It is no good giving an individual rights if he does not have the capacity to exercise them. The question of mental capacity is one of fact, though the correct legal test must be applied. This may vary according to the circumstances, and is either determined by

---

1    Since 1945 there have been approximately 50 statutes containing reference to specific rights for physically disabled people, but very few dealing with mental handicap.

2    s.25(i). This was signed in 1948 and provided the basis for the European Social Charter in 1965.

3    Adopted by the UN General Assembly 1971, 26th Session, Resolution 2856. There are variations in different translations.

statute (which may be interpreted by case law) or settled by common law. Ultimately the question can only be decided in legal proceedings, and the judge makes his determination not as medical expert but as a lay person influenced by personal observation and on the basis of evidence not only from doctors but also those who know the individual. Less formal assessments are made by a variety of people but those in relation to more serious matters are generally made by doctors, usually because the need arises whilst a person is under their care, and assessments in relation to aspects of daily life are frequently made by carers on an instinctive basis.[4]

## Presumptions

Because of the importance of personal freedom and autonomy there is a long established legal presumption, at least as regards mental illness, that adults are capable until the contrary is proved,[5] but this may be rebutted by a specific finding of incapacity. If a person is proved incapable in contract generally, the law presumes such condition to continue until it is proved to have ceased although a lucid interval may be proved.[6] The longer the time that has elapsed since an act which it is sought to set aside on grounds of mental incapacity, the stronger will be the evidence required to establish this. In civil proceedings if an act and the manner in which it was carried out is rational, there is a strong presumption that the individual was mentally capable at the time.[7]

## Evidence

Evidence of conduct at other times is admissible, and the general pattern of life of the individual may be of great weight, although it is the state of mind at the time of the act that is material. Legal capacity depends upon understanding rather than wisdom so the quality of the decision is irrelevant as long as the person understands what he is deciding. General reputation is not admissible in evidence, but the treatment by friends and family of a person alleged to be suffering from mental disorder may be admissible as between them respectively. Medical evidence is admissible and usually important, but it is for the court to decide

---

4    There has been little research into the skills and abilities needed to determine legal capacity. Assessment is not a medical or psychiatric diagnostic art, but rests on a judgment of the type that an informed lay person may make using a relatively simple check-list.

5    "In all cases every man is presumed to be sane unless the contrary is proved, and it must be clearly proved, that, at the time of committing or executing the act, the party was labouring under such a defect of reason from disease of the mind as not to know the nature and quality of the act he was doing; or if he did know it, that he did not know that he was doing what was wrong" - Tyndal LCJ (1843).

6    One should be careful about seeking to declare incapacity in all things, because this is to take away all rights and that shows a lack of respect for the individual and understanding of the true nature of mental handicap.

7    This is an outcome test as distinct from a function test and whilst convenient it may not produce a just result and may discriminate against persons who have been taught to behave in a socially acceptable manner.

whether the opinion of a medical witness has been formed on sufficient grounds and on the basis of the correct legal test. In England an Order of the Court of Protection based upon a finding of lack of capacity to manage affairs by reason of mental disorder is admissible as *prima facie* evidence of this fact.

### Children

The legal right to make decisions arises for most persons at 18 years (the age of majority) in England, and (subject to certain qualifications) at 16 in Scotland. Up to these ages a mentally handicapped child is generally speaking treated by both legal systems in the same way as any other child.

# PART I - RIGHTS AND CAPACITY

We consider in this Part the legal rights of a person with a mental handicap in relation to normal transactions, and the extent to which the individual is capable of exercising those rights.

## CONTRACT

### General

The general principle is that anyone may enter into a contract provided he has the necessary contractual capacity which means that he understands what he is doing and is capable of agreeing to it. There are several elements in this:
- did he understand the transaction?
- was he capable of deciding whether to reach the agreement?
- was he aware of any choices and able to make them?
- was he capable of committing himself to the transaction?

The extent of such understanding depends upon the implications of the particular contract. Capacity must be judged for each individual in respect of each transaction at that particular moment, (an individual may have a lucid interval). No-one should be regarded as legally incapable in the total sense (although as we shall see, some persons may have certain of their legal powers taken away from them).

In England a contract may be set aside at the option of a party if it can be shown that he did not understand its nature and the other party knew (or should have been aware) of this.[8] In Scotland the contract is void if the party lacked the capacity to understand and transact the business in question, the state of knowledge of the other party being irrelevant.[9] In neither country is the question of whether the contract was fair relevant. In England, but not in Scotland, the court must decide whether the other party was aware of the incapacity. It will often be apparent on meeting a mentally

---

8　　*Hart* v. *O'Connor* [1985] 2 All ER 880. Thus the protection of the individual is subordinated to the need to avoid prejudicing the other party.

9　　*John Loudon & Co.* v. *Elder's Curator Bonis* 1923 SLT 226. But see "necessaries" below.

handicapped person that there is limited capacity, but the lack of real understanding may be disguised by a convincing manner. In most cases the individual will not have control of any financial resources so will not be worth suing, but problems arise if personal possessions are sold at an undervalue and it is desired to recover them.

## Necessaries

Contracts for the purchase of items that are deemed to be necessary for the individual will not be set aside for lack of capacity. This includes the purchase of ordinary food, drink, clothing or other items or services that are considered necessary in everyday living. The common law obligation to pay a reasonable price was converted into a statutory obligation in 1893 in the following terms[10]:

> Where necessaries are sold and delivered to an infant ... or a person who by reason of mental incapacity or drunkenness is incompetent to contract, he must pay a reasonable price therefor.

This principle will apply to expenditure on professional services necessary to preserve the property of a person who lacks mental capacity, though it is not clear whether it would also apply to steps taken to enhance the value thereof.

## Court of Protection (England)

If the individual (the patient) is subject to the jurisdiction of the Court of Protection a contract involving the patient's money may only be made under the authority of that Court, which may have been delegated to a receiver.[11] The patient cannot enter into a contract or make a gift and this can have serious consequences, as illustrated by the following case (unreported):

> An elderly lady resided in a residential care home where her fees were paid by a Receiver appointed by the Court of Protection. He arranged for some of her antique furniture to be placed in her room for her use but she purported, without his knowledge, to give an oak chest to a nurse who promptly sold it and spent the proceeds. The nurse was convicted of theft. Despite the persistence of the lady who appeared to know what she wanted, the nurse knew of the appointment of a receiver and should have known that only he could have authority to make a gift.

In suitable cases the Court will authorise the patient to have the conduct of a bank account, under the supervision of the receiver, so as to have personal freedom in small financial transactions.

## Curators bonis (Scotland)

Similarly, in Scotland where a curator bonis has been appointed to a person (the ward), the curator bonis takes over entirely the administration of the ward's affairs, and the ward is deemed to

---

10 Sale of Goods Act 1893, s.2. "Necessaries" mean goods suitable to the condition in life of the person and to his actual requirements at the time. The burden of proof is on the person supplying the goods. This provision was re-enacted in the Sale of Goods Act 1979, s.3.

11 See Chap.10A.

have lost all capacity to contract,[12] even though by the normal tests described above he might otherwise have been considered to have had capacity for at least some transactions. Increasingly, however, in well-run curatories, and where appropriate, the curator will arrange to make available to the ward money which the ward may in practice manage and spend himself.[13]

*Facility and Circumvention (Scotland)*
A contract may be set aside where someone has taken unfair advantage of a person with a mental handicap, even though the contract would have been valid by the tests of capacity described above. Three elements must be present. Firstly, the handicap must be such that the person was liable to be intimidated, misled, or imposed upon, and the person's ability to resist such tactics must have been seriously impaired. Secondly, someone must in fact have taken unfair advantage of the mentally handicapped person. Thirdly, the resulting transaction must have been to the detriment of the mentally handicapped person. All three elements must be present, but the court assesses the whole picture, so that (for example) the contract may be set aside if the degree of susceptibility is moderate, but the level of intimidation or unfair persuasion considerable - or vice versa.[14]

## Banking accounts

The conduct of a bank account involves entering into contracts, so capacity is required. It is usual for banks to make inquiries about prospective customers to ensure that they are suitable to enter into banking transactions, but this depends upon the type of account to be opened and current banking practice. If a banker wishes to explain a transaction to a person who is known to have limited mental capacity it is wise to have a carer present who can ensure that the explanation is both fair and properly understood, and who can repeat it later when required. Similar principles may apply to building societies.

*Capacity*
An individual who understands basic banking transactions (*i.e.* the implications of paying money into and out of an account) and who is able to produce a consistent signature should be entitled to open a personal account. The safest course is for the person with a mental handicap to be introduced by a parent or carer who is already known at the branch. At a small branch he may be accepted and treated with consideration thereby receiving the service needed and gaining independence. If it becomes apparent that an account holder does not understand the transactions involved an account will be frozen until directions are given by

---

12  *Mitchell and Baxter* v. *Cheyne* (1891) 19 R 324. See Chap.10B.
13  There is a possible argument, not judicially tested, that under such arrangements the curator's authority gives validity to the ward's transactions within that authority.
14  *Morrison* v. *Maclean's Trs* (1862) 24 D 625.

the Court of Protection (in England) or a curator bonis is appointed (in Scotland). This could cause delay and expense in a borderline case where helpful staff at a local branch have been replaced by others who take a less tolerant view.

The need to produce a consistent signature may deprive a person who has contractual capacity but not the physical ability to sign of freedom to conduct transactions through a bank account, whereas a person with low understanding but no physical limitations may pass the usual tests. Care must be taken to support the rights of the former and to protect the latter from exploitation.

*Deposit accounts*

Few inquiries are made on opening a deposit account and all that is required may be completion of a form giving name and address with a specimen signature. The depositor may not even need to attend at the branch concerned, so the effective test will be ability to produce a signature on demand. Having received the money the bank will be concerned to ensure that it has a valid receipt in respect of money paid out and problems arise if the customer cannot satisfy the bank in this respect.

*Current accounts*

Here a cheque book is issued so the bank will be more concerned about the status of the customer especially if an overdraft is authorised. In England a person under the age of 18 years (a minor) may open a current account but whether an overdraft may be recovered is a matter for common law.[15] It has been said that the disability of minority goes no further than is necessary for the protection of the minor[16] and the position may be the same for a person who lacks mental capacity; in each case it is a question of balancing the degree of capacity against the amount of money involved.

In Scotland, a child under 16 may validly enter transactions of a kind commonly entered by such a child and on terms which are not unreasonable.[17] Deposit accounts customarily operated by children are thus validated, but an overdraft would probably be invalid, though money lent and expended to the benefit of the child's estate is recoverable under the principle of recompense.[18] Prejudicial transactions by 16 and 17 year olds may be set aside if the person applies before reaching the age of 21.[19] As there could be doubt about whether overdrafts were prejudicial or not, banks may sometimes be wary about granting them. However, some transactions may not be set aside in this way, including transactions by 16 and 17 year olds in the course of their trades,

---

15 The Infants Relief Act 1874, s.1 rendered such overdraft irrecoverable but this was repealed by the Minors' Contracts Act 1987.
16 See *Pearce* v. *Brain* [1929] 2 K.B. 310.
17 Age of Legal Capacity (Scotland) Act 1991, s.2(1).
18 *Scott's Trustee* v. *Scott* (1887) 14 R 1043.
19 Age of Legal Capacity (Scotland) Act 1991, s.3(1).

businesses or professions, transactions validated after reaching 18, and transactions validated by the court.[20] However, all of these provisions are overriden if the young person in fact lacks capacity through mental disability,[21] and likewise in Scotland the validity of banking transactions by adults is determined by the normal general principles of capacity described above,[22] though - as with children - money which is lent and expended to the benefit of the person's estate would be likely to be recoverable under the principle of recompense.

The duty and authority of a bank to pay a customer's cheque is determined by notice of mental disorder where this is of a sufficient degree to prevent an understanding of the transaction.[23] The size and nature of the cheque is relevant, and if it is only for a small sum in keeping with the balance normally held in the account or in payment for necessaries the bank may not be on enquiry, but if it is unusual and disproportionate in amount the bank should refuse to accept it.

### National Savings Bank accounts

Special rules exist for the receipt and repayment of deposits in the NSB. Deposits may be made on behalf of and in the name of persons of unsound mind and there are regulations which cover this.[24] The use of an ordinary or investment deposit account may therefore be suitable for persons with a mental handicap just as they are in common use in respect of very young children. The account may actually be in the name of the individual but administered by someone else.[25]

### Credit cards

It may not be wise to issue a credit or charge card to a person with limited mental capacity, but the general principles outlined here in regard to current accounts no doubt apply.

### Bank loans, interest and charges

Customers may borrow from a bank by way of loan or overdraft. A loan is a matter for specific agreement and the bank must satisfy itself that there is sufficient understanding for this to be binding on the customer. By custom a bank is entitled to charge simple interest at a reasonable rate upon overdrafts, and if the bank has concluded that a customer has sufficient capacity to conduct an account it follows that capacity to submit to interest and charges will be assumed. It has been held that a banker was not entitled to

---

20   s.3(2).
21   s.1(3)(b).
22   For advice on the prudent course for bankers to adopt, see *Stair Memorial Encyclopaedia*, Vol.2, para.1258.
23   *Drew* v. *Nunn* (1878) 4 QBD 661.
24   National Savings Bank Act 1971, s.8(1)(f);    National Savings Bank Regulations 1972, regs.6 and 7.
25   Similar rules applied to Trustee Savings Banks until 1985 when they were absorbed in the TSB Group which acquired the status of a full bank.

interest and bank charges in respect of an overdraft where the money had been applied for the maintenance of a person of unsound mind but the implications of this are not clear.[26]

*Guarantors*

In England, at common law a guarantor of a minor's overdraft was not liable if the fact of such minority was known to all parties, unless the guarantor made himself liable as principal debtor, the reason being that there cannot be a guarantee of an unenforceable debt. This rule may apply in the case of an adult who is known to lack mental capacity to take a loan. The position is reversed in respect of minors since 1987[27] but this appears to leave the law unchanged for other forms of incapacity. In practice, banks providing loans or overdrafts for persons of doubtful mental capacity may require the willing carer to enter into a separate contract of indemnity.

In Scotland, by contrast, the common law position is that the guarantor of a child's overdraft is liable under the guarantee even though the child's transactions are void through lack of capacity.[28] This principle is equally applicable to guarantees in respect of adults who lack capacity.

*Duty of care*

In regard to the operation of a current account the customer owes a duty of care to the bank not to draw a cheque in a manner that facilitates fraud or forgery and to notify any fraud or forgery. A bank would be justified in refusing to open an account for a person likely to be incapable of fulfilling this duty, but would it be sufficient if an assurance were given that the chequebook would always be handled by a responsible person and that the customer would merely add his signature to properly drawn cheques? This might be relevant where the customer can neither read nor write but is nevertheless capable of making decisions on money matters after receiving proper explanations.

*Confidentiality and supervision*

If an individual is able to conduct a personal banking account, all transactions should be treated as confidential, although in particular cases it may be appropriate for a degree of discretion to be exercised especially where a carer has assisted in the opening of the account and provided an indemnity.

In those cases where some supervision is felt necessary the account may be opened in joint names with a carer. If the individual does not have the capacity or ability to conduct a personal account an account may be opened in the name of the carer as nominee or agent, but in that event the relevant tax office should be notified to avoid misunderstandings as to the tax liability on any interest.

---

26 *Re Beavan* [1912] 1 Ch 196.
27 Minors' Contracts Act 1987, s.2.
28 *Stevenson* v. *Adair* (1872) 10 M 919.

## Investments

Where more than small sums of money are involved other forms of investment may be desired. The reality of mental handicap may be overlooked initially, especially in borderline cases, and if problems later arise in England an application to the Court of Protection must be made unless an Enduring Power of Attorney can be completed. In Scotland, appointment of a curator bonis will have to be considered, unless the person has sufficient capacity to grant a Power of Attorney.[29]

### Stocks and shares

Where securities are offered for sale directly to the public all that is required is the completion of a signed form and payment of the price so there is no enquiry as to the capacity of the investor. Problems may arise in regard to the banking of dividends or on the disposal of the investment. Other investments may be made through a financial intermediary who is obliged to give best advice and accordingly to "know the client", so the mental capacity of the potential investor must be considered. The intermediary could be liable for any loss made on an investment by a person incapable by reason of mental disorder of handling his affairs, yet if the investment proves successful it is likely to be adopted and the profit retained. Parents or others with access to the money of a handicapped person may make investments in their own names but this leads to problems of ownership, taxation and inheritance.

### Property ownership

In English textbooks on real property it is not unusual to find the phrase "mental disorder" used as if this by itself connotes incapacity, whereas it merely refers to a condition which may have some influence upon capacity. Property transactions will be binding unless the unsoundness of mind is known at the time by the other party. If the owner of real property is incapable by reason of mental disorder of handling his property and affairs the only way of dealing with that property is under the authority of the Court of Protection. In the absence of a clear, universal test of capacity there is room for different opinions and this raises the prospect of an individual being permitted to own a property on proper advice and later being considered incapable of administering such property.

In Scotland, mental handicap, however severe, does not disqualify a person from owning heritable property (land and buildings), but incapacity at the time of entering a contract or granting a deed renders the contract or deed void,[30] regardless of whether any other parties to the transaction were aware of the incapacity.[31] It is necessary to have a curator bonis appointed to carry through any

---

29   A full explanation of this topic will be found in Chaps.10A and 10B.
30   See *Sivewright* v. *Sivewright's Trs* 1920 SC(HL) 63.
31   *John Loudon and Co.* v. *Elder's Curator Bonis* 1923 SLT 226.

dealings with heritable property on behalf of a person lacking sufficient capacity to do so himself. Scots law applies to heritable property in Scotland, even though the mentally handicapped adult dealing - or purportedly dealing - with it is domiciled elsewhere.[32]

## Insurance

An insurance policy is a form of contract so capacity is necessary. The existence of a relevant disability should be disclosed when proposing for a policy and also on renewal if there has been any change in the nature or degree of handicap. A policy could be void for such non-disclosure. In some cases, especially for health or holiday policies, there may be an express declaration that there is no pre-existing medical condition or disability, so the proposal form should be carefully examined.

### Life insurance

Some insurance companies take a more relaxed view than others about capacity to take out a life policy. If a mentally handicapped individual wishes to take out a policy the signature of the parent or carer may be required and, although this is unlikely to affect its validity, the insurer is then less likely to question the policy before paying out. Policies covering funeral expenses may be useful and a receiver in England, or curator bonis in Scotland, may be expressly authorised to take out such a policy.

Life policies for the benefit of a mentally handicapped individual can cause problems. The insurers may insist upon the appointment of a receiver (in Scotland, a curator bonis) before paying out and the receipt of such money could affect other funding. If it is desired to provide a fund to support the individual, this is best done by appointing trustees of the policy and creating a settlement of the proceeds.[33]

### Car insurance

Any material disability must be disclosed when taking out motor insurance and medical evidence may then be required before a policy is issued. The question of whether a driver who regularly takes mentally disabled passengers should disclose this to the insurers is dealt with in Chapter 3, Part II, at page 149.

## Agency

Only a person with contractual capacity can appoint an agent, so although a physically disabled person may choose to operate through an agent, this facility is not available to those who lack mental capacity. A Power of Attorney is an agency appointment so these limitations apply, but in England there is scope for the use of an Enduring Power of Attorney if the mental disability is not too

---

32  Gordon, *Scottish Land Law*, para.11-01.
33  The trustees may be given a discretion as to the settlements to which they credit the monies, and in what proportions, thereby enabling the providers to make new settlements during their lifetimes as circumstances change.

severe.[34] In Scotland a Power of Attorney validly granted on or after January 1, 1991, remains in force even though the granter subsequently loses capacity.[35]

## OCCUPATIONS

Only those with a moderate mental handicap are likely to find or retain any form of employment and few will become partners in businesses or company directors. Some legal implications are dealt with here.

### Employment

The situation of disabled persons in employment, and some special schemes to encourage employers to provide jobs for them, are considered in Chapter 6, Part II, pp.327 *et seq.*

### Partnership

Partnership is a contract to which the general principles outlined above apply, but it concerns both the liability of partners to one another and to persons dealing with them. "Unsoundness of mind" is not itself a bar to entry into partnership unless the individual lacks sufficient capacity to enter into the contract, nor does it operate as immediate dissolution, but it is a ground for asking the court to decree a dissolution.[36] If the person lacked sufficient capacity when purportedly entering the partnership, he may still be bound as a partner if the other partner did not know of the incapacity (in Scotland he will not be bound regardless of such knowledge). However, in dealings with third parties, even if there is in fact no valid partnership, a purported partner could be liable under the principle of "holding out" if he represents himself, or knowingly allows himself to be represented, as the partner of the incapacitated individual.[37] If that individual does have sufficient capacity to enter a valid partnership, the partnership remains in force even though there is a subsequent deterioration in capacity (unless this triggers a specific termination provision in the partnership agreement), until steps are taken to terminate the partnership .

### Directorships

There is no general disqualification of directors based on mental incapacity and it is open to any registered company to impose such conditions as are deemed to be necessary in its Articles of Association. Many older companies include a provision that a director shall vacate office if he "is found lunatic or becomes of

---

34   See generally Chap.10A, Part I.
35   Law Reform (Miscellaneous Provisions) (Scotland) Act 1990, s.71; but see criticisms in McCusker *Continuing Powers of Attorney - Continuing Problems?* 1991 JLSS 255-257.
36   Partnership Act 1890, s.35. This may arise where a person becomes of unsound mind during the subsistence of a partnership.
37   Partnership Act 1890, s.14(1).

unsound mind" but this begs the question what such phrases mean. It is now usual to refer to "mental disorder" since this is defined in the Mental Health Acts, and to qualify this in the following way[38]:

"he is, or may be, suffering from mental disorder and either:
(i) he is admitted to hospital in pursuance of an application for admission for treatment under the Mental Health Act 1983 or, in Scotland, an application for admission under the Mental Health (Scotland) Act 1960 [*sic*]; or
(ii) an order is made by a court having jurisdiction (whether in the United Kingdom or elsewhere) in matters concerning mental disorder for his detention or for the appointment of a receiver, curator bonis or other person to exercise powers with respect to his property or affairs."

Thus some step is required in addition to the existence of mental disorder which also deprives the director of his personal freedom or financial powers. If the situation falls short of this but the director behaves in an inappropriate manner, the other directors or the shareholders can seek to remove him using one of their other powers.

Careful thought should be given to this provision in the Articles when a guarantee company is being formed to work in the field of mental handicap, because it may be desired to include persons with a mental handicap on the committee.[39] An alternative is:

"he suffers from mental disorder, unless it is demonstrated to the satisfaction of the other Directors that his disorder is not such as will affect the discharge by him of any of his duties as a Director."

## HOUSING

Housing, including the legal right and capacity of the individual to become a tenant or purchase a house with a mortgage, is dealt with in Chapter 7, Part II, page 338 *et seq.*

## SUCCESSION

Subject to certain restrictions,[40] an individual has freedom by Will to direct who shall inherit any savings or assets owned at death, and intestacy rules specify who is entitled in the absence of a Will.

### Wills

It should not be assumed that a person with a mental handicap is incapable of making a Will. Any desire expressed as to the disposal of possessions after death is entitled to be respected, and the execution of a Will should be seriously considered. An individual who does not have significant savings or assets but expresses a clear desire (*e.g.* "I want my friend to have my stereo when I die") should be enabled to record this instruction in a Will which is then treated as valid despite limited mental capacity.

---

38  Companies (Tables A to F) Regulations 1985, Table A.
39  In such case the committee members will be the directors.
40  Inheritance (Provision for Family and Dependants) Act 1975 in England and Wales, and legal rights in Scotland.

### England and Wales

*Capacity*

In order to make a valid Will it is necessary to have attained legal majority (*i.e.* 18 years) and have *testamentary capacity* at the time when the Will is made, which means that the testator understands:
  - that he is giving his property to persons of his choice;
  - the extent of the property being dealt with;  and
  - the nature and extent of the obligations that he has to relatives and others.[41]

This test is not the same as that for contractual capacity. In addition to passing the ordinary test of *understanding* the testator must also pass a *memory* test and show a sufficient *awareness* of moral obligations. In cases of doubt it is wise to obtain a medical opinion on capacity and even to arrange for the medical attendant to witness the Will. Testamentary capacity is presumed unless it is contested, in which case the onus of proof is upon the person putting forward the Will. Circumstances may outweigh the presumption, such as a previous finding that the testator was suffering from mental disorder, as would be the case if a receiver had been appointed of his affairs by the Court of Protection.[42] It may still be shown that the Will was made during a lucid interval.

*Execution*

It is not essential that the Will is actually signed by the testator, so inability to produce a signature is not by itself an obstacle. A testator may instead make his mark (*e.g.* a cross) and this will be witnessed by, or acknowledged to, the persons who sign as witnesses. Another person may even sign on behalf of the testator provided that this is in his presence and by his direction, and the testator should confirm this to the witnesses.[43] It is advisable for the signature to be at the end of the Will to avoid dispute, although this is no longer essential provided that the testator intended the signature to give effect to the Will. An incomplete signature will only be sufficient if it can be established that the testator was unable to finish it for physical reasons, and not because of a change of mind. If the testator could not read the Will it is necessary to establish that he knew its contents before signing.

*Revocation*

A Will is not revoked by supervening incapacity and may only be revoked by the testator (*e.g.* by making a later Will). The capacity required for revocation is the same as that needed to make a Will.

---

[41]  The most often quoted test of testamentary capacity is found in the judgment of Cockburn C.J. in *Banks* v. *Goodfellow* (1870) LR 5 QB 549.

[42]  In this context the definition of "mental disorder" in the Mental Health Act is usually adopted. It is only the presumption that is rebutted; a person for whom a receiver has been appointed may still have testamentary capacity.

[43]  Wills Act 1837, s 9 substituted by Administration of Justice Act 1982, s 17.

*Statutory wills*
If an individual has substantial assets and is not capable of making a Will, it may be possible to arrange for a statutory Will to be made by the Court of Protection.[44] Failing this the assets will pass to the next of kin on an intestacy. The high cost of a statutory Will should be taken into account when considering whether intestacy is to be avoided.

*Green Form legal advice*
The cost of preparing a Will is not usually covered under the green form scheme but an exception is where the client is disabled which includes a person "who suffers from mental disorder of any description, or who is substantially and permanently handicapped by illness, injury or congenital deformity".[45] Having decided that the client suffers from mental disorder to the extent that he is within the scheme creates another problem, namely deciding whether the client has the mental capacity to make a Will.[46] Notes should be kept to justify the decision in case the existence of the costs claim is used as evidence to challenge the validity of the Will.

# Scotland

*Capacity*
In order to make a valid Will it is necessary to have attained the age of 12[47] and to have testamentary capacity at the time when the Will is made. To have testamentary capacity, the person must comprehend what a Will is and what would be the consequences of making one.[48] Also likely to be relevant are the English tests mentioned above of understanding of factors such as the extent of the property being dealt with, and the nature and extent of obligations to relatives and others. Valid Wills may be made by long-stay hospital patients[49] or by persons with a curator bonis.

*Facility and circumvention*
A Will may be set aside on grounds of facility and circumvention.[50]

*Execution*
Scottish forms of execution are appropriate where:
- the Will is executed in Scotland, or
- the testator has Scottish domicile or is resident in Scotland, or
- the Will deals solely with immoveable property situated in

---

44  This topic is dealt with in Chap.10A, Part IV.
45  Legal Advice and Assistance (Scope) Regulations 1989, reg. 4(2)(*b*). Under reg.2(1) "mental disorder" has the meaning assigned to it in the Mental Health Act 1983, s.1.
46  The statutory definition of "mental disorder" does little more than record a fact, and does not involve any assessment of degree of incapacity.
47  Age of Legal Capacity (Scotland) Act 1991, s.2(2).
48  *Sivewright* v. *Sivewright's Trs* 1920 SC(HL) 63.
49  *Nisbet's Trs* v. *Nisbet* (1871) 9 M 937.
50  See above under "Contract", p.24.

Scotland.[51]
A Will is validly executed if:
- it is wholly in the testator's handwriting, and signed by the testator, or
- adopted as being in the testator's handwriting, by writing "Adopted as holograph" in his own handwriting immediately above his signature, or
- signed by the testator on each page, the signature being attested by two witnesses who sign on the last page,[52]   or
- notarially executed on behalf of the testator (see below).

The testator must sign at the end. If he has physical difficulty in signing, his wrist may be supported, but his hand may not be guided. A signature by initials or other abbreviated form may suffice if that can be shown to be the testator's normal signature,[53] but a mark is not sufficient.[54]

*Notarial execution*
If the testator is blind or unable to write, but has testamentary capacity, the Will may be signed for him by a notary public, solicitor, justice of the peace or any Church of Scotland minister acting in his own parish, who reads the Will over to the testator, obtains authority to sign, writes a prescribed docquet, and signs, all in the presence of two witnesses who also sign.

*Revocation*
A Will does not lose validity if the testator subsequently loses capacity. Provided that the testator has capacity to do so, he may revoke the Will by destroying it or by expressly revoking it by deed executed with testamentary formalities. A subsequent Will without express clause of revocation supersedes an earlier Will to the extent that the two are inconsistent.

*Statutory wills*
There is no provision in Scotland for a Will to be made on behalf of a person lacking testamentary capacity.

*Legal advice and assistance*
In Scotland the costs of preparing a Will are covered by the legal advice and assistance scheme.[55]

---

51  Wills Act 1963.
52  The witnesses do not require to see the testator sign provided that he acknowledges his signature to them, and they do not need to sign in presence of each other.
53  "Mum" at the end of a letter to a daughter was held to be a sufficient signature in *Rhodes* v. *Peterson* 1971 SC 56, 1972 SLT 98.
54  Halliday, *Conveyancing Law and Practice*, Vol.I, para.3-06 and cases there cited, though in *Stair Memorial Encyclopaedia*, Vol.25, para.725 it is suggested - without any authority being quoted - that a mark may be a usual signature.
55  Legal Aid (Scotland) Act 1986, s.6(1).

## Trusts and Estates

### *England*

#### *Inheritance*

There is no reason in law why a person with a mental handicap should not inherit substantial wealth, though this situation may be best avoided. Where property is to be left to a person who would not be capable of managing his own financial affairs it is desirable to create a trust otherwise a receiver must be appointed.[56]

#### *Variation of trusts*

The court has power to approve an arrangement varying or revoking trusts, or enlarging the powers of trustees, on behalf of a person who by reason of incapacity is incapable of assenting, but only if this would be for the benefit of such person.[57] This power is usually exercised in respect of infants, and whilst it also applies in the case of a "mentally defective beneficiary" the proper course where a receiver has been appointed is to apply to the Court of Protection for approval on behalf of the patient.[58] That Court will endeavour to do what the patient (*i.e.* the beneficiary) would have done had he been of sound mind.

#### *Grants of Probate and Administration*

Some textbooks state that if a person who is appointed an executor is suffering from mental disorder such person is regarded in law as incapable not only of carrying out the duties of the office, but also of determining whether or not to assume the office.[59] But the statutory definition of mental disorder does not take into account the degree of incapacity and this may be of more relevance in this context than the mere question whether the individual has "arrested or incomplete development of mind". In practice it will not be known by the Probate Court if mental disorder exists unless the application for a Grant is challenged. If there had been no previous finding of mental disorder the issue would have to be tackled, presumably on medical evidence, by that Court. It is unlikely that a person incapable of acting would apply for a Grant, but this could arise where that person was under the influence of others wishing to misappropriate an inheritance, and there is nothing to prevent this if such person appears capable of swearing the oath.

#### *Trustees*

The persons with power to appoint new trustees have power to do so in place of a trustee who is "incapable of acting".[60] It is not clear what test of incapacity should be applied, but text books on

---

56  These topics are dealt with in Chaps.9 and 10A respectively.
57  Variation of Trusts Act 1958, s.1(1).
58  s.1(3); *Re Sanderson's Settlement Trusts* [1961] 1 WLR 36.
59  The same principle would presumably apply to a person entitled to take out a Grant of Letters of Administration.
60  Trustee Act 1925, s.36.

the law of trusts indicate that this could be by reason of lunacy, age or infirmity, and that a person suffering from mental disorder could be replaced, though this term does not indicate the degree of incapacity. Where the trustee is also entitled to a beneficial interest in possession in the trust property and is incapable, by reason of mental disorder within the meaning of the Mental Health Act 1983, of exercising his functions as trustee, no appointment of a new trustee in his place shall be made unless leave has been given by the Court of Protection.[61] The court has power to appoint a new trustee in substitution for a trustee who is incapable by reason of mental disorder but will only do so where this is necessary.[62] There are also provisions entitling the court to vest trust property in trustees on various occasions, including where a person entitled is under disability.[63]

## Scotland

### Inheritance
Estates may be left to a person with a mental handicap, however severe the mental disability, but the beneficiary may then require a curator bonis to administer the bequest. Alternatively, a trust may be created so that trustees will manage the bequest.[64]

### Variation of trusts
The Inner House of the Court of Session may approve a variation of trust purposes on behalf of a person who lacks capacity to consent, provided that in the opinion of the court the proposed variation is not prejudicial to that person. The court may also authorise the variation or revocation of an alimentary provision.[65]

### Executors
In the absence of authority to the contrary, the test of capacity to act as an executor is probably the same as for trustees (see next section). A mentally handicapped person who lacks sufficient capacity is unlikely to be nominated in a Will to act as executor, but where there is no executor-nominate,[66] such person may be the one who would normally be appointed executor by the court, because he is entitled to the estate on intestacy, or is sole or residuary beneficiary under a Will. In such cases, if he has a curator bonis, or if the inheritance justifies appointment of a curator, the curator may apply to the court to be appointed executor.[67] Alternatively some other person qualified to do so may

---

61   Trustee Act 1925, s.36(9) as substituted by Mental Health Act 1959.
62   *e.g.* where the sole trustee is incapable and there is no-one else with power to make the appointment, s.41(1).
63   s.44(ii)(*a*).
64   These topics are dealt with in Chaps.10B and 9 respectively.
65   Trusts (Scotland) Act 1962, s.1.
66   An executor-nominate is an executor appointed in a Will; an executor-dative is appointed by the court.
67   The curator is appointed executor-dative qua curator bonis. See Currie, *Confirmation of Executors* (7 ed.), p.92 for reasons why this procedure is

instead petition for appointment.

*Trustees*

Anyone who lacks capacity to deal with his own property is disqualified from acting as a trustee in a trust governed by Scots law. Where an existing trustee loses capacity, if he has a curator bonis the curator bonis may apply to the court to resign the trusteeship on his behalf. When a sole trustee loses capacity, the court may appoint new trustees.[68]

## CIVIL PROCEEDINGS (England)

There are special rules dealing with proceedings by and against a person under a disability, which in this context means a person who is an infant or a "patient", defined as[69]:

> "a person who, by reason of mental disorder within the meaning of the Mental Health Act 1983, is incapable of managing and administering his property and affairs".

We are concerned with patients, but an infant who is mentally handicapped would come within both categories. In certain respects the rules treat infants differently from patients, because the disability of infancy ceases on attaining legal majority whereas that of a patient may last a lifetime (and generally does in cases of mental handicap).

### General

The court hearing the proceedings has power to decide whether a party is a patient, but if that decision has already been made by the Court of Protection it should be followed and that Court will normally decide who shall conduct the proceedings on behalf of the patient.[70]

*Service*

Where a defendant is a patient, proceedings must be served on the person authorised by the Court of Protection (if any) or "on the person with whom the patient resides or in whose care he is".[71] Service upon the patient is technically invalid, but may bring the appropriate response.

*Costs*

If costs are awarded against a next friend or a guardian *ad litem* then, in the absence of misconduct on his part, he is entitled to recover such costs from the property of the patient. Costs awarded in favour of a patient will usually be on the standard basis with a further order for legal aid taxation if appropriate. The costs of the

---

to be preferred.

68  Trusts (Scotland) Act 1921, s.22.

69  RSC, Ord.80, r.1. The words "minor" and "infant" both mean a person who has not attained 18 years. The modern practice is to use minor (as in the County Court Rules) but infant is used in Rules of the Supreme Court.

70  *Re S (FG) (Mental Health Patient)* [1973] 1 All ER 273.

71  RSC, Ord. 80, r.16; CCR, Ord. 10, r.4(*b*). There may be deemed service.

patient's own solicitor must also be taxed and this will usually be on the standard basis, but taxation may be dispensed with if the court is satisfied that the costs will be met by a third party without recourse to the patient (*e.g.* the solicitor undertakes to take no more than is recoverable from the other party though the court will usually wish to be told the amount).

*Appeals*

As an additional safeguard the Official Solicitor has been given power to appeal to the Court of Appeal in any case concerning a patient where he deems it in the patient's interest that the case be so considered and this may not otherwise happen and the Court of Appeal gives leave.[72]

## High Court

A person under disability may not be involved in any proceedings except by his next friend or guardian *ad litem*. and if a party becomes a patient during the course of proceedings an application must be made for an appropriate appointment. Subject to this, anything which might normally have been done in the proceedings may be done by the next friend or guardian *ad litem*, who must act by a solicitor.[73]

*Next friend*

A person under disability may not bring, or make, a claim in any proceedings except by his next friend and once a court decides that a plaintiff is under a disability all further proceedings must be stayed unless and until a next friend is appointed.[74] It is doubtful whether any steps taken on behalf of a patient without a next friend are valid. A plaintiff's solicitor may be personally liable for the additional costs if he commences or continues proceedings for a patient without a next friend.[75] A defendant on whom proceedings are served who considers that the plaintiff is incapable by reason of mental disorder should give notice of intention to defend and then take out a summons asking that a next friend be appointed or the writ set aside, although this step could also be taken at a later stage in the proceedings if the defendant was not initially aware of the disability.

The patient should not be so described in the writ or originating summons and the title to the proceedings will be *AB by CD his next friend* but the fact that the plaintiff is a patient suing by a next friend should be alleged in the pleadings. A defendant who wishes to challenge the use of this procedure should not seek to plead that it is not justified; the proper course is to apply for the stay or dismissal of the action and the issue as to whether a next friend is

---

72   *Practice Direction (Lord Chancellor's Department) (Mental Health: Appeal)* [1989] 1 All ER 764.
73   Ord.80, r.2.
74   In this context "proceedings" includes every form of civil litigation.
75   *Yonge* v. *Toynbee* [1910] 1 K.B. 215.

appropriate will then be heard.[76]

*Guardian ad litem*

A person under disability may not acknowledge service, defend, make a counterclaim or intervene in any proceedings, or appear in any proceedings under a judgment or order notice of which has been served on him, except by his guardian *ad litem*. Any acknowledgment filed or pleading served in contravention of this is ineffective.[77] Once a proper acknowledgment has been filed, or an Order made appointing a guardian *ad litem*, the title to the action should be amended to *EF by GH his guardian ad litem*.

*Counterclaims, etc.*

A guardian *ad litem* is appointed in respect of a counterclaim even though this is a cross-action, but where third party proceedings are to be taken a next friend is required. Thus a party may have both a next friend and a guardian *ad litem* in the same proceedings, although usually the same person would be both!

*Appointment*

An Order is not necessary for the appointment of a next friend or a guardian *ad litem*, except when the appointee is to be changed or a party becomes a patient after proceedings have been begun, or no acknowledgment is filed by a guardian *ad litem*.[78] A person authorised by the Court of Protection (who will usually be the patient's receiver) is entitled to be appointed unless the court dealing with the proceedings actually appoints someone else.[79] Any person seeking to be appointed on commencing proceedings or filing an acknowledgment must file the following documents:

(a) a written consent to be appointed;   and

(b) an office copy of any authorisation from the Court of Protection;   or

(c) a certificate by the solicitor to the patient that:

(i) he believes the person is a patient, giving the grounds of such belief[80];

(ii) there is no person authorised as aforesaid;   and

(iii) the proposed appointee has no interest in the cause or matter in question adverse to that of the patient.[81]

Where a proper acknowledgment is not filed following service of proceedings upon a patient, the plaintiff must apply to the court for the appointment of a guardian *ad litem* before taking any further steps in the proceedings.[82] The application, which may

---

[76]  *Richmond* v. *Branson* [1914] 1 Ch 968.

[77]  The solicitor concerned may be personally liable for the costs wasted even though ignorant of the incapacity, see *Yonge* v. *Toynbee* (supra).

[78]  Ord.80, rr.3 and 6.

[79]  The rules do not allow for an attorney under a registered Enduring Power of Attorney.

[80]  Any medical opinion relied on should be annexed to the certificate.

[81]  This requirement does not apply in the case of the Official Solicitor.

[82]  Ord.80, r.6. Similar provisions apply in respect of third party proceedings.

only be made after the time limited for acknowledging service has expired, must be supported by evidence proving that[83]:

    (a) the person served is under a disability;
    (b) the person to be appointed is willing and a proper person to act, and has no interest in the proceedings adverse to that of the patient;
    (c) the proceedings were duly served on the patient;   and
    (d) the notice of application was also duly served.

*Who is appointed*

One of the persons encouraging the bringing of a legal action by a mentally handicapped individual will usually be the next friend. Actions against such individuals are rare if only because of a lack of funds to meet any damages awarded and the difficulty of proving liability, but difficulties may arise in finding a guardian *ad litem* and, if a social worker or probation officer is not available the court will refer the matter to the Official Solicitor who may be willing to act. As a last resort a District Judge may be appointed and there are procedures for dealing with this.

Parents or carers may find themselves in conflict with social workers or advocates as to the course that any litigation should take and thus as to who should have conduct thereof. The court then has to decide what is in the best interests of the patient in appointing the appropriate nominee. If recovery of a substantial sum of money is involved it is wiser for this issue to be dealt with by the Court of Protection which has more experience in this area and has responsibility at a later stage so should dictate policy from the inception of the claim.

The substitution of another person can only be effected by court order, and a parent acting for a mentally handicapped son or daughter will only be removed on the application of another person if it can be shown that the parent is not acting properly in his or her interest.[84]

*Compromises, etc*

Where in any proceedings money is claimed by or on behalf of a person under a disability, no settlement, compromise or payment and no acceptance of money paid into court is valid without the court's approval.[85] There is a procedure whereby the court can approve a settlement reached before the commencement of proceedings,[86] which is intended to protect minors and patients from lack of skill or experience on the part of their legal advisers, and provide a means whereby the defendant can obtain a valid discharge from the claim. It also ensures that the solicitors

---

83    An Affidavit is usually filed and served in support of the application and the consent of the proposed appointee may be exhibited.

84    *Re Taylor's Application* [1972] 2 All ER 873, CA. In the new climate of community care a social worker or advocate may take a different view to parents as to the conduct of proceedings and seek to take over control.

85    Ord.80, r.10(1).

86    Ord.80, r.11.

involved are paid their proper costs and no more, and that the money recovered is properly looked after and wisely applied.

Special procedures apply to the administration of damages awarded to patients. These are dealt with in Chapter 10A, Part III.

## County Court

Broadly similar rules apply in the County Court[87] and although the expression *mental patient* is used, this is defined in the same terms as *patient* in the High Court.[88] A person under a disability may not bring or make a claim except by his next friend, or defend or make a counterclaim except by his guardian *ad litem* and in each case this shall be any person who may have been so authorised by the Court of Protection, unless some other person is appointed by the court. Any step which might normally be taken in the proceedings may be taken by the next friend or guardian *ad litem*, but unlike the High Court Rules there is no requirement that such person must act by a solicitor.[89]

### Commencement of proceedings

On the commencement of proceedings the next friend must deliver to the court either an authorisation from the Court of Protection or a written undertaking to be responsible for any costs ordered to be paid by the patient. If this procedure has not been followed the court has power on application to appoint as next friend a person who has such authority or gives the undertaking, or to strike out the proceedings.[90]

### Defence

If a person seeking to be guardian *ad litem* delivers to the court with the admission, defence (and counterclaim if appropriate) or answer either an appropriate authority from the Court of Protection, or a certificate that he is a fit and proper person to so act and has no interest in the matter adverse to that of the defendant, no order appointing such person to act is necessary. Failing this, the person bringing the proceedings must apply for an order that the person named in the application or some other proper person be appointed guardian *ad litem*, and the application is supported by an Affidavit showing that the person proposed is a fit and proper person, has no adverse interest and consents to act.[91] The court may appoint the person proposed or, if not satisfied that he is suitable, any other person willing to act and in default the District Judge of the court.[92] A guardian *ad litem* will not be personally liable for any costs not occasioned by his

---

87  CCR, Ord.10.
88  CCR, Ord.1, r.3. "Mental patient" is inappropriate because it fails to allow for persons with a mental handicap who are included in the definition.
89  CCR, Ord.10, rr.1 and 12.
90  CCR, Ord.10, rr.2 and 3.
91  CCR, Ord.10, rr.5 and 6. See Forms N237, N238, N239.
92  Formerly known as the Registrar. The Official Solicitor should first be considered, but must be consulted before being appointed.

personal negligence or misconduct.[93]

*Termination of proceedings*

No compromise or settlement of proceedings involving a person under a disability will be valid without the approval of the court. and there are provisions whereby an action may be brought solely for the purpose of obtaining the court's approval.[94] Taxation will usually be required of any plaintiff's solicitors costs. Where in any proceedings money is recovered by or on behalf of a patient it must be paid into and remain in court where it will be invested and applied as the court from time to time directs, usually on the application of any person interested, although the court will consider whether it is appropriate to pass the money over to the Court of Protection for supervision and should do so when that Court is already involved in the affairs of the patient.[95]

## Court of Protection

The jurisdiction and procedures of the Court of Protection are considered in Chapter 10A, but the question here is at what stage that court should become involved in a claim on behalf of a patient. For small claims it may not be necessary to refer to this Court at all as the procedures outlined above will be adequate, but where substantial damages are likely to be recovered (as in brain injury cases) it is wise to consult the Court of Protection at the outset and certainly before any offer is accepted. The Court sends out a long explanatory letter to solicitors as soon as it hears of such litigation and it is as well to set up the procedure for receiving and investing damages before they are actually paid into court otherwise there could be long delays.

*Effect on damages*

When formulating a claim for damages on behalf of a patient it is appropriate to include an element for the fees and costs that will be involved in administering those damages through the Court of Protection. Guidance on the costs of administering awards should be obtained and produced as many courts do not allow for this when awarding damages.

## Limitation of actions

If on the date when any right of action accrued for which a period of limitation is prescribed the person to whom it accrued was under a disability, the action may be brought within six years (or three years for personal injury claims) from the date when the disability ceased or the person died (whichever first occurs) even though the period of limitation has expired. A person is treated as under a disability while he is an infant or of unsound mind. A person is of unsound mind if he is incapable by reason of mental disorder (within the Mental Health Act 1983) of managing and

---

93   CCR, Ord.10, r.9.
94   CCR, Ord.10, r.10.  See Form N292.
95   CCR, Ord.10, r.11.

administering his property and affairs, and this is a question of fact to be decided in each individual case. A person who is liable to be detained or subject to guardianship under the Mental Health Act 1983 (or receiving in-patient treatment in any hospital within the meaning of that Act immediately thereafter) is conclusively presumed of unsound mind for these purposes.[96]

It is not necessary to be under the jurisdiction of the Court of Protection to be found under a legal disability, but a person who is under that jurisdiction must be presumed to be under a disability because that Court will have found him to be mentally incapable. That finding is likely to have been made on the basis of a single medical report on an uncontested written application and it seems unjust that a defendant in subsequent litigation is thereby denied an opportunity of disputing the incapacity. Although it would be possible to argue that the disability arose subsequent to the cause of action, such argument is unlikely to succeed in a case of mental handicap where the disability will not vary.

## Legal Aid

Legal aid is available in the normal way based upon the financial circumstances of the patient, but the application will be submitted by the person acting (or proposing to act) for the patient in the proceedings. In some cases a disabled person may be eligible for support which is not generally available.

### Green Form

Advice may be given to, or on behalf of, a person with a mental handicap under the green form scheme. It is provided that[97]:

> (3) A solicitor may accept an application for advice and assistance on behalf of a child or patient from:
> (a) in the case of a child, his parent or guardian or other person in whose care he is; or
> (b) in the case of a patient, a receiver appointed under Part VII of the Mental Health Act 1983 or the patient's nearest relative or guardian within the meaning of Part II of the Mental Health Act 1983; or
> (c) in the case of a child or patient, a person acting for the purposes of any proceedings as his next friend or guardian *ad litem*; or
> (d) in the case of a child or a patient, any other person where the Area Director is satisfied that it is reasonable in the circumstances and has given prior authority for the advice and assistance to be given to such other person on behalf of the child or patient.

### ABWOR (Assistance by Way of Representation)

Part III of the Legal Aid Act 1988 applies to ABWOR given to a person in proceedings before a Mental Health Review Tribunal under the Mental Health Act 1983 whose case or whose application to the Tribunal is or is to be subject of the proceedings.[98]

### Certificate

A legal aid application may be made by a next friend or guardian

---

96   Limitation Act 1980, ss.28(1), 38(2) and 38(3) as amended by 1983 Act.
97   Legal Advice and Assistance Regulations 1989, reg.14.
98   Legal Advice and Assistance (Scope) Regulations 1989, Part III, reg.9.

*ad litem* on behalf of the person under disability. If proceedings have not actually been begun, the person intending to act in one of these capacities may apply. The Certificate will not be issued unless the person applying signs an undertaking to pay to the Board (if required to do so) any sums which an assisted person of full age and capacity may be required to pay upon the issue or during the currency or upon the discharge or revocation thereof. The Certificate is in the name of the person under disability but states the name of the person who has applied for it who in any matter relating to the issue, amendment, revocation or discharge thereof is treated for all purposes as his agent.[99] The Area Director may, where the circumstances appear to make it desirable, waive all or any of these requirements. It is the financial circumstances of the person under disability that are relevant, and children under 16 years are now assessed on the basis of their own means rather than that of their parents.

## Claims for damages

### Child born disabled

A cause of action existed at common law for pre-natal injuries, but this was replaced with statutory liability by the Congenital Disabilities (Civil Liability) Act 1976.[100] The Act provides that a person responsible for an occurrence affecting the parent of a child (either the father or the mother) causing the child to be born disabled, will be liable to the child if he would have been liable in tort to the parent affected. There is no liability if the parent knew of and accepted the risk, and a professional person is not liable for treatment or advice given according to prevailing professional standards of care. The right to damages may be excluded or reduced by the consent or contributory negligence of the parent.

The Act has rarely been relied upon, but there may be more scope for it to be used in the case of a child born mentally handicapped. The defendant's duty to the child is contingent upon there having been a duty to the parent, breach of which led to the child's injuries, so a medical procedure carried out to enhance the mother's health which causes damage to the foetus may not be actionable. The mother is not answerable for any injuries she may cause to her child in utero, except by negligent driving, so the effects of smoking, drinking or drugs will not result in a claim. The position may have been otherwise at common law, although it does not appear to have been tested.

### Medical negligence

There are many brain damaged children awaiting settlement of claims for medical negligence and awards can be between £500,000 and £1 million. Since April 1990 children under 16 years have been assessed on the basis of their own means and not

---

99   Civil Legal Aid (General) Regulations 1989, reg.16. The person under a disability is described here as a "minor or patient".

100  Amended by the Human Fertilisation and Embryology Act 1990, s.44.

that of their parents in determining whether or not they should be granted legal aid to bring civil actions and this could result in a significant upsurge in the number of applicants for legal aid to bring actions where brain damage occurred at birth and a major increase in the number of medical negligence cases.[101] In order to succeed in such cases it is necessary first to establish the liability of the health authority, and then to prove that it was negligent action by the hospital staff which caused the condition. Only a limited legal aid certificate is granted initially and a reasonable chance of success must be shown before the limitation is removed. The cost of a preliminary investigation, involving the review of medical records and obtaining counsel's opinion, can be substantial.

## CIVIL PROCEEDINGS (Scotland)

### Capacity.

Three categories can be distinguished[102]:
- people who have a curator bonis, or a tutor with relevant powers;
- people who lack capacity but have neither a curator bonis nor a tutor with relevant powers;   and
- actions of divorce and separation (where special rules apply).

Questions of capacity to sue and be sued are separate from the question of whether a person can give evidence, which is considered later. A party who cannot himself "appear" as pursuer or defender may nevertheless be able to give evidence as a witness.

*Curator bonis, or tutor with relevant powers*
A mentally handicapped person who has a curator bonis can neither sue nor be sued in his own name, and may not himself appear either as pursuer or defender. Proceedings may be brought by or against the curator bonis.[103] Likewise, where the person has a tutor with unlimited powers, proceedings may be brought by or against the tutor. Where a tutor-dative is appointed as personal guardian only, with specified powers, only proceedings within the scope of those powers may be brought by or against the tutor-dative. Customarily the power of a tutor-dative to commence, compromise or settle proceedings is limited to proceedings that do not relate to the person's estate.

*No curator bonis*
If the person has no curator bonis or tutor but in fact lacks sufficient capacity to sue or appear, then he cannot competently do

---

101  Previously in many cases it was necessary to wait till the child attained 16 years before legal aid could be obtained and a claim contemplated, and then difficulty was encountered in tracing medical records, witnesses, etc.
102  Even respected modern texts, such as MacPhail's *Sheriff Court Practice*, describe the law only in relation to "insane persons". The same principles would appear to apply to all categories of mental disability.
103  *Anderson's Trs* v. *Skinner* (1871) 8 SLR 325; *Latta* 1977 SLT 127.

so himself.[104] Subject to the exception mentioned below, it will be necessary for a curator bonis or curator *ad litem* to be appointed. Proceedings may be served upon the person, if he has no curator, but the court should then be advised of the incapacity. The court will thereupon either sist the action pending appointment of a curator bonis, or appoint a curator *ad litem*.[105] For these purposes, capacity or incapacity is a question of fact to be resolved by evidence. There is a presumption in favour of capacity, therefore the onus of proof is upon the party alleging incapacity. There are no detailed procedural rules, but if the matter is disputed the court will fix a preliminary proof.[106]

There is danger of prejudice when proceedings are served upon a mentally handicapped person who does not understand the significance of the papers which he has received, and ignores them. If the pursuer is unaware of the incapacity, or chooses to ignore it, an undefended decree will be obtained. If the matter subsequently comes to light, the position can be retrieved by the procedure known as reponing, but reponing is not competent once the decree has been implemented in full, or after six months following personal service of the action or of a charge.[107] Thereafter an action of reduction is necessary. It is unsatisfactory that special provisions for intimation of proceedings against people with a mental disability are limited to actions of divorce and separation (see below).

The exception to the above is that proceedings within the scope of a management appointment other than as curator bonis or tutor are sometimes in practice conducted in name of the mentally handicapped person upon the instructions of the manager. For example, a social security appeal may be taken in name of the person, upon the instructions of the DSS appointee.[108]

### Curator bonis or curator ad litem?

A curator bonis takes over entire management of a person's estate on a long-term basis,[109] whereas a curator *ad litem* is appointed solely to conduct the litigation in question. The existing rule appears to be that normally a curator bonis will be appointed to conduct proceedings, but in some cases the court may instead

---

104 *Reid* v. *Reid* (1839) 1D 400, followed in *McGaughey* v. *Livingstone* 1992 SLT 386, though in the latter case Lord Coulsfield suggested (at p.387) that there "might be room for a different approach" where an incapax would otherwise suffer prejudice.

105 *Moodie* v. *Dempster* 1931 SC 553.

106 *AB* v. *CB* 1937 SC 408. See also *Gibson* v. *Gibson* 1970 SLT (N) 60.

107 Sheriff Court Ordinary Rules 28 and 26.

108 This occurred in *Moffat* v. *Secretary of State for Social Services*, October 25, 1991 (see 1992 SLT 393) in which an appellant with Down's Syndrome succeeded in an appeal to the Court of Session, after unsuccessful appeals to a Social Security Appeal Tribunal and a Social Security Commissioner. Strictly speaking, proceedings commenced in name of an incapax purser are normally incompetent. See cases in footnote 104.

109 See Chap.10B.

appoint a curator *ad litem*. It is believed that the court may appoint a curator *ad litem* in special circumstances and in actions affecting status[110] (and as we shall see, under Sheriff Court Rules a curator *ad litem* is appropriate in actions of divorce and separation).

It would be reasonable, and it is submitted appropriate, for the courts to develop these principles with greater clarity. In modern practice and conditions, the appointment of a curator bonis can result in disadvantages as well as advantages. In particular, appointment of a curator bonis deprives a person of all legal capacity to manage his own affairs, a step which should never be taken lightly. Curatory may be inappropriate where estate can be managed satisfactorily by other means and the size or nature of the estate does not justify or require a curator bonis. Clearly, a curator bonis should be appointed if it is in fact appropriate that the mentally handicapped person should have one, and normally that will include cases where success in the litigation would render a curatory appropriate, as where the mentally handicapped person is suing for payment of a substantial sum or possession of substantial property. However, it is submitted that a curator bonis should not be appointed solely because the mentally handicapped person happens to have become involved in litigation, and where otherwise - even following success in the litigation - a curatory would not have been considered appropriate. In such circumstances, a curator *ad litem* should be appointed, though at present this can only be done after proceedings have commenced. In some cases it may be possible and appropriate to avoid this dilemma by having a tutor appointed, particularly if there is time to do so before the proceedings commence.

Curators bonis are described in Chapter 10B and tutors in Chapter 3, Part II. Curators *ad litem* are described below.

*Divorce and separation*

Ordinary Cause Rule 11A applies to Sheriff Court actions of divorce or separation where the defender has a "mental illness or mental handicap however caused or manifested".[111] The action must be served upon every daughter of the marriage over 12, every son over 14,[112] one of the defender's next-of-kin who has reached these ages, and any curator bonis. If the address of any of these people is not known to the pursuer, the pursuer should say so in the initial writ, and then service on that person is not required. Any person who does receive intimation under these provisions

---

110 *Moodie* v. *Dempster* 1931 SC 553, *Drummond's Trs* v. *Peel's Trs* 1929 SC 484, *Finlay* v. *Finlay* 1962 SLT (Sh.Ct.) 43.

111 This being the definition of "mental disorder" in the Mental Health (Scotland) Act 1984, s.1(2) referred to in Rule 11A(1). This appears to apply regardless of the effect, if any, of the mental disorder upon capacity.

112 These were the old ages at which pupillarity ended, and Rule 11A was not amended by the Age of Legal Capacity (Scotland) Act 1991, which under, s.1(3)(*d*) does not affect any age limit expressed in years.

may seek leave to enter the proceedings.

There are additional requirements under Rule 11A(4) where the defender "suffers or appears to suffer from a mental disorder and is resident in a hospital or other similar institution".[113] The defender is cited by sending the service copy initial writ and warrant by registered or recorded delivery post to the medical officer in charge. The medical officer must either deliver the writ and accompanying items to the defender, or certify that such delivery would be dangerous to the health or mental condition of the defender. The medical officer must also either explain the contents to the defender, or certify that such explanation would be dangerous to the health or mental condition of the defender. The medical officer must do these things regardless of the defender's actual capacity to understand the writ.

Under Rule 11A(5) the sheriff may at any time prior to granting decree order further medical enquiry, and order further service, as the sheriff may think fit, where the writ has not been served because it would be dangerous to do so. The sheriff apparently has no such powers where the defender could not or may not have understood the writ.

While it has been generally assumed that a person lacking capacity could not be pursuer in an action of divorce, at time of writing an application for special powers to do so was under consideration where there was evidence of the person's intentions prior to losing capacity.

## Curator *ad litem*

A curator *ad litem* may be appointed only in proceedings already before the court, not in anticipation of proceedings. The appointment is made by the court, either on its own initiative or upon the application of any interested party. Except for mandatory appointment in actions of divorce and separation (see above), the court may take a broad view of the circumstances, including the interests of the parties to the action and others, and exercise its discretion in deciding whether justice requires that a curator *ad litem* be appointed.

The curator *ad litem* is an officer of court. He need not be a lawyer, but usually is, in which case he may either conduct the proceedings himself or appoint another lawyer to do so. He takes an oath,[114] and thereafter acts independently to safeguard the interests of the incapacitated person in the litigation. He must decide whether to continue to pursue or defend the action. He reports his decision to the court, and continues to report to the court as he thinks necessary or as the court requires. He may ratify anything done in the action prior to his appointment, and

---

[113] The Rules give no guidance as to what is or is not a "similar institution", except that it would appear to be limited to an institution which has a medical officer in charge (but some mental handicap institutions do not).

[114] The oath *de fideli administratione*.

may settle or compromise the action.

His powers are strictly limited to conducting the action in question. He has no powers of management or guardianship.[115] He cannot be made personally liable for any expenses. To cover his own costs, he may if necessary and appropriate require to apply for legal aid, although there would appear to be some doubt about the competency of this (see under "Legal aid" below). If there is difficulty over covering his costs, the court will endeavour to secure his expenses from any available funds: the court may order an appropriate party to provide funds, and even where the curator *ad litem* has been unsuccessful in the litigation the court may order the expenses to be borne by the party who required the curator's appointment, or whose actings brought it about.

The appointment ceases upon conclusion of the proceedings. The consent of the court is required to terminate the appointment sooner.

## Administration of damages

The sheriff courts have power to receive and administer damages awards.

## Prescription

A large category of obligations are extinguished if no "relevant claim" is made, and the obligation is not "relevantly acknowledged", for five years.[116] Excluded from computation of the five-year period is any period during which the person entitled to enforce the obligation was under legal disability by reason of "unsoundness of mind".[117] Mental disability does not interrupt the running of the twenty year prescriptive period which extinguishes obligations and rights relating to property.[118]

Actions for damages for personal injuries must be brought by the injured person within three years of the date when the injury was sustained (or in case of continuing neglect or default, when the neglect or default ceased). In the case of claims arising from someone else's death, the three years run from date of death. If when the right of action accrued the person was under legal disability by reason of "unsoundness of mind", and not in the custody of any parent, step-parent or grandparent, the three-year period does not commence unless and until capacity is regained.[119] An adult living with a parent is not in the parent's custody,[120] but might be if the parent is also tutor-dative. When the claimant (or parent with custody) was unaware of decisive facts, and could not reasonably be expected to have ascertained them or be put on

---

115 For example, he cannot consent to a blood test upon the mentally handicapped person, *Docherty* v. *McGlynn* 1983 SLT 645.
116 The Prescription and Limitation (Scotland) Act 1973, s.6, and Sched.1.
117 ss.6(4)(*b*) and 15(1).
118 s.14(1)(*b*).
119 s.17(2).
120 *Kirkby* v. *Leather* [1965] 2 QB 367.

enquiry about them, until less than three years previously, then the claim is not time-barred.[121] None of these provisions affords protection where a person loses capacity during the three-year period.

## Legal aid

In Scotland, legal aid is administered by the Scottish Legal Aid Board. It is available to people with mental handicaps, the only specialities being as to the way in which applications are made. There are two relevant methods of application under identical provisions for civil legal aid, and for criminal legal aid in summary proceedings. Firstly, where cause is shown why the applicant cannot sign the application, but the applicant has sufficient capacity to authorise someone else to sign, the application may be signed by the person authorised by the applicant. Secondly, an application may be signed on behalf of a mentally disabled person by the person's curator bonis, tutor, judicial factor or guardian. Surprisingly, curators *ad litem* are not included.[122]

Applications for criminal legal aid in solemn proceedings "shall be made in writing and shall be in such form as the court may require".[123] In the case of mentally handicapped applicants, one would expect the court, when determining the form of application, to have regard to the provisions mentioned above.

Where an application for legal aid is made by a person for appointment in a representative or fiduciary capacity (an example being an application for appointment as tutor-dative), the proposed appointee is treated as the applicant, but the means assessment is concerned only with the means of the mentally handicapped person.[124] Where there is more than one proposed appointee, each completes a form CIV1, but not a financial statement. A financial statement (usually Form L20) is completed in respect of the mentally handicapped person.

The Scottish legal advice and assistance regulations provide that a person who for good reason cannot make application may authorise someone else to apply,[125] but this provision would appear to require the person to have capacity to give such authority, and mentally disabled people in Scotland would seem to be disadvantaged by the absence of provisions for applications by nearest relatives, guardians, or other specified representatives such

---

121  ss.18 and 22.
122  Civil Legal Aid (Scotland) Regulations 1987, regs.3 and 5(1)(*a*); Criminal Legal Aid (Scotland) Regulations 1987, regs.2 and 8(1)(*a*). The regulations refer to the definition of mental disorder in Mental Health (Scotland) Act 1984, s.1(2) which is "mental illness or mental handicap however caused or manifested".
123  Criminal Legal Aid (Scotland) Regulations 1987, reg.6.
124  See determination by Scottish Legal Aid Board quoted in *The Power to Act*, p.48 (see Appendix II).
125  Advice and Assistance (Scotland) Regulations 1987, reg.5(1).

as are contained in the equivalent English regulations.[126]
Assistance by way of representation ("ABWOR") is available for
advice and assistance in instructing and conducting appeals to the
sheriff under the Mental Health (Scotland) Act 1984.[127]

## CIVIL RIGHTS

### Driving licences

It is an offence to drive a motor vehicle on a road unless the
driver holds a licence authorising him to drive a vehicle of the
class being driven.[128] An applicant for a driving licence must state
whether he is suffering from a "relevant disability", which means
either a disability prescribed by the Secretary of State or any other
disability which is likely to cause the driving of a vehicle by the
applicant to be a source of danger to the public.[129] Severe mental
handicap is a prescribed disability, as is being subject to a
guardianship order under the Mental Health Acts or in the care of
the local health authority.[130] It should not be assumed that persons
who might come within the general description of "mentally
handicapped" are necessarily unable to obtain a driving licence. A
person suffering from cerebral palsy who has severe problems of
movement and communication may nevertheless be able to
demonstrate an ability to drive a suitably modified car quite
safely. A right of appeal lies to the magistrates court for the petty
sessional area in which the aggrieved person resides (or in
Scotland to the Sheriff) against a refusal to grant a driving licence.

### Passports

Where a person is unable to sign a passport application form
through mental disability, a declaration signed by a person
responsible for the applicant's welfare may be accepted. The
signatory could be, for example, a parent, doctor, social worker
or officer-in-charge of a residential care home. The signatory
should explain in the "Other Information" section of the form, or
in a separate letter if preferred, that the applicant is mentally
handicapped and that the signatory (as parent or in some other
relevant capacity) has signed on the applicant's behalf.

### Firearms

It is an offence for a person to sell or transfer any firearm or
ammunition to, or repair, prove or test any firearm or
ammunition for, any other person whom he knows or has
reasonable cause for believing to be of unsound mind. A firearm

---

[126] Legal Advice and Assistance Regulations 1989, reg.14; see under Green
Form on p.43.
[127] Advice and Assistance (Assistance by way of Representation) (Scotland)
Regulations 1988, reg.3.
[128] Road Traffic Act 1988, s.87(1).
[129] s.91(1).
[130] (SI 1987 No. 1378), r. 24(1)(b).

certificate shall not be granted to a person whom the chief officer of police has reason to believe to be of unsound mind.[131]

## Access to Information

During recent years several statutes have been passed giving individuals the right to inspect information held about them. These are considered under the rights of parents and carers in Chapter 3, Part II, but certain aspects are relevant here.

### Access by the Individual

People may only have access to information about themselves, so a person with a mental handicap who is not capable of making an application is in effect precluded from having access to such information notwithstanding that he is likely to feature in reports and documents maintained by the authorities.[132] Care must be taken before releasing information to other persons, and it must not be assumed that parents should automatically be entitled to inspect information relating to their son or daughter.

The most recent Act attempts to address the problem by providing that where a person is incapable of managing his own affairs, any person appointed by a court to manage his affairs may make application for access to a health record.[133] In England, this means a person authorised by the Court of Protection, but that court only deals with financial affairs and most people with a mental handicap will not have sufficient funds to make involvement with that court necessary. In Scotland, this appears to have the strange result that the curator bonis, appointed only to manage affairs, may apply, but that a tutor-dative, with the role of personal guardian, may not.[134] It is customary for tutors-dative to be granted powers to exercise all rights and powers competent to the person under statute, and in particular under the statutes relating to access to information.

### Access by others

Difficulties arise where other persons require a medical report upon a mentally incapable individual. Thus where a man suffers a serious brain injury and is likely to remain permanently incapable, his employers will need a medical report from his usual doctor in order to decide whether to pension him off. There is no provision in the Access to Medical Reports Act for such circumstances, but a series of consents is required, first to request a report, then

---

131 Firearms Act 1968, ss.25 and 27(1). The Act does not define "unsound mind".

132 The guidance circulars seem to envisage access by third parties in some circumstances.

133 Access to Health Records Act 1990. The original Bill contemplated that when the relevant section of the Disabled Persons (Services, Consultation and Representation) Act 1986 was in force, an "authorised representative" appointed under that Act would be able to apply on behalf of a person with a mental disorder.

134 In practice, tutor-dative petitions seek authority to exercise this right of access, but there could be doubt as to the effect of this.

whether the patient wishes to see the report, and finally whether the report once seen is to be sent unamended. Who, if anyone, can give these consents? In Scotland, the answer is that a tutor-dative can give such consent.

# PART II - CIVIL RESPONSIBILITY

It has to be assumed that a person with a mental handicap has the same legal responsibilities as other members of the community unless there is a rule of law to the contrary. We now consider some special provisions.

## TAXATION

### Income tax

Mentally disabled people must pay income tax in the same way and to the same extent as everyone else; there are no special allowances or reliefs available to them. Personal income will usually be from state benefits, most of which are not taxable, and other forms of support provided by local authorities and charities are also not taxable. An individual with an investment income of any size who is not capable of completing a Tax Return will also be unable to handle his affairs, so the procedures for delegation of financial affairs will apply (see Chapters 10A and 10B).

*Allowances*
There are no longer specific income tax allowances for dependent members of a family. The former tax allowances and reliefs for a housekeeper, daughter or son's services and dependent relatives were abolished by the Finance Act 1988.

### Capital taxes

There are special provisions in regard to Capital Gains Tax and Inheritance Tax for trusts for the benefit of disabled persons, and these are dealt with in Chapter 9, Part II, page 483 *et seq.*

### Community Charge

Until April 1993 adults must pay the Personal Community Charge ("poll tax"), though certain persons are exempt including:
- people resident in hospital or subject to detention there;
- people looked after in residential care homes, nursing homes and hostels providing a high level of care[135];
- the severely mentally impaired;
- volunteers working on low pay for charities.

*Severely mentally impaired*
The exemption applies to an individual who on a particular day[136]:

---

[135] This includes those detained in hospital under the Mental Health Acts.

[136] It is not clear why there is such emphasis upon the time of the assessment when mental handicap is a lifelong condition and the definitions themselves make express mention of its permanence.

    (a)  is severely mentally impaired (at any time of the day);

    (b)  has a certificate of a registered medical practitioner to this effect; and

    (c)  fulfils one or more of a number of conditions, namely is entitled to Invalidity Pension, Attendance Allowance, Severe Disablement Allowance or some other benefits.[137]

The conditions are designed to provide a filter through which the applicant must pass before it becomes necessary for a medical practitioner to become involved. Doctors are given little guidance as to what this legal definition means, and a letter from the Department of Health to GPs states "exemption does not flow from any specific medical diagnosis" but that doctors must use their clinical judgment. This exemption got off to an unfortunate start because the definition of *severely mentally impaired* in the Local Government Finance Act 1988[138] was similar to that used in other legislation and as a result there was a reluctance to apply for the exemption for fear that this automatically imposed restrictions upon the individual. The Secretary of State was given power by the Act to amend the definition, and substituted[139]:

> "A person is severely mentally impaired if he has a severe impairment of intelligence and social functioning (however caused) which appears to be permanent".

This new definition is wider and includes people with a mental illness which is likely to be permanent (*e.g.* dementia).

*Procedure*

An application for exemption must be made to the Community Charge Registration Officer by or on behalf of the individual, though those living in a residential care home or similarly treated establishment are automatically exempt. Practice Notes set out the procedure to be followed for claiming exemption.[140] If the Registration Officer refuses to accept the exemption a right of appeal lies to the *Valuation and Community Charge Tribunal*.

*Rebates*

There is a rebate scheme (*Community Charge Benefit*) for those on low incomes. Those on Income Support pay only 20 per cent. of the charge

---

137  Local Government Finance Act 1988, Sched.1, para.4(1) and (2) (England); Abolition of Domestic Rates *Etc.* (Scotland) Act 1987, Sched 1A (added by Local Government Finance Act 1988). There is anxiety lest someone who is severely mentally impaired loses the exemption by seeking work and transferring to the new Disability Working Allowance.

138  1988 Act, Sched.1, para.4(3) (England). For Scotland, see next footnote.

139  The Personal Community Charge (Exemption for the Severely Mentally Impaired) Order 1990, Art.2(2) which puts a new para.4(3) in Sched.1. For Scotland, see the Personal Community Charge (Exemptions) (Scotland) Regulations 1989 and the Personal Community Charge (Exemption for the Severely Mentally Impaired) (Scotland) Regulations 1989 and 1992.

140  Community Charge: Practice Note No. 19 (England).

## Council Tax

This new tax, replacing the Community Charge from April 1993, is basically a property tax which assumes that two people live in a dwelling and assesses properties in valuation bands attracting different levels of tax. If there is only one person there is a 25 per cent. discount, and this discount will also apply to a person in an exempt category but only if one of the two people living in the house is liable for the tax. The exempt categories include "severely mentally impaired" persons as defined for the Community Charge, and some carers will also be exempt if caring for 35 hours a week.[141] Any householder on Income Support has a 100 per cent. rebate, and there will be Council Tax Benefit for those on low incomes.[142] There are also special reductions for some houses adapted for people with disabilities.

## National Insurance contributions

National Insurance contributions are intended to be paid during a normal working life, so they are not payable by those under the minimum school leaving age or by those over pensionable age. There are different classes of contribution depending upon the status of the individual, namely:

| | |
|---|---|
| Class 1 | Earnings related - paid by employers and employees in respect of anyone in employment. |
| Class 2 | Flat rate - paid by the self employed. |
| Class 3 | Flat rate - paid voluntarily by those who wish to enhance an incomplete contributions record. |
| Class 4 | Profit related - paid by self employed persons whose profits exceed a defined maximum. |

Persons with a mental handicap who are in normal employment are liable to make contributions, but those who are not capable of employment usually receive Severe Disablement Allowance which provides contribution credits.

## CIVIL DUTIES

### Voting

An entitlement to vote arises in local government, Parliamentary and European elections, but legal capacity remains unclear.[143] The registration form completed by the householder in October each year does not raise questions of mental capacity so a mentally handicapped resident's name should be included and will then appear on the electoral register.[144]

---

[141] A house with only one carer and a severely mentally impaired person will get a 50 per cent. discount.

[142] Local Government Finance Act 1992.

[143] At common law an "idiot" did not have capacity but a "lunatic" might vote during a lucid moment.

[144] In practice, some registration officers will not enter on the register people who are not eligible to vote.

*Personal voting*

It remains for the presiding officer to challenge the individual when he requests a ballot paper at the polling booth if lack of mental capacity is suspected, and to decide as a question of fact whether he at that moment is sufficiently *compos mentis* to discriminate between the candidates and to answer certain statutory questions in an intelligible manner.[145] These questions include "Are you the person whose name appears on the Register as ....?" and "Have you already voted?" and are inappropriate for determining mental capacity, but no further questions may be put. This procedure is unsatisfactory because it depends more upon ability to communicate unaided than upon actual mental capacity.

*Postal voting*

Some electors are entitled to vote by post. Where an elector applies for this facility, and provided that all other requirements are fulfilled, it must be granted by the registration officer[146]:

    (a) for an indefinite period, if he is satisfied that the elector cannot reasonably be expected to go in person to the allotted polling station or to vote unaided there by reason of blindness or other physical incapacity; or

    (b) for the particular election, if he is satisfied that the elector's circumstances on the date of the poll will be or are likely to be such that he or she cannot reasonably be expected to vote in person at the allotted polling station.

If the individual votes as an absent voter there appears to be no means whereby the vote could be questioned.

*Proxy voting*

An elector who satisfies the postal voting qualifications may also apply to the registration officer for the appointment of a proxy to vote for him at a specific election or for an indefinite period. This must be granted if it meets the prescribed requirements and the registration officer is satisfied that the elector is or will be registered as an elector and the proxy is capable of being and willing to be appointed.[147]

*Mental hospitals*

There are special rules relating to persons in mental hospitals.[148] If they are detained patients they are not treated as resident there,[149] but will not be resident anywhere else and, as it is necessary to be resident in a constituency to be on the electoral register they are effectively disenfranchised. Voluntary patients

---

145 Parliamentary Election Rules, r.35(1). A candidate or the election/polling agent may require the questions to be put to the prospective voter.

146 Representation of the People Act 1985, ss.6 and 7. The new provisions were intended to help carers as well as disabled people.

147 ss.8 and 9.

148 It seems that this includes mental handicap hospitals.

149 Representation of the People Act 1983, s.7(1). This also appears to apply to persons subject to guardianship orders under the Mental Health Acts.

are entitled to register but only if they are able to, and actually do, make a declaration without assistance other than that necessitated by blindness or physical incapacity, and this must be attested by a member of the hospital staff authorised for that purpose by the managers who must be satisfied that the particulars recorded are true.[150] Clearly sufficient mental capacity will be required to overcome this hurdle.

## Jury service

In England the following are ineligible for jury service:
  (a) anyone who suffers or has suffered from mental illness, psychopathic disorder, mental handicap or severe mental handicap and because of that is either resident in a hospital or similar institution, or regularly attends for treatment by a medical practitioner;
  (b) anyone under guardianship;
  (c) anyone whose property and affair are administered by the Court of Protection.[151]

In Scotland, the following are ineligible:
  (a) anyone receiving medical treatment for mental illness or mental handicap who is resident in hospital for such treatment, or attends more than one day of each week to receive it;
  (b) anyone who has a curator bonis;
  (c) anyone under statutory guardianship.[152]

Severely handicapped people who are living in the community and not receiving regular medical treatment are not automatically ineligible, but if such a person is called for jury service and is not thought fit to sit on a jury, the jury office (or clerk of court) should be informed and the summons will usually be withdrawn. A judge may discharge a person who reports for jury service but is considered unable to understand the nature of the oath or the evidence.

## COURT PROCEEDINGS

The involvement of persons with a mental handicap in court proceedings is dealt with elsewhere,[153] but some specific points concerning the liability of such persons are mentioned here.

### Service and admissions

In England, where a document is to be served upon any person who is known to be a patient, the document must be served upon the person, if any, who is authorised to conduct in the name of the patient or on his behalf the proceedings in connection with which

---

150 s.7(4).
151 Juries Act 1974, s.1 and Sched.1 as amended by Mental Health Act 1983.
152 Law Reform (Miscellaneous Provisions) (Scotland) Act 1980, Sched.1, Part.I.
153 See Chap.2, Part I "Civil Proceedings" and Chaps.10A and 10B.

the document is to be served. If there is no such person it must be served upon the person with whom the patient resides or in whose care he is.[154] A patient must not be taken to admit the truth of any allegation of fact made in the pleadings of the opposite party by reason only that he has not in his pleadings either stated that he does not admit it or denied it expressly or by implication.[155]

## Stay of execution

If judgment is obtained against a defendant under mental disability an English court would be sympathetic towards an application for a stay of execution to enable steps to be taken on the defendant's behalf, and should grant a stay to enable an application to be made to the Court of Protection for the appointment of a receiver or for a receiver to pay the liability out of the patient's estate.

## Injunctions and Interdicts

It has been held in England that the fact of disability is not itself a bar to the granting of an injunction against a person suffering under a disability, but that in the case of mental incapacity the question is whether such person understood the proceedings and the nature and requirements of the injunction. If he was incapable of understanding what he was doing or that it was wrong, an injunction ought not to be granted because he would not be capable of complying with it and the injunction would not have a deterrent effect and, furthermore, any breach would not be subject to effective enforcement proceedings since he would have a defence to an application for committal to prison for contempt.[156] The appropriate way of restraining unsocial behaviour by a person under a disability by reason of mental incapacity is the use of the powers under the Mental Health Act 1983 of admission and detention for assessment and treatment, but a limited interlocutory injunction might be appropriate while the mental condition of the person concerned is investigated.

Similar principles would be likely to be applied in Scotland in the event of interdict being sought against a person with a mental disability. The dominant consideration would probably be that of enforceability. Moreover, it is settled law that interdict may only be granted against a wrong, and it is doubtful whether a court would regard conduct as wrongful for this purpose if the necessary mental element were lacking (see section on delict below). In addition, the court has an equitable jurisdiction to grant or refuse interdict, and has for example refused interdict where rights were infringed unintentionally.[157]

---

154 RSC, Ord.80, r.16(2). In this context, patient means "a person who, by reason of mental disorder within the meaning of the Mental Health Act 1983, is incapable of managing and administering his property and affairs".

155 RSC, Ord.80, r.8.

156 *Wookey* v. *Wookey* [1991] 3 All ER 365, CA.

157 See generally *Hay's Trustees* v. *Young* (1877) 4R 398 at 401, and other cases cited in Walker's *Civil Remedies*, pp.215 and 216.

## Tort and Delict

### England

There is little case law on the extent to which mental incapacity affects liability in tort. The question appears to be whether the individual has the requisite state of mind for the particular tort for which he is to be held responsible, and he must behave as would be expected of a person of normal intelligence in the situation. It is no defence that he acted to the best of his own judgment if this is below that of the reasonable man. There is some indication that a lower standard of care is required from an infant, and it may be that this should also be applied to a person who has a mental handicap. In the case of negligence, which depends upon damage arising from breach of a duty of care, the personal characteristics of the defendant do not appear to be relevant save that a higher duty of care may be required from an expert (*e.g.* a professional person in the conduct of his business). Mental incapacity may not therefore be a defence to an action in negligence because the test is objective, but there is no direct authority on the point. Some torts involve strict liability and the mental capacity of the defendant will then be irrelevant, although if the acts complained of were involuntary there may be a defence. If a person who is mentally disordered but who knows the nature and quality of his act commits a tort, it is no defence that he does not know that what he is doing is wrong.[158]

### Scotland

The test of delictual liability of a mentally handicapped person is in each case a factual one dependent on the nature of the alleged wrongdoing and the capacity of the person. The person will have no liability if he lacked rational control of the actions complained of, or if he was not capable of foreseeing possible harmful consequences. Where the delict complained of requires a particular state of mind (such as intent, malice or negligence), the person will not be liable unless he was capable of that state of mind, and in fact had it in relation to the matter complained of. Where the person is liable by these tests, his liability cannot be mitigated on grounds of his handicap. If he was capable of foreseeing that his conduct could have harmful consequences, it is no defence that he was less able than a non-handicapped person to foresee the likely extent of such harm, or the harm which in fact occurred.

Where civil liability is imposed by statute, it is necessary to look to the precise terms of the relevant statute. In some such cases absolute liability is imposed, in which case the mental state of the defender is not relevant. Likewise, mental handicap would not be a defence in cases of strict liability at common law, but the pursuer would have to prove that the requirements for such liability

---

[158] *Morris* v. *Marsden* [1952] 1 All ER 925.

existed, and that despite his handicap the defender was in the position of being the person who incurred the liability in question.

## Evidence in Court

*England*

A mentally disordered adult is in a similar position to a child when giving evidence in court, but there is no statutory provision allowing evidence to be given in criminal proceedings without taking an affirmation or oath.[159] Thus evidence may only be given if the individual understands the nature and consequences of an oath and the duty to tell the truth, but lack of such understanding does not necessarily mean that he or she is unable to give an account of what happened. This is considered further in Part III.

As regards the giving of evidence in civil proceedings, which may include a claim brought by the mentally handicapped person or an attempt to give evidence in support of someone else (*e.g.* a carer), the question of competence will still arise but the oath is not obligatory, and the approach of individual judges to the evidence varies depending upon knowledge of mental handicap, tolerance, understanding and prejudice.

*Scotland*

In neither criminal nor civil procedure in Scotland is it essential that a witness with a mental handicap or other mental disability be capable of understanding and taking the oath. The witness may give evidence if "shown to be capable of making a correct and truthful statement respecting facts as to which he or she is not likely to be mistaken".[160] As with young children, the witness may be admonished to tell the truth, rather than put on oath. The oath will be administered if it is shown that the witness "has a sufficient appreciation of the solemnity of the occasion and the added responsibility to tell the truth, which is involved in taking an oath" over and above the normal social duty of truthfulness.[161] A mentally disabled witness may be examined under reservation of all questions as to the effect of the witness's evidence.

---

[159] *Cf.* Children and Young Persons Act 1933, s.38; Children Act 1989, s.96.

[160] *H.M. Advocate* v. *Skene Black* (1887) 1 White 365.

[161] *R.* v. *Hayes* (1976) 64 Cr. App. R.194.

# PART IIIA - CRIMINAL RESPONSIBILITY AND VICTIMS OF CRIME (England)

## Introduction

There is much concern about involvement of people with a mental handicap with the criminal justice system. They may be accused of or commit criminal offences and they may be victims of criminal acts. Both these topics are dealt with here.[162] Special treatment is needed for those who are suspected or accused of crimes or are convicted because:

- they may not understand the process of investigation and prosecution so need *safeguards*[163];
- they may be found to be under a disability in relation to the trial (*unfit to plead*) so that the trial cannot proceed;
- they may wish to plead that they were insane at the time of the offence and pursue a verdict of not guilty by reason of insanity (*special verdict*). An alternative plea when charged with murder is *diminished responsibility*;
- there will be concern about *detention* in prison while awaiting trial or when sentenced.

Those who are victims of crime may find themselves at a severe disadvantage.

## SAFEGUARDS

There exist certain safeguards for the person with a mental handicap:

- the policy is that people who are mentally disordered should not be prosecuted unless it is in the public interest;
- procedures for the treatment of detained persons make allowances for children and persons of limited intelligence;
- there is a police complaints procedure which may be available in cases of improper treatment.

## Place of safety

Powers are given by the Mental Health Act 1983 to remove a person who suffers from a mental disorder to a place of safety.[164]

*Removal from a public place (s.136)*

A constable who finds a person in a public place who appears to

---

162 Material for this Part was contributed by **Lydia Sinclair**, solicitor and legal officer to MENCAP.

163 The police need training so that they do not accept at face value an admission of guilt obtained from a person with a mental handicap under the stress of being in a hostile environment or as a result of the desire to please and be able to go home.

164 *Mental disorder* in this context it means "mental illness, arrested or incomplete development of mind, psychopathic disorder and any other disorder or disability of mind" and this includes mental handicap and brain damage; Mental Health Act 1983, s.1(2).

suffer from mental disorder can in the interest of that person or the protection of others remove the person to a place of safety. The detention may be for a maximum of 72 hours to enable an assessment and examination by a registered medical practitioner[165] and an approved social worker (ASW) and to allow arrangements to be made for treatment and care in hospital.

This allows a policeman to intervene in a public place, to make a decision that the person is mentally disordered and to detain the person on the basis of that judgement. Practice varies with regard to the use of this section, particularly the location of the place of safety[166] which can be a police cell, residential accommodation, hospital or some other place. There is considerable variation between police districts about the length detention and how quickly an assessment is carried out, and co-operation between police, health and social services is crucial. If an individual is assessed and found to be in need of medical treatment in hospital then an admission under the Mental Health Act may follow.[167] An informal admission may also follow if treatment in hospital is recommended and the individual consents.

Where the assessment results in a decision that no medical treatment as an in-patient is required then the police may be left with a detained person who has possibly committed an offence and who may need some form of community support and/or care. In some cases the police will discharge the person from police custody and it is essential there is planning with social services with regard to such a discharge. The *Code of Practice* under the Mental Health Act 1983 provides guidance on the use of this provision and recommends that a local policy between health, social services and police be written to:

(a) enable competent and speedy assessment;

(b) define the responsibility of police officers while the patient is in a place of safety; and

(c) ensure that there is satisfactory return to the community of the person assessed under section 136 but not admitted to hospital or immediately placed in accommodation.[168]

The Code recommends monitoring of section 136, identification of a place of safety, immediate contact between police, hospital and social services and recording of police action. An individual arrested under the provision is entitled to have another person of his choice informed of his arrest and whereabouts, and the detained person also has a right to legal advice when detained in the police station and where detained elsewhere should be given access to legal advice.[169]

---

165  A psychiatrist approved under Mental Health Act 1983, s.12.

166  Defined in Mental Health Act 1983, s.135.

167  See Chap.4, Part II.

168  Code of Practice, para.10.

169  Police and Criminal Evidence Act 1984, ss.56 and 56 and Code of Practice under the Mental Health Act 1983, para.10.9.

*Entry to premises and removal (s.135)*
An application may be made by an approved social worker (ASW)
to a magistrate for a warrant to authorise a constable to enter
specific premises and remove to a place of safety (as defined
above) a person reasonably believed by the ASW to be suffering
from mental disorder and who has been or is being neglected, ill
treated or not kept under control. This also relates to someone
living alone who is unable to care for himself. The warrant
authorises forced entry by a constable and removal to a place of
safety for up to 72 hours with a view to further assessment and
admission under the Mental Health Act.[170]

## Alternatives to prosecution

A Home Office Circular[171] draws the attention of the courts and
those services responsible for dealing with mentally disordered
persons who commit, or are suspected of committing, criminal
offences to the legal powers which exist and the desirability of
ensuring effective co-operation between agencies to ensure that the
best use is made of resources. The overall aim is to divert
mentally disordered people from the criminal justice system and
keep them out of prisons where this is appropriate. Wherever
possible they should receive care and treatment from the health
and social services, and the use of Mental Health Act powers is
encouraged. This policy can be effective only if the courts and
criminal justice agencies have access to these services and this
requires consultation and co-operation. Additional facilities may
be required if the objectives are to be achieved, and the
Department of Health contributed to the Circular and sent copies
to all health and social services authorities with a letter drawing
attention to their responsibilities for ensuring that sufficient
facilities are available for the care of mentally disordered
offenders.

*Police*
The first point of contact with the criminal justice system is often
the police who should establish close working relationships with
local health, probation and social services to assist them in
exercising the range of powers available to them. Where there is
evidence to show that a mentally disordered person has committed
an offence, consideration should be given to whether prosecution
is required by the public interest, taking into account alternatives
such as cautioning, admission to guardianship or to hospital (if the
person's mental condition requires hospital treatment), or
informal support in the community by social services departments.

*Bail and remands*
Where prosecution is appropriate the individual has the same right
to bail after charge as any other person, and if his mental state or

---

170 See Chap.4, Part II.
171 *Provisions for Mentally Disordered Offenders*, Circular 66/90.

other factors (*e.g.* homelessness) give rise to difficulties, arrangements should be made with health, probation or social services to ensure that appropriate support is provided. Police bail cannot be subject to conditions of residence or medical treatment, but voluntary arrangements may facilitate release rather than detention pending appearance before the magistrates' court. Mentally disordered persons should never be remanded to prison simply for medical treatment or assessment, and courts should receive professional advice at as early a stage as possible on facilities which may be available to assist. Alternatives to custody are considered below under the heading "Hospital and non-custodial outcomes".

*Assessment*

Arrangements should be made with health, probation or social services for assessment to ensure that medical treatment is received if necessary and that the Crown Prosecution Service (CPS) and court can be advised of any particular bail conditions or, after conviction, disposal that may be appropriate. Any information provided by the police with the papers regarding the person's mental condition, or discussions held with other agencies, will be taken into account by the CPS, and where it is satisfied that the probable effect upon his mental health outweighs the interests of justice in the particular case, it will consider discontinuing the proceedings. Where mental disorder is present without there being any indication that proceedings will have an adverse effect, the CPS will take account of the public interest in attempting to ensure that the offence will not be repeated as well as having regard to the welfare of the accused.

The probation service works with other agencies including the voluntary sector, and information about facilities for treatment, accommodation, education and supervision should be pooled. It should provide information to the courts for bail and sentencing decisions and to the CPS in connection with bail information schemes, provide bail and probation hostels, supervise offenders on probation orders and provide for the care and supervision of offenders released from prison on licence and parole. In these ways the service plays its part in diverting mentally disordered persons from custodial remand and keeping them out of prison.

## Code of Practice (PACE)

When any person is detained by the police there are procedures to be followed under the Police and Criminal Evidence Act 1984 (PACE). A *Code of Practice* provides guidance for the police as to the treatment and questioning of detainees and interviewees and *Notes for Guidance* contain specific provisions dealing with mentally disordered and mentally handicapped people. A breach in circumstances which are regarded as unreasonable would raise questions about the validity of police evidence, particularly statements made by vulnerable people in the absence of an appropriate adult or confessions given in circumstances of discomfort and duress.

The Code states that "all persons in custody must be dealt with expeditiously and released as soon as the need for detention has ceased to apply".[172] The general provisions regarding appropriate and considerate treatment of individuals by the police relate also to those voluntarily attending police stations to assist with investigations.[173] The definition of detention includes persons who are mentally disordered and detained at a police station as a place of safety.[174]

### Identifying mental handicap

Special safeguards for persons with a mental handicap are found in paragraph 1.4 of the Code which states:

> "if an officer has any suspicion, or is told in good faith, that a person of any age may be mentally disordered or mentally handicapped, or mentally incapable of understanding the significance of questions put to him or his replies, then that person shall be treated as a mentally disordered or mentally handicapped person for the purpose of this code."

The language used distinguishes between mental disorder and mental handicap and the Notes further clarify the difference.[175]

### "Appropriate adult"

When a detained person has been so identified, a third party, described as an *appropriate adult,* must be brought in to safeguard the rights of the person by being present at interviews and having certain other functions. The appropriate adult in this context is:

(a)  A relative, guardian or other person responsible for his care or custody;
(b)  Someone who has experience of dealing with mentally disordered or mentally handicapped persons but is not a police officer or employed by the police (such as an ASW as defined by the Mental Health Act 1983 or a specialist social worker); or
(c)  Failing either of the above, some other responsible adult aged 18 or over who is not a police officer or employed by the police.

Thus someone with experience in caring for mentally handicapped people is present during interviews and at other times in the police station, but it is recognised that there may be times when a relative without such qualifications would be appropriate if this is the wish of the detained person. A solicitor in the police station in a professional capacity may not act as an appropriate adult.[176]

### Rights of detained persons

Mentally handicapped people have the same general rights when in police custody and being questioned as other detained persons

---

172  Code of Practice, para.1.1.
173  *Notes for Guidance*, para.1a.
174  *I.e.* under the provisions of Mental Health Act 1983, ss.135 and 136; *Notes for Guidance*, para.1.11.
175  *Notes for Guidance*, 1G.
176  See *Notes for Guidance*, 1E and 1F. In cases where communication is very difficult then a carer, parent or teacher with specific skill and experience should be found to act as the appropriate adult.

including the right to[177]:
- be given information about and notice of their rights;
- have someone informed of their arrest;
- be told that free independent legal advice is available;
- consult privately with a solicitor;
- consult the Code and other codes of practice.

### Notice of detention

When a person is brought to a police station under arrest or is arrested at the police station having attended there voluntarily, the custody officer must inform him clearly of his right, which may be exercised at any stage during the period in custody, to have someone informed of his arrest. This can be someone known to the detained person or someone likely to have an interest in his welfare and this person must be informed at public expense as soon as practicable of the detained person's whereabouts. If the person cannot be contacted the detained person can choose two alternative people to be informed and if they cannot be contacted the officer in charge of the detention has discretion to allow further attempts to inform another person. The right can only be delayed in exceptional circumstances and may be exercised each time a person is moved to another police station.

### Consulting a solicitor

A detained person has the right to consult a solicitor and to be told that independent legal advice is available free of charge. The consultation must be in private, either in person or on the telephone. The custody officer must act promptly to secure advice without delay except when the interests of the police investigation would be hindered. No attempt must be made to dissuade the individual from seeking legal advice and when he has requested this he may not be interviewed or continue to be interviewed until his solicitor arrives.[178] Where a solicitor is not available or the detained person does not wish to instruct the duty solicitor then the enquiry can continue without legal representation. In cases where the appropriate adult has been informed of the person's right to legal advice and considers that such advice should be taken, the Code applies as if legal advice has been requested and prompt action to secure such advice must be taken.[179]

### Consulting the Code

There is a right to consult this and other codes of practice, and a detained person who is mentally handicapped will probably need assistance to read and understand these codes.

### Functions of the Appropriate Adult

A custody officer who authorises the detention of a person who is

---

177  Code of Practice, para.3.1.
178  There are exceptions to this which generally cover delays which would cause risk or harm to persons or unreasonable delay to the investigation.
179  See generally para.6.

mentally handicapped must as soon as practicable inform the appropriate adult of the grounds of the detention and ask the adult to come to the police station to see the person. If the appropriate adult is already present in the police station when the detained person's rights are stated to him this must be in the presence of the appropriate adult, but if not then present the rights must be repeated in the presence of the appropriate adult.[180]

### Cautioning

If there are grounds to suspect that the detained person committed an offence, he must be cautioned before being questioned. If he is mentally handicapped and questioned without an appropriate adult present this caution must be repeated in the presence of an appropriate adult. If there is concern that the caution has not been understood it should be explained by the officer in his own words and if necessary further explanation of the significance of the caution must be given.[181]

### Interviews

Interviews with detained persons must be conducted fairly and with particular reference to confessions the Police and Criminal Evidence Act states[182]:

> "... where ... it is represented to the court that the confession was or may have been obtained ... (b) in consequence of anything said or done which was likely, in the circumstances existing at the time, to render unreliable any confession which might be made by him in consequence thereof, the court shall not allow the confession to be given in evidence against him except in so far as the prosecution proves to the court beyond all reasonable doubt that the confession in court (notwithstanding that it may be true) was not obtained as aforesaid".

The Code provides that an accurate record of the interview including place, time of beginning and end, breaks and names of those present must be made. Such record must be read and signed by the detained person, and an appropriate adult or solicitor present at the interview should also read and sign the record.[183] A juvenile or person who is mentally handicapped (whether or not a suspect) must not be interviewed or asked to provide a written statement in the absence of an appropriate adult.[184] This adult is not present at the interview simply as an observer and must be asked to participate as an adviser to the individual being questioned and as an observer that the interview is conducted properly and fairly. If necessary the appropriate adult will be asked to assist communication with the person being interviewed.

---

180  Para.3.11.
181  Para.10.6 and *Note for Guidance*, paras.10C and 10D.
182  s.76(2).
183  Code of Practice, paras.11.5 and 11.11.
184  Para.11.14. There are special provisions with regard to interviewing juveniles and an appropriate adult is also required here. In cases where the detained person is a juvenile who is also mentally handicapped it is important that family and carers are informed immediately and an appropriate adult found as soon as possible.

*Review of detention, charging and searches*

An appropriate adult available at the time of review of the detention must be given an opportunity to make representations to an officer or superintendent about the need for continuing detention.[185] If a custody officer charges a mentally handicapped person with an offence this must be done in the presence of the appropriate adult to whom a written notice is given.[186] A search of a mentally handicapped person can only be conducted in the presence of an appropriate adult of the same sex unless there is a specific request for a particular adult of the opposite sex.[187]

*Implications for mental handicap*

A mentally handicapped person detained in custody is particularly vulnerable so it is important that another person (*i.e.* family member, carer, social worker) be informed as soon as possible of his whereabouts. It is also important that an appropriate adult be found without delay. The following case illustrates this:

> A mentally handicapped person died by committing suicide while on remand in prison. The police had made some attempt to contact an appropriate adult and his father but were unsuccessful. A solicitor had attended the police station in his professional capacity and took the place of the appropriate adult, but as a result no-one was present during questioning and charging to inform the police of his background or his problems.

The Notes for Guidance state that if no-one is identified to be contacted for advice, support or help, the custody officer should consider local voluntary bodies or other organisations who may be able to offer help. This is particularly important for people of no fixed abode or who live in a hostel or are unable to give the name of a contact person or family member. *PACE* seeks to minimise the risk of mentally disordered or handicapped persons giving evidence without intending to do so and without being fully aware of the significance of this and their rights. It is recognised that evidence given in such circumstances may be unreliable, misleading or self-incriminating and the guidance notes emphasise the importance of appropriate and sensitive questioning and in particular the importance of corroboration of any fact admitted. There is provision for interview of detained persons or suspects to be carried out in the absence of an appropriate adult when an officer of the rank of superintendent or above considers that further delay will cause risk to personal property, but this should only be exercised in exceptional cases.

The Court of Appeal has held that the mere fact that there was a breach of *PACE* does not mean that evidence has to be rejected, as it is no part of the court's duty to rule a statement inadmissible simply to punish the police for failure to observe the Code[188]:

---

185 Paras.15.1 and 15.2.
186 Paras.16.1 to 16.3.
187 Annex A, para 5.
188 *R.* v. *Dalaney, The Times*, August 30, 1988.

Following an alleged assault of a young girl the appellant was subject to a 90 minute interview after which he confessed that he had committed the offence. Further admissions were later made. This was the whole basis of the prosecution case and the Judge was asked to rule whether the confession should be admitted in evidence. The Judge's ruling to admit the evidence was overturned on appeal and the conviction quashed. The Court of Appeal recognised that the confession was inadmissible, particularly because of the appellant's age (17 years) and his backward mentality.

The appropriate adult is not governed by the same duty of confidentiality as a solicitor, so it is suggested that the solicitor should not take instructions in the presence of the appropriate adult but should instead tell him what the instructions are so that if they are then related to anyone else the hearsay rules would apply.

## Police Complaints Code

A victim or witness of alleged police misconduct may lodge a formal complaint, but this must relate to the action of identifiable officers and not to police action in general. "Misconduct" means any breach by a police officer of the Police Discipline Code[189] which is extensive and should be consulted before deciding whether to lodge a complaint. Offences under the Code which may arise in respect of a person with a mental handicap include:
- any breach of the Code of Practice;
- failing to react promptly to a request for assistance from a member of the public;
- being abusive or oppressive to any member of the public;
- racially discriminatory behaviour.

The "member of the public" could, of course, be a person with a mental handicap and the complainant could be the parent or carer.

*Procedure*
The complainant, or somebody acting on his behalf, simply writes a letter addressed to the Chief Constable (the Commissioner of Police if in London) setting out the circumstances. The letter should give the date, time and place of the incident and identify the officers involved by name, number or description. It should describe the incident including details of any damage or injuries sustained and also give details of any witnesses. There is an *informal* procedure for conduct which would not justify a criminal or disciplinary charge, and where the complainant agrees that the matter can be resolved informally. An interview with the investigating officer follows. If the complaint cannot be resolved informally, it may be investigated formally either by an *Internal Formal Investigation* or, for the most serious complaints, by the Police Complaints Authority.[190]

*Outcome*
There are three possible findings from the investigation:
- there has been no breach of the Police Discipline Code;

---

[189] Police Discipline Regulations 1985 (SI No.518), Sched.1.
[190] 10 Great George Street, London SW1P 3AE.

- there has been a breach but no action will be taken;  or
- there has been a breach and disciplinary action or criminal proceedings will be initiated against the officer involved.

There is no provision for the payment of compensation.

## FITNESS TO PLEAD

### Criminal Procedure (Insanity) Act 1964[191]

In Crown Court proceedings a person who is judged unable to:
- understand the proceeds of the trial;
- conduct a proper defence;
- challenge a juror to whom he may wish to object;  or
- understand the substance of the evidence

is considered to be "under a disability in relation to the trial" and special provisions apply.[192]

*Background*
Until January 1, 1992, where the accused was found to be under a disability the trial did not proceed and the court would order him to be admitted to a hospital specified by the Secretary of State to be detained subject to restrictions without limit of time.[193] The accused was then in the same position as a patient detained under the Mental Health Act 1983,[194] but had a right for the case to be referred to a Mental Health Review Tribunal and the Secretary of State had power to refer the case back to the court for a trial if satisfied that the accused could be properly tried.[195] The fact that cases were seldom referred back to court in future years was a cause of concern for those detained for long periods in hospital after a finding of unfitness. The accused may never be able to stand trial for the offence yet may not be in need of hospital treatment or custodial care. People with a mental handicap may never have capacity to stand trial and not be "treatable" within the meaning of the Mental Health Act, yet the issue of treatability did not arise when evaluating fitness for trial. The question of a balance between allowing a defendant the right to appear in court and challenge a prosecution case, and protecting a mentally disordered defendant from the trauma of trial was considered by the Butler Committee in 1975 which stated that if the individual was unable to participate in the trial this should be decided as soon as possible to protect the individual from unnecessary stress.[196]

---

[191] As amended by the Criminal Procedure (Insanity and Unfitness to Plead) Act 1991.

[192] The phrase *unfit to plead* has been commonly used.

[193] 1964 Act, ss.4(5) and 5, Sched.1.

[194] *I.e.* under ss.37–41, a Hospital Order with restrictions.

[195] 1964 Act, s.5(4). This only tended to be used in cases where the mental state of the individual improved quickly.

[196] *Report of the Committee on Mentally Abnormal Offenders*, Command Report No.6244 (1975), HMSO, para.10.12.

*Criminal Procedure (Insanity and Unfitness to Plead) Act 1991*
This statute tackles the inappropriate deprivation of liberty that
could arise under the 1964 Act,[197] and the Home Office has issued
a Circular providing guidance to the courts, police, probation
service and health and social services departments.[198] The main
changes introduced are:

(a) where an accused has been found unfit to be tried there will
be a "trial of the facts" to determine whether the jury is
satisfied beyond reasonable doubt that he did the act or
made the omission charged;

(b) where the accused has been found unfit to be tried (but
following a trial of the facts to have done the act or made
the omission) or not guilty by reason of insanity, the court
is given a wider range of disposal options;

(c) the evidence of two or more medical practitioners (one of
whom must be duly approved by the Secretary of State
under the Mental Health Act 1983) is required before an
accused can be found unfit to be tried or not guilty by
reason of insanity.

*Determination and appeal*
The question of disability in relation to trial or fitness to plead can
be raised by the defence, the prosecution or the court and should
normally be determined as soon as it arises, although the court
may postpone this until the defence opens its case which enables
the prosecution case to be tested.[199] A jury must determine the
question of disability,[200] and if this is on arraignment (*i.e.* when
the indictment is read out to the accused and he is asked whether
he pleads guilty or not guilty) and the trial proceeds, a different
jury must then try the case. Where the determination is to be made
at the end of the prosecution case, the court can direct that this be
by the same jury which has been trying the case or a separate jury.
There is a right of appeal for the accused against a finding of
unfitness,[201] but there is no appeal against a finding of fitness to
plead though the accused retains the right to appeal against any
subsequent conviction and sentence.

*Burden of proof*
If the question is raised by the defence it must be proved on a
balance of probabilities and if it is raised by the prosecution it
must be proved beyond all reasonable doubt. It must be decided on

---

197 It was promoted by the Law Society's Mental Health & Disability Sub-
Committee and came into force on January 1, 1992.

198 Home Office Circular No.93/1991, dated November 20, 1991.

199 The detailed provisions are set out in s.2 of the 1991 Act. It follows that the
accused may be acquitted without the issue of fitness to be tried being
considered and without a finding of mental disability being recorded.

200 1964 Act, s.4(4).

201 Criminal Appeal Act 1968, s.15 which provides that the appeal is on a
question of law and with leave of Court of Appeal on either a question of
law or mixed law and fact.

the basis of medical evidence presented to the court. In cases where the issue is postponed to allow the defence to present its case, the question of determining trial at that stage is one for the Judge to be made on the basis of the medical evidence presented and a review of the prosecution case.

*Test of disability*
What constitutes disability is not set out in the statute and is described as "any disability such that apart from the act it would constitute a bar to his being tried ...." This means any disability which by virtue of common law would bar the trial.[202] In *R* v. *Pritchard* the following questions were put to the jury[203]:

> "Is the accused of sufficient intellect to comprehend the course of the proceeding in the trial so as to make a proper defence - to know that he might challenge any of (jury) to whom he may object, and to comprehend the details of the evidence."

There is authority that an accused person who is unable to communicate with his legal adviser should be found unfit to plead.[204] The test of disability is not identical to the categories of mental disorder in the Mental Health Act 1983 or in clinical literature, and the presence of such mental disorder will not automatically mean that a defendant will be found unfit to plead. The finding of a disability is based upon the capacity of the individual to understand the proceedings, and an individual with a mental handicap may be able to do so even though his evidence in defence will as a result be poor.

*Trial of the facts*
If the accused is found unfit to be tried, a trial of the facts follows in which a jury examines the evidence, if any, already given and any further evidence adduced by the prosecution or the defence, and determines whether the accused did the act or made the omission charged. The prosecution must prove this beyond reasonable doubt, but such a finding is not the equivalent of a conviction, and if the jury is not so satisfied the accused is acquitted. The court will not look at the intentions of the accused as this is meaningless for someone who is unfit to plead.
If the question falls to be determined when the accused first appears in court and he is found so fit, the trial proceeds in the normal way but with a new jury. If found unfit, the trial of the facts takes place but again with a different jury. However, where at a later stage in the trial the accused is found unfit to be tried, the ensuing trial of the facts will continue with the same jury.
An accused found unfit to be tried should always be legally represented during the subsequent trial of the facts. If, because of

---

202  For further discussion see Nigel Walker, *Crime and Insanity in England*, University Press Edinburgh, Chap.14, vol.1 (1968).
203  (1836) 7 C and P 303.
204  *R* v. *Burles* [1970] 1 All ER 643, CA. For further discussion see Gostin, *Mental Health Services Law and Practice* Shaw and Sons Ltd (1986), paras.14.05 to 14.07.

mental disorder, the accused repudiates his legal representative the court should appoint a person whom the court considers may properly be entrusted to pursue the accused's interests to put the case for the accused.[205] The Official Solicitor will be appointed where no-one else is able or willing to act and usually then instructs a solicitor in private practice to act on his instructions.[206] Legal aid is not available in these cases but costs are payable from central funds.[207] If on a trial of the facts the accused is found to have done the act or made the omission charged, and admission to hospital is directed, the Secretary of State retains the power to remit the accused to stand trial if while still detained in hospital he subsequently becomes fit to plead. This is unlikely in a case of mental handicap.

## Disposal options

The court is no longer required to order detention in hospital subject to a restriction order without limitation of time of a person found unfit to plead or not guilty by reason of insanity, unless the offence is one for which the sentence is fixed by law (*i.e.* murder). Additional disposal options are now available where the court thinks this appropriate, namely:

(a) an order that the accused should be admitted to such hospital as may be specified by the Secretary of State. The court may also direct that the accused be treated as though subject to a restriction order without limit of time or for a specified period;

(b) a guardianship order;

(c) a supervision and treatment order, requiring the accused to co-operate with supervision by a social worker or a probation officer for a period of not more than two years and with treatment (for all or part of that period) by a registered medical practitioner;   or

(d) an order for the absolute discharge of the accused.

# INSANITY DEFENCE

## Special verdict

If a jury finds beyond all reasonable doubt that a defendant committed an offence for which he is charged, but on the balance of probability that he was insane at the time of the offence and not responsible for his actions, the jury must return a *special verdict*. This is that the defendant is not guilty by reason of insanity.[208]

---

205 This may be the previous advocate or any other solicitor known to the court to have experience in such matters.

206 Such solicitor should be experienced in both criminal law and the law relating to mental health.

207 Prosecution of Offences Act 1985, s.19(3) inserted by 1991 Act, Sched.3, para.8.

208 Trial of Lunatics Act 1883, s.2(1) amended by the Criminal Procedure Insanity Act 1964.

Insanity is a defence which is usually raised by the defence, but in some cases the judge can raise the matter, or the prosecution if the defence claims diminished responsibility.

*Test of insanity*

It is the defendant's state of mind at the time he committed the offence that is important, not his state of mind since the offence or at the time of trial, although information about this may be relevant to the medical expert's judgement about his state of mind at the time of the act. The test of insanity is found in the *McNaghten Rules* of 1843 under which the defence must establish:

> "at the time of the committing of the act, the party accused was labouring under such a defect of reason, from disease of the mind, as not to know the nature and quality of the act he was doing, or if he did know it, that he did not know what he was doing was wrong ...".

The defendant is required to show that his ability to comprehend his actions was affected or that he did not know these actions were unlawful. Disease of the mind is a question of fact based on medical evidence presented to the court during trial. The fact that an individual suffers from a mental illness or handicap will not automatically fulfil the test; this may not actually impair a person's reason to the extent required unless it is very severe. Each case will depend on the facts and the specific medical evidence presented to the court about the defendant's comprehension and understanding of his acts at the time of the offence.[209]

*Sentence*

A finding of not guilty by reason of insanity previously resulted in an automatic order that the defendant be admitted to a hospital designated by the Secretary of State.[210] Such a defendant is detained on a restriction order without limit of time but in certain circumstances a Mental Health Review Tribunal may consider the legality of continuing detention,[211] and the Secretary of State has power to order the patient's discharge from hospital. The sentence categorises the individual as a patient who can be detained either in a special hospital, a county hospital or secure unit and the court has the authority to place such a patient without the consent of the receiving hospital. The patient has then the same rights as other patients under the jurisdiction of the Mental Health Act 1983 with regard to review by Tribunal.

Since January 1, 1991 the court has had the further range of disposal options set out above.[212]

---

209 The Butler Report (see above) recommended a review and amendment of the *McNaghten Rules*. They have been criticised for being vague and unclear and psychiatric evidence does not easily relate to their requirements.

210 An admission must be within two months of the date of the order. Criminal Procedure (Insanity) Act 1964, s.5 amended by the Courts Act 1971, s.56 and Sched.11.

211 Mental Health Act 1983, ss.69(2a), 42, 71(1) and 71(5).

212 Criminal Procedure (Insanity and Unfitness to Plead) Act 1991.

## Automatism.

The special verdict must be distinguished from the defence of *non-insane automatism* which is available when it is proved that a defendant acted unconsciously in doing the act for which he is charged.[213] The result of a successful plea is that the defendant is acquitted, and not held criminally responsible or in need of continuing custodial care. This state of unconsciousness is different from "a disease of the mind" as defined by the *McNaghten Rules*. A court trying to distinguish between "disease of the mind" and other malfunctions which would allow a defence of "non-insane automatism" held that[214]:

> "a malfunctioning of mind of transitory effect caused by application to the body of some external factor such as violence, drugs ... alcohol and hypnotic influences cannot fairly be said to be due to a disease."

This distinction has been much debated in cases involving epilepsy. In one appeal the House of Lords considered whether epilepsy was "a disease of the mind" for the purposes of the *McNaghten Rules*. The defendant who committed an offence of assault and at the time of the offence was suffering from a post-epileptic state wished to plead non-insane automatism. The court held that epilepsy was a disease of the mind and that he would be able to invoke the special verdict as defined under the *McNaghten Rules*.[215]

## Diminished responsibility

The doctrine of diminished responsibility was introduced into English law by the Homicide Act 1957.[216] This is a plea made on behalf of an accused charged with murder. The jury can find that the accused suffered from impaired judgement at the time of the offence and if this plea is successful it will allow conviction for manslaughter and not for murder. The Act provides:

> "where a person kills or is party to the killing of another he shall not be convicted of murder if he was suffering from such abnormality of mind (whether arising from a condition of arrested or retarded development of mind or any inherent causes or introduced by disease or injury) as substantially impaired his mental responsibility for his acts and omissions in doing or being a party to the killing."

The plea must be raised by the defence unless it raises the plea of insanity in which case the prosecution can bring evidence to prove that the defendant was not insane but suffered from diminished responsibility. The defence must prove diminished responsibility on the balance of probabilities, but if the plea is introduced by the prosecution it must prove this beyond all reasonable doubt. The finding of diminished responsibility is one of fact for the jury.

The court can take into account all the facts and circumstances

---

[213] Examples are acts done while in a state of concussion, hypoglycaemia or a drug induced state.

[214] *R v. Quick* [1973] 3 All ER 347, CA.

[215] *R v. Sullivan* [1983] 2 All ER 673.

[216] s.2(1).

relating to the offence, not just the medical evidence, and the judge must explain to the jury the statutory provisions. The success of the plea will depend on the medical evidence presented in support, and if no medical evidence is presented the judge is not required to put the issue to the jury.[217] If the medical evidence is clear in support of the plea the Judge can find without reference to the jury.[218]

The phrase "abnormality of mind", which has been much criticised by psychiatrists and lawyers, has been defined as follows[219]:

> "... a state of mind so different from that of ordinary human beings that the reasonable man (*i.e.* a man with a normal mind) would term it abnormal. It appears to us to be wide enough to cover the mind's activities in all its aspects, not only the perception of physical acts and matters, and the ability to form a rational judgement as to whether the act was right or wrong, but also the ability to exercise will-power to control physical acts in accordance with that rational judgement."

It is interpreted widely by the courts and is much wider than "defective reason" under the *McNaghten Rules*. It includes the defendant's knowledge, understanding, freedom to act and will-power, and is not synonymous with categories of mental disorder defined under the Mental Health Act 1983. A finding of mental disorder will not therefore necessarily mean a successful plea of diminished responsibility.

*Sentencing*

The judge has wide discretion as to sentence and the medical reports submitted to the court will be crucial. If these recommend treatment for a mental disorder in hospital the judge will probably make a hospital order.[220] A prison sentence can be imposed if no need for treatment is shown but such environment is generally recognised to be inappropriate for persons with a mental handicap. A non-custodial sentence may be imposed if the court is satisfied that there is no danger to the public and that appropriate support and care are available in the community. It is therefore important that all the relevant and social information is available.

## HOSPITAL AND NON-CUSTODIAL OUTCOMES

### Preliminary

The police can divert a person with a mental handicap into the hospital system or the community without pursuing a prosecution when such prosecution is not considered to be in the public interest and medical treatment and/or alternative care is thought to be appropriate. Where such a person is convicted of an offence the

---

[217] *R* v. *Dicks* (1982) 74 Cr App R 306.

[218] *R* v. *Cox* [1968] 1 All ER 386, CA. Medical reports should be sought from a specialist in mental handicap with experience and knowledge of forensic psychiatry.

[219] *R* v. *Byrne* [1960] 3 All ER 1.

[220] *I.e.* the patient is detained in hospital and subject to the Mental Health Review Tribunal provisions of the Mental Health Act 1983.

courts have powers to impose sentences which do not involve custody in prison.

When charged with a serious offence it may be necessary to remand the accused in custody. In the case of mentally disordered persons an application for bail with a condition for treatment may be appropriate, and alternatives to prison custody should be considered such as residence on a hospital ward as a condition of bail, or residence in a bail hostel with a condition for medical treatment. Solicitors, carers and other representatives should monitor the progress of such persons detained in prison, whether on remand or following sentence, and press for transfer to a hospital where their mental health is deteriorating, because they are unlikely to receive appropriate medical care in prison.

## Powers

Various powers are granted by the Mental Health Act 1983.

*Remand for reports (s.35)*

The court may remand the accused to hospital for a report on his mental condition. This is available:

(a) to a Crown Court for any person awaiting trial for an offence punishable with imprisonment or who has been arraigned for such an offence and not yet sentenced;

(b) to a magistrates' court for any person convicted of an offence punishable on summary conviction with imprisonment and any person charged with such an offence if the court is satisfied that he did the act or made the admission charged or has consented to the exercise by the court of its powers.

The court must be satisfied, on the written or oral evidence of a registered medical practitioner (RMP) that there is reason to suspect that the accused person is suffering from mental illness, psychopathic disorder, severe mental impairment or mental impairment and that a report on the person's mental condition would be impracticable if the person were remanded on bail.

*Remand for treatment (s.36)*

The Crown Court may order that the accused be remanded to hospital for treatment instead of in custody. This is available when the court is satisfied on the written or oral evidence of two RMPs that the person suffers from mental illness or severe mental impairment of a nature or degree which makes it appropriate for him to be detained in hospital for medical treatment (these criteria are referred to again below). It can be used for an accused person in custody awaiting trial before the Crown Court for an offence punishable with imprisonment (other than an offence with a fixed sentence) or who prior to sentence is in custody during the course of the trial. The court must be satisfied that a bed will be available for the person within seven days beginning with the date of remand. Further remands are possible for not more than 28 days at a time or 12 weeks in all.

*Transfer to hospital (ss.48 and 47)*
A remand (unconvicted) prisoner can be transferred from prison to hospital if the basic criteria for section 36 are satisfied and he is in urgent need of treatment.[221]
A convicted person who is serving a sentence of imprisonment can be transferred from prison to hospital if broadly similar criteria are satisfied (though the mental impairment need not be severe) and the treatment is likely to alleviate or prevent a deterioration of his condition.

*Alternative sentences (ss.37)*
In the case of a person convicted:
  (a) before a Crown Court of an offence punishable with imprisonment (other than one with a fixed sentence); or
  (b) by a magistrates court of an offence punishable on summary conviction with imprisonment,
the court may authorise admission to and detention in such hospital as may be specified in the order or place the person under guardianship of the local social services authority. This order can be made if the above criteria are satisfied and (in the case of mental impairment) the treatment is likely to alleviate or prevent a deterioration of his condition or (in the case of an offender who has attained the age of 16 years) the mental disorder is of a nature or degree which warrants his reception into guardianship. The court must be satisfied, taking into account the circumstances of the offence and the character and antecedents of the offender, that this is the most suitable method of disposing of the case.
The above orders for hospital detention and guardianship may be imposed on a person charged before a magistrates court where the above criteria are satisfied without convicting him.

*Interim hospital orders (s.38)*
In the above circumstances the court can make an interim hospital order if there is reason to suppose that the mental disorder from which the offender is suffering is such that it may be appropriate for a hospital order to be made in his case, and the court is satisfied that a bed will be made available. The order can be made for a period not exceeding 28 weeks and can be renewed for further periods of not more than 28 days at a time but not more that six months in all.

*Availability of hospital bed (s.39)*
The court cannot generally make a hospital order unless satisfied that a bed will be made available to the individual within the required time period (seven or 28 days), so the accused's solicitor should ensure that appropriate medical reports are available and that the hospital has committed a bed to that person. While the

---

221 This applies to persons detained in prison or remand centres, persons remanded in custody by a magistrates' court, civil prisoners and persons detained under the Immigration Act 1971.

court cannot compel a hospital to admit a particular person, it can require the Regional Health Authority for the region in which the person resides or last resided (or any other RHA that appears appropriate) to provide information about hospitals in the region at which arrangements could be made for an admission of that person. This provision allows courts to put some pressure on RHAs to explain their bed provision and with particular reference to individuals who in the court's view require hospital care.

## VICTIMS OF CRIME

Victims and their carers require support, information about the criminal justice system, and advice on remedies for injury or damage suffered and compensation schemes available. They do not qualify for legal aid.[222]

## Prosecution

When an individual alleges that an offence has been committed against him, there must be an immediate decision about involving the police and any serious offence should be reported. The victim may go to the police direct or with help from a parent, carer or other person. The staff in a residential care home or hospital may wish to report the matter to the police direct but this often depends on the ability of the victim to speak up. The victim should be consulted and where possible consent to a referral to the police. Once the matter is reported the victim is asked whether he wishes to press charges and after that the police investigation takes over.

### Investigation

The police are concerned with gathering evidence and taking statements. They have a discretion whether to prosecute and the decision is based on the seriousness of the offence, the wishes of the victim and the public interest, but the final decision is made by the CPS who review the police file. The victim will not be involved in this process except as a witness providing a statement and any other evidence to support a prosecution case. A statement can be taken immediately the offence is reported or left until later, especially is the victim is upset or confused, but he has a right to a copy.[223] There is no legal requirement for a statement to be taken before the complaint is noted and investigated. The victim may be asked to be photographed to provide evidence of bruising or other physical damage, and to take part in identification of suspects either informally or by means of a formal identification parade, and to identify photographs.

In cases of physical or sexual abuse, immediate police involvement is important to enable them to collect corroborative forensic evidence and conduct a physical examination of the victim. The enquiry can be distressing to the victim so training is provided for

---

222 The *National Victim Support Scheme* provides advice and support for victims in both England and Wales, and Scotland.

223 Home Office Circular 82/1969.

police and specialist teams to undertake this with sensitivity.

*Press coverage and information*
The police regularly report crimes to the local press and reports of an offence, particularly an assault, can be upsetting for the victim. Practice varies on how much information about victims is given and in cases of vulnerable victims a request should be made to withhold name and address. There will also be press coverage of a trial and the victim may be subjected to considerable media attention, though rape victims must not be identified.[224]
Policy varies as to information given to victims. Increasingly the practice is to tell them of an arrest, of a decision to prosecute or not, and of the outcome of a trial. Many victims feel excluded from the process and require advice and support to clarify their role as a prosecution witness and not as a party to proceedings.

## Evidence

The victim may be a major witness and his capacity to give clear evidence and to cope with cross examination and the trauma of a public appearance in the witness box will be crucial to the success of the trial. In some cases there will be no prosecution because of lack of reliable evidence or corroboration.

*Pigot Report*
The Report of the Pigot Committee on Video Evidence concluded that children should be kept away from criminal trials as much as possible, and give their evidence at an informal preliminary hearing which would be video-recorded and shown at the eventual trial which the child would not attend. Only the judge, counsel and the child, with a supporter, would be physically present at this hearing which the defendant would view through a television link with an audio link to his counsel.[225] The Committee could see no reason in principle why measures designed to reduce the stress experienced by witnesses and so ensure that the court receives clearer and fuller testimony should be restricted to children. The Report concluded that vulnerable adult witnesses should eventually be able to give evidence on the same general basis as proposed for children, but that judges should have considerable discretion both in determining the eligibility of vulnerable witnesses to testify and the techniques to be allowed in individual cases. A vulnerable witness would be one who, in the view of the court, would be likely to suffer "an unusual and unreasonable degree of mental stress" if required to give evidence in open court. The court would have regard to the physical and mental condition of the witness, and the nature and seriousness of the offence charged and of the evidence which the witness was to give. It would take account of information from those responsible for the health or welfare of

---

[224] Sexual Offences (Amendment) Act 1976.
[225] This would apply to a child under 14 years, or under 17 years in the case of an offence of a sexual nature.

the witness and hear objections from the opposing party before reaching its decision.

*Competence*
It is for the judge to examine potential witnesses to ascertain whether they have the necessary understanding of the concepts of truth and duty and the burden of proving this rests with the party calling the witness. If the judge is not satisfied beyond reasonable doubt that a prosecution witness has the requisite understanding he will not be allowed to give evidence. It has been stated that it is "ridiculous" to suppose that any value could be attached to the evidence of a 5 year old witness,[226] and in consequence evidence is seldom given by young children unless they seem to have the understanding normally expected of a child of about 8 years.[227] This makes it virtually impossible to convict offenders who molest very young children in private.

The Pigot Committee considered that the unofficial age restriction could not be justified, that young children were no more likely to give inaccurate or untruthful evidence than other witnesses and that it was wrong for the courts to refuse to consider any relevant understandable evidence. Judges and juries should weigh matters such as the demeanour of the witness, his or her maturity and understanding and the coherence and consistency of the testimony, in deciding how much reliance to place upon it. Some of the proposals of this Report concerning the giving of evidence by children and young people in criminal proceedings have been implemented.[228] The evidence of a child (under 14 years of age) in criminal proceedings shall now be given unsworn, and provision is made for a video recording of an interview with a child or young person[229] to be admitted in evidence with the leave of the judge in certain criminal proceedings. There has been criticism that these provisions do not go far enough, and represent the minimum to reduce the stress of child witnesses. The Government resisted amendment but undertook to "monitor the implementation and operation of what are important reforms", and to support the provision with an advisory Code of Practice.[230]

*Implications for mental handicap*
Problems arise for mentally disordered people in three areas:
  - it is difficult, especially if their evidence cannot be given, to obtain convictions for offences against them because evidence in corroboration is seldom available;
  - they may suffer unacceptable levels of stress when giving

---

226  Lord Goddard in *Wallwork* (1958) 42 Cr.App.R.153, approved by Court of Appeal (Criminal Division) in *Wright and Ormerod* (1987) unreported.

227  In Scotland where there is a similar formal competence requirement, it is not unusual for children as young as 4 years to give evidence.

228  Criminal Justice Act 1991, ss.42 and 44. These respectively insert new ss.33A and 32A in the Criminal Justice Act 1988.

229  *I.e.* under 17 years. The age at the time of the video recording counts.

230  Hansard (House of Lords), April 22, 1991, col.83.

evidence;
- judges and juries tend to regard their evidence with suspicion through unfamiliarity with the nature and effects of particular kinds of disability.[231]

Because people with a mental handicap are often expressed as having a mental age which equates to that of a young child, they may be denied an opportunity to give evidence in a criminal court, yet be even more vulnerable to physical and sexual abuse than a child. Whereas the child no longer needs to take and understand the oath, this remains a hurdle for the mentally handicapped witness.[232] The individual may also have difficulty communicating his evidence and this can produce a stressful situation exacerbated by any impatience shown. Is it sufficient for the judge to decide whether the individual is capable of giving evidence without hearing evidence as to actual competence and reliability? The recommendations in the Pigot Report are a step in the right direction, but until implemented the law which has hitherto applied to children will continue to apply to persons with a mental handicap even though it no longer applies to children!

## Compensation

The victim of a crime may obtain compensation for damage to his property or person as a result of a crime in one of three ways:
1. a criminal compensation order;
2. a claim for damages in the civil courts;
3. a claim to the Criminal Injuries Compensation Board.

*Criminal compensation order*
The court which convicts an individual of an offence can make an order for compensation in addition to or instead of another sentence.[233] If the offender cannot pay both adequate compensation and fine, the compensation should be given priority. The amount will reflect the damage resulting to the victim from the offence for which the accused is convicted or any other offence taken into consideration by the court in deciding on sentence.[234] The courts have laid down the following guidelines for such an order:
- it is not an alternative to sentence;
- it should take into account the defendant's finances;
- the amount must not be oppressive and take into account that discharged prisoners are often short of money and if ordered to pay compensation might commit further offences;
- the amount must be realistic and an order for payment by

---

231 Psychiatric evidence as to capacity could sometimes be helpful, but there is doubt about whether such evidence may be admitted.

232 Public disquiet has been expressed over a 1990 case where a young mentally handicapped woman was not allowed to give evidence in a case of alleged rape because she was assessed as having a mental age of seven years.

233 Powers of the Criminal Courts Act 1973 as amended by the Criminal Justice Act 1982.

234 The maximum amount in the magistrates court is £2,000.

instalments over a long period should be avoided;
- an order should only be made when it is clear that the
  defendant is under a legal liability to compensate.

In England there are few compensation orders and awards tend to
be very low. In Scotland there is a system to allow the prosecution
to obtain information on a regular basis about injuries suffered by
victims and loss of property; a form is provided by the prosecutor
for the individual to complete and there is a more systematic
approach to identifying a need for compensation of victims.

### Civil action for damages

A victim will have a civil action in assault in cases of personal
violence and in trespass for loss of or damage to property. The
decision about a civil action will depend on whether the offender
has means to pay compensation or is insured, and the victim must
be able to fund the action or qualify for legal aid. The standard of
proof in civil courts is "on the balance of probabilities" and in
criminal courts is "beyond all reasonable doubt", so a civil claim
may be pursued in a case where a criminal trial did not take place
or the defendant was acquitted.

## Criminal Injuries Compensation Scheme

*The material under this heading relates also to Scotland.*

Anyone who has been injured as a result of a crime of violence
can apply to the Criminal Injuries Compensation Board[235] for
payment of compensation even if the injuries were caused by
someone who is unknown, or has not been prosecuted or could not
be held responsible under the criminal law (*e.g.* because insane).
The incident must have been reported to the police without delay
and the claimant must have helped the police in bringing the
offender to justice and not have been responsible for the incident
(otherwise the award may be reduced or even refused). Motoring
offences are not included. The claimant's character and way of life
are taken into account.

### Procedure and time limits

A claim can be made on behalf of a person with a mental handicap
and will be accepted if the application form is completed by a
parent or other responsible person even if the claimant is an adult.
However, if an award is made it may be necessary to apply for the
appointment of a receiver or curator bonis to whom the money
will be paid, though the Scheme provides that arrangements such
as payment to trustees may be established.[236] Legal aid is not

---

[235] Address in Appendix I.

[236] Para.9. In England this may be necessary for an infant (as the Court of
Protection has no jurisdiction) and it may also be preferred for adults
especially in the case of small sums (though the short procedure order is
then available - see p.552). In Scotland it is clearly more appropriate to
establish such a trust than to set up a curatory for an uneconomically small
amount - see p.612. As payments are *ex gratia* it is suggested that payment
can be made to anyone the Board considers suitable, and the question of a
valid receipt should not arise.

available but advice and assistance can be given by solicitors under the green form scheme[237] and applications can be made for extensions for this work.

There is a time limit of three years from the date of the injury for submitting the claim, but late claims may be accepted if there is good reason for the delay as shown in the following case:

> The parents of a mentally handicapped woman instructed solicitors to make any appropriate claims on behalf of their daughter following an assault in which she sustained personal injuries. They obtained claim forms from the Board but did not submit these and the time limit expired. Another firm of solicitors was then instructed and when they gave an explanation the claim was accepted out of time.

The mental condition of the victim, leading to delayed disclosure[238] or delay in making the claim, could amount to good reason for a late claim, and possibly also ignorance of the scheme.

### Awards and appeals

Awards are of an *ex gratia* nature representing what a court would award for the injury with a minimum level below which an award will not be made.[239] The award will include the following:

- compensation for pain and suffering;
- loss of earnings to date as a result of injury;
- loss of future earnings and a sum to reflect difficulty in obtaining future employment.

The award is usually paid as a lump sum, but will be reduced to take into account any other compensation received for the same injury and social security payments must be deducted in full. It must be repaid to the extent that compensation is subsequently received from another source.

There is no right of appeal but if not satisfied with the decision initially made by a Board member the claimant may ask for a hearing which would be in private before three other members who have the power to make an award, reject the application, or increase or decrease the amount. The members of the Board are all experienced lawyers.

### Implications for mental handicap

It may be possible for a claim to be made on behalf of a person with a mental handicap who is the victim of sexual abuse although special rules apply in this type of case. The following case illustrates a situation in which a claim may be appropriate:

> A 25 year old mentally handicapped woman was being looked after in a local authority hostel during a period of respite care when, in the temporary absence of a member of staff, another resident thrust a glass in her face causing scarring and a consequent fear of returning to any form of residential care. The incident was reported to the police who felt unable to prosecute because of the difficulty of getting evidence. The parents contemplated taking proceedings against the local authority for damages for negligence on behalf of their daughter but were reluctant to do so because this would involve

---

237 In Scotland, legal advice and assistance.
238 *e.g.* in the case of physical or sexual abuse of a mentally disabled person.
239 £1,000 from January 6, 1992.

making allegations which could prejudice their future relationship with the authority. Instead the father submitted a claim to the Criminal Injuries Compensation Board and an Award was made without difficulty. A short procedure Order was made by the Court of Protection in favour of the father to enable him to handle the compensation.

# PART IIIB - CRIMINAL RESPONSIBILITY AND VICTIMS OF CRIME (Scotland)

## Introduction

Concerns in Scotland about the involvement of people with a mental handicap with the criminal justice system are similar to those in England as described in Part IIIA, but in some significant areas the response to those concerns is less well developed.[240] Scottish readers may accordingly find it helpful, when considering some of the topics described below, to refer also to the equivalent sections of Part IIIA.[241]

Here we consider ways in which account may be taken of a person's mental handicap at the various stages of reporting and investigating a suspected crime, detention and arrest, trial and disposal, and we also consider the mentally handicapped witness and victim. Except in circumstances where medical examination takes place as normal routine in all cases, initial identification of a mental handicap and of its possible relevance necessarily depends upon non-medical people. This can result in delay or even failure in identifying a significant mental handicap, particularly where there are no very obvious physical manifestations of the handicap and (as is increasingly the case with improved training and normalisation programmes) superficial social and communication competence masks the true degree of intellectual disability. Conversely, there are some cases where people with a relatively mild mental handicap have learned to attract sympathy and special treatment when it would be better for their long-term development that they should have to face up to the consequences of at least some of their actions: for some, this may be a necessary part of "normalisation". It is often unsafe to rely upon lay assessment of such matters, and important to obtain expert assessment at an early stage.

*Principal legislation*
  Police (Scotland) Act 1967
  Criminal Procedure (Scotland) Act 1975

---

[240] *e.g.* Where England has the Code of Practice (PACE) described on pp.64 *et seq.*, Scotland has only the unpublished guidance referred to below, and Scotland has no legislation equivalent to the Criminal Procedure (Insanity and Unfitness to Plead) Act 1991 even although there is equal need in Scotland for such provisions. (Developments in the two jurisdictions are in general uneven - *cf.* the Scottish development of the tutor-dative as personal guardian, which has as yet no counterpart in England - and each could perhaps be more ready to learn from and apply the experience of the other).

[241] See *Mentally Disturbed Offenders: The Report of a Working Party*, SACRO

Criminal Justice (Scotland) Act 1980
Mental Health (Scotland) Act 1984
Referred to as the 1967 Act, 1975 Act, 1980 Act and 1984 Act.

*Definitions*
For definitions of nearest relative, mental health officer and responsible medical officer see Chapter 4, page 205. References below to detention in hospital and to guardianship should be read in conjunction with the relevant sections of Chapter 4, Part IIB.

## SAFEGUARDS

### Suspects and witnesses

Scots law has no equivalent to the English Code of Practice described in Part IIIA,[242] but similar safeguards are recommended in unpublished guidance from Scottish Office Home and Health Department to Chief Constables. The English Code includes certain specific rights, such as the right to consult the Code in case of detention: it is unfortunate that Scottish safeguards are not similarly published and made available, and that there seems to be marked reluctance by individual police forces to disclose their own guidelines.[243]
The Scottish guidance applies where a mentally handicapped (or mentally ill) person comes into contact with the police either as a suspect or as a witness (including a witness who is a victim). The provisions of the guidelines are in addition to normal rights and duties which by law apply to all people, handicapped or not. In the case of mental handicap, the guidelines apply if an officer has any suspicion, or is told in good faith, that a person of any age may be mentally handicapped, or may be mentally incapable of understanding the significance of questions put or of his replies. In such circumstances the officer should immediately have an "appropriate adult" informed why the person is with the police and requested to attend at the police station.

*Appropriate adult*
The Scottish definition of an appropriate adult is similar to the English definition, and is as follows:
  (a) A relative, guardian or other person responsible for [the handicapped person's] care or custody;
  (b) Someone who has experience of dealing with mentally ill or mentally handicapped persons but who is not a police officer or employed by the police; or
  (c) Failing either of the above, some other responsible adult who is not a police officer or employed by the police.
It is envisaged that the appropriate adult should be someone who

---

242 See pp.64-68.
243 The Crown Office plans shortly to issue detailed advice to procurators fiscal on witnesses who have mental handicaps. See "Advice on interviewing techniques" below.

has appropriate experience or training rather than someone such as a relative who may lack these, but where practicable a clearly expressed preference by the person for a relative will be respected, even if the relative is less well qualified, though the appropriate adult should not be a person who is suspected of involvement or is a victim. The function of the appropriate adult is to provide support and reassurance to the person and where possible to facilitate communication. The appropriate adult should not seek to exercise an active role, for example by objecting to questions or advising the person whether or how to answer them beyond the extent necessary to facilitate communication.

### Interviews

The guidance points out that people with a mental handicap may often be able to provide reliable evidence, but may also be prone to providing information which is unreliable, misleading or self-incriminating, and stresses the importance of obtaining independent confirmation and of having the appropriate adult present throughout the interview with the handicapped person, except where an inspector or higher officer considers that delay would involve immediate risk to persons or property or would prejudice the interests of justice or the person's wellbeing. Even in such exceptional circumstances, questioning should cease as soon as it has elicited enough evidence to avert the envisaged risk.

Wherever possible the appropriate adult should be present when information about rights and entitlements is given[244] and when the person is cautioned and charged. If an appropriate adult is not there, such steps should be repeated in the appropriate adult's presence. The appropriate adult may see documents signed and statements made, and should be invited to sign them and to note any points of disagreement. An appropriate adult of the same sex should be present during an intimate search.

If a case goes to trial, the court should take account of a person's mental disability in considering whether an interview was fair, and thus whether evidence concerning it is admissible. In one case it was held that the interview was unfair because it was conducted in such a friendly manner that the person would not have realised the seriousness of the situation.

### Comment

Guidance is not given as to how a police officer might identify that a person has a mental disorder. The role of the appropriate adult is more restricted than under the PACE Code of Practice: for example, under the English Code he participates as an adviser and observer to ensure a fair interview (see page 65 *et seq.*).

The guidance does not explore the reasons why interviewers unskilled in dealing with mentally handicapped people may elicit

---

244 *e.g.* Information to a detained person about the nature of the offence suspected, the reason for detention and the right to have a solicitor and some other person informed (1980 Act, ss.2 and 3).

only incomplete or misleading information. There may be difficulties of comprehension or communication. The person may focus unduly on aspects which others consider less important. Many have been conditioned to try to please, and will give the response which they think is expected or hoped for, avoiding a reply which in their view might lead to conflict. They will answer questions literally, and are unlikely to answer implied questions which are not specifically spelled out.

> Andrew was charged with breach of the peace by running up behind two girls in the street, and continuing to run behind them when they fled in alarm. Throughout police interview, with a social worker present, the only answer which he gave to the question "why were you running" was that he was in a hurry. No-one explicitly explored why he was in a hurry. He agreed that he probably frightened the girls. He told his solicitor that he had missed an earlier bus, and was running back to his hostel because if he missed a deadline he would lose pocket-money. This explanation was verified and reported to the procurator fiscal, who took no further action.

*Advice on interviewing techniques*

Advice on interviewing techniques and procedures, with helpful background information on relevant aspects of mental handicap, is contained in a forthcoming paper to be issued by the Crown Office to procurators fiscal, but which - when published - should be studied by police officers and by lawyers dealing with mentally handicapped people as witnesses and in other contexts.[245]

## ALTERNATIVES TO PROSECUTION

Most commonly, a suspected crime is either reported by the public to the police or detected or witnessed by the police themselves. The police investigate; may detain a person for up to six hours for the purpose of investigating an offence[246]; may obtain a warrant to arrest, or arrest without warrant when necessary in the interests of justice; has various powers to search, take fingerprints and conduct identity parades; may caution and charge; and report offences to the procurator fiscal. The procurator fiscal, or in some cases the Crown Office, decide whether to prosecute. We consider here various outcomes other than prosecution, and the routes by which a person with a mental handicap may reach such an outcome, by considering the roles of public, police and prosecutor. The remainder of this section assumes that a mentally handicapped person has committed an offence, or has done something which, if done by a person of unimpaired capacity, would be an offence, or is suspected of one of the foregoing.

---

245 Bull and Cullen *Witnesses who have mental handicaps*. The Scottish author is grateful to the Crown Office for making a draft available to him and for permission to refer to it in this work.

246 A constable must have reasonable grounds for suspecting that the person has committed (or is committing) an offence punishable by imprisonment; 1980 Act, s.2(1).

## Public

Possible courses of action by members of the public include
- *informal action*, such as ignoring the incident, or remonstrating with the mentally handicapped person, or escorting him home, and so forth;
- *reference to other agencies*, such as putting the person in touch with medical help or referring the matter to the social work department (who may in turn initiate one of the Mental Health Act procedures described in Chapter 4, Part IIB);
- *common law detention*, under which a member of the public may impose temporary restraint upon a mentally disordered person "who has run amok and is a manifest danger to himself or to others" and detain him for long enough to hand him over "to proper authority"[247];
- *citizen's arrest*, by a private citizen who has witnessed a serious crime, who must hand the person over to a police officer as soon as possible;
- *report to the police*.

Under the last three options, any decision whether to follow an alternative to prosecution is passed to others, usually in the first instance the police.

## Police

The police view of their own role has been described as that of providing "the only real twenty-four hour service of social help",[248] and in relation to people with a mental handicap who get into trouble they may follow the alternatives of *informal action* or *reference to other agencies* described above. Other courses open to the police, not necessarily mutually exclusive, include those described below.

*Removal from public place*
A constable may remove to a place of safety[249] a person whom he finds in a public place, and who appears to be suffering from a mental disorder and in immediate need of care and control, if the constable thinks that such removal is necessary in the interests of the person or for the protection of others. The purpose of this action is to enable medical examination to be carried out and any necessary arrangements to be made for treatment and care. As soon as practicable after removing the person to the place of safety, the constable must inform someone responsible who resides with the person and also the nearest relative.[250]

*Medical examination*
The police have a duty to take every precaution to ensure that any

---

247 *B.* v. *Forsey* 1988 SLT 572 (HL).
248 Chiswick *et al. Prosecution of the Mentally Disturbed*, p.30.
249 1984 Act, s.118. See p.61 for definition of a "place of safety". The person may be detained there for up to 72 hours.
250 For definition of "nearest relative", see Chap.4, p.205.

person charged with an offence is not unreasonably and unnecessarily detained in custody.[251] Such precautions include obtaining medical advice if it is possible that by reason of a mental disorder the person is not fit to be detained in police custody. Following medical examination the person may be kept in custody; or formal Mental Health Act procedure may be followed; or the person may voluntarily accept treatment; or may simply be released.

### Report to prosecutor

Where an offence has been committed, the duty of the police is to report the matter to the appropriate prosecutor so that the offender can be brought to justice with all due speed.[252] Thus, whether the person has been kept in custody or released, where the police are satisfied that an offence has been committed the decision whether to proceed with prosecution will pass to the procurator fiscal (or the Crown Office).

## Prosecutor

The procurator fiscal has the duty to make enquiries into alleged offences within his area. Once he has before him all necessary and available information and evidence, he or an advocate depute in the Crown Office must decide whether to prosecute. We consider first the circumstances in which a prosecutor may seek psychiatric advice in the course of discharging the first of these duties, and then relevant principles which may guide his decision in discharging the second.

### Medical reports

Procurators fiscal generally obtain psychiatric reports in all cases of alleged murder, sexual offences and fire-raising. In other cases they will seek reports if they have reason to believe that there is or could be an element of mental disorder which could be relevant to the decision whether to prosecute. Factors prompting such a decision include evidence of unusual behaviour by the accused or information that the accused has or may have a mental disorder or psychiatric history. Such information may come from records of previous cases (such as a previous hospital order) or may be provided by the defence or accused. It is entirely appropriate for anyone concerned for the welfare of a person with a mental handicap to ascertain whether a report has been made to the procurator fiscal and, if so, to ensure that the procurator fiscal is aware of any relevant information concerning the mental handicap. In relation to minor offences it may be possible to give the procurator fiscal existing medical information which may suffice for his purposes.

### Decision whether to prosecute

The prosecutor must first decide whether the evidence shows that

---

[251] 1967 Act, s.17.
[252] 1967 Act, s.17.

a crime has been committed and is sufficient to justify criminal proceedings. If so, the prosecutor still has a fairly broad discretion to decide whether it is in the public interest and in the interests of justice that a prosecution should proceed.[253] Evidence of a mental handicap or other mental disorder will be taken into account, but in the context of the whole circumstances and consequences of the alleged offence, and other relevant factors such as the accused's record and the likely sentence for the offence, rather than in isolation. It would be a relevant consideration, for example, that the offence would probably not have been committed had the person been receiving appropriate care, treatment or guidance, and that following the offence this was being provided. The prosecutor may decide to take no proceedings, and may leave the matter at that, or may in addition arrange for alternative procedure (such as a Mental Health Act procedure) to be initiated, or for the accused to be guided towards appropriate help, for example by directing him to a social work or psychiatric diversion scheme.[254] Where it is thought that counselling or support might prevent a repetition of the offence, the decision whether to prosecute may be deferred to enable the accused to co-operate: after a set period the case is reviewed, and if the accused has co-operated the prosecutor may then decide to take no proceedings. The prosecutor may also issue a warning, which can be a valuable course where a prosecution is considered inappropriate but on the other hand the person is capable of understanding a warning that his conduct was unacceptable and that he cannot expect to be able to repeat it with impunity. Here also, it is appropriate for those concerned for the welfare of the person to ensure that relevant considerations and possible alternative disposals are drawn to the attention of the prosecutor: they can expect a sympathetic response provided that their contribution is presented in an informative and reasonable way, and that they recognise that full responsibility for any decisions rests with the prosecutor.

### Prosecution
In the following sections we consider matters which may be relevant if the prosecutor decides to initiate proceedings.

## "INSANITY"

### Definition and defences
Although antiquated concepts of "insanity" are difficult to apply in the context of many forms of mental illness, and quite inappropriate to mental handicap, use of this term persists in

---

253   For discussion of such considerations in relation to s.106 of the 1984 Act, see *The Power to Act*, Chap.IX (see Further Reading).

254   There are several social work diversion schemes, and a few psychiatric diversion schemes, including those in Inverness and in Glasgow, where the scheme at the Douglas Inch Clinic involves psychiatrists, psychologists and social workers.

relation to any situation where some form of mental disability (including mental illness and mental handicap) affords a defence to a criminal charge.[255] We consider below the two distinct pleas of insanity in bar of trial (unfitness to plead) and insanity as a defence.[256]

## Fitness to plead

A plea of insanity in bar of trial is concerned with the mental state and capability of the accused at time of trial.[257] The defence will succeed if it is shown that, due to mental disability, the accused is not capable of making a decision to plead guilty or not guilty, or of instructing his legal advisers so that his defence can be properly conducted.[258]

### Plea prior to trial

To enable the accused to be psychiatrically examined, he is either liberated on bail with a condition that he attends for such examination, or is remanded in custody in prison or hospital.[259]

### Procedure at trial

A plea of insanity in bar of trial should be intimated at least ten days before the trial (solemn procedure) or before the calling of the first witness (summary procedure), but the matter may in practice be raised at any time, even during the trial, and if it appears that the accused cannot give instructions the prosecutor is obliged to raise the matter with the judge if the defence does not. The judge himself may also raise the matter. However it is raised, the issue of insanity in bar of trial is normally determined on the basis of separate examinations by two psychiatrists (or psychologists may be more appropriate in mental handicap cases).

## Insanity defence

The defence of insanity is concerned with the mental state and capability of the accused in relation to the alleged crime. In the case of mental handicap, the defence is likely to succeed if it is established that the accused's handicap deprived him of rational control of his conduct or reactions in relation to the criminal act which he is alleged to have committed, or deprived him of proper appreciation of the circumstances and of the ability to act or react on the basis of such appreciation.[260] If the plea is successful, the

---

255 For discussion of the problems of definition, see Blackie & Patrick, *Mental Health: A Guide to the Law in Scotland,* para.5.1:4.

256 For legislation see 1975 Act, ss.174, 375 and 376.

257 Though the plea may be tendered at any time during the proceedings.

258 Both the High Court and the Sheriff Court may deal with such a plea, but District Courts may not, so that District Court cases require to be transferred to the Sheriff Court, 1975 Act, s.376(4).

259 Remand in a psychiatric hospital is often preferable to prison, but the court must be satisfied that a suitable bed is available, and lack of a suitable bed can lead to inappropriate detention in prison or police cells. See "Outcomes" below and 1975 Act, ss.25 and 330.

260 *HM Advocate* v. *Kidd* 1960 JC 61.

accused is acquitted, but the plea is rarely taken because the outcome is often regarded as more serious than the likely penalty upon conviction. Moreover, the static nature of most mental handicaps (contrasting with the fluctuations of many mental illnesses) means that in most cases where an insanity defence would be likely to succeed the accused will be found unfit to plead. However in some cases an accused with a mental handicap may also have a mental illness, and if the degree of handicap is relatively mild the person may be fit to plead, but the question of an insanity defence may arise because of the combined effects of the handicap and the illness in relation to the alleged criminal act.[261]

## Outcomes

If the accused is found unfit to plead due to insanity, or succeeds in a defence of insanity, then in solemn procedure the judge must order him to be detained without limit of time in the State Hospital at Carstairs (or in another hospital, if there are special reasons for sending the accused there). The accused may only ever be discharged by the Secretary of State, or by appeal to the Sheriff.[262] Under summary procedure, in the case of unfitness to plead the accused is also ordered to be detained in hospital, but not necessarily in the State Hospital nor without limit of time; and the court will proceed similarly in the case of a successful defence on grounds of insanity where the "insanity" arises from mental handicap.[263]

These outcomes will occur, and the accused will find himself committed to hospital, notwithstanding that the court will not have made any decision as to whether the accused in fact did what he was charged with having done, and notwithstanding that some other disposal which would have been available on conviction might have been more appropriate. This situation has been addressed in England by the Criminal Procedure (Insanity and Unfitness to Plead) Act 1991.[264] It is not known why that Act did not include appropriate equivalent provisions for Scotland, but it is understood that Scottish Office Ministers are now reviewing the law in Scotland in the light of the changes made in England.

## Diminished responsibility

The defence of diminished responsibility applies only in relation to a charge of murder. If the plea succeeds, the accused will be convicted of culpable homicide rather than murder. In the case of mental handicap, it must be shown that while the handicap is not sufficient for a defence of insanity, responsibility and

---

261  There is evidence that the incidence of mental illness is higher than average among mentally handicapped people.

262  See also Chap.4, Part IIB.

263  But in *Smith* v. *M.,* 1983 SCCR 67 the court held that it could not order hospitalisation when the accused had recovered.

264  See Part IIIA above.

accountability for the person's actions are impaired.[265]

## HOSPITAL AND NON-CUSTODIAL OUTCOMES

This section describes outcomes which might occur by reason of mental handicap where the mentally handicapped accused has been prosecuted and convicted, *i.e.* where no alternative to prosecution has been followed, there has been no successful plea of insanity in bar of trial or as a defence, and the accused has pled or been found guilty.

### Remand for report

Before passing sentence the court may remand the person in custody or on bail for up to three weeks (renewable for up to three weeks at a time) for the purpose of obtaining a psychiatric report prior to passing sentence.[266]

### Interim hospital orders[267]

Before making a final decision as to the disposal of the case, the High Court or Sheriff Court may order the person to be detained in the State Hospital at Carstairs, or for special reasons in another hospital, for up to 12 weeks (renewable for up to four weeks at a time, up to a maximum total period of detention of six months) if
- the person has been convicted of an offence punishable with imprisonment (other than murder, for which life imprisonment is mandatory); and
- the court is satisfied on the evidence of two doctors that the person has a mental disorder which could be treated in hospital.

If the court makes such an order, it may not at that stage order imprisonment, impose a fine or make a probation or community service order, but may impose a driving disqualification or order forfeiture of goods where appropriate. When the interim hospital order ceases to have effect, any disposal which was competent at time of conviction may be applied, other than another interim hospital order.

### Hospital and guardianship orders - general

The High Court and the Sheriff Court may make a hospital or guardianship order if
- the person has been convicted of an offence punishable with imprisonment; and
- the court is satisfied on the written or oral evidence of two doctors that the Mental Health Act criteria for detention or guardianship[268] apply, provided that the doctors agree that

---

[265] For definition of diminished responsibility see *HM Advocate* v. *Savage* 1923 JC 49, per Lord Alness at p.51.

[266] 1975 Act, ss.180 and 381.

[267] 1975 Act, ss.174A and 375A.

[268] See "Persons liable to be detained", Chap.4, p.209, and "Criteria for guardianship", Chap.4, p.214.

the relevant criteria apply and agree as to the form of mental disorder; and

- the court is of the opinion that the order in question is the most suitable disposal, having regard to the nature of the offence, the character and antecedents of the person, and other available disposals.

If the court makes a hospital or guardianship order it may not imprison or fine the person, or make a probation or community service order, but may impose a driving disqualification or order forfeiture of goods where appropriate.[269]

## Hospital orders

An additional requirement before a hospital order may be imposed is that the court must be satisfied that the hospital can admit the person within 28 days. The court may commit the person to the State Hospital at Carstairs, but only if satisfied on the medical evidence that special security is required and that suitable care is not available in another hospital. Following admission, the person is in the same position as a patient detained under the Mental Health Act "formal procedure" described in Chapter 4,[270] and the same renewal provisions apply, but the patient may not be discharged by the nearest relative.[271]

*Restriction orders*

A restriction order may be made for a specified or unlimited period, and while it is in force the person may only be discharged by appeal to the Sheriff[272] or by the Secretary of State.[273] The other methods of discharge (by the responsible medical officer, Mental Welfare Commission or nearest relative) only become available if the person remains a detained patient after expiry of a limited restriction order. A restriction order can only be made if a psychiatrist gives oral evidence to the court, and if it appears to the court that the order is necessary to protect the public from serious harm, having regard to

- the nature of the offence,
- the person's antecedents, and
- the risk of further offences resulting from the person's mental disorder should he be set at large.[274]

When a person is subject to a restriction order the normal provisions regarding duration, renewal and expiration of detention do not apply; the consent of the Secretary of State is required for

---

269  1975 Act, ss.175, 176, 376, 377.
270  Part IIB, pp.209 *et seq.*
271  1984 Act, s.60 and Sched.2, Part I; see also s.34(3).
272  The person may appeal to the Sheriff between the sixth and twelfth months of detention and in any subsequent period of 12 months. The Sheriff may order absolute or conditional discharge. See 1984 Act, ss.63 and 64.
273  1984 Act, s.68. See s.62(2) regarding provision of periodic reports by the responsible medical officer to the Secretary of State.
274  1975 Act, ss.178 and 379.

leave of absence and for transfer to another hospital; if leave of absence is granted the Secretary of State (as well as the responsible medical officer) may recall the patient; and there is no time-limit for detaining and re-admitting a patient absent without leave.[275]

## Guardianship orders

In addition to the general requirements described above, a guardianship order may only be made if the court is satisfied
- having considered the evidence of a mental health officer, that the order is necessary in the interests of the person's welfare; and
- that the proposed guardian is willing to act as such.

Once the person has been received into guardianship the normal provisions for statutory guardianship apply except that the nearest relative cannot discharge the person from guardianship.[276]

## Appeal

A person may appeal against an interim hospital order (but not renewal thereof), a hospital order, a restriction order or a guardianship order in the same way as he may appeal against sentence.[277]

## Probation orders

If the court is satisfied on the evidence of a psychiatrist that a person's mental condition requires and may be susceptible to treatment, but detention in hospital is not warranted, then the court may make a probation order with a requirement to submit to medical treatment for up to 12 months. The treatment may be as an in-patient[278] or out-patient, or by a specified doctor. The court must be satisfied that necessary arrangements have been made (including availability of a bed for in-patient treatment). The category of treatment may be altered if the doctor treating the patient thinks this appropriate and the patient and probation officer both agree.[279]

Non-compliance with the treatment condition may result in having to give an explanation in court, or in arrest, and may be followed by a sentence. However refusal to undergo particular treatment is not a breach of the probation order if the court considers that the refusal was in the whole circumstances reasonable.[280]

## Deferred sentence

The court may defer sentence subject to such conditions as the court may determine, and may accordingly impose a condition that the person undergo treatment. Breach of such a condition cannot

---

[275] 1984 Act, s.62(1) and Sched.2, Part II.
[276] 1984 Act, Sched.2, Part III, para.7(c). See Chap.4, Part IIB, p.217.
[277] 1975 Act, s.280.
[278] But not in the State Hospital.
[279] 1975 Act, ss.186 and 387.
[280] 1975 Act, ss.186 and 387.

result in sentence prior to expiry of the deferment, but will be taken into account then, when the court may still impose any sentence which could have been imposed at time of conviction.[281]

## TRANSFER

We deal here with procedures for transfer to hospital of a person in prison awaiting trial, or awaiting sentence, or after sentence. In all cases the person may only be transferred from prison to hospital if it appears to the Secretary of State that the statutory criteria for detention apply.[282]

### Before trial or sentence

The Secretary of State may apply to the Sheriff for a *transfer order* transferring the person to hospital. Two medical reports must be submitted to the Sheriff. The Sheriff may make the order if satisfied that the statutory criteria for detention apply. The order has the same effect as a hospital order with an unlimited restriction order (see above), but the Secretary of State may transfer the person back to prison if the responsible medical officer reports that treatment for mental disorder is no longer required, and in any event the order lasts only until the case against the person is disposed of by the court or dropped. If the person is still in hospital when sentenced, he will continue as a detained patient (as if admitted under the normal procedure described in Chapter 4, Part. IIB) if the court does not imprison him or make a hospital, guardianship or probation order.[283]

### After sentence

In the case of a person serving a sentence of imprisonment,[284] if the Secretary of State is satisfied on the basis of two medical reports that the criteria for detention apply, he may make a *transfer direction* transferring the person to hospital. The effect is the same as that of a hospital order (see above). Within one month the person may appeal to the Sheriff, and if the Sheriff is not satisfied that the criteria for detention apply the person is returned to prison.[285]

The Secretary of State may also make a *restriction direction*, which has the same effect as a restriction order (see above), but may last only as long as the remaining period of the prison sentence.[286] The same provisions for appeal to the Sheriff apply,

---

[281] 1975 Act, ss.219 and 432.

[282] See "Persons liable to be detained", Chap.4, p.209.

[283] 1984 Act, ss.70 and 73.

[284] And also civil prisoners and persons detained under the Immigration Act 1971.

[285] 1984 Act, s.71.

[286] See 1984 Act, s.74(5) and (6) for assessment within last 28 days before the restriction direction expires, and procedure to continue to detain the person in hospital thereafter, failing which the person must be released when the restriction direction expires (s.74(4)).

but if the appeal is successful the person may be returned to prison, or released on licence or subject to supervision, or remain as a detained patient.[287]
The Secretary of State must return the person to prison or (if the prison could have done so) may release him on licence, if the Secretary of State is satisfied (a) that the person no longer suffers from a mental disorder requiring treatment as an in-patient or (b) that such treatment is not necessary for the person's health and safety or the protection of others, and (in either case) that the person need not be liable to recall for hospital treatment. If (a) or (b) applies but the person may need to be recalled to hospital for treatment, the Secretary of State has a discretion to return him to prison, release him on licence or keep him in hospital.[288]

## VICTIMS OF CRIME

### Cross-references

See "Victims of crime" in Part IIIA (England) (page 79 *et seq.*) for general discussion of relevant issues, and for coverage of the operation of the Criminal Injuries Compensation Scheme in both England and Scotland (page 83). The section on "Safeguards" above (page 86 *et seq.*) describes provisions applicable both to suspects and to witnesses, including witnesses who are victims. The giving of evidence in court by a mentally handicapped person is dealt with on page 60.

### Compensation order

When an individual is convicted of an offence the court may make an order for compensation in addition to or instead of dealing with him in some other way, provided that the court does not proceed by way of absolute discharge, probation or deferred sentence. The amount of compensation may not exceed the maximum level of fine which the court could have imposed (which means that there is no limit upon conviction on indictment of a common law offence). If the offender cannot pay both adequate compensation and fine, the compensation should be given priority: if both are imposed, the compensation is paid first from payments received. Payment and enforcement are dealt with by the court, not by the victim. A compensation order may not be made in relation to a road accident, or in relation to the death of any person, but otherwise compensation may be ordered for any injury, loss or damage resulting directly or indirectly from the offence, though the court must have regard to the means of the offender when assessing compensation. The amount actually paid under the order is deducted from any civil damages for the same loss.[289]

---

287  1984 Act, ss.63, 65, 72 and 74(3).
288  1984 Act, s.74. Amendment to ss.74 and 75 is proposed in the Prisoners and Criminal Proceedings (Scotland) Bill 1992.
289  1980 Act, ss.58-67.

## Civil action for damages

Crimes of violence and against property will usually give rise to a right of civil action for reparation. Legal advice and assistance is available to investigate such claims, and legal aid to pursue them, subject to the relevant financial qualifications and, for proceedings, to the Scottish Legal Aid Board being satisfied that there is a probable cause. Failing legal aid or legal expenses insurance, the claimant must be able to fund costs himself, except to the extent that costs may ultimately be retrieved from the defender, and must bear in mind the risk of having to meet the defender's expenses if unsuccessful. As the standard of proof in civil claims is "on the balance of probabilities" rather than the criminal standard of "beyond all reasonable doubt", a civil claim may succeed even though there was no prosecution, or an unsuccessful prosecution.

# PART IV - PERSONAL RELATIONSHIPS

*Preliminary*

It is usually inappropriate for decisions to be made by others in regard to personal relationships, so it is important to determine whether the individual can, or should be allowed to, make such a decision and carry it into effect because if not the individual is deprived of a fundamental freedom. It is not unusual for persons with a mental handicap to want to marry and they should have this right like anyone else,[290] although until recently every effort was made to dissuade them. The first obstacle may be for them to make their wishes known to persons who will take them seriously, but assuming that they can overcome this obstacle, the legal implications of marriage must be considered.

## MARRIAGE (England)

## Capacity

Marriage is a simple contract, which it does not require a high degree of intelligence to understand.[291] The consent of a parent is only required for a person aged between 16 and 18 years. The parties must truly consent to the marriage and understand the nature of marriage and the duties and responsibilities it creates.[292] The fact that a party is totally unfit for marriage would appear to be irrelevant, though it may result in resistance by others to the marriage in the first place, and could render the marriage voidable. Consent will not be validly given if it was given under

---

[290] European Convention on Human Rights, Article 12 states: "Men and women of marriageable age have the right to marry and to found a family, according to the national laws governing the exercise of this right".

[291] *Durham* v. *Durham* (1885) 10 P D 80 at p. 82, per Sir J. Hannan P.

[292] *Re Park* [1953] 2 All ER 1411.

duress or there was mistake as to the person being married or the nature of the ceremony. However, lack of consent only makes a marriage *voidable* and not *void*.

*Caveat*

If someone believes that a party to a proposed marriage does not have the necessary capacity, they can enter a *caveat* at the relevant registration office or church and this puts the registrar or clergyman on notice and creates a requirement to investigate the matter.[293] The burden of proof of lack of capacity falls on the person seeking to oppose the marriage and medical evidence may be required. The Superintendent Registrar will give the person who gave notice of marriage an opportunity to answer the objection and to produce evidence in rebuttal, and there is a right of appeal to the Registrar General against a refusal to issue a certificate of marriage because a caveat has been entered.

*Banns*

Most Anglican weddings take place after the reading of banns in church and this may give an opportunity to concerned persons to record an objection to the proposed marriage causing an enquiry to be made as to capacity of the parties to enter into the ceremony.

*Detained patients*

It is now possible for a marriage ceremony to take place in a mental hospital for a detained patient.[294] Previously it was difficult for a patient compulsorily detained in hospital to arrange a ceremony of marriage due to restrictions on being allowed outside the hospital. These provisions only relate to the location of the marriage ceremony and do not give anyone the right to marry who did not already possess that right. Hospitals should arrange careful counselling for any detained patient who wishes to marry, and possibly for the prospective spouse. Anyone, including the doctor in charge of the patient's treatment, who does not believe that the patient is capable of giving valid consent, may enter a caveat with the Superintendent Registrar before the ceremony.[295]

## Nullity

Marriages may be void or voidable.

*Void marriages*

Since the Nullity of Marriage Act 1971 a marriage will be void only if certain of the necessary formalities have not been complied with, the parties are within the prohibited degrees of relationship or not respectively male and female, or one of them is under 16 years of age or already married. In all other circumstances the marriage will be voidable only.

---

[293] Marriage Act 1949, s.29. A doctor or anyone else may take this step, but there must be good grounds for doing so, because if not a liability could arise for the registrar's costs and damages to the couple.

[294] Marriage Act 1983, s.1.

[295] DHSS Circular LAC (84) 9.

## Voidable marriages

There are several grounds upon which a marriage may be voidable at the instance of one of the parties[296] but the following are relevant to situations where one party has a mental handicap:
- incapacity by either party to consummate the marriage;
- wilful refusal by respondent to consummate the marriage;
- either party did not validly consent to the marriage;
- at the time of the marriage either party, though capable of consenting, was suffering from mental disorder within the meaning of the Mental Health Act 1983, of such a kind or to such an extent as to be unfitted for marriage.

There must be apparent consent for the ceremony to take place, so the question is whether this is accompanied by the necessary intention. Mental handicap only vitiates consent if the party was, at the time of the ceremony, incapable of understanding the nature of the marriage and the duties and responsibilities it creates.[297] The fact that the party is totally unfit for marriage is irrelevant in the context of consent, but the fourth ground above was introduced to cover the case where the afflicted party is capable of giving a valid consent but has a mental disorder which makes him or her incapable of carrying on a normal married life. Such person may even petition on the basis of his or her own mental disorder.

## Bars to a decree

There are no bars to the granting of a decree if one of the grounds on which a marriage is void is established. However, proceedings on the basis of lack of consent must be commenced within three years of the marriage, though the court may give leave for the proceedings to be instituted at a later date if the petitioner has at some time during the three year period suffered from mental disorder and it is in all the circumstances just to do so. In addition the court may not grant a decree in the case of a voidable marriage if the respondent satisfies the court that:
   (a) the petitioner, with knowledge that it was open to him to have the marriage avoided, so conducted himself in relation to the respondent as to lead the respondent reasonably to believe that he would not seek to do so; and
   (b) it would be unjust to the respondent to grant a decree.[298]

## Conclusion

Severe mental handicap which prevents a party consenting to the marriage merely makes it voidable, and a petitioner may obtain a decree of nullity on the basis of the respondent's mental disorder even though he or she knew of that condition at the time of the marriage. This presumably allows for the situation where the mental disorder becomes worse after the marriage, but in the case

---

[296] The Matrimonial Causes Act 1973 consolidated the earlier legislation, but has been amended by the Marriage Act 1983, s.2(4).

[297] *Re Park* [1954] P 112.

[298] Matrimonial Causes Act 1973, s.13(1).

of mental handicap the condition is usually static so it is questionable whether a party can seek to have a marriage annulled because he or she asserts that the reality is worse than he expected.

## Divorce

We consider here the divorce of a person with a mental handicap, and in the next chapter we shall look at the implications of the mental handicap of a child upon the divorce of parents. Until the Divorce Reform Act 1969 the dissolution of marriage was based upon the concept of the matrimonial offence,[299] but an exception to this was introduced in 1937 when unsoundness of mind became a ground for divorce available to the other party subject to certain severe limitations. Mental subnormality which, though not mental illness, rendered a patient incapable of looking after himself or his affairs outside an institution, or of standing up to the ordinary problems of married life, could constitute unsoundness of mind.[300]

### Irretrievable breakdown

The 1969 Act provided that "the sole ground on which a petition for divorce may be presented to the court by either party to a marriage shall be that the marriage has broken down irretrievably". However, the court may only be satisfied of this if the petitioner establishes one of five "facts", namely[301]:

(a) that the respondent has committed adultery and the petitioner finds it intolerable to live with the respondent;
(b) that the respondent has behaved in such a way that the petitioner cannot reasonably be expected to live with the respondent;
(c) that the respondent has deserted the petitioner for a continuous period of at least two years immediately preceding the presentation of the petition;
(d) that the parties to the marriage have lived apart for a continuous period of at least two years immediately preceding the presentation of the petition and the respondent consents to a decree being granted;
(e) that the parties to the marriage have lived apart for a continuous period of at least five years immediately preceding the presentation of the petition.

### Behaviour

Before 1969 when cruelty was one of the grounds for a divorce, it was necessary to show wilful conduct, or that the cruel conduct was aimed at the other party. This made it difficult to obtain a divorce on this ground where the intended respondent was incapable of appreciating the effect of his or her behaviour. It is now the effect of behaviour on the petitioner that is relevant.

### Consent

The validity of a mentally disordered respondent's consent to a decree of divorce following two years' separation depends on whether he or she has the capacity to understand the nature of the consent and to appreciate the effect and result of expressing it.[302]

---

299 Adultery, cruelty and desertion.
300 *Robinson* v. *Robinson* [1964] 3 All ER 232.
301 Matrimonial Causes Act 1973, s.1(2).
302 *Mason* v. *Mason* [1972] 3 All ER 315.

If the respondent is incapable of managing his or her property and affairs so that a guardian *ad litem* must be appointed, a divorce may not be obtained on the basis of consent.

## Judicial separation

The grounds for obtaining a judicial separation are the same as for a divorce, so the points noted above are relevant.

## Financial provision

When considering what orders to make dealing with the finances of the parties following a divorce, it is the duty of the court "to have regard to all the circumstances of the case". First consideration is given to the welfare of any minor child of the family, but there is a list of matters to which the court should in particular have regard and this includes[303]:

(a) the income, earning capacity, property and other financial resources which each of the parties to the marriage has or is likely to have in the foreseeable future, including in the case of earning capacity any increase in that capacity which it would in the opinion of the court be reasonable to expect a party to the marriage to take steps to acquire;
(b) the financial needs, obligations and responsibilities which each of the parties to the marriage has or is likely to have in the foreseeable future;
(c) the standard of living enjoyed by the family before the break down of the marriage;
(d) the age of each party to the marriage and the duration of the marriage;
(e) *any physical or mental disability of either of the parties to the marriage*;
(f) the contributions made by each of the parties to the welfare of the family, including any contribution made by looking after the home or caring for the family;
(g) the conduct of each of the parties, if that conduct is such that it would in the opinion of the court be inequitable to disregard it
(h) . . . . . .

There is little evidence of para.(e) above having been considered as a separate matter by the courts and it may not add much to the other matters, but is worthy of further consideration by lawyers. As regards para.(g) it is unlikely that the conduct of a spouse with a mental handicap would be taken into account especially if (as is likely) such handicap was known and accepted by the other spouse at the time of the marriage.

## Welfare of children

When considering whether to make orders in regard to a child of the family the welfare of the child is the paramount consideration, but amongst the other matters to be taken into account are[304]:

(a) the ascertainable wishes and feelings of the child . . . . ;
(b) his physical, emotional and educational needs;
(c) the likely effect on him of any change of circumstances;
(d) his age, sex, background . . . ;
(e) any harm which he has suffered or is at risk of suffering;

---

303 Matrimonial Causes Act 1973, s.25 as amended by Matrimonial and Family Proceedings Act 1984.
304 Children Act 1989, s.1(3). For the Orders that can be made see s.8 and Chap.3, Part II.

(f) how capable each of his parents...is of meeting his needs.

Clearly a mentally handicapped parent is at a disadvantage when it comes to questions of continuing care for the child, and if both parents are handicapped the possibility of care being transferred to others cannot be excluded. However, the range of orders now available is much more flexible and this should enable handicapped parents to have as much contact with their child as is consistent with the child's welfare.

## Procedure

The Family Proceedings Rules 1991 make special provision in respect of parties in matrimonial proceedings who are incapable by reason of mental disorder of managing and administering their property and affairs.[305] Such persons are deemed to be under a disability and commence proceedings by a next friend and defend them by a guardian *ad litem*.[306] The Rules provide how such representatives are to be appointed and interaction with the Court of Protection is provided for. Where proceedings have been commenced against a person who there are reasonable grounds to believe is under a disability and no notice of intention to defend has been given, an application must be made to the District Judge for directions before any further steps are taken. In certain circumstances documents will be served on the carers of the person under a disability.

## MARRIAGE (Scotland)

To be valid, a marriage must conform to the formalities of the law of the place where it is celebrated. A regular marriage in Scotland may be either civil or religious. Marriage may also be constituted irregularly by cohabitation with habit and repute.

## Capacity

For a marriage to be valid, both parties must be capable of understanding the nature of and consenting to marriage, and be over the age of 16. Parental consent is not required. Neither may be already party to a subsisting marriage. The parties must be male and female, and must not be related within degrees prescribed by statute.[307] On any of the foregoing grounds, an intended marriage may be objected to, and a purported marriage may be declared void. An intended marriage may also be objected to if one or both parties is not of Scottish domicile and the marriage would be void by the law of the domicile.

### Objections

Each party to an intended marriage must submit a marriage notice to the registrar for the district where the marriage is to be

---

305 See Part IX, r.9.1-9.5.
306 See Part I of this chapter, at p.37 *et seq.*
307 See Marriage (Scotland) Act 1977, Sched.1.

solemnised (whether by civil or by religious ceremony). Birth certificates, documentary evidence of termination of any previous marriage and certain certification where the parties are related must be produced, but no other evidence of capacity is required, except that a party domiciled abroad must if practicable produce a certificate that he or she has no known legal incapacity by the law of domicile. The names of the parties and proposed date of marriage are displayed, normally for at least 14 days. An intending objector may examine the entries in the marriage notice book, and anyone may state objections. Unless the objection is trivial, it is referred to the Registrar General for determination. The statutory grounds of objection include that "one or both of the parties is or are incapable of understanding the nature of a marriage ceremony or of consenting to marriage".[308] In construing this provision, the Registrar General would be likely to have regard to the heavy onus of proof upon anyone challenging validity of a marriage on such grounds (see below).

*Celebration of regular marriage*
If the district registrar is satisfied that there is no legal impediment, he makes up the marriage schedule and the marriage may take place. A civil ceremony normally takes place in the registrar's office, but he may on application celebrate the marriage elsewhere if either party is unable to attend the registrar's office "by reason of serious illness or serious bodily injury" and there is good reason why the marriage cannot be delayed until attendance at the registrar's office is possible.[309] It could be argued that the phrase quoted does not cover mental handicap, but one would expect the phrase to be given a broad construction where the person does have sufficient capacity to marry and one of the consequences of the handicap is inability to attend the registrar's office. A religious marriage may be celebrated by an authorised celebrant, upon production of the marriage schedule, and there is no legal restriction as to precisely where within the registration district it may take place. Marriage by proxy is not possible in Scotland.

*Marriage by cohabitation with habit and repute*
If the requirements for marriage by cohabitation with habit and repute are met, the law presumes that the parties have tacitly agreed to marry and thus are married, unless it is proved that they never intended to be husband and wife. The requirements are that the parties must live together as husband and wife, in Scotland, for long enough to infer tacit agreement to marry, and must be uniformly regarded to be husband and wife. The parties must also have legal capacity to marry, but if an initial impediment subsequently ceases to apply, the parties may thereafter become married by this method. It is possible that a mentally handicapped

---

[308] s.5(4)(*d*).
[309] s.18.

person might have difficulty in communicating or otherwise demonstrating sufficient comprehension and capacity on any one occasion in advance of a proposed regular marriage, yet might be seen to have developed sufficient understanding and commitment over a period of cohabitation. Without such capacity, the fundamental proposition of tacit agreement would of course be lacking. While there is some authority that a marriage void for lack of effective consent may be validated by the parties continuing to live together as husband and wife, it has been suggested that the better view is that this situation is covered by the doctrine of cohabitation with habit and repute.[310]

## Void marriages

Where there is a legal impediment or defective consent, the purported marriage is void and of no legal effect, whether or not proceedings are taken to have it declared void. Where such proceedings are taken, the onus of proof is upon the party seeking to establish that the marriage is void. It was held in *Long* v. *Long*[311] that there is a very heavy onus upon a person seeking declarator of nullity on grounds of lack of capacity through mental illness or mental handicap. This approach is now reinforced by the assertion of the right to marry in Article 12 of the European Convention on Human Rights.[312] A marriage is likely to be void if consent were induced by force or fear. While no relevant precedents exist, it is generally considered that the test would be the subjective one of whether the will of the party was in fact overcome by such duress, which need not be physical.[313] This principle could be relevant where a mentally handicapped person has sufficient capacity but is believed to have been pressurised.

An action for declarator of nullity may be brought in the Court of Session by a party to the marriage, or by anyone with a legitimate interest.[314] The validity of a marriage may be asserted in an action of declarator of marriage before the Court of Session.

## Voidable marriages

If at the time of the ceremony one or both parties was permanently and incurably impotent, a party to the marriage may have it annulled. Unless and until either does so, the marriage remains valid. This is the only ground on which a marriage is voidable, rather than void.

---

310  *Stair Memorial Encyclopaedia*, Vol.10, para.826.

311  1950 SLT (N) 32.

312  "Men and women of marriageable age have the right to marry and to found a family, according to the national laws governing the exercise of this right".

313  Clive, *The Law of Husband and Wife in Scotland*, (2 ed.), pp.100-101, *Stair Memorial Encyclopaedia*, Vol.10, para.824.

314  There is a paucity of precedent as to who has a legitimate interest, see Clive, *op. cit.,* p.123. The Accountant of Court has refused to sanction challenge by a curator of a marriage entered by his ward.

## Divorce[315]

The Divorce (Scotland) Act 1976 established irretrievable breakdown of marriage as the only ground of divorce. Irretrievable breakdown may be established in five ways: by adultery; by behaviour such that the pursuer cannot reasonably be expected to live with the defender; by wilful desertion for two years; by two years non-cohabitation, with consent of both parties; and by five years non-cohabitation.

### Behaviour

It must be established that the defender has behaved in such a way that the pursuer cannot reasonably be expected to cohabit with the defender, whether or not the behaviour results from mental abnormality, and whether the behaviour was active or passive.[316] The meaning of "mental abnormality" is not defined, but is presumably intended to be at least as broad as mental disorder, and thus to include mental handicap.

Where the pursuer has a mental handicap, it would be relevant to prove conduct rendering it unreasonable to expect that a person with a handicap of that nature and degree should continue to live with the defender, even though the same conduct might not have been unreasonable in relation to a non-handicapped person.[317]

### Desertion

The desertion must be wilful. Detention in hospital is not desertion nor, probably, is necessary voluntary admission. However, intention is not relevant to non-cohabitation.[318]

### Consent to divorce

In cases based on two years non-cohabitation, consent is required. It has been held in England that for a party's consent to be valid, he (or she) must have the capacity to understand the nature of the consent and to appreciate the effect and result of expressing it.[319]

## Judicial separation

The grounds for obtaining a judicial separation are the same as for establishing irretrievable breakdown for purposes of divorce.[320] The points noted above in relation to divorce are accordingly relevant also to judicial separation.

## Financial provision

In dealing with an application for financial provision on divorce

---

[315] The divorce of the parents of a mentally handicapped person is considered in Chap.3, Part II at p.150.

[316] Divorce (Scotland) Act 1976, s.1(2)(b).

[317] Clive, op. cit., p.447 comments that the question is a compromise between a subjective and an objective test: "whether the pursuer, with his or her characteristics, can reasonably be expected to cohabit with the defender".

[318] Clive, op. cit., pp.467-469.

[319] Mason v. Mason [1972] 3 All ER 315, see p.102.

[320] Divorce (Scotland) Act 1976, s.4(1).

the court makes such order, if any, as is justified by certain statutory principles and is reasonable having regard to the resources of the parties.[321] There is no direct equivalent of the English principle that regard should be had to any physical or mental disability of either spouse, but such disability could be relevant to the application of the following of the five statutory principles[322]:

> (b) fair account should be taken of any economic advantage derived by either party from contributions by the other, and of any economic disadvantage suffered by either party in the interests of the other party or of the family;
> (d) a party who has been dependent to a substantial degree on the financial support of the other party should be awarded such financial provision as is reasonable to enable him to adjust, over a period of not more than three years from the date of the decree of divorce, to the loss of that support on divorce;
> (e) a party who at the time of the divorce seems likely to suffer serious financial hardship as a result of the divorce should be awarded such financial provision as is reasonable to relieve him of hardship over a reasonable period.

## Custody of children

In any proceedings regarding custody or any other parental rights the court must have regard to the child's welfare as the paramount consideration, and may not make any order unless satisfied that to do so will be in the child's best interests.[323] There are no specific principles equivalent to those in England (see above). The Scottish approach would discriminate neither for nor against a mentally handicapped parent, but would require an objective view to be taken of the likely effect of the handicap upon the child's welfare, in conjunction with all other factors which might be relevant to the individual case. Upon breakdown of a marriage, the courts will not lightly conclude that it is in a child's best interests to sever all contact with a parent, and it is difficult to visualise a case in which this would be justified by a mental handicap alone.

It is a statutory ground for reception into local authority care that the parent of a child under 17 is temporarily or permanently unable as a result of physical or mental illness "or any other circumstances" to provide proper accommodation, maintenance and upbringing. A mental handicap could be a "circumstance" in this context. The local authority has a duty to give assistance if this is likely to diminish the need to take the child into care.[324]

### SEXUAL RELATIONSHIPS

A person has not only the right to live, but also the right to a sex life, though sexual activity involves responsibilities and risks. The other side of the equation is the right of persons with mental

---

[321]  See generally Family Law (Scotland) Act 1985, ss.8(2) and 9(1).
[322]  Principles set out in s.9(1).
[323]  Law Reform (Parent and Child) (Scotland) Act 1986.
[324]  Social Work (Scotland) Act 1968, ss.15(1) and 12.

limitations to protection from exploitation.[325] We are concerned here with the balance between personal freedom and protection of vulnerable individuals from abuse.[326] Sexual relationships are a matter for personal choice, so that if individuals are incapable of making the decision, no-one may make it for them. The common law test of capacity to consent to sexual activity in general follows the usual form, that the person concerned must be capable of understanding what is proposed and its implications and of exercising choice. The age at which a woman may consent to sexual intercourse is 16 years,[327] and in England a man is deemed to be incapable by law of having sexual intercourse until he is 14 years of age regardless of his actual capacity.[328] Limitations have been imposed upon the capacity of people with a mental handicap to give a valid consent with the aim of protecting them from exploitation and abuse. However, some of these people may be quite capable of consenting to sexual activity.

## Protection

There are several criminal and civil wrongs which might arise where someone engages in sexual activity with a person with a mental handicap. Whether such activity is unlawful may depend on whether the person with a mental handicap has consented to it, but statute makes certain activities unlawful, generally where a person is severely mentally handicapped or the other party is in a position of trust, *e.g.* as a carer.

### Abuse

Sexual abuse is sexual activity without the consent of one of the parties or when one party appears to be exploited. This might arise in a family, residential care, training or other context, but sexual activity does not automatically mean that abuse is occurring. Much depends upon whether the activity is exploitative or injurious to the handicapped individual, but if it is then steps should be taken to protect that individual from further exposure. Where sexual abuse is suspected, the appropriate course of action will vary depending on the circumstances, but it is often advisable to inform the police since the surprise element may result in evidence to support the allegations of abuse. Any evidence from the victim or carers should be recorded.[329]

---

[325] The European Court of Human Rights has ruled that the Netherlands was in breach of the Convention in failing to provide such protection in its criminal law - *X and Y* v. *The Netherlands* March 26, 1985, Appl.16/1983/72/110.

[326] For a review of these issues in a Scottish context see C. McKay, *Sex, Laws and Red Tape* (SSMH 1991). In England: David Carson, *The Sexuality of People with Learning Difficulties* 1989 JSWL No.5 p.355; Mike Gunn, *Sex and the Law: A Brief Guide for Staff* (FPA).

[327] Sexual Offences Act 1956, s.6(1) (England); Sexual Offences (Scotland) Act 1976, s.16.

[328] But not in Scotland - *Fulton* (1841) 2 Swin. 564.

[329] MENCAP produce a pamphlet entitled *The Law on the Sexuality of People with a Mental Handicap*, and SSMH produce *Sex, Laws and Red Tape*.

*Prosecution*

An activity of doubtful legality may never be tested in the courts. If relations between the individual, parents and staff of any residential home involved are good, it is unlikely that a situation would be brought to the attention of the police. If it is, the police will investigate and report to the Crown Prosecution Service (in Scotland, to the Procurator Fiscal) who decide whether to bring charges, and that decision is based upon a number of factors including whether any purpose is served by a prosecution and whether there is sufficient evidence for conviction.[330] Where the purpose is to prevent exploitation, charges are unlikely to be brought if there is no evidence of this.

*Civil proceedings*

If a wrong is done to the individual a civil remedy may be available even if the police will not prosecute. Proceedings for trespass (in Scotland, assault[331] and rape are both delicts) or negligence may be appropriate, and proof will only be required "on the balance of probabilities" which is less onerous than the criminal test. Legal Aid may be available, and in addition to the recovery of damages an injunction (in Scotland, interdict) may be available.[332] The Criminal Injuries Compensation Scheme provides another possible remedy.

## Special criminal offences

We consider here some special offences against or relating to a person who is mentally handicapped.[333]

*England*

Several specific offences can be committed in respect of a person who is a *defective,* which means "a person suffering from a state of arrested or incomplete development of mind which includes severe impairment of intelligence and social functioning".[334] In each case it is a defence for the person charged to prove that he did not know and had no reason to suspect that the victim came within the definition of those protected, and in this context *unlawful* means "outside marriage". It is an offence for[335]:

---

330  It will be necessary for the evidence of the mentally handicapped individual (if such evidence can be given) to be corroborated by that of another person, and the case must be proven "beyond all reasonable doubt".

331  There does not need to be physical contact or physical harm, if the person is seriously threatened, frightened or affronted. See Walker, *The Law of Delict in Scotland* (2 ed.), pp.488-492.

332  This will be appropriate if someone is harassing the individual perhaps following a relationship that has ceased, and it is desired to stop this.

333  Offences by such persons are covered in Parts IIIA and IIIB which deal with their criminal responsibility.

334  Sexual Offences Act 1956, s.45, as amended.

335  Sexual Offences Act 1956, ss.7, 9, 14, 15, 21, 27 and 29. The Sexual Offences (Amendment) Act 1992 makes provision for the extension of anonymity to any person against whom certain sexual offences are alleged to have been committed, including most of those mentioned below.

- a man to have unlawful sexual intercourse with a woman who is a defective[336];
- a man to procure a woman who is a defective to have unlawful sexual intercourse;
- a person to take a woman who is a defective out of the possession of her parent or guardian[337] against his will, if she is so taken with the intention that she shall have unlawful sexual intercourse with men or with a particular man;
- a person to make an indecent assault on a woman or a man, and a defective (or a girl or boy under the age of 16 years) cannot in law give any consent which would prevent an act being an assault;
- a person who is the owner or occupier of any premises, or who has, or acts or assists in, the management or control of any premises, to induce or knowingly suffer a woman who is a defective to resort to or be on those premises for the purpose of having unlawful sexual intercourse with men or a particular man[338];
- for a person to cause or encourage the prostitution in any part of the world of a woman who is a defective.

## Homosexuality

A homosexual act in private between consenting parties both of whom have attained the age of 21 years is no longer an offence. If more than two people are present it would not be in private. A man who is suffering from "severe mental handicap" cannot in law give the necessary consent.[339]

## Sexual relationships with staff

It is an offence for a male member of staff or manager of a hospital or mental nursing home to have unlawful sexual intercourse with a woman (or to commit acts of gross indecency on a male patient) who is for the time being receiving treatment for mental disorder or is an out-patient at the hospital or home. Similarly, for a man to have unlawful sexual intercourse with a woman who is a mentally disordered patient and who is subject to guardianship or otherwise in his custody or care under the Mental Health Act 1983, or in NHS premises, Part III accommodation or a residential home for the mentally disordered.[340] Any such

---

336 The Law Commission in a Report on the codification of the criminal law proposed that it should not be an offence if the man is mentally handicapped himself (1989).

337 "Guardian" means anyone having the lawful care or charge of the woman.

338 This offence causes concern to staff at residential care homes and hospitals who may be aware of sexual relationships by residents or patients. Hopefully the courts would interpret the phrase "knowingly suffer" to mean cause or encourage, but could it be said that the defective was on the premises "for the purpose of" sexual intercourse?

339 Sexual Offences Act 1967, s.1 amended by the Mental Health (Amendment) Act 1982.

340 Mental Health Act 1959, s.128. Sexual Offences Act 1967, s.1(4).

offence must be reported to the Chief Constable, who refers it to the Department of Health and the Director of Public Prosecutions without whose consent there can be no prosecution.[341] There are no equivalent offences for female members of staff, but a sexual relationship with a patient could be indecent assault.

### Aiding and abetting

A person may be guilty of aiding, abetting, counselling or procuring an offence who causes or assists another to commit one.

## Scotland

In each case, an offence is only committed if the victim comes within the definition of those protected by the relevant provision, and as in England it is a defence for the person charged to prove that he or she did not know and had no reason to suspect this.

### Mental Health (Scotland) Act 1984, s.106

Three offences relate to sexual intercourse outside marriage with a woman who "is suffering from a state of arrested or incomplete development of mind which includes significant impairment of intelligence and social functioning". These are:
- for a man to have such intercourse with such a woman;
- for anyone to "procure or encourage" any such woman to have such intercourse;
- for anyone who owns, occupies, manages or controls premises, or assists in their management or control, to induce such a woman to be on the premises (or to resort to the premises) for the purpose of such intercourse.

The interpretation of these provisions, which date originally from legislation of 1885,[342] presents problems in modern conditions. The offences concentrate upon the fact of intercourse, rather than upon whether it is exploitative, and have caused concern in relation to the provision of education, counselling and accommodation. The Lord Advocate has however indicated that the prosecuting authorities would have regard to the purpose of the section, being to protect mentally handicapped women from exploitation, and it is likely that the courts would adopt the same approach. Before encouraging or supporting a relationship, those concerned should be careful to follow the normal good professional practice of considering whether the woman has sufficient intelligence and general understanding of relationships to make a genuine and informed choice to enter or continue a particular relationship. If this test is satisfied, then the woman probably will not come within the definition of those protected.[343]

---

341 DHSS Memorandum on the Mental Health Act 1983. Even if the member of staff is not prosecuted, there may be a breach of the contract of employment which justifies instant dismissal.

342 Criminal Law Amendment Act 1885.

343 See *The Power to Act*, Chap.IX. The need for law reform, in relation to ss.106 and 107 (see below) is considered by the Scottish Law Commission in Discussion Paper No.94, *Mentally Disabled Adults*, paras.2.102-2.110.

*Criminal Justice (Scotland) Act 1980, s.80*

This provision legalises homosexual acts in private between consenting males both aged over 21. Mentally handicapped men are protected by provisions broadly similar to those set out above, but the definition of those protected is different. Section 80 protects a man "who is suffering from a mental deficiency of such a nature or degree that he is incapable of living an independent life or of guarding himself against serious exploitation". It is an offence for a man to participate in a homosexual act with a man protected by this section. The definition of those protected is clearer than under section 106. It refers to capability of independent living (not whether the man in fact is living independently), and capability of safeguarding himself from serious exploitation (though the question of whether the relationship was in fact exploitative is not addressed).

*Mental Health (Scotland) Act 1984, s.107*

This section relates both to sexual intercourse outside marriage with a woman, and to homosexual acts with a man.

Under section 107(1)(*a*) those protected are patients receiving treatment in a hospital or nursing home for mental disorder (*i.e.* mental illness or mental handicap however caused or manifested). Acts on the premises with people attending as out-patients are included. Acts are an offence if committed by any man who is an officer or staff-member, or is a manager of the hospital, or carries on the nursing home.

Section 107(1)(*b*) concerns people with a mental disorder in the following circumstances:
- if the person is under statutory guardianship, acts by the guardian are an offence;
- if the person is in the custody or care of a man under any provisions of the Mental Health (Scotland) Act 1984, acts by that man are an offence;
- if the person is in the care of a local authority under the Social Work (Scotland) Act 1968 or resident in a house provided by a local authority under that Act, acts by any man are an offence.

Someone may have a mental disorder, yet be capable of valid consent and of protecting herself (or himself) from exploitation but under section 107 such matters are irrelevant. The absurdity of this is demonstrated by considering the situation of an unmarried couple in a stable, loving and non-exploitative relationship, where one has a mental disorder, and is then housed by the local authority social work department. If intercourse, or homosexual acts, continue, the other, if a man (but not if a woman) is then committing an offence. He does so if he knows of the mental disorder, even if he does not know that his partner's housing is provided by the social work department.

*Comment*
There is no statutory protection equivalent to any of the foregoing provisions for men in heterosexual relationships or women in lesbian relationships.

*Conclusions (England and Scotland)*
An examination of these special criminal offences leads one to the following practical conclusions:

(a) prosecutions relating to moderately handicapped persons will be rare because the accused could say that he (or she) did not know and had no reason to suspect that the victim was a defective;

(b) two people both with a severe mental handicap may have sexual intercourse without risk of prosecution, if it can be argued that the man cannot recognise the degree of impairment of his partner;

(c) a man with a severe mental handicap may legally have sexual intercourse with any woman because the law only refers to female defectives. The woman could be charged with indecent assault, but this is only likely if there is exploitation;

(d) a woman with a severe mental handicap may only have sexual intercourse with a man without risk of him being prosecuted if he can show that he did not know and had no reason to suspect that she was a defective;

(e) if the parties are married sexual intercourse cannot be an offence however serious the mental handicap, because it will not be "unlawful",[344] provided (in Scotland) that the marriage is not void (see page 106);

(f) two men both with a severe mental handicap may have a homosexual relationship without risk of prosecution, if neither could be expected to recognise the degree of impairment of his partner;

(g) a man may have a homosexual relationship with a man with a severe mental handicap without risk of prosecution if it can be shown that he did not know and had no reason to suspect the degree of impairment of his partner.

## Sex Education

Professional carers may be asked to provide sex education to people with a mental handicap, but the law in this area is not clear so it is difficult to identify the limits of acceptable involvement beyond basic hygiene and facts of life education. A careful and properly recorded assessment is essential, and multi-disciplinary case conferences should examine strategies for sex education for a particular individual, and careful records should be kept with all

---

[344] It would appear to be still an indecent assault because the defective cannot by law consent to the act even in marriage but prosecution is unlikely unless the defective really did not acquiesce in the act (*cf.* rape within marriage).

decisions being documented. Psychological and medical advice should be sought and recorded where appropriate. To avoid problems carers should only provide sex education as part of a formal and structured programme and always act within general written guidelines. Any personal programme should not only identify the means by which it is to be implemented, but also the member of staff who is to implement it, and should be monitored and assessed regularly. Personal (as distinct from group) counselling is particularly open to misunderstanding by the recipient or others.[345]

*Birth control*

It may be necessary for a carer to decide whether to give advice on birth control or provide contraceptives to a person who is in law incapable of consenting to sexual intercourse. The carer may know that sexual intercourse will take place in any event. Although there are differences between this situation and that of contraceptives being provided for a girl under 16 years of age,[346] it is suggested that such advice or provision is, by itself, too remote from any act of sexual intercourse to constitute an offence.

## Conclusions

The manner and extent to which persons who have a mental handicap may enjoy a sexual relationship with others is one of the principle areas of uncertainty in the law. Cases reaching the courts concentrate on the issues of sterilisation and abortion, and a degree of sensitivity tends to ensure that the more day to day issues do not become the subject of legal scrutiny. Nevertheless, those working with and attending to the daily needs of handicapped persons need to know where they stand and where the line is drawn between behaviour on their part which is acceptable, and behaviour which is a criminal offence.

The problem was officially recognised in 1985 when the Second Report of the Social Services Committee on Community Care recommended that the DHSS institute an independent expert review of law and practice on sexuality and contraception in relation to mentally disabled people. The law relies on a series of sexual offences defined in past generations when attitudes were different, with the result that even the well intentioned carer may be vulnerable to the suggestion that criminal offences are being committed. Conversely, the handicapped person may be vulnerable to all kinds of physical and sexual abuse because it is not possible to produce evidence that would satisfy a court.

---

[345] Organisations such as the British Institute of Learning Disabilities and The Association to Aid the Sexual and Personal Relationships of People with a Disability offer courses and conferences on personal relationships and sex education.

[346] see *Gillick* v. *West Norfolk & Wisbech Area Health Authority* [1985] 1 All ER 533, CA; [1985] 3 All ER 402, HL.

## CHILDREN

A person with a mental handicap is entitled to have children but there may be cases where, on medical grounds, pregnancy and parenthood are inadvisable. The rights of parents can subordinate to those of a child even before the child's birth and the court always treats the welfare of the child as the paramount consideration. (But note that a doctor may decide that an abortion is in a woman's best interests, and the welfare of the child is not then considered). Thus if parents are mentally handicapped and there are doubts about their ability to cope, care proceedings may be commenced and the child taken into care. In considering what is in the best interests of the child, the court will take account of the advantage to a child of being brought up by its natural parents. However this may not be sufficient to persuade the court that the child should remain with mentally handicapped parents.

In some cases a local authority has taken wardship proceedings (in Scotland, has taken the child into care) immediately following the birth of the child. In England, proceedings under the Children Act 1989 will now be appropriate. The court should appoint a guardian (or curator) *ad litem* for the mother if she is not capable of giving adequate instructions to a solicitor, so as to ensure that her interests are adequately expressed. The underlying problem may be not that the mother is totally inadequate, but that the local authority is unable or unwilling to give her the level of support that she needs, and steps should then be taken to secure adequate support rather than deprive her of the child. If the wider family is supportive the court may give care and control to the local authority but with liberty to place the child with a relative of the mother with whom the mother resides, and direct an independent family assessment (perhaps by the NSPCC or RSSPCC).

# PART V - CONCLUSION

The law normally applies without modification to persons with a mental handicap, though in many instances the question of capacity arises. The aim is to provide such degree of autonomy for the individual as would be available to any other person of the same age, but this approach must be modified to provide protection for the handicapped person who is, by his or her very nature, vulnerable to being taken advantage of by others. There are many instances where rights of supervision or control are given to others, and this inevitably results in a withdrawal of or restriction upon the rights of the individual. These instances are considered in later chapters dealing with the powers and responsibilities of other persons and bodies, but the fact that the rights of the individual may be and often are lawfully overridden in this way must be taken into account throughout consideration of this chapter.

There is no universal test of capacity to enter into legal

relationships with others, and a different test of capacity may be applied in each situation. Many statutes dealing with capacity borrow Mental Health Act definitions, but this tends to apply a uniform test to different situations for which they were not designed. When it comes to applying the tests in practice lawyers rely on the medical profession, but the average doctor or consultant has little knowledge of or training in mental capacity in the context of legal definitions. We are not concerned with diagnosis of a condition, but judging the effect of the condition upon the individual. The question to be asked is: *"Is he capable of taking this step?"*, not *"Has he a disability which brings his capacity into question?"*. The views of a carer or social worker may be of more assistance than those of the medical practitioner who will only see the individual for short consultations usually in the presence of a carer.

Whilst the law is concerned with what is going on in the mind, society tends to be concerned with the outward physical manifestations. The method of assessment, whether formal or informal, may become of more significance than the legal test to be applied. Ability to communicate (and being able to sign one's own name) are significant and whilst some carers may develop these skills in the handicapped person, others may neglect to do so in order to retain control. This is where a personal advocate becomes important.

## LAW REFORM (England)

### Decision-making

The question of decision-making and mental incapacity is being considered by the Law Commission which has produced a Consultation Paper.[347] One of the problems is how to reconcile the conflict between the need to provide a quick, inexpensive and accessible form of delegation and the need for effective supervision to prevent abuse. Consideration is being given to the best way of choosing alternative decision-makers, and whether overhauling and expanding the existing provisions for guardianship and property management are a more practical starting point than the creation of a new statutory institution.

### Advocacy

The new concept of advocacy involves having someone to speak for and on behalf of the individual and is considered on page 7. The role of an independent advocate may be particularly useful where the individual is capable of making decisions but not of communicating them, or where there is merely capacity to choose from a range of options and these should not be restricted so as to achieve a desired result.[348] There is no legal basis for advocacy

---

[347] Consultation Paper No.119: *Mentally Incapacitated Adults and Decision-Making: An Overview*, May 1991.

[348] For further information see the Advocacy Alliance Handbook: *Guidelines*

schemes and these depend upon the co-operation of all concerned, but if law reform is to extend to decision-making the role of a properly trained and constituted advocate should not be overlooked.[349]

### Authorised representatives

The Disabled Persons (Services, Consultation and Representation) Act 1986 provides for the appointment of an *authorised representative* on behalf of a disabled person who has rights of representation in connection with the provision of local authority services. These provisions have not been, and are unlikely to be, brought into force.

### Adult guardianship

An adult guardianship law has been proposed, perhaps on the lines of legislation in Alberta, Canada[350] which has been followed in South Australia, Victoria and New Zealand. The whole subject is under debate in Europe where some countries have guardianship laws that go beyond the protection of property which heretofore has been the primary objective. In England, a Working Party[351] has drafted a Bill which provides for the appointment by the Court of a partial guardian who would only have defined powers given on the appointment and these would be subject to review at any time on the application of either the dependent adult or any interested person on his or her behalf. The partial guardian would be directed in particular to exercise those powers in the best interests of such dependent who should be encouraged to become capable of caring for himself or herself and to make his or her own judgments. The guardian should act in the manner least restrictive to the rights of the dependent in respect of decisions on one or more of the matters for which appointed.

Some professionals consider that an adult guardianship law is restrictive of the right of adult handicapped persons to be like anyone else and prefer to concentrate on advocacy, assistance and representation. The ultimate question may be whether or not any system designed to help the adult mentally handicapped should be subject to judicial control.[352]

### An Agenda for the 1990's

The Disability Manifesto Group[353] sets out in this document a number of recommendations which would enable disabled people to move closer to exercising their full rights of citizenship. The

---

*for One-to-One Advocacy in Mental Hospitals.*

349 *Citizen Advocacy: A Powerful Partnership* is a handbook written for people setting up schemes. Available from National Citizen Advocacy, 2 St. Paul's Road, London N1 2QR. (formerly Advocacy Alliance).

350 The Dependent Adults Act 1976 and Amendment Act 1985.

351 Law Society's Group for the Welfare of People with a Mental Handicap.

352 Adult guardianship is considered in *The Power to Act* -see Further Reading.

353 Comprising 13 organisations including MENCAP, MIND, The Spastics Society and Disability Alliance.

type and severity of disability and level of need experienced by these individuals varies and the Manifesto is concerned with both physically and mentally disabled persons, but it is pointed out that it is not necessarily disability that handicaps people, but the way in which they are treated by society. People with the same level of disability should be treated equitably and provision should be made for them regardless of race, gender and age. All people should have equal rights, equality of income and participation, and be afforded equal respect and opportunities.

The difficulties disabled people experience often result from reinforcement of their disability by a society which discriminates against them. This may be direct, such as the withholding of employment opportunities, or indirect, such as inaccessible buildings or inadequate transport, or imposing conditions which a disabled person will be less able to fulfil. Unlike those facing discrimination due to race or sex, disabled people who experience unfair discrimination have no redress in the UK. The Manifesto proposes that there should be legislation to combat unfair discrimination on the grounds of actual or perceived disability, and that this should cover employment and training, education, housing, transport, provision of goods, services and facilities, communication, and access to places used by the public. An enforcement agency would be needed, with some monitoring of the way in which society meets the needs of disabled people.

*Civil Rights (Disabled Persons) Bill 1992*
This private member's Bill is designed to introduce anti-discrimination legislation covering employment, access to buildings, transport facilities, services, education, insurance, recreation and housing.

## LAW REFORM (Scotland)

In matters of personal guardianship and personal decision-making, Scotland has benefited from experience gained from the revival and development of tutors-dative. This is not however a perfect solution, but rather a stopgap pending law reform.

In September 1991 the Scottish Law Commission published Discussion Paper No 94 on *Mentally Disabled Adults - Legal Arrangements for Managing their Welfare and Finances*. Options for reform include a new statutory code in respect of personal decision-making including new statutory personal guardians, and a new code for financial management. There is discussion of clarification or amendment of the law concerning medical treatment and related matters (such as research and organ transplantation or donation). The need to reform offences concerned with protection from sexual exploitation is addressed.

The Scottish Law Commission has also recently recommended abolition of marriage by cohabitation and repute.

# CHAPTER 3     SITUATION OF PARENTS AND CARERS

## INTRODUCTION

The English and Scottish Law Commissions have pointed out that parenthood is a matter of responsibilities rather than rights,[1] and the House of Lords has emphasised that the parental power to control an infant child exists not for the benefit of the parent but for the benefit of the child.[2] This role must be recognised in the relationship between carers (including parents) and a mentally handicapped adult, and the emphasis in this chapter is on responsibilities. In practice carers find informal ways of dealing with situations as they arise and the practical solution is usually of more significance than the legal one (if there is a legal solution). Carers are concerned about their right to make decisions on behalf of the person cared for, especially as they will be taking (or at least communicating) such decisions on a daily basis. Parents are in the same position as unrelated carers, because the relationship by itself does not confer any additional legal rights upon them once their child has become an adult, though this change in legal status is seldom realised.

*Scope of chapter*
We consider first who the carers are and their needs, and then their authority and obligations, and finally the remedies available to them. It will usually be left to carers to ensure that the rights of the handicapped individual are not overlooked, but the individual will be expected to conform to the norms of society and this may place duties upon carers which they find it difficult to fulfil. The responsibilities imposed upon carers by the mere fact of caring must therefore be considered.

## PART I - CARERS

*Preliminary*
The parents will usually be the first carers, but when do they cease to be carers and who then takes over that role and in what circumstances? Increasingly parents are coming to realise that it is often better for their handicapped child to move away from home in a carefully planned way at a chosen time, when a package of care facilities has been arranged. It is as normal for a handicapped child to want to move out of the family home as for any other child, and with greater life expectancy the alternative is an abrupt

---

1    *Guardianship and Custody*, Law Commission (1988), No. 172, Part II.
2    *Gillick* v.*West Norfolk and Wisbech Area Health Authority* [1985] 3 All ER 402, HL.

ill-prepared change of lifestyle when the parents either die or
become too infirm to continue coping. Thus when we consider
carers we are not just thinking of parents or relatives.

## DEFINITION

There is no specific meaning of "carer" in this context. A person
may be a carer for an afternoon or even for a few minutes, but the
word is generally used to describe someone who takes on a
commitment to care either for a particular individual or for a
class of persons in the community. The former may be described
as an *informal carer* and could be a parent looking after a
mentally handicapped son or daughter. The latter is likely to be a
*professional carer*, examples being a social worker dealing with
the handicapped or a community mental handicap nurse. This
chapter considers informal carers.

### Informal carers

The significant point about being an informal carer is that the life
of the carer is restricted, usually to a substantial extent, by the
need to be responsible for the person cared for. The distinction
between this type of caring and the normal caring that we all do
for short periods is that it is a one-way commitment that may last
for the life of the person being cared for, or of the carer. Anyone
may become an informal carer, and seldom is this by choice. With
parents it just happens, but a brother or sister may take over the
role out of a sense of duty or because there is no-one else to do so.
Often this is a gradual process, though many parents go to great
lengths to ensure that their other children do not take on the
burden of caring that has fallen upon them for most of their lives.
Circumstances vary enormously, according to the condition of the
person cared for, economic circumstances and the support
available. The level of care varies from occasional help to
virtually continuous caring, and the level of dependency similarly
varies. As the majority of carers are women, the greatest single
factor which may affect informal care in the future is the level of
employment of women; depending upon personal priorities and
choice, either caring will restrict availability for employment or
employment will restrict ability to provide care.

### Involuntary carers

Informal carers have not necessarily chosen this role and
sometimes resent it. They may be referred to as involuntary carers
and, although dedicated to the welfare of the person cared for, the
mixture of emotions involved can be intense and may not always
be recognised.

### Statutory definition

The Disabled Persons (Services, Consultation and Representation)
Act 1986 uses the word carer for the first time in a statute dealing
with handicap. It means a person who provides a substantial

amount of care on a regular basis for a disabled person living at home,[3] and a duty is imposed on the local authority to take into account the ability of the carer to continue to provide such care when deciding what services should be provided.

## CARING FOR CARERS

It helps for the adviser to recognise the complex mixture of emotions felt by carers and to identify their needs.[4]

### Understanding

Involuntary carers (especially parents) often feel:

| | |
|---|---|
| Inadequate | - because they cannot cope; |
| Isolated | - by the commitment to caring; |
| Frustrated | - by the lack of understanding; |
| Angry | - about the whole situation; |
| Resentful | - at their predicament; |
| Bewildered | - by a role that they feel ill-prepared for; |
| Embarrassed | - by the tasks that they have to perform; |
| Guilty | - that they are not doing enough; |
| Anxious | - about continuing care in the future. |

These feelings are aggravated by conflict between these emotions.

### Birth of handicapped child

A lawyer is unlikely to be consulted soon after parents realise that their child has a mental handicap, but guidance and support at that stage may be of immense value. Initially they cannot face reality, but feelings of sorrow, grief, anxiety, guilt and aggression then come to the surface. It helps just to listen, so that they may rationalise their feelings by talking things through, but eventually they ask questions about what can be done, and then the listening role must change to one of giving informed advice. If legal advice is not appropriate, at least parents should be encouraged to make contact with the other professionals who can help them. The social services (or social work) department should be contacted and financial benefits should not be overlooked.

### Effect on family

A handicapped child means a handicapped family, and a common outcome is withdrawal into the family unit leading to social isolation. Only a strong family can withstand the pressures and warning signs of breakdown in the personal relationships should be watched for. Mother may become over-protective to the child causing father to feel rejected, in addition to the personal loss that he feels; whilst she feels under pressure and unsupported, he may become withdrawn, and an emotionally explosive situation develops. If a solicitor is consulted in the context of marriage

---

3    s.8. A person employed to provide care by a local authority or similar body in the exercise of its functions under any enactment is not included.

4    This topic is dealt with in greater detail by Jill Pitkeathley, *It's My Duty, Isn't It? The Plight of Carers in Our Society* (Souvenir Press) (1989).

breakdown, counselling and practical support should be arranged and divorce may be avoided if the parties can be encouraged to recognise their own emotions and develop a new relationship with each other.

*Leaving home*

Parents have differing views about when their handicapped son or daughter should leave home.[5] Some desperately desire this, either because they cannot cope or wish their child to be independent; others strive to hold the family together as long as possible. Some are uncertain as to what is best; they doubt that their child will be happy elsewhere, and they don't know how they themselves will cope after many years of caring. A substantial loss of state benefits to the household may arise. Parents need help in coming to terms with the decision that may need to be taken, and their son or daughter should be consulted and needs information and training.

## Needs

It is easy for involuntary informal carers to feel that no-one cares (*i.e.* about them caring), and they need:

| | | |
|---|---|---|
| recognition | - | of their contribution and needs; |
| relationship | - | with someone who understands; |
| reliable information | - | about services and benefits; |
| relevant services | - | according to their circumstances; |
| resources | - | to cover the cost of caring; |
| respite | - | from caring for periods; |
| relief | - | from caring in the long term; |
| reassurance | - | that others will care when they can't. |

The need to keep coping and the lack of time or energy to think rationally about the situation frequently results in an inability to consider changes or act on advice. Advisers should not be put off by this and need to be persistent with their advice and offer encouragement for this to be followed up.

There is a danger that professional carers along with the rest of society concentrate so much upon the needs of the handicapped person that they overlook the needs of the carer. The effect of a handicapped child upon the family should not be overlooked.

## Cost of caring

The true cost of being a carer is seldom recognised and is not covered by weekly state benefits. A study concludes that families with a mentally handicapped dependant incur substantial extra costs and carers suffer major loss of earnings.[6] The earnings of the father are often reduced and the main problems of mothers wishing to work are finding a suitable substitute carer or a job

---

5    The dilemma facing parents is sympathetically considered by Ann Richardson and Jane Ritchie, *Letting Go* (Open University Press) (1989).

6    Judith Buckle, *Mental Handicap Costs More* (published by Disablement Income Group Charitable Trust of Attlee House, 28 Commercial Road, London E1 6LR) (1984).

with convenient hours and holidays. The strain of combining care and work is often too great, and the promotion prospects of a parent with a handicapped child may be affected.[7] Regular extra expenditure may arise,[8] and heavy wear and tear may result in regular replacement of items such as washing machines and driers. Thus care of a mentally handicapped dependant results in three separate financial consequences: lack of earnings for the handicapped person, loss of earnings for the carer(s), and higher living costs.

*Provision*

The cost of caring should be borne in mind when administering a trust fund set up for the benefit of a handicapped person. It is all too easy to conclude that such a person has few financial needs when in reality this is because the carers are providing an entire environment at great financial and emotional cost to themselves. Provision of extra facilities in the home, respite care and holidays not only for the handicapped person but also for the carers should all be considered as worthwhile objects of the trust.

It is worth checking that all available state benefits are being claimed by both the handicapped individual and the carers. Maximising income for the family is a positive step that can be taken and if the adviser does not have this expertise he should refer the client to a welfare rights office (if one is available in the community) or to a citizens advice bureau which will have access to up-to-date information at no charge.

## COMMUNITY CARE

The policy of community care means providing the services and support which disabled and infirm people need to be able to live as independently as possible in their own homes, or in homely settings in the community.[9] In its wider concept it is not a new policy, but the emphasis now is away from care provision in hospital (for those who do not need medical treatment) and other forms of institutionalised care. The key role in securing the delivery of services is given to local authorities and we consider this in Chapter 5, but here we identify the implications of the policy upon parents and carers.

### Recognition

In its White Paper the Government recognised that most care is

---

7   In some police forces, the parent of a child with a significant problem has his personnel file marked to indicate that he has a "welfare problem", and this can be a block to promotion.

8   *e.g.* from unprescribed medicines and creams, incontinence aids, special diets, special or additional clothing and shoes, extra heating and washing, mobility and transport problems and necessary toys and play equipment.

9   *Community Care: Agenda for Action* (Griffiths Report) 1988; White Paper *Caring for People: Community Care in the Next Decade and Beyond* (1989).

provided by family, friends and neighbours who need help to manage what can become a heavy burden. Their lives can be made easier if the right support is there at the right time, and statutory services providers should do all they can to assist and support carers. Help may take the form of providing advice and support as well as practical services such as day, domiciliary and respite care. The Minister for Health in her evidence to the Social Services Committee acknowledged the importance of carers and their need for practical help. She stated that, although not enshrined in legislation, the role of carers would be given the priority it deserves in all guidance about assessment, community care plans and other aspects of the proposals.[10] The Committee concluded that the Government must recognise more fully the value to society and to the taxpayer of the work done by carers, and provide proper support for them despite the cost implications if the community care policies are to succeed.

### Information

The Committee recommended that social services departments should make it a prime objective to bring together and disseminate information about statutory and voluntary services in their areas which would be of assistance to carers and their dependants. Where appropriate, this should be available in Welsh or Gaelic and in the languages of the main ethnic minority groups in the area, as well as in English. Professionals involved also need information, especially general practitioners who are given a gatekeeping role in regard to the provision of services. The White Paper recognises that GP's are well placed to ensure that factors which affect the quality of life other than medical ones are taken into consideration, and their new contract imposes an obligation to refer on patients where there are problems needing specialist services and provide advice to enable patients to take advantage of local authority social services. However, whilst familiar with the problems of the elderly they may have few patients with a mental handicap, so do not have the incentive to become familiar with the services available for such persons in their area. It does not follow that because a patient has a mental handicap there will be increased need to consult the doctor on health grounds, and long periods may elapse between visits.

### Services

#### Assessment
The first step is to assess the needs of the person cared for and to see how these needs may be best fulfilled. A carer's needs and wishes will not always be the same as those of the person cared for, but should also be taken into account and services should be

---

10 *Community Care: Carers* - Fifth Report of the House of Commons Social Services Committee, Session 1989-90. This conflicts with the evidence of MENCAP that "... the White Paper does not address the needs of carers".

designed to meet the needs of carers as well as those cared for. Local authorities are made responsible for assuring these needs, nominating a case manager to review them and ensuring that resources are managed efficiently and that each service user has a single point of contact. The needs of each individual will be different, so assessments should lead to an Individual Programme Plan, which is a personal package of care.

### Respite services
Respite care can be of considerable benefit to carers, whether this be on a regular basis or for holidays, and may be provided in different ways. The Social Services Committee identified a wider range of respite services which should be available in all areas:
- in-patient accommodation for the most severely disabled;
- hospice care for the terminally ill;
- residential care and nursing home places near to home;
- placement with an alternative family and other types of placement schemes (*e.g.* supported lodgings);
- overnight respite care;
- day care facilities of many sorts with flexible hours;
- sheltered employment;
- holidays for both the person cared for and carers.

It also recommended that carers and their organisations should be involved in designing different types of respite facilities, and that information about these should be made available to carers and their dependants when needs assessments were made. Respite care is more than just crisis intervention.

### Communication
Problems of communication often arise, sometimes unknowingly, between professionals and carers. Professionals use language which is misunderstood, or simply not understood, by the people they are talking to. Community care is creating its own jargon and this should be discouraged; advisers who come across phrases and concepts that they do not understand should seek an explanation and encourage their clients to do likewise.

# PART II - RIGHTS AND RESPONSIBILITIES

### Preliminary
We consider first such legal rights or authority as parents have in respect of their child. In general such authority ceases when the child attains legal majority,[11] but in so far as any identifiable rights continue they are mentioned here. We then consider the legal obligations of parents and, though most of these also cease when their child attains legal majority, some may continue or arise if they continue as carers thereafter. At that stage parents have the same legal status as any other informal carer, in most instances no

---

11   Unless some specific appointment, such as appointment in Scotland of a tutor-dative, is made.

more and no less, so although this chapter relates to the parents of a child it covers all carers of that child when an adult.

## STATUS

### Abortion

The question may arise whether a pregnant woman is entitled to have an abortion if she is aware, or has reason to believe, that her child would have a serious abnormality.

*Legislation*
The Abortion Act 1967 sets out the circumstances in which the medical termination of a pregnancy shall not be an offence, and these include: "that there is a substantial risk that if the child were born it would suffer from such physical or mental abnormalities as to be seriously handicapped".[12] Two registered medical practitioners must be of this opinion, formed in good faith, but a husband has no enforceable right to stop his wife having a legal abortion in these circumstances. In England it is an offence to destroy the life of a child capable of being born alive (*i.e.* 28 weeks or more) unless this is done in accordance with the provisions of the 1967 Act.[13]

*Ethical issues*
It is pointed out that people are not always clear about the difference between prevention of handicap, treatment of handicap, and avoiding the problem of handicap by destroying the embryo.[14] This last form of treatment has been facilitated by recent medical advances making it possible to detect handicap at an earlier stage, and the current medical practice of many doctors is based on the view that if the handicap is detected early enough there is no ethical objection to abortion. At present the existence of defective genes indicating a disorder can be detected though not the extent of the likely handicap. The view is held that not enough emphasis is placed on prevention of handicap, and that the ability to destroy the embryo when potential handicap is detected removes the incentive for research on prevention.[15]

There are two categories of handicap, but many of those that can be discovered *in utero* are not disabling:

(i) *congenital abnormalities* which appear during the growth

---

12 1967 Act, s.1(1)(*d*) as amended by the Human Fertilisation and Embryology Act 1990, s.37(1). The period for an abortion is now reduced to 24 weeks except in certain cases (such as that quoted) where there is effectively no time limit.

13 Infant Life (Preservation) Act 1929, s.1 as amended by the 1990 Act. This covers the possible gap between abortion and murder which exists in Scotland - see Gordon, *Criminal Law* para.23.02.

14 *The Association of Lawyers for the Defence of the Unborn* of 40 Bedford Street, London WC2E 9EN.

15 Instead research is concentrating upon detection of abnormalities at the earliest possible date.

of the child before birth (such as Down's Syndrome and spina bifida)[16];

    (ii) *genetic disorder* which is capable of being inherited according to the laws of genetics. Although the genes of parents can be examined to see if they are defective, defects can arise spontaneously in a child due to genetic mutation even where parents do not have the defective gene.[17]

A group of voluntary organisations recommends that genetic counselling should be offered to all potentially affected parents to enable them to make an informed choice (*i.e.* before conception). If a genetic condition is identified, the parents should be given clear and practical information.[18]

### Damages claims

The possibility of a mother bringing a claim for damages when not informed of the possibility that her child may be handicapped was considered in a recent case[19]:

> A mother sued a consultant radiologist for failing to ascertain from an ultrasound scan that her child was suffering from spina bifida. The mother was 26 weeks pregnant when she had the scan, and although the radiographer thought that the scan showed a possible abnormality and discussed this with the consultant radiologist, no further action was taken and the mother was not told. The mother claimed that the radiologist had been negligent in not ascertaining whether the foetus was abnormal when that possibility was raised by the radiographer and she had thereby been deprived of the possibility of having the pregnancy terminated.
>
> It was held the foetus had reached that stage in its development where it was capable if born, of living and breathing through its own lungs without any connection to its mother, so was a child "capable of being born alive" within section 1(2) of the Infant Life (Preservation) Act 1929. Accordingly an abortion at that stage would have been unlawful even if carried out within the period of 28 weeks referred to in the Act, so it was not possible to found a cause of action for failing to advise of the possibility of termination. The consultant radiologist had not been negligent in failing to direct a re-scan since by then it was too late to carry out a lawful termination.

## Disputes between parents

### England

When parents split up or are in dispute, the court has power to decide who shall look after any minor child of the family so we

---

16    The normal method of detecting these before birth is by amniocentesis, which is a method of obtaining a specimen of the fluid surrounding the child, but there are dangers to the mother and child and the defect cannot be discovered much before the 20th week of pregnancy when an abortion is much more dangerous and traumatic for the mother.

17    About 200 genetic disorders have been recognised, of which about 150 can be discovered by amniocentesis and others by examining specific genes and seeing if they are defective.

18    *An Agenda for the 1990's* published by the Disability Manifesto Group.

19    *Rance* v. *Mid-Downs Health Authority* [1991] 1 All ER 801. Significant damages may be awarded on the basis that the child would have been aborted, and this places the parents in a quandary because they must prove that they would not have had the child but are now accepting long term responsibility.

consider any special rules that can apply where there is a mentally handicapped child. There is no power to resolve disputes between parents of an adult child so obstruction by a parent looking after a mentally handicapped child who has attained 18 years can mean that the other parent is denied contact with the child without any legal remedy.

*Divorce*
All "children of the family"[20] must be identified in the Petition but if they have attained the age of 18 years this fact should be stated and no further details need to be given. However, it is desirable to include information about any child whose special circumstances will require the court's attention even though an adult (*e.g.* a mentally handicapped child). The existence of a handicap must also be disclosed on the Statement of Arrangements for minor children filed with the Petition and served upon the other spouse who may, if desired, respond with his or her own Statement. The District Judge may order a medical report so that the court is aware of the nature and extent of the handicap and this will be taken into account when considering the arrangements for the children.[21] Traditionally the court has made orders for custody to one parent with reasonable or defined access to the other, or (by agreement) custody to both parents with care and control to one and reasonable access to the other.

*Orders relating to children*
The approach to children under the age of 18 and the types of order that may be made have been radically changed by the Children Act 1989. The modern concept is *parental responsibility* which declines as the child grows older (though perhaps not in the case of a child with a mental handicap) and is defined as[22]:

> "... all the rights, duties, powers, responsibilities and authority which by law a parent of a child has in relation to the child and his property".

This would seem to include the rights to physical possession and personal contact, and to impose discipline, administer property, represent in legal proceedings and consent to medical treatment or marriage, and also the power to control education and choose religion.[23]

---

20    This includes a child who has been treated by the parties as a child of the family, but not a child boarded out with them by a local authority.

21    Before October 14, 1991, a Decree Absolute could not be issued until there was a Certificate of Satisfaction in regard to the arrangements for all minor children of the family, but from that date the Children Act 1989 only requires the court to consider whether it should exercise its powers in respect of such children though it may delay the decree absolute until satisfied.

22    s.3(1). Both married parents, or the mother if not married, will normally have parental responsibility but an unmarried father may acquire parental responsibility by agreement or court order.

23    These are the same areas that need to be provided for in respect of an adult who lacks the capacity to make decisions.

Following the separation or divorce of parents the emphasis is now on agreement being reached as to the future upbringing of the children, and the court will not make an order unless it considers that doing so is better for the child than making no order at all.[24] A wider range of orders can now be made as follows[25]:

**contact order** - an order requiring the person with whom a child lives, or is to live, to allow the child to visit or stay with the person named in the order, or for that person and the child otherwise to have contact with each other;

**prohibited steps order** - an order that no step which could be taken by a parent in meeting his parental responsibility for a child, and which is of a kind specified in the order, shall be taken by any person without the consent of the court;

**residence order** - an order settling the arrangements to be made as to the person with whom a child is to live;

**specific issue order** - an order giving directions for the purpose of determining a specific question which has arisen, or which may arise, in connection with any aspect of parental responsibility for a child.

No order is to be made which will have effect after a child attains 16 years unless the court is satisfied that the circumstances of the case are exceptional, but this is likely to include mental handicap.[26]

*Who may apply*

Any parent or guardian of the child, or anyone in whose favour a residence order is in force with respect to the child, may apply for an order; other persons can apply without leave in certain circumstances and anyone can apply with leave. The intention is to enable anyone who is concerned about any aspect of the child's welfare to ask the court to consider it, but the requirement to ask for leave aims to protect families from unwarranted interference in their lives. The court has a general power to make an order even if no application has been made.[27]

*Matters to be taken into account*

When a court determines any question with respect to a child the welfare of the child is the paramount consideration but the court must have regard in particular to[28]:

   (a) the ascertainable wishes and feelings of the child;

   (b) the physical, emotional and educational needs of the child;

   (c) the likely effect on the child of a change of circumstances;

   (d) the age, sex, background and any characteristics of the child which the court considers relevant;

   (e) any harm which the child has suffered or is at risk of suffering;

   (f) how capable each of the child's parents (and any other person) is of meeting the child's needs;

---

24  s.1(5).

25  These are known as "section 8 Orders", being under that section of the Act.

26  s.9(6). Orders will in any event cease when the child attains 18 years.

27  See generally, s.10. A child who has sufficient understanding to make the application may apply with leave.

28  s.1(3).

(g) the range of powers available to the court.

There is thus scope to take into account all relevant factors in regard to a mentally handicapped child, but if harm is being caused due to lack of provision to meet exceptional needs rather than the inadequacies of the parents, the court may not have power to order that extra support be provided.

## Scotland

### Children

Sheriff courts have jurisdiction to make decisions about custody and access in respect of children under 16,[29] and in relation to parental rights other than custody and access in respect of children under 18.[30] Any person claiming interest may apply for an order relating to parental rights, and the court may make such order as it thinks fit,[31] but only a parent, tutor, curator or guardian may be granted custody (except where certain special requirements are met).[32] In actions of divorce (and also judicial separation and nullity) the court may not grant decree unless satisfied in relation to children of the marriage under 16 that arrangements have been made for the care and upbringing of the child and that those arrangements are satisfactory or are the best which can be devised in the circumstances; or alternatively that it is impracticable for the party or parties appearing before the court to make any such arrangements.[33] There are no special statutory provisions relating to children with mental handicaps or other disabilities.

### Adults

None of the foregoing provisions applies to adults. A dispute as to who should care for a mentally handicapped adult can be resolved by appointing a statutory guardian, who has power to require the adult to reside at a place specified by the guardian.[34] Following divorce or separation, one parent may seek appointment as tutor-dative, and the appointment will normally include power to determine place of residence and who should have access. The court would require to resolve any competition between parents for appointment: the Scottish author is not aware of any case where this has yet happened.

## Guardianship

### England

In certain circumstances a *guardian* may be appointed who will

---

29 A petition for custody of a 16 or 17 year-old can be brought in the Court of Session.

30 Law Reform (Parent and Child) (Scotland) Act 1986, s.8.

31 *Ibid.* s.3(1).

32 Children Act 1975, s.47(2).

33 Matrimonial Proceedings (Children) Act 1958; where granting of decree is urgent, the court may instead accept an undertaking to return to court regarding arrangements for the children within a stipulated period.

34 Mental Health (Scotland) Act 1984, s.41(2)(*a*).

have parental responsibility for the child.[35]

*Testamentary*
A parent who has parental responsibility for a child under the age of 18 (or a guardian of such a child) may, by a signed and dated document which includes a Will, appoint another individual to be the child's guardian in the event of the parent's (or guardian's) death. The appointment will not usually take effect whilst there is another parent with parental responsibility for the child unless there was a residence order in favour of the deceased, and the guardian can disclaim within a reasonable time of the appointment becoming effective. An appointment usually revokes any earlier appointment made in respect of the same child.

*Court order*
The court may, on the application of any individual or of its own initiative, appoint a guardian of a child under the age of 18 if there is no parent with parental responsibility for the child or a residence order had been made in favour of a parent or guardian who has died.

*Adult*
There is no similar provision in respect of an adult, but there can be no harm in appointing by Will a guardian of an adult mentally handicapped child "in so far as the law allows" and this may be a useful step to take in case the law changes. It is evidence of the wishes of the parent which are entitled to some respect especially if the parent looked after the child up to the time of death. Many parents believe that they continue as their child's guardian after the age of eighteen, but guardianship in English law does not apply to adults, regardless of their mental age or capacity, so a mentally handicapped adult cannot have a guardian.

### Scotland
Parents may not appoint a guardian by Will to a person over 16, and they retain no guardianship powers or statutory parental rights beyond 18, however severely their son or daughter may be handicapped. Apart from statutory guardianship, referred to below, guardianship powers may only be conferred by appointment of one or more tutors-dative, or service of a tutor-at-law. These forms of personal guardianship have no equivalent in England, and are described separately in the next main section "Tutors to adults - Scotland", page 136 *et seq*.

### Control of an adult

*Statutory guardianship*
The Mental Health Act 1983[36] and the Mental Health (Scotland) Act 1984[37] offer a limited form of guardianship, but in England it

---

35   Children Act 1989, ss.5 and 6.
36   s.8. The procedures are dealt with in Chap.5. The power is seldom used, perhaps because it is so limited.
37   ss.36-52.

applies to very few people with a mental handicap since it only relates to those who are abnormally aggressive or seriously irresponsible. However, a parent or member of the family may be appointed. The powers of this type of guardian are limited to three specific rights, namely to require:

(a) the patient to live in a specified place;

(b) the patient to attend at specified times and places for the purpose of medical treatment,[38] occupation, education or training; and

(c) access to the patient by the social worker, doctor or other specified person.[39]

There is no power over the property of the patient. A private guardian has various duties which relate to notification of the local authority and the appointment of a medical practitioner. It is an offence to illtreat or wilfully neglect a person subject to a guardianship order.

## Restraint

Carers may need to impose restraint to prevent the person causing harm to either himself or someone else. There are many types of restraint, including physical force, locked doors, intimidation and using equipment or furniture which restricts movement. The degree of restraint used is important, as any act of touching another person's body is technically an assault if there is no consent. Providing it was not a hostile act it will not generally be treated as an assault, and if reasonable force is used an act will not be hostile. It is difficult to provide guidelines as reasonableness in each case will depend upon the particular circumstances, and in practice one may be forced to make snap decisions where there is little time to judge the reasonableness of the action required. Circumstances will be taken into account.[40] In any setting where physical restraint is likely to be needed from time to time, guidelines and training should be provided to protect everybody's interests.[41] In Scotland restraint is justifiable to prevent someone from harming himself or others, unless restraint is exercised quite unnecessarily or unjustifiably, or with excessive force, or for an unreasonable time, or maliciously and without probable cause.[42] This is a power of last resort, to be exercised where it would be impracticable to obtain authority by appropriate legal procedures.

---

[38] There is no power to compel the patient to have such treatment, nor can the guardian consent to treatment on the patient's behalf.

[39] In Scotland, any doctor, mental health officer or other person.

[40] e.g. emergency action to stop someone walking in front of a car may have to be rough by ordinary standards.

[41] The Mental Health Acts give protection from civil or criminal proceedings for anything done in pursuance of the Acts, unless done in bad faith or without reasonable care; 1983 Act, s.139 and 1984 Act, s.122. In one Scottish case a sheriff held that this covered throwing cold water on patients and striking them to control conduct: *Skinner* v. *Robertson* 1980 SLT (Sh Ct) 43 - criticised in *Scots Law and the Mentally Handicapped*, pp.52-54.

[42] Walker, *The Law of Civil Remedies in Scotland,* p.40.

If restraint for any duration is necessary, appropriate detention or other procedures should be initiated as soon as possible. If a pattern develops of repeated need to exercise restraint, then again appropriate authority (such as appointment of a tutor) should be obtained.[43]

*Financial control*

Parents usually supervise the finances of their young child, but on attaining 18 (Scotland 16) the child will have the full right to control his financial affairs without parental interference, unless some specific appointment is made. This is of concern to parents who consider their son or daughter not to be mature enough to take such responsibility, but the provision of continuing support often gives them some influence. Where there is mental handicap some degree of control over money may be essential, if only because despite having attained that age the child is incapable of handling financial affairs. The problem is that in law either the child is treated as incapable with the consequence that all financial powers can be taken away, or is not incapable, in which event no restrictions are imposed and there is no delegation to others.

*Foster parents*

Under local authority schemes a handicapped child may be placed with foster parents and this relationship may continue for many years. Once the child attains legal majority foster parents have no continuing legal status in regard to the child, unless (in Scotland) they are appointed tutors-dative. They may merely continue as voluntary informal carers with no legal right to be consulted when formal decisions are taken as to the future of the child.

## Burial

Parents of a young severely mentally handicapped child may not feel able to cope and allow the child to be placed in the care of the local authority, or a residence order may be made in favour of a third party. If the child later dies it seems that any vesting of parental responsibility in another party ends, and that in England the natural parents have a right to bury the child (and are obliged to provide for the burial if they have the means to do so).[44]

In the case of an adult, the court is reluctant to interfere with any decision of the executors as to funeral arrangements at the suit of a near relative, and in the case of a deceased who was mentally handicapped and incapable of appointing executors this approach will presumably apply to the persons entitled to be administrators who will be the next of kin (in Scotland, the person entitled to be

---

[43]   *cf. B.* v. *Forsey* 1988 SLT 572 (HL) where it was held that the common law right to detain was not available to hospitals, and hospital staff, as the statutory provisions of the Mental Health (Scotland) Act 1984 had been provided to them by parliament in place of the common law rights.

[44]   *R.* v. *Gwynedd County Council* (1991) CA, reported in *Family Law*, September 1991. This decision was prior to the Children Act 1989 but may not be affected thereby.

appointed executor-dative).[45] However, where the deceased leaves no money to pay for a burial arrangements will be made by those prepared to pay, or the Environmental Health Department..

## Interference with rights

### England

Parents have no right of action or remedy in damages against a stranger who interferes with their rights in respect of or their relationship with their child. There is a statutory code for the welfare of young children under which local authorities exercising an administrative function can interfere with parental rights, but breaches of this by an authority do not give rise to a private right by parents to claim damages for interference with their rights and only give rise to public law remedies to protect the welfare of the child and the remedy of damages for the tort of misfeasance in a public office. It has been held that to acknowledge the existence of a tort of interference with parental rights based on an unjustifiable interference with legal rights would adversely affect the duties of local authorities under the statutory code to protect the welfare of infant children.[46]

### Scotland

There is a right to continuance of unimpaired domestic relations, and parents probably have a claim in damages against anyone who takes or entices away their child under the age of majority.[47] However, no such liability attaches to public authorities or their officials acting with statutory authority, provided that they act in good faith and within the scope of their authority.[48]

## Legal Aid

Children are now assessed on the basis of their own means, and in relation to appointment in a representative or fiduciary capacity eligibility is assessed on the basis of the mentally handicapped person alone.[49] There are no special procedures in relation to applications by the parents or carers of a handicapped person in their own right.

### Wills

In England, the cost of preparing a Will is not usually covered under the green form scheme, but one of the exceptions is where the testator has a disabled child and wants to make provision for that child in the Will.[50] It is then appropriate to consider eligibility

---

45  See *Re Grandison (Dec'd), The Times,* July 10, 1989.
46  *F.* v. *Wirral Metropolitan Borough Council* [1991] 2 All ER 648, CA.
47  Walker, *Delict* (2nd ed.), p.713.
48  The Mental Health (Scotland) Act 1984, s.122(1) provides specific protection from liability for acts purporting to be done in pursuance of the Act or regulations thereunder, unless done in bad faith or without reasonable care.
49  Procedures for applying for legal aid on behalf of people with mental handicaps are described in Chap.2 at p.43.
50  Legal Advice and Assistance (Scope) Regulations 1989, Part II,

for green form assistance and to apply for an extension, as the normal limit on costs is likely to be exceeded.[51] The Regulations appear to anticipate that a more complicated Will than usual is needed (*i.e.* making trust provision), and presumably provision is made for the child even if it is only on a discretionary basis.

In Scotland, legal advice and assistance is available for preparing a Will.

## TUTORS TO ADULTS (Scotland)

### Background

The appointment of a suitable guardian, where needed, is a right of the individual, not of the parents or carers.[52] However, the revival and development of the tutor-dative as a personal guardian since 1986, and recent interest in revival of the tutor-at-law, have been almost entirely parent-driven. In practice the need for such personal guardianship is almost always identified and addressed on the initiative of parents or carers,[53] and it is for this reason that these procedures are for convenience described here rather than in Chapter 2. "Tutor" is the legal term for the person having the full rights of the parent of a young child (formerly termed a "pupil child"). Statutory guardians had all the personal guardianship powers of the parent of a pupil child until 1984, when the powers were restricted to the narrow interventionist powers described above.[54] This created a requirement for a form of true personal guardianship, and the gap was filled by the revival of the old common law procedure of appointment of tutors-dative.[55] "Dative" means appointed by a court. A tutor-dative is accordingly a person appointed by a court to hold and exercise the powers of a parent of a young child.

### Tutors-dative

*Persons to whom tutors-dative may be appointed*
In modern practice the outdated and meaningless concepts of insanity and unsoundness of mind have been abandoned in relation to tutor-dative procedure. Relevant factors now are that a mentally

---

reg.4(2)(*b*). This includes a person "who suffers from mental disorder of any description, or who is substantially and permanently handicapped by illness, injury or congenital deformity" and by reg.2(1) "mental disorder" has the meaning assigned to it in Mental Health Act 1983, s.1.

51   This situation may arise quite frequently, *e.g.* in the case of a parent who is in receipt of income support but is a homeowner. For an explanation of the pitfalls involved in making a Will in these circumstances, see Chap.9.

52   "The mentally retarded person has a right to a qualified guardian when this is required to protect his personal wellbeing and interest", United Nations Declaration on the Rights of Mentally Retarded Persons (1971), Article 5.

53   But not always. On at least one occasion the Mental Welfare Commission for Scotland suggested appointment of a tutor-dative when the statutory criteria for a statutory guardian ceased to apply.

54   Under "Control of an adult", pp.132 *et seq.* above

55   See A.D. Ward, *Revival of Tutors-dative*, 1987 SLT (News) 69; A.D. Ward, *The Power to Act*, Chaps.III-VII.

handicapped person:
- requires supervision in some or all aspects of everyday life;
- requires help and guidance in making reasonable judgements in many or all of the things involved in the process of daily life; and
- is unable continuously to care for himself or herself.

*Powers of tutors-dative*
It is still competent to seek appointment of a tutor-dative simply with all of the powers of a tutor, but the Scottish author is not aware of any modern case where this has happened. Firstly, powers have been limited to personal guardianship powers, and have excluded management powers, but this would seem to be because the person's needs have in each case been adequately met by an existing curator bonis or DSS appointee, or by hospital management,[56] except for one recent case where a tutor-dative was appointed solely to carry out a single act of management.[57] Secondly, in practice the minimum necessary intervention principle is applied, and powers are limited to those necessary in each individual case. Even where comprehensive powers are necessary, they are normally listed in some detail in the appointment. The following list of powers, which should be used selectively and adapted as necessary in each individual case, is based on current practice:
(a) To decide where he is to live, whether permanently or temporarily;
(b) To decide with whom he is to live and with whom he is to consort;
(c) To decide whether he should (or should be permitted to) engage in social activities and, if so, the nature and extent thereof and matters related thereto;
(d) To decide whether he should (or should be permitted to) work and, if so, the nature or type of work, for whom he is to work and matters related thereto;
(e) To decide whether he should (or should be permitted to) take or participate in any educational, vocational or other training and, if so, the nature and extent thereof and matters related thereto;
(f) To decide whether he should (or should be permitted to) apply for any licence, permit, approval or other consent or authorisation required by law;
(g) To commence, compromise or settle any legal proceeding that does not relate to his estate and to compromise or settle any proceeding taken against him that does not relate to his estate;
(h) To exercise all rights and powers competent to him under statute, and in particular under the Data Protection Act

---

[56] Under Mental Health (Scotland) Act 1984, s.94.
[57] *Queen* (1992), unreported.

1984, Access to Personal Files Act 1987, Access to Medical
Reports Act 1988, Environment and Safety Information
Act 1988 and Access to Health Records Act 1990;
(i)  To consent to any health care that is in his best interests;
(j)  To make normal day-to-day decisions on his behalf
     including as to his diet and dress.

Where decisions of particular importance or gravity are
necessary, the court may be requested specifically to authorise
them in the appointment. For example, the court may authorise an
operation to sterilise the person, where that is shown to be
appropriate.

*Persons who may be appointed*

Any suitable person, not just a parent or relative, may be
appointed. More than one person may be appointed: appointments
of two or three joint tutors-dative are normal. Recent appointees
have included both parents; both parents and a sibling; a widowed
parent and an unrelated family friend; a divorced parent plus a
sibling; and a curator bonis. Other appointments sought in current
cases include a single parent; a separated parent plus a sibling; and
a mother, aunt and sibling (where the father worked abroad).
Siblings and others frequently feature because of parents' anxiety
to provide continuity in event of their own death or incapacity. In
one case[58]:

> Appointment was sought of parents, together with a sister as substitute, to
> take over in event of death of both parents. Lord Caplan was reluctant to
> make such appointment, and the family were happy to accept joint
> appointment of all three. This case does not however entirely rule out the
> possibility of applying for appointment of a substitute.

It would be competent to seek appointment of unrelated carers,
which in some circumstances could be helpful in formalising and
recognising the relationship between carers and a mentally
handicapped person.

*Duration and review*

In early petitions[59] appointment was sought for a limited duration,
on the basis that justice required that the appointment be reviewed,
and in the absence of any mandatory review procedure this was
best achieved by limiting the duration of the appointment. In other
cases, where there was certification that no significant change in
capacity of the mentally handicapped person was foreseen such as
to warrant limiting the duration of the appointment, the
appointment was granted without such limitation.[60] It is now
doubtful whether the courts will continue to do this[61]:

> In a 1991 petition seeking appointment of unlimited duration, supported by
> appropriate medical certification, Lord Penrose took the view that the court

---

58  *Morris No 2* (1991), unreported.
59  For example *Morris No 1* (1986), unreported, where the initial appointment
    was for five years (renewed in *Morris No 2* (1991), for 10 years).
60  *e.g. Buchanan* (1989), unreported.
61  *Emslie* (1991), unreported.

ought to be in a position to monitor the appointment, and granted the petition subject to there being a review within 10 years.

Modern tutor-dative procedure has now developed to the point where it is appropriate for the courts to adopt Lord Penrose's approach. When many petitioners consider it appropriate, in the interests of the mentally handicapped person, voluntarily to ask the court to limit the duration of appointment, the court cannot be sure that such a safeguard will never prove to be necessary in cases where petitioners do not invite the court to impose it upon them. This approach recognises that while some people do require this form of guardianship, the appointment is a significant - albeit necessary - limitation of the rights of the mentally handicapped person. A further safeguard is that under the normal form of appointment the tutors-dative themselves, or any other person claiming an interest, may apply to the court for variation of the appointment at any time.

*Procedure*
Procedure is by way of petition to the Court of Session, dealt with by a single judge in the Outer House. Sheriff courts do not have jurisdiction to appoint tutors-dative. The petition is supported by medical evidence, commonly two medical certificates.[62] The petition states who are the nearest relatives, and is served on them. It is also served on the mentally handicapped person, unless the medical certificates give good reasons for not doing so (which rarely occurs). Service might also be appropriate on others, such as unrelated carers with whom the person resides, or any curator bonis. The petition briefly describes the person's handicap and medical condition, and the history of accommodation, care and training, up to and including present and any proposed future arrangements. The petition states whether the person has any assets or income. If so, they are specified, with a statement of present and any proposed future arrangements for administration of them. The petition concludes by setting out the proposed duration and precise terms of the appointment. The petition may be opposed by anyone on whom it has been served, including the mentally handicapped person, or by anyone else showing interest to do so. Unlike statutory guardianship, there is no requirement for social work input, or for notification of appointment to the Mental Welfare Commission.[63]

*Legal aid*
Eligibility to legal aid is assessed on the basis of the means of the mentally handicapped person, not those of the petitioner or proposed appointees. The proposed appointees (whether petitioners or not) are however each required to submit a legal aid

---

62  For an appropriate style of certificate, see *The Power to Act*, pp.48-49.
63  Though a substantial proportion of appointees have voluntarily assisted a recent research study by the Mental Welfare Commission of tutors-dative.

application form.[64] Unfamiliarity of legal aid officials with the
procedure sometimes gives rise to delay and difficulty.

*Effect of appointment*
Following appointment tutors-dative have legal authority to make
decisions and exercise guidance and supervision within the scope
of the powers contained in the appointment. They should
remember that in exercising powers conferred by the court they
are responsible and accountable to the court. They should
therefore exercise their powers in the best interests of the mentally
handicapped person, which includes using them to foster the
development of that person as far as possible, and to encourage
responsibility and self-reliance. Failure to do so may result in
removal, or non-renewal of the appointment. Anyone seriously
concerned about the conduct of tutors-dative should consider
whether their concerns ought to be drawn to the attention of the
court (appointments usually permit this). Local authorities, health
boards and others do of course require to consult tutors-dative in
any matters within the scope of the appointment. Tutors-dative
may grant authority to others within the scope of the appointment:
for example, they may authorise hostel staff to supervise diet and
dress, or to take the person for regular dental checks.

*Comment*
Tutor-dative procedure is an example of the inherent flexibility of
Scots law, which enables existing common law principles to be
applied to meet modern needs in ways which accord with
contemporary social circumstances and perceptions. After initially
sanctioning the refinements of limitation of powers and duration,
following the principle of minimum necessary intervention, the
courts are now moving towards insisting upon those refinements.
That sheriff courts cannot make appointments, that social work
departments are not notified of applications, and that appointments
are neither notified to nor supervised by the Mental Welfare
Commission, are all seen as disadvantages, which the Scottish Law
Commission propose should be rectified even if a new form of
statutory guardianship is not introduced to replace tutors-dative.[65]
More generally, there are concerns that appointment tends to
reinforce the parental role in an indiscriminate way.[66] The most
satisfactory further development of this area of law will be for
accumulated experience of the developing use of tutors-dative to
be carried forward into a new statutory form of personal
guardianship in the context of a comprehensive modern code of
private law provision for mentally disabled adults.

**Tutors-at-law**

At time of writing a petition to appoint a tutor-at-law is before the

---

64   See Legal Aid (Scotland), p.50.
65   Discussion Paper No.94 *Mentally Disabled Adults*, paras.2.29-2.33.
66   *The Power to Act*, p.53.

court, and other such petitions are contemplated. The nearest male agnate (*i.e.* relative on the father's side) is entitled to be served as tutor-at-law, though there is uncertainty as to the degree of incapacity warranting appointment. If appointed, the tutor-at-law has all the guardianship and management powers of the parent of a young child, and automatically supersedes any curator bonis. Although the procedure is in some ways antiquated and unsatisfactory, it has been considered as a possible solution in cases where carers are seriously dissatisfied with curatory, and where it is thought that it would be helpful for personal guardianship and management to be integrated in the same person. The case at present before the court is supported by the family and professional advisers, but opposed by an existing curator bonis.

## INFORMATION

During recent years several statutes have been passed giving individuals the right to inspect information held about them. Parents or carers who seek information relating to themselves will be able to exercise their statutory rights, but more often they will require information relating to the individual being cared for and then difficulties may arise. The most recent Act relating to health records attempts to address the problem and is considered below.

### Data Protection

Since the Data Protection Act 1984 came into force in November 1987 individuals have had the right to see most information stored about themselves on a computer. A Data Protection Registrar keeps a Register of computer users who hold personal information about individuals and this may be inspected by the public, but a direct approach may also be made to anyone who is believed to hold information on computer about the applicant, including departments of local authorities. A fee may be charged but time limits are laid down for a response and failure to reply to a request, although not a criminal offence, may result in a court order to comply (with costs) or enforcement by the Registrar leading on non-compliance to an offence. There are exemptions for certain types of data some of which (in particular medical and social records) are dealt with by regulations.

An individual who suffers damage because of inaccurate personal data held by a computer user is entitled to apply to the courts for compensation, but this will not be awarded if the computer user can prove that all reasonable care was taken to ensure accuracy. There is a right to have incorrect or misleading information corrected or erased.

### Local government

The Local Government (Access to Information) Act 1985 has considerably extended the right of members of the public to information from and about local government.[67]

## Personal files

The Access to Personal Files Act 1987 enables ministers to make regulations giving people a right of access to information about themselves on manually held local authority housing records and social work records.[68] The individual may obtain copies of such information and require amendment where appropriate. It is doubtful whether regulations could give authority for another person to have access to records on behalf of the individual to whom they relate, but some records may be treated as relating to the family. The Act states that "any obligation to give access to information is an obligation to give access to the individual who is the subject of it or is, under (the) Schedule, to be treated as such",[69] and the Schedule provides that "information about any member of the individual's family held for any purpose of that relationship or potential relationship shall be treated as information of which he is the subject and accessible by him accordingly".

### Social Services files

The Access to Personal Files (Social Services) Regulations 1989 now give individuals (including children) the right to see their manually held social services files. Provided that an individual applies in writing, pays the appropriate fee and supplies sufficient information to establish his identity and enable the local social services authority to locate the information, the authority is obliged to tell him whether they hold any information on him and to give him access to that information.[70] If the information for which an application has been received refers to another individual, the authority must within the specified time seek his or her consent to the information being disclosed. The information supplied must be that held at the time the request is made and must be supplied within the specified time. Provision is made for certain information to be exempt from disclosure,[71] for inaccurate information to be rectified or erased, and for the review of decisions by members of the local social services authority.[72]

## Medical reports

Under the Access to Medical Reports Act 1988 people have a right, in respect of a medical report about them prepared after

---

67    This topic is more conveniently covered in Chap.5 at p.225.

68    No right of access to any records exists under the Act unless regulations are made, and these will not relate to information prior to the date thereof.

69    s.2(3).

70    Regs.2, 3 and 4.

71    The decision of the European Court of Human Rights in the case of *Graham Gaskin*, July 7, 1989 is likely to result in new procedures.

72    Regs.5-11. For Scotland, see Access to Personal Files (Social Work) (Scotland) Regulations 1989, and Social Work Services Group Circular SW2/89, para.42.

January 1989 for an employer or insurance company, to see the report before it is sent and for six months afterwards. Reports by a doctor (including a consultant or psychiatrist) who has treated them are included but not those by an independent doctor acting purely for the employer or insurer. Before applying for a report the employer or insurer must obtain the individual's written consent and inform him of these rights. The individual is asked to say if he wishes to see the report before the doctor submits it, and if the answer is yes the doctor is notified and must wait for up to 21 days before releasing it so as to allow for access. If no contact is made within this period the doctor is free to submit the report. There is no charge for inspecting a report but a reasonable charge may be made for a copy. If the individual believes that the report is incorrect or misleading he can ask the doctor to correct it and, if the doctor refuses, to attach a written statement of his own views about the disputed matter.

*Exemptions*
A doctor can withhold information about any third party (including the identity of someone who has supplied information) but the identity of another doctor or health professional cannot be concealed. Information likely to cause serious harm to the individual or other persons can also be withheld. The doctor must notify the individual if any exempt information is withheld, and if it is felt that information is being wrongly withheld or that there is a breach of the statutory provisions an application can be made to the court for compliance. This can be ordered by the County Court in England, and by the Sheriff Court in Scotland.

**Education records**

*England*
Since September 1, 1989 there has been a duty to keep a manual curricular record for each pupil in local education authority maintained schools, grant maintained schools and special schools (whether or not so maintained), and provisions dealing with disclosure, correction and transfer came into effect a year later. The person entitled to see the record following a written request is the parent (for a pupil up to age 17) and also the pupil (from the age of 16), and it seems that a parent who does not have day-to-day care of the pupil has the right. There are certain exceptions, including where disclosure would, in the opinion of the record holder, be likely to cause serious harm to the physical or mental health or emotional condition of the pupil or any other person, and also statements of special educational needs under the Education Act 1981. Provision is made for the correction or removal of any inaccuracies found, and arrangements must be made by the governing body for appeals. If a pupil transfers from one school to another the record will usually be transferred.[73]

---

[73]   Education (School Records) Regulations 1989 made under the Education Reform Act 1988, ss.218 and 232. DES Circular No. 17/89.

*Scotland*

Pupils have the right of access to information, but require parental consent if they are under 16. Parents have right of access in respect of pupils under 18, and pupils over 18 unable (in the opinion of the education authority) to understand the information. The information which may be obtained is personal information kept as part of the pupil's progress record in education authority schools or kept in any other education (but not further education) records of the authority. The regulations list exceptions, and circumstances where disclosure depends on the opinion of a health professional, health board, or Reporter to a Children's Panel. Information must be given free of charge within 40 days of written request for it. The authority must either rectify any inaccuracy or note the complaint of inaccuracy. Refusal to disclose, or to correct an error, can be appealed to a sub-committee of the education committee.[74]

## Environment and safety

The Environment and Safety Information Act 1988 requires authorities who enforce four major safety, fire and environment laws to set up public registers containing details of enforcement notices that they have served. These are:

Fire Precautions Act 1971 - fire authorities;

Health and Safety at Work Act 1974 - Health and Safety
    Executive inspectorates;

Safety of Sports Grounds Act 1975 - local authorities;

Food and Environment Protection Act 1985 - agricultural
    inspectorate.

## Health records

Under the Access to Health Records Act 1990, people are allowed to see and copy information which has been manually recorded on their health records since November 1991. A health record is one which[75]:

> "(a) consists of information relating to the physical or mental health of an individual who can be identified from that information, or from that and other information in the possession of the holder of the record; and
> (b) has been made by or on behalf of a health professional in connection with the care of that individual."

Both the NHS and the private sector are covered, and though medical reports for social security purposes supplied by the regional medical service are not included, the government has given an undertaking that they will be made available. Health records held on computer are accessible under the Data Protection Act 1984 so are specifically excluded. A record not made in connection with the care of an individual does not fall within the

---

74    School Pupil Records (Scotland) Regulations 1990.
75    s.1(1). "Health professionals" include medical practitioners, dentists, opticians, pharmacists, nurses, midwives, health visitors, occupational therapists, physiotherapists and clinical psychologists.

definition, and in this context care is defined as including "examination, investigation, diagnosis and treatment". Thus the Act will not apply to a record about the physical or mental health of an individual made in connection with the investigation of a crime, and it is doubtful if it applies to a medical report prepared in connection with the education or residential care of the individual.[76]

*Applications*

Applications must be made in writing to the holder of the record, usually the GP or health authority, and access must usually be given within 40 days. Applicants can inspect the record in person or authorise a representative to do so, and they can have photocopies on payment of postage and photocopying costs. Any unintelligible terms must be explained. An access fee of up to £10 may be charged except for information added to the records in the previous 40 days.

*Persons under disability*

Provision is made as to who may be an applicant[77]:

"An application for access to a health record, or to any part of a health record, may be made to the holder of the record by any of the following:
(a) the patient;
(b) a person authorised in writing to make the application on the patient's behalf;
(c) where the record is held in England and Wales and the patient is a child, a person having parental responsibility for the patient;
(d) where the record is held in Scotland and the patient is a pupil, a parent or guardian of the patient;
(e) where the patient is incapable of managing his own affairs, any person appointed by a court to manage those affairs;
(f) where the patient has died, the patient's personal representative and any person who may have a claim arising out of the patient's death."

Parents wishing to see their child's record need the child's consent unless the child is incapable of understanding the nature of the application in which event access depends upon whether the record holder is satisfied that access is in the child's best interests.[78] Infants (in Scotland, children under 16) may be able to see their own records if the record holder is satisfied that there is sufficient understanding of the nature of the application.[79]

In the case of people who lack mental capacity, the person appointed by the court to manage their affairs is entitled to apply on their behalf. This provision is not as adequate as it may appear, because in England and Wales such appointment can only be made by the Court of Protection and then only when there are financial

---

[76]  If supplied to social services (work) department, it may be accessible under access to social services (work) files after consultation with the health professional.

[77]  s.3(1).

[78]  Information which, in the record holder's opinion, has been provided by the child in the expectation that it would be kept confidential from the parents will not be revealed.

[79]  s.4.

affairs that need to be managed. People with a mental handicap seldom have funds or assets which make the involvement of that court necessary, so may be denied their rights under the Act when the request can only be made by a parent or carer.

In Scotland, this Act appears to have the strange and unsatisfactory consequence that although access to medical records will almost always be required for personal rather than management reasons, a tutor-dative appointed as personal guardian is not given authority to apply for access, but a curator bonis (who is a manager, not a personal guardian) is. The answer may be that the statute should not be interpreted as employing the customary modern terminology which contrasts management of affairs with personal decision-making, but rather as meaning "affairs of a property or personal nature", in which case a tutor-dative appointed as personal guardian would be included. That the courts might take this approach is perhaps indicated by the customary inclusion in the specific powers conferred by the court upon tutors-dative of power to exercise rights under this statute. Another way of putting the argument would be to say that by conferring such powers the court appoints the tutor-dative as a manager of affairs within the meaning of this Act (whatever that meaning might be!).

*Exemptions*

Information which in the record holder's opinion is likely to cause serious harm to the physical or mental health of the patient or someone else need not be disclosed.[80] Also, information recorded before November 1991 will not have to be disclosed unless in the record holder's opinion it is necessary to make some later part of the record intelligible. Applicants have no right to be told if information has been withheld, but anyone who suspects this may appeal.

*Corrections*

A person who believes that part of a record is incorrect, misleading or incomplete can apply for it to be corrected. If the record holder accepts that the information is inaccurate, it must be corrected, but otherwise a note describing the applicant's views is added to the record. In either case a copy of the correction or note must be supplied to the applicant without charge.

*Appeals*

An applicant who considers that a record holder is failing to comply with the Act, for example by improperly withholding information, refusing to correct information which is inaccurate or acting on the basis of a wholly unreasonable opinion, must first go through an internal complaints procedure which will be set up by regulations. If still dissatisfied an application may be made to the court to order compliance.

---

80   Information identifying third parties may not be disclosed without consent.

## RELATIONSHIPS

Informal carers may encounter difficulties in their relationships with others, including those who may be classed as professional carers. Despite their contribution, informal carers often have no right to be consulted and their role is often taken for granted. We now consider the relationship between such professionals and the informal carers of a mentally handicapped adult.

### Social workers

Parents of a mentally handicapped child should be known to their local Social Services Department (in Scotland, the Social Work Department)[81] and have a social worker allocated to them, though many do not. Many of the services which people with a disability need are provided by or through this department, and a satisfactory relationship with a social worker can be supportive and the gateway for contact with other service providers. Under community care policies local authorities through their social services departments take on an increasing role in providing for disabled people, including assessment of need, preparation of care packages and funding. They must identify members of the local community who need special provision so that advance planning can take place.

### Problems

Difficulties can arise where the relationship with the social worker breaks down. Parents may feel threatened if the social worker takes a different view of a situation, and care must then be taken to avoid a breakdown in the relationship. In some cases there may be a failure by the social services department to distinguish between the situation of a problem family and that of a problem child in an otherwise stable family environment, and policies within this relatively new profession appear to be still evolving often at the expense of parents as the following 1985 case history shows:

> Parents who had approached social services for practical help in coping with an extremely active mentally retarded child discovered that, although no such help was given, the child had without their knowledge been placed on the "at risk" register and case conferences held by professionals concerned with the child. After observing the secret official monitoring for some time the parents protested but the social worker seemed more concerned at how they had found out than the effect it was having upon them. Access was requested to the files because the parents could not identify anything to justify this treatment, but this was refused and the reason stated for inclusion on the register was "The mother admitted to smacking him on occasions". The parents felt that they had been denied an opportunity to participate in the concern shown about their child, despite the fact that they were left to cope on their own, and that they had been prejudiced in their relationship with the various professionals. This undermined their confidence in themselves and in the authorities responsible for helping them.

---

81   In England and Wales this is a department of the County (or Metropolitan) Council. In Scotland it is a department of the Regional (or Islands) Council. Usually found in the telephone directory under the name of the Council, sub-heading Social Services (or Social Work) Department.

The Court of Appeal has recently held that parents have no legal right to attend a case conference, but that they should be given a proper opportunity to comment on any allegations that may have been made.[82] The decision to place a child's name on the child abuse register will be subject to judicial review if it can be shown to be utterly unreasonable, but this will be rare because the welfare of the child is paramount and the interest of an adult accused of abuse may have to be subordinated to the child's interest. The local authority is not carrying out a judicial process since an entry in the register as an abuser is neither a finding of fact nor a finding of guilt. A similar approach was adopted in a later case, when it was stated that recourse to judicial review in respect of decisions which did not involve removing a child from the care of a parent ought to be rare and adopted only in exceptional cases.[83]

*Advice*

Parents should be advised to keep a file containing, preferably in chronological order, all letters and documents relating to their child, and also a brief note of all meetings with social workers and other professionals, summarising matters discussed and decisions reached. In the event of conflict social services and any other departments will refer to their own file in which contact with parents is noted and discussions recorded, often with the writer's comments. This will be produced at any case conference or court hearing, and the parents will be at a disadvantage if they can only rely upon their memory when faced with such evidence.

## Other professionals

Personal contact with the headteacher and child's teachers should be maintained as valuable support and information can be obtained from this source. Considerable practical help may also be available from a health visitor, especially if specially trained in regard to mental handicap, and regular contact including home visits should be encouraged. At a relatively early stage, when parents have become aware of the special educational needs of their child and consideration is being given to the ways that these can be met, contact will be made by an educational psychologist employed by the local education authority. Positive advice is available from this source, although this may need to be carefully weighed against the views of the parents and any independent professional advice, because the psychologist's views may be influenced by the provision that the authority has available.

---

82   *R.* v. *Harrow London Borough Council, ex p. D* [1990] 3 All ER 12.

83   *R.* v. *East Sussex County Council, ex p. R* [1991] 2 FLR 358. As to the balancing act to be performed before deciding whether to disclose the name of a suspected child abuser, see *R.* v. *Lewisham LBC, ex p. P.* [1991] 3 All ER 529. The child's interests do not totally over-ride those of others.

## RESPONSIBILITIES

Various duties and responsibilities are imposed by statute upon professional or paid carers, often involving registration with and supervision by the local authority. We concentrate here on the informal carer who will usually be a parent or relative. Carers will be liable for damages in respect of any assault upon the person cared for, and in serious cases could be prosecuted if a criminal offence has been committed which can include neglect or ill-treatment.

### Insurance

An informal carer may need to make special insurance arrangements by reason of the provision of care for an adult with a mental handicap. It is advisable to read the small print to see if any pre-existing medical condition or disability must be declared. The contract of insurance depends upon full disclosure of any matters which may affect the risk and in default the policy may be void. It is not usually necessary to disclose the existence of children when submitting an insurance proposal, but the presence of a person with a mental handicap may be different. The correct approach may be to consider not the mere existence of a mental handicap, but whether the ability and behaviour of the individual materially affects the risk to a greater extent than the presence of any other member of the household, such as a child. If past history shows that it does, or several handicapped persons are involved, it will usually be desirable to disclose this.

*Property insurance*

Most household insurance policies cover the proposer and other members of the household against legal liability to pay damages as a result of an accident causing injury to another person or damage to property. This will not extend to injury to a member of the household or domestic employee or the property of such a person, but liability to a domestic employee may be covered, so if a nanny or domestic help is employed this point should be checked. The policyholder is expected to take all reasonable precautions to prevent a claim and to ensure that every member of the household complies with the policy terms, and this may create some vulnerability where the mental handicap is relevant unless it has been disclosed.

*Motor insurance*

Concern has been expressed as to whether drivers who regularly carry passengers with a mental handicap should disclose this to their motor insurers. The above approach would seem to apply and in each case it may be a matter of degree. It is suggested that the implications rather than the existence of the handicap are relevant. Care workers who regularly drive disabled persons in their cars should consider whether to disclose this to the insurers, especially if disruptive behaviour is a possibility. They should also discuss this with employers, since it will be necessary to clarify whether doing so is within the course of employment and therefore a potential claim on the employers liability insurers. The taxi firm that transports a group of such passengers under contract should make full disclosure and carry an escort when necessary. The situation of the individual parent or carer may be different. The occurrence of a potentially dangerous incident in a vehicle may give rise to a need to disclose, yet many children display irrational and disruptive behaviour during certain periods of their lives and it is not suggested that the mere existence of a child must be disclosed. Few insurers would wish to load the premium in such circumstances unless there have been problems and proposal forms only ask about other drivers and not regular passengers. Clearly there is a difference between a passenger who is physically incapable and one who displays unpredictable behaviour (*e.g.* may try to leave the car whilst it is in motion or interfere with the driver). In some cases it might be unwise to take an individual in a vehicle without an escort, but this could be difficult for a family already struggling to cope with a handicapped member yet needing mobility.

### Death and incapacity

Many severely handicapped individuals now outlive their parents and it should not be assumed that other members of the family will take over the caring role, so parents have a responsibility to make provision for this eventuality. An abrupt change is not in the best interests of the person being cared for and opportunities are increasingly available for parents to let go before a crisis arises. The legal adviser should be aware of the need to face realities, but great tact is required in discussing this topic with those parents who of necessity have had to bring up their son or daughter with little outside help and are unable to contemplate a new situation. In Scotland, parental anxieties about what will happen in the event of their death or incapacity can to some extent be alleviated by having a younger person appointed as joint tutor-dative with them.

### FINANCIAL RESPONSIBILITIES

### Marriage breakdown (England)

*Infant child*
On any application made by a parent or guardian of a child under 18 years of age, or by any person in whose favour a residence order is in force with respect to such a child, the court may make one or more of the following orders against a parent[84]:
  (a) a periodical payments order;
  (b) a secured periodical payments order;

---

84    Children Act 1989, Sched.1. The High Court, county court and magistrates court all have jurisdiction, but the magistrates may only make periodical payments and lump sum orders.

    (c) a lump sum order;

    (d) a settlement of property order;

    (e) a transfer of property order.

"Parent" includes a party to a marriage in relation to whom the child is a "child of the family". In each case the order may be in favour of the applicant or the child, and for such amount as the court thinks fit. Periodical payments orders will be for a period fixed by the court and may later be varied or discharged, but will not continue beyond the age of 17 years unless the child is:

    - receiving instruction at an educational establishment or undergoing training for a trade, profession or vocation;  or

    - there are special circumstances justifying the order.

Such orders (unless secured) will cease on the death of the paying parent or if that parent lives with the other parent for more than six months.

### Relevant matters

In deciding whether to exercise its powers and if so in what manner, the court has regard to all the circumstances including:

    (a) the income, earning capacity, property and other financial resources which each relevant person[85] has or is likely to have in the foreseeable future;

    (b) the financial needs, obligations and responsibilities which each relevant person has or is likely to have in the foreseeable future;

    (c) the financial needs of the child;

    (d) the income, earning capacity (if any), property and other financial resources of the child;

    (e) any physical or *mental disability of the child*;

    (f) the manner in which the child was being, or was expected to be, educated or trained.

In deciding whether to exercise its powers against a person who is not the mother or father of the child (*i.e.* a new spouse who has accepted the child as a "child of the family") and if so in what manner, the court also has regard to the extent to which that person has assumed responsibility for the child knowing that the child was not his, and the liability of the natural parent to maintain the child.

### Maintenance agreements

An agreement may be reached without the need for a court order, but this must be on the statutory form.[86]

### Adult child

The question arises whether mental handicap amounts to special circumstances justifying the making of a periodical payments order against a parent for the life of the child. In view of the implications of state and local authority funding it may be unwise

---

[85] *I.e.* the parents (as defined), applicant and recipient.

[86] See Children Act 1989, Sched.1, para.10.

for parents to agree to or invite the court to make such an order.[87] Even a nominal order may keep alive the right to increase the amount later.

A child who has attained 18 years may apply at any time for a new periodical payments or lump sum order against either or both parents if one of the conditions set out above is satisfied and the parents are not living with each other in the same household.[88] This raises the doubtful possibility that if the parents of an adult mentally handicapped child are living apart and no periodical payments order has previously been made in respect of the child, the local authority can cause an application to be made in the name of the child and thereby establish liability on the part of a parent to contribute towards the cost of the accommodation or services provided for the child. If this was intended, it is strange that the power only exists in such restricted circumstances, as apart from this statutory provision there would be no liability on the part of the parent to contribute. If the court finds special circumstances to make the order then the means-tested support otherwise available to the child would not appear to be one of the matters to be taken into account, whereas the existence of the mental handicap and the needs of the child must be taken into account.

**Parental aliment obligations (Scotland)[89]**

Both parents have an obligation to aliment their children, and their marital status is irrelevant. Anyone who has accepted[90] the child as a child of the family has a similar obligation: this could cover a step-parent, or a relative who brings up the child. The obligation extends to all children up to the age of 18 and to those up to 25 who are reasonably and appropriately undergoing instruction at an educational establishment, or training for employment or for a trade, profession or vocation. These provisions may be difficult to interpret in relation to some mentally handicapped people in the 18-25 age-group (*e.g.* it is not certain that attendance at an adult training centre qualifies them) but unless they come within the definition the parents' obligation to aliment ceases at 18. Parents have no obligation to aliment their sons or daughters over 25, however great their needs.

The obligation is to provide such financial support as is reasonable in the circumstances. Relevant factors are the needs and resources of both the parent and the child, the earning capacities of both, and all the circumstances of the case.[91] The child's mental handicap and the financial and other consequences of the handicap can

---

87   This topic is considered in Chap.9.
88   Sched.1, para.2. The child may not apply if immediately before attaining 16 years a periodical payments order was in force with respect to the child, para.2(3).
89   See Family Law (Scotland) Act 1985.
90   For difficulties caused by use of *accepted* rather than *treated*, see J.M. Thomson, *Family Law in Scotland*, p.153.
91   1985 Act, s.4(1).

accordingly be relevant factors; but the needs of a child aged 18-25, however great, are irrelevant if the child does not meet the "instruction or training" test described above.

## Voluntary support

Usually parents wish to provide support for their adult mentally handicapped child but need to be careful how they do so. If the child is eligible for means-tested state benefit and local authority support, any money paid to the child, especially if on a regular basis, may be counter-productive unless substantial. It will usually be more beneficial for parents to provide the use of facilities (including perhaps the right to occupy a home), and clothing and personal effects by way of gift.

### Income tax allowances

The policy now seems to be to provide financial assistance for carers through the social security system rather than by way of tax allowances. There are no longer any tax reliefs or allowances specifically targetted at carers, save that certain social security benefits are not taxable. An additional personal allowance (bringing the personal allowance up to the level for a married couple) is available to single parents who have living with them their child (including a step-child or adopted child), or any other child under the age of 18 whom they are maintaining, and in either case such child is in full-time education or training for at least two years for a trade or profession. This provision appears to discriminate against parents of a handicapped child who has left school to attend a special training establishment.

## PART III - REMEDIES

### Preliminary

When a parent or carer alleges that his rights have been infringed, or that he or the person cared for is not receiving all appropriate services, it is necessary to consider the remedies (if any) that are available and whether these are adequate. We now look at some of these remedies.

## CHALLENGING DECISIONS

Parents and others who have become, or chosen to be, informal carers may have difficulty in obtaining an adequate package of care provision. Appropriate handling of the matter may be more productive than single-minded reliance on legal rights.

### Entitlement to Services

One of the questions likely to be asked is "What am I entitled to?" This may relate to education or training, financial support, housing, domiciliary or day services, or residential care. Assessments and case conferences form an essential part of the procedures involved in the provision of support and services, and parents or carers should participate in these. Good practices may be of more importance than legal rights, but these depend upon the availability of adequate services and funding. It is desirable to provide entitlement to at least a minimum level of provision, but most legislation is qualified in its terms so as to deny the individual legal redress.

*Decision or indecision?*
It is first necessary to decide whether a decision has been made by the relevant authority which should be challenged, or whether the problem is that no decision has been (or is to be) made, and then to ascertain whether this is a request which the authority is under an obligation to consider even if the outcome may be difficult to challenge. Delay by the authority may be the most effective way of avoiding providing services when shortage of funds or lack of facilities make it difficult to fulfil a request.

## Complaining

Carers who feel that they are receiving inadequate services will wish to complain. Those who complain the most persistently or emotionally often get priority, but others with greater needs may not be able to behave in that way until they have actually passed breaking point. Complaints should be in an appropriate form to the right person and in some instances it may be more effective for a group of disadvantaged persons to put forward a common complaint. It is desirable to identify who would be responsible for providing the service, and to contact that person preferably in writing with a carefully reasoned case. Whenever possible ask for a review of a decision and be prepared to accept a compromise, as this is usually quicker than adopting any appeal procedure and less damaging than an unsuccessful appeal. The legal position should however be checked at an early stage, especially in relation to any enforceable duties or time limits for taking action.

*The press*
Airing a complaint in the press should be seen as a last resort for an individual, but where the complaint is of a lack of services generally, or the withdrawal of a valuable facility, and there are many motivated persons in the community, the local press may be interested in taking up the campaign in a constructive manner and this may be very effective. Any lawyer involved should ensure that the press are adequately briefed and that all facts put forward are correct. It is usually best to present the arguments in a moderate manner and avoid an excess of emotion, because the press look for a headline and this may deflect from the real issue.

In 1991 a media campaign was launched in Scotland about provision of educational speech therapy. There was a good coverage in the press and on radio and television. Great care was taken in the choice of families put forward for interview. A solicitor briefed all journalists and radio and TV researchers to ensure legal accuracy and that coverage concentrated on the lack of provision rather than apportioning blame, thus enabling politicians to become involved in a positive way. When the Minister promised to investigate individual cases drawn to his attention, it was ensured that he was inundated with letters and also that a radio phone-in was jammed with calls. The outcome was a rapid improvement in services and long-term measures being taken to maintain this.

## Appeal procedures

Whilst negotiations are continuing, check if there is an appeal procedure. The authority will usually be under an obligation to provide details and in some cases there will be a complaints procedure.[92] Most people who make administrative decisions are reluctant to see these challenged, so further negotiation may then become possible. Green Form legal advice (in Scotland, legal advice and assistance) may cover this.

## Default orders

In England, Ministers have in certain cases specific powers of control over authorities that fail to carry out statutory functions. They may issue directions or transfer the powers of the defaulting authority to themselves or to another authority. These powers are seldom used.

In Scotland, complaint may be made to the Secretary of State (or any appropriate minister) that a local authority has failed to do something which by statute it is required to do. On receipt of such a complaint (or on his own initiative) he may cause a local inquiry to be held into the matter and if then satisfied that the authority is in default, may make a default order specifying the steps to be taken by the local authority to remedy the default, and setting a deadline. If the authority fails to comply by the deadline, the Secretary of State or minister may (through the Lord Advocate) apply to the Court of Session to order specific performance and do whatever else the court considers just. This is a general procedure in addition to, and not in place of, other more specific provisions regarding enforcement of statutory duty.[93]

## COURT PROCEEDINGS

Mental handicap does not deprive an individual of the ability to have his legal rights enforced through the courts, though usually the need for proceedings will be identified by the parents or carers who then initiate the necessary steps on behalf of the individual. One of the first decisions to be made is whether the claim is that of the parents or carers or that of the person cared for, and this will depend upon the nature of the claim. The rights of handicapped individuals and the manner in which they may conduct court proceedings have been considered in the previous chapter. We consider here some remedies that parents and carers may wish to

---

92 *e.g.* to a user committee of some public undertaking. This is appropriate in the event of dissatisfaction with facilities for travel by rail, or the supply of water, gas or electricity, or the use of the telephone. The statutory social services (or social work) complaints procedure is another example.

93 Local Government (Scotland) Act 1973, s.211.

consider when not satisfied with the conduct of the authorities or the policies that are applied.

## Judicial review

### England

One of the most rapidly developing remedies in the field of provision for disabled persons is the judicial review procedure which may be used to force a local authority to do something it is legally obliged to do or to prevent it from a particular course of action. The procedure is based on the common law remedies of declaration and the prerogative writs which have now been consolidated.[94] Proceedings must be commenced in the High Court and a series of complicated rules has been developed to govern the circumstances in which the procedure is available. There may be long delays in a case being heard, although urgent cases can be expedited. Even if a case is made out, the relief is discretionary and the court will not necessarily grant a remedy.

### Scope

Relief is available where the decisions of inferior courts, tribunals and public bodies are unlawful. This could be for one of several reasons, namely that the decision is:

(a) *ultra vires* (*i.e.* outside the powers of the body making it);

(b) contrary to the rules of natural justice;

(c) made in a way that is procedurally incorrect;

(d) based on a misinterpretation of the law;

(e) unreasonable or irrational (*e.g.* a material consideration was not taken into account, or matters have been taken into account which ought not to have been).

The courts tend to concern themselves with the decision-making process rather than the merits of the decision. In order to be upset on the irrational ground a decision must be "so outrageous in its defiance of logic or of accepted moral standards that no sensible person who had applied his mind to the question to be decided could have arrived at it".[95]

The *Wednesbury principle* is relevant in this context[96]:

> "a person entrusted with discretion must ... direct himself properly in law, he must call his own attention to the matters which he is bound to consider ... Similarly, there may be something so absurd that no sensible person could ever dream that it lay within the powers of the authority."

Examples of situations in which the remedy might be appropriate in the interests of persons with a mental handicap are:

> A local authority imposes charges for services which it is under a general duty to provide for disabled persons, and these charges are far in excess of the actual cost.
>
> An education authority proposes to close a special school without

---

94 Supreme Court Act 1981, s.31 and RSC, Ord.53.

95 *CCSU* v. *Minister for Civil Service* [1985] AC 374, *per* Lord Diplock.

96 *Associated Provincial Picture Houses Ltd* v. *Wednesbury Corporation* [1947] 2 All ER 680.

complying with the full statutory procedures (*e.g.* no consultation or the authority did not state in advance its proposals for all existing children attending the school).

A decision to close a special school is made by the chairman of the education committee rather than by the committee itself.

An education authority fails to provide a Statement of special educational needs in respect of a handicapped child when this is required, or fails to make the educational provision specified in a Statement.

## Leave to apply

The applicant must first obtain leave to apply for judicial review from a High Court judge on a written application although a hearing may be held especially if the matter is urgent. All that is required is a statement of the details of the decision to be challenged, the relief sought and the grounds for doing so, and an Affidavit will be lodged in support. The application for leave must be made promptly and in any event within three months from the date when the grounds for the application arose. An applicant must have sufficient interest in the matter to which the application relates and must normally have used all existing internal appeal procedures before leave will be given.[97]

## Procedure

If leave is granted the applicant serves an originating summons on the respondent and any other person affected, each of whom will file affidavits in response. Such affidavits are usually relied upon as evidence at the hearing although oral evidence may be given. Discovery is not often required and hearings are often short and in consequence not necessarily expensive.

## Remedies

The orders that can be made are:

| | | |
|---|---|---|
| *mandamus* | - | to compel the performance of a public duty imposed by law; |
| *prohibition* | - | to restrain an inferior court from acting unlawfully in the future; |
| *certiorari* | - | to review and if necessary quash a wrong decision; |
| *injunction* | - | to require a party to do, or refrain from doing, a particular act; |
| *declaration* | - | a finding of the court on a question of law or rights. |

## Legal aid

Legal aid is available for judicial review but will only be granted if the Legal Aid Committee considers that there is a reasonable chance of success and that legal action would be justified in terms of the likely cost.

## Scotland

Judicial review is intended as a relatively simple and expeditious

---

[97] In an application involving a local authority this could involve using an existing appeal procedure to the Secretary of State.

procedure by which the Court of Session now exercises its supervisory jurisdiction to review the acts, omissions and decisions of a judicial, quasi-judicial or administrative nature of a wide range of bodies with judicial and administrative powers.[98] Judicial review is only available where there is no statutory appeal or review procedure which would provide an adequate remedy. The bodies whose acts, omissions or decisions may be reviewed include the Crown, ministers and their servants (with some limitations); local authorities, health boards, Scottish Homes, Scottish Enterprise, the Mental Welfare Commission for Scotland, inferior courts and tribunals, and many other public boards and bodies.

*Grounds of challenge*

Acts and decisions may be challenged on grounds that:
- they are *ultra vires* (outwith the powers of the body in question);
- they are so unreasonable that no reasonable authority would have so acted or decided;
- in making a decision the authority has taken into account matters which it ought not, or failed to take account of matters which it should;
- a discretionary power has been exercised for an improper purpose;
- there has been improper delegation of decision-making;
- there has been adherence to a fixed policy and failure to treat a matter on its merits;
- the body has acted contrary to natural justice;
- there has been failure to follow procedure correctly.

Mere exercise of managerial powers (as opposed to administrative acts) and exercise of the Royal Prerogative are not reviewable.

*Procedure*

There is a prescribed form of petition and matters which require to be set forth in the petition include:
- particulars of the parties;
- the title and interest of the applicant to bring the petition;
- the act, omission or decision to be reviewed;
- the remedies sought;
- the grounds of challenge;
- the legal arguments, with enactments and cases to be founded on; and
- relevant legal pleas.

All relevant documents must be listed and lodged, with an affidavit as to essential matters not apparent from the documents. The application is dealt with by a single judge who immediately makes a first order for intimation and service, and may grant an interim order at that stage. He sets a date for the first hearing, when he may either decide the matter, or make an interim order or order

---

98    The procedure is governed by Rule of Court 260B. See generally J. St Clair and N.F. Davidson, *Judicial Review in Scotland*.

for further procedure, as he thinks fit. If the matter goes to a second hearing, he may then adjourn the hearing, continue it for further procedure, or decide the matter.

*Remedies*
The court may make such orders as it thinks fit, interim or final, and whether or not sought in the application. The whole range of civil remedies is available, including orders for reduction, declarator, suspension, interdict, implement, restitution and payment (of damages or otherwise).

## European Court of Justice

This Court, based in Luxembourg, is the ultimate appeal court on matters relating to the Treaty of the European Community. Its decisions, which are binding upon the courts of the United Kingdom, are becoming increasingly important in shaping our law. In particular there have been a number of significant appeals by pressure groups[99] and more are likely in the future. The role of this court may be of particular interest in cases involving discrimination against handicapped persons. An example of an unsuccessful attempt to establish sex discrimination in a case involving state benefits for a carer illustrates this[100]:

> A widow claimed Invalid Care Allowance for the care of her daughter. She was eligible but also received a widow's pension which was greater, so no part of the allowance was paid. She claimed that this was unlawful sex discrimination as it was the widow's pension which rendered her unable to receive the care allowance thus causing her to be treated less favourably than a male. It was held that this was not caused by discrimination but resulted from the fact that she started from a different situation from that of any man, who may not receive a widow's pension.

*Preliminary rulings*
Where an issue of European Community law arises before a national court, questions of interpretation or validity can be referred to the Court for a preliminary ruling.[101] The procedure is available to national courts, not to the parties appearing before the court, and it is the court which decides the question to be referred. In social security matters, a reference can be made by a Social Security Appeal Tribunal, a Commissioner or the courts. Where a party is legally aided the Certificate may be extended to cover the reference, but the Court itself may grant legal aid in special circumstances for "the purpose of facilitating the representation or attendance of a party".

## European Court of Human Rights

It is possible to take a case to this Court in order to protect an individual's fundamental rights against government misuse of power, and this may be relevant to people with a mental handicap

---

99  *e.g.* the successful challenge by CPAG of the refusal by DSS to pay Invalid Care Allowance to women who were married or co-habiting.
100  [1990] 2 CMLR 399.
101  Article 177 of the Treaty of Rome.

whose rights are vulnerable to being overridden.[102]
In 1950 the Council of Europe formulated the *European Convention on Human Rights* which, although not legally enforceable in member states, sets out certain fundamental human rights concerned with liberty, natural justice, respect for privacy, freedom of expression and from discrimination, and including the right to marry. By Article 1 all countries which ratify the Convention agree that they shall secure to everyone within their jurisdiction the rights and freedoms contained in the Convention. Various *Protocols* have followed some of which have been ratified by the United Kingdom.

### The Commission

The European Commission of Human Rights hears complaints that individual's rights under the Convention have been violated by a member state. It comprises one member for every state which is a party to the Convention, sits in camera and is governed by Rules of Procedure. The staff are helpful and speak English, and may be contacted at the address in Appendix I.

### Case Reports

Reports on cases are published in *Decisions and Reports* which appears four times a year.[103] *European Human Rights Reports* are also published bi-monthly by The European Law Centre at Sweet & Maxwell.[104]

### Complaints

Complaints can only be made to the Commission if one or more of the fundamental rights has been violated, all available remedies in the member state concerned have been exhausted, and the application is made within six months of the final decision of the highest competent court or authority.[105] A complaint may initially be by letter containing a summary of the complaint, details of the Convention rights violated and of the remedies used or attempted, and a chronological history of the case. Details of all decisions of the courts or the authorities should be provided.

The complaint letter will be acknowledged by the secretary and further information may be asked for. If the complaint is capable of registration as an application a set of forms will be supplied and these must be completed and submitted as the formal application. The Commission then considers whether the application is *admissible* (*i.e.* whether a *prima facie* case has been made out) and may refer to the relevant government for its observations, but the

---

102   This material is based on an article by Luke Clements in Legal Action, January 1991. For further information contact the Legal Officer, Interights, 5-15 Cromer Street, London WC1H 8LS.

103   Copies may be obtained from HMSO, Agency Section, 51 Nine Elms Lane, London SW8 5DR. Information sheets are issued free of charge by the Commission giving details of recent decisions.

104   ITPS Ltd., Cheriton House, North Way, Andover, Hampshire SP10 5BE.

105   Absence of legal aid is not an acceptable excuse, but the position might be otherwise if the applicant is mentally incapable of acting in person.

applicant is given an opportunity to comment thereon. If the application is admissible the Commission endeavours to secure a friendly settlement, which may involve an agreement to amend the law or procedures, or the payments of costs or compensation.

### European Court of Human Rights

If a friendly settlement cannot be achieved the case is referred to the Court. The Commission prepares a report detailing the facts of the case and giving its view on whether the case constitutes a violation of the Convention. The Court comprises one judge for every state which is a party to the Convention and is governed by Rules of Procedure. Most cases are heard by a chamber composed of seven judges whose names are drawn by lot, together with the judge from the state concerned and the president (or vice-president). In some cases the entire court sits. The Court usually considers written observations first and then fixes a hearing date. Hearings may be in public and the state concerned is a party with one or more commissioners appearing as delegates to assist the Court in the capacity of "defenders of the public interest". The main issue is between the Court and the state, to establish whether a violation has occurred, but the applicant may also on request be represented by an advocate at the hearing. An advocate must be either a solicitor, barrister or advocate, or other person approved by the president. Proceedings once before the Court can take up to two years, and judgment is always reserved.

### Legal Aid

The Commission may grant legal aid, which is funded by the Council of Europe, either at the applicant's request or of its own volition, but only if satisfied that this is essential for the proper discharge of its duties and the applicant has insufficient means. The applicant must fill in forms for this purpose which are then certified by DSS (Policy Section at Preston), and if granted fixed payments are specified for each stage of the proceedings.

### Relevance to mental handicap

Although there have been a number of cases involving mental health, problems caused by mental handicap have featured far less frequently. In a recent application[106] the Commission has requested written observations from the UK government on the admissibility and merits of a case concerning a father's access to his mentally handicapped daughter:

> The daughter was placed in care in 1979 and sent to a special school, but the father had access to her until 1987. Such access had to be terminated because of, *inter alia,* the daughter's negative reactions to the father's visits. In March 1988 the daughter reached 18 years of age and, although the care order had expired, the local authority continued to refuse access.

## OMBUDSMEN

The concept of an *ombudsman* has grown during the last 25 years,

---

[106] No.14247/88.

this being an independent person who can investigate and report on complaints by members of the public about the way they have been treated by particular public bodies. Reference to an ombudsman may be a suitable way of seeking redress in situations where there is no legal remedy and procedures which unfairly discriminate against handicapped persons are an example. The bringing of a complaint does not necessarily provide an adequate remedy, but may discourage similar administrative action in subsequent cases.

*Maladministration*
Complaints dealt with relate to bad administration, which is usually referred to as *maladministration*. This term has not been defined, but refers to the way in which a matter has been handled rather than the actual merits of a decision, and thus includes administrative action (or inaction) based on or influenced by improper considerations or conduct. It is much wider than illegality, though it includes failure to comply with a legal obligation. It may take many forms including unjustifiable delay, incompetence, neglect, discourtesy or harassment, bias or unfair discrimination, mistakes in the handling of claims, and failing to give proper advice or follow recognised procedures or take account of representations. There is no power to question the merits of a decision where there is no maladministration.[107]
The person complaining must usually have suffered injustice as a result of maladministration. This may range from disappointment or a lost opportunity to a serious financial loss, and frustration in not having received replies to letters may be enough.

## Parliamentary Commissioner for Administration

This Commissioner (referred to here as "PCA" but commonly known as the *Parliamentary Ombudsman*) is someone completely independent of the government who can investigate complaints by members of the public about the way they have been treated by government departments and certain non-departmental public bodies.[108] The Office was set up in 1967 for England, Wales and Scotland, and there is a separate Commissioner for Northern Ireland.[109]

*Complaints*
The individual must have suffered injustice as a result of maladministration and the actions giving rise to the grievance must

---

[107] See the judgment of Lord Denning in *R* v. *Local Commissioner for Administration, ex p. Bradford MCC* [1979] 2 All ER 881.

[108] Inland Revenue, Legal Aid Boards, Scottish Office, Lord Chancellor's Department, and the Departments of Social Security, Transport, Environment and Employment. Also bodies such as the Arts Council, Data Protection Registrar, Countryside Commissions, Equal Opportunities Commission, Commission for Racial Equality, Medical Practices Committee, Housing Corporation, Sports Councils, the Tourist Boards and various Industry Training Boards.

[109] Parliamentary Commissioner Act 1967.

be administrative in nature, and have affected the complainant personally or, in the case of a group of persons such as a society or association, they must affect the specific interests of that group and its members. Complaints about government policy or the content of legislation are matters for Parliament itself and may not be dealt with. The complainant must either be resident in the UK or have been resident there when the actions complained of took place, unless it can be shown that the complaint concerns rights and obligations arising in the UK. There are certain matters which the PCA cannot investigate,[110] and he cannot look into complaints against the police, nationalised industries or similar bodies such as the Post Office, British Rail or the Civil Aviation Authority.

Before a complaint can be investigated, all existing means of seeking redress must first be exhausted. If a remedy may be available in the courts the PCA may only become involved if he considers it unreasonable to expect the complainant to go to court, and the cost is not normally regarded on its own as a good reason. Once a matter is being dealt with by the court there remains no discretion for the PCA to investigate it.

*Procedure*

The PCA will only become involved in a complaint if asked by a Member of Parliament,[111] who effectively acts as a barrier for trivial or inappropriate complaints and presumably will consider whether a complaint is properly brought on behalf and in the best interests of a person who lacks mental capacity. A person who is ill or otherwise unable to make a complaint may get a member of the family or a friend to do it for him and a professional person such as a solicitor may also present the complaint. The PCA must be satisfied that the person with the grievance actually wants the matter to be investigated and this may cause problems when that person is incapable of forming such intent.

The complainant must offer some evidence that he has personally been affected by bad administration, and this will usually involve producing correspondence and documents, though these will be returned when the investigation is over. The MP may try to sort the matter out by approaching the department concerned before refering to the PCA. The complaint must usually be brought within a year of the grievance arising though there is a discretion to allow a longer time.

After considering the complaint the PCA will either write to the MP confirming that he has accepted it, or give reasons for not being able to take it up. He does not usually see complainants personally, though in some cases further information may be requested and this could involve a visit to the complainant's home. There is provision for expenses to be paid where these must be

---

110  *e.g.* personnel matters matters in the public service and armed forces, the investigation of crime, conduct of proceedings by government departments.

111  This does not have to be the complainant's own MP but in most cases this will be the appropriate person to approach in the first instance.

incurred as part of the investigation.

*Powers*
The PCA has powers similar to those of the High Court (in Scotland, the Court of Session), but does not operate formally and proceedings are always in private. He may inspect government files and papers and can summon anyone to give evidence in an investigation.

*Decision*
When the investigating officers have collected all the relevant information the PCA personally considers the case and decides whether to uphold the complaint, in which event the body concerned is invited to offer a suitable remedy for the injustice caused. A full Report will be sent to the MP who referred the case and a copy will be passed on to the complainant. The PCA has no power to compel the body to comply with his recommendations, but may report the matter to Parliament. There is no right of appeal against his decision. The process is confidential and information is not given to the press or the public about particular cases in a way which would identify the complainant.

*Statistics*
The Annual Report 1989 gives some indication of the number and type of complaints dealt with. A majority involve the Department of Social Security, mostly of delay causing serious consequences to the claimant, and although compensation frequently arises as an issue in these cases the scheme provides for this to be paid by DSS on an *ex gratia* basis. Next come complaints against Inland Revenue, followed by the Home Office and Lord Chancellor's Department (*i.e.* administration of courts). Client groups that frequently feature in investigations are the young, the elderly, families under stress and single parents so it appears that disabled people are not yet making full use of this facility.

## Local Commissioners

The *Commissions for Local Administration* were set up for England and Wales in April 1974 when the new authorities were created there, and the following year in Scotland.[112] Their addresses are contained in Appendix I. Local Commissioners have been appointed (sometimes referred to as *Local Ombudsmen*) and there are three for England, each responsible for a specific area of the country. Anyone who considers that they have suffered injustice since April 1974, or in Scotland since May 15, 1975, because of maladministration by a local authority (other than a parish council) or certain other authorities (including police authorities) may be able to have a complaint looked into.

*Complaints*
The actions giving rise to the grievance must be administrative in

---

[112] Local Government Act 1974; Local Government (Scotland) Act 1975.

nature, and have affected the complainant personally, or the specific interests of a group of persons. Normally the complaint is made by the person who claims to have suffered injustice, but where he is for any reason unable to act for himself, it may be made by a member of his family or "some body or individual suitable to represent him".[113] It is then in the discretion of the Commissioner to decide who is properly speaking for and in the best interests of the complainant.[114]

*Jurisdiction*
Complaints must normally be made in writing within 12 months of the day when the matter complained of came to the notice of the aggrieved person. Any matter which has been appealed to a tribunal or the subject of court proceedings or referred to a Government Minister may not be investigated, and usually all existing remedies or rights of appeal must be used unless the Commissioner is satisfied that it is not reasonable to expect the complainant to use these rights.[115]

*Procedure*
The Commissioner can only become involved in a complaint after it has been brought to the attention of the relevant authority either by the complainant or a member of the authority. Complaints are first directed to the department involved or chief executive and it is only if the grievance is not removed that a request is made to a member of the authority for help in pursuing the complaint. A formal request should then be made for it to be considered, although a letter will be sufficient, and only if the member fails to refer the matter in this way should the complaint be sent direct. The service is free and a booklet is available giving an explanation of the procedures with a detachable form on which a complaint may be made.

If the complaint passes initial screening it will be taken up in correspondence, but there is power to examine the authority's internal papers and to take written and oral evidence from anyone who can provide relevant information.[116] The complainant may be visited at home or asked to attend for an interview. All parties will be informed that there is to be an investigation and the authority is given an opportunity to comment on the allegations, but the

---

113 Local Government Act 1974, s.27(2); Local Government (Scotland) Act 1975, s.25(2).

114 Conflict may arise in the case of adults with a mental handicap, because the social worker concerned may oppose a complaint against an authority which is his or her employer, whereas parents may wish a complaint to be made.

115 Local Government Act 1974, s.26(6), Sched.5; Local Government (Scotland) Act 1975, s.24, Sched.5 and Local Government Administration (Matters Subject to Investigation) (Scotland) Order 1988, (S.I.1988 No.1306). As judicial review is such an uncertain remedy the complainant will not usually be required to seek it.

116 The Commissioner has all the powers of the High Court (in Scotland, the Court of Session) to question witnesses and see documents, s.29(2). (Scotland, s.27(2)).

investigation is conducted in private. An attempt is usually made to achieve a settlement without a formal investigation, and many complaints are resolved in this way.

*Legal representation*
It is not usually necessary for parties to be represented by lawyers, as the procedures are as informal as possible. The Commissioner decides whether such representation will be permitted, and may consider a payment towards legal costs. Where a serious complaint is brought on behalf of a mentally handicapped person and it is observed that the authority is dealing with this through its legal department, it may be appropriate to draw this to the attention of the Commissioner and seek assistance. This is especially so if the dispute is between carers and a social services department, because of the conflict of interest within that department which is otherwise responsible for acting in the best interests of the handicapped person.

*Report*
When the investigation has been completed a draft Report is prepared setting out the relevant facts and the complainant is given an opportunity to comment on this. The full Report will then be prepared giving the findings and a copy sent to all parties, but this does not normally identify the complainant. The authority must make the Report available to the public and the press and, where injustice has been found, inform the Commissioner what action it proposes to take. There is no legal sanction but if not satisfied with the proposals the Commissioner issues a further report, and this usually gets considerable publicity.[117] Usually a remedy is sought for the particular injustice found, and also a change of administrative procedures to prevent a recurrence as this is often the main concern of the complainant. Payment of compensation may be recommended and councils have specific power to make payments in these circumstances.[118] Examples of relevance to a person with a mental handicap are:
- unreasonable refusal to install a lift in a disabled person's home;
- delay in special education statementing process, or appeal committee not following correct procedure;
- giving misleading information to applicants for a housing grant;
- failure to advise a tenant of the storage of his possessions when he was made homeless;
- failure to take into account all the circumstances when deciding about free transport to school;

---

[117] s.31(2) (Scotland, s.29(2)). If the council still does not comply it must in England pay for a statement in an agreed form to be published in the local press, Local Government and Housing Act 1989.
[118] Local Government and Housing Act 1989, s.31(3) (Scotland, 1975 Act, s.29(3) as amended). Compensation may vary from a few hundred to several thousand pounds.

- failure to give a full explanation of the outcome of an investigation about treatment of residents in a private residential care home.

## Health Service Commissioner

There are Health Service Ombudsmen in each country who can investigate certain types of complaint about the NHS.[119] They are independent of the NHS and government, though responsible to Parliament which lays down what they can and cannot do and to whom they make reports about their work. A helpful explanatory leaflet is issued free by the relevant office and this should be obtained before a complaint is pursued.

### Complaints

A free complaints service is provided by the ombudsman, but the source of the complaint must first be taken up with the appropriate NHS authority who should provide a leaflet explaining how to make complaints and how these are dealt with. Sometimes the matter may be resolved informally, but in any event a reasonable opportunity should be given to the authority to respond. Only if satisfaction is not gained in this way should the complaint be referred to the ombudsman, and this is done by letter outlining the complaint and enclosing copies of all relevant documents and correspondence. There is a time limit of one year from the date when the matter first came to the notice of the complainant, though the ombudsman has a discretion to look at earlier matters.

### Jurisdiction

Complaints can be investigated about failure by a NHS authority to provide a service which it has a duty to provide, failure in a service that is provided, or maladministration connected with action taken by or on behalf of the authority. Complaints may be about attitude as well as actions of members of staff. The complainant must personally have suffered injustice or hardship as a result of the authority's failure or maladministration, but a complaint on behalf of a mentally incapacitated person can be investigated if the ombudsman is satisfied that it comes from an appropriate source and it is in the best interests of the individual to investigate. The ombudsman cannot investigate a complaint which could be dealt with by a court or tribunal unless he thinks it reasonable to do so, nor can he investigate clinical decisions about care or treatment of a patient,[120] or complaints about services provided by family doctors, dentists, opticians or pharmacists and certain other matters.

### Procedure

The ombudsman first decides whether to start or continue an investigation and each complaint is considered on the merits. If the

---

119 The addresses will be found in Appendix I.
120 There is a special *clinical complaints procedure* which provides for the care or treatment to be reviewed by two independent consultants

complaint is accepted, a letter with a summary of what is to be investigated is sent to the complainant and the authority. An officer may visit the complainant to discuss the matter and he will explain what happens. The investigation is conducted in private and will usually be informal so legal representation is seldom necessary, but if it is help may be given with the costs. A written Report is sent to the complainant and the authority, and if a complaint is upheld this will state whether the authority has agreed to remedy any injustice or hardship caused, perhaps by offering an apology or agreeing to policy changes or new procedures.

## Family Practitioner Services

Although the Health Service Commissioner cannot investigate complaints about the independent practitioners mentioned above, they have a contract with the local *Family Health Services Authority* (in Scotland, the relevant *Health Board*) which have informal and formal procedures for dealing with complaints. These are designed to find out whether the practitioner's terms of contract have been broken, and there is a right of appeal to the Secretary of State for Health (or Secretary of State for Scotland).

## MENTAL WELFARE COMMISSION

### Scotland

In addition to specific functions in relation to detained patients and people subject to guardianship, the Mental Welfare Commission for Scotland has a general duty to exercise protective functions in respect of people who may be incapable of adequately protecting themselves or their interests because of a mental handicap (or mental illness).[121] The Commission has a duty to make enquiry into any case where it appears to them that there may be ill-treatment, deficiency in care or treatment, or improper detention of any person who may have a mental handicap (or be suffering from a mental illness). They must also make enquiry where the property of any such person may be at risk, by reason of mental handicap or illness.

Where the Commission consider it desirable for any hospital or local authority to exercise their functions to secure the welfare of a mentally handicapped person, they must bring the facts of the case to the attention of the managers or authority. They must do this for the purpose of preventing ill-treatment, remedying any deficiency in care or treatment, terminating improper detention, or preventing or redressing loss or damage to property. For the purpose of exercising these duties, the Commission may interview in private any person who has or appears to have a mental handicap. A medical commissioner or medical officer of the Commission may examine any such person in private, and may require production of, and inspect, the medical records of any

---

121  Mental Health (Scotland) Act 1984, s.3(1). Address in Appendix I.

such person. The Commission can arrange formal enquiries, with power to require witnesses to attend and give evidence on oath.

Anyone with a significant concern about the welfare or interests of a mentally handicapped person which cannot readily be resolved should consider contacting the Commission. Initially, contact by telephone may be helpful and perhaps reassuring. The Commission is often well-placed to cut through red tape and resolve matters informally, but where necessary has significant powers to investigate and report.

### England

There is no comparable body in England, and this may be a serious omission. The Mental Health Act Commission (see Chapter 4) does not have the scope of its Scottish equivalent, being mainly concerned with detained patients in hospitals. In 1986 the Commission asked for its responsibilities to be extended to include those who lacked capacity but did not come within compulsory procedures and the Royal College of Psychiatrists support this.

# PART IV - CONCLUSION

In past generations the family of a person with a mental handicap has had to provide unsupported care, or accept institutionalised care. We are now part of a more caring society in which the role of the family is reduced and that of society increased. Conflicting with the carer's responsibility is the need for the person cared for to enjoy as great a degree of personal independence as possible. When parents provided care with little outside support, any opposition by others to the regime that they adopted was viewed by them as interference, but now that state agencies are involved on a more active basis the needs of the individual can be considered independently of those of the parents. Whilst parents should be encouraged to take advantage of the services and financial assistance to which they are entitled, the converse of this is that they alone are not entitled to make all decisions affecting the well-being of their son or daughter. A partnership with the state agencies should arise, with responsibility gradually shifting away from the parents as the child becomes an adult, as would be assumed in the case of other children.

### Responsibility of parents and carers

If the law is to recognise the role of parents and carers, it must define their responsibilities as regards both obligations and entitlements.

*Parental responsibility*
In England, the Children Act 1989 has radically altered the legal relationship between parents and children. It is now appropriate to refer to "parental responsibility" rather than rights.[122] This

---

122  The Law Commission in its Report on Illegitimacy in 1982 stated that it was

expression can imply either that parents have duties towards their children, or that they rather than the state are responsible for care. The balance between the responsibility of the parents and that of the state is a delicate one and tends to shift according to prevailing attitudes of society and the age of the child, but in most respects there is a cut-off point when the child attains the age of majority. Those who consider that a mentally handicapped son or daughter should always be treated as a child, perhaps on the basis of mental age, regard this cut-off point as inappropriate and would wish to retain the legal status of child. A White Paper[123] stated that the prime responsibility for the upbringing of children rests with parents and that the transfer to the local authority of parents' legal powers and responsibilities for caring for a child should only be done by a full court hearing following due legal process, yet in the case of a mentally handicapped person such transfer in effect takes place automatically when the child attains legal majority.

*Rights to support and services*
The provision by the state of financial support for disabled people and their carers is regulated by legislation, and potential claimants are usually able to adopt independent appeal procedures if they consider that they are not receiving the benefits to which they are entitled. However, in many situations it has proved difficult to define the circumstances in which entitlement arises, and there has been a trend to withdraw appeal procedures and put regional cash limits upon the total amount of money available.[124]

Parents and carers also need to know their rights to services and to have a procedure for enforcement. The law tends to give agencies the authority to provide a service, sometimes with an obligation to do so in general terms, but without giving the intended recipients power to enforce such provision in individual cases. This may be because the law is not capable of defining when particular services are required, but is more likely to be because society cannot face the cost of giving enforceable legal rights to the provision of services. It is the delivery of services that is important, and with strong competition for public funds there remains the danger that in the absence of legally enforceable rights essential services will not be provided even if they are deemed to be available. Any reform in the law should concentrate upon ensuring that monies made available for the provision of services can only be spent on such provision, and that proper procedures are applied in regard to the delivery of care even if the decisions made are not themselves subject to the legal process. Such procedures should involve the parents or carers and the individual in all decisions to

---

"more appropriate to talk of parental powers ...authority ...responsibilities, rather than rights" and this was confirmed by the House of Lords in *Gillick* v. *West Norfolk and Wisbech Area Health Authority* [1985] 3 All ER 402.

123  *The Law on Child Care and Family Services* 1987, which preceded the Children Act 1989.

124  As in the case of the Social Fund, see Chap.8.

the same extent as the professionals, and any assessments of need should be based upon the views of all those having relevant involvement in the life of the individual.

It would be intolerable to impose a lifelong obligation on parents to look after their child just because he or she was mentally handicapped, and this would be a retrograde step so far as personal freedom of the child is concerned, but if the law neither gives parents rights nor imposes responsibilities, there are dangers that they will prematurely reject their natural role as carers through a lack of recognition and support.

*Guardianship and advocacy*

The issue of adult guardianship for England[125] has been covered in the previous chapter because the appointment of a suitable guardian is a right of the individual, not of the parents. It must not be assumed that the parents are the most suitable choice (though they may be the only persons available), or that they would be the choice of the mentally handicapped individual, if able to choose. Parents may tend to be over-protective and not to allow sufficient risk-taking in areas of personal development. Whilst they usually wish that their son or daughter could live independently, they may not recognise the ability to do so. It is here that the concept of advocacy, someone speaking on behalf of the individual, becomes significant. This also falls to be considered amongst the rights of the individual.

## LAW REFORM

Existing legal procedures and concepts in regard to mental incapacity tend to be outdated, unhelpful and fragmented, with gaps and inconsistencies. This is increasingly being realised, and there are signs of a new, positive and co-ordinated approach in both jurisdictions in the future.

*England*

The Law Commission has taken an overview of the situation of mentally incapacitated adults and published a consultation paper which highlights the inadequacies of the law.[126] It is not yet known whether any consequent law reform will be comprehensive or merely tackle specific problems.

*Scotland*

The need for comprehensive review of private law provision has been recognised and addressed by the Scottish Law Commission in a discussion paper[127] which should prove to be the first step towards a new comprehensive and co-ordinated statutory code replacing and rationalising all existing procedures which modify

---

[125] For Scottish equivalent, see "Tutors to Adults (Scotland)", p.136 above.

[126] Consultation Paper No.119: *Mentally Incapacitated Adults and Decision-Making: An Overview* (May 1991).

[127] Discussion Paper No.94: *Mentally Disabled Adults - Legal Arrangements for Managing their Welfare and Finances* (September 1991).

the legal status of people with mental disabilities of all kinds (including mental handicaps) and which confer decision-making and supervisory powers upon others. The new regime should include unified one-door procedures for obtaining personal orders (including appointment of personal guardians, and decisions about medical procedures) and property orders (including appointment of managers, and other management techniques). It is to be hoped that the opportunity will be taken to rationalise the inconsistent diversity of procedures and concepts found across various areas of the law.

# CHAPTER 4 HEALTH AUTHORITIES AND LEGISLATION

## INTRODUCTION

In this chapter we consider the provision of medical treatment with reference to the needs of and problems presented by persons with a mental handicap, and then summarise the mental health legislation involving health authorities (separately for England and Scotland).

### Terminology

The Secretary of State for Health has announced the adoption, within the Department of Health, of the phrase "people with learning disabilities" instead of "mentally handicapped people".[1]

### Management

#### England

The NHS is managed locally by:

*Family Health Services Authorities*[2] - arrange the services provided by family doctors (*i.e.* general practitioners), dentists, opticians and pharmacists.

*District Health Authorities* - responsible for the hospital and community health services provided in the district.

*Regional Health Authorities* - mainly concerned with planning but also provide ambulance and some other services direct to the public.

*Special Health Authorities* - manage certain specialist hospitals or have particular functions including the Special Hospitals Service Authority and the Disablement Services Authority.

*NHS Trusts* - set up to own and manage certain NHS hospitals or other units.

#### Scotland [3]

The NHS is managed locally by:

*Health Boards* (of which there are 15) - responsible in their areas for hospital and specialist services; services provided by general practitioners, dentists, opticians and pharmacists; school and community health services; and other functions.

*NHS Trusts* - set up to own and manage certain NHS hospitals or other facilities.

Most functions administered nationally are delegated to the

---

1  Press release from Department of Health, June 25, 1991.
2  Formerly *Family Practitioner Committees*.
3  The principal legislation is the National Health Service (Scotland) Act 1978 as amended (including amendments in the National Health Service and Community Care Act 1990). Provisions regarding the management of the State Hospital at Carstairs are in Mental Health (Scotland) Act 1984, ss.90 and 91.

*Common Services Agency* which is responsible for provision of accommodation, procuring equipment and supplies, providing various technical services, health education, ambulance services, blood transfusion services, prescription pricing, legal services, and various other co-ordinating and servicing roles.[4]

## Supervisory role

In England, the registration and control of nursing homes and mental nursing homes in the private sector is the responsibility of District Health Authorities. In Scotland, the registration and supervision of nursing homes is the responsibility of the Health Board. This topic is dealt with in Chapter 7, Parts IIIA and IIIB.

## Community Care

Under the new formal policies of care in the community, the role of health authorities is to be restricted to the provision of health care, though it will take a long time to wind down completely their previous role of providing residential care. We deal with Community Care in Chapter 5, but some key points that relate to health authorities are mentioned here.

### Mental handicap hospitals

The Government now acknowledges that people with a mental handicap mainly need social rather than health care and the aim is stated to be to continue to reduce the numbers of people in specialist mental handicap hospitals, and to ensure that no child requiring long term residential care grows up in such hospital.[5] As a result people with a mental handicap are being moved out of these hospitals, which are being closed.[6]

### Joint planning

Agreement on joint strategies should be reached between health and local authorities for the resettlement of hospital residents. In Scotland "planning agreements" are now largely in place but in England few are in place and working satisfactorily. This has been contributed to by a lack of mutual trust and the requirement for health authorities to transfer funding with patients to provide for their long term care.[7] Problems also arise over the transfer of hospital staff as their pay, training and conditions of service differ in material respects from those of local authority employees. Health authority areas do not coincide with those of local authorities so they may need to negotiate with several authorities.

---

4    The *State Hospital Management Committee* manages the State Hospital at Carstairs on behalf of the Secretary of State.

5    White Paper *Caring for People: Community Care in the Next Decade and Beyond* (November 1989) which resulted in the passing of the National Health Service and Community Care Act 1990.

6    The Secretary of State has stated that he will not approve closure of any such hospital unless satisfied that proper alternative services are in place.

7    This is often referred to as a *dowry*, see Chap.5. Local authorities decline to accept patients unless all costs are refunded whilst health authorities are reluctant to pay dowries in perpetuity.

*NHS community units*

Although patients may be transferred to local authority social services departments or homes in the private or voluntary sector, some health authorities have set up small community units to which they move patients from the wards. These are sometimes in the grounds of existing hospitals and are criticised by local authorities as merely being an extension of the hospital. They also pose problems with social security funding which was not designed to cope with such provision and run counter to the policy of giving local authorities the key role in the delivery of community care, but result from problems in implementing joint strategies.

# PART I - MEDICAL TREATMENT

The medical needs of people with a mental handicap may be no different from those of other members of the community, and their rights to health care and treatment are the same. Problems do arise, however, in regard to consent to treatment especially where this is of a type where personal choice is normally exercised, and behaviour or communication problems may make it difficult to provide routine health care.

## NHS REFORMS

The changes made by the National Health Service and Community Care Act 1990 were designed to produce a more efficient service that puts the patient first, reinforcing the main aim of the NHS which is to help people live longer and enjoy a better quality of life.

*Doctors*

General practitioners now offer a wider range of services, with more emphasis on the promotion of good health and the prevention of disease, on the basis that prevention is better than cure. For adults, regular life-style check-ups are available with more health promotion clinics, and for children under five years a programme should be offered either by the GP or a local health authority clinic for following the development of the child. These services should be available to all, regardless of any mental handicap. Directories are produced of local GP's giving details of their practices and the services that they provide, and the practices themselves should produce leaflets giving this information. In order to change your GP it is now only necessary to call at the surgery of the chosen GP and ask to be registered.

*Hospitals*

In England, health authorities have a legal duty to ensure a comprehensive range of health services to meet the needs of the local population, and should aim to provide maximum choice. They assess the state of health of the local population and decide what services are needed. In Scotland, the provision of a comprehensive and integrated health service, of general medical and other services, and of hospitals and other facilities is the duty of the Secretary of State, who determines the functions of health boards in the administration of the health services provided by him. Health authorities and boards are funded according to the size of their local population, with allowances for their age and health, and the relative cost of providing services for them, and use their allocation of money to arrange the services needed. They make agreements with a range of hospitals and other units in order to provide comprehensive services for the local population, and targets to reduce waiting times for operations are built into these agreements. Both the patient and GP should be involved in any decision about where to go for treatment which will not be restricted to hospitals within the health authority area. The GP will be aware of the range of local hospitals offering services, and will be able to recommend the hospital where the best and most appropriate care is available. Each health authority retains money to pay for referrals by GPs to hospitals which are not covered by their existing agreements.

The NHS reforms aim to encourage hospitals to provide an environment in which the patient feels welcome and cared for as an individual. That means a high standard of clinical care, a personal service, pleasant waiting areas, reliable appointment times, adequate information, effective procedures for discharge, simple complaints procedures and efficient methods of communication.

*NHS Trusts*

Since April 1991 hospitals have been allowed to become NHS Trusts when they are judged to be ready to make the best use of these freedoms.[8] They then remain part of the NHS but are run by their own boards of directors (rather than the health authority) which are able to own their assets, employ their own staff, set their rates of pay and borrow money to develop their services. This is intended to allow local management and staff with knowledge of the needs of local people to have more control over the running of their hospital and enables them to improve standards and the quality of care.

Although NHS Trusts have control over the services they provide, where a service must be provided locally an NHS Trust can be obliged to provide it if it is the only hospital able to do so, thereby ensuring the continued provision of essential local services.

## COMPLAINTS

The NHS has declared that everyone should have equal access to the health care services they need, and it is important to ensure that these objectives are fulfilled also in ways that cater for the

---

8    In Scotland, there is to be the Royal Scottish National Hospital and Community Trust which has various community-based units.

needs of those with a mental handicap. Where a complaint relates to such a patient there seems no reason why it may not be presented by someone with a sufficient connection to the patient, and hospitals should have a procedure to recognise a parent or carer (or advocate) for an adult who is mentally handicapped and who cannot easily speak for himself.

Any patient who is unhappy with the treatment received under the NHS should first discuss the problem with the health professional concerned. A solicitor should be consulted at an early stage if there is a possibility of seeking legal redress, for example by claiming damages for some loss or harm. If it appears that a crime has been committed (*e.g.* that a handicapped person may have been assaulted) it may be necessary to report the matter to the police: if so, it should be reported promptly. If a discussion does not resolve the matter, the next step depends on which part of the NHS is involved.

*Clinical judgement complaints procedure*
If the complaint relates to clinical judgment, there is a three stage complaints procedure involving first the consultant, secondly the Regional Medical Officer (or equivalent) and thirdly (for complaints of a substantial nature) two independent consultants. This is the only way, without taking legal action, to ensure an independent review of medical decisions. The following procedures should be considered for other types of complaint.

## England

*GP, dentist, pharmacist or optician*
A complaint should be made to the local Family Health Services Authority and may lead to a formal investigation as to whether or not the health professional complied with his or her terms of service. If necessary it may be decided by a committee made up of an equal number of health practitioners and members of the public, with a chairman who is not a health practitioner.

*Hospital or community health service*
A complaint is made to a specially appointed officer whose name and location should be available in the hospital, and a written reply will be received once the complaint has been looked into. The local Community Health Council, which plays a part in representing the interests of local patients, can provide help and advice, and if still not satisfied the patient may refer the complaint to the Health Service Commissioner.[9]

*Professional misconduct*
Complaints of this nature may include rudeness and clinical mistakes. If against GP's or hospital doctors they are made to the General Medical Council (which is the disciplinary body), and

---

9    Address in Appendix I. This topic is dealt with in Chap.3, Part III at p.167. See the Hospital Complaints Procedure Act 1985 and Directions made thereunder.

those in respect of the conduct of nurses, dentists, pharmacists and other professional groups are made to the professional association concerned.

## Scotland

The Mental Welfare Commission[10] should be contacted if the complaint concerns ill-treatment, deficiency in care or treatment, or improper detention of anyone with a mental handicap or mental illness. Other complaints procedures fall into the following broad categories.

*Family doctors, dentists, pharmacists and opticians*
These professionals provide services under contract to the health board. Complaints should be made to the health board, who will either try to settle the matter informally, or alternatively follow a formal procedure designed to determine whether the practitioner's terms of contract have been broken (and under which there is right of appeal to the Secretary of State). Local health councils can provide guidance about procedures.

*NHS authorities*
Each should have a leaflet explaining its procedure for dealing with complaints, which should be available at all hospitals and clinics. If guidance or assistance is required, the local health council should be contacted and failing satisfactory response from the relevant authority, complaint may be made to the Health Service Commissioner for Scotland.[11]

*Professional misconduct*
As in England (see above), complaints may be made to the General Medical Council or other relevant professional organisation.

## Information

Under the Access to Health Records Act 1990, from November 1991 people are allowed to see and copy information which has been manually recorded on their health records from that date, and other legislation relates to information held on computer.[12]

## CONSENT TO TREATMENT - England[13]

Persons over the age of 18 must consent to their own medical treatment. Treatment which involves touching the patient without consent is a trespass to the person (assault and battery), but consent can be express by signing a consent form or giving verbal consent, or may be implied by actions or conduct. The legal right to consent to medical treatment has traditionally depended on whether the individual has attained legal majority, but recent case

---

10   Address in Appendix I.
11   See footnote 9 above.
12   This topic is dealt with in Chap.3, Part II at p.144.
13   The English author is indebted to **Lydia Sinclair**, solicitor and Director of the Legal Services Department of MENCAP for her contribution.

law complicates the law in this area especially in regard to young persons between the ages of 16 and 18.

## Nature of consent

The consent of the patient to the medical treatment proposed must be specific and valid. This means that the patient:

- has the capacity to give consent;
- is given appropriate information prior to consent;
- consents to the particular treatment that is given; and
- gives consent voluntarily.

### Capacity

The first question is whether the patient has the necessary understanding of the proposed treatment to consent thereto. The patient must give consent to a particular treatment and continue to do so. The assessment of a patient's ability to consent will usually be made by the doctor proposing the treatment, his decision being based on judgement of the patient's understanding of the particular treatment concerned and the information provided by the doctor. Ability to consent and capacity to consent will be different depending on the nature of the decision. The complexity of the proposed treatment and the degree of understanding required will be different in each case and capacity should therefore be assessed on each occasion and be continually re-assessed with each particular treatment and at each stage of treatment.

### Information

There is no duty on the doctor to inform the patient of all likely risks and advantages of the treatment, and what to tell the patient is within the doctor's discretion. This matter was considered by the House of Lords in 1985 when Lord Templeman stated[14]:

"if the doctor making a balanced judgement advises the patient to submit to the operation, the patient is entitled to reject that advice for reasons which are rational or irrational, or for no reason. The duty of the doctor in these circumstances, subject to his overriding duty to have regard to the best interests of the patient, is to provide the patient with information which will enable the patient to make a balanced judgement if the patient chooses to make a balanced judgement."

If the patient asks questions these should be answered, but the doctor has a discretion as to the amount of information he should volunteer and can withhold information for good reason but this will need to be justified. In the above case Lord Bridge stated:

"When questioned specifically by a patient of apparently sound mind about risks involved in a particular treatment proposed, the doctor's duty must, in my opinion, be to answer both truthfully and as fully as the questioner requires."

### Voluntary consent

Consent must be freely given and no threat or implied threat should be used. Threats such as the use of compulsory section if treatment is not accepted or that discharge may result from failure

---

14    Sidaway v. Bethlem Royal Hospital Governors [1985] 1 All ER 643.

to agree to treatment, would nullify the consent. Whether consent is voluntary will depend on what information is given to the patient and how this is presented.

*Implications of lack of consent or information*
Lack of consent may result in an action in assault. A total failure to inform the patient may amount to lack of consent, but wrong or misleading information may give rise to an action in negligence if this breach of duty causes an injury directly resulting from the failure to inform. The patient must show that he would not have consented to the treatment had he been properly informed and that the damage directly resulted from this failure to inform and the subsequent treatment.

*Implications to mental handicap*
It is necessary to assess understanding and capacity very carefully. Good practice would be to do this in consultation with those persons who know the patient well, including parents, carers, teachers, psychologists, nurses and others. The information must be provided in a way which encourages understanding and involves the patient at every stage of treatment. The fact that a person is mentally handicapped does not necessarily mean that he cannot consent to proposed medical treatment, and every effort should be made to overcome any communication difficulties, to present information in a simple and non-threatening way and to involve carers and others in the presentation of this information. A broad understanding of the treatment proposed is what is required, and it is good practice to record the procedure for assessment and the decision in the medical record.

## Treatment without consent

Lawful authority to give medical treatment without the consent of the individual is provided by common law and statute in the following circumstances:

1. In the case of a child under the age of 16, the person who has parental authority (*i.e.* guardian, parent, High Court, local authority) can consent on behalf of the child;
2. Where a patient is unconscious emergency treatment can be given to save his life[15];
3. Where the patient is suffering from a mental disorder and his behaviour may be a danger to himself or others. In this situation the common law defence of self-defence and use of reasonable force is warranted;
4. Where the patient is mentally incapable of giving consent and the treatment is considered by the treating doctor to be in his best interest;
5. Where the patient is detained under the treatment

---

15    There are exceptions in cases where it is known the patient would not wish to be treated because of religious or other beliefs. The general view is that such treatment would not be given in these circumstances.

provisions of the Mental Health Act 1983 medical treatment for a mental disorder can (subject to the safeguards) be given without the patient's consent.[16]

*Best interests*

Best interest means necessary to save life or prevent deterioration or ensure improvement in the patient's physical or mental health.[17] In deciding whether a treatment is necessary the doctor must act in accordance with a practice accepted as proper by a responsible body of medical practitioners, skilled and experienced in the relevant speciality.[18]

*Limitations*

Although several statutes make provision for the welfare of persons with a mental handicap, they do not enable treatment to be given without consent. Thus the National Assistance Act 1948 provides for the removal from a place of persons who are in need of care and attention because they are "suffering from a grave and chronic disease or, being aged, infirm or physically incapacitated or living in insanitary conditions and are unable to devote to themselves and are not receiving from other persons proper care and attention". Removal is to a "suitable hospital or other place", but although the purpose is "to secure the necessary care and attention" for the person it does not authorise medical treatment without consent. Common law rules of necessity would apply to treatment in this situation where the patient was refusing or unable to consent.

# Children

In the case of proposed medical treatment for minors who are incompetent (under the age of 18 years), the courts have clarified the law and stated that parents or others acting *in loco parentis* (*e.g.* guardian, local authority, High Court) can consent to the child's medical treatment. The court may need to resolve any dispute between parent and child, and can give consent to medical treatment of a ward.

*Appropriate treatment*

Parents have a duty to act in their child's best interests, as illustrated in the following case[19]:

> B. was a baby with Down's syndrome suffering a heart defect and surgery had been proposed. Without this she would die within a few days. Her parents did not consent to this surgery and argued that "nature had made its own arrangements to terminate a life which would not be fruitful and nature should not be interfered with". The child was made a ward and the court had to decide whether the operation should go ahead giving the child a possibility

---

16  See Part IIA at p.195.
17  *F.* v. *West Berkshire H.A.* [1989] 2 All ER 545, see below.
18  *Bolam* v. *Friern Barnet Hospital Management Committee* [1957] 2 All ER 118.
19  *Re B. (a minor)(wardship: medical treatment)* [1990] 3 All ER 927, CA, (the case was actually heard in 1981).

of 20 or 30 years of life. The Court of Appeal decided that the child must live and that the duty of the court was to decide this on the basis of the child's interest.

In a later case[20] the Court of Appeal considered the treatment appropriate in the case of a terminally ill child. Rather than give directions as to specific treatment, the court would accept the opinions of the medical staff looking after the ward if they decided that the aim of nursing care should be to ease suffering rather than achieve a short prolongation of the child's life. More recently the Court of Appeal considered the case of a profoundly mentally and physically handicapped child whose life expectancy was uncertain and who would on occasions require painful ventilation treatment to survive.[21] The issue was therefore whether it could ever be justified to withhold life-saving treatment whatever the quality of life being preserved. It was held that, although the court would never sanction positive steps to terminate life, where disabilities were so grave that life would be so intolerable for the individual that he would choose to die if able to make a judgment, then the court could direct that treatment to prolong life need not be given. The court had to perform a balancing exercise in the best interests of the child, looked at from his point of view.

*Testing for AIDS*

Circumstances may arise where it is desired to test the blood of a mentally handicapped child for the HIV virus. Taking a blood sample involves physical contact and although a competent child must consent it seems that parents (or others authorised by law) may consent on behalf of an incompetent child. In doing so they must act in the child's best medical interests, so much may depend upon whether a responsible body of medical opinion would consider it to be in the child's health interests. It is the interests of the child and not of other persons that are to be taken into account, and in view of the sometimes adverse consequences that may follow a positive test it will usually only be justified if it is believed that the child is already HIV positive and decisions are immediately needed on future medical care.

## Young persons

*Capacity to consent*

Section 1 of the Family Law Reform Act 1969 provides:

> "the consent of a minor who has attained the age of 16 years to any surgical, medical or dental treatment which, in the absence of consent, would constitute a trespass to his person, shall be as effective as it would be if he were of full age, and where a minor has by virtue of this section given an effective consent to any treatment it shall not be necessary to obtain any consent for it from his parent or guardian."

The situation is not as clear cut as this, because the House of Lords

---

20   *Re C. (a minor)(wardship: medical treatment)* [1989] 2 All ER 782, CA.
21   *Re J. (a minor)(wardship: medical treatment)* [1990] 3 All ER 930, CA.

in the *Gillick* Case[22] established the principle that a child's capacity to give consent to medical treatment depended upon understanding and maturity rather than age, and that a young person under the age of 16 years could give valid consent. Lord Scarman stated:

"I would hold that as a matter of law the parental right to determine whether or not a minor child below the age of 16 will have medical treatment terminates if and when the child achieves a sufficient understanding and intelligence to enable him or her to understand fully what is proposed. It will be a question of fact whether a child seeking advice has sufficient understanding of what is involved to give a consent valid in law. Until the child achieves the capacity to consent, the parental right to make the decision continues save only in exceptional circumstances."

## Capacity to refuse consent

The Act does not address the situation where there is a conflict between parents or guardians and the young person, and does not specifically state that the young person can refuse treatment where parents or guardians consent. This conflict arose recently when the Court of Appeal considered the case of a 15 year old ward of court who was refusing consent to specific medication for mental illness.[23] The court considered whether she was of sufficient maturity to understand the nature and importance of the treatment proposed, and also whether the wardship jurisdiction was wider than parental right to consent to treatment on behalf of a minor. She was not held to be competent in the sense defined in the Gillick case, but the court considered that even if she had been the judge was correct in consenting to the treatment.

This case raises the issues of whether a young person under the age of 16 who suffers from mental impairment could ever be considered to be competent in the Gillick sense, and also whether any child under 16 has an absolute right to refuse treatment where parents or the High Court consent to it. Lord Donaldson stated:

"both in this case and in Re. E the judges treated Gillick as deciding that a Gillick competent child has a right to refuse treatment. In this I consider that they were in error. Such a child can consent, but if he or she declines to do so or refuses, consent can be given by someone else who has parental rights or responsibilities. The failure or refusal of the Gillick competent child is a very important factor in the doctor's decision whether or not to treat, but does not prevent the necessary consent being obtained from another competent source."

Lord Donaldson summarised the position as follows:

"1. No doctor can be required to treat a child, whether by the court in the exercise of its wardship jurisdiction, by the parents, by the child or anyone else. The decision whether to treat is dependent upon an exercise of his own professional judgement, subject only to the threshold requirement that, save in exceptional cases usually of emergency, he has the consent of someone who has authority to give that consent. In forming that judgement the views

---

22  *Gillick* v. *West Norfolk & Wisbech Area Health Authority* [1985] 1 All ER 533, CA; [1985] 3 All ER 402, HL.

23  *Re. R. (a minor) (wardship: medical treatment)* [1991] 4 All ER 177, CA. This may reflect a shift away from an assessment of the patient's purported wishes to one of refusing to over-ride doctors' clinical judgment as to appropriate treatment.

and wishes of the child are a factor whose importance increases with the
increase in the child's intelligence and understanding.
2.   There can be concurrent powers to consent. If more than one body or
person has power to consent, only a failure to, or refusal of, consent by all
having that power will create a veto.
3.   A 'Gillick competent' child or one over the age of 16 will have a power
to consent, but this will be concurrent with that of a parent or guardian.
4.   'Gillick competence' is a developmental concept and will not be lost or
acquired on a day to day or week to week basis. In the case of mental
disability, that disability must also be taken into account, particularly where it
is fluctuating in its effect.
5.   The court in the exercise of its wardship or statutory jurisdiction has
power to override the decision of a 'Gillick competent' child as much as
those of parents or guardians.
6.   Waite J. was right to hold that R. was not 'Gillick competent' and, even
if R. had been, was right to consent to her undergoing treatment which might
involve compulsory medication."

## Sterilisation

In cases where the proposed treatment is sterilisation the courts
have recommended that application be made to the High Court
under the wardship jurisdiction. The House of Lords has held that
the court should consider expert and other evidence before coming
to a decision about the proposed sterilisation and in doing so must
treat the welfare or best interests of the minor as the paramount
consideration.[24] A recent case has established that a sterilisation
proposed on the basis of therapeutic reasons (*i.e.* medical need)
can be carried out without application to the High Court for a
declaration.[25] The Official Solicitor has made a practice direction
relating to the procedure to be adopted in applications for both
minors and adults.[26]

## Adults

The common law basis for treating an incompetent patient is the
doctrine of necessity, namely that medical treatment can be given
if the doctor considers this treatment to be in the best interests of
the patient. Medical treatment for a mental disorder can be given
under the provisions of the Mental Health Act 1983 (see Part II
below). After some uncertainty the High Court decided that there
was no power to give consent to medical treatment on behalf of an
incompetent adult, but that the court could declare a proposed
operation not to be unlawful.[27] The cases referred to the courts
relating to the carrying out of an abortion upon or the sterilisation

---

24   *Re B. (a minor)(wardship: sterilisation)* [1987] 2 All ER 206.
25   *Re E. (a Minor)* TLR, February 22, 1991. Parents were able to give valid
     consent to a proposed hysterectomy to be performed for therapeutic reasons
     on their 17 year old mentally handicapped daughter notwithstanding that the
     incidental result would be sterilisation. A declaration by the court was not
     necessary. A similar decision was reached in the case of a 29 year old
     mentally handicapped woman in *F.* v. *F.*, TLR, April 29, 1991.
26   This was amended pursuant to the judgement of Thorpe J. in *Re C.*, TLR,
     February 13, 1990.
27   *Re T., The Times,* May 26, 1987 (Latey J.); *T.* v. *T.* [1988] 1 All ER 613
     (Wood J.).

of women who are mentally handicapped have raised questions relating to all medical treatment when the patient is unable to consent. The issue was ultimately considered by the House of Lords in *Re F.* in 1989.[28]

*Principles*

In considering the position of an adult without capacity to consent to a proposed sterilisation the House of Lords concluded that:

1. No court or judge has jurisdiction comparable to wardship jurisdiction to give or withhold consent to an operation;
2. The court has jurisdiction to declare the lawfulness of such an operation proposed to be performed on the ground that it is in the best interest of the patient and, although such a declaration is not necessary to establish the lawfulness of the operation, in practice the court's jurisdiction should be invoked whenever such an operation is to be performed;
3. In determining whether the proposed operation was in the best interests of the patient the court should apply the established test of what would be accepted as appropriate treatment at the time by a reasonable body of medical opinion skilled in that particular form of treatment;

*Best interests*

In deciding that this particular operation should be carried out Lord Brandon further stated the common law provisions in cases where the patient is unable to consent to medical treatment:

"in my opinion, the solution to the problem which the common law provides is that a doctor can lawfully operate on or give other treatment to, adult patients who are incapable, for one reason or another, of consenting to his doing so providing that the operation or other treatment concerned is in the best interests of such patient. The operation or other treatment will be in their best interests if, but only if, it is carried out in order either to save their life, or to ensure improvement or prevent deterioration in their physical or mental health . . . when persons lack the capacity, for whatever reason, to take decisions about the performance of operations on them, or the giving of other medical treatment to them, it is necessary that some other person or persons, with the appropriate qualifications, should take such decisions for them. Otherwise they would be deprived of medical care which they need and to which they are entitled ...."

*Procedure*

The procedure to be adopted in these cases was outlined in *Re F.*:

- application for a Declaration should be by way of originating summons issued out of the Family Division of the High Court;
- the applicants should normally be those responsible for the care of the patient, or those intending to carry out the proposed operation or other treatment if it is declared to be lawful;
- the Official Solicitor and the patient should always be parties and will normally be respondents;
- with a view to protecting the patient's privacy, but subject to

---

[28]   *F.* v. *West Berkshire H.A.* [1989] 2 All ER 545.

the Judge's discretion, the hearing will be in chambers, but
the decision and the reasons will be given in open court.

## Abortion

In the case of proposed abortions for adults who are incapacitated
it has been held that, as the Abortion Act 1967 provides adequate
safeguards for the doctors involved, it is not necessary that
specific approval of the High Court should be obtained but the
provisions of the Act must be complied with.[29]

## Other medical treatment

With regard to all other medical treatment which would include
courses of medicine, surgery, general medical care and testing of
various kinds (*e.g.* HIV, hepatitis B, mamography, cervical
smears) the best interest test is the basis for treatment where the
adult patient is unable to consent. The procedure must be within
the definition of medical treatment and necessary for the person's
best interests.

## Testing for AIDS

Unlike the situation of an infant, no-one has authority to consent
on behalf of a mentally incompetent adult to the taking of a sample
of blood for the purpose of testing for the HIV virus. However, it
has been held in relation to medical touching that[30]:

> "... in these exceptional circumstances where there is no provision in law for
> consent to be given and therefore there is no-one who can give the consent,
> and where the patient is suffering from such mental abnormality as never to
> be able to give such consent, a medical adviser is justified in taking such
> steps as good medical practice 'demands'...."

Applying this test to the taking and testing of blood one would
conclude that the act is not unlawful if the health interests of the
incompetent adult would otherwise be adversely affected. This
would not justify adopting the test simply to find out if the adult
was HIV positive in order to protect other persons with whom he
may have physical contact to the extent that there was a risk of
infection. It is the health of the individual to be tested that is
relevant rather than the best interests of others. The position
becomes more complicated if a test is possible of some bodily
substance obtained without the need to have physical contact with
the individual.

## Use of drugs

Anti-psychotic drugs are sometimes prescribed for long-term
patients resident in hospitals, both on an everyday basis and when
needed to calm down disturbed behaviour. They may be helpful in
the short term but their long-term effects are not known, yet they
tend to be prescribed for mentally handicapped people based upon
habit rather than scientific evidence. It is important for the family
to ask what drugs are being prescribed and what these are for and

---

29    *Re G. (Mental patient: termination of pregnancy)*, TLR, January 31, 1991.
30    *T* v. *T* [1988] 1 All ER 613, Wood J. Subsequent cases have developed this
       principle further.

to insist upon regular reviews. From a legal point of view the problem may be who has the right to ask such questions in respect of an adult, and the answer is by no means clear. It is good practice for hospitals/doctors to consult with the family or carers of a person with a mental handicap when planning treatment and prescribing medication.

## CONSENT TO TREATMENT - Scotland[31]

### Introduction

"Consent to treatment" is convenient shorthand for consent to, or authorisation of, any health care examination, treatment or other procedure. Any such procedures would be likely to be assaults, unless there is implied consent, or they are covered by the principle of necessity, or there is valid consent (of the patient, or of someone with legal authority to consent on behalf of the patient), or they are authorised by statute. For some procedures it is wise, and possibly necessary, to obtain authorisation from the court.

*Comparison with English law*
It is not safe to rely indiscriminately upon English authorities for two principal reasons. Firstly, English law has no equivalent to the tutor-dative (who can grant valid medical consent on behalf of an adult) and in consequence has had to stretch the principle of necessity to cover this gap. Secondly, the English courts appear (for reasons which are not entirely clear) to equate necessity with the test for medical negligence,[32] and the tests for medical negligence differ in the two countries.[33]

*Implied consent*
Consent may be implied provided that a person has capacity to consent. Thus if someone consults a doctor about a complaint, consent to necessary examination may be implied, even if not expressly given.

### Necessity

Consent is not required in relation to people with or without the capacity to give it if the proposed procedure is covered by the principle of necessity, and it is not in fact possible to seek consent. This principle thus covers both the person who has capacity but is unconscious or cannot communicate, and the person who may be

---

[31] For more detailed discussion see Ward *The Power to Act,* Chap.VIII, and Blackie and Patrick *Mental Health,* Chap.4, but note Age of Legal Capacity (Scotland) Act 1991, s.2(4).

[32] *F.* v. *West Berkshire Health Authority* [1989] 2 All ER 545.

[33] In England "a doctor is not negligent if he acts in accordance with a practice accepted at the time as proper by a responsible body of medical opinion" (*Bolam* v. *Friern Hospital Management Committee* [1957] 2 All ER 118), whereas in Scotland the question is whether a doctor "has been proved to be guilty of such failure as no doctor of ordinary skill would be guilty of if acting with ordinary care" (*Hunter* v. *Hanley* 1955 SC 200).

conscious and able to communicate but who lacks sufficient capacity to give valid consent. A procedure is only justified on grounds of necessity if it is in the best interests of the patient and if (but only if) it is necessary to save life or to ensure improvement or prevent deterioration in physical or mental health.[34]

### Examination

Authorities on necessity are generally concerned with operative or other treatment. The principle of necessity probably covers examination where the proposed examination is the only practicable way of checking whether essential treatment of any kind is required, and where reasonable care and concern for the person's wellbeing indicates that such examination should be carried out.

## Consent: children under 16

### Consent by child

A child under 16 may validly consent to any surgical, medical or dental procedure or treatment where the child is (in the opinion of a qualified medical practitioner attending the child) capable of understanding the nature and possible consequences of the proposed procedure or treatment.[35]

### Consent by guardian

The guardian of a child under 16 may give valid consent on behalf of the child. The guardian may delegate the power to consent - parents often do so when someone is put temporarily in charge of their children.

## Consent: adults and children over 16

References in this section to adults include children of 16 and 17.

### Consent by adult

Medical treatment normally proceeds on the basis of the adult's consent, provided that the adult is able to communicate and has adequate capacity to give valid consent. Legal capacity to give medical consent is tested by criteria similar to those for other purposes. It is essential that the adult has reasonable understanding of the nature and possible consequences of the proposed procedure. Where a doctor would normally explain to a patient the risks or relative advantages and disadvantages of alternative courses, the adult must be able to understand those factors to a sufficient degree to make a reasonably informed choice and decision. A proposed procedure cannot be authorised by apparent consent, if the person lacks capacity to give it validly.

---

34    This is the English test in *F.* v. *West Berkshire Health Authority* (above). While this test may be referred to in Scotland, the Scottish courts may interpret it more restrictively: they are most unlikely to go further than the English test.

35    Age of Legal Capacity (Scotland) Act 1991, s.2(4).

*Consent by tutor-dative*
A tutor-dative appointed with unlimited powers may consent (and delegate) in the same way as the guardian of a child under 16. In modern practice tutors-dative are usually appointed with express power to consent to any health care that is in the person's best interests. Only a tutor-dative with the necessary powers may give medical consent on behalf of an adult. For example, a statutory guardian may not (despite having powers to require attendance for health care, or access by health care professionals).

## Detained patients[36]

The provisions described in this section apply only to patients detained under 28-day short-term detention and patients detained under formal detention procedure. They do not apply to patients detained under the shorter emergency procedures, or to voluntary patients.[37]

*General rule*
For detained patients to whom these provisions apply, the general rule is that consent is not required for any medical treatment for the patient's mental disorder, if the responsible medical officer is in charge of the treatment - though mental handicap is arguably untreatable.[38] There are two groups of exceptions, described below, to which special procedures apply.

*Consent and second opinion required*
Both consent and three certificates are required for surgical destruction of brain tissue or its functioning, and for surgical implantation of hormones to reduce male sexual drive.[39] The patient's consent must be obtained, and three persons appointed by the Mental Welfare Commission (a doctor and two non-doctors) must certify that the patient is capable of understanding the nature, purpose and likely effect of the treatment and has consented to it. The doctor must also certify that the treatment should be given, having regard to the likelihood of the treatment alleviating the patient's condition or preventing deterioration. The doctor must first consult those primarily concerned with the patient's treatment and care. There are provisions about reporting, and as to circumstances in which the treatment must stop.

*Consent or second opinion required*
Consent or a second opinion are required for administration of drugs over a period of three months or longer, and for electro-convulsive therapy. If the patient consents, a medical certificate is required confirming that the patient has consented and is capable of understanding the nature of the treatment and its purpose and

---

36   Mental Health (Scotland) Act 1984, Part X.
37   For detention procedures see Part IIB below.
38   It has been suggested that this does not cover treatment of a mentally handicapped person as the handicap itself cannot be treated.
39   The Secretary of State may add categories by regulation.

likely effects. The certificate may be issued by the responsible medical officer, or by a doctor appointed to do so by the Mental Welfare Commission. If the patient does not consent, or is not capable of giving valid consent, a medical certificate is required from a doctor appointed by the Commission that the treatment should be given, having regard to the likelihood of the treatment alleviating the patient's condition, or preventing deterioration.

**Approval of court**

There are circumstances where it is wise to obtain the approval of a court. [In Scotland it may be included in a petition for appointment of a tutor-dative, or by a tutor-dative subsequently to appointment, or by declarator by any person showing cause, or (in relation to children) by an order relating to parental rights under the Law Reform (Parent and Child) (Scotland) Act 1986]. It is doubtful whether procedures such as sterilisation, and others of similar gravity, may safely be undertaken without such approval. The question has not been tested in Scotland. In England, the House of Lords has only gone as far as describing such approval as highly desirable as a matter of good practice (see pages 178-186), but was probably constrained from going further because of the need in England to stretch the necessity principle to cover the lack of an equivalent to tutor-dative procedure. If the court is declaring the treatment to be necessary, it is confirming an existing state of affairs. In Scotland, it is more easily open to the courts to separate out questions of approval from questions of consent or necessity. It is recommended that, at least as a matter of good practice, approval of a court should be sought:
- where there is doubt whether proposed treatment may lawfully be given without consent on grounds of necessity;
- where a tutor is in doubt whether to consent or not (except in relation to simple and minor procedures);
- in any case where sterilisation or other serious procedure is proposed (except in cases of urgent medical necessity which are clearly justified within the necessity principle).

# PART IIA - MENTAL HEALTH LEGISLATION
# England

*Introduction*
Much of our mental health legislation[40] does not relate to the "typical" individual with a mental handicap so is outside the scope of this book. However, some will be affected, particularly those with disturbed or anti-social behaviour or those who also suffer from a mental illness and need restraint or treatment. In addition, references to the Mental Health Act (other than in the context of financial arrangements) may result from a failure to distinguish between *mental illness* and *mental handicap* and lead to an

---

[40]    A list of books on the topic is included in Appendix II.

inappropriate threat to implement laws which have no application. In the event of law reform it is possible that aspects of mental health legislation will be extended to cover associated problems of mental handicap, but the general view is that separate legislation is required. For these reasons, a basic summary of existing legislation and practice is now set out.

## THE MENTAL HEALTH ACT 1983

### Scope

This Act applies to persons suffering from a mental disorder as defined (referred to as *patients*) and provides for:
- their compulsory admission to and detention in hospital;
- their medical treatment in hospital without consent;
- review of their detention and treatment by a tribunal;
- their reception into guardianship in the community;
- management of their property and affairs by the Court of Protection[41]; and
- special treatment when they are involved in criminal proceedings or sentenced by the courts.[42]

Not all of the provisions apply to Northern Ireland, and only a few minor provisions apply to Scotland.

*Arrangement*
The Act is divided into Parts which deal with separate topics:

Part 1       - application of the Act, including definitions;
Part II      - compulsory admission to hospital and guardianship;
Part III     - criminal proceedings and sentencing;
Part IV     - consent to treatment;
Part V      - Mental Health Review Tribunals;
Part VI     - removal and return of patients within UK;
Part VII    - management of property and affairs;
Part VIII - functions of local authorities and Secretary of State;
Part IX     - offences;
Part X      - miscellaneous and supplemental.

### Approved social workers (ASW)

Local social services authorities have to appoint a sufficient number of approved social workers (ASW), with appropriate competence in dealing with persons who are suffering from mental disorder, for the purpose of discharging the functions conferred on ASWs by the Act.[43]

*Functions*
The ASW has various statutory powers and duties, including a right in limited circumstances to enter and inspect premises and to

---

41   This topic is separately dealt with in Chap.10A.
42   These provisions are dealt with in Chap.2, Pt.IIIA.
43   s.114. Authorities must have regard to such matters as the Secretary of State may direct, see DHSS Circular LAC 86/15.

interview and examine a person, but he must believe the person to be suffering from a mental disorder. It can be an offence to obstruct the ASW in the performance of his duties. One of the roles of an ASW is to prevent the need for compulsory admission to hospital, but a personal duty is imposed to make application for admission or guardianship in certain circumstances so the ASW has a key role in the procedures under the Act.[44]

## Definitions

There are a number of terms defined in the Act which are of key importance throughout any consideration of mental health law and those of relevance to mental handicap are set out here.[45]

"**mental disorder** means mental illness, arrested or incomplete development of mind, psychopathic disorder and any other disorder or disability of mind and 'mentally disordered' shall be construed accordingly;
**severe mental impairment** means a state of arrested or incomplete development of mind which includes severe impairment of intelligence and social functioning and is associated with abnormally aggressive or seriously irresponsible conduct on the part of the person concerned and 'severely mentally impaired' shall be construed accordingly;
**mental impairment** means a state of arrested or incomplete development of mind (not amounting to severe mental impairment) which includes significant impairment of intelligence and social functioning and is associated with abnormally aggressive or seriously irresponsible conduct on the part of the person concerned and 'mentally impaired' shall be construed accordingly;
**psychopathic disorder** means a persistent disorder or disability of mind (whether or not including significant impairment of intelligence) which results in abnormally aggressive or seriously irresponsible conduct on the part of the person concerned".

"**nearest relative** in relation to a patient has the meaning given in Part II of the Act, namely, the first of the following persons surviving[46]:
    (a) husband or wife;
    (b) son or daughter;
    (c) father or mother;
    (d) brother or sister;
    (e) grandparent;
    (f) grandchild;
    (g) uncle or aunt;
    (h) nephew or niece".

"**medical treatment** includes nursing, and also includes care, habilitation and rehabilitation under medical supervision;
**mental nursing home** has the same meaning as in the Registered Homes Act 1984;
**patient** ... means a person suffering or appearing to be suffering from mental disorder".

Nothing in these definitions is to be construed as implying that a

---

44   See generally ss.115, 129 and 13. The offence of obstruction may apply to a relative or friend who prevents an ASW from seeing a mentally handicapped person.

45   The definitions are found in Part 1, ss.1(2), 26 and 145(1) (as amended).

46   See s.26 which clarifies and sets out in detail the treatment of relatives of the whole and half-blood, and competing members of the same class by age. The county court has power on application by *any* relative, a person with whom the patient was residing or an approved social worker to replace the nearest relative by any such person who is willing to act, see generally s.29.

person may be dealt with under the Act as suffering from mental disorder by reason only of promiscuity, immoral conduct, sexual deviancy or dependence on alcohol or drugs.[47]

*Interpretation of terms*
The overall definition of *mental disorder* is very wide, and where this term is the basis for admission to hospital under the Act both mentally ill patients and patients with mental handicap/learning disability will be admissible. People who have suffered organic brain damage can also be included.

Three categories of mental disorder are further defined, namely:

*Severe mental impairment* - the effect of this definition is to limit the application of the Act to those persons with mental handicap/learning disability who need treatment in hospital and who have a behavioural problem. This is a specific diagnosis.

*Mental impairment* - the difference between severe mental impairment and mental impairment is one of degree.

*Psychopathic disorder* - the word persistent means that the disorder must have existed for some time before actual diagnosis. This diagnosis is based on observations of behaviour which can be but are not necessarily associated with mental illness or mental impairment.

## Compulsory admission to hospital

The term *section* is often used to refer to the authority under which a person is detained in a mental hospital.

*Admission for assessment (section 2)*
This can be made for a patient diagnosed as suffering from mental disorder of a nature or degree which warrants detention in hospital for assessment and this is in the interests of the patient's health or safety or for the protection of other persons. Two medical recommendations are necessary and the period of detention is for up to 28 days which cannot be renewed. Although such detention is for assessment, treatment can be given without the patient's consent. Because the legal term mental disorder is used as a basis for such admission , persons with a mental handicap can be admitted even if there is no "abnormally aggressive or seriously irresponsible conduct". (This diagnosis is only necessary when the term mental impairment or severe mental impairment is the basis for admission).

*Admission for treatment (section 3)*
This can be made if the patient is diagnosed as suffering from a specific condition, namely mental illness (which is undefined), severe mental impairment, psychopathic disorder or mental impairment, and it is appropriate to receive medical treatment in hospital. The grounds are that it is necessary for the health or safety of the patient or for the protection of other persons. In the case of mental impairment the treatment must be likely to be

---

[47]  s.1(3).

positive for the patient, *i.e.* alleviate or prevent a deterioration of his condition. Two medical recommendations are required and detention is for up to six months in the first instance, renewable for another period of six months and then for periods of one year at a time.

*Admission for assessment in emergency (section 4)*
In cases of urgent necessity the patient can be admitted on the grounds set out in section 2 on the recommendation of one doctor, but the detention is for a period of up to 72 hours. At the end of that time the section can be converted to a section 2 on provision of a second medical recommendation.

The basis for admission here is a diagnosis of mental disorder, so this section could apply to a person with a mental handicap who did not exhibit abnormally aggressive or seriously irresponsible conduct.

*Further short term powers (section 5)*
Under section 5(2), an in-patient in hospital may be detained for up to 72 hours by a doctor in charge of treatment. This can be in any hospital including a medical or surgical ward of a general hospital and this provision could apply to all persons with a mental handicap.

Under section 5(4), a patient receiving in-patient care for a mental disorder can be detained by a nurse for up to six hours if the nurse considers that he is suffering from mental disorder and it is necessary for his health or safety or the protection of others that he be restrained (*e.g.* the patient tries to leave the hospital against advice). Persons with a mental handicap who do not have abnormally aggressive or seriously irresponsible conduct could be detained under the provision.

## Powers of the police

A police constable has the following powers under the 1983 Act to detain an individual, and these provide for short term detention with a view to early examination and assessment and if necessary further treatment in hospital either under section or voluntarily. The term used is mental disorder and therefore persons with a mental handicap will be eligible for detention and can be assessed for further treatment.

*Warrant (section 135)*
A constable, accompanied by an ASW and a registered medical practitioner, can remove a person to a place of safety[48] for up to 72 hours on issue of a warrant by a magistrate if an ASW has reasonable cause to suspect that he is suffering from a mental disorder and is ill treated, neglected or out of control or unable to care for himself and living alone.

---

48  *I.e.* local authority residential accommodation, a hospital, a mental hospital, a police station or "any other suitable place the occupier of which is willing temporarily to receive the patient", s.135(6).

*Removal from public place (section 136)*
A constable can remove from a public place to a place of safety a person who appears to the constable to be suffering from a mental disorder and to be in immediate need of care and control if he thinks it is necessary to do so in the interests of the person or the protection of others. The person may be detained there for up to 72 hours.

## Effect of admission under section

Once an application has been made under a section of the Act the applicant or person authorised by him can legally convey the patient to hospital using reasonable force if necessary.

*Freedom of Movement*
Detention under section means that the patient cannot leave the hospital or mental nursing home or place of safety without the authority of the responsible medical officer or until a full assessment is completed. The responsible medical officer can grant any patient a leave of absence from the hospital with conditions attached if necessary (section 17). However absence without leave will mean that the patient is subject to compulsory return to hospital if necessary by force (section 18).

*Right to Vote*
The right of patients to vote is dealt with in Chapter 2, Part II at page 55.

## Medical treatment

*Compulsory treatment*
A patient detained for assessment and/or treatment under section 2 or 3 is subject to compulsory treatment for his mental disorder, which may be given by the responsible medical officer without his consent.[49] This does not include general medical care, for which treatment can only be given with consent or under the common law rules as stated in Part I of this chapter. Compulsory treatment can include living in the general environment of the ward, drug treatment, behaviour therapy, psychotherapy, ECT and any other forms of treatment given directly to address the mental disorder of the patient.

*Serious treatments*
Part IV of the Act provides safeguards for certain treatments regarded as serious. The first group currently includes surgical operations for destroying of brain tissue (psychosurgery) and "surgical implantation of hormones for the purpose of reducing the male sex drive", but the categories can be extended by the Code of Practice issued by the Secretary of State and by

---

[49]   s.63. This does not apply to patients detained under short term sections including ss.4, 5(2), 5(4), 135 and 136. These patients cannot be given medical treatment either for a mental disorder or for general medical care unless they consent.

regulation. These treatments can only given if the patient consents
and the treatment is endorsed by an independent panel of three
people and with certification of the patient's ability to understand
the "nature, purpose and likely effects of the treatment".[50] The
responsible medical officer must certify that the treatment is likely
to alleviate or prevent a deterioration of the patient's condition.

The second group presently includes electro-convulsive therapy
(ECT) and a course of medication which has continued for three
months or more. These treatments cannot be given unless either
the patient has consented and is certified as being capable of doing
so, or (if the patient does not or cannot consent) an independent
(second opinion) doctor endorses treatment stating that it is likely
to alleviate or prevent a deterioration in the patient's condition.[51]

Both groups are subject to an urgent treatment provision which
provides that the treatment can be given without the safeguards
stated above if the treatment is not irreversible and is immediately
necessary to alleviate suffering or prevent deterioration.[52]

## Guardianship

Statutory guardianship for adults in its present form is a lesser and
more appropriate form of intervention than detention in hospital
for those with mild mental disorders. It is quite distinct from
guardianship of minors.

### Background

The Mental Health Act 1959 gave to the guardian powers
equivalent to those of the father of a child aged 14. When its
operation was reviewed in 1978 the essential powers approach was
adopted and the guardian's powers reduced to the minimum
needed to secure medical treatment, social support and training
and access. The categories of people who could be received into
guardianship were also restricted. It was intended that
guardianship would be useful for a small number of patients with
a mild or chronic form of mental illness for whom detention in
hospital was not appropriate, but in practice it has been used
mainly for people who are mentally handicapped and is often
viewed as a way of protecting those who are at risk living in the
community. It has recently been stated that the purpose is to enable
patients to receive community care where it cannot be provided
without the use of compulsory powers.

Guardianship enables the establishment of an authoritative
framework for working with a patient with a minimum of
constraint to achieve as independent a life as possible within the
community. Where it is used it must be part of the patient's
overall care and treatment plan.[53] It has been little used but may

---

50    s.57. This section applies to both detained and voluntary patients and the
      treatment can never be given if the patient does not or cannot consent to it.
51    s.58.
52    s.62.
53    Code of Practice, para 13.4 - see p.201.

yet prove important in the implementation of community care for people with a mental handicap.

*Applications*

A patient who has attained the age of 16 may be received into guardianship provided certain statutory criteria are met[54]:

    (a) the patient must suffer from one of the four specific categories of mental disorder[55];

    (b) this must be of a nature or degree which warrants guardianship; and

    (c) guardianship is necessary for the welfare of the patient or the protection of others.

Application is made to the local authority social services department by an ASW or the patient's nearest relative and supported by two doctors, but the nearest relative can object to the application or subsequently discharge the patient. Guardianship initially lasts for six months, but may be renewed for a further six months and thereafter annually. The guardian may be either the social services department or a private individual with the approval of the local authority. There is a right of appeal to a Mental Health Review Tribunal.[56]

*Powers*

The guardian has three main powers, namely to require that[57]:

    - the patient resides at a specific place;

    - the patient attends at places and times specified for the purpose of medical treatment, occupation, education or training;

    - access to the patient be given at the patient's residence to any medical practitioner, ASW or other person specified.

The guardian is not obliged to use all these powers and should only use those which are necessary to achieve the specific purposes envisaged for the individual patient. It is important to bear in mind that guardianship is a restriction of a patient's liberty.

*Limitations*

These powers are subject to significant limitations and it is these which have persuaded some social services departments to be reluctant to make use of guardianship, namely:

    - the treatment provisions of the Act do not apply so the patient cannot be given medical treatment without consent;

    - there is no power enabling anyone to physically remove an unwilling patient into guardianship;

    - the guardian can require the patient to reside at a specific place, but not with a specific person;

    - the guardian has no power to detain the patient and cannot

---

[54] s.7.

[55] *I.e.* mental illness, severe mental impairment, mental impairment or psychopathic disorder.

[56] On these points see ss.11(4), 23(1), 29, 20(1) and (2), and 69(1)(*b*).

[57] s.8.

restrict his movements. If a residence requirement is
imposed then all that the guardian can insist upon is that the
patient ordinarily resides at the place specified.

Thus although the patient can be compulsorily returned to a place
where he is living if he absconds, the patient is not liable to be
detained there.[58]

### Duties and sanctions

The duties of a guardian are governed by regulations.[59] There
must in all cases be fairly close supervision by social services,
even where a private individual is appointed, and this may
discourage use of the guardianship procedure by carers seeking to
create a legal basis for the provision of care. There is seldom any
advantage to social services in adopting these legal procedures in
the absence of effective legal sanctions, and in most cases they can
provide services without guardianship.

For guardianship to be successful there must be a recognition by
the patient of the authority of the guardian and a willingness to
work together. The only real sanction the guardian has is where
the patient leaves any place where he is required to live without
the consent of the guardian; in these circumstances the patient can
be taken into custody and returned to that place within 28 days of
leaving. If the patient is not returned or taken into custody within
that period then the guardianship ceases.

### Use by Tribunals

Despite these limitations, guardianship can be a useful option in a
number of cases. Whenever a Tribunal decides not to discharge a
hospital patient from a section it may consider, with a view to
facilitating discharge on a future date, whether to recommend that
the patient be transferred to guardianship. Tribunals should not
hesitate to explore the issue of guardianship fully with the social
worker and may adjourn for further information if necessary.
They may also reconvene if they make the recommendation and it
is not complied with within an appropriate period of time.[60]

The following example illustrates this use:

> Michael is 30 and mildly mentally handicapped. When he was only 16 he
> was convicted of a serious sexual offence against a young boy and made the
> subject of a Hospital Order under section 37. He was placed in a psychiatric
> hospital specialising in mental handicap and has been there ever since. He
> has begun to acquire limited social skills and greater self confidence and is
> also behaving in a more responsible fashion although he remains inadequate
> and unpredictable. He applied for his discharge and the Tribunal refused this
> but recommended that guardianship should be considered. As a result,
> although he remains on section, Michael has been placed in a hostel on a trial
> basis. If all goes well, guardianship will be invoked with appropriate

---

58   s.18(3).
59   Mental Health (Hospital, Guardianship and Consent to Treatment)
     Regulations 1983.
60   Concern has been expressed about cases where such recommendations have
     been thwarted by local authorities unwilling to accept the patient, see Mental
     Health Act Commission in its 3rd Biennial Report (November 1989).

conditions and the section discharged. There is a real prospect that rehabilitation into the community might be successfully achieved in due course as a result of the Tribunal's initiative.

### Use by criminal courts
A guardianship order may be made by a criminal court which considers it a suitable disposal after convicting a person of any offence punishable with imprisonment. The medical criteria and effects of the order are the same as for civil guardianship, except that the patient's nearest relative has no power of discharge.[61]

### Implications for mental handicap
A positive use of guardianship might be to protect a mentally handicapped adult from a relative who was unable or failing to provide adequate care, or who was exploiting the relationship, but it is doubtful if this can be done in the absence of severe behaviour problems. It could in any event be vetoed by the nearest relative, who may be the person involved, and whilst application can be made to the county court for the removal and replacement of the nearest relative on the ground that an objection is unreasonable, this delays the whole process and more urgent steps might be needed. Guardianship does not confer parental powers or give the guardian authority to make personal decisions on behalf of a person who cannot make those decisions for himself.

## Discharge

Detention or guardianship ceases if a written order for discharge is made.[62] The order in respect of a hospital patient detained under section 2 or 3 may be made by the responsible medical officer, the managers or the nearest relative of the patient, and in respect of guardianship also by the responsible social services authority. Where the nearest relative wishes to take the initiative he must give at least 72 hours notice in writing to the hospital managers[63] and the responsible medical officer may then within that time provide a Report to the managers that in his opinion the patient, if discharged, would be likely to act in a manner dangerous to himself or to some other person. If such Report is made the order for discharge by the nearest relative will be of no effect and a similar order cannot be made within the next six months. A patient who is detained under section 2 or 3 or received into guardianship has a right to have the detention or guardianship reviewed by the Mental Health Review Tribunal.[64]

---

61   s.37. A magistrates court can make the order in respect of a severely impaired person without a conviction if satisfied that the individual did the act charged, s.37(3).

62   s.23.

63   The responsible social services authority in the case of guardianship.

64   s.66(1). Application must be made within the relevant period which is defined in s.66(2).

## Mental Health Review Tribunals

The Mental Health Act 1959 provided for the setting up of this Tribunal which was continued by the 1983 Act.[65] It is an independent tribunal comprising three members appointed by the Lord Chancellor including a president (a lawyer), a psychiatrist and a lay member. It is governed by the Council on Tribunals and administered regionally by the Department of Health with offices in London, Nottingham and Liverpool. The Tribunal hears the case in the hospital where the patient is detained.

*Who can apply for a Tribunal*
The patient can apply where he is detained for assessment or treatment, or is under guardianship, and also in cases where the mental disorder has been reclassified and where the authority to detain has been renewed.[66] A patient detained for treatment or transfer to hospital for treatment who has not applied for a Tribunal within six months of such detention or transfer will have the case referred to the Tribunal by the hospital managers.[67] There is an overriding power for the Secretary of State to refer to a Tribunal the case of any patient who is liable to be detained or subject to guardianship.
The nearest relative can apply for a Tribunal in cases where he has demanded the discharge of the patient and the responsible medical officer has barred this, and where an order is made in the county court directing that the functions of the nearest relative be carried out by an acting nearest relative.[68]

*Time limits*
Patients who are detained under section 2 for assessment must apply for a Tribunal within 14 days of the date of the admission to hospital under section and patients who are detained under section 3 for treatment or section 7 guardianship must apply within six months of the date of admission under section or the application for guardianship.

## *Powers of Tribunals*
The Tribunal may discharge the patient, or decline to do so, or may make certain other orders. Decisions are by majority, with the presiding member having a casting vote when necessary.[69]

*Discharge immediately*
The Tribunal will direct the discharge of a patient detained under section 2 if they are satisfied that he is not suffering from a mental disorder which warrants his detention in hospital for assessment or that the detention is not justified for his own health or safety or the protection of others.

---

65   s.65 and Sched.2.
66   ss.16 and 20.
67   s.68.
68   s.25 and s.29 respectively. See s.66 for specific provisions and time limits.
69   These powers are found in s.72.

Discharge of a patient detained under section 3 should be directed if the Tribunal is satisfied he is not suffering from mental illness, psychopathic disorder, severe mental impairment or mental impairment of a nature or degree which makes it appropriate for him to be detained in hospital for treatment or that it is not necessary for his health or safety, or the protection of others, for him to receive treatment. Even if these conditions are not fulfilled the Tribunal can exercise its discretion in discharging the patient and in doing this should consider:

- whether medical treatment will alleviate or prevent a deterioration in his condition; and
- if the patient suffers from mental illness or severe mental impairment, whether the patient can care for himself, obtain the care he needs or guard against exploitation on discharge.

It is important to present to the Tribunal a care package for the patient to fulfil this requirement. These provisions are particularly important for persons with a mental handicap, where the decision to discharge may depend on their ability to care for themselves and be protected.

For patients received into guardianship the Tribunal shall direct discharge if satisfied that the patient is not suffering from a specific form of mental disorder or that it is not necessary in the interests of his welfare or for the protection of others to continue in guardianship.

*Discharge at a future date, leave or transfer*
The Tribunal can also:
- order discharge on a specific date in the future;
- recommend leave of absence to home;
- recommend transfer to another hospital; or
- recommend transfer to guardianship.

A Tribunal can re-convene at a future date to consider the outcome of any recommendation.

If no discharge is ordered the Tribunal can also direct that the form of mental disorder be substituted for another form.

*Legal representation*
Legal representation before the Tribunal is encouraged. The Law Society maintains a panel of solicitors, legal executives, trainee solicitors and solicitors' clerks who are willing to prepare and conduct cases personally and who have the necessary training and experience.[70] Legal aid is not available, but Green Form advice and ABWOR are available in England or Assistance by way of representation in Scotland.

## Code of Practice

A Code of Practice prepared by the Department of Health and the

---

[70]  Those wishing to be considered should contact the Panel Administrator, Professional Standards and Development Directorate, The Law Society, Ipsley Court, Berrington Close, Redditch, Worcestershire B98 0TD.

Welsh Office pursuant to section 118(4) of the 1983 Act was laid before Parliament in December 1989. It offers detailed guidance on how the Act should be implemented and is not legally binding, but failure to follow the Code could be referred to in evidence in legal proceedings. Much of the Code may already have been standard practice in many places, but it is acknowledged that in some areas there will be significant resource implications to adopting the recommendations and that this can only be done as resources permit. The Code is primarily aimed at the needs, rights and entitlements of mentally disordered persons who are detained under relevant mental health legislation, but much of its guidance also applies to informal patients, so it may be referred to as a good practice document for the care and management of all mentally disordered patients. It deals with matters such as assessment prior to admission, admission to hospital or guardianship, treatment and care in hospital, leaving hospital, people with mental handicap and children and young people under 18.

The Code sets the following broad principles for treatment of people to whom the Act applies, They should:

- receive respect for and consideration of their individual qualities and diverse backgrounds - social, cultural, ethnic and religions;
- have their needs taken fully into account though it is recognised that, within available resources, it may not always be practicable to meet them;
- be delivered any necessary treatment or care in the least controlled and segregated facilities practicable;
- be treated or cared for in such a way that promotes to the greatest practicable degree, their self determination and personal responsibility consistent with their needs and wishes;
- be discharged from any Order under the Act to which they are subject immediately it is no longer necessary.

Thus patients should be as fully involved as possible in decisions about their care and treatment, and be made aware of their legal rights within the limits of their understanding. They should be restricted as little as possible for as short a period as possible, taking into account their own individual needs.

## Mental Health Act Commission

The 1983 Act also establishes the *Mental Health Act Commission*, provided for under the National Health Service Act 1977. This is a Special Health Authority which began its statutory duties on September 30, 1983 with the implementation of the Act.[71] The Commission consists of a Chairman, a Vice Chairman and approximately 92 other members. There is a Chief Executive and the central office is in Nottingham. All Commissioners are part time and spend one or two days per week on the work. They are

---

[71]  s.121.

drawn from a multi-disciplinary group[72] and appointed by the Secretary of State for up to four years and, whilst eligible for re-appointment, may also be removed at any time and for any reason.[73] They work in teams to visit on a regular basis all hospitals and mental nursing homes with detained patients. The Commission meets as a national body twice yearly and its professional work is conducted by National Standing Committees.

*Functions*

The Commission has several statutory functions which include protecting the interests of detained patients by reviewing their care and treatment, or any aspect of thereof, in hospitals and mental nursing homes.[74] It will:

- visit and interview patients in private in hospitals and mental nursing homes;
- investigate complaints by and about detained patients;
- keep under review the way in which the powers and duties under the Act are carried out;

and can require the production and inspection of any records relating to the treatment of any person who is or has been a patient in a mental nursing home. Further functions are[75]:

- appointment of "second opinion" doctors for the purpose of reviewing medical treatment for a mental disorder;
- review of treatment plans given to patients[76];
- review of any decision to withhold a postal packet from a detained patient in a special hospital[77];
- publication of a bi-annual report of its activities to be laid before Parliament;
- to monitor the implementation of the *Code of Practice* and advise Ministers on amendment. The Commission was charged with the production of the Code.
- to advise Ministers on matters falling within its remit.

Most patients who are mentally handicapped are not detained in hospital under section, and the Commission is concerned that its protection be extended to them because they may lack capacity to consent to treatment or to choose to continue to live in a hospital. Its influence in this area is presently limited.

**Receivership**

The Court of Protection has power under Part VII of the 1983 Act

---

[72] Including doctors, nurses, social workers, lawyers, academics, psychologists, other specialists and lay members.

[73] Mental Health Act Commission Regulations 1983, regs.3, 4 and 5.

[74] Mental Health Act 1983, s.121. The Commission has no jurisdiction to do the same for informal (non-detained) patients although it has sought for this to be extended to include informal patients, see Second Bi-Annual Report MHAC 1985-1987.

[75] See generally s.121.

[76] *I.e. under* ss.57 and 58, as provided under s.61.

[77] See s.134. This decision is made in the interests of safety of the patient, protection of others or to avoid distress or danger to other persons.

to make orders dealing with the financial affairs of certain persons and often a receiver will be appointed. These provisions are dealt with in Chapter 10A, Part II, but some general points are mentioned here. The Court only has powers to manage the financial affairs of an individual who has been found unable to do so by reason of mental disorder, and such finding is based upon a medical report by one doctor (not necessarily a psychiatrist). This finding is entirely separate from the assessment to detain a patient for treatment or receive a patient into guardianship under Part II of the Act. Patients do not automatically become subject to the Court of Protection jurisdiction by reason of being detained, and many patients whose affairs are managed by the Court are not living in hospital or subject to compulsory detention powers.

# PART IIB - MENTAL HEALTH LEGISLATION Scotland

## INTRODUCTION

### Mental Health (Scotland) Act 1984

Described below are the main relevant provisions of the following Parts of the Mental Health (Scotland) Act 1984:

Part I     - application of the Act, including definitions
Part II    - Mental Welfare Commission
Part V    - admission to and detention in hospital, and guardianship
Part VII - removal and return of patients within UK, etc.
Part IX   - miscellaneous and general: ss.117 and 118 (place of safety orders, etc.)

Described elsewhere are:

Part III   - local authority services (see Chapter 5)
Part IV   - private hospitals (see Chapter 7)
Part VI   - detention of patients concerned in criminal proceedings, etc. and transfer of patients under sentence (mentioned briefly below, but see Chapter 2, Part IIIB)
Part VIII - state hospitals (see Chapter 4, Introduction)
Part IX   - protection of property of patients (see Chapter 10B)
Part X    - consent to treatment (see Chapter 4, Part I)
Part XI   - miscellaneous and general: ss.106 and 107 (sexual offences) (see Chapter 2, Part IV)

*1991 Act*

The 1984 Act is described with amendments up to and including those in the Mental Health (Detention) (Scotland) Act 1991, which was brought into force on March 9, 1992.

*Code of Practice*

The Secretary of State has issued, and from time to time must revise, a Code of Practice for the guidance of members of relevant professions and others in relation to detention and discharge of patients under the 1984 Act, and in relation to medical treatment of people with a mental disorder.

## Mental disorder

The 1984 Act refers repeatedly to "mental disorder", which means mental illness or mental handicap however caused or manifested. This bracketing of people suffering from mental illness and those who have a mental handicap has historical origins, and has become increasingly inappropriate. However, some procedures conceived principally in terms of mental illness do apply to people with a mental handicap, and sometimes require to be applied to them. Moreover, mentally handicapped people, like every other section of the population, are not immune to mental illness.

## Persons with authority

### Relatives and nearest relative

Relatives, and in particular the nearest relative, have various roles under the 1984 Act. A relative is anyone on the following list, and the nearest relative is the first person on the list caring for the person (or who was doing so immediately prior to detention or guardianship):

(a) spouse;
(b) child;
(c) father or mother;
(d) brother or sister;
(e) grandparent;
(f) grandchild;
(g) uncle or aunt;
(h) nephew or niece.[78]

The sheriff may appoint an acting nearest relative where there is no nearest relative within the statutory definition, where the nearest relative is incapable of acting, or where the nearest relative applies on grounds that he is unwilling or considers it undesirable to continue acting. The legislation is deficient in that unless the nearest relative himself applies, the sheriff cannot disqualify the nearest relative and appoint an acting nearest relative however desirable it may be to do so (*e.g.* where the nearest relative is an abuser).

### Mental health officers

Mental health officers have various important functions under the 1984 Act, and local authorities have a duty to appoint a sufficient number to discharge those functions. In practice, mental health officers are usually experienced social workers who undertake further training to qualify for appointment. Before making the

---

[78] Siblings of the full blood take precedence over those of the half blood, and among relatives in the same category the eldest takes precedence. Exceptions include separated or deserting spouses, and persons (other than spouses) under 18.

appointment, the local authority must ensure that the appointee has such qualifications, experience and competence in dealing with persons suffering from mental disorder as the Secretary of State may direct.[79]

*Responsible medical officer*

The responsible medical officer is a medical practitioner authorised to act as such by the managers of a hospital (in relation to detention) or by the local authority (in relation to guardianship).

## MENTAL WELFARE COMMISSION

The Mental Welfare Commission for Scotland plays a major role in protecting the persons and interests of people with mental disorders. As well as dealing with individual cases, the Commission addresses issues of general concern. It has, and exercises, a wider range of functions than the Mental Health Act Commission in England.

## Duties

The primary duty of the Commission is generally to exercise protective functions in respect of people incapable of adequately protecting their persons or interests because of mental disorder. This duty applies to people in the community as well as those in hospital or other institutions.

*Enquiries*

The Commission must make enquiry into any case where (in relation to a mentally disordered person) it appears to them that there may be ill-treatment, deficiency in care or treatment, or improper detention, or where property may be exposed to loss or damage. Such an enquiry may be carried out by an individual member of the Commission, or a committee of members, or an advocate or solicitor of not less than five years standing appointed for the purpose. Such enquiries can exercise the powers and privileges of a court of law: witnesses can be compelled to attend and give evidence, and can be put on oath. This duty, like the Commission's primary protective duty, applies in relation to all mentally disordered people, whether in hospitals or other institutions, or in the community.

*Visiting*

The Commission has various duties to visit patients who are detained or under guardianship. In the case of restricted patients[80] the Commission must advise the Secretary of State if they consider that the patient should be discharged.

---

79   The local authority must also have regard to such other matters as the
     Secretary of State may direct. For relevant provisions, see 1984 Act, s.9.
80   See p.214 below; also Chap.2, Part IIIB, p.95.

*Notification*

The Commission must bring to the attention of hospital managers or the local authority the facts of any case where the Commission consider it desirable for those bodies to exercise their functions to prevent ill-treatment, remedy deficiency in care or treatment, terminate improper detention or prevent or redress loss or damage to property. Where the Commission consider that they ought to bring to the attention of the Secretary of State, a health board, local authority or any other body any matter concerning the welfare of any mentally disordered person, they have a duty to do so. For these purposes a medical commissioner or medical officer of the Commission may examine any patient, and the Commission may interview any patient, in private.

*Annual reports*

The Commission is required to publish annual reports, and to submit them to the Secretary of State (who lays copies before parliament). The reports are valuable documents for reference purposes.

## Powers

In addition to powers mentioned above in conjunction with duties, the Commission's powers include the following.

*Patients' records*

A medical commissioner or medical officer of the Commission may require production of the medical records of any patient, and may inspect them.

*Detained patients, guardianship*

The Commission has powers and functions in relation to detained patients and persons under guardianship as described in the next two main sections.

## Duties of others

The Secretary of State must afford the Commission all facilities necessary to enable them to carry out their functions in respect of any patient in a hospital (other than a private hospital). The relevant local authority, and the guardian, must afford the Commission all facilities necessary to discharge their functions in respect of persons under guardianship.

## DETENTION

The relevant provisions are contained in Part V of the 1984 Act. References to the 1991 Act mean the Mental Health (Detention) (Scotland) Act 1991.

## Two-hour detention by nurse

This emergency procedure applies where a voluntary patient tries to leave hospital, but it is necessary to stop him going for the sake of his own health or safety, or for the protection of others. If a doctor is not available to make an immediate "emergency recommendation" (see below), then a suitably qualified nurse can detain the patient for up to two hours, pending the arrival of a doctor who can make an emergency recommendation. The nurse must record the details in writing. The record is passed to the managers of the hospital, and by them to the Mental Welfare Commission. This procedure may be followed by emergency detention or release of the patient.

## 72-hour emergency detention

A single doctor may examine a person and that day make an "emergency recommendation" if compulsory admission is urgently necessary for the patient's health or safety, or for the protection of others, and if more formal procedures would involve undesirable delay. Where practicable, the consent of a relative or of the mental health officer must be obtained.[81] The emergency recommendation authorises the patient's removal to hospital at any time within three days, and (in relation to patients so removed, or patients already in hospital) detention for up to 72 hours. The managers of the hospital must if possible notify the nearest relative of the admission, and they must notify the Mental Welfare Commission. Unless the person was already in hospital as a voluntary patient, some responsible person residing with the patient must also be notified. This procedure may be followed by either 28-day short-term detention or formal procedure (see below for both), or by release of the patient, but not by another 72-hour emergency detention.

## 28-day short-term detention

This procedure applies where the patient has been admitted on an emergency recommendation, and the patient's condition is such that it is appropriate to detain him at least for a limited period, and necessary to detain him for his own health or safety, or for the protection of others. Where practicable, consent must be obtained from the nearest relative or from the mental health officer. A psychiatrist examines the patient and makes out a report that the above requirements apply. If consent of the nearest relative or mental health officer has not been obtained, the reason must be included in the report. The report is passed to the managers of the hospital, and they must notify:
- the nearest relative (where practicable, but not if the nearest relative has already consented),
- the local authority (unless their mental health officer has consented), and
- the Mental Welfare Commission.

During the last week of the 28-day period of detention the mental health officer must interview the patient and report on his social

---

81    This "where practicable" formula, and a similar provision in relation to 28-day short-term detention, presents unresolved difficulties of interpretation; for example, where only a few relatives can be contacted and none consents.

circumstances. This procedure may be followed by either interim detention or formal procedure (see below for both), or by release of the patient, but not by 72-hour emergency detention or another 28-day short-term detention.

*Interim detention (1991 Act)* [82]
Under this procedure short-term detention may be extended for a further three working days[83] where a relapse occurs so late in the 28-day period that a formal application cannot be prepared and lodged before expiry. A doctor approved for the purpose by the health board personally examines the patient and prepares a report that in his opinion the patient suffers from mental disorder making it appropriate for him to be detained for at least a limited period, and that he ought to be detained for his own health or safety or the protection of others. Where practicable, the consent of the nearest relative or mental health officer must be obtained, and the reason for any failure to obtain it must be included in the report. The medical practitioner lodges the report with the sheriff clerk and informs those persons and bodies listed above.

*Appeal to sheriff*
The patient may appeal to the sheriff to order his discharge from 28-day short-term detention, or any extension under interim detention procedure.

*Further extension (1991 Act)*
Where a patient is detained under short-term or interim detention and an application for formal detention is lodged with the sheriff clerk, the patient may be further detained for up to five working days from lodgement of the application. Within the five working days the sheriff must either approve the formal application or hold a hearing, but may adjourn the hearing, in which case detention may continue until the application is finally determined.

## Formal procedure

*Persons liable to be detained*
A mentally handicapped person may be detained if all of the following requirements are satisfied:
   (a) The mental handicap is of a nature or degree which makes it appropriate for the person to receive medical treatment in a hospital.
   (b) The person's intelligence and social functioning are either "severely" or "significantly" impaired, and (in either case) the person's conduct is abnormally aggressive or seriously irresponsible.
   (c) Where intelligence and social functioning are "significantly" but not "severely" impaired, medical treatment in hospital must be likely to alleviate the person's

---

82   For guidance on provisions of 1991 Act see Scottish Office circular SOHHD GEN 1992/6 dated March 4, 1992.
83   The definition excludes Saturdays, Sundays and court holidays.

condition or likely to prevent deterioration.

(d) Medical treatment in hospital must be necessary either for the health or safety of the person or for the protection of others.

(e) Such treatment cannot be provided unless the person is detained under Mental Health Act provisions.[84]

## Application

An application naming the hospital to which compulsory admission is sought is made by either the nearest relative or the mental health officer. The application is addressed to the managers of the hospital, and requires the approval of the sheriff.

## Role of mental health officer

If relatives feel that detention is necessary, the nearest relative should contact the social work department, who then have a duty to have the case considered by the mental health officer. If the mental health officer decides that detention is not necessary, he must give the nearest relative his reasons, in writing. In any case where the mental health officer proposes to make an admission application he must interview the person during the fortnight before the application is submitted to the sheriff. He must tell the nearest relative about the proposed application, and about the nearest relative's right to object.[85] If the mental health officer receives two medical recommendations (see below) and if one of the doctors asks him to make an application for admission, he must do so, whether he agrees with the application or not. He must say in the application whether in his opinion the application should be granted, and he too must give his reasons.

## Application by nearest relative

The nearest relative must have seen the person during the fortnight before the application is submitted to the sheriff.

## Medical recommendations

All applications require two medical recommendations.[86] The two medical examinations may take place together unless the mentally handicapped person or the nearest relative objects, in which case they must take place separately, but not more than five days apart. The examinations (or the second, if they are done separately) must take place during the week before the application is submitted to the sheriff. Both medical recommendations must confirm that the person has a mental disorder, and they must say which of the

---

84  In relation to "mental illness", that term should be substituted in (a), and for (b) and (c) is substituted a requirement that where the mental disorder is a persistent one manifested only by abnormally aggressive or seriously irresponsible conduct, medical treatment in hospital is likely to alleviate the person's condition or likely to prevent deterioration. (d) and (e) both apply.

85  Any objections are heard by the sheriff, who may order that the proceedings should be in private.

86  There are detailed provisions as to which doctors can provide these recommendations. If possible, one recommendation is given by a specialist and the other by a general practitioner who knows the person.

criteria for detention apply. Reasons must be given.

*Involvement of patient*

There is a statutory duty to try to take steps to ensure that the person understands the proceedings. However, the sheriff may exclude the person from the proceedings if satisfied that involvement would be prejudicial to health or treatment.

*1991 Act*

Within five working days of lodgement of the application for admission with the sheriff clerk, the sheriff must approve the application or hold a hearing, but may adjourn the hearing.

*Procedure before sheriff*

The sheriff may make enquiries and hear the person or others. He must give an opportunity to be heard to the person or nearest relative if objecting, or to the mental health officer if applying for but recommending against detention, and must not withhold approval without giving an opportunity to be heard to the applicant and any witnesses for the applicant. He may hold the proceedings in private, and must do so if the patient or applicant so wishes.

*Procedure following approval*

If the sheriff approves the application, the approval authorises removal of the patient and compulsory admission to the hospital named in the application, at any time within seven days of the approval being granted. Within the same seven day period:

- the local authority for the area where the hospital is situated must be notified (unless the application was made by their mental health officer), and
- the Mental Welfare Commission must be notified.

During the fourth week after admission, the case must be reviewed, and if the criteria for detention no longer apply, the patient is discharged. If the criteria still apply, and detention is to continue, notification must be given to the Mental Welfare Commission, the nearest relative, the local authority, and the managers of the hospital. The detention will then continue until six months after it began.

*Renewal*

Detention can be renewed for another six months, and annually thereafter. The patient is assessed during the last two months of each period of detention, and if the grounds for detention still apply, a report is made to the managers of the hospital and to the Mental Welfare Commission, and detention is renewed. Renewal does not involve approval by the sheriff, but the patient may at any time following renewal appeal to the sheriff, who will discharge the patient if he finds that grounds for detention no longer exist.

*Treatment*

Detained patients may be given medical treatment for mental

disorder without consent, except for specified categories of treatment to which special requirements apply (see page 187-190).

*Religion*
In arranging detention, "regard shall be had" to the religious persuasion of the person.

*Correspondence*
Sections 115 and 116 of the 1984 Act contain detailed provisions and procedures regarding circumstances in which mail to or from detained patients may be opened and inspected, or withheld.

*Right to vote*
Voting rights of patients are dealt with in Chapter 2, Part II at page 55.

## Discharge

A detained patient may be discharged
- by the responsible medical officer or Mental Welfare Commission, and
- by the nearest relative after giving seven days written notice to the managers of the hospital (unless within the seven days the responsible medical officer certifies that the grounds for detention (see page 209) still apply).[87]

If the patient does not suffer from mental disorder of a nature or degree which makes detention appropriate, or if treatment in hospital is not necessary for the health or safety of the patient or the protection of others:
- the responsible medical officer or Mental Welfare Commission must discharge the patient, and
- the sheriff must order discharge upon appeal by the patient, or by the nearest relative, against a responsible medical officer's certificate halting discharge, if the sheriff is satisfied that the above criteria apply.[88]

## Absence and removal

The responsible medical officer may grant and (in certain circumstances) revoke leave of absence. A patient absent without leave may be taken into custody and returned to hospital, but only within 28 days of going absent. The 1984 Act also contains provisions regarding removal of patients to and from England and Wales, Northern Ireland, and elsewhere.

---

87  In which case the nearest relative has 28 days to appeal to the sheriff, but otherwise may not seek to discharge the patient again for six months. Discharge by nearest relative does not apply to State Hospital patients.

88  For the purpose of such an appeal, the appellant may have the patient visited and examined in private by a medical practitioner, who may require production of and inspect relevant records.

## Place of safety orders [89]

*Entry and removal*

A right of entry arises in cases of suspected ill-treatment or neglect of a person with a mental disorder, or if it is suspected that the person is not being kept under control, or is living alone and uncared for and is unable to care for himself, in any place. If a mental health officer or medical commissioner of the Mental Welfare Commission has reasonable cause to believe that one of these criteria apply, he may demand admission to the place.[90]

If admission is not refused, he may enter and inspect the place: in this event, there are no other specified procedures, but procedures such as an emergency recommendation, formal detention or guardianship may be initiated if appropriate. If admission is refused, or refusal is apprehended, sworn information to that effect may be submitted to a justice of the peace, who may grant a warrant to enter the premises, if necessary by force: and the person may then be removed to a place of safety.

*Removal from public place*

A constable may remove to a place of safety a person whom he finds in a public place, and who appears to be suffering from a mental disorder and in immediate need of care and control, if the constable thinks that such removal is necessary in the interests of the person or for the protection of others.

*Place of safety*

In these provisions a place of safety means a hospital or residential home for people with a mental disorder, or any other suitable place where the occupier is willing to receive the person temporarily. A police station may only be used in an emergency, when no other suitable place is available.

The person may be kept in the place of safety for up to 72 hours so that he can be medically examined and any necessary arrangements made for treatment or care. Such detention in a place of safety may be followed by an emergency recommendation or formal application for detention.

## Criminal procedure

Procedures applicable to persons with a mental handicap who are accused or convicted of an offence are described more fully in Chapter 2, Part IIIB, page 85 *et seq.* A summary follows.

*Hospital orders*

This procedure applies when a person has been convicted of an offence (other than murder) punishable with imprisonment, and the person meets the criteria for "persons liable to be detained" described on page 209. The court may make a hospital order if satisfied that this is the best way of dealing with the case. The

---

89   1984 Act, ss.117 and 118.
90   He must produce authentication if asked.

effect of the order is similar to admission under the formal detention procedure described above.

### Restriction orders

The court may make a restriction order if that is necessary to protect the public from serious harm. The restriction order may be of fixed or indefinite duration. The effect is that the person may only be discharged by the Secretary of State, or by appeal to the sheriff.

### Transfer orders

Transfer orders also apply to persons meeting the criteria for "persons liable to be detained". The Secretary of State may ask the sheriff to order the transfer to hospital of a prisoner awaiting trial or sentence. The effect is the same as a hospital order with an unlimited restriction order. Unless the court passes a custodial sentence,[91] following sentence the person will remain in hospital as if detained under formal procedure.

In the case of a prisoner serving a custodial sentence, if the detention criteria apply the Secretary of State may order transfer to hospital, and may impose a restriction direction (equivalent to a restriction order for the remainder of the custodial sentence). The person may within one month appeal to the sheriff to be returned to prison.

The Secretary of State must keep under review the condition of prisoners transferred to hospital, and if certain discharge criteria apply, must return the person to prison or release him on licence or under supervision.

## STATUTORY GUARDIANSHIP

Statutory guardianship was introduced in Scotland in 1913. Until 1984 statutory guardians had the same powers of personal guardianship as the parent of a young child,[92] and thus effectively the same powers as a modern tutor-dative with unlimited personal powers. Statutory guardians now have limited interventionist powers, and are not true personal guardians. The relevant provisions are contained in Part V of the 1984 Act.[93]

### Criteria for guardianship

A person aged 16 or over may be received into guardianship if suffering from a mental disorder of a nature or degree which warrants reception into guardianship, and if guardianship is necessary in the interests of the person's welfare.

### Powers of guardian

Statutory guardians have only the following powers:

---

91    Or makes a hospital, guardianship or probation order.
92    Except that power to inflict corporal punishment was specifically excluded.
93    See also the Mental Health (Specified Treatments, Guardianship Duties, etc) (Scotland) Regulations 1984, (S.I.1984 No.1494).

- power to require the person to reside at a place specified by the guardian;
- power to require the person to attend at places and times specified by the guardian for the purposes of medical treatment,[94] occupation, education or training;
- power to require access to the person to be given, at any place where the person is residing, to any medical practitioner, mental health officer or other person specified by the guardian.

Management powers are specifically excluded. Administration of corporal punishment is prohibited, and is an offence.

## Duties

### Guardian

A guardian who is an individual must provide any required reports to the social work authority, and must notify the social work authority of any proposed permanent change of address by the person or the guardian, particulars of the person's general practitioner (and any change), the person's death, any absence without leave, and any return from absence without leave (whether voluntary or because the person is brought back).

### Social work authority

The social work authority (whether itself the guardian or not) must appoint a responsible medical officer to the person, exercise general supervision of the person, arrange for the person to be visited at least every three months, and notify the Mental Welfare Commission of any of the matters listed in the preceding paragraph.

## Procedure

### Guardians

The guardian may be the local authority,[95] or a person chosen by the local authority, or any other person accepted as suitable by the local authority.[96]

### Application

The application to appoint a guardian is made either by the nearest relative or by the mental health officer. The proposed guardian is named in the application, and the applicant may propose himself. The application is addressed to the local authority, and requires to be approved by the sheriff court.

### Role of mental health officer

If relatives feel that guardianship is necessary, the nearest relative should contact the social work department, who then have a duty to have the case considered by the mental health officer. If the

---

94  But the statutory guardian, unlike a tutor-dative, may not consent to treatment (see p.189 above).

95  Such impersonal guardianship is undesirable, and not to be recommended.

96  In arranging guardianship, "regard shall be had" to the religious persuasion of the person.

mental health officer decides that guardianship is not necessary, he must give the nearest relative his reasons, in writing. In any case where the mental health officer proposes to make a guardianship application he must interview the person during the fortnight before the application is submitted to the sheriff. He must tell the nearest relative about the proposed application, and about the right to object.[97] The application must be accompanied by a recommendation from the mental health officer confirming, with reasons, that guardianship is necessary in the interests of the person's welfare. The mental health officer must disclose any personal relationship or personal pecuniary interest.

*Application by the nearest relative*
The nearest relative must have seen the person during the fortnight before the application is submitted to the sheriff.

*Medical recommendations*
All applications require two medical recommendations.[98] The two medical examinations may take place together unless the mentally handicapped person or the nearest relative objects, in which case they must take place separately, but not more than five days apart. The examinations (or the second, if they are done separately) must take place during the week before the application is submitted to the sheriff. Both medical recommendations must state the form of mental disorder and confirm that it warrants guardianship, and must give reasons. Any relationship to the person, or financial interest, must be disclosed.

*Involvement of the person*
There is a statutory duty to try to take steps to ensure that the person understands the proceedings. However, the sheriff may exclude the person from the proceedings if satisfied that involvement would be prejudicial to health or treatment.

*Procedure before sheriff*
The sheriff may make enquiries and hear the person or others. He must give an opportunity to be heard to the nearest relative, if objecting, and must not withhold approval without giving an opportunity to be heard to the applicant and any witnesses for the applicant. He may hold the proceedings in private, and must do so if the person or applicant so wishes.

*Procedure following approval*
If the sheriff approves the application, it must be forwarded to the local authority, and they must notify the Mental Welfare Commission, all within seven days. The initial guardianship order lasts for six months.

---

97    Any objections are heard by the sheriff, who may order that the proceedings should be in private.
98    There are detailed provisions as to which doctors can provide these recommendations. If possible, one recommendation is given by a specialist and the other by a general practitioner who knows the person.

*Renewal*

Guardianship can be renewed for another six months, and annually thereafter. The person is assessed during the last two months of each period of guardianship, both medically and by the mental health officer. If the grounds for guardianship still apply, reports are made to the local authority and to the Mental Welfare Commission, and guardianship is renewed. Renewal does not involve approval by the sheriff, but the person under guardianship may at any time appeal to the sheriff, who will terminate the guardianship if he finds that grounds for guardianship no longer exist.

## Discharge

The responsible medical officer, social work authority or the Mental Welfare Commission must discharge the person from guardianship if either of the criteria for guardianship[99] no longer applies. The nearest relative may discharge the person after giving at least 14 days written notice to the local authority (unless within the 14 days the local authority and the responsible medical officer certify that both criteria for guardianship still apply).[100]

The sheriff must order discharge upon appeal by the person against renewal, or by the nearest relative against certification halting discharge by the nearest relative, if the sheriff is satisfied that either of the criteria for guardianship no longer applies.

Guardianship ceases if the person is absent without leave for 28 days from the place where he is required by the guardian to reside, and ceases upon detention in hospital under formal procedure.

## Absence

A person under guardianship absent without leave from the place where he is required by the guardian to reside may be taken into custody and returned within 28 days of going absent. This may be done by the guardian, any local authority officer, any constable, or anyone with written authorisation from the guardian or the local authority.

## Transfer

The local authority may transfer guardianship to a new guardian if the new guardian consents, and the existing guardian consents or (if the existing guardian refuses consent) the sheriff approves. The local authority automatically becomes guardian if an individual guardian dies or relinquishes the guardianship and may then transfer guardianship to a new guardian. During incapacity of a guardian, the guardianship functions may be exercised by the local authority or by a person approved for the purpose by the local authority. Where guardianship is transferred under any of these

---

99 See p.214.
100 In which case the nearest relative has 28 days to appeal to the sheriff.

provisions, the local authority must intimate such transfer within seven days to the nearest relative and to the Mental Welfare Commission.

### Guardianship order

This procedure applies when a person has been convicted of an offence (other than murder) punishable with imprisonment, and the person meets the criteria for guardianship described above. The court may make a guardianship order if satisfied that this is the best way of dealing with the case. The person is then received into guardianship and all of the provisions described above apply, except that the nearest relative cannot discharge the person from guardianship. (See also Chapter 2, Part IIIB, pages 94-96).

# PART III - CONCLUSION

## Medical treatment

Concerns about procedures and practice relating to medical treatment include withholding of treatment, and failure properly to evaluate capacity and consult with carers about capacity or proposed treatment. There is concern that decision-making about medical treatment should be based on statute rather than case law.[101] The possible conflict between the patient's wishes (actual or perceived) and clinical judgment has yet to be resolved, and there is concern that the doctor who decides on the patient's ability to consent is the same person who decides that treatment is in the patient's best interests, with the obvious temptation to find someone who disagrees with the doctor to be incapable of rational decision.

### *Consent or decision?*

When considering medical treatment the courts consider the ability of the patient to *consent*, and recently they have had to cope with the implications of a refusal to consent by a person who had not attained legal majority but might otherwise have been treated as able to consent. When considering other matters the question is the capacity of the individual to *make decisions*. The difference in approach is probably due to the fact that the medical profession is concerned to have a valid consent for any surgical procedure or course of treatment, but by restricting consideration to the ability of the patient to consent to the proposed treatment those concerned (and ultimately the court) may fail to consider other options. Medical treatment does not always involve a simple yes/no decision, which is implied by asking whether the patient consents, and it is suggested that the correct approach is to enquire whether the patient is capable of considering all the relevant options and making a rational choice between them.

---

[101] The current reviews by the Law Commissions in England and Scotland include the issue of decisions about medical treatment.

*Implications to mental handicap*

In England, the position now is that medical treatment for incapacitated adults can be given on the basis of best interests, the ultimate decision being that of the treating doctor. In Scotland, recent English cases have received much attention, but there has been no test before the courts of the effect of the distinction that English law has developed in the absence of any form of personal guardianship such as the tutor-dative provides in Scotland. In both countries, there is concern about the use of medical discretion and how best interests are decided. In England, all the treating doctor needs to do is show that there is a responsible body of medical opinion that would have approved of the treatment given, even if this is a minority view. Confusion may arise, such as where the surgeon is prepared to proceed but the anaesthetist is not. There is also uncertainty as to the categories of medical treatment where it is unwise to proceed without court approval.

There is some concern that an application to the High Court under the English provisions is expensive and the parents as applicants may not qualify for legal aid. It is understood that in such cases the applicant could be the patient and a legal aid certificate could be applied for on behalf of the patient as applicant. It is important to monitor the award of legal aid in these cases.[102]

## Mental Health Acts

The majority of patients are, at least technically, voluntary but unlike patients in detention there is little obligation to explain their rights to them. The following areas are also of current concern in regard to mental health legislation:

*Guardianship*

Amendments proposed include widening guardianship provisions to include a power to convey the patient to a place of residence (which may include a hospital). Presently guardianship is under-used and many social workers do not feel that it provides any real power to assist with the care of the patient. In England, possible extension of the eligibility of people to be received into guardianship would allow the procedure to be used for people who are learning disabled but do not have abnormally aggressive or seriously irresponsible conduct.

*Treatment in the community*

The issue of compulsory treatment in the community has been considered by many, including the Law Society, the Royal College of Psychiatrists and the British Association of Social Workers. The concern has been about patients who are discharged from hospital and released from liability to detention, and then stop taking medication. Proposals for compulsory treatment in the community have been made to include a form of community treatment order

---

102 In Scotland, the legal aid position appears to be clearer: eligibility will be assessed on the basis of the means of the patient alone (see Chap.2, p.50).

with a power to compel medication and to insist on a possible recall to hospital if necessary. The debate about this continues.

### Community Care

The after-care provisions of the Mental Health Acts place duties on the District Health Authority and local social services authority (in Scotland, health boards and social work authorities) to provide, in co-operation with relevant voluntary agencies, aftercare services for certain patients who have been detained. After-care is not defined, but this is an area in which legal action on behalf of the individual to enforce the duty could be useful, depending on the facts of any individual case and how the discharge assessments are made. Most hospitals and social service departments have now developed joint policies which should be available to the patients and their representatives.

In England, the Mental Health Act *Code of Practice* and the Fourth Bi-Annual Report of the Mental Health Act Commission addressed management and care of patients with a mental handicap. There is particular concern about patients who are difficult to manage and the use of behaviour therapy. The Commission remit does not extend to patients who are not formally detained but the Commission continues to seek to extend this remit. The question of behaviour therapy remains of some concern and particularly as this is not a treatment identified as one of special concern under sections 57 and 58 the English Act (sections 97 and 98 of the Scottish Act). Behaviour therapy may be implemented as part of a treatment plan in consultation with a clinical psychologist and the programme may involve withholding of privilege or reduction of quality of life for the patient.

# CHAPTER 5    COMMUNITY CARE

## INTRODUCTION

The emphasis in this chapter is not on the legal rights of the individual, because these are very limited in the context of services provided for the benefit of people with a mental handicap, but on the range of services that may be available and the procedures and statutory authority under which these are provided. The law imposes an obligation on local authorities to provide certain services, but many others are either provided wholly at the discretion of the authority or on the basis of a general requirement to provide a service rather than to provide it for a particular person. In such cases, either no action can be taken to insist upon those services being made available or enforcement depends on the relevant Secretary of State stepping in. A lawyer may be able to assist in a particular case in securing a package of care, but an awareness of the type of services that may be required or available is needed. It could be argued that failure by a local authority to provide a care package amounts to a denial of the right of the individual to receive support and assistance and of the authority's duty to provide this, but it may first be necessary to identify the authority which has a duty where each potential authority is seeking to pass responsibility to another.

### Funding

The biggest problem is usually the lack of public funding for the needs of disabled persons, with the result that even if an authority has the will to provide services it seldom has the means. This may exhibit itself in a lack of the services which authorities have power to provide, or inadequate general provision of facilities which they have a duty to provide, but more serious is a failure to provide a service to which an individual is legally entitled. This is where the law must be identified and used. Too often authorities fail to carry out their legal obligations and this remains unchallenged by the handicapped individual and the family (if there is one). Sometimes authorities make their own rules and no-one thinks to question them, and all too often assessments of need are influenced by the cost of fulfilling those needs or simply not made at all.

As a result, many authorities operate on the basis of crisis management rather than forward planning, and this has serious implications for the future. Where assessments are made they may be influenced more by resources than needs, and the picture of care provision painted by policy documents is seldom reflected in reality. Figures produced by MENCAP indicate that in England alone, at least 20,000 people with a mental handicap do not get a day service of any kind, and many others only benefit from a part-time or inadequate service. In some areas the outlook is bleak for the school leaver who may have stayed on in an inappropriate

special school until almost 20 years of age simply because nothing
was available thereafter.

In Part I we outline the structure of local authorities and how they
operate and offer guidance on dealing with them; in Part II we
consider the policy and legislation behind care in the community;
in Part III we identify the services that are provided. The specific
topics of education, training and employment, and of housing and
residential care are dealt with in the following chapters.

# PART I - DEALING WITH LOCAL AUTHORITIES

## Preliminary

The first problem faced by an individual needing services may be
to identify the local authority, department and officer responsible
for providing them, so a general introduction to local government
is given, followed by some guidance on how to secure any
necessary service which is not provided. The principal statutes
dealing with such matters are the Local Government Act 1972 (as
amended) and the Local Government (Scotland) Act 1973.[1]

## STRUCTURE

### Councils

In England and Wales there are three tiers of local government:
county councils, district (or borough) councils and parish (or
town) councils. It is usually county councils with which the
handicapped individual will be involved in regard to the provision
of services, save that district councils are responsible for housing
and environmental health. In metropolitan areas[2] the Metropolitan
District Councils through their social services departments have
responsibility for the handicapped, and in Greater London it is the
Borough Councils.

In Scotland, there are two tiers, regional councils and district
councils, except for the three single-tier islands councils.
Education, social work and transport are included in the functions
of the nine regions; housing, environmental services and
recreation are among the functions of the 53 districts. Both tiers
have planning functions.[3] Community councils do not have local
authority status.

## Councillors

Councillors are elected, usually for a four year period, and tend to
be collectively responsible for policy decisions and seeing that
these are implemented. They have no particular training or

---

1    Though there is separate legislation dealing with principal functions such as
     education, social work and housing.
2    Greater Manchester, Merseyside, South Yorkshire, Tyne and Wear, West
     Midlands and West Yorkshire.
3    Local Government (Scotland) Act 1973. See also Local Government and
     Planning (Scotland) Act 1982. Reform to a single tier is proposed.

expertise and receive advice from their officers.

*Officers*

An authority must appoint such officers as it thinks necessary for the proper discharge of its functions.[4] They are paid officials, usually experts in their own particular field, who carry out policy decisions and are responsible for administration. They may also be given delegated powers in particular areas. The most senior officer is usually the Chief Executive.

## Departments

The administration of local authorities is divided into various departments, each of which has a senior officer, including:

*Social Services,* headed by a Director of Social Services,[5] whose responsibilities and powers are found in numerous statutes and include welfare of vulnerable people such as children, the elderly and persons who are physically disabled or mentally incapable.

*Education,* under a Director of Education (or Chief Education Officer), which deals with schools and other educational establishments and comprises the local education authority.

*Housing,* under a Director of Housing, which deals with the provision of housing.

*Environmental Health,* headed by a Chief Environmental Health Officer, which covers all matters of public health and has responsibilities as regards the environment.

## Social workers

In England, since 1970 local authorities[6] have been obliged to establish a Social Services Committee which must appoint a Director of Social Services and employs social workers.[7] Whilst the legislation sets out the framework for the provision of social services it is not specific about how they are organised.

In Scotland, the modern social work regime was introduced by the Social Work (Scotland) Act 1968,[8] creating a general duty to promote social welfare.

*Role*

Social workers have clients whose welfare and interests they seek to look after by providing support, guidance and advice, and an introduction to services. In addition they have a statutory role which may oblige them to use statutory powers to protect the client. A conflict can arise between these two roles. In the case of decisions having an adverse effect on the client, the first step is to

---

4   (England) Local Government Act 1972, s.112; (Scotland): power in Local Government (Scotland) Act 1973 s. 64(1), duties in various provisions.

5   In Scotland, *Social Work* headed by a Director of Social Work. The appointment of these officers is mandatory.

6   Metropolitan boroughs and county councils.

7   Local Authority Social Services Act 1970, s.2; Local Government Act 1972, s.101(8).

8   See also Social Work (Scotland) Act 1972.

know who made the decision (*i.e.* which authority, department, official, etc.) and problems of conflict of interest, or lack of true independence, may arise where the social worker is employed by the same authority that the client wants to challenge. When the social worker has reached the limits of his legal knowledge the client should be referred to a solicitor (possibly on legal aid) or to a law centre (or welfare rights office) if there is one in the area.

Some social workers have special knowledge, training and responsibilities (*e.g.* they concentrate on child care or child abuse), and there are also *approved social workers* (in Scotland, *mental health officers*) under the Mental Health Acts who have certain statutory powers.

### Social Services Inspectorate (England)

The function of this Inspectorate is to assist local authorities to obtain value for money through efficient and economic use of available resources. It helps to secure the most effective use of professional and other resources, normally by identifying good practice. Inspections may be initiated under the Secretary of State's formal powers, or undertaken outside these either:

(a) in relation to issues of general concern, by agreement with a number of local authorities in accordance with a programme agreed by the local authority associations; or

(b) at the request of, or in agreement with, an individual local authority in relation to specific services or activities of that authority.

### Social Work Services Group (Scotland)

The Secretary of State has powers relating to regulation, inspection, training and research, and his authorised officers have powers of entry and inspection.[9] These functions are exercised by the Social Work Services Group, which was established as a central professional advisory service whose role has been described as less directly inspectorial than that of the Inspectorate in England.[10] In April 1992 the *Social Work Services Inspectorate* was established within the Group, and it is anticipated that its role will be closer to that of the English Social Services Inspectorate.

## Procedures

Most of the powers and duties of councils are vested in the elected councillors as a body and not in individual councillors or officials. Many are delegated to committees or sub-committees which deal with specific areas of responsibility and are advised by officers, and some powers are delegated to officers. Each committee has a chairperson who will be the link between the officers and members between meetings. Committees operate according to standing orders laid down by the council which are available for public inspection, and decisions are made by a majority of those

9    Social Work (Scotland) Act 1968, ss.5 and 6.
10   *Stair Encyclopaedia*, Vol.22, para.7.

present and voting.

A *National Code of Local Government Conduct* lays down further rules by which councils must operate and covers a wide range of matters affecting councillors, including standing orders, public duty and private interest, disclosure of pecuniary and other interests, membership and chairmanship of committees, use of information, gifts and hospitality, expenses and allowances, and use of council facilities.[11]

## Central control

Many statutes vest supervisory powers in government Ministers, and Codes of Guidance may be issued by the relevant government department. Some statutes conferring powers or duties on local authorities authorise the Minister to make Regulations prescribing how they shall exercise those powers or perform those duties, or require authorities to prepare schemes setting out how they will perform those duties which the Minister may then approve or reject.[12] In some situations a right of appeal against a decision of a local authority lies to the Minister. Control may also be exercised through the system of grants and the giving of consent to borrowing and capital expenditure.

## Audit Commission (England)
## Commission for Local Authority Accounts in Scotland

These Commissions are responsible for the audit of local authority accounts. They are appointed by the respective Secretaries of State after certain consultation.[13] In addition to the usual duties of financial audit, the Commissions must undertake or promote comparative studies concerning economy, efficiency, effectiveness and financial or other management of bodies subject to audit. A number of Reports are referred to in this chapter.

## REMEDIES

Duties of local authorities are found in statute but are not always enforceable in the courts. Parents or carers who demand their rights are often the ones who receive the most help and support, but they are not always the most needy. This is an area where lawyers are able to provide assistance, even if this only amounts to assisting the client to write a suitable letter to the right agency.

## Information

The workings of local authorities should be both visible and intelligible[14] and most now have Information Departments which should on enquiry indicate which department or office is

---

11   See *Report of the Redcliffe Maud Committee* 1974, HMSO Cmnd.5636.
12   A recent development is for Directions to be made by Ministers which are binding on local authorities but not subject to parliamentary scrutiny.
13   See Local Government Finance Act 1982 (England); Local Government (Scotland) Act 1973 as amended by Local Government Act 1988.
14   *Report of the Redcliffe Maud Committee*, 1974.

responsible for a service.

*Access to information*

Recent legislation has considerably extended the right of members of the public to information about local government.[15] Minutes of meetings are available for public inspection and these reveal the names of the councillors and officers present. Councils have a statutory duty to provide the following information on request:

- details of forthcoming meetings of committees and sub-committees (including agenda, copies of any reports to be publicly discussed and background papers)[16];
- similar details of meetings that have taken place together with the minutes;
- a register of councillors, including their address and the ward or division they represent;
- identity of members of committees and sub-committees;
- details of any powers that have been delegated for more than six months to an officer and the rank of that officer;
- the housing allocation policy.

As a result of further legislation[17] council tenants have the right to see their housing records, social services (and social work) clients have access to their social work records, and parents have a right of access to their children's school records.

*Access to meetings*

A member of the public has the right to attend any meeting of the council or a committee or sub-committee unless the council has exercised its power to exclude the public from all or part of the meeting. It may only do so if the presence of the public would result in disclosure of confidential information[18] or exempt information.

*Exempt information*

Certain categories of information are exempt from disclosure, including that relating to recipients of services or financial assistance from the council, the financial affairs of a particular person, or the care or education of a particular child.[19] Any documents disclosed under the above provisions should have such information excluded.

---

15 Local Government Act 1972, Part VA, ss.100A-K and Local Government (Scotland) Act 1973 Part IIIA, ss.50A-K as inserted (in both cases) by Local Government (Access to Information) Act 1985. Applies in England, Wales and Scotland but not Northern Ireland.

16 A reasonable fee may be charged.

17 Access to Personal Files Act 1987 - and see also Data Protection Act 1984. Such legislation is considered in Chap.3, Part II.

18 *I.e.* information furnished by a government department on terms forbidding its disclosure and where disclosure is prohibited by court order or statute.

19 There are lists in the Local Government (Access to Information) Act 1985 - see Part I of Sched.12A to the 1972 Act (England) and Part I of Sched.7A to the 1973 Act (Scotland).

# Complaints

Complaints should in the first instance be to the officer concerned, and if this does not resolve matters to the line manager or head of department. The most serious complaints may be directed to the Chief Executive. If the complaint relates to policy it may be made to the chairperson of the relevant committee.

## Councillors

Members of the public may also complain to their local councillor, who can check that policies and decisions are being carried out, but it is important to approach the correct authority. Thus a district councillor should not be contacted if a county or regional function is involved, and *vice versa*. Any request by an individual councillor for access to a file must be justified.[20] If a complaint is made about an officer there is a duty upon the councillors to investigate and in doing so they may inspect any relevant files. This does not necessarily mean that they may disclose the contents to the complainant.

## Complaints procedure

A responsibility is now placed upon local authorities to establish a procedure for considering any representations or complaints with respect to the discharge of their social services functions or the failure to discharge those functions.[21] Some had already set up a formal complaints procedure in recognition of the rights of users and carers. Any such procedure must provide a definition of a complaint and identify who can bring a complaint, and provide for the role of the *independent person*, and support for persons who need assistance in bringing a complaint. These procedures should be used before reference to the ombudsman.

## Petitions, etc

Where a complaint affects a large number of people it may be desired to submit a petition or to send a deputation to address a meeting. Procedures for dealing with this are usually laid down in standing orders of the council.

# Enforcement

Policies, practice and more often lack of available funding, will frequently be quoted as reasons why a particular service is not available or provision cannot be made. It may only be when carers are desperate for assistance or feel discriminated against that they turn to a solicitor for help, and a crisis or confrontation may already have arisen.

---

20  A councillor is entitled by virtue of his office to have access to all written material in the possession of the authority if he has good reason for access - *R* v. *Birmingham D. C., ex p. O* [1983] 1 A.C. 578.

21  Children Act 1989; National Health Service and Community Care Act 1990 (in Scotland, amending Social Work (Scotland) Act 1968: see also Social Work (Representations Procedure) (Scotland) Directions 1989, Annexe to Circular SW5/1991).

*Instructions*

At the initial interview a wide range of problems may be mentioned and to establish a positive relationship it is necessary to adopt a listening role and show understanding, but the specific problem to be dealt with must be identified in order that a course of action can be determined. An understanding of the needs of the client as well as a broad knowledge of the services that can be provided and their source is needed.

*Tactics*

Many problems arise from ignorance of the legal position, because the client is seldom told his rights by the authority, and if negotiations are involved it is as well to know the strengths and weaknesses of one's position. But knowing where and how to complain may be just as significant. A letter is often the first step, but the client may not be capable of writing a suitable letter. It may be best to help the client write a personal letter, because this is likely to receive serious consideration and produce a reply on the basis of which the next step can be considered. If the solicitor uses his own letterheading any reply will probably be approved by the legal department, so be delayed and guarded in its terms.

*Councillors*

If correspondence and contact with officers fail to produce results it may be worth enlisting the active support of one or more councillors, and at this stage threats of legal action are probably unwise. On grounds of cost and delay, and also because it may be counter-productive, recourse to legal remedies should not be seen as the first step.

## Legal entitlement

The impression may be gained that a local authority is obliged to provide certain services and that an individual may enforce such provision, but the situation is not as simple as this. It is first necessary to draw a distinction between those duties which create rights that may be enforced by the individual, and those which are expressed in general terms and not enforceable other than, perhaps, in the event of a total failure to perform them. It is then necessary to consider whether any duty is qualified in its terms so that an authority may be excused from performance if, for example, there is a lack of resources. Such duties may amount to little more than statements of intent which may be ignored or overridden by the authority for any politically acceptable reason.

*Social Services (England)*

The National Health Service Act 1977 provides that social services departments are obliged to provide residential accommodation and day care facilities, and authority is given to the Secretary of State to make directions. As we shall see when these specific services are considered, the Secretary of State has given general approval to local authorities for the provision of residential accommodation and training and occupation facilities, and has directed them to make these arrangements.[22] Whilst authorities must make some provision they are not specifically directed to make adequate provision. It could be argued that by implication the provision made must be sufficient, but if the matter were tested in the courts it is likely that the authority could only be required to provide facilities within the resources available.[23] This is the view of the government, yet the resources available are a matter solely under the control of the authority concerned!

*Social Work (Scotland)*
Social work authorities in Scotland have a general duty to promote social welfare by making available advice, guidance and assistance on such a scale as may be appropriate to their areas. In relation to facilities, including residential and other establishments, their obligation is to make such provision as they may consider suitable and adequate; thus they define the extent of their own duty in these matters.[24] Included in their specific duties are duties to provide domiciliary services (formerly home help service), to provide or ensure provision of such residential or other establishments as may be required for their functions,[25] to ascertain persons in need of social work services in relation to chronic illness and disability (and to ascertain needs for such services),[26] to provide after-care services,[27] and to provide (or ensure provision of) suitable training and occupation for people with a mental handicap over school age.[28]

*Education*
The statutory provisions in both England and Scotland that deal with education are much firmer, and impose clearly defined duties upon local education authorities which are not limited by the adequacy of resources. For example, in England schools must be "sufficient in number, character and equipment" to afford all pupils opportunities for education, so parents of a mentally handicapped child may enforce the duty to provide a suitable education; but as soon as the child leaves school they cannot enforce the provision of replacement services.[29]

---

22 Circular 19/74.
23 When interpreting another provision in this statute Lord Denning added the words: "such as can be provided within the resources available" and stated that the Secretary of State was not under an absolute duty to provide services but could take financial resources into account - *R.* v. *Secretary of State for Social Services, West Midlands R.H.A. and Birmingham A.H.A., ex p. Hincks* (1979) 123 SJ 436.
24 Social Work (Scotland) Act 1968, s.12(1).
25 ss.28 and 59.
26 Chronically Sick and Disabled Persons Act 1970.
27 Mental Health (Scotland) Act 1984, s.8.
28 *ibid*, s.11.
29 In Scotland, duties under 1984 Act, s.11 may well be enforceable by individuals. For education authority duties generally, see Chap.6.

*Summary*
In regard to health services, residential accommodation and day services the authority responsible has only to state that it does not have further or adequate resources available and there is little that can be done to require such provision for an individual. However, it should not be overlooked that the Minister responsible does have default powers enabling him to instruct a local authority to take action which he considers it has failed to take.

## Legal remedies

Circumstances arise in which a local authority will not carry out its functions and consideration must then be given to legal remedies, though these may not prove adequate.

*Secretary of State*
Under default powers in England the Secretary of State may call an authority to account for failure to exercise its functions, direct the authority to comply and take over the authority's functions.[30] It is rare for these powers to be exercised, but the threat to refer a matter to the Minister may be a useful tactic. If the issue is the level of resources these default powers may be the only remedy available. There is a general power to declare local authorities in default if they fail to comply with their social services duties[31] and this may prove to be an essential ingredient of making community care work, fuelled by persistent complaints by disabled persons about the performance of particular authorities. If a direction is not complied with it may be enforced by an order for mandamus from the High Court, but it is not clear whether this remedy is available to an individual. Similar powers exist as regards the provision of services for children.[32] The sanction of making the authority perform its duties may encourage the Secretary of State to exercise his default powers more often, compared with the original default powers under which he had to take over the duty.
In Scotland, the Secretary of State or an appropriate minister may order a local inquiry, and if then satisfied that the local authority is in default, may direct compliance, and in event of non-compliance may obtain a court order for specific performance, or other appropriate order.[33] The Secretary of State may also issue directions which are binding on social work authorities.[34]

*Ombudsman*
A Commissioner for Local Administration investigates allegations by members of the public that they have suffered an injustice as a

---

30  National Assistance Act 1948, s.36; see also Mental Health Act 1983, s.124, National Health Service Act 1977, s.85.
31  Local Authority Social Services Act 1970, s.7D, inserted by National Health Service and Community Care Act 1990, s.50.
32  Children Act 1989, s.84, *i.e.* children under the age of 18 years.
33  Local Government (Scotland) Act 1973, ss.2(10) and 2(11).
34  Social Work (Scotland) Act 1968, s.5(1A) (inserted by 1990 Act, s.51).

result of maladministration in local government. The scope of this remedy and the procedure to be followed are outlined in Chapter 3, Part III, page 161 *et seq.*

### Breach of statutory duty

The first question may be whether the statute confers a power or imposes a duty, and if the latter, whether this is merely a general duty or a specific duty towards the particular individual. It seems that the courts will not allow private individuals to bring actions for breach of statutory duty unless the legislation expressly or by implication makes this possible. It has been held in England that where an authority fails to discharge its functions the only proper legal procedure is to ask the Secretary of State to exercise his default powers.[35]

### Contract and tort (or delict)

The contracts of local authorities are governed by general principles and may be enforced through the courts in the usual way. Although the more important contracts may be under seal, a contract may be signed by an authorised person and may even be verbal. General principles of implied authority apply.

An action in tort for damages or an injunction[36] may also be brought against a local authority under general legal principles. This may include employer's liability, and liability for the acts of an agent where the authority has expressly authorised them or subsequently ratifies them.

### Judicial review

These are procedures whereby the High Court in England and the Court of Session in Scotland may review the legality of a course of action, and the remedies may include requiring an authority to do something that it is legally obliged to do, or preventing it from taking a particular course of action. A series of rules has been developed to define the circumstances in which the court will intervene and this topic is considered in Chapter 3, Part III, at p.156. There are instances in which the courts have intervened[37]:

> A disabled individual sought assistance with the cost of a privately arranged holiday under the Chronically Sick and Disabled Persons Act 1970. The council adopted a blanket policy whereby it would only sponsor holidays which it had itself organised, and the Secretary of State refused to exercise his default powers. The court held that it had no power to award damages, but declared that by applying a blanket policy indiscriminately the council had not acted fairly and reasonably and had thereby acted *ultra vires*.

If the Secretary of State fails to act when asked to use his default powers and the authority has acted unlawfully it may be possible to seek judicial review of that failure.[38] The potential for judicial

---

35  *Wyatt* v. *Hillingdon L.B.C.* 76 LGR 727 applying *Southwark L.B.C.* v. *Williams* [1971] 2 All ER 175. This may not be followed in Scotland.

36  In Scotland, actions of reparation or interdict.

37  *R.* v. *London Borough of Ealing, ex p. Leaman* (1984), unreported.

38  See *dicta* of Simon Brown J. in *R* v. *Kent C.C., ex p. Bruce* (1986) *The Times*, February 8, 1986.

review is likely to increase by reason of the additional obligations upon local authorities to assess the needs of disabled individuals for services provided in the community.

## PART II - POLICY AND LEGISLATION

### Preliminary

Care in the community is not a new concept, but has been seen as the ideal by an increasing number of people during the past 30 years. It follows from the desire to reduce institutional care and provide alternative services in a community setting, but is more than just the provision of a home in the community for former hospital patients; a whole range of support and services must be provided for all persons needing care, including those already living with parents in their own family homes. The Social Services Committee expressed this as follows[39]:

> "There is a great need to provide community based facilities for the social and everyday needs of all people with a mental disability, not just those being discharged from hospital. Like all other members of the community, they need somewhere to call home and something meaningful to do in the way of education, work and recreation."

We concentrate upon the policies that are relevant to persons with a mental handicap, but the new approach to care provision is not limited to such persons and is often overshadowed by the needs of other larger or more vociferous groups.[40] For many, care in the community has been the reality, but this has meant care within the family with little support from the state in an indifferent society. When the individual or the family could no longer cope the alternative has been institutionalised care in hospitals or residential care homes, hidden away from the rest of society where standards have not always been those which society would have wished.

There has during recent years been ever increasing pressure from concerned people and organisations to recognise the rights and freedoms of these underprivileged members of society, and this has now found expression in new policies which are symbolised by the phrase *community care*. The Government has stated that it is firmly committed to a policy of community care which enables people in need of care to achieve their full potential, but whilst problems in the provision of community care have been well documented, similar attention has not been given to the rights of those involved and the legal remedies available.

---

39   Eleventh Report to the House of Commons, Session 1989-90, para.109. In its Second Report 1984-85 the Committee said that it was vital that the pressing problems confronting those mentally disabled people already living in the community be more fully taken into account in developing policies of community care.

40   Children and the elderly, mentally ill and physically disabled have all been included as categories of people in need of care, and more recently drug abusers, alcoholics and Aids sufferers have been added to the list.

# GENERAL

## Definition

Although community care has no precise definition, the Social Services Committee has referred to the provision of care for individuals in such a way as to enable them to lead as normal an existence as possible given their particular disabilities and to minimise disruption of life within their community.[41] The disruption element does not feature expressly in later interpretations, though it may be implicit. The Audit Commission took a wider view when it regarded community care as providing clients with a full range of services, and a wide range of options; bringing services to people, rather than people to services; the adjustment of services to meet the needs of people, rather than the adjustment of people to meet the needs of services.[42] A more recent definition by the Government is[43]:

> "Community care means providing the services and support which people who are affected by problems of ageing, mental illness, mental handicap or physical or sensory disability need to be able to live as independently as possible in their own homes, or in homely settings in the community."

## Background

The environment in which local authorities are developing services is changing. More disabled people are outliving their parents, and the closing of hospitals means the transfer of residents into the community and more people remaining in the community who would previously have been looked after in hospital. There is also a growing awareness that people with a mental handicap have potential for development and need services that fulfil their own requirements. There is thus a need for more accommodation in the community, with training and other day time opportunities for people to achieve their full potential.[44]

*Numbers*

According to the Audit Commission there are about 124,000 adults with a mental handicap in England.[45] The number of NHS mental handicap hospital places peaked in the late 1960's at 60,000 and by 1989 had fallen to about 30,000 with more reductions in progress. Between 1980 and 1986 the number of hospital places for them fell by 14,000 whilst the number in residential care homes rose by only 11,000 and places in Adult Training Centres by a similar number.

---

[41]  Second Report to the House of Commons, Session 1984-85 para.11.

[42]  *Making a Reality of Community Care*  (Report of 1986).

[43]  *Caring for People: Community care in the next decade and beyond* 1989.

[44]  Audit Commission, occasional paper *Developing Community Care for Adults with a Mental Handicap,* October 1989.

[45]  Figures such as this are misleading because they depend upon the criteria adopted. Many more will need community care services than are officially classed as mentally handicapped.

In Scotland, information published by Social Work Services Group[46] on places for people with a mental handicap shows that long-stay hospital places reduced from 6,680 in 1980 to 4,542 in 1990, and that residential care home places increased from 1,093 in 1980 to 2,501 in 1990. The number of day centre places rose from 5,096 in 1980 to 7,721 in 1990.

### Costs

Figures quoted by the Audit Commission show that small staffed homes are more expensive to run than large community based homes or hospitals. The cost per person of a place in a small hospital based home seems to be fairly well controlled but could be 25 per cent. more than in the hospital itself and up to twice as much as in a large home in the community. On the other hand, the cost of a place in a small home in the community varies enormously, perhaps according to the severity of the handicaps catered for, but can extend from being the cheapest residential provision to by far the most expensive.

## Reports

There have been many reports on the provision of services for persons with a mental handicap and others in need of care, but it is only as we move into the 1990's that the Government has taken the initiative in actively promoting reforms.

### Better Services for the Mentally Handicapped

This 1971 White Paper set out a 20 year plan to shift provision from hospital based to community based services. Prominence was given to developing co-ordinated health and social services provision in each local area according to individual needs with increasing responsibility for service provision being given to local authorities. The development of adult training centres, residential accommodation and the need to employ and train more staff were identified. Together with the 1980 review *Mental Handicap: Progress, Problems and Priorities* it is still relied upon to indicate the required scale of provision.

### Day Services for Mentally Handicapped Adults

This 1977 pamphlet sets out the required content and standard of services.[47]

### All Wales Strategy

The All-Wales Working Party on Services for Mentally Handicapped People was set up in 1981 by the Secretary of State for Wales and produced a report which resulted in this Strategy being published in March 1983. It provided guidance on new patterns of services for mentally handicapped people and in particular for the preparation of detailed plans for provision at local level, and resulted in further funding being available. The

---

46   Bulletin, December 1991.
47   National Development Group's 1977 Pamphlet No.5.

underlying principles are that mentally handicapped people:
- should have a right to normal patterns of life within the community;
- should have a right to be treated as individuals;
- require additional help from the communities in which they live, and from professional services if they are to develop their maximum potential as individuals.

Review Reports have been prepared and these, together with the original strategy document, make valuable reading and have had an influence upon the development of community care policies.

*Audit Commission Reports*
In a 1986 review of community based care services,[48] the following problems were identified by the Audit Commission:
- a mismatch of resources to meet the requirements of community care policies;
- the need for short-term bridging finance to fund the transition to community care;
- social security policies provided a perverse incentive for residential rather than domiciliary based care;
- there was fragmented organisation, and lack of effective joint working and planning between the different agencies involved in the provision of services;
- there were inadequate arrangements for training and providing opportunities in community services for existing staff in long-stay hospitals, and for training sufficient numbers of community-based staff.

A paper in 1987[49] dealt with the resettlement of hospital patients in the community and identified concerns over the transfer of skilled staff and the absence of adequate financial adjustment for those who would in the past have been admitted to hospital but now remain in the community.

An occasional paper in 1989[50] highlighted the following points in regard to the new community care policies:
- existing local authority services for people with a mental handicap are under pressure (as a result of closure of hospitals, changing ideas on support, the ageing population and greater expectations from users);
- well-managed community care, especially in domestic-sized houses, provides a higher quality of life than hospital care but there has been little progress in joint resettlement programmes;
- support for those living in the community is inadequate;
- there has been a rapid and unplanned growth in independent residential care homes promoted by the state benefits system, and this care may be both unsuitable and more expensive

---

48  *Making a Reality of Community Care.*
49  *Community Care: developing services for people with a mental handicap.*
50  *Developing Community Care for Adults with a Mental Handicap.*

than is necessary.

It was recommended that local authorities should take advantage of the delay in introducing community care to negotiate with local health authorities, improve co-operation and collaboration with other agencies, and develop the reality of care management with budgetary arrangements and organisational adjustment to match.

### Social Services Committee Reports[51]

In 1985 the Committee pointed out[52] that a policy of community care for people with a mental disability involves a lot more than reducing the number of hospital beds. It means the creation of a wide variety of alternative facilities, and providing supportive services for those many disabled people who currently have little contact with statutory services and for their families. It means that the rest of the community has to be prepared to accept people with a mental disability in its midst, the redeployment of staff and a switch of capital resources.

During the 1989-90 Session the Committee also produced a series of Reports on aspects of community care of which the following are later referred to:

> Community Care: Future Funding of Private and Voluntary Residential
>     Care (2nd Report)
> Community Care: Funding for Local Authorities (3rd Report)
> Community Care: Carers (5th Report)
> Community Care: Quality (7th Report)
> Community Care: Services for People with a Mental Illness and People
>     with a Mental Handicap (11th Report)

### Community Care:  Agenda for Action

The most recent review in 1988, referred to as the *Griffiths Report,*[53] is of great significance to the future delivery of services. In a statement to the House of Commons on July 12, 1989 the Secretary of State for Health announced the Government's proposals for the future organisation and funding of community care, which largely accepted the recommendations in the Report.[54]

### Caring for People: Community Care in the Next Decade and Beyond

The Griffiths Report was followed by the publication of this White Paper in 1989 which resulted in the passing of the National Health Service and Community Care Act 1990. It reaffirms the belief that people with a mental handicap mainly need social rather than health care, and acknowledges the need to promote:

> "the provision of services to individuals, developed from a multi-disciplinary assessment of their needs and made with proper participation of the individuals concerned, their families and other carers."

---

51   Social Services Committee of the House of Commons.

52   *Community Care with Special Reference to Adult Mentally Ill and Adult Mentally Handicapped People*, Second Report, Session 1984-85.

53   Report to the Secretary of State for Social Services by Sir Roy Griffiths.

54   The Secretaries of State for Scotland and Wales made similar statements.

The aim is to continue to reduce the numbers of people in specialist mental handicap hospitals, and to ensure that no child requiring long term residential care grows up in a mental handicap hospital, but the needs of those already in the community must not be overlooked. The policies are aimed at improving social care services by ensuring that they are properly tailored to the needs of individuals, but this requires a clear, locally determined, set of priorities and effective collaboration between public, private and voluntary agencies. The proposals are linked to changes in the financial arrangements for people needing public support in residential care and nursing homes, and local authorities will take over a new responsibility to assess the needs of people and meet the costs of residential or domiciliary care. The Government rejected the recommendation in the Griffiths Report for a specific (or ring-fenced) community care grant, even though the Social Services Committee also recommended this.

*Government statement*
The new policies were intended to come into effect from April 1991, but in a statement to the House of Commons in July 1990 the Secretary of State for Health announced that they would be phased in.[55] In April 1991, the inspection units within local authorities and complaints procedures would be introduced, with development work to continue on the new procedures and responsibilities within social services departments. From April 1992 the new planning arrangements for local authorities and health authorities would be implemented, with the new system, including the new benefit arrangements, being fully implemented from April 1993. The reason given was the problems posed by the community charge, but the delay was also intended to give local authorities time to prepare for their substantial new responsibilities. It was recognised that local authorities need adequate resources to enable them to discharge their new responsibilities, and the monies which would otherwise have been provided to finance care through social security payments to people in residential and nursing homes are to be transferred to the authorities.

## Legislation

*National Assistance Act 1948, Part III*
Imposes on local authorities duties to make arrangements for promoting the welfare of disabled persons as defined therein.

*Disabled Persons (Employment) Act 1958*
These provisions are considered in Chapter 6, Part II where employment rights of disabled persons are dealt with.

*Chronically Sick and Disabled Persons Act 1970* [56]
Introduced as a private members Bill, this Act caused a revolution

---

55   The Secretaries of State for Scotland and Wales made similar statements.
56   Also an amendment Act in 1976. The Chronically Sick and Disabled Persons (Scotland) Act 1972 extended the provisions to Scotland.

in services for people with disabilities by requiring local authorities to keep a register of disabled people in the area, assess the needs of such persons for a range of services, and satisfy those needs to the extent that they are not being met. Some of the services referred to are of more relevance to people with physical handicaps, though practical help, holidays, transport *etc.* may all be relevant to the mentally disabled. Although there may be legal entitlement, there is no adequate procedure for enforcement (other than judicial review) and problems arise in implementation largely due to lack of resources.

*Housing (Homeless Persons) Act 1977 - England*
*Housing (Scotland) Act 1987, Part II*
Imposed duties on local housing authorities to provide, secure or help to secure accommodation for homeless persons and those threatened with homelessness. Disabled people have priority need.

*National Health Service Act 1977*
Requires health and local authorities to co-operate to secure and advance the health and welfare of people in England and Wales.

*National Health Service (Scotland) Act 1978*
Health boards, social work authorities and education authorities must co-operate to secure and advance the health of the people of Scotland.

*Disabled Persons Act 1981*
Amends, and inserts provisions into, various Acts in order to ensure that better provision is made for the needs of disabled persons using highways, buildings, etc.

*Health and Social Services and Social Security Adjudications Act 1983*
Local authorities are permitted to charge for services including those for people with a mental handicap.

*Disabled Persons (Services Consultation and Representation) Act 1986*
Introduced as a private members Bill with considerable support from voluntary organisations to impose administrative reforms on local authorities in line with current good practice on assessment and service provision. The principle of personal advocacy and the needs of carers receive statutory recognition for the first time. Many of the key provisions have not been brought into effect and the government has now indicated that it does not intend to implement these because it claims that their objectives are reflected in the community care provisions.[57] This is not regarded as satisfactory by organisations concerned with disability because the Act would have provided absolute rights whereas the community care provisions are no more than codes of practice. The Act refers to *welfare enactments* and these are:

---

57   Mainly those relating to advocacy and representation. The community care provisions merely introduce complaints procedures.

National Assistance Act 1948, Part III;
Chronically Sick and Disabled Persons Act 1970, s.2;
National Health Service Act 1977, Schedule 8 (in England);
National Health Service (Scotland) Act 1947, s.27;
Social Work (Scotland) Act 1968;
Mental Health (Scotland) Act 1984, ss.7 and 8.

*National Health Service and Community Care Act 1990*
Parts III (England) and IV (Scotland) implement the 1990 White
Paper proposals. Though the Act received the Royal Assent on
June 29, 1990, its key provisions are only being brought into
effect in stages and rely upon regulations that have yet to be made,
so it will be April 1993 at the earliest before these apply. Those
relating to persons with a mental handicap are:

*Part III (England)*
s.42 extends the role of local authorities in the provision of
residential accommodation and welfare services, and
enables them to make agency arrangements with other
organisations and persons;
s.43 restricts the power of local authorities to provide
accommodation;
s.44 amends the provisions as to charges for residential
accommodation;
s.45 deals with recovery of charges due to local authorities for
residential accommodation;
s.46 requires local authorities following consultation with
health and housing authorities to prepare and publish a
community care plan;
s.47 requires local authorities to carry out an assessment of
care needs of any person who may require community
care services, and to decide what services need to be
provided;
s.48 deals with the inspection of certain premises used for
community care services and provides for access to
information;
s.49 provides for the transfer of staff from health authorities
to local authorities;
s.50 requires local authorities to comply with directions from
the Secretary of State in carrying out their social services
functions, and provides for a complaints procedure, the
holding of inquiries, and default powers.

*Part IV (Scotland)*
s.51 empowers the Secretary of State to give directions to
social work authorities, with which they must comply;
s.52 requires social work authorities to prepare, publish and
annually review community care plans. They must consult
health boards, district councils as housing authorities, and
representatives of service users (presumably drawn from
the voluntary sector);
s.53 confers on the Secretary of State additional powers to

> inspect facilities and services, and all relevant records, and additional powers to obtain information and to interview and examine residents;
>
> s.54 empowers the Secretary of State to initiate enquiries into social work functions of local authorities in relation to adults;
>
> s.55 requires local authorities to carry out an assessment of care needs of any person who may require community care services, and to decide what services need to be provided;
>
> s.56 empowers local authorities to arrange for provision by other bodies of residential accommodation where specialised nursing care is provided, and extends to such homes the inspection powers of the Secretary of State;
>
> s.57 prevents local authorities from financially supporting accommodation costs of people benefiting from transitional provisions;
>
> s.58 empowers the Secretary of State to make grants towards community-based services for people with a mental illness.

Despite the wide ranging reforms proposed in the White Paper, the Act only contains nine sections for England, and eight for Scotland, dealing with community care, which is an indication that most of the reforms depend upon regulations and policies rather than primary legislation.

### Circulars and Directions

Many aspects of an authority's powers and duties are controlled by government circulars and it may be desired to quote these and seek to compel an authority to comply with them. An English authority is only obliged to take account of advice contained in circulars, and having done so is not under a positive duty to comply with it.[58] Where an appeal to the Secretary of State is provided for it may be expected that he will follow his own advice. It seems likely that considerable guidance will be issued to local authorities under the new community care policies and the Secretary of State may issue Directions which must be observed, the sanction being the use of default powers[59]:

> (1) ... every local authority shall exercise their social services functions in accordance with such directions as may be given to them under this section by the Secretary of State.
> (2) Directions under this section:-
>    (a) shall be given in writing; and
>    (b) may be given to a particular authority, or to authorities of a particular class, or to authorities generally.

The equivalent provisions in Scotland require local authorities to perform social work functions under the general guidance of the Secretary of State who is empowered to make regulations, and also

---

58  Local Authority Social Services Act 1970, s.7.
59  s.7A, added by the 1990 Act, s.50.

to give directions with which social work authorities must comply.[60] In the Scottish provisions, directions need not be in writing, may be issued to local authorities individually or collectively, and may relate to any functions under a range of social work legislation.[61]

## DISABLED PERSONS

### Definition

For the purposes of the Chronically Sick and Disabled Persons Act 1970, disabled means "substantially or permanently handicapped by illness, injury or congenital deformity or suffering from mental disorder of any description". The Disabled Persons (Services, Consultation and Representation) Act 1986 uses the definition of disabled persons found in National Assistance Act 1948, s. 29, namely people who are:

"blind, deaf or dumb, and other persons who are substantially and permanently handicapped by illness, injury or congenital deformity or who are suffering from a mental disorder within the meaning of the Mental Health Act".

In England, this definition has recently been elaborated upon in the Children Act 1989[62]:

"... a child is disabled if he is blind, deaf or dumb or suffers from mental disorder of any kind or is substantially and permanently handicapped by illness, injury or congenital deformity or such other disability as may be prescribed; and ...
'development' means physical, intellectual, emotional social or behavioural development; and
'health' means physical or mental health."

The definition of mental disorder has previously been considered but will include the typical individual with a mental handicap.[63]

### Registers

*Local authority*

Under the 1970 Act people qualify for additional help if their handicap is substantial and permanent. The individual can be registered with the local authority and may become eligible for various forms of help, though whether these are actually provided depends upon economic constraints and the consequent policy of the authority, which may be the social services department, or the housing department or the health authority. Local authorities are under a duty to keep a register of disabled persons in their area.[64]

---

60  Social Work (Scotland) Act 1968, s.5(1); s.5(2) and (3); and s.5(1)(A), added by the 1990 Act, s.51.
61  The 1968 Act, the enactments listed in s.2(2) thereof, and the 1990 Act.
62  s.17(11). This has been criticised as being based on the now outdated definition of the 1948 Act which does not integrate with the 1970 Act.
63  The Scottish definition includes mental handicap however caused or manifested - Mental Health (Scotland) Act 1984, s.1(2).
64  (England), National Assistance Act 1948, s.29(4)(*g*); DHSS Circular LAC13/74, para.8. Note also register of children in need mentioned below.

*Department of Employment*
The separate voluntary register maintained for the purpose of employment is considered in Chapter 6, Part II, at p.326.

## POWERS AND DUTIES

The powers and duties of local authorities have been developed on a piecemeal basis and are found in a variety of provisions introduced by both primary legislation and government circulars. We identify some of these in respect of both children and adults.

### General duties

There is a mass of legislation relating to adults and the 1990 Act has done nothing to assist in this respect. Persons with a mental handicap will be within the definition of disabled but are not singled out for any special treatment. A local authority must[65]:
- identify disabled persons and the number within its area;
- measure and assess the need to provide community care services;
- prepare community care plans.

*Information*
Social services departments are required to publish general information as to the services available in their area and to inform disabled persons receiving any service from them of relevant services provided by the local authority or by any other authority or organisation of which the department has particulars.[66] Hence charities providing services for the disabled should notify relevant authorities in the areas in which they operate of the nature and extent of those services and ensure that this information is being passed on to those who may benefit from it. Otherwise some departments may be reluctant to obtain information for fear of prompting demand that they cannot meet or do not wish to fund.

*Ordinarily resident (England)*
The duties of a local authority apply to an individual who is ordinarily resident in its area.[67] Two elements are important in determining ordinary residence:
   (i)  it must have been voluntarily adopted;
   (ii) there must have been a degree of settled purpose in relation to that decision.

Where an adult is not capable of deciding where to live and it is unreal to talk of a settled purpose, the ordinary residence may be

---

65  1948 Act, s.29 (England); 1970 Act, s.1 (England and Scotland); DHSS Circular 13/74. An authority cannot in law save on resources by simply not telling disabled persons what help may be available to them if only they had known. These duties also apply in England in respect of disabled children, Children Act 1989, Sched.9, para.16.

66  1986 Act, s.9, amending 1970 Act, s.1 which only referred to other local authority social services.

67  This requirement is deleted from the application of the 1970 Act to Scotland - see s.29(2) of 1970 Act (as amended).

that of the parents.[68] Everyone is ordinarily resident in the area of some local authority, and if a person has no fixed abode he is reckoned to be ordinarily resident in the place where he happens to be when the need for services arises.[69]

*Adjustments between authorities (Scotland)*
Where a social work authority in Scotland in performing various specified functions incurs expenditure in relation to a person ordinarily resident in the area of another local authority (in Scotland, England or Wales) the expenditure is recoverable from that other authority. Questions as to ordinary residence are determined by the Secretary of State.[70]

## Welfare of the disabled

*England*
Section 29 of the National Assistance Act 1948 is still one of the key provisions dealing with disabled persons and this states[71]:

(1) A local authority shall have power to make arrangements for promoting the welfare of persons to whom this section applies, that is to say persons [aged 18 or over] who are blind, deaf or dumb or who suffer from mental disorder of any description and other persons [aged 18 or over] who are substantially and permanently handicapped by illness, injury or congenital deformity or such other disabilities as may be prescribed by the Minister.
(2) In relation to persons ordinarily resident in the area of a local authority the authority shall, to such extent as the Minister may direct, be under a duty to exercise their powers under this section.

The Secretary of State has approved the following provision[72]:
- social work service and such advice and support as may be needed to support a person in their own home or elsewhere;
- facilities, at centres or elsewhere, for social rehabilitation and adjustment to disability including assistance in overcoming communications or mobility problems;
- facilities, at centres or elsewhere, for occupational, social, cultural and recreational activities and, where appropriate, the making of payments to persons for work undertaken by them;
- payment of any specialist fees in respect of advice given as to whether a person is within s.29;
- hostels for persons undertaking training or employment and the provision of holiday homes;
- free or subsidised travel for all or any persons who do not receive concessionary travel from some other source;
- assistance in the finding of suitable and supportive lodgings;

---

68  R. v. *Waltham Forest, ex p. Vale* (1985) *The Times,* February 25, 1985. This is similar to the test adopted in respect of an infant.
69  Baroness Blatch in a debate on the National Health Service and Community Care Act 1990.
70  Social Work (Scotland) Act 1968, s.86.
71  Words in square brackets inserted by Children Act 1989, Sched.13, para.11(2).
72  DHSS Circular LAC 13/74. There is a general duty to provide items (a)-(d) and a power to provide the remainder.

- arranging for the provision of such services by another local authority or voluntary organisation.

*Scotland*

In Scotland the equivalent provision is section 12 of the Social Work (Scotland) Act 1968, which refers to persons in need (who are defined as including the disabled) and does not make specific reference to the disabled, but contains a general duty to promote social welfare by making available advice, guidance and assistance. The Chronically Sick and Disabled Persons Act 1970 (see pages 237 and 241) in its application to Scotland does specifically refer to persons suffering from mental disorder, the definition of which includes mental handicap.[73]

## Prevention, care and after-care

*England*

Under the National Health Service Act 1977, social services departments may make provision for the prevention of illness and for the care and after-care of persons suffering from illness, including mental illness.[74] The following types of provision are to be made to assist persons with a mental disorder[75]:

- care for persons ordinarily resident in the area of the authority and for those in that area who have no settled residence;
- centres (including training centres and day centres) or other facilities (including domiciliary facilities) whether in premises managed by the authority or some other body and used for the training or occupation of such people;
- social work support and other domiciliary and care services to people living in their homes and elsewhere;
- home helps for households where help is required owing to the presence of a person handicapped as the result of illness or by congenital deformity.

The provision of meals, and social and recreational activities has been authorised. Authorities are directed to arrange for training and occupation facilities, and general social work support and to provide for guardianship and the appointment of approved social workers. They may use accommodation, facilities and services provided by another authority, voluntary body or person on agreed conditions, but this should be as near to the person's home as practicable. In deciding what provision to make for a person living at home and receiving substantial care from another person, the authority must have regard to the ability of that other person

---

73    1970 Act, s.29(2) as inserted by the Chronically Sick and Disabled Persons (Scotland) Act 1972, s.1(1) and amended by the Disabled Persons (Services *etc.*) Act 1986, s.12(1).

74    s.21 and Sched.8. This provision does not apply to persons under the age of 18 (Children Act 1989, Sched.12, para.34).

75    DHSS Circular LAC 19/74. The 1990 Act abolished the power to provide accommodation under the 1977 Act - but see the 1948 Act below.

to continue to provide care.[76]

Some of these services overlap with those under the National Assistance Act 1948 (as above) but provision is generally made under the 1977 Act.[77]

*Scotland*

Under the Social Work (Scotland) Act 1968, social work departments may make provision for the prevention of illness and the care and after-care of persons suffering from illness, and they must provide and maintain such residential and other establishments as may be required for their functions under the Act.[78] In relation to mentally handicapped people (and the mentally ill), under the Mental Health (Scotland) Act 1984[79] they may arrange provision, equipment and maintenance of residential accommodation, the care of residents in such accommodation, and the provision of ancillary and supplementary services; and they must provide after-care services (in co-operation with health boards and the voluntary sector, where appropriate). They may also arrange for the supervision of mentally handicapped people who are neither detained patients nor under statutory guardianship, and they must arrange for provision of suitable training and occupation for mentally handicapped adults.[80] As in England, when assessing needs they must have regard to the ability of a carer to continue to provide substantial care on a regular basis.[81]

## Provision of accommodation

*England*

Also under the National Assistance Act 1948, local authorities are under a duty to provide residential accommodation for persons who by reason of age, [illness, disability] or any other circumstances are in need of care and attention which is not otherwise available to them.[82] This is known as *Part III accommodation*. Regard must be had to the welfare of all persons for whom accommodation is provided so the different needs of each category must be considered. The concept of ordinary residence is relevant, but persons without a settled residence and those in urgent need may come within the duty.[83] Accommodation may be provided in premises managed by the local authority or by

---

76  This rider was added by the 1986 Act, s.8(1).
77  See DHSS Circular LAC 17/74, para.14.
78  s.13B, inserted by the 1990 Act , s.56; and s.59.
79  ss.7 and 8.
80  s.11.
81  1986 Act, s.8.
82  s.21(1)(*a*). The 1990 Act substituted "illness, disability" for "infirmity" and extended the power to cover nursing homes as well as residential care homes - s.42(2).
83  Persons will generally keep the ordinary residence they had before entering such accommodation or going into hospital.

another authority in which event terms should be agreed for reimbursement of the cost. Arrangements may also be made with residential homes managed by voluntary organisations or in the private secto.. A person for whom accommodation is provided may be required to pay all or part of the cost.[84]

Under Directions issued by the Secretary of State the following provision must be made[85]:

- accommodation for persons ordinarily resident in the area of the authority or for other persons in urgent need, who come within the above statutory provision;
- temporary accommodation for those who are in urgent need of it either as a result of circumstances which could not reasonably have been foreseen, or in such circumstances as the authority may in any particular case determine;
- for the welfare of all persons for whom it provides accommodation, and for the supervision of the hygiene of that accommodation;
- to enable residents in accommodation provided by it to obtain medical attention, nursing attention during an illness of a kind which is normally nursed at home, and the benefit of NHS provisions;
- other services, amenities and requisites as the authority considers necessary in connection with any accommodation provided;
- regular review of the above provisions and any necessary improvements.

and the following further provision is authorised:

- accommodation (of the above nature) in premises managed by another local authority;
- such accommodation, to an extent which it considers desirable, for persons ordinarily resident in the area of another authority;
- such accommodation by making arrangements with voluntary organisations, or persons in charge of registered homes;
- so far as it considers it to be appropriate, the provision of transport to and from any accommodation provided.

*Scotland*

The equivalent provisions in Scotland are contained in Part IV of the Social Work (Scotland) Act 1968, and accommodation thus provided is accordingly known as *Part IV accommodation* in Scotland. It is the duty of Scottish local authorities to provide and maintain such residential and other establishments as may be required for their functions under the Act, or to arrange such provision jointly with other local authorities, or to secure such provision by the voluntary sector. The Scottish legislation does not specify a requirement for ordinary residence, but see provisions

---

84    This topic is dealt with in Chap.8, Part II.
85    DHSS Circular LAC 13/74.

described above (page 243) regarding financial adjustments between authorities.

## Guardianship

Statutory guardianship[86] should not be overlooked when considering the powers of the local authority because a social worker will be involved. In England it seldom applies to people with a mental handicap because the element of abnormally aggressive or seriously irresponsible conduct will not be present.[87] The purpose of guardianship is to enable an adult to receive community care where this cannot be provided without the use of compulsory powers and to remove people who are at risk of abuse, but it has been little used by social workers, perhaps because of reluctance to adopt an authoritarian role, and because the powers of a guardian are very limited.

## Removal

A magistrates court (in Scotland, the sheriff court) may authorise removal of persons to suitable premises for the purpose of securing necessary care and attention if they are[88]:

(a) suffering from grave chronic disease, or being aged, infirm or physically incapacitated, are living in insanitary conditions; and

(b) unable to devote themselves, and are not receiving from other persons, proper care and attention.

Application is made by the appropriate authority for the area in which the person is residing,[89] and it is the court for that area which has jurisdiction. Before an application is made, a medical officer of health must certify in writing to the authority that, after thorough inquiry, he is satisfied that in the interests of the person concerned, or of preventing injury to the health of, or serious nuisance to, other people it is necessary to remove the person from the premises. The order names an officer of the authority responsible for carrying it out and removal is to a hospital or other specified place within a convenient distance. Seven clear days notice must be given to the person concerned and also to the manager of the hospital or other place named who will have an opportunity to be heard. Detention may be authorised for up to three months and extended for similar periods.

### Emergency application

The requirement for seven days notice caused unacceptable delay in urgent situations so an emergency procedure was introduced.[90]

---

86  *I.e.* under the Mental Health Act 1983, ss.7-10 and the Mental Health (Scotland) Act 1984, Part V. See Chap.4, at pp.196 and 214.

87  But in Scotland these elements are not required (see p.214) and many people under guardianship are mentally handicapped.

88  National Assistance Act 1948, s.47.

89  District council or London borough in England; regional or islands council in Scotland.

90  National Assistance (Amendment) Act 1951.

Notice is waived if a medical officer of health and a registered general practitioner certify that in their opinions it is necessary to remove the person without delay. In England, a single justice may alone deal with the application, *ex parte* if necessary. The order will only last for three weeks.

*Implications to mental handicap*
Some persons with mental handicaps may fall within these powers but such detention does not attract Mental Health Act powers especially as regards consent to medical treatment. The provision is most often used in respect of elderly persons who are not coping at home but will not accept help.

## Protection of property

A local authority has a duty to take reasonable steps to prevent or mitigate loss or damage to the moveable property of a person admitted as a patient to any hospital, or who is admitted to Part III (in Scotland, Part IV) accommodation or removed to suitable premises by the local authority.[91] In performing this duty the authority has power to enter the patient's home, and may recover reasonable expenses from the patient.

## Children (England)

The Children Act 1989 creates a single unified regime for children[92] based upon a voluntary partnership between local authority and the family with emphasis upon support in keeping the family together as a unit.[93] Where that is not possible, parental responsibility[94] and contact should still be maintained. When a court considers any question concerning the upbringing or property of a child the welfare of the child is the paramount consideration.[95] Children should be listened to in making plans for their future.

*Children in need*
The Act introduces a concept of *children in need*. A child is to be taken to be in need if[96]:

> (a)  he is unlikely to achieve or maintain, or to have the opportunity of achieving or maintaining, a reasonable standard of health or development without the provision for him of services by a local authority ...;
> (b)  his health or development is likely to be significantly impaired, or further impaired, without the provision for him of such services; or
> (c)  he is disabled.

---

91   1948 Act, s.48; in Scotland, see also Mental Health (Scotland) Act 1984, s.92.

92   In this context a child means a person under 18 years of age, but some of the provisions only apply at a younger age.

93   Part III of the Act indicates the services that a local authority may or must provide and replaces provisions in the Child Care Act 1980, National Assistance Act 1948 and National Health Service Act 1977 which, although continuing in respect of adults, no longer apply to infants.

94   This is a concept introduced by the Act - see Chap.3, Part II at p.129.

95   Children Act 1989, s.1.

96   s.17(10).

Children who are disabled are thus one category of children in need.[97] There is a general duty upon local authorities to assess the needs and promote the welfare of children in need living within the area and to promote their upbringing by their families. This involves providing a range and level of services appropriate to their needs, and is supported by specific duties such as the facilitation of the provision by others (including voluntary organisations) of services which may include respite care and other support services for the families of disabled children.

*Role of the Authorities*
The Act provides that[98]:

> Every local authority shall have services designed:
> (a) to minimise the effect on disabled children within their area of their disability; and
> (b) to give such children the opportunity to lead lives which are as normal as possible.

The ordinary life approach to special needs and the integrationist principle underly these provisions, and the various authorities with a role to play[99] should work together to meet the needs of children in need, but most of the duties are placed on social services departments. The local authority must[100]:

- identify the extent to which there are children in need in the area;
- support and develop links with families;
- consider a child's racial, cultural and religious background;
- provide day care for children in need under five;
- provide day care for school age children during out-of-school hours and during school holidays;
- set up procedures to consider representation about provision of services.

Every social services department must identify children with disabilities in its area, open a register of such children[101] and make the following services available (they do not have to provide them all themselves, though they must publish information about the services that are provided):

(a) services to safeguard and promote their welfare and give them the opportunity to lead lives which are as normal as possible;
(b) support to enable them to live at home with their parents, if this is possible and appropriate, including:
  (i)  advice, guidance and counselling;
  (ii)  occupational, social, cultural or recreational facilities;

---

97  The definition of *disabled* in the Children Act 1989 is set out at p.241.
98  Sched.2, para.6.
99  Including social services, housing, education and health authorities.
100  See generally Part III and Sched.2 for the support to be given.
101  Registration is optional and not a pre-condition of receiving services but parents should be encouraged to register because this enables authorities to plan for the future and it may be a passport to services.

(iii) help in the home (*e.g.* laundry facilities);
(iv) facilities for, or assistance with, travel to get to and
from services;
(v) help to enable the child and his family to have a holiday.
Where possible services should be provided in settings with
children who do not have disabilities. This new provision should
improve the range of holiday, sitting and other services for those
living at home or with foster families.

## Enforcement

There are increased controls upon the local authority, including
case reviews and complaints procedures. Of importance in the case
of a handicapped child is the extent to which parents and others
may enforce the duty to provide support. The Secretary of State is
given default powers where he is satisfied that the authority has,
without reasonable cause, failed to comply with a duty under the
Act, and may then direct the authority to do so within a specified
period and enforce this by applying to the High Court for judicial
review. It is not clear to what extent the courts will permit parents
to by-pass the default procedures and apply for judicial review.

## Provision of accommodation

Support should be available to enable parents to bring up their
child, but if children need to live away from the family in
accommodation provided or arranged by the local authority,
whether by agreement or under a court order, the person with
parental responsibility should not lose this. The emphasis is then
upon provision of accommodation and the child is no longer taken
into care. So far as reasonably practicable and consistent with the
child's welfare, due consideration should be given to the child's
wishes having regard to his age and understanding.

## Care proceedings [102]

There is now a single ground for compulsory care. The court may
only make a care or supervision order in respect of a child under
17 years if it is satisfied that the child is suffering or is likely to
suffer significant harm.[103] Social services departments will be able
to obtain care orders only where the courts are satisfied that the
harm or likely harm is attributable to the standard of care either
given, or likely to be given, to the child being "below that which it
would be reasonable to expect the parent of such a child to give"
or to "the child's being beyond parental control". In the case of a
child with a mental handicap the comparison must be with a child
having a similar handicap in order to see whether his health or

---

[102] See Part IV of the Act (care and supervision) and Part V (Protection of
children).

[103] s.31. Harm is widely defined and includes impairment of health (physical or
mental) or development and ill-treatment, including sexual abuse and
emotional ill-treatment. Where it depends upon health or development the
court must compare with that which could reasonably be expected of a
similar child - s.31(10).

development is being impaired as a consequence of the home environment. This may divert attention onto whether the child's special needs are being adequately catered for, and the standard of care expected of the parents will be that of parents coping with such special needs.

A *supervision order* puts the child under the supervision of a local authority or a probation officer who will have the duty to advise, assist and befriend the child. A *care order* gives the local authority parental responsibility for the child and power to determine the extent to which a parent or guardian may meet his or her parental responsibility but the authority may only exercise this power if satisfied that it is necessary to safeguard the child's welfare. When a child is in care there is a presumption that the child should have reasonable contact with the parents, but this can be restricted or refused by the court or, on an emergency basis, by the local authority. There are provisions for an assessment of the child to be made and this may be important where problems have arisen as a result of the mental handicap of the child and the parents' ability to cope with this.

## Children (Scotland)

The general local authority duty to promote social welfare by making available advice, guidance and assistance also applies to children under 18, and includes a duty to children requiring assistance in kind (or in exceptional circumstances in cash) where it appears to the local authority that such assistance is likely to diminish the need to take the child into care (or keep the child in care) or to refer the child to a children's hearing, under the provisions described below.[104]

### Local authority care

The local authority has a duty to take into its care a child under 17 who has no parent or guardian, or who is abandoned or lost, or whose parents or guardians are unable to care for him, if the local authority consider it necessary for the welfare of the child. The criteria include cases where the parent or guardian is temporarily or permanently prevented from providing proper accommodation, maintenance and upbringing because of illness, mental disorder (including mental handicap), bodily disease or infirmity, or other incapacity or circumstances. Having taken the child into care, the local authority must try to find a parent or guardian, or other suitable person, to care for the child. Failing that, the local authority must itself care for the child for as long as may be necessary, up to the maximum age of 18.[105]

### Local authority taking parental rights

The local authority may resolve to take parental rights over a child, or to confer parental rights on a voluntary organisation

---

[104]  Social Work (Scotland) Act 1968, s.12(1) and (2).
[105]  ss.16 *et seq.*

which itself has care of the child, if the child is already in the care of the local authority (or the voluntary organisation) and if certain grounds exist. The grounds include a situation where the parent or guardian has a mental disorder (including a mental handicap) which renders him or her "unfit to have the care of the child". Other grounds are where the parent or guardian has abandoned the child, is incapable of caring for the child through some permanent disability, or is unfit to have the care of the child because of habits, mode of life or persistent failure (without reasonable cause) to discharge parental obligations (or where one of these grounds has already been applied to a parent who is, or is likely to become, a member of the same household as the child). Further grounds include cases where the parents are deceased and there is no guardian, and where the child has been in care (under the provisions described in the preceding paragraph) for three years.

The parents may object to the local authority resolution by applying to the sheriff, in which case the onus is upon the local authority to show that proper grounds have been made out and continue to exist, and that the resolution is in the best interests of the child.

This taking of parental rights does not terminate access by the parents or guardian unless the parents are first given a prescribed notice of termination or refusal, which is appealable to the sheriff. Following taking of parental rights, the parents remain liable to contribute towards the maintenance of the child; they may still determine the religion in which the child is to be brought up; and their consent is still required for adoption.[106]

*Children's hearings* [107]

Children's hearings consider the cases of children who may be in need of care and protection. The Reporter arranges hearings, brings cases before them, and has other duties. Children may be brought before a hearing if one of a list of grounds of referral exists. If the ground of referral is not accepted (including cases where the child or parent is not capable of accepting it) the case is referred to the sheriff to determine whether the alleged ground of referral has been established. If so, the case goes back to the children's hearing to deal with it. The grounds of referral include cases where lack of parental care is likely to cause the child unnecessary suffering or seriously to impair the child's health or development, and cases where the behaviour of a child in local authority care requires special measures to achieve adequate care and control. Other grounds of referral include being beyond parental control, falling into bad associations, exposure to moral danger, persistent truancy without reasonable excuse, solvent abuse, commission of an offence, and various circumstances where

---

[106] s.15.
[107] Part III.

offences have been committed against the child or someone in the same household. There are also provisions covering children transferred from elsewhere in the United Kingdom.

Various disposals are available to children's hearings, including requiring the child to go to an assessment centre, putting the child under the supervision of a social worker, putting the child into certain kinds of homes and schools, making some other voluntary arrangement, or simply taking no action. If the hearing consider that the child is seriously mentally disturbed or handicapped, the child may be sent to hospital, though this must be done by the sheriff, not by the children's hearing.

Parents of children under 16 who are subject to supervision may be required to contribute towards maintenance, but such requirements seem to be rare in practice.

# PART III - PROVISION OF SERVICES

## GENERAL

We now consider the services that local authorities should provide to people with a mental handicap. The emphasis is upon services because, although some need to be cared for, most need the provision of services so that they can achieve their own potential.

## Assessment

There is a duty imposed upon local authorities to assess the needs of disabled persons for *welfare services*, and they must do so on the request of the disabled person or any person who provides a substantial amount of care on a regular basis.[108] Authorities must now assess a person for whom they may provide, and who in their view may need, *community care services*, even if not asked to do so, and then decide whether provision should be made.[109] If whilst doing so it appears to the authority that the person being assessed is a disabled person it must proceed to assess the need for *welfare services* without being asked and inform the person of his rights in that respect.[110]

The Secretary of State may give directions as to the manner in which an assessment is to be carried out or the form that it shall take but, subject to this, it shall be as the authority considers appropriate. In cases of urgency, services may even be provided without an assessment but this should follow as soon as possible. The person should be informed of any assessment and of his statutory rights. The district health authority (in Scotland, the health board) or local housing authority may be invited to assist in

---

108  1986 Act, s.4. This provision was enacted because local authorities were not carrying out assessments. For welfare services, see p.258.

109  For community care services, see p.259.

110  1990 Act, s.47(2); Social Work (Scotland) Act 1968, s.12A(4) .

the provision of services and in the assessment.[111] Provisions
intended to enable the disabled person or an authorised
representative to make representations as to the needs of the
disabled person and, following receipt of a written statement of
services to be provided and the basis of the assessment, to ask for a
review, have not been brought into effect.[112]

### Establishing need

Where a local authority is satisfied in the case of a person
ordinarily resident in its area that it is necessary in order to meet
the needs of that person to make arrangements to provide *welfare
services*, it is the duty of the authority to do so regardless of
resource constraints.[113] This does not mean that the authority must
be satisfied beyond reasonable doubt, but merely that it must make
up its mind in the specific case and this necessarily means making
an assessment of need.[114] The obligation to provide community
care services appears to be less stringent because the assessment is
in two stages, an assessment of need and a statement of services,
and it has been made clear that the first stage is not resource
dependent but the second stage is. The shortfall in total need
should then be addressed in the next Community Care Plan.

### Carer's needs

When assessing the needs of a disabled person who is living at
home the local authority must have regard to a carer's ability to
continue providing care on a regular basis.[115] It is suggested that
this includes physical, emotional, practical and financial abilities.
The social services department cannot use the presence of a carer
as an excuse for not looking critically at the needs of the disabled
person and for failing to provide the services that are needed.
There is no requirement to provide services for the carer, but
authorities should "as part of normal good practice have regard to
the possible need for such services, and to the desirability of
enabling the disabled person to continue living at home for as long
as possible if this is what he or she wishes to do."[116] A carer who
needs services is entitled to his own assessment of need.

### Policies

The local authority cannot fetter its discretion in regard to an
individual by introducing and imposing a blanket policy regarding
disabled people in general. Each case must be dealt with on its
merits, but in practice standard criteria tend to be applied. Thus

---

111 See generally s.47 of the 1990 Act (England) and s.12A of the 1968 Act
     (Scotland) where assessments relate to all community care services.
112 1986 Act, s.3
113 1970 Act, s.2(1). Welfare services are set out therein and aimed at
     physically disabled persons, see below.
114 *Blyth* v. *Blyth* [1966] 1 All ER 524, HL.
115 1986 Act, s.8 - carer means someone who is providing a substantial amount
     of care on a regular basis but is not employed to do so by a statutory body.
116 DHSS Circular 6/87.

adopting strict criteria because of a lack of funds is probably not permissible, although the Secretary of State does not appear to have taken authorities to task over this when asked to use his default powers. Although the local authority may be under an obligation to provide the particular welfare service once a need is established, it seems that this must be within a reasonable time thus implying that a waiting list is permissible. An excessive delay would no doubt be open to challenge, unless it could be justified due to other factors outside the control of the local authority.

## Provision

Care services may be provided by health authorities, charities and private agencies as well as local authorities, and usually revolve round the care already being provided by family, friends and neighbours. The significance of the new regime of community care is that local authorities are given responsibility for arranging and co-ordinating the package of care needed by an individual and will get funding from central government to buy in care services. The role of the health authority will be restricted to health care. A social services (or social work) department cannot generally give money as distinct from providing services, but there are ways round this for the benefit of those who prefer self-help.[117]

When the provision of care is being organised, people with a mental handicap should never be regarded as a group with the same attributes. Quite apart from the fact that such handicap is wide ranging in its nature and severity, different languages, religions and cultures must be catered for.

### Role of other agencies

The Secretary of State has emphasised that local authorities should not seek to provide all services themselves, but make use of the voluntary and commercial sectors.[118] Housing authorities and associations, education departments, charities and other associations, and the private sector all have an important role to play in the delivery of community care. Planning is needed to ensure that the contribution from these agencies is part of a co-ordinated service making the best use of available resources in meeting individual needs.

### Contracts

Contracts that spell out who is going to do what and on what terms are an important aspect of community care, and these must be negotiated. The parties to the contract will usually be the local authority and the care provider, yet it is the fate of the person with a mental handicap that is being determined and often his money that is to be spent. There should be some procedure to ensure that the wishes of this person are not overlooked in the

---

117 *e.g.* the individual may place an order for some form of help and the cost is then paid for by the department, perhaps on a voucher system.

118 Statement to the House of Commons on July 12, 1989.

desire to create a tidy package of service provision. Skills have to be developed by officers of local authorities in drawing up and placing contracts for the provision of services as they move to the enabling role from that of being providers. If there are no regulatory or quality assurance mechanisms there is the danger that community care contracts will be awarded primarily on costs grounds even if the quality of services provided is inferior.

*Training*

It is suggested that training of staff include the following:[119]

1. Knowledge of carers' needs, benefits systems and local voluntary sectors;
2. Skills in advocacy, negotiating and counselling;
3. Changing attitudes from provider role to partner role;
4. Offering carers training in the practical skills of caring and help in gaining information about their rights and also how to assert those rights.

## Obligations

When considering whether there is an obligation on the part of an authority to provide services it should be noted that there are two different types of obligation:

*legal obligations* - failure involves a breach of statutory duty, but the question must be asked whether the duty is owed to an individual or only generally. In the latter event no action may be brought by the individual to enforce the duty in a particular case. It is not always easy to determine if a legal obligation has been imposed;

*political (or social) obligation* - the authority has powers to provide the service and is expected to do so, but there is no legal requirement. Such services are not enforceable by law, though action may be taken if there is discrimination on grounds of sex or race (but not disability) or the authority blindly follows a particular policy without considering individual circumstances or makes a decision which is unreasonable.[120]

## Community Care Plans

All local authorities must now prepare, in consultation with health and housing authorities and voluntary organisations, and publish their plans for community care, thereby enabling public scrutiny both as to the adequacy of the plan and the extent to which it is being fulfilled.[121] Plans should be in a readily understandable form and must be modified at intervals as directed by the

---

119 *Community Care: Carers.* Social Services Committee, 1989/90 Session.

120 *I.e.* on the Wednesbury principles (failing to take all relevant facts into account etc., see p.156).

121 1990 Act, ss.46 and 52. In addition, district health authorities and Family Health Service Authorities are encouraged to prepare and publish plans (and in Scotland health boards are instructed to do so).

Secretary of State. They should contain a balanced consideration of the needs of different groups and will be monitored by the Social Services Inspectorate (in Scotland, the Social Work Services Inspectorate). The government will be looking to local authorities in preparing their community care plans to assess the needs of the populations they serve and, where provision is inadequate, to specify how they plan to improve the availability of services. The Secretary of State for Health has announced[122]:

- publication of draft circulars to health and social services authorities on the provision of social care for people with learning difficulties;
- the issuing of draft guidance on the development of day care services;
- the adoption, within the Department of Health, of the phrase "people with learning disabilities" instead of "mentally handicapped people".

and set the following timetable for implementing plans in England:

*by September 1991* - prepare a population profile and identify needs; identify existing services, including the voluntary sector; establish procedures to work with the voluntary sector and involve users and carers in planning.

*by April 1992* - publish Community Care Plans; identify services to contract out; agree on joint commissioning of services.

*by September 1992* - negotiate assessment role of voluntary sector; encourage new service provision by voluntary and private sectors; develop service specifications to meet identified needs.

Planning agreements or joint plans should also be drawn up between health and local authorities, specifying who does what, who pays, contract specifications and ways of ensuring continuity of care.

The timetable in Scotland was:

*by July 1991* - local authorities and health boards to submit planning agreements.

*by April 1992* - local authority community care plans to be published, health boards to submit community care plans linked to local health strategies.

## TYPES OF SERVICES

When considering the services that are, or might be, available it is easy to lose sight of the objective of providing a full and satisfying way of life. The Social Services Committee considered that people with a mental disability need somewhere to call home and something meaningful to do in the way of education, work and recreation,[123] and this should be without placing too great a

---

122  Press release from Department of Health, June 25, 1991.
123  Eleventh Report to the House of Commons, Session 1989-90, para.109.

burden on informal carers. Education (including formal training beyond school leaving age) and housing (including residential care which is housing plus the other elements in a single package) are dealt with in the next two chapters, and other services or facilities provided or promoted by local authorities are considered here.

## Classification

Care services may be classified in many ways, and services may be specifically for the benefit of the disabled person (including those necessary to promote independent living), or may be to assist the informal carer to provide continuity of care.

### General categories
The following general categories may be identified:

> **Domestic help** - a home help visiting every day, or for a few hours per week, to provide assistance with cooking, cleaning and shopping; the provision of meals-on-wheels or a laundry service;
> **Personal care** - a care assistant providing help with bathing, washing, or other jobs around the house, or even night time care;
> **Transport** - to day care facilities; schemes for the disabled (usually those with physical disability) include car adaptations, motability,[124] and a parking badge[125];
> **Financial** - state and local authority benefits are dealt with in Chapter 8;
> **Equipment** - aids available through the health service (bedpans, incontinence pads, walking aids and wheelchairs) or social services (domestic equipment and adaptations to the home);
> **Training** - for the disabled person and for the carer;
> **Respite care** - anything from an occasional sitting or minding service at home to residential care for a holiday or on a regular basis;
> **Residential care** - permanent accommodation in a residential care home for those who need this;
> **Health care** - the full range of health services provided under the NHS which includes home visits by doctors, nurses, dentists, opticians and chiropodists, and also in-patient and out-patient hospital treatment.

### Care categories
Care providers often see the provision of care as falling into three broad categories:

> *domiciliary*  -  services provided inside the home[126];
> *day*          -  services provided outside the home;
> *residential*  -  residential services (short or long term).

In addition there is assistance for the physically disabled with appliances and with the home either in the form of adaptations or the provision of a suitable home.

## Welfare services

Some services for a disabled person were specifically identified by statute in 1970[127]:

---

124 Use of mobility allowance to buy or lease a car or electric wheelchair.
125 Enables the user to park in otherwise restricted places - usually issued free by social services or social work departments. This is a statutory scheme under the Chronically Sick and Disabled Persons Act 1970.
126 The help usually provided is assistance with bathing, dressing and eating, but it may extend to cleaning, shopping, etc., aids or appliances.
127 Chronically Sick and Disabled Persons Act 1970, s.2.

(a) practical assistance in the home;
(b) provision of, or assistance in obtaining, wireless, television, library or similar recreational facilities;
(c) provision of lectures, games, outings or other recreational facilities outside the home or assistance in taking advantage of educational facilities;
(d) provision of facilities for, or assistance in, travelling to and from home for the purpose of participating in services;
(e) assistance in arranging for the carrying out of any works of adaptation in the home or the provision of any additional facilities designed to secure greater safety, comfort or convenience;
(f) facilitating the taking of holidays, whether at holiday homes or otherwise and whether provided under arrangements made by the authority or otherwise;
(g) provision of meals whether in the home or elsewhere;
(h) provision of, or assistance in obtaining, a telephone and any special equipment necessary for its use.

## Community care services

These are defined as services which a local authority may provide or arrange under any of the following provisions:

*In England*
    National Assistance Act 1948, Part III
    Health Services and Public Health Act 1968, s.45[128]
    National Health Service Act 1977, s.21 and Sched.8
    Mental Health Act 1983, s.117
*In Scotland*
    Social Work (Scotland) Act 1968[129]
    Mental Health (Scotland) Act 1984, ss.7,8 and 11

## Day services

Community based facilities for the social and everyday needs of the individual are an essential component of community care, and must be adequate to enable the individual to have a purposeful life in keeping with the education which is provided as of right.[130] Personal choice should be offered where possible. If training or employment cannot be provided the availability of day services is a minimum requirement in order to provide variation in the pattern of life and relief for carers.[131] Social services departments have an obligation to provide training and occupation facilities for

---

[128] This is not dealt with because it relates to the welfare of old people. The other provisions have all been covered in the text.

[129] As amended by National Health Service and Community Care Act 1990, Part II.

[130] There is a stark contrast between the entitlement to education up to the age of 19 (in Scotland, 18) and that which is available thereafter.

[131] *Caring for People* recognises this but does not indicate how day care facilities for people with a mental handicap should be provided.

adults with a mental handicap.[132] Such provision is used by many, but the way in which this obligation is met varies markedly from one local authority to another. Authorities will not be able to deliver all the services required, but are given a co-ordinating responsibility by the 1986 Act. Community based services which are generally available should be used with support as necessary, though in many cases separate services will be provided. The Social Services Inspectorate (in England) may promote agreement as to what constitutes satisfactory day service provision and what this should achieve, and national guidelines should emerge, but the emphasis in the policy statement on available resources will inhibit the development of services however necessary they may be.

### Duration and choice

Day services must be seen as something more than daytime activities on weekdays. Facilities of some sort should be available during evenings and weekends, though to some extent this can be achieved by using existing community facilities.[133] Instead of depending on whatever the department decides to provide, the individual should be able to enter into a formal agreement setting out a lifelong entitlement to day services as and when these are required. Attempts may then be made to try something different or take advantage of educational opportunities without prejudicing the future availability of services presently being provided.

### Day Centres

Adult Training Centres (increasingly referred to as Social Education Centres or Adult Resource Centres) have traditionally formed the basis of day service provision. In some areas there is little else, and there are seldom enough places for all those who need them.[134] Unfortunately, this means that they must be all things to all people: not only do they cope with a wide range of mental (and often physical) disabilities, but also they seek to provide work, education and leisure (i.e. something meaningful to do) for those who attend. This dilutes each function and leaves staff confused as to their objectives. It may therefore be better to develop other services and encourage these centres to become more specialised and selective.[135]

### Community facilities

Community facilities should be available and accessible to persons

---

132 National Health Service Act 1977 and DHSS Circular 13/74. In Scotland, the duty of social work departments is to arrange provision of suitable training and occupation - Mental Health (Scotland) Act 1984, s.11.

133 See the Social Services Committee Second Report, Session 1984-85.

134 The 1971 White Paper set a target of 74,500 places to be provided by 1991 in England, but in 1989 there were less than 55,000, a shortage of 27 per cent.

135 The Audit Commission felt that the shortfall may not be a bad thing if it leads to more places in further education, work experience, employment and other activities outside centres, though the shortfall is unlikely to be made up in these ways - Occasional Paper No.9 (1990).

with a mental handicap. These include libraries, swimming pools, leisure centres, cinemas, theatres, museums, sports events, etc. Some progress has already been achieved in ensuring that such facilities can be used by physically disabled persons, but informal carers tend to be inhibited from visiting such places or events by reason of the attitudes of staff and members of the public, and embarrassment exacerbated by their emotional attachment to the person being cared for. Disabled persons may be encouraged to use these facilities in several ways, for example:
- special times when they attend together;
- support clubs which encourage them to show an interest in the activity;
- reduced admission prices or other special terms;
- assistance with transport;
- special rooms or areas where they may (not must) go;
- training of staff to be especially considerate towards their needs, thereby showing carers that they are welcome;
- availability of care staff to supervise, thereby creating short regular periods of respite care.

Local authorities should ensure that their own facilities do not adopt policies which discourage use by disabled persons. Where the facility is provided commercially they can promote use by such persons but care must be taken not to discriminate by discouraging them from using the facilities on a normal basis.

*Day nurseries*
Day nurseries may be provided by local authorities, but many are provided by private institutions, and there is a scheme for the regulation and supervision thereof.[136] The need for day nurseries providing for handicapped children has reduced since local education authorities became obliged to provide special education for such children at any age, even though compulsory education only starts when the child is five years old.

*Summer Playschemes*
In some areas playschemes are available for mentally handicapped children during the school summer holiday, often organised and funded by the voluntary sector. Whilst some social services departments provide this facility, they are not obliged to do so. Such playschemes represent good value compared with the cost of respite care, and enable available money to be spread more evenly amongst a wider group of parents. Parents can usually manage with less respite care during this period if they have relief of this nature during the day and their children benefit from the varied group activities.

---

136 Nurseries and Child-Minders Regulation Act 1948 has been replaced by new provisions under Children Act 1989, Part X, ss.71-79 and Sched.9. Part X applies to both England and Scotland. See also the Disqualification for Caring for Children Regulations 1991.

## Home assistance

Housing is a vital component of community care and it is often the key to independent living. A range of possible residential facilities is available for people with a mental handicap, but whilst the ideal is to be supported in their own homes, this can never be feasible for all. The role of the local authority in the provision of housing and residential care is considered in Chapter 7.

## SPECIAL SITUATIONS

### Children in homes (England)[137]

Local authorities must be informed by health and education authorities, and residential care, nursing or mental nursing homes of any child who spends at least three months in their care. The social services department within whose catchment area the child lives must "take such steps as are reasonably practicable to enable them to determine whether the child's welfare is adequately safeguarded and promoted" while he stays in the accommodation and "consider the extent to which (if at all) they should exercise their functions under (the) Act with respect to the child".[138]

### Leaving school

This topic is covered in Chapter 6, Part IA for England and Part IB for Scotland, in each case under the heading "Transition".

### Leaving hospital

As we have seen, people with a mental handicap are being moved out of hospitals and these are being closed. The Secretary of State has stated that he will not approve closure of any mental handicap hospital unless satisfied that proper alternative services are in place, but whether this objective is being fulfilled is open to doubt.

*Financial arrangements*
Individuals can be moved to small community units run by the NHS, or transferred to local authority social services departments or to private or voluntary sector accommodation. When they cease to be the responsibility of the health authority a sum of money or *dowry* is transferred with them, the amount or terms for payment being negotiated between that authority and the transferee and paid by the authority.[139] A 1983 Circular states that as vacancies arise in community care facilities supported from NHS funds in this

---

137 For supervision of children's homes in Scotland see: Social Work (Residential Establishments - Child Care) (Scotland) Regulations 1987, S.I. 1987/2233 as amended by S.I. 1988/1091.

138 Children Act 1989, ss.85 and 86.

139 In Scotland the dowry system is legally possible but has not so far been used. Health boards may transfer resources to social work departments and voluntary and private agencies to provide community services for former hospital patients (see 1985 circular NHS(Gen)18) but there is no obligation or sufficient incentive for them to do so.

way for people moving out of hospital, the vacancies may be filled by other people moving from hospital or by people who would otherwise imminently need to be admitted to hospital.[140] Although this suggests that the transfer of funds is to be in perpetuity, not all health authorities are willing to pay dowries on that basis. This system is not therefore coping with the financial implications of the transfer of patients, and local authorities are increasingly having to meet the cost of provision previously made by health authorities without more money being made available to them for that purpose.

*Transfer of staff (England)*

In connection with arrangements relating to community care services the Secretary of State may make regulations with respect to the transfer to employment by a local authority of persons previously employed by a NHS body.[141] Nurses may be reluctant to transfer and local authority staff wary of accepting them. NHS pay, training and conditions of service differ in material respects from those of local authorities and lengthy negotiations are required to resolve the problems.

*Joint planning*

Delays have arisen in the agreement and implementation of joint strategies between health authorities and local authorities for the resettlement of hospital residents. These have been contributed to by a lack of mutual trust and unwillingness by local authorities to accept such residents unless all costs are refunded whilst health authorities are reluctant to pay dowries in perpetuity. An added problem is that health authority areas do not coincide with those of local authorities so they need to negotiate with several authorities. It should not be assumed that just because a hospital patient has been discharged the health authority has funds available to support the former patient in the community; it is only when sufficient patients have left to enable a ward or hospital to be closed that appreciable funds are released, but the local authority needs the funding as soon as it takes over responsibility. There is thus a period when it actually costs more, and outside funding is not available for this. Where joint strategies do not exist health authorities tend to resettle patients in their own units or private or voluntary homes, thereby not relying directly upon the local authority, though this may deprive others still living with their family of places in care homes and lead to a lack of day care facilities for such persons.[142]

---

[140] *Health Service Development: Care in the Community and Joint Finance* DHSS Circular HC(83)6 and LAC(83)5.

[141] 1990 Act, s.49.

[142] The availability of Income Support residential care allowance until April 1993 encourages this, as the health authority only needs to provide top-up to meet the fees. The problem of day care is emphasised where large numbers move into residential care homes in an area without any advance arrangement with the social services department.

Longer term problems arise where health authorities avoid the formal transfer of patients to local authorities in these ways. The numbers in hospitals decline through such transfers and deaths and there being no new admissions to make up for it, so the care of the next generation shifts to local authorities without a commensurate transfer of funds. Also, local authorities are having to care for the more severely disabled who would previously have been admitted to hospital, yet they do not have the staff or expertise to cope with them. These problems hit local authorities as soon as a mental handicap hospital closes its doors to new admissions, and they must take on the increased responsibility with neither the extra funding nor additional staff to enable them to do so.

*After care of patients*
When a detained patient leaves a mental hospital, a duty is imposed on the district health authority and social services department in co-operation with voluntary agencies to provide after care services until satisfied that these are no longer needed.[143] Further provisions intended to ensure that a co-ordinated health and social services assessment is made of the needs of a person who is to be discharged after receiving in-patient treatment for mental disorder for at least six months have not been brought into effect.[144]

## CARE PACKAGES

A mentally handicapped person (the client) relies upon a package of services and resources which changes in content throughout his life. This package is made up of formal and informal components, some of which cover special needs, and these may be designed to support the parents or carers and prevent the break-up of the family. The co-ordinator should be a social worker, but while social services may have statutory power, and in some cases a qualified duty, to provide or secure appropriate support, the individual components can seldom be obtained by the client as a legal right.

## Codes of Practice

Much will depend upon codes of practice, and the first of these is *Community Life: a Code of Practice for Community Care,*[145] though this deals with all persons who may need care, not just those with a mental handicap. The Code amplifies the White Paper in stating the purpose of Community Care as being:

> "to restore to and sustain in decent life those who, for whatever reason, require more than normal assistance to enjoy that right. It should not be forgotten that carers may often, in turn, be incapacitated in their everyday living by the onus of their commitment."

---

143  Mental Health Act 1983, s.117 (England); Mental Health (Scotland) Act 1984, s.8.
144  1986 Act, s.7. These provisions are unlikely to be implemented.
145  Published by Centre for Policy on Ageing of 25-31 Ironmonger Row, London EC1V 3QP (1990) and with a Foreword by Sir Roy Griffiths.

Partnership is the key, and it is pointed out that for the proper delivery of care, two levels of partnership are necessary:

  (i)  between the public, commercial and voluntary sectors, all of whom may be concerned in the provision of care;
  (ii) between the provider and the consumer.

Consumers (*i.e.* disabled people) should have as much choice and control as is compatible with the public interest, but carers should also have a say in what is provided because, although they share the role of providers, they are also users of services.

*Information*

Information is the lifeblood of consumerism, and the Code recommends that every effort be made to provide the public (*i.e.* disabled persons and their families, carers, care workers and agencies) with regularly updated and accurate information about services that are available and how to request them. Social services departments should encourage requests for assessment not only from those in need of care but also from carers, members of the public and professionals.

*A Care Charter*

The Code recommends that social services departments adopt a *Community Care Charter* and that representatives of consumers and carers participate in drafting this. It would provide that published information is in plain language, readily accessible and widely disseminated, and that there is a written agreement between provider and consumer. The provision of community care should be monitored on a regular basis, with participation by consumers and carers, and social services departments should prepare an annual report made available as part of the information service.

## Care management

Sound management is as important as the availability of adequate resources. Referrals to the department concerned, assessment of care needs, availability, provision and financing of services needed, and review and monitoring of those services are all fundamental. At all stages the views of the individual and family or informal carers should be ascertained and taken into account.

*Assessment*

Local authorities are responsible for assessing individual need and designing care arrangements, but there are no nationally agreed standards and these vary from one area to another. Although they must establish and make public their criteria of eligibility for assessment, they will also have to decide whether to assess in each particular case and to see if any other assessment already done can be used for community care purposes. The aim is to decide whether services should be provided and in what form, taking into account what is available and affordable. There are dangers in giving responsibility for assessment to the body that is responsible for funding, because this can lead to resource-led assessments, where the needs of the individual are determined according to what is (or is made) available.

The Code anticipates that assessment will be based upon an informal discussion with the person in need of care, of which a record will be retained and copies made available. In the case of persons with a mental handicap the family or other carers will be closely involved. There should be an emphasis on abilities and interests rather than merely problems, and a social profile should be built up of consumer and carers. The Code sets out a list of questions to be asked and emphasises that it is important to ask not only "Can you?", but also "Do you?" It is also necessary to assess the ability and willingness of carers to provide continuing care, and the level of support that they need in order to do so. Assessment should not be elaborate and bureaucratic and simplicity is the key, with regular re-assessment.

### Provision

If assessment is to be worthwhile there must be a choice of care services available and resources must be provided to meet the needs identified. It will be the responsibility of the social services department to design care arrangements in line with individual needs, in consultation with the consumer and other care professionals, *and within available resources*. This proviso, which does not appear in regard to education, is likely to result in resource-led provision.[146] Social services departments will have to establish priorities and a clear statement thereof should be available to the public. Provision may be in the form of services or environmental improvement, and the latter should never be overlooked especially in the case of physically disabled persons because it may be the least expensive option.[147]

### Agreements

Consumers need to know what to expect and what is expected of them, and a written agreement between provider and consumer would purport to identify rights and responsibilities on each side.[148] According to the Code this would:
- identify the parties and give information about them;
- detail the package of care agreed, and its duration;
- specify any costs involved;
- provide a date for re-assessment;
- outline a complaints procedure.

### Challenging inadequate provision

The following questions should be asked if problems are encountered in securing adequate care provision:

---

146  This is preferable to resource-led *assessments* because at least the shortfall in provision can be identified.

147  Adaptations to a house or provision of equipment may enable the individual to continue to be cared for at home without needing residential care.

148  In the case of people with a mental handicap it may be necessary for someone to enter into the agreement on their behalf, but written agreements are perhaps less likely to be favoured by providers in such case. An outline of an Agreement is included as an Appendix to the Code.

- Has an assessment of needs been made?
- If so, what is the result; if not, why not?
- What provision is being made to meet the assessed need?
- What provision is available to meet these needs?
- Can the needs be re-assessed?
- Why is any restriction or condition being imposed? Is it necessary? What purpose is it intended to fulfil, and can that purpose be fulfilled in some other way?

## Complaints procedures

There is no formal or independent appeal system, but complaints procedures must be introduced for clients who think they have been treated badly and the Code makes suggestions as to how these may operate. The Secretary of State may by order require authorities to establish a procedure for considering any representations or complaints which are made to them by a qualifying individual or anyone acting on his behalf, in relation to the discharge of, or any failure to discharge, any of their social services functions in respect of that individual.[149] A qualifying individual is one for whom the authority may provide a service and whose need has come to the attention of the authority.[150]

## Case conferences

A case conference attended by concerned people from different disciplines is a valued contribution towards solving problems and devising a well balanced package of care. It is now good practice to invite parents and/or the handicapped individual, and they should be encouraged to attend (perhaps with a friend) and express their views and ask for explanations of matters that they do not understand.[151] Notes or minutes of the conference should be circulated to those who attend with an opportunity to submit comments in writing if they do not accept them, and if this is not done, those attending should retain their own notes. It should be borne in mind that the more senior people present, whose views are likely to be more influential, may have the least personal knowledge and a care worker with close personal contact with the individual may be represented by a more senior official who will express views based upon secondhand information.

A case conference is required to act fairly when making a decision to enter a name on the child abuse register and if it acts unfairly or unreasonably the court may grant judicial review. An authority will have acted unfairly, unreasonably and in breach of natural justice if it fails to consider whether the complainant's accusations

---

149 Such an order has been made, and the related Directions include an appeal to an internal committee.

150 *England*: Local Authority Social Services Act 1970, s.7B as added by the 1990 Act, s.50. The Secretary of State may give directions as to procedure to be adopted and action to be taken, and is given default powers.*Scotland*: Social Work (Scotland) Act 1968, s.5B as added by the 1990 Act, s.52.

151 In the case of children, this is confirmed by the DoH guidance *Working Together under the Children Act 1989* .

might be a fantasy or fabrication, and decides on guilt after a brief and one-sided investigation without giving the accused person the opportunity of objecting.[152]

### Persons involved

*Case manager (or care manager)*
Clients assessed as being in need of care will usually be put in the charge of a social services case manager responsible for planning the package of care. Some may have their own limited budgets, but this confuses the roles of pressing for adequate care and rationing care provision. It is important to separate the roles of case manager and service provider so that the varying needs and wishes of clients may be taken into account. Ideally a three-way arrangements between manager, provider and client is required.

*Key-workers*
A professional involved in caring for the handicapped person, *e.g.* a care assistant or community nurse, may be treated as the key-worker and become a contact point for help and advice. The key-worker should have a working knowledge of state benefits and care services and take an active role in identifying what is needed after taking into account at a personal level the views and wishes of the handicapped person. There is potential for a keyworker to develop a close personal relationship with the individual whilst at the same time being a source of information and of access to the many services and agencies available.

*Authorised representative*
Statutory provisions intended to encourage the appointment by or on behalf of a disabled person of an authorised representative are now unlikely to be brought into effect.[153] These provisions only dealt with relationships with social services, but were expected to be extended to health services and other local authority services. They would for the first time have given a legal framework to the concept of advocacy, though they may not have ensured that the advocate was independent of the authority providing the services. The scheme provided that the disabled person, or local authority in the case of a person who appeared unable to do so, might appoint a representative who would have certain powers to speak on behalf of the disabled person. For a person under the age of 16 the appointment could be made by the parents or guardian.

The authorised representative was to be permitted to act as the representative of the disabled person at his or her request in connection with the provision by the local authority of social services and also to accompany the disabled person to any meeting or interview held by or on behalf of the authority in connection with the provision of such services. The authorised representative

---

152  *R.* v. *Norfolk County Council, ex p. M* [1989] 2 All ER 359.
153  1986 Act, ss.1, 2 and 3. Failure to implement these provisions has been criticised by organisations concerned with the welfare of disabled persons.

would also have a right of access to the disabled person at all reasonable times, and to the information that the disabled person was entitled to have including inspection of documents. In any assessment the representative would make representations as to the needs of the disabled person and following receipt of a written statement thereof could ask for a review. In Scotland, there is scope for tutors-dative with appropriate powers to exercise at least some of these roles.

### Community Mental Handicap Teams

These teams are being set up to provide specialist support of a multi-disciplinary nature, involving staff from both health and local authorities.

### District Handicap Teams

The Court Report (1976) recommended that local services for handicapped children could best be co-ordinated by the formation of District Handicap Teams which would have a core membership of a consultant community paediatrician, a nursing officer for handicapped children, a specialist social worker, a principal psychologist and a teacher. In practice membership varies from district to district, but the team investigates and assesses individual children and arranges and co-ordinates their treatment.

## Individual Programme Plans

Care plans should be prepared on an individual basis and seen as the basis for the planning and the eventual provision of services appropriate to the needs of the individual. The plan should be reviewed regularly, and at least once a year. As there is a tendency for authorities to develop plans on the basis of what is available (so that they can claim that they are providing appropriate care), it is essential to ensure that plans reflect what the individual needs even though concessions then need to be made according to what is available. Only then can the parents press for more provision when this is potentially available and will a true overall picture of the adequacy of the care being provided by the authority emerge.

### Policies

Much of the service provision depends upon policies which may be difficult to identify or interpret and are subject to constant change. Parents often comment that the emphasis is upon services that are being developed for tomorrow (if funds can be found) whereas their need is today. When seeking to identify good practice the response is often an indication of a new approach being developed rather than that which is presently applied. Carers and voluntary organisations should not have imposed upon them, without question, the views of good practice of the person in authority when there are variations throughout the country or between different disciplines or authorities.

The Code identifies various principles to be taken into account in assembling a care plan. The preferred solution should:

- favour environmental rather than service provision;

- reflect the informed choices and wishes of the consumer and carer;
- be publicly funded rather than personally charged;
- name one care worker for consumer liaison, and where there are several services being provided one person should have a co-ordinating role;
- favour domiciliary rather than day care services, though day facilities may be required as well.

## FUNDING

Adequate funding is essential if community care policies are to be more than an ideal, yet there do not appear to be any official calculations of the cost of implementation. Local authorities are expected to make the policies work without any guarantee that sufficient funding will be provided. We now identify the principle sources of revenue available to authorities for their community care budgets, administered by the social services departments.

### Sources

Resources for community care come from a variety of sources, but the four main sources are[154]:

(a) community charge (or council tax) raised locally;
(b) Revenue Support Grants paid from the Department of the Environment Vote, or in Scotland from the Exchequer (previously rate support grants);
(c) NHS funding, mainly from the Hospital and Community Health Services Budget[155];
(d) DSS Votes paid as social security benefits to disabled people.[156]

The following further types of funding should also be mentioned:

- sums earmarked by health authorities for development of specific community care projects following hospital closures (bridging finance or dowry payments for specific patients);
- joint finance allocations of district health authorities intended to pump-prime social services and voluntary sector activities;
- specific grants to local authorities from the DoH for particular community care initiatives;
- payments to voluntary organisations by the DoH for experimental projects and to help with central administration costs of national bodies.[157]

### Application

As regards local authority expenditure, a budget is determined for

---

154 Social Services Committee's 3rd Report, 1989/90 Session, *Community Care: Funding for Local Authorities*.

155 Paid from DoH Votes via district health authorities and family health service authorities.

156 See Chap.8, Part I.

157 In Scotland, similar funding from the Scottish Office. This type of funding may include Urban Aid or European Social Fund payments.

social services departments which in turn decide how to spend this. Other calls upon this budget include services for children which in England are likely to increase considerably as a result of the implementation of the Children Act 1989. The budget may include monies received from health authorities for the re-settlement of former hospital patients. NHS funding is spent, in addition to hospital services, on the community nursing services and family health services. Social security benefits are claimed mainly by the handicapped person rather than the carer, but taken into account by local authorities in assessing community care needs.

### The future

The new community care policies do not include any specific grants from the government for people with a mental handicap.[158] The only substantial change is to be the transfer to local authorities of that part of social security benefits which previously covered the care element, this being the excess of the Income Support residential care allowance over and above the normal board and lodging allowance. It will be added to the Revenue Support Grant. Transitional provisions preserve the entitlement of those already receiving support under the existing system, so for many years the two bases of funding may continue side by side, adding to the already over-complex funding arrangements.

## Ring-fencing

It was an essential part of the proposals in the Griffiths Report, supported by virtually every voluntary organisation, that monies made available by central government to local authorities for community care should be ring-fenced (*i.e.* should be paid direct to social services departments and not spent on anything else). The Government has decided not to accept this proposal and to leave it up to authorities how they allocate the funds that they receive. They are expected to exercise discretion in allocating such funds between services in the light of local needs and priorities, so there is no certainty that the money to be transferred from the DSS Votes will actually be used for community care.

## Adequacy

Apart from concerns about the absence of ring-fencing, there is no certainty that monies actually made available for community care will be adequate. There is no single community care budget, and future expenditure is likely to be larger as areas of unmet need are identified and costs are incurred in implementing the changes. Until April 1993 social services departments must prepare for the full implementation of community care without any additional resources. They will have to fight for their budgets along with

---

158 The Griffiths Report recommended a system of targetted specific grants but this was not accepted. There are grants for the social care of people with a mental illness and drug and alcohol misusers (starting from April 1991) but none for mental handicap.

other departments which may have higher priorities in the eyes of elected councillors (*e.g.* highways, the police), and financial pressures on local authorities generally will be reflected in the budget for community care. An injection of funds from central government is inevitable if local authorities are to avoid imposing an additional burden upon local chargepayers because authorities cannot be expected to absorb the extra cost. As an indication of the widespread concern about the adequacy of funding for community care, the Association of County Councils has stated to the Social Services Committee:

> "It is unlikely that the resources eventually identified by Government as the care element within the present income support allowances will begin to meet the additional cost of implementing the White Paper proposals."

### All Wales Strategy

The Strategy, implemented in 1983 for Wales and based upon eight multi-disciplinary County Planning Forums, has a commendable record of achievement in both fostering new services and identifying unmet needs. Each county forum consists of local authority, health authority and voluntary sector representatives, together with people with a learning disability and their parents. Funding from the Welsh Office is based upon local needs properly researched by these forums. The key to the success of the strategy has been the guarantee (ring fencing) of funding for the services identified. With the transfer of social security funding to the direct control of local authorities planned for 1993 it is feared that funding for these services may no longer be reliably available.

# PART IV - CONCLUSION

*Preliminary*
Persons with a mental handicap need services and support which will generally be provided or arranged by departments of their local authority. As a basic minimum this should consist of:
- individual assessment including the need for support services;
- assessed needs being met with a range of options in education, employment and recreation;
- a clear indication as to who has statutory responsibility for providing such services;
- an adequate procedure for joint consultation and planning between the three statutory services, the handicapped individual and the carers.

Although statutory responsibilities may be imposed to provide essential services, there is inadequate machinery to enforce such provision in individual cases and much depends upon funding which is frequently inadequate to meet identified needs. There is a serious risk of *resource-led* assessments as distinct from provision being influenced by available resources.[159] It is only if needs are correctly identified that the extent of unmet need in an area can be quantified, and then perhaps something can be done about this.

## Changing trends

The trend is towards community care, which involves enabling people with disabilities to live as normal a life as possible with a minimum of necessary interference, whilst minimising the disruption that they may cause to the rest of the community. Life in a small home in the community makes such people more visible and thus more vulnerable to abuse or exploitation, and the dangers are enhanced if resources are insufficient to meet the demands upon them and the necessary degree of support and supervision is not available. Other trends are:

increased mobility has contributed to the breakdown of the wider family living in the same vicinity so the burden placed on parents as primary carers has become heavier;

- fewer potential family carers because more married women are in employment;
- more mentally handicapped people outlive their parents;
- the increase in the pace and complexity of life makes it more difficult for the mentally disabled individual to cope;
- an increasing appreciation of the rights of disabled adults.

Mentally handicapped people should have a real choice between independent living and residential care, and the right to fully participate in their communities. Many already live in the community but are denied independent lives because support services are non-existent or not suitable to meet their needs.

### Recommendations

A group of voluntary organisations recommends in this context[160]:

- a statutory duty on social services and health authorities to co-operate in assessing and providing services;
- disabled people or their representatives must be consulted when their community care needs are assessed;
- statutory funding for residential care should be increased to meet the real costs;
- the funds available for community care should be ringfenced to ensure they are spent in this area and not elsewhere;
- the high costs of meeting the needs of people with mental handicap should be recognised and sufficient funds allocated for the specialist provision required;
- information should be provided through an advocate.

---

[159] Consumers may accept a situation where their needs are acknowledged but cannot be met for the time being because of financial constraints, but they cannot tolerate being told that they do not have a need when they know full well that they do.

[160] *An Agenda for the 1990's* published by the Disability Manifesto Group.

## Attitudes and education

Community care requires changed attitudes on the part of all concerned. It will only work if there is a true partnership between the social services (or social work) department responsible for co-ordinating a care package, those involved in providing the components (including informal carers, the private sector and voluntary organisations) and the consumer. There must also be acceptance by society of its new relationship with disabled people and responsibilities to them.

### Care staff and professionals

Training is needed to equip professionals and staff at all levels for their new responsibilities, not merely in regard to procedures but also the way they see consumers. Care staff accustomed to thinking for their patients must be taught to recognise them as individuals and to accept and encourage the concepts of personal choice, independence and advocacy. Those involved in provision must be flexible in their approach, and concentrate upon fulfilling the needs of consumers rather than administrative convenience, whilst making maximum use of available resources.

### Consumers

Consumers themselves need not be deterred from asking pertinent questions, and their advisers should assist them in doing so. Even though the individual appears to have few legal rights in many areas, there are hitherto unexplored opportunities for developing the role of the law, and the skills of the lawyer in identifying the questions to ask, and how and of whom to ask them, are of great value to those in need of care who may otherwise be overlooked.

### Society

The longer term problem is that members of the community need to change inherited attitudes, and to recognise their prejudices for what they are. Society cannot be trained in the same way as employed staff, and it may take a whole generation before mentally disabled people are treated with the respect that they deserve, so it is up to a reforming government to enact laws which are ahead of the prevailing views of society today.[161] We have seen this with legislation relating to discrimination on grounds of race and sex.

## LAW REFORM

Law reform in this area is a matter of public policy. With the notable exception of education the law has been largely restricted to an enabling and regulating role; the actual provision of care and facilities becomes a matter for administration controlled by political factors and resources and the individual has few rights, however severe the need. There are many aspects of care

---

161   This is not just a government responsibility; voluntary bodies and the media can do much to achieve improved attitudes.

provision which are best left to codes of conduct, but the disabled individual must have certain basic rights and should not be left at the mercy of administrators or dependent upon society's varying willingness to fund. General duties imposed upon authorities may satisfy society but are of little comfort to the individual whose needs are not provided for, and prove to be ineffectual when not backed up by adequate financial resources. Even where specific duties are imposed upon authorities they are not always complied with, usually because of funding pressures. The experience of lawyers is that any rights must be supported by adequate appeal procedures and remedies - without these they are rights in name only. This does not necessarily mean involving the courts, except when the legal procedures are not being complied with. In other areas of welfare provision (*e.g.* social security benefits) well respected procedures have been developed and the provision of care in the community should not be an exception to this.

The law ought not to concentrate merely upon additional areas where controls or restrictions should be imposed for the protection of vulnerable people. Consumers welcome safeguards against abuse or profiteering from the care business and to that extent such safeguards are necessary, but too many controls can stifle enterprise and render it too expensive or complicated to provide new facilities.[162] What is needed is full implementation of the Disabled Persons (Services Consultation and Representation) Act 1986, stronger requirements for co-operation between health authorities/boards and social services/work departments (including an obligation or incentive for the former to transfer resources into community care), and registration of day services. The emphasis should shift from restrictions to rights for disabled persons.

---

[162] There are many instances of small groups, often set up as local charities, being frustrated in their efforts to provide respite or full-time care by the need to comply with the unco-ordinated requirements of many officials each concerned with their own aspect.

# CHAPTER 6    EDUCATION, TRAINING AND EMPLOYMENT

## Introduction

In this chapter we consider first the provision of education and training for people with a mental handicap, increasingly in this context referred to as learning difficulties or disabilities. The law in England and Wales, and Scots law, are different and are dealt with separately.[1] Under the Education Act 1981, English education authorities are obliged to provide education for people with a handicap, if requested, up to the age of 19, and the obligation under the Education (Scotland) Act 1980 continues up to 18. Above those ages, although many authorities provide training centres or an equivalent, they are not obliged to provide places for particular people.[2] We then consider employment and some special schemes that have been introduced, although there are no laws to prevent direct or indirect discrimination against mentally or physically disabled people seeking employment.

### European Convention on Human Rights
Our education systems must abide by this Convention, and an individual whose rights have been denied may complain to the European Commission of Human Rights in Strasbourg, and thence to the Court if a settlement cannot be agreed.[3] Several of the Articles setting out fundamental human rights are capable of being breached in schools (*e.g.* use of corporal punishment), but Article 2 of Protocol 1 is the most significant regarding mental handicap:

> "No person shall be denied the right to education. In the exercise of any functions which it assumes in relation to education and to teaching, the State shall respect the right of parents to ensure such education and teaching in accordance with their own religious and philosophical convictions."

### UN Convention on the Rights of the Child
A disabled child has the right to special care, education and training to help him enjoy a full and decent life in conditions which ensure dignity, promote self-reliance and facilitate active participation in the community. This is subject to available resources, but assistance given to the child and to carers should be appropriate to the child's condition and the circumstances of the carers. Preparation for employment and recreation opportunities is specifically mentioned.[4]

---

1    The legal framework of education law in Northern Ireland is also different but is not dealt with here.

2    In Scotland, local authorities have a duty to ensure provision of suitable training and occupation for people with a mental handicap who are over school age and not in hospital.

3    This is considered in Chap.3, Part III.

4    Article 23, ratified by the UK Government on December 16, 1991.

# PART IA - EDUCATION AND TRAINING (England)

We consider here the rights of a child with learning difficulties to a suitable education and the special provisions that apply.[5] There has been substantial reforming legislation during the past decade.

## BACKGROUND

### Definitions

*Child* is used here to refer both to an infant and a young person. *Parent* in this context includes a guardian and the person with whom the child lives, either temporarily or permanently.[6] Thus in addition to the biological parents, those living with the child share the rights and duties which parents have in education law. When a child is in care, the biological parents may lose some or all of their rights (depending whether it is voluntary care or not), and the care authority acts as parent; thus foster parents, or the key worker in a children's home, should also be treated as parents for the purpose of the child's education.

### Secretary of State

References to the Secretary of State in this Part mean, in England, the Secretary of State for Education and Science[7] and in Wales the Secretary of State for Wales.[8]

### Legislation

#### Education Act 1944

This Act provides the foundations for the modern system of education. Compulsory education now ceases at 16, but all young people have the right to full-time education between the age of five and their 19th birthday if they ask for it before leaving school. Local education authorities must ensure that in their area there are sufficient schools to provide "full-time education suitable to the requirements of both junior and senior pupils", which means that they are sufficient in number, character and equipment to afford all pupils opportunities for education offering such variety of instruction and training as may be desirable in view of their different ages, abilities and aptitudes, including practical instruction and training appropriate to their respective needs.[9]

---

5　Further information may be obtained from the Advisory Centre for Education which publishes a series of ACE booklets, and The Children's Legal Centre which publishes an Education Rights Handbook (addresses in Appendix 1).

6　Education Act 1944, s.114(1) as amended by Education Act 1981.

7　Department of Education and Science, Elizabeth House, York Road, London SE1 7PH. Booklets may be obtained from Publications Despatch Centre, Honeypot Lane, Stanmore, Middlesex HA7 1AZ, 081-952-2366.

8　Welsh Office, Cathays Park, Cardiff CF1 3NQ.

9　1944 Act, s.8; Education (Miscellaneous Provisions) Act 1948, s.3. A senior pupil is defined as a person "who has attained the age of 12 years, but has not attained the age of 19 years" - s.114.

Authorities should have particular regard to:

> "the need for securing that provision is made for pupils who suffer from any disability of mind or body by providing, either in special schools or otherwise, special educational treatment, that is to say education by special methods appropriate for persons suffering from that disability"

and must keep arrangements for children with special educational needs under review.[10] Although considerable changes have since been made these principles still form the basis of the duties of education authorities.

*Education (Handicapped Children) Act 1970*
Prior to April 1971 children with severe mental handicaps were considered unsuitable for education at schools and excluded from the education system.[11] Instead they attended Junior Training Centres run by local authority health departments and no teaching qualifications were required for those employed in these centres. This Act required all children to be included in the education system and the centres were replaced by special schools for which education authorities were responsible. Children were classified into one of the categories of handicap defined by the Secretary of State, which included "educationally sub-normal" (ESN).[12]

*Warnock Report*
It was then enacted that special education should be provided in ordinary schools except where this was "incompatible with efficient instruction in the schools or involved unreasonable expenditure".[13] This was followed by the Warnock Report[14] which identified the wider need of one in every five children to some form of special educational provision at some time in their school career, and recommended that classification should be abandoned in favour of the identification of *special educational needs* which should be met by appropriate provision. The term "children with learning difficulties" was thought more appropriate for those with a mental handicap, who should (subject to exceptions) be educated alongside other children in ordinary schools. A White Paper followed.[15]

*Education Act 1981*
This Act makes provision with respect to children with special educational needs. It creates a framework under which they should, subject to certain conditions being satisfied, be educated in ordinary schools and special educational provision is usually left to the school which the child attends. For a small number (including

---

10   1944 Act, s.8(1) and (2);   Education Act 1981, s.2(4).
11   1944 Act, s.57.
12   Two sub-categories emerged: moderate - ESN(M),  and severe - ESN(S).
13   Education Act 1976. This provision was never implemented.
14   *Report of the Committee of Enquiry into the Education of Handicapped Children and Young People* (Warnock, 1978) Cmnd. 7212, HMSO.
15   *Special Educational Needs* (1980), Department of Education and Science, Cmnd. 7996, HMSO.

most children generally regarded as mentally handicapped)[16] the education authority must determine by a set procedure the special educational provision to be made.

## Education (No. 2) Act 1986

This Act defines new responsibilities for school governing bodies, extending their role and prescribing their composition. Many new opportunities arise for parent participation.

## Education Reform Act 1988

This substantial legislation[17] restructures the education service yet relies substantially upon the foundations laid down in 1944 and makes very few changes to the Education Acts of 1944 to 1986. It creates new rules about the admission of pupils to schools which limit the power of the education authority to restrict the operation of parental choice, and introduces a National Curriculum. There are also changes which relate to children who have disabilities.

## Children Act 1989

This Act, which makes fundamental changes to child law, affects educational provision in three areas: the relationship between local authorities and local education authorities, the securing of a child's attendance at school, and the safeguarding of the welfare of children in independent schools.

## The National Curriculum

All state schools must provide a balanced and broadly based curriculum which promotes the spiritual, moral, cultural, mental and physical development and prepares pupils for opportunities, responsibilities and experiences of adult life. There are three *core* subjects (English, mathematics and science), and seven *foundation* subjects (technology, history, a modern language, geography, art, music, and physical education). The curriculum applies to children aged 5 to 16 and specifies attainment targets, programmes of study and arrangements for assessing pupils. Each pupil has a legal right to such a curriculum which is also relevant to his personal needs, and all children should follow the curriculum to the maximum extent possible. It is intended to provide wide scope for teachers to deal with the full range of an individual pupil's needs. Information about pupils' programmes and their attainments as individuals and collectively must be made available to parents and others, and arrangements established for the consideration of complaints.

## Modification

The curriculum may be modified or excluded on a general basis where certain groups of children would find it inappropriate.[18] Also in respect of individual children:

(i) the headteacher may modify or disapply the curriculum for

---

16    Estimated at 2 per cent., part of the "1 in 5" identified in the Warnock Report.

17    The Act has 284 sections, some very complex, and 13 Schedules.

18    The Secretary of State may make regulations to this effect; 1988 Act, s.17.

a short period or periods in respect of pupils for whom it is temporarily inappropriate[19];

(ii) the education authority may modify or exclude the curriculum in respect of a particular child in a Statement of special educational needs.[20]

Any modification or exclusion must deal not only with the core and foundation subjects, but also the attainment targets and programmes of study, although the assessment procedures will still be of benefit to the child with learning difficulties.

*Assessment*

The curriculum has a built-in method of assessing progress which should include specifications of goals for change and of a child's requirements. It should state what services are required and take into account the wishes and perceptions of the parent and child. The annual review should examine how any extra help provided has helped the child make progress, and if there is not sufficient progress, what changes, if any, are needed. The views of parents are important, and they have the right to be kept informed at all times in clear and concise terms, and to appeal to the school governing body or to a local committee if all the negotiation fails.

*Implications for mental handicap*

MENCAP considers that the curriculum should be applicable to all children, whatever their degree of learning difficulty, and that each subject syllabus needs to be extended to include pupils with learning difficulties. There should be no reason to exclude any child from every aspect of the curriculum, but care should be taken to ensure that children's learning needs which are outside the curriculum can be met.

## Parent's Charter

The Department of Education and Science has published a Parent's Charter which purports to give new rights to individual parents and to give them new responsibilities and choices. The general booklet is entitled *You and your child's education* but there is a separate booklet *Children with special needs*. These helpful publications should not be relied on solely, because they do not give any new rights and merely draw attention to some (but not all) of the statutory rights described below. In some respects (*e.g.* moving to another area) the information is misleading and in others (*e.g.* reference to the Ombudsman) it is incomplete.

---

[19]  s.19. If the child does not have a Statement and is experiencing difficulty with the curriculum, it can be suspended for up to six months whilst assessment and statementing take place.

[20]  This will usually be appropriate in the case of a mentally handicapped child. The assessment procedures are dealt with below.

## SPECIAL EDUCATION

### Special educational needs (SEN)

A child has *special educational needs* if he has a learning difficulty which requires special educational provision to be made for him.[21] A child with a *learning difficulty* is one who:
   (a) has a significantly greater difficulty in learning than the majority of children of that age;   or
   (b) has a disability which either prevents or hinders him from making use of educational facilities of a kind generally provided in schools, within the area of the local authority concerned, for children of that age;   or
   (c) is under the age of five and is, or would be if special educational provision were not made, likely to fall within either of the above cases when over five.[22]

*Identifying*

Every local educational authority has a duty to exercise its powers with a view to securing that, of the children for whom it is responsible, those with SEN which require the authority to determine the special educational provision which should be made for them are identified by the authority.[23] The extent to which a learning difficulty hinders a child's development depends not only upon its nature and severity but also upon the other abilities of the child and the help available at home and school.[24] The deciding factor is whether the child has severe learning difficulties which require the provision of extra resources in ordinary schools, and a formal assessment will always be appropriate where the child is in a special school or a special unit attached to an ordinary school. It should also be initiated where there are prima facie grounds to suggest that a child's needs are such as to require educational provision additional to, or otherwise different from, that made generally in local maintained schools.

*Responsibility*

An authority is responsible for a child in its area who either:
   (a) is registered at a school maintained by it;   or
   (b) has been brought to its attention as having, or probably having, SEN and is registered at a school (otherwise than as above) or not so registered but between age two and compulsory school age.[25]

### Special educational provision (SEP)

In relation to a child who has attained the age of two, *special*

21   1981 Act, s.1(1).
22   s.1(2).
23   s.4(1).
24   DES Circular 1/83.
25   s.4(1) and (2). This does not include a child above school leaving age who is no longer a registered pupil (*i.e.* has left school).

*educational provision* means "educational provision which is additional to, or otherwise different from, the educational provision made for children of [the child's] age in schools maintained by that local educational authority".[26] Care must be taken to avoid the ambiguity of this definition. If only a limited assessment is carried out, a difficulty in a major skill such as reading may be identified, but as tuition in reading is generally available in schools this would not be a special provision so the child would not be assessed as having SEN. In reality the child may have a more general problem in learning which exhibits itself most conspicuously in reading, and it is that learning problem that requires special provision.

### Duties

Governors must use their best endeavours to secure that SEP is made for any registered child requiring it, and must ensure that where the headteacher has been informed by the education authority that a child has SEN, these are made known to all who are likely to teach the child and they are aware of the importance of identifying and providing for those needs.[27] There is a statutory obligation to make SEP but this only arises where there are SEN which means that the child must have learning difficulty within the meaning of the above definition. Such a child must be educated in an ordinary school if account has been taken of the views of the parent and this is compatible with receiving the SEP required, the provision of efficient education for the other children in the school and the efficient use of resources. The child must engage in the activities of the school together with children who do not have SEN so long as this is reasonably practicable.[28]

### Information

Education authorities have to publish information about their policy and arrangements for education of children with SEN, and about maintained schools including special schools.[29]

### Speech therapy

It has been held that speech therapy can constitute a SEP which must in appropriate cases be provided by the authority[30]:

> A mother complained about the small amount of speech therapy being received by her son, and the education authority tried unsuccessfully to persuade the health authority to provide the level necessary to meet his needs. She applied for judicial review of the appeal committee's decision that

---

26    s.1(3)(*a*). Under that age it means educational provision of any kind.

27    s.2(5). This duty to use best endeavours applies to the wider class of pupils whose needs do not require formal assessment, and is not restricted to those who have been assessed as needing a statement.

28    1981 Act, s.2. The authority is constrained by its duty to make provision in an ordinary school where possible, see *R.* v. *Surrey C.C. ex p. H.* (1985) 83 LGR 219, CA *per* Slade LJ at p.235.

29    Education (School Information) Regulations 1981, as amended by Education (School Information)(Amendment) Regulations 1983.

30    *R.* v. *Lancashire County Council, ex p. CM* , *The Times*, March 27, 1989.

speech therapy was not SEP. The Divisional Court held that: (i) speech therapy could be SEP; (ii) the education authority had to consider on a case by case basis whether a need for speech therapy was an educational or non-educational need; (iii) once it had been decided that a child's need was educational the authority was under a duty to make appropriate provision. This was upheld by the Court of Appeal which considered that speech therapy stood between medicine and education. At one end of the scale it could be akin to teaching, for example, to teach a child who had never been able to communicate by language - due to either a chromosomal disorder or social causes - was just as much educational provision as teaching a child to communicate through writing. At the other end of the scale was treatment for an adult who had lost his larynx due to cancer. This child had SEN and speech therapy was part of the SEP which he needed to enable him to be fully understood by others. A local education authority could employ speech therapists itself, or elicit help from the district health authority or private sector. The fact that the authority did not employ speech therapists did not mean that speech therapy was not SEP. The council's duty was to arrange that SEP was made for the child even though the people who were to supply it were not in its direct employ.

This has removed much uncertainty over the responsibilities of education authorities towards children with learning difficulties who need speech therapy, because among such children it will usually be a SEN requiring SEP, but it does not automatically follow that speech problems by themselves amount to a learning difficulty such that the child has SEN.

A speech therapist is a person with specialist knowledge of how we communicate with one another, and what goes wrong if difficulties are experienced. The therapist works closely with teachers, GPs, medical officers, psychologists, occupational and physio-therapists, social workers, health visitors and families. Help may be given with difficulties in the following areas: pre-verbal skills, understanding language, developing and using speech sounds, voice disorders, stammers, alternative means of communication, listening and attention skills.

## Assessment

Where, in the case of a child for whom the local education authority is responsible, the authority is of the opinion that the child has, or probably has, SEN which require the authority to determine the SEP that should be made the authority must make an assessment of the educational needs.[31] In the case of a child under two the assessment may only be made with the consent of the parents and must be made if they so request.[32] Failing the above, an assessment is required if the authority considers that the child needs exemption from the National Curriculum.[33]

### Parent's request

If the parent of a child over two for whom a local education

---

31   1981 Act, s.5(1). The child will probably have been identified by monitoring at school.

32   s.6(1). For a child under two years the assessment may be made in any manner the authority considers appropriate; the procedures outlined below do not apply.

33   1988 Act, s.18.

authority is responsible, but for whom no Statement is maintained, asks the authority to assess the child's SEN, the authority must comply with the request unless it considers it unreasonable.[34] If the parent of a child for whom an authority maintains a Statement asks the authority to re-assess the child's educational needs and such assessment has not been made within six months prior to the request, the authority must comply unless satisfied that this would be inappropriate.[35]

### Health Authority request

If an area or district health authority, in the course of exercising any of its functions in relation to a child under the age of five, forms the opinion that the child has, or probably has, SEN the authority must inform the parent of its opinion and of its duty in relation to the child and, after giving the parent the opportunity to discuss that opinion with the authority's officer, must bring it to the attention of the appropriate local education authority.[36]

### Refusal to assess

No appeal is provided for against a refusal by an education authority to assess a child following a parent's request, though the only issue would be whether the request was unreasonable. Faced with an outright refusal (or delay in proceeding with the assessment) the main remedy for the parents is an application to the High Court for judicial review. Legal Aid is available to the child for this, so the financial circumstances of the parent will not be taken into account.

### Procedure

The procedure is governed by a Circular which sets out in an Annex a checklist to be followed in every assessment.[37] It is suggested that to enable the child's needs to be determined and documented the vital question to be asked is: "How does this child learn at present?" Learning itself is a learned skill, and the aim should be to teach the child in the way that he can actually learn so as to develop competence in learning.[38] The authority must decide in its discretion whether the child's needs call for determination and a Statement or whether they may be met in some other way.

---

34　1981 Act, s.9(1). DES Circular 22/89: *Assessments and Statements of Special Educational Needs*, para.33. The authority will normally be bound to assess. Unreasonable means "conduct which no sensible authority acting with due appreciation of its responsibility would have decided to adopt", *Secretary of State for Education and Science* v. *Metropolitan Borough of Thameside* [1976] 3 All ER 665, HL.

35　s.9(2). Inappropriate has not been judicially defined in this context, but if a change of circumstances can be shown it must be appropriate to re-assess.

36　s.10(1) and (2). The health authority must also inform the parents of any voluntary organisations which may be able to help.

37　DES Circular 22/89 *Assessments and Statements of Special Educational Needs: Procedures within the Education, Health and Social Services*.

38　These ideas are amplified in *Children with Special Needs. Assessment, Law and Practice - Caught in the Act* ; details in Appendix II.

Some needs may be met through provision determined by the school, such as remedial teaching. If the authority proposes to make an assessment it must notify the parent of this.[39] The notice must state the procedure to be followed, the officer from whom further information may be obtained and the right to make representations. A parent cannot object to the carrying out of an assessment, but may submit written evidence to the authority within the period specified in the notice.[40] The service of the notice should never be the first indication to the parent that the child has learning difficulties, and efforts should be made by the authority to effect contacts between the teachers, any other professional involved and the parent.

The parent should be given the name of an officer from whom further information is available, and be notified in straightforward language of the right to make representations within a minimum period of 29 days after the date of notification. When notifying parents of this right, authorities should encourage representations, pointing out the importance of their contributions, and may invite them to indicate formally if they do not wish to make or add to representations, in which case they should be told that the authority understands that the right is not to be exercised and assessment can proceed without delay. Where parents do wish to make representations, they may need help in doing so, and where these are made orally to the named officer a written summary should be agreed with the parent. Alternatively, the authority may suggest to the parent the name of a voluntary organisation or educational welfare officer who could help.

Wherever possible, assessments should take place in surroundings familiar to the child, either at home or at school. A supported mainstream placement may be appropriate for assessment, and in exceptional circumstances the use of a special school placement for assessment purposes may, if parents agree, be appropriate, but children should not remain for long periods in such placements and their progress should be monitored. When the period for representations has expired, the authority may decide to determine the educational needs of the child in which event it must notify the parents and give reasons for the decision. If it decides not to do so it must notify the parents in writing.[41]

*Examination*

An examination of the child will form part of the assessment. The

---

[39]  s.5(5). DES Circular 22/89 advises that any guardian, person with whom the child is living, or local authority (where the child is in care) should be notified. Copies of the notice must be sent to the local social services department and the district health authority - Education (Special Educational Needs) Regulations 1983, reg.3.

[40]  s.5(3). DES Circular 22/89 states: "The parental contribution, based on informal, intimate and detailed knowledge of the child's personal characteristics and needs forms an important and essential complement to the professional advice".

[41]  s.5(6) and(7).

authority may serve a notice on the parents requiring the child's attendance for examination and this must state the purpose, time and place of the examination, the officer from whom further information can be obtained, and the parent's right to submit information and be present at the examination.[42] It is an offence for a parent without reasonable cause to fail to comply with this notice if the child is of compulsory school age.

*Delay*

Draft assessments should be available for production to the parents within six months of the commencement of the procedure, but differences of opinion between parents, schools and education authorities about the severity of a child's needs and how those may be met has resulted in a large number of disputed cases and delay in completing assessments. There are also cases where authorities have delayed assessments because of a reluctance to fund the special provision that these would reveal.[43]

*Decision*

If after making an assessment, or before this is completed, the authority decides not to determine SEP for the child, it must inform the parents of this and of their right to appeal to the Secretary of State who may direct the authority to reconsider.[44] Otherwise the statementing procedure applies.

**Representations and advice**

When making an assessment, the authority should take into account any representations made or evidence presented in response to its previous notice, and any information relating to the health or welfare of the child provided by any district health authority or social services department. It must also seek and take into consideration educational, medical and psychological advice about the child as well as any other advice which it considers desirable, and this advice must be presented in writing.[45] The advice should relate to:

(a) the educational, medical, psychological or other features of the case which appear to be relevant to the child's present and future educational needs;

(b) how those features affect those needs; and

---

42   1981 Act, Sched.1. Parents should be made aware that some forms of psychological testing might best be carried out without others being present, although they may insist on attending.

43   This may arise where a 16-year old should be considered for residential schooling, and if the assessment is delayed long enough it may become too late for this need to be satisfied.

44   s.5(6),(7) and (8). This does not mean that the child receives no specialist teaching, but simply means that the responsibility is placed upon the school to make arrangements to satisfy the child's needs.

45   Education (Special Educational Needs) Regulations 1983, S.I. 1983 No.29 as amended by S.I. 1988 No.1067. See Regs. 4-8. The wider the advice, the more likely it is to provide an accurate picture of the child's abilities and learning difficulties and the more appropriate the provision will be.

(c) the special education or other provision rendered necessary by those features if the child is to benefit properly from the education.

Advice must be written advice on the features of the case which are relevant to and affect the child's SEN and on the ways of meeting those needs. The authority must provide all professionals with copies of any representations or evidence submitted by or on behalf of the child's parent, including any written summary of oral representations. It falls to the professional advisers to consult others, including any persons specified by the authority, and to collect and collate any relevant information obtained from their area of responsibility and to submit it to the authority. There is no prescribed form in which advice should be presented. Some authorities have already provided checklists or profiles for parents to use to help them contribute to assessments, and these can be helpful although they should not restrict parents from giving evidence in some other form.

*Educational advice*

Advice should normally be obtained from the headteacher of any school which the child has attended during the previous 18 months and the teacher who has actually taught the child should be consulted. Failing this, a person with experience of teaching such children should be consulted. Evidence from assessments made under the National Curriculum arrangements may be relevant.

*Medical advice*

Advice must be obtained from a registered medical practitioner who is either designated for the purpose or nominated for the child. This will usually be the school doctor, but he should co-ordinate advice from all other doctors involved and indicate who they are in his report. There is no reason why the parent should not supplement this advice by obtaining and submitting a report from the family's general medical practitioner who will have experience of the child in the home environment. If the child has been referred to a consultant a report may be produced from that source, though this may only be necessary if the parent disagrees with the outcome of the assessment. Medical advice should be concise and relevant to the child's educational needs, but in some cases District Health Authorities will be involved so as to strengthen the multi-disciplinary approach.

*Psychological advice*

This advice will usually be the most important and will be sought from a person regularly employed or engaged by the education authority as an educational psychologist, who should consult any other psychologist known to have some knowledge of the child. Parents who do not accept the advice tendered will usually need to employ their own independent expert in this field.

*Social Services*

A copy of the notification to the parent should be sent to an officer nominated for this purpose by the social services department so that they may consider whether they know of any problems affecting the child and indicate whether they have information relevant to the assessment. Any advice furnished will be included in an Appendix to the Statement. The authority may also seek advice from this source where it has not been volunteered.

*Co-operation*
Professional advisers may submit their evidence separately, copying their advice to others involved, and it may be desirable for this to proceed in sequence, educational advice being followed by medical advice and then by psychological advice, but this is not obligatory. In some cases a case conference may help professional advisers identify the child's needs, and various groupings of professionals may take place. Although parents have no legal right to attend, their trust and cooperation is more likely to be maintained if they are invited to take part, with a friend or adviser. Where consolidated advice is provided in consequence, the contributions of individuals must be identifiable and any reservations must be recorded. Advice should not be influenced by consideration of the eventual school placement for the child, but discussions about the child's needs should cover the various options without pre-empting the decision about the provision and placement to be made.

The ultimate responsibility for formulating an assessment of the child's SEN rests with the education authority which must coordinate and summarise the advice, evidence, representations and information received about the child. Where there is conflict in the advice, or where it is clear that further consideration is required, the authority should arrange further discussions, and where it proves impossible to reconcile differences the authority must determine the SEP and clearly set out the reasons for the decision in the draft Statement.

## Statements

Where an assessment has been made in respect of a child aged two or older, the local education authority responsible for the child must, if it is of the opinion that it should determine the SEP which should be made, make and maintain a Statement of SEN for the child.[46] This can include a modification or exclusion of the National Curriculum in the child's particular case.[47]

*Contents*
The Statement must be in the prescribed form and contain the prescribed information.[48] It includes:
    (a) details of the child and the parent or guardian (*Section I*);

---

[46] The authority may decide whether and in what manner to maintain a Statement for a child under two; the statutory provisions do not apply.

[47] 1988 Act, s.18.

[48] 1981 Act, Sched.1, Part II, para.3. The form is specified in a Schedule to the Education (Special Educational Needs) Regulations 1983.

(b)  the SEN as assessed - *Section II*;
(c)  the SEP which the authority considers appropriate to meet these needs - *Section III*[49];
(c)  the type of school (or any other arrangements), naming any particular school which the authority considers appropriate for the child - *Section IV*[50];
(d)  details of any additional non-educational provision which is considered advantageous to the child and which is to be made available by the education authority or some other body - *Section V*.[51]

The educational, medical, psychological and other advice, and parental evidence, on which the decision was based will be set out in Appendices.[52] Where the advice of the professional advisers is in accord and the authority adopt this as their assessment, this should be stated in Section II, but if there is any doubt or conflicting advice the authority should state its decision about SEN, and the reasons for it. The child's needs must be analysed carefully and in detail, and the provision must be specified in detail.[53] The provision must deal fully with the needs and deal with the child as an individual.[54]

*Procedure*
Before making a Statement the authority must serve on the parents a copy in draft form with a written explanation of the provisions that apply if they do not accept it. A parent may within 15 days make representations about the content of the Statement or require a meeting with an officer of the authority to discuss the draft. Further meetings may be requested and the authority must arrange such meetings as it considers will enable the parent to discuss the

---

49   This must be specified in terms of facilities and equipment, staffing arrangements, curriculum or otherwise; Education (Special Educational Needs) Regulations 1983, reg.10. It should take into account the needs expressed in Section II and provide a programme to meet these needs. Any modification to the National Curriculum should also be specified.

50   Authorities will wish to observe the parents' choice of school where they can, but are not obliged to do so and the Statement will determine the issue. If it is considered that education should be provided other than at school particulars must be given.

51   This is provision that must be made if the child is to benefit from the SEP specified in the Statement. It is not legally enforceable, but not to provide it would frustrate the educational provision so there are strong arguments that it should be provided. The 1988 Act amends s.7 of the 1981 Act to give education authorities a discretion to fund non-educational provision.

52   Education (Special Educational Needs) Regulations 1983, reg.10(1)(*d*). These should be complete and if anything material (*e.g.* representations made by the parents) has been omitted the parents may reject the Statement and ask for a new one. In default the remedy may be judicial review.

53   Circular 22/89, paras.18, 60 and 61. Vague guidelines are not sufficient.

54   *R. v. Secretary of State for Education, ex p. E, The Times*, January 17, 1991. The child was assessed as having difficulty with numeracy skills but the Statement failed to make any SEP for this. Nolan J. held that if the need was serious enough to be included in the Statement it must qualify for provision. Part III had to deal fully with Part II.

relevant advice with the appropriate persons.[55] Parents should take advantage of every opportunity to negotiate, and before agreeing the final document should make sure it complies with the statutory requirements, clearly spells out what their child's difficulties are and meets the child's needs.

Many disputes between parents and education authorities are resolved at these meetings, which give the parents an opportunity to justify their view by explaining the problems of the child, the family and the home. The presence of an educational psychologist or lawyer on behalf of the parents can assist especially where there are severe problems which may justify the child being sent to a specialist school.

### Completion

After considering any representations made, the authority may make a Statement in the form originally proposed, or in a modified form, or determine not to make a Statement. The parents must be notified of the decision. Where a Statement is made a copy signed by a duly authorised officer of the education authority must be served on the parents with notice of the right to appeal, and of the name of the person who can give information and advice about the child's SEN.[56]

### Confidentiality

Statements are confidential and should not be disclosed without the parent's consent except where the authority considers this to be in the child's educational interests and some other circumstances.[57] This extends to all documents included in the Appendices.

### Interpretation

Education authorities have exercised considerable discretion when deciding whether a child's needs are sufficiently great to justify maintaining a Statement. This is illustrated by a recent case[58]:

> Parents requested an assessment of a girl who had been accepted to be a slow learner with SEN but the authority considered that her needs could be met in an ordinary school and that no Statement was necessary. The Secretary of State declined to intervene on the parents' behalf and on appeal against an unsuccessful judicial review application the Court of Appeal held that the authority was entitled to come to such a decision. A distinction was drawn between a child who has SEN, and one whose SEN are such that the authority considers that it should determine the SEP that should be made for the child.

There has been a wide diversity of policies on statementing, and in

---

55    1981 Act, s.7(3)-(6). This means the person who gave the relevant advice or any other person who may be appropriate.

56    s.7(8) and (9). Sched.1, para.6(4) deals with amendments to Statements.

57    Reg.11. This includes for appeal, educational research, under a court order, for criminal proceedings or for a maladministration investigation, but has since been extended to permit disclosure to the child's social services department, S.I. 1988 No.1067.

58    R. v. Secretary of State for Education and Science, ex p. Lashford [1988] 1 F.L.R. 72.

consequence a Circular[59] emphasises that authorities would be expected to statement all children with severe or complex learning difficulties which require special provision, over and above that normally provided in ordinary schools, or where placement in a special school for all or most of the time is considered necessary. A Statement would not generally be necessary in other cases. The discretion has now been virtually eliminated in the case of a child with severe learning difficulties following the introduction of the National Curriculum, as this will need to be modified in respect of the child and that can only be done, other than for a short period of time, by a Statement. If the child is to be sent to a special school, a Statement will certainly be required.

*Re-assessment*

Parents can request a re-assessment at any time if there has been a significant change of circumstances, and headteachers may also institute a re-assessment.[60] This may result from an annual review. The child must be re-assessed between ages 13 years and six months and 14 years and six months unless he has been assessed since age 12 years and six months.[61] This provides the opportunity for the child, and all concerned with his future, to consider the arrangements to be made for the remainder of the child's time at school and for preparation for transition to adult life; and to determine the nature of further education, vocational training, employment or other arrangements to be made.

*Review*

Just as assessment of a child's progress is continuous, Statements must be reviewed at least once a year by the authority to ensure that the provision is appropriate to the child's needs.[62] Unlike a re-assessment, a review does not require the authority to follow the procedure outlined above. Reviews are normally based on reports from the child's school, including the views of teachers and other professionals involved, and the National Curriculum assessments, but the views of parents and the child should be taken into account and attendance at review meetings encouraged. The aim is to check whether the provision being made is meeting the stated aims and objectives for the child and whether the school placement remains appropriate.[63] Any amendments should be notified to parents.

*Amendment*

An amendment is a change to the Statement which can be made

---

59 Circular 22/89 (replacing Circular 1/83). The difficulty only needs to be severe or complex, not both.

60 *I.e.* under Education Reform Act 1988, s.19 if he or she considers it essential to modify or disapply the National Curriculum while a reassessment is carried out - see DES Circular 15/89 *Temporary Exceptions from the National Curriculum.*

61 Education (Special Educational Needs) Regulations 1983, reg.9.

62 1981 Act, Sched.1, Part II, para.5.

63 For those in special schools the option of a supported mainstream placement should be considered.

without re-assessment. If an authority proposes to amend or cease to maintain a Statement, it must give notice in writing to the parent who may within 15 days make representations and there is a right of appeal after the decision has been notified.[64] If the authority is in effect making a re-assessment it must do so fully.

*Transfers*

Irrespective of review or reassessment, authorities and schools should be sensitive to the changing needs or circumstances of pupils, and allow for the possibility of transfers between schools to meet such changes. If a child moves to the area of a different authority the Statement is to be transferred and must be complied with although the new authority may cause a full re-assessment to be made.[65] If it is not transferred the old authority remains under an obligation to make the provision until replaced since the Statement and not the residence places the obligation.

## Appeals

There are several means whereby decisions of the authority during the assessment and statementing process may be challenged, but disputes should be resolved informally at local level if possible.

*Appeal Committee*

Every local education authority must make arrangements for appeals by parents to an independent Appeal Committee.[66] The Committee should consist of three, five or seven persons and include at least one member with relevant knowledge who could be a parent (but seldom is), and authority members should not exceed others by more than one. Any reports presented to the Committee must also be made available to the child's parent who may seek disclosure of documents, and any further evidence provided by the parent must also be made available to the authority who should ensure that it is passed to the Committee.

Appeals may be against the SEP proposed in Statements following a first or any subsequent assessment of their child, or against any amendment to a Statement.[67] The Committee may confirm the Statement or refer it back for reconsideration in the light of its observations, and must give proper reasons for its decision.[68] The

---

64    Sched.1, Part II, para.6. The right of appeal where a Statement has been amended was not explicit but has been confirmed by 1988 Act, Sched.12, para.85.

65    Reg.12 of 1983 Regulations as amended by Education (Special Educational Needs) (Amendment) Regulations 1988.

66    Constituted under 1980 Act, Sched.2, para.1. Part II thereof (as modified) deals with procedure. Committees should be convened and conducted in accordance with a *Code of Practice on Appeals* prepared by the Council on Tribunals and the Local Authority Associations.

67    1981 Act, s.8 as amended by 1988 Act, Sched.12, para.84. The appeal is always against SEP, but if the SEN are not properly identified the provision is unlikely to be adequate.

68    *R.* v. *Surrey C.C., ex p. H., supra, per* Waller LJ at p.221. The Committee is subject to the jurisdiction of the Council on Tribunals.

time limit for appeal is in the discretion of the education authority, and although normally stated to be 14 days it could be extended for good reason. Copies of all letters, reports and documents to be relied upon should be sent to the Clerk to the Committee at least 14 days before the hearing for circulation in advance to the Committee and the authority's representative.

*Appeal to Secretary of State*

The parent has a further right of appeal to the Secretary of State who, after consulting the authority, may confirm or amend a Statement or direct the authority to cease to maintain it.[69] Such appeal should be seen as a last resort, but is appropriate where the Committee confirms the decision of the education authority or remits it for reconsideration by the authority and the parents are not satisfied with the outcome. This appeal is also available where, after making an assessment, the authority decides not to determine the SEP by making a Statement.[70]

Meetings may be arranged at which parents, experts and lawyers can attend and this opportunity should be utilised where possible. There is a duty to give a fair hearing and allow each party to put its case. The Secretary of State has also adopted a practice of obtaining his own independent evidence and not always advising the parties of this, but as he is acting in a judicial capacity the rules of natural justice apply and any such failure to disclose may well be a breach thereof. These appeals take on average nine months and in some cases over a year. It has been held that the Secretary of State's powers only extend to the future and cannot be retro-spective, so if parents have incurred expenditure on some educational provision there is no power for this to be refunded on the basis that the authority should have made that provision.[71]

*Judicial Review*

Another option for dissatisfied parents is judicial review proceedings if the authority or the appeal committee has made an error of law or has acted unreasonably or in breach of natural justice. This may be particularly appropriate where the correct interpretation of the law is in doubt. It is also an option to consider if the authority refuse to assess, or having assessed refuse to make a Statement, or if a proposed Statement is based upon a wholly inadequate assessment or materially incorrect information and the authority refuse to prepare a complete new one.

*Ombudsman*

In recent years the Ombudsman has increasingly been involved in

---

[69]   ss.8(6) and (7). The decision can only deal with the provision to be made and will not have retrospective effect.

[70]   s.5(6). See also 1944 Act, ss.68 and 99 for the right to complain to the Secretary of State when the LEA acts unreasonably or fails to fulfil a duty.

[71]   *R. v. Secretary of State for Education and Science, ex p. Davies The Times,* January 6, 1989. This conflicts with earlier authorities, so the point may not yet be resolved. Actions for judicial review or negligence may be possible.

disputes under the Education Act 1981 where there has been maladministration.[72]

## Implications to mental handicap

Many children need extra help for a short period only, and this may be available within the school, so no Statement is necessary. Children with a mental handicap have an ongoing need for SEP which is more extensive than that which can routinely be provided in an ordinary school, so the education authority becomes involved and the assessment process will usually result in a Statement being prepared.[73]

### Advice to parents

Parents do not have to accept a place at a special school for their child until a Statement has been made and all appeal procedures exhausted. In the meanwhile they can still insist upon the provision of education that does not prejudice the outcome of the assessment procedures. It is not unknown for education authorities to cheat on the assessment and statementing procedures. In some cases only a short Statement is provided which does not set out the advice of the professionals that have to be consulted, or the authority may provide annual reviews without ever having made the initial Statement. In other cases the Statement may be delayed or deferred almost indefinitely, especially when it would indicate provision which the authority is not in a position to make from its own resources. Parents have the right to see, and to comment on, the independent professional advice which the authority is obliged to obtain, and to have a Statement at the times and on the occasions laid down in the legislation, and this right should be enforced where necessary. This is the basis upon which SEP must be made for their child. Parents should be advised to keep letters received and copies of letters that they send and notes of interviews and telephone conversations, noting the date, who they spoke to, the subjects discussed and what was said. If anything important was said it should be confirmed in writing.

### Identifying the issue

Although the procedures and the involvement of so many people may be confusing, the issue is what is best for the child and this can be addressed by asking two simple questions:
- what is the problem (*i.e.* the child's needs); and
- what provision should be made to deal with the problem?

For a child whose behaviour is very demanding, it may not be possible to separate the child's needs from those of the family, and the conclusion could be that residential schooling is appropriate.

### Resource-led Statementing

Statements may be slanted so that the child cannot be said to have

---

72  Reference should be made to Chap.3, Part III.
73  The use of the word Statement has been criticised as stigmatising the child and being too similar to Section as used in mental health.

needs which the authority is unable to meet. Pressure may be put on professionals involved, especially the educational psychologist (employed by the authority) not to recommend provision which the authority is not able to make from its own resources and which would be expensive to buy in from elsewhere.[74] The authority may have a policy not to fund out of county, yet may not have any residential special schools. Parents may be told that there is only so much funding available and that if their child is to be provided with a particular type of schooling there would be less money for other children who would in consequence suffer. This should be firmly resisted: it is the needs of the child, rather than those of the local education authority, that should be identified and met.

## Coping with delay

Parents may be concerned that delay by the authority in carrying out the statementing procedures, or in the appeal process, is depriving their child of essential SEP and that it may be too late to remedy this by the time the issues are resolved. Those who can afford to place their child at a specialist school (e.g. at a boarding school when the policies of the authority do not include this type of provision) may choose to do so immediately. In that event they should notify the authority in writing that this is a temporary provision and that they are still looking to the authority to make SEP but that it had become necessary to take immediate action.[75] In other cases parents can request temporary interim provision. The authority has an overriding duty to educate a child in accordance with his age, aptitude and ability and the child's SEN, and the Secretary of State has confirmed that placements can be made on a provisional basis as part of the assessment.[76]

## Independent reports

It may be desirable to obtain an expert's report, and this should deal with the legal and other issues involved and not be merely in general terms. Thus if the issue is the provision to be made, the report should deal with the aspects specified in the regulations, namely: "facilities and equipment, staffing arrangements, curriculum or otherwise". The basic questions to be addressed are always (i) what are the needs, and (ii) what provision is required to satisfy these needs, but any report should also deal with (iii) the question of the school, or type of school, that is appropriate for

---

[74] Professionals may be asked to submit two reports (a secret one for the file and another for the parents), or to submit a draft report which the authority then amends. An interview with the professional may confirm suspicions in this respect, and the parents may commission a report from an independent professional which identifies these dual standards.

[75] Even if this type of provision is ultimately confirmed in the Statement, the parents may be in some difficulty recovering the fees already paid because the statementing process is not retrospective. There is some authority to the contrary - see H. Chasty & J. Friel, *Children with Special Needs*.

[76] 1944 Act, s.8(2)(c). Circular 22/89, para.64. The examples given relate to severe emotional or behavioural problems or where the assessment is likely to be protracted.

the child,[77] (iv) any non-educational provision that is needed and (v) any modification of the National Curriculum. It may be helpful to follow the checklist in the government Circular, but the report should reach a clear conclusion.[78] An independent educational psychologist will usually be the best person to assist with a report, and panels are available.[79] For a child with severe disabilities a report from the doctor or consultant may be more relevant, and most doctors are willing to co-operate by producing a short report without a fee. Where a child has severe behavioural problems the extent and implications of these should be covered in a report and taken into account in the recommendations made.

*Legal aid*

It may be possible to obtain a report from an independent expert under the *Green Form* scheme (with an extension), but if the fees cannot be afforded the only alternative is to ask the authority or the school for a re-assessment. Legal Aid is not available for the appeal process, though it would be for judicial review. There may also be the prospect of an action in negligence against the professional adviser involved in the education appeal process, whether or not he is employed by the education authority.

*Behavioural difficulties*

A Circular deals with pupils with emotional and behavioural difficulties, which may include mentally handicapped children.[80] A Report is referred to which indicated that, while these pupils present considerable difficulties, there were sufficient examples of good practice to confirm that their educational, emotional and care needs can be met through appropriate curricular planning, sound organisational arrangements, and effective teaching and care.[81] Special schools for these pupils tend to be small and to cater for a wide range of age, ability and social functioning, so it is necessary for the National Curriculum to be planned along with the other provision to be made for the education, care and personal development of the individual pupil and contact with ordinary schools is normally appropriate. It is not unreasonable for these pupils to be educated together, but separate primary and secondary schools should be available where possible. Most education authorities place some of these pupils in non-maintained special schools or independent schools, and boarding schools have an important part to play in the provision that should be available.

---

77　If a particular school is considered to be most suitable this should be stated and the reasons given. The parents, and the expert, may wish to visit several schools before reaching a conclusion.

78　DES Circular 22/89 - *supra*.

79　See addresses in Appendix I.

80　DES Circular 23/89, dated November 8, 1989.

81　*HMI National Survey of Provision for Pupils with Emotional/Behavioural Difficulties in Maintained Special Schools and Units 1983-1988.* Report 62/89 available from DES Publications Despatch Centre, Honeypot Lane, Canons Park, Stanmore Middlesex.

## SPECIAL SCHOOLS

Special schools are those which are specifically organised to make SEP for pupils with SEN and which are approved as such by the Secretary of State.[82]

## Integration

Integration in education is a controversial subject, especially among parents, but much may depend upon the nature and degree of the child's handicap. The authority's general duty, subject to certain exceptions, is to ensure that the child is educated at an ordinary school but account has to be taken of the views of the parents. Each form of provision has advantages and disadvantages, and most parents consider that their views are important and that they should be offered choice.

*Advantages of special schools* are that they:
- cater well for their pupils' SEN because they are small, allowing for small classes and tutorial groups;
- have a good teacher to pupil ratio, allowing for individual attention and close relationships between staff and pupils;
- provide a sheltered and supportive environment in which children can learn at a pace which suits them;
- are run by specialist staff;
- are well supported by the local community;
- have a clearly focused curriculum, and a commitment to the educational success of children with special needs.

*Advantages of integrated education* are that:
- children with mental handicap are kept in touch with local children, an arrangement which can benefit everyone;
- the child can build up a network of local friends;
- other children grow up with an awareness, and acceptance, of those with handicaps;
- a child attending a neighbourhood school is more likely to feel accepted as a member of the local community than a child taken daily to a distant special school;
- the children have access to a wider curriculum and range of facilities, and to subject specialist teachers.

Although integration of children with learning difficulties into ordinary schools is the policy behind the present legislation, it has to be recognised that some children present challenges that cannot be coped with or catered for in ordinary schools, and some form of special education is then needed.

*Primary and secondary*

Primary and secondary education need not be provided in separate schools so far as special schools are concerned, but the Secretary

---

82  1944 Act, s.9(5) as substituted by 1981 Act, s.11(1). Regulations may set out the requirements for school approval - ss.12(1), (2) and 13(1), see Education (Approval of Special Schools) Regulations 1983.

of State can require a special school to be organised either as a primary school or a secondary school.[83]

## Types

### Independent schools

Special needs education can be provided at a grant maintained[84] or independent school,[85] but the local education authority will retain its duties in respect of the pupils at the school. The authority must pay the fees for the education provided, and if board and lodging is included and the child could not otherwise receive education suitable to his needs, the authority must also pay the cost of accommodation.[86] An authority may not make arrangements for SEP for a statemented child at an independent school unless the Secretary of State has approved it as suitable or consents to the particular child being educated there. An approval or consent may be subject to conditions imposed upon the authority and may be withdrawn if these conditions are not complied with.[87] Such schools are not to be conducted for profit, and their premises must normally conform to the standards prescribed for maintained special schools. The Children Act 1989 provides additional safeguards for children at independent schools: social services departments must take all reasonably practical steps to enable them to decide whether the child's welfare is adequately safeguarded and promoted in the school, and if they consider this not to be the case they must notify the Secretary of State.[88]

### Boarding schools

A parent or an authority may consider that a child's SEN can only be met in a residential school or at a particular school which is not within reach of daily travel. As part of their duty to provide sufficient schools authorities must have regard "to the expediency of securing the provision of boarding accommodation, either in boarding schools or otherwise for pupils for whom education as boarders is considered by their parents and by the authority to be desirable".[89] Authorities may provide boarding accommodation and some maintain their own boarding schools, both special and

---

83  1944 Act, s.33(3). 1981 Act, s.12(3).
84  *I.e.* taken out of local authority control under Education Reform Act 1988.
85  This means any school at which full-time education is provided for five or more pupils of compulsory school age . . . not being a school maintained by a local education authority, a grant-maintained school or a special school not maintained by a local education authority: 1944 Act, s.114(1) as applied by Children Act 1989, s.105(1).
86  Education (Miscellaneous Provisions) Act 1953, s.6.
87  1981 Act, s.11(2)-(4).
88  Children Act 1989, s.87. They may enter the school and inspect the premises, the children and the records.
89  1944 Act, s.8. A child should not be placed in a boarding school without the parents' approval, so if this is proposed in a draft Statement and the parents do not agree they should ask for it to be deleted.

ordinary, though independent boarding schools may be used.[90] Authorities may require parents to pay towards the cost of the accommodation unless the authority is providing this because in its opinion education suitable to the age, ability and aptitude or SEN of the child could not otherwise be provided.[91]

*Other provision*
If the education authority is satisfied that it would be inappropriate for the SEP to be made in a school it may, after consulting the child's parents, arrange for this to be made elsewhere.[92] The authority has power to pay for a child to attend a specialist establishment outside England and Wales, and this includes paying travelling fees for the child and a person accompanying the child.[93] Even if a child is in hospital, the authority is under a duty to provide full-time suitable education, and the idea of going out to school should be preserved even for children who are severely handicapped physically and mentally, by arranging for them to leave the ward for their education.[94]

## Closure

A local education authority may only cease to maintain a special school in accordance with proposals approved by the Secretary of State. It must serve written notice of its proposals on the Secretary of State, the parent of every child who is a registered pupil of the school at the time, any other local education authority which has arranged for SEP to be made at the school for a child in its area and such other persons as the authority considers appropriate. The notice must specify the time at which the authority intends to implement the proposals and a period (not less than two months from the date when the notice is served) during which objections may be made to the authority. Within one month from the expiry of that period the authority must send to the Secretary of State copies of all objections, together with its observations on them. After considering proposals and any objections and observations, the Secretary of State may approve or reject the proposals.[95]

## GENERAL

### Statutory duties

The education authority is under a duty to ensure that the SEP specified in a Statement is actually made for the child unless the parent has made suitable arrangements.[96] This duty may have to be

---

[90]   s.50.   Education (Miscellaneous Provisions) Act 1953, s.6.
[91]   s.52.
[92]   1981 Act, s.3.
[93]   *e.g.* the Peto Institute in Hungary.  1981 Act, s.3A inserted by Children Act 1989, Sched.12, para.36.
[94]   DES Circular 5/74.
[95]   These provisions are found in 1981 Act, s.14.
[96]   1981 Act, s.7(1) and (2).  In a case involving a 13-year old boy with

performed by sending the child to an appropriate specialist independent school. Cost is not a factor though the authority is under a duty to see that its resources are used efficiently. This does not mean that second best will do just because it is cheaper, nor that parents can insist on the best in all cases. A balance must be struck, and if the parents can show that the child needs a certain form of expensive provision and that the authority cannot provide this then cost is an irrelevant factor.[97] The authority may arrange for any non-educational provision specified in the Statement to be made in such manner as it considers appropriate.[98]

### Grant-maintained schools

Grant-maintained schools are expected to follow the policy towards admission of pupils with SEN which operated prior to their change of status, and the governors and headteacher must observe the requirements of the 1981 Act in respect of all their pupils. Where a statemented child is admitted, the education authority is responsible for providing any additional support specified, and this may be in the form of grant to the school to enable it to make the necessary provision, direct provision of staff, equipment, etc., or assistance by the educational psychologist service on the same basis as to maintained schools.[99]

Schools which opt out of local education authority control under the Education Reform Act 1988 create an additional problem. Hitherto the receiving schools of statemented children have not been involved in the statementing process, but under the new scheme the headteachers and governors of locally maintained schools will have greater powers over the admission of children to their schools. The following questions arise:

(a) if the education authority issues a Statement naming an opted-out school, will that school be obliged to take the child?

(b) if the authority provides funds for special education within the school, who will control those funds and ensure that they are actually directed to special education?

(c) who will ensure that the provision specified in the Statement is actually enforced?

---

dyslexia and discalcula (problems with letters and numbers) the education authority insisted upon a local school with additional support in spelling and writing, and was upheld on appeal to the Education Secretary. The Court of Appeal (May 1991) held that the authority was legally obliged to make provision for all learning difficulties identified in the Statement, and that the authority should reconsider its decision because it had failed to deal with the numeracy issue.

97  R. v. *Secretary of State for Education and Science, ex p. Davies, The Times,* January 6, 1989.

98  Education authorities now have power to pay for non-educational provision (1988 Act, Sched.12, para.83), and attendance at an establishment outside England and Wales (1981 Act, s.3A inserted by Children Act 1989, Sched.12, para.36).

99  DES Circular 22/89, para.84.

(d) what action and against whom can a parent take to ensure duties are being carried out?

*Co-operation between authorities*

Health and local authorities (including both education and social services) are required to co-operate in exercising their respective functions, and provision is made for the establishment of joint consultative committees.[100] A local education authority may be requested to give assistance to the local authority in the performance of its obligations to provide support for children and families, and education authorities are under a statutory duty to comply with such a request if this is compatible with their duties and would not unduly prejudice the discharge of their functions.[101] However, there is a reciprocal duty on local authorities to assist with the provision of services for a child with SEN within its area. A local authority which is looking after a child whom it proposes to accommodate in an establishment where education is provided must normally consult the education authority before doing so, and notify the arrangements made for the child's accommodation and subsequently when the child ceases to be so accommodated.[102] Similar provisions apply for notification of the local authority where accommodation is provided by an education authority or health authority, or in a residential care or nursing home, for more than three months. The local authority (usually through its social services department) is then under an obligation to consider whether the child's welfare is being adequately safeguarded and promoted, and whether it should exercise any of its functions under the Children Act 1989.[103]

## Provision

*Grants*

Education authorities have power to make grants towards the whole or part of the cost of a placement at a specialist school, and the use of this power may be appropriate pending a Statement or where there is a strong but not definite case for a child to attend a specialist school and the parents are prepared to pay towards this.[104] Although authorities may develop policies in these matters, they must always give individual consideration to each case and they may depart from any policy in their discretion.

*Fees*

No fees can be charged for education provided in schools,[105] but authorities may charge for non-advanced further education (*i.e.* at

---

[100] National Health Service Act 1977, s.22.
[101] Children Act 1989, s.27. This is especially so in the case of day care and child minding - see Sched.9, para.8.
[102] s.28(1)-(3). Where the child has SEN this will be the local education authority who maintain the Statement thereof - s.28(4)(*b*).
[103] ss.85 and 86.
[104] Education (Miscellaneous Provisions) Act 1953, s.6.
[105] 1944 Act, s.61.

or below GCE A-level or its equivalent). The only restraint, other than that of unreasonableness, is that fees should not differ substantially from the corresponding fees charged for similar courses in neighbouring authorities.[106] It was initially not the practice to charge for further education courses broadly similar in content to those provided in schools, but some authorities have departed from this.[107]

### Travelling

Authorities are required to make arrangements for the provision of transport for school pupils, or to pay for transport, where they consider it necessary or as directed by the Secretary of State.[108] Walking distances are generally two miles up to the age of eight years and three miles thereafter with bus or train fares being paid if they exceed this, but in the case of mentally handicapped pupils assistance may be required in transporting them to schools and the distance to the nearest special school will usually be such that the authority is obliged to provide door to door transport.

### School meals

There is no longer any statutory obligation to provide meals or free milk in schools, and this is in the discretion of the authority. It must make such provision as seems to be requisite (*i.e.* to the authority) free of charge to families on Income Support or Family Credit, and must provide to all pupils facilities for them to eat food brought from home.

## Enforcement

We have seen that appeal procedures are available in certain circumstances. The Secretary of State also has a general power to direct local education authorities or school governors where he is satisfied, on receipt of a complaint or otherwise, that they are in default of duty, and if necessary may enforce his directions by applying to the court.[109] In addition, if the Secretary of State is satisfied, following a complaint or otherwise, that a local education authority has acted, or is proposing to act, unreasonably with respect to the exercise of any power or the performance of any duty, he may give such directions as appear to him to be expedient.[110] A complaint to the Secretary of State may thus be made when it is alleged that an authority is acting unreasonably, but judicial review proceedings in the courts will be appropriate where the authority has not complied with the law.

---

[106] Education (Schools and Further Education) Regulations 1981, r.17(2).
[107] *e.g.* by charging employed young people for part-time and evening courses.
[108] 1944 Act, s.55 (as amended).
[109] s.99.
[110] s.68; Education (No 2) Act 1968, s.3(3)(*b*). For an interpretation of this power see *Secretary of State for Education and Science* v. *Metropolitan Borough of Tameside* [1976] 3 All ER 665.

*General duties*

It should not be assumed that all statutory duties can be enforced by judicial review proceedings. A distinction must be made between a duty owed to an individual and one owed to the community. If of the latter type, such as the general duty to provide sufficient schools, the authority would not necessarily be held to be in breach of the duty if the desired standards were not being met, and even if there was a breach the courts in their discretion might not intervene if the authority was doing all it reasonably could to remedy the situation. A general duty, intended to be for the benefit of the public and not to give the individual a cause of action, is not absolute.[111]

*Effect of wardship*

Although the court retains jurisdiction over a ward with SEN it should decline to intervene in the education of the ward if this would create a conflict, or risk of conflict, between the roles of the court and the local education authority. However, the court may intervene when this is desirable in order to assist the authority to perform its statutory duties, and ought to intervene when invited to do so by the authority. If the court in the exercise of its wardship jurisdiction decides what educational provision should be made for the ward, the education authority is then entitled, in the exercise of its discretion, to conclude that there is no need for it to prepare a Statement of the child's needs.[112]

## Parental role

The parent of a child of compulsory school age is under a duty to cause the child to receive sufficient full-time education suitable to his age, ability and aptitude, and to any SEN the child may have, either by regular attendance at school or otherwise.[113] Failure to comply with this duty may be a criminal offence. Parents who have strong convictions as to their child's educational needs may refer to the duty imposed upon them when they are taking steps to ensure that those needs are provided for. Unlike the position of children in ordinary schools, the parent of a child of compulsory school age in a special school cannot withdraw the child without the consent of the education authority, but if such consent is refused the parent can refer the matter to the Secretary of State who may make such direction as he thinks fit.[114]

---

111  R. v. *Inner London Education Authority, ex p. Ali, The Times,* February 14, 1990.

112  *Re D. (a minor)* [1987] 3 All ER 717, C.A. This wardship application was made by parents who disagreed with the authority's decision to send their child to a residential special school, but on the evidence the Court committed the child to the care of the local authority and recommended that he should attend that school.

113  1944 Act, s.36; 1981 Act, s.17.

114  1981 Act, s.11(2).

*Choice of school*

There is a general duty on education authorities to educate pupils in accordance with the wishes of their parents, but this is only "so far as is compatible with the provision of efficient instruction and training and the avoidance of unreasonable public expenditure".[115] An authority may accept an application from outside its area for a school place, and recoupment (*i.e.* the payment of out county fees between authorities) is automatic.[116] In allocating school places, authorities must comply with preferences expressed by parents from outside their area unless this would "prejudice the provision of efficient education or the efficient use of resources".[117]

*Access to records*

Parents have a legal right to see reports prepared for an education authority as part of a formal assessment.[118] Where any educational records held by education authorities or schools are computerised, the persons referred to in them have rights of access under the Data Protection Act 1984.[119] Since September 1989 there has been a duty upon schools to keep a curricular record for each pupil, and since September 1990 further provisions relate to disclosure, correction and transfer of records.[120] These apply to manual records held in local education authority maintained schools, grant-maintained schools and special schools (whether or not so maintained). An entitled person on making a written request has a right to see the pupil's record within 15 days and to receive a copy subject to payment of the cost of reproducing this.

*Parents' dilemma*

There is a conflict between the desire of many parents to preserve their existing segregated special schools and the more generally accepted philosophy of integration. This can often be explained by the difference between proposals and reality. Parents of the more profoundly handicapped children tend to feel protected by their special school, and fear that if this is closed a shortage of funding will result in satisfactory alternative provision not being made. Another problem is the lack of public acceptance of people with a mental handicap. The speed of progress towards integration is inevitably linked to the attitude of the public at large. The first children in a newly integrated environment may have many additional difficulties to overcome, and parents are aware of this.

---

[115] 1944 Act, s.76. This is only a general provision and whilst the authority must take into account the parent's wishes it is not obliged to comply with them, though it may only reject them for the reasons stated.

[116] 1980 Act, s.31.

[117] s.6.

[118] 1981 Act, s.5.

[119] A pupil dealt with in a Statement of SEN which is computerised does not have any rights under this Act, and only has access to the record through the parents who have their own rights in this instance.

[120] 1988 Act, ss.218 and 232. Education (School Records) Regulations 1989. DES Circular No. 17/89. See also Chap.3, Part II.

## Starting school

Although local education authorities have the power to provide nursery schools or pre-school playgroups, they are not under an obligation to do so. A child normally has the right to start school at the beginning of the term following the fifth birthday, and some authorities allow children to start at an earlier age. However, they have a legal duty to provide education for children under five years who have been identified as having SEN. A child under two years may be assessed but the full procedures do not apply and SEP under this age means any kind of educational provision including support and advice to parents to help their children. The full statutory requirements must be complied with between the ages of two and five years.

Early identification is crucial for the young child with disabilities since prompt and appropriate provision can enhance the child's future progress. Priority to children with SEN should be given in admitting children to nurseries, and careful observation and recording at that stage assists in later provision. Liaison between the school health services, social services, family doctor, health visitor, therapist, any other specialists, the parent, any voluntary organisation involved, and the teacher is important.

## School attendance

Parents will usually be concerned to ensure that the best possible educational provision is made for their child, but there may be cases where they are so concerned about the suitability of that which is being insisted upon by the education authority that they refuse to send the child to the specified school. We therefore consider the implications of the enforcement procedures, but it is assumed that the parents will be taking steps to secure what they consider to be suitable educational provision by means of the appeal procedures rather than stubbornly refusing to do anything.

*Education supervision orders*

The court may on the application of the education authority make an *education supervision order* where a child is of compulsory school age and is not receiving efficient full-time education suitable to his age, ability and aptitude and any SEN the child may have. There must first be consultation with the social services department of the appropriate local authority (*i.e.* for the area in which the child lives), which may decide to provide support for the child and the family, or to apply for the compulsory admission of the child to care or for an ordinary supervision order.[121] A child may only be placed in compulsory care on the application of the local authority where he is suffering or likely to suffer significant harm which is attributable to a lack of reasonable parental care, and not where lack of intellectual development at school may be a school problem rather than a parenting problem.

---

121  Children Act 1989, s.36 and Sched.3.

Parents who keep the child away from school because they are not satisfied with the educational provision being made are unlikely to be vulnerable to the child being taken into care.

An education supervision order lasts for up to one year initially but may be extended for up to three years at a time, though it may not last beyond the child's compulsory school leaving age. It is the duty of the supervisor to advise, assist and befriend and give directions to the child and the parents in such a way as to secure that the child is properly educated.[122] Before giving any directions he must, as far as practicable, ascertain and give due consideration to the wishes and feelings of the child and parents and in particular their wishes as to the place at which the child should be educated. Where any direction has not been complied with, the supervisor must consider what further steps he should take, which include making new directions, applying for a discharge of the order, or referring the matter to the relevant social services authority. A parent who persistently fails to comply with a direction under an education supervision order may be prosecuted, and the education authority must notify the local authority of the failure to comply so that it may investigate the child's circumstances with a view to considering the necessity to use their powers.[123] The order may be discharged on the application of the child, the parent or the education authority and, in that event, the court may direct the local authority to investigate the child's circumstances.

*School attendance orders*
A parent who fails to comply with a school attendance order in respect of a child or the parent of a child who fails to attend regularly at the school at which registered as a pupil commits an offence. Proceeding may be brought only by a local education authority but, before instituting proceedings the authority must consider whether it would be appropriate, instead or in addition, to apply for an education supervision order.[124]

## TRANSITION

## Future Needs Assessment

The Disabled Persons (Services, Consultation and Representation) Act 1986 is designed to help young people with significant disabilities and their parents or carers by ensuring that the education authority and social services department work together to help such young people when they leave school.

*Education authority duties*
A thorough review and assessment of continuing educational needs

---

[122] Parent has the same meaning as in the Education Act 1944 (as amended by Sched.13 to the Children Act 1989) so includes any person who has parental responsibility for or care of the child - Sched.3, para.21.

[123] *I.e.* under Parts III and IV of the Act (Sched.3, para.19).

[124] 1944 Act, ss.37-40., Children Act 1989, Sched.13 para.8.

should be undertaken about two years before a statemented student leaves school. As part of the first annual review or assessment or reassessment after the 14th birthday the education authority must seek from the social services department an opinion as to whether the student is a disabled person within the terms of the 1986 Act. If so, the authority must then inform social services eight months before such student's date of leaving full-time education, if he is under 19, and social services must undertake an assessment. The authority must keep under review the expected leaving dates of disabled students so that they are able to comply with this.[125] This provides the framework for assessment and provision of services for those leaving full-time education, and unlike some provisions of the Act they have been brought into force.

### Social services duties

There must be an assessment of welfare services needed within five months of notification of leaving school, subject to parental agreement.[126] Parents and child both contribute to the assessment. A letter should then be sent which includes a description of identified needs and a statement of intent as to whether the social services department is able to meet those needs. If parents are dissatisfied a review may be requested. Assessment should be completed at least three months before the child leaves school and take into account the stress level of parents and other carers to cope with the demands of caring on a continuing basis. Not participating at this stage does not prevent seeking assistance later if circumstances change.[127]

### Disclosure

Disclosure is now permitted by an education authority to a social services department of the child's Statement of special educational needs. This is restricted to those in the department who need to know for the purpose of assessing the needs of that child with respect to the provision of statutory services under the welfare enactments. Where information likely to prove distressing to the child is included, such as limited life expectancy or a prognosis of deteriorating powers, officers are asked to treat that information in strict confidence. Whilst the contents of the statement when held on a computer do not need to be revealed this applies only to the education authority and cannot be relied upon by the social services department.[128] In these circumstances the withholding of

---

125  1986 Act, ss.5 and 6.

126  This assessment should cover all services under the welfare enactments and not just the welfare services - 1986 Act, s.5(5).

127  1986 Act, ss.5 and 6. DHSS Circular LAC(88)1, DES Circular 2/88 and Welsh Office Circular 3188 detail the impact on disabled young people leaving school.

128  Data Protection (Miscellaneous Subject Access Exemptions) Order 1987. The provisions of the Data Protection (Subject Access Modification) (Social Work) Order 1987 may be relevant where the statement is held on computer for social work purposes.

information, on the grounds of potential harm to the physical or mental health or emotional condition of the child, is allowed.[129]

## Provision

Parents and child should be informed in writing of the reasons for recommending a particular placement after school, and should be involved in the decision-making process. All educational possibilities should be considered, and although the decision must be made on the basis of what is best for the child this will involve taking into account the needs of the family and the ability of the parents to cope, because it is in the best interests of the child that the family continues to cope and remains together.

Where a move to a full-time course at a college of further education is proposed, the curriculum should be examined to ensure that it includes, as appropriate:

    (a) reading, writing and numeracy;
    (b) development of personal and independence skills, including facilities outside the college;
    (c) access to classes with other students;
    (d) instruction in leisure activities;
    (e) speech therapy;
    (f) access to all departments;
    (g) orientation to future possible placements.

Free transport should be provided where necessary, and access to the full range of courses should be available without an upper age limit.

### Remedies

If no school place is available after age 16 and a suitable alternative is not offered, parents should make a written request for continuing education to the local education authority quoting the legislation referred to above, and if the authority is unable to offer a place a letter should be requested confirming this. A formal complaint may then be made to the Secretary of State for Education asking him to use his powers[130] to direct the authority to fulfil its legal obligations. A joint complaint by a number of parents in the area is likely to be more effective.

## Young persons

The local education authority is obliged on request to provide continuing education for those who remain registered pupils at school after completing their compulsory education (*i.e.* at the age of 16) up to the age of 19. However, alternatives may be available.

### Adult Training Centres.

In some cases the individual may be offered a place at an Adult Training Centre (sometimes known as Social Education Centres) at an earlier age. It may be in his interests to make the move at that

---

129  As a result of the passing of the 1986 Act, the 1983 Regulations were amended by S.I.1988 No.1067
130  *I.e.* under Education Act 1944, ss.68 and 99.

stage, but parents who disagree are in a dilemma because there is no obligation upon the local authority to offer such a place and if it is turned down there is no certainty that the offer will be repeated on subsequently leaving school. Although these centres run by social services departments may include some educational work, they do not meet the educational authority's responsibilities to provide education.

*Further education.*
Education authorities must also provide adequate facilities for further education for their area, and the question arises whether this may be used as a substitute for school provision. The view of the Department of Education and Science is that education must be provided either in a school or a further education college for all in the age-group who want to continue full-time education, but not necessarily in whichever of the two the individual prefers. Another view is that education authorities are obliged to secure sufficient provision in schools for all those under 19 who seek continuing education, and that the offer of a place in a further education college would not be sufficient.

## ADULTS

### Further education

Where people with severe learning difficulties have taken part in further education there have often been considerable benefits in the form of increased employability, development of advocacy skills and general improvement in the quality of life.

*Entitlement*
For many years local education authorities have been required to secure the provision of adequate facilities for further education for their area, though not necessarily in their area. This means full-time or part-time education for those over compulsory school age and leisure time occupation for those over that age who are able and willing to profit from it.[131] Colleges of Further Education can provide courses for young people with learning difficulties who have left school, but there is no specific obligation upon them to do so and no specific entitlement for an individual.

*Curriculum*
Education authorities which provide such courses will wish to develop their own curriculum aims and content, but this should be in consultation with health and social services, schools, parents, voluntary organisations and professionals. Aims should include:
  - creating an awareness of self, others and the environment;
  - developing communication, social and motor skills;
  - training for daily living and leisure;
  - enhancing practical and vocational abilities;

---

[131] s.41.

- decision making and autonomy;
- promotion of personal dignity;
- opportunities for extending and re-inforcing experiences.

It should not be left to education authorities to meet these needs alone and their role will primarily be in organising and evaluating programmes in which other agencies play a part.

### White Paper

In May 1991 the Government issued a White Paper describing its plans to improve and develop the education and training system for 16 to 19 year olds.[132] The first volume describes policies and implementation, and the second puts forward plans for establishing a new college sector for post-16 education and training. From April 1, 1993 colleges of further education and sixth form colleges will be removed from local authority control and funded directly by the Government through Councils appointed by and responsible to the Secretaries of State for Education and Science and for Wales. These will be responsible for a new funding regime designed to provide incentives to recruit additional students and reduce unit costs, and will be under a duty to ensure that enough further education is provided and suitable full-time courses are available for all young people who want them. Their structure and intended powers and duties are described, and they are to have a general duty to have regard to the requirements of students with learning difficulties, but the provisions of the Education Act 1981 relating to school age pupils will not extend to the Councils and no further detail is given as to how they should fulfil their duties towards young people with disabilities.[133] The aims are summarised in Chapter 1 of Volume 1, but these concentrate upon the attainment of skills and qualifications for future careers rather than the more limited objective of independent living. It is only in Volume 2 dealing with the duties of Councils that mention is made of people with learning difficulties.

### Further and Higher Education Act 1992

This Act follows the White Paper and the following concerns have been identified, apart from the fact that the opportunity has not been taken to extend the right to full-time education for those with special needs beyond the age of 19:

1. the Further Education Funding Councils for England and Wales will be made up of educationalists, professionals and persons with experience in commerce and finance, but there

---

132 *Education and Training for the 21st Century*. The Disability Consortium argues that the proposals are a backward step, missing the opportunity to establish crucial rights for students with disabilities, and calls for the right (i) for education up to 25 years (ii) to choice of funding in integrated or specialist colleges and (iii) to a full assessment of needs and achievements.

133 This may result in parents insisting upon their children remaining in the otherwise less appropriate special schools so as to have the benefit of the legally enforceable Statementing procedures.

is no requirement for someone with experience of disability to be on the Council;

2. no relevant duties are imposed on the Councils, which are merely to have regard to the requirements of students with learning disabilities and may make provision to allow such students to attend residential courses;

3. the list of further education courses does not include many of those taken by people with learning disabilities.

## Continuing education

Classes in a range of subjects are available at Adult Education Institutes or Centres and Continuing Education Centres for people not involved in full time education. These allow adults to develop individual interests and skills and make new social contacts in their own community. There is no obligation to make this provision available to adults with a mental handicap in a way which meets their individual needs.

## Day Centres

The need for education and training does not cease on leaving school, and there is also a continuing need to provide purposeful activities for people with a mental handicap who may not be suitable for permanent employment in a commercial sense. Services vary from one part of the country to another and legal remedies are seldom available.[134] There are minimum standards that the authorities should seek to provide, and parents and others should seek to achieve, in Day Centres in their areas.[135]

### Adult Training Centres
Many mentally handicapped young people now move to a local Adult Training Centre (or Social Education Centre) when they leave school. This continues the work of the special school in training them to take part in the life of the community and provides social training and classes in subjects like art, handicraft, woodwork and physical education as well as continued general education. Trainees also learn to do simple jobs like packing, laundry work and operating light machinery, and the more able students may be encouraged to try and find a job, though most will stay on at the Centre. These Centres provide daytime activities five days a week in a building designed or adapted for the purpose.

---

134 The MENCAP Report: *Day Services - Today & Tomorrow* highlights the problem for those leaving school. 20,000 more places are needed at Adult Training Centres, existing places are under-funded and under-staffed, and there is little staff training leading to low morale, with no system to cover sickness or holidays. More people are threatened with charges for transport, meals and attendance although their only income may be social security benefits. Access to professionals, *e.g.* speech therapists, is poor and often it is the most difficult and dependent young people who are denied services.

135 See Stamina Paper No. 2 *Services for People with Mental Handicap over 16 (Education, Training and Day Care)* issued by the Royal Society for Mentally Handicapped Children and Adults in 1986.

*Resource Centres*
In some areas the development of day services has moved away from the use of training centres as a base to the idea of individual programmes of activities being planned and co-ordinated from a Resource Centre.

*Entitlement and assessment*
There is no statutory obligation upon local authorities to provide a place for an adult at a particular centre, or at all.

When a new trainee is admitted to a centre a full report should be provided by the previous educational establishment with a copy of its final assessment, and this should be followed by regular re-assessments within the centre taking into account educational, social, vocational and physical aspects. Parents and staff should both be involved, and where possible trainees should be aware of and agree to the assessments, and a copy provided to the parents.

*Programmes*
Programmes should be based primarily on education and training (including matters such as personal hygiene and self-care) rather than being concerned with production. The emphasis should be upon developing personal independence and dignity aimed at integration in the community, with trainees being involved in decision-making so far as possible. Individual programmes will be developed for the trainees with both long and short term aims, and staff should be involved, with parent participation, and where possible trainees being aware of and agreeing to them. Programmes should be in writing and available to staff and parents, and regularly monitored, recorded and up-dated. Further education should be available to those in these centres.

*Code of Practice*
There is no uniformity, but a Code setting out the following policy objectives has been suggested:
- centres should encourage user participation in management giving users the right to express their views without fear of recrimination;
- a users' committee be formed;
- assertiveness training be offered to users;
- assessment to take place when a user enters a centre;
- there be a balance and variety of choice between work and other activities;
- advocacy schemes should be available;
- there be standardisation of structure and pay for staff;
- a contract between the centre and sponsoring authority be introduced.

*Resources and cost*
The curriculum should be structured on a multi-disciplinary basis involving educators, social workers, craftsmen, therapists and other caring staff, with teaching staff seconded from the local education authority and a continuous programme of staff training.

Physiotherapy, speech therapy and non-verbal communication should be part of the treatment and training where required, with adequate resources for social training and opportunities for physical education and sport, where possible using community facilities. Transport facilities are needed.

It should not be assumed that a place at one of these day centres will be provided without a means-assessment of the individual involved, and charges may be introduced for those who have the means to pay. Travelling expenses will usually be paid or supervised transport provided to and from the centre, but a contribution towards the cost may be required.

# PART IB - EDUCATION AND TRAINING (Scotland)

*Preliminary*

Scotland has its own distinct education system and separate body of education law. This Part describes those aspects of this legal regime most likely to concern children and adults with a mental handicap. Much of the general material and comment in Part IA is relevant, and will be of assistance if read in conjunction with the description in this Part of the somewhat different legal framework in Scotland.

This Part is dealt with under four main headings. The first considers children below school age[136] and children of school age.[137] The second deals with the transition at school leaving age, and the remaining headings deal with the education and training of "young persons" over school leaving age, and of adults.

## Law and organisation

*Legislation*

Well over 50 statutes and statutory instruments are relevant to education and training in Scotland, and there are even more Scottish Education Department circulars and memoranda.[138] Most of the law described here is to be found in:

Education (Scotland) Acts 1980 and 1981

Mental Health (Scotland) Act 1984

Disabled Persons (Services, Consultation and Representation) Act 1986

Self-Governing Schools etc. (Scotland) Act 1989

---

[136] Children reach school age on the "school commencement date" (usually in August) on or next after the child's fifth birthday - 1980 Act, s.32 (though parents may opt for children born in approximately the first half of the school year actually to start school at the commencement date preceding the child's fifth birthday).

[137] School leaving age is reached on May 31, or the start of the Christmas holidays in the half-year in which the child reaches 16 (the half-years being those starting on March 1 and October 1) - 1980 Act, s.33.

[138] For a complete list of educational provisions up to 1986 see *The Law of the School* (Scottish Consumer Council), pp.227-231.

Education (Record of Needs) (Scotland) Regulations 1982
Further and Higher Education (Scotland) Act 1992[139]
These are referred to in this part as "the 1980 Act" etc. The law of
special educational needs described below is, except where
otherwise indicated, to be found in sections 59-65 and Schedule A2
of the 1980 Act, as substantially amended by the 1981 Act, the
1986 Act and the 1989 Act.

*Organisation*
Education is the responsibility of the nine regional and three
islands councils, each of which is the education authority for its
area, but the 1992 Act transfers responsibility for further
education to the Secretary of State. The provision of education is
supervised by the Scottish Education Department, part of the
Scottish Office, which is headed by the Secretary of State for
Scotland (referred to in this part as the Secretary of State).[140] One
of the Scottish Office ministers is allocated responsibility for
education, usually along with other duties. The regional and
islands councils are also responsible for social work functions,
supervised by the Secretary of State through the Social Work
Services Group.[141] Social work functions are particularly relevant
to the transition from school provision, and to adult provision.

## CHILDREN

### Educational provision

*Definition of "parents"*
In this section parents are referred to for simplicity, but the term
includes single parents, guardians, anyone liable to maintain the
child, and anyone having custody of the child.[142]

*General duties*
Parents of every school-age child have a duty to provide efficient
education for the child.[143] Education authorities have a duty to
secure that there is made for their areas adequate and efficient
provision of school education.[144] These duties apply to all
children, whether handicapped or not, and are the basis of the
entitlement of every child to an efficient education. Likewise, all
of the other general duties of education authorities apply to all
children, including handicapped children. Among these duties are:
  - the duties regarding choice of school;
  - parents' rights to information;
  - rights to consultation about school closures and certain other
    changes;

---

139 Not in force at time of writing.
140 University education is outwith the responsibilities of education authorities
    and the Scottish Education Department. For 1992 Act, see p.325.
141 Attached to Scottish Education Department until recently, but no longer.
142 1980 Act, s.135(1).
143 s.30.
144 s.1(1).

- provision of adequate books, equipment and materials;
- keeping progress records for each child;
- safeguarding against sexual and racial discrimination[145];
- offering bi-lingual education in Gaelic-speaking areas;
- provision of certain types of care;
- provision of proper safety and supervision; and
- the duty to enforce school attendance.

## Special Educational Needs (SEN)

Many children require extra help with their education, at least at some stage. Provisions regarding the special educational needs (SEN) of such children are also generalised. Many mentally handicapped children come within those provisions, but they are not put in a special category because of their mental handicap. The provisions are designed to apply to any child whose educational needs cannot be met unaided by the classroom teacher in an ordinary school.

The school education which education authorities must provide is defined as including provision for SEN.[146] A child has SEN if, because of a learning difficulty, he requires educational provision additional to, or otherwise different from, the provision made generally for children of the same age in the authority's schools. The child has a learning difficulty if he has significantly greater difficulty in learning than the majority of children of the same age, or if the child suffers from a disability which prevents or hinders use of educational facilities generally provided for children of the same age in the authority's schools. A child under school age with similar learning difficulties is also defined as having SEN.

*Duties in relation to SEN*

Education authorities have various duties in relation to SEN:

1. Within their general duty to make "adequate and efficient" provision of school education, there is a duty to make general provision for SEN. This duty covers children from two years old up to school leaving age.

2. Education authorities must publicise the importance of early discovery of SEN and the right to assessment.

3. Where children over two have SEN which are "pronounced, specific or complex", the education authority has duties to assess and where necessary record.[147] By this method a child's SEN are identified, and the manner in which the education authority will meet its obligation to make adequate and efficient provision for those needs is established. In this context "record" means opening and keeping a Record of Needs. These procedures are described below.

---

[145] But not discrimination on grounds of handicap.

[146] s.1(5).

[147] s.60(2).

4. When a child has a Record of Needs, the education authority has a duty to secure that the child receives the provision identified as needed in the Record of Needs.[148]

*Psychological service*
Education authorities have a duty to provide for their areas a psychological service in clinics or elsewhere.[149] The service provided must include the study of children with SEN; giving advice to parents and teachers about the education of such children; provision in clinics for the SEN of such children (in suitable cases); and advising social work departments regarding assessment of needs for social work or other statutory purposes.[150]

## Enforcement

Many duties of education authorities are described above. Only if they are duly performed in relation to all children, will all children receive the adequate and efficient education (including provision for any SEN) to which they are entitled. It is necessary for those concerned about the education of children with special needs, particularly parents, to be vigilant. Not infrequently general provision for special needs is found to be deficient, the importance of early discovery of special needs is not adequately publicised, there is reluctance (or undue delay) in recording, records do not specify needs sufficiently clearly, or the provision set out in the Record is not delivered. If a breach of duty is encountered, it is normally best to draw this to the attention of senior management in the education authority. If that does not produce reasonably prompt and satisfactory results, two possible courses of action are open. The first is to take the education authority to court under judicial review procedure[151]; the second is to request the Secretary of State to take action under section 70 of the 1980 Act.

*Section 70 procedure*
This section confers powers upon the Secretary of State if "on complaint by any person interested or otherwise" he is satisfied that an education authority (or others) have failed to discharge any duty imposed on them by or for the purposes of the 1980 Act or any other education legislation. The Secretary of State may make an order declaring the authority to be in default and setting a deadline to remedy the default, and on failure to discharge the duty in question by the deadline, two courses are open to the Secretary of State. He may himself make such arrangements as he thinks fit for the discharge of the duty, and charge the cost to the education authority; or he may obtain an order for specific

---

[148] ss.1 and 62(3).
[149] Termed the "regional psychological service" or the "islands authority psychological service".
[150] 1980 Act, s.4 (as amended).
[151] See Chapter 3, Part III, p.156.

performance of the duty from the Court of Session. If it is thought that an education authority is in breach of duty, all that is required is to write to the Scottish Education Department[152] giving details of the alleged breach of duty and asking that the Secretary of State exercise these enforcement powers. Usually, the Secretary of State's expert advisers investigate and report to him. If there appears to be a breach of duty, the reports are made available informally to the education authority and the matter is often resolved at that stage.

The fact that section 70 procedure has been initiated does not of course stop informal negotiation and discussion with the education authority while the complaint is under consideration, and not infrequently the matter can be resolved by agreement, and the complaint simply withdrawn. In practice, the Scottish Office will generally respond effectively if a complaint is well-founded. In 1991 the then Minister of State responsible for education, Mr Michael Forsyth, stated[153]:

> "When complaints are made we do follow them up very vigorously, and it is quite unacceptable that children with special needs do not get the support which they require".

## Record of Needs

The assessment procedures described below are concerned with deciding whether a child requires a Record of Needs, making it up, and reviewing it. In about the last year of compulsory schooling the education authority carries out a "future needs assessment" of recorded children, and this is described under Transition below. In relation to children over two and up to school leaving age, the education authority must establish which children require a Record of Needs, and if necessary open and maintain one.[154] They may do these things, but are not under a legal duty to do so, in relation to children under two and young persons who are still at school after school leaving age up to the age of 18.

*Form and content*

The form of the Record of Needs is laid down in regulations[155]:

**Part I** contains the full name, current address, date of birth and sex of the child; and various certificates for completion upon the opening, transfer, discontinuance and preservation of the Record of Needs;

**Part II** contains details of the parents and Named Person[156];

**Part III** contains the *assessment profile* describing the child's

---

152  The Scottish Office Education Department (address in Appendix I).

153  Scottish Television, *Scottish Questions*, June 27, 1991.

154  In relation to children from two up to school age, the duty arises if they come to the attention of the education authority as having SEN (or appearing to have them).

155  Education (Record of Needs) (Scotland) Regulations 1982.

156  See under "Named Person", below.

strengths and weaknesses (as identified in the assessment procedure) and lists the specific impairments giving rise to SEN, with the implications which each has for every aspect of education;

**Part IV** lists the SEN themselves, under the categories: sight, hearing and communication; intellectual/curricular; social/emotional; and physical/medical.

**Part V** lists the ways in which the education authority proposes to meet those needs, under two headings:
> A. education authority services; and
> B. other services.

**Part VI** specifies the school to be attended;

**Part VII** sets out the parents' views.

**Part VIII** is a record of re-assessment and any resulting alterations to the Record of Needs.

**Part IX** records any disclosure of the contents of the Record of Needs (which are confidential - see below).

*Education authority duty*
It is the duty of the education authority to ensure that the child receives all of the educational provision in Part V of the Record of Needs whether the authority has indicated an intention to provide it themselves, or through some other agency. The Scottish Record of Needs has no equivalent of the additional non-educational provision in section V of the English Statement.[157] This must be borne in mind when considering English cases dealing with whether particular provision is educational or non-educational. The provision identified in both Parts VA and VB of the Scottish Record of Needs is all educational, and thus within the statutory duty of the education authority.[158]

**Assessment**

*Request by parent*
If the parent of any child requests the education authority to arrange for the child to be assessed, the authority must comply with the request unless in their opinion it is unreasonable.

*Initial notices to parents*
Formal recording procedure is initiated by a written notice from the education authority to the parents inviting them to allow observation and assessment of the child. The notice must explain that the purpose of the observation and assessment is to help the education authority decide whether the child should have a Record of Needs. If medical or psychological examinations are proposed, the notice must say when and where they are to be held, and the parents have the right to be present at any medical examination. The notice must state the name of someone in the education authority who is available to give the parents advice and

---

157  See Part IA of this chapter.
158  See *The Power to Act*, pp.152-155.

information.[159] The notice must also give the parents at least 21 days to write in to the education authority with their own views regarding the child's SEN, and what should be done about them. A Scottish Education Department circular stresses that it is the duty of the named official in the authority to assist the parents, if such help is needed. If the parents wish to make a placing request, it should be made not later than this stage. Only if the parents have made a written placing request can they appeal about the school to be attended under the appeal procedures described below.

In relation to children aged from two to school leaving age, a second notice may be submitted to the parents if following the first notice they have failed to submit the child for assessment, without reasonable excuse. This notice requires (rather than invites) the parents to submit the child for assessment. If they fail to comply without reasonable excuse they are guilty of an offence, and even if there was a reasonable excuse the education authority are no longer obliged to proceed with the assessment.

*Decision to record*

The authority must obtain a report from any teacher employed by it who is involved in the child's education, or has been. If the child has ever attended a school not managed by the education authority, the authority may seek a report from the managers of that school. The authority may obtain reports or information about the child's educational needs from any other source. The authority must consider the parents' views, the advice given to it as a result of the process of observation and assessment, and all the other reports and information which they have obtained. The authority then decides whether the child should have a Record of Needs, and intimates its decision to the parents, with reasons.

## Preparation of record

*Draft Record of Needs*

If the authority has decided that the child should have a Record of Needs, it prepares this in draft form and sends it to the parents with the notice intimating the decision to record. Within 14 days thereof the parents may comment upon the contents of the draft.[160]

*Record of Needs*

In making the final decision as to the content of the Record of Needs, the education authority must have regard to any such comments by the parents. The authority then sends yet another notice to the parents intimating the final content of the Record of Needs and telling the parents about their rights of appeal (see below). Unless the parents have requested the education authority not to appoint a Named Person, this notice must give the name and address of the Named Person. The education authority must send a

---

159 This person is **not** the Named Person.
160 For some reason the education authority is not obliged to tell the parents of this right, but it is good practice to do so.

copy of the Record of Needs to the parents, and tell them where the original may be inspected.

## Placing requests - recorded children

Some special provisions apply to placing requests for children with special needs. Placement of such children may be requested in a school which is within one of the following three categories:

(i) schools managed by the same education authority;
(ii) private (fee-paying) special schools anywhere in Scotland: this covers schools which make provision wholly or mainly for recorded children, and also special classes in primary schools, secondary schools and psychological service clinics;
(iii) schools in England, Wales or Northern Ireland which make provision wholly or mainly for children with pronounced, specific or complex SEN.

The education authority may refuse the placing request if it can show that it is able to provide for the child's SEN in a school of its own, and that it is not reasonable to place the child elsewhere, having regard to comparison of both cost and suitability of the education authority's own school and the other school. Accordingly, even though an education authority has offered a place at a school of its own which could cater for the child's needs at less cost, the authority will still have to meet the cost of educating the child at a special school if the special school is more suitable, and if the advantages as regards suitability outweigh the cost disadvantages.

### Education abroad

Parents cannot request placement in establishments outside the UK, but education authorities are empowered to arrange for children to attend schools or other establishments abroad. The school or establishment must be one which makes provision wholly or mainly for persons with pronounced, specific or complex SEN. The education authority may make such provision as it thinks fit, including meeting some or all costs of fees, travel, maintenance and other expenses. The authority may meet the costs of one or both parents, or some other person, if the authority thinks that their presence would be to the child's advantage.

## Appeal

Parents have the right to appeal against the decision to record or not to record. If a Record of Needs has been issued they may appeal against the details therein regarding the child's impairments or SEN. If they have made a placing request, they may also appeal about the school to be attended.

### Time limit

Any such appeal must be lodged with the appeal committee within 28 days of receipt of notice of the education authority's decision. The notice is presumed to have been received the day after it was posted, weekends excepted. A late appeal may be accepted.

*Appeals (other than choice of school)*
If the appeal concerns the decision to record, or not to record, or the details regarding which appeal is competent (see above), it is submitted to the appeal committee, but referred by the committee to the Secretary of State for decision. He must consider the parents' views and must notify his decision to them, to the appeal committee, and to the education authority.

*Appeals (choice of school)*
Appeal as to choice of school is only competent if the parents have made a placing request. Two methods of appeal are possible: the parents may appeal against the nomination by the education authority of the school to be attended, or against refusal of the placing request. Neither method is permitted within 12 months of a previous appeal of either type.

The appeal committee decides the appeal, but if their decision depends on matters referred to under the preceding heading, they may refer any of those matters to the Secretary of State for him to decide. They must notify their decision, with reasons, to the parents and to the education authority. A decision by the appeal committee refusing the parents' choice of school can be appealed to the Sheriff,[161] who may refer to the Secretary of State any of the matters which may be referred to him by the appeal committee. Where the Sheriff decides that the child should attend a fee-paying school, he can order the education authority to pay the fees and other costs of attending.

## Review and transfer

The education authority must keep under consideration the cases of all children who have a Record of Needs. The authority must carry out reviews whenever it thinks them necessary, and the parents may request a review of the decision to have a Record of Needs, or of the main information therein, but may not request a review of any matter until at least 12 months after that matter was last decided or reviewed. The procedure for reviews is substantially the same as for the original assessment, as described above, and the same rights of appeal are available. Whenever the Record of Needs is altered, following appeal or review, the education authority must intimate the change to the parents, and update all copies.

If a recorded child moves permanently from the area of one education authority to that of another, the Record of Needs must be transferred to the new authority as soon as practicable.

## Confidentiality, destruction

*Rights of access*
The parents must be given a copy of the Record of Needs, and

---

161 *Lamont* v. *Strathclyde Regional Council* 1988 SLT (Sh.Ct.) 9 is an example of such an appeal, though the decision itself has been superseded by the 1989 Act.

have the right to examine the original at any time during normal business hours. They need not be told of disclosure to anyone mentioned below, but may examine Part IX, which records all disclosures. The Named Person, civil servants concerned with the provision made for the SEN of the child, and the Reporter to the Children's Hearing, all have the right to see the Record of Needs, to ask for a copy or extract, and to ask for information from it.

*Discretionary access*
The education authority has a discretion to permit the following categories of people to see the Record of Needs (but not Part VII, containing the parents' views):

    (a) teachers and others involved in identifying the child's SEN, or providing for them;
    (b) social workers involved with the child; and
    (c) health board officers for the area.

They may be given information from the Record of Needs (except for Part VII), but may not be given a copy or extract. The authority may also disclose the Record for purposes of research or studies, but must not disclose the child's identity unless the education authority considers it essential for the research or studies.

*Confidentiality*
The education authority must not disclose the Record of Needs to anyone not mentioned above unless the parents consent in writing, and may demand return of copies sent to anyone other than the parents.

*Destruction*
The Record of Needs is kept for five years after discontinuation (upon review, or because the child has left school) and must then be destroyed. If it has been discontinued as a result of an appeal decided by the Secretary of State, or discontinued on request in the case of a young person over school leaving age, the parents can opt for it to be destroyed, or kept for five years. They must be sent a written notice asking for their decision in writing within 21 days, and if they do not respond, the Record is destroyed. They must be notified of destruction under any of the above provisions.

## Named Person[162]

Every recorded child has a Named Person, unless the parents have opted not to have one, but they may not insist upon their choice of person or appeal against the education authority's selection. The education authority must however have regard to any views expressed by the parents about the draft Record (which will include particulars of the proposed Named Person), and it would be most unusual for the education authority to insist upon a Named

---

162 For comment, and further information, see *Scots Law and the Mentally Handicapped*, pp.72-74 and *Information for the Named Person* (SSMH, 1987).

Person not acceptable to the parents.

The Named Person is defined as the person to whom application may be made for advice and information about the child's SEN, and his (or her) name, address and telephone number (if any) must be entered in the Record of Needs. He is entitled to inspect the Record of Needs, to ask for a copy of it, and to ask for an extract or information from it. His copy must be updated whenever information in the Record of Needs regarding SEN is altered, and must be returned on demand, though he may immediately ask for another.

## TRANSITION

Problems can be experienced in ensuring provision of necessary facilities and services at the age when, for most purposes, people cross over from educational responsibility to social work responsibility. The 1981 Act, which brought in recording procedures, also introduced the Future Needs Assessment in about the second last year of compulsory schooling. The 1986 Act strengthened the Future Needs Assessment procedures by linking social work departments into them.[163]

### Future Needs Assessment

The education authority must carry out a Future Needs Assessment of recorded children not more than two years nor less than nine months before the child reaches school leaving age.[164] The procedure is substantially the same as for preparing and reviewing the Record of Needs, and may be carried out in conjunction with such review. Following the Assessment, the education authority must prepare a report which must include a recommendation as to whether it would benefit the child to stay on at school after school leaving age, and, if so, whether the Record of Needs should be continued. Copies of the report are sent to the parents and (when the education authority considers it appropriate to do so) to the social work department and to the health board. If the education authority thinks that provision from any other bodies would benefit the child, copies are also sent to those bodies, provided that the parents agree.

### Opinion from social work department

The education authority must in various circumstances seek an opinion from the social work department as to whether a child or young person is a "disabled person".[165] It must do this:

(a) before completing a Future Needs Assessment; or

(b) if it decides to open a Record of Needs for a child or young person already beyond the age of Future Needs Assessment; or

---

163  s.13. For prospective changes under 1992 Act, see p.325.
164  See "Preliminary" at beginning of Part IB, p.313.
165  See "Disabled Persons" in Chap.5, p.241.

(c) if the child or young person was not a disabled person when a Future Needs Assessment was prepared, but there has been a subsequent change which causes the education authority to believe that he is now a disabled person.

In response, the social work department must give an opinion as to whether the person is a disabled person. If the social work opinion is that he is a disabled person, the following duties of both education and social work authorities arise.[166]

## Education authority duties

The education authority must enter in the Record of Needs and in the Future Needs report the opinion that the person is a disabled person. It must enter in the Future Needs report the date on which the person is to leave full-time education, or (if there is no such report) it must give the social work authority at least six weeks notice of the date on which the person is to leave full-time education. If for any reason these requirements have not been followed at the proper time, the education authority must follow them as soon as is reasonably practicable.

## Social work duties

The social work authority must carry out its own assessment of the person's needs for services under "welfare enactments", and prepares a report.[167] If the opinion that the person is a disabled person is given in conjunction with a Future Needs Assessment, the social work assessment must be carried out not less than nine months before the person reaches school leaving age. Otherwise, it must be carried out within six months from when the education authority asked for the social work opinion. However, the social work authority does not have to follow the procedures described in this paragraph if specifically asked not to by the person's parents, or by the person (if over 16 and able to do so).

## Continuing review

Both education and social work authorities must keep under consideration the cases of all persons who have had reports prepared following either a Future Needs Assessment or a social work assessment. Both authorities must review the information in the report "at such times as they consider appropriate". In the case of reports following a Future Needs Assessment, these review provisions apply whether or not the person has been noted as being a disabled person. Although a report may have been prepared by only one authority or the other, both must keep the case under consideration and carry out reviews.

---

166 These procedures do not in themselves place duties upon the health board, but where appropriate the Future Needs Assessment is submitted to the health board (see above).

167 *Welfare enactments* include various provisions of social work, health, chronically sick and disabled, and national assistance legislation - see 1986 Act, s.16.

## YOUNG PERSONS

Assessment under educational recording procedures of young persons[168] is voluntary, and where possible the young persons are themselves involved in the procedures. Accordingly, the provisions and procedures regarding assessment and preparation of a Record of Needs, as described above in relation to children, apply subject to the following modifications.

### Assessment

The provisions regarding formal notices inviting or requiring participation in assessment do not apply. The education authority may devise whatever assessment process it considers necessary. If the young person is able to express his own views, he must be invited to do so. If the education authority is satisfied that the young person cannot express his own views, the parents must be invited to give their views. Either way, the invitation must be in writing and allow at least 14 days for submission of views about the young person's SEN, how those needs should be met, and whether the young person should have a Record of Needs.

### Notices

If the young person is able to express his own views, notices are sent to the young person rather than to the parents, and it is the young person who may take the various steps which may be taken by parents in relation to children under school leaving age. If however the education authority is satisfied that the young person cannot express his own views, the parents act for him, just as they do for a child under school leaving age.

### Discontinuance

The young person (or the parents acting for him) may request that the Record of Needs be discontinued. If they do so, it must be.

## ADULTS

The remainder of this section describes duties of education and social work authorities in respect of all people over school age, including adults. Only legal duties are described, and for further information on the types of provision which may be available see Part IA, above.

### Further education

*Further and Higher Education (Scotland) Act 1992*
When the 1992 Act is brought into force further education colleges will be run by independent Boards centrally funded by the Secretary of State, and universities will be brought under the Higher Education Funding Council. Local authorities will cease to be responsible for further education, but will remain responsible

---

168 Pupils who remain in education from school leaving age up to 18.

for community education. Further education colleges will have a duty to provide vocational education, and will be required to assist in future needs assessments by providing information or advice reasonably required by the local authority to facilitate the assessment (s.27). In exercising their powers under the Act, both the Secretary of State and Boards must have regard to the needs of students with learning difficulties, and the definition of further education includes programmes of learning for people with a learning difficulty [ss.1(2) and 12(3); s.6(1)(c)].

## Social work duties and statutory powers

### Duties under Mental Health Act 1984, s.11

Social work authorities have a duty to provide suitable training and occupation for people with a mental handicap, or to secure the provision of such training and occupation. These must be provided for people over school age who are not in hospital. Authorities must make such provision as they think necessary for transport for people wishing to use such facilities. They may discharge their duties by making arrangements with voluntary organisations, to whom they may make financial contributions.

### Powers under Social Work (Scotland) Act 1968, s.12

Social work authorities may provide *inter alia* "advice" and "guidance" to persons in need, who are defined as including persons with any kind of mental disorder. This power may reasonably be construed as including appropriate instruction and training. (Compare the more specific provisions of the equivalent English statute, National Assistance Act 1948, s.29).

# PART II - EMPLOYMENT

### Preliminary

Provision of some form of employment is as important to people with a mental handicap (where appropriate) as it is to anyone else, because it provides a structured week and improves self esteem. It also provides opportunity for wider social contacts and financial independence. The performance of persons who have a mental handicap can be excellent if supervisors and instructors ensure that they are given tasks within their capabilities, but only persons with moderate mental handicaps are likely to find or retain any form of employment. Many acquire skills and are painstaking in their work thus making extremely reliable and useful employees. Schemes for people with disabilities have tended to concentrate upon sheltered employment or diversionary activity, but supported employment is now becoming a further option.

## Registration

To register as disabled for purposes of employment, a person must be substantially handicapped in obtaining or keeping employment, or in undertaking work on his own account, of a kind which apart from his injury, disease or deformity would be suited to his age, experience and qualifications. The disability must be likely to persist for at least 12 months.[169] This voluntary registration scheme is separate from that adopted by social services (or social work) departments[170] and persons who are registered carry a "green card" issued by the Disablement Resettlement Officer at the local Job Centre. In practice many people who could register choose not to do so because production of the card is seen as a disincentive for employers to take them on. *Committees for the Employment of Disabled People* have been set up under this legislation to advise the Secretary of State on local matters relating to employment of people with disabilities.

### Powers of local authority

A local authority may make provision for sheltered employment training and assistance in finding work for those who are registered as disabled with the Department of Employment and are unlikely, because of the nature or severity of their disablement, to obtain employment at any time or for a considerable time, or to work on their own account, and who are ordinarily resident in its area.[171]

### Unfair dismissal

Some protection is afforded to an employee who is registered as a disabled person under the employment legislation. It has been held that an employer should not expect a normal standard of work or output from such an employee.[172] Dismissal would only be fair if it can be shown that the standard of work was below that which could reasonably be expected from the particular employee, and the employer would also need to show that the case had been given special consideration and that the needs of the business made dismissal necessary.[173]

### Company obligations

Companies employing more than 250 people are required to include in their directors' report a statement describing the policy operated in the previous financial year towards the recruitment, training, career development and promotion of people with disabilities and the retention of newly disabled employees.[174] This is not restricted to persons registered as disabled and whilst it does not apply to public sector employees it is in practice adopted.

## Quota schemes

There is a statutory duty on a firm employing over 20 people to ensure that three per cent. of its employees are registered disabled

---

169 Disabled Persons (Employment) Act 1944, s.1.
170 *I.e.* under the Chronically Sick and Disabled Persons Act 1970.
171 Disabled Persons (Employment) Acts 1944 and 1958.
172 *Kerr* v. *Atkinson's Vehicles Ltd* [1974] IRLR 36.
173 *Pascoe* v. *Hallen & Medway* [1975] IRLR 116.
174 Companies Act 1985, s. 235 and Sched.7, Part III.

people.[175] Although this includes persons who have a mental handicap, they must be actively looking for work with some prospect of finding it. An employer who is below quota must not engage anyone other than a registered disabled person without first obtaining a permit to do so from the local Job Centre, nor discharge such a person without reasonable cause. Employers who are subject to quota are obliged to keep records of the number and names of registered disabled persons and to produce these for inspection when required. Certain occupations are reserved for people with disabilities *e.g.* car park and lift attendants.

In practice the quota scheme is not enforced,[176] and each year some 20,000 permits are issued allowing employers to ignore the quota, although this is on the understanding that they will notify details of vacancies to the Job Centre and consider sympathetically any suitable registered disabled person who is available. The statutory scheme does not apply to public sector employers and whilst it is adopted by them, few meet the quota.

### Employment schemes

The *Employment Service*[177] provides a series of leaflets which deal with disabilities and their effect on employment. This includes a booklet entitled *Code of Good Practice on the Employment of Disabled People* which provides information and guidance though this is primarily concerned with those who can compete fully in the normal open employment market. For those with severe disabilities sheltered employment is more suitable.

The *Disablement Advisory Service* gives practical help and advice on integration of people with disabilities into a workforce and can arrange for expert advice on medical, psychological and technical aspects.[178]

The *Employment Medical Advisory Service* gives detailed advice on the medical aspects of employing disabled persons.

The *Employment Rehabilitation Service* provides an assessment service for workers who become disabled and employers who seek advice, and makes recommendations about future employment. It also runs courses which aim to restore confidence and abilities.[179]

The *Pathway Employment Service* offers a free service run in conjunction with many local authorities and the Employment Service which introduces employers to people with learning disabilities, and helps recruitment and training for a trial period before there is a commitment. (Pathway is for England and Wales

---

175 Disabled Persons (Employment) Acts 1944 and 1958.

176 Since 1944 there have been less than 10 prosecutions with fines averaging £62, the last in 1975. In 1989 the Department of Employment made only 2,050 quota inspections.

177 Address in Appendix I.

178 May become part of PAC (Personal Assessment and Counselling Team) following re-organisation.

179 May also become part of PAC. Rehabilitation is provided through agents, *e.g.* SSMH in Scotland.

only; in Scotland refer to SSMH for advice). There is assessment of the individual's abilities and aptitudes and employer's requirements, and support given to each. A foster worker may be allocated to the prospective employee and paid a gratuity for providing support and assistance. The aim is to place people with a mental handicap in regular jobs earning the going rate for the work that they do. Funding comes from local authorities and health authorities, and sometimes from other sources.

### Special Schemes

The *Special Aids to Employment Scheme* and *Adaptations to Premises and Equipment Scheme* are available to both employers and employees who are unable to provide equipment or modifications to premises at their own expense.

The *Job Introduction Scheme* provides financial help to enable a disabled person to be taken on for a trial period where there is doubt about ability to do a particular job.

The *Sheltered Placements Scheme* is a government run programme designed to help people with disabilities who are unable to work at the required speed. It enables a severely disabled employee to be paid only for the work actually done whilst a sponsoring organisation makes up the remuneration.

*Fares to Work* provides assistance for taxi costs for disabled people who cannot travel independently.

# PART III - CONCLUSION

There seems to be a reluctance to give disabled people legal rights which can be enforced in the courts. General duties prove to be ineffectual when not backed up by adequate financial resources, and the needs of the disabled do not generally fare well when balanced against other needs of society. Even where specific legal duties are imposed upon authorities, as in the case of special education, experience shows that they are not always complied with, usually because of funding pressures, but at least legal remedies are available in the field of education, even if not widely used. Those in the context of employment are not even enforced.

### Provision of special education

Many lawyers in England feel that the intentions of the Warnock Committee and the 1981 Act are not being fulfilled, and that parents are having to resort to the courts with increasing frequency to try to obtain the provision which they consider their child requires, as the following quote shows[180]:

> Difficulties arise in relation to the identification of need and the making of provision. Certain authorities seem only prepared to identify need where they already have the provision available to meet that need, and there is a

---

[180] Memorandum of the Law Society's Group for the Welfare of People with a Mental Handicap to the House of Commons Education, Science and Arts Committee 1986/87.

reluctance to identify need if the provision for that need is likely to require additional resources not previously budgetted for. Where an authority does not have available, or does not wish to have available, a particular provision there seems to be ample opportunity to avoid the intentions of the legislation, and regrettably, the cases brought before the courts appear to have found justification for supporting the authority's approach. Dispute between parents and their advisers and education authorities, particularly where support for the parents' views are forthcoming, if not actually stimulated by, other professionals dealing with the child give rise to feelings of bitterness and resentment on the part of parents at a time when they are already under tremendous psychological and emotional strain. It is appreciated that proposals for reform in this area are tied up with questions of the overall funding of resources for the handicapped. Unless steps are taken to ensure that the Act is implemented in a considerate and consistent manner and in such a way that the fulfilment of the needs of the child is seen as the predominant consideration then amending legislation will be necessary in order to eliminate the discretions available to local education authorities and to enforce compliance by them with the primary intentions of the legislation.

## Recommendations

A group of voluntary organisations has made recommendations in regard to education which include the following[181]:

(a)  Children with special needs should have the right to an appropriate education in the setting which is correct for their needs and in line with their parents' choices;

(b)  Local Education Authorities should be allowed to retain central funding of Special Educational Needs support services as a mandatory exception within the Local Management of Schools formulae;

(c)  Co-operation between special and mainstream schools should be improved through increasing flexibility in the special schools budgets;

(d)  Statements of Special Educational Needs should be expanded to include non-educational services (such as speech therapy), with local education authorities made responsible for ensuring that these services are provided;

(e)  The appeal system should be changed to introduce an effective independent review structure, and the appeal procedure brought in line with the 1980 Education Act;

(f)  The extent to which children with Special Educational Needs receive modified curricula or are exempted from subjects should be monitored, and exemption should be the exception rather than the norm;

(g)  The assessment and statementing procedure should be extended to require local education authorities to provide for the Special Educational Needs of students throughout adult life where appropriate.

(h)  Funding for Further Education colleges should provide greater incentives for them to accept students with Special Educational Needs.

## Leaving school

The transition from school to adult and/or working life is particularly significant to persons with disabilities because of the implications upon the quality of the rest of their life. The aim should be to achieve personal autonomy, productive activity leading to economic self-sufficiency, equal opportunities for leisure and community participation, and meaningful relationships with others. These are the qualities of adult status, though such status may be physically defined by bodily changes and legally defined as the age of 18 years. Persons with a mental handicap have difficulty achieving adult status because their disability

---

181  *An Agenda for the 1990's* published by the Disability Manifesto Group.

prevents them from achieving the necessary level of competence and denies them access to learning experiences, and also because such competence as they may have is seldom recognised by others. Preconceptions about the effects of a disability should not increase the personal handicap or limit choice or opportunity, and though specific schemes may concentrate on one aspect of transition it should not be assumed that other aspects of the individual's development automatically take place. Transition is slower for those with mental disabilities so education, training and support is needed for a longer period. The statutory right to an education ceases on leaving school, but continuing education should be available to all, regardless of their age or degree of handicap. Opportunities vary from area to area, and there is no national programme for school leavers.

## Discrimination in employment

Discrimination comes in many forms and may be unintentional rather than through prejudice, but three types may be identified:

*direct* - treating the individual less favourably because of his or her disability;

*indirect* - imposing non-essential conditions which make it harder for disabled people to qualify; or

*inequality* - failing to remove a barrier which otherwise exists in the environment and which may make it impossible for the disabled person to compete.[182]

There is no law against discrimination against disabled people in the workplace, but a major difficulty is that disability, unlike race or sex, can be relevant to job performance and what to some might seem like discrimination may in reality be recruitment based on legitimate preferences and likely performance. This is particularly so in the case of mental disabilities. Employers often take on non-disabled people on the basis of general character assuming that they will learn the job, whereas they tend to require disabled people to show that they can do the job before they will take them on. Three factors give impetus to the campaign for anti-discrimination laws in this context:

- legislation against discrimination on grounds of race and sex[183];
- assertion by groups of disabled people of their own rights[184];
- new laws to prevent discrimination against disabled people in the United States and other countries.[185]

As long as the law is based upon freedom of contract in the workplace, discrimination against disabled people will continue. Legislation is needed, but the policy of recent governments has been against giving rights to the individual and even the quota

---

[182]  *e.g.* a building that is inaccessible to a physically disabled person.

[183]  Sex Discrimination Act 1975; Race Relations Act 1976.

[184]  The civil rights movement has grown to the extent that there are now organisations *of* disabled people rather than just *for* disabled people.

[185]  Americans with Disabilities Act 1990, coming into force in 1992.

system introduced by the Disabled Persons (Employment) Act 1944 has not been enforced.[186] Instead of new legislation aimed at securing good practice through sanctions a voluntary approach is preferred, as embodied in the 1984 *Code of Good Practice*, but grants and incentive schemes for employers remain inadequate to make any real inroads into the problem especially in times of high unemployment. Despite the recommendation of the House of Commons Employment Select Committee that "the Government should explore urgently the possibility of equal opportunities legislation for the employment of people with disabilities"[187] the Minister for Disabled People expressed the view that "the most constructive and productive way forward is through raising awareness in the community as a whole".[188] A private member's Bill promoted in 1992 is designed to introduce anti-discrimination legislation covering not only employment but also access to buildings, transport facilities, services, education, insurance, recreation and housing.[189]

---

[186] The Government proposed abolition in a consultation paper, *Employment and Training for People with Disabilities*, (1990). Other reforms were also proposed which may affect the employment schemes described above.

[187] First Report for Session 1990-91.

[188] For more material on this topic see *Equal Rights for Disabled People* by Ian Bynoe and others, Institute for Public Policy Research, 30 Southampton Street, London WC2E 7RA.

[189] Civil Rights (Disabled Persons) Bill 1992.

# CHAPTER 7   HOUSING AND RESIDENTIAL CARE

## Introduction

Some people with a mental handicap are able to establish independent lives in the community, but the majority are looked after within the family and when the stage is reached when parents or voluntary carers die or can no longer cope it may be necessary to rely upon professional care. Residential care may be needed on a long term basis or for short periods as respite care. Until recently people with a severe mental handicap were looked after in special hospitals which were the responsibility of the health authorities. Now their care is seen as being under the auspices of social services departments of local authorities (in Scotland, social work departments) and even long stay patients in hospitals are being moved out. At the same time local authorities are moving away from the concept of institutional care in residential homes to small homes in the community.

Residential care may be seen as housing plus the other elements of care (education, work and recreation) in a single package. However, total dependence upon a care establishment should be avoided as it is this which leads to an institutionalised existence. Residents of care homes are encouraged to have contact with outside agencies for daytime activities and to benefit from as much care in the community as possible. A care home that enables a resident to move out into his own home, even if on a supported basis, will have achieved its objective far better than by providing a protected environment for life.

The problem may be enabling people with a mental handicap to establish a home, either alone or with others. There is an obligation on housing authorities[1] to provide housing for vulnerable people who are homeless and those with a mental handicap may come within this definition, but this does not necessarily mean accommodation of a particular type or best suited to an individual's needs. Most authorities seek to cater for special needs, but the accommodation available may not be suitable and whilst moral pressure can be applied in such circumstances there is no legal remedy.

In this chapter we consider first the types of care provision that may be made and then housing for mentally disabled people. The framework of controls that apply to registered homes in England and registered establishments in Scotland is then identified separately because the legislation is different, and finally we point

---

1   *I.e.* district councils, or (in England) borough councils or (in Scotland) islands councils.

to some of the implications of registration in both countries.
Funding remains the controlling factor and this is considered in
Chapter 8.

# PART I - CARE PROVISION

## Background

The Mental Health Act 1959 allowed local authorities to provide,
equip and maintain suitable residential accommodation or hostels
for the care or after-care of mentally handicapped people.[2] A
White Paper in 1971 made the provision of local authority hostels
a priority.[3] These were to provide long-term residential care for
those people who could not live at home but did not need hospital
care. As a result many new purpose-built hostels came into
existence in the 1970's. The inability of local authorities to cope
with increased demand coupled with the incentive provided by the
availability of state funding in the form of Income Support
residential care allowance produced an unplanned explosion in the
provision of residential care homes for the elderly in the private
and voluntary sectors, which resulted in limits being placed on the
amount of the allowance. Homes for people with a mental
handicap needed a "top-up" if they were to be economically viable,
and they came under pressure to become larger in order to remain
viable. This resulted in institutionalised hospital care being
replaced by care of an institutional nature in large care homes, but
the policy is now for small homes in the community.

## Forms of care

*Residential care*
Full time care in a residential environment may be provided in
different ways. What is required depends largely upon the needs
and abilities of the individual, but that which is actually provided
may depend more upon what is available and can be financed.
Some homes provide a range of activities during the daytime, but
others rely upon local authority provision for residents during the
week, such as attendance at adult training centres.

*Respite care*
This is short term care, often on a regular basis, to give parents or
carers a break from caring. It represents not only an opportunity
for them to live a normal life with other children, but also a
beneficial break from routine and change of environment for the
individual cared for. Respite care may also be used as a way of
preparing a handicapped person for a move from the family to
permanent residential care and this is especially important when
the carer is becoming old or infirm. The care may be provided in
a local authority hostel, a private or charitably maintained home,

---

2    This provision remains unchanged by the 1983 Act. See Mental Health
     (Scotland) Act 1984, ss.7 and 8 for equivalent Scottish provisions.
3    *Better Services for the Mentally Handicapped* - DHSS.

or by a family under a local authority supervised scheme. Family support or fostering schemes operate in many parts of the country, usually run by social services (or social work) departments but sometimes by voluntary organisations. Support families are recruited and training is given before they are matched with a "handicapped family" with information being exchanged so that the child can experience continuity between the two households. A longer term placement may also be arranged.

### Day care
Some residential establishments provide care during the daytime for non-residents and in many cases this is all that is required, though in other cases it may be all that is available.

## Adult homes

Various types of home provide residential care for adults.

### Residential care homes
Many disabled and infirm people live in homes which are specially set up to care for their needs. These may be run by individuals or companies on a commercial basis with a view to profit, or by societies or charities which charge fees to cover weekly expenses but do not seek to make a profit. Homes of this nature are also administered by local authorities, though the policy is now for them to buy in such services rather than seek to provide them. There is a registration system, but this does not apply to local authority homes though inspection procedures have been introduced. Residential care homes vary from small houses to large establishments, and some village communities have also been established, often with a strong individual philosophy.

### Nursing homes
Those with very severe physical as well as mental disabilities may need full time nursing care which can only be provided in a hospital or private nursing home so the regulatory procedure which applies to nursing homes is included here for the sake of completeness. There is a sub-class known as *mental nursing homes* which provide for those with a mental illness and these may on occasion accommodate people with a mental handicap simply because no other suitable provision is available.

### Group homes
This term generally relates to establishments providing residential services for people with present or past mental disorder. They may live together in an ordinary house and look after themselves with or without resident support, the aim being in some cases to prepare them for living independently in the community. Homes arranged on a "core and cluster" basis may be particularly suitable for those with a mental handicap.

### Adult Placement Schemes
Some local authorities developed arrangements (otherwise known as *boarding-out schemes*) whereby one or more individuals with a

mental handicap are accommodated as paying tenants of a suitable private householder who lives in the same premises and provides care and attention which is monitored by the social services department. A variation is *Life Share* where the disabled person lives with a non-disabled person and they jointly have a tenancy of a house or flat; the sharer is responsible for organising the daytime and leisure activities of the disabled person and receives a salary from the local authority.

### Children's homes (England)[4]

The legislation relating to homes for children was consolidated by the Children Act 1989 which identifies three types of home in addition to fostering arrangements.[5] It is the duty of any organisation or person carrying on such a home to safeguard and promote the child's welfare, and the relevant local authority is under a duty to ensure that this is being done. This legislation relates to all children, but homes specifically for handicapped children come within the Registered Homes Act 1984 rather than the 1989 Act.[6]

*Community homes*

Local authorities have a duty to make such arrangements as they consider appropriate to ensure that community homes are available for the care and accommodation of children looked after by them and for the welfare of children whether or not looked after by them.[7] The authority does not necessarily provide and manage the home, and there are two sub-categories[8]:

*Controlled:* provided by voluntary organisation but managed, equipped and maintained by the authority.

*Assisted:* provided and managed by voluntary organisation but equipped and maintained by the authority.

Provisions relating to the management and conduct of all types of community homes are contained in the 1989 Act, which also gives the Secretary of State power to make regulations on a wide variety of matters concerned therewith.[9] A community home with which a voluntary organisation is concerned may not be run at a profit.

*Voluntary homes*

A home or other institution providing care and accommodation for children which is carried on by a voluntary organisation is known as a voluntary home.[10] Such a home may not be run for

---

4    For registration of homes in Scotland see Part IIIB below.

5    Children Act 1989, Parts VII and VIII, repealing and in part re-enacting Child Care Act 1980 and Children's Homes Act 1982.

6    See Part IIIA below.

7    Children Act 1989, s.53(1).

8    s.53(4) and (5) respectively.

9    Sched.4.

10   s.60. This does not include a nursing home, mental nursing home, residential care home or a school and certain other exempted homes (including community homes).

profit, and there is a registration procedure with rights of appeal to the Registered Homes Tribunal. The Secretary of State has power to make regulations.[11]

### Registered children's homes

There is regulation of the private placement of children either in a children's home or with foster parents.[12] Children's homes which are privately run for profit, other than those which are controlled by other parts of the Act or other legislation, are subject to controls. A children's home means a home which provides (or usually provides or is intended to provide) accommodation and care wholly or mainly for more than three children at any one time.[13] Registration is compulsory, conditions may be imposed and there is a right of appeal to the Registered Homes Tribunal.[14] Failure to register is a criminal offence, and persons may be disqualified from carrying on or being employed in such homes.

## Types of provision

The provision of homes may be organised by different bodies and financed in various ways.

### Health Authorities

Until the 1950s the only provision made by the state for the care of people with a mental handicap was in long stay mental hospitals. The financing of hospital care has always been the responsibility of health authorities, but as it has become apparent that mentally handicapped people do not need hospital care such authorities have developed forms of care which do not involve living in a hospital and are now authorised to make capital and revenue funding available for schemes to help people move out of hospital or provide an alternative to admission. These schemes overlap with the provision made by local authorities. However, the incidence of mental illness is higher amongst those with a mental handicap than the rest of the community, so for some a mental hospital is still the only answer. Others with profound physical disabilities need nursing care that currently can only be given in a suitable hospital.

### Joint planning

Health authorities are increasingly handing over care of suitable patients to social services departments who thereupon become responsible for providing long term care in the community. Joint planning is necessary, and a transfer of money must be made from the health authority to reflect the cost to the social services department of taking over the financial obligations.[15]

### Local Authorities

Local authorities may either provide care themselves or buy it in

---

11  Sched.5.
12  Parts VIII and IX respectively.
13  s.63(3)(a). The numbers distinguish this from private fostering.
14  Sched.6.
15  In Scotland the resources are more often transferred to a voluntary body.

from other agencies, and are now being encouraged to arrange
and supervise care rather than actually to provide it.

*Voluntary bodies*
Voluntary bodies have an important part to play in the provision
of all kinds of supported housing and residential care. Those
working with housing associations must have a legal status, but
being a registered charity or a limited company is sufficient.

*Housing Associations*
Housing associations are involved in the provision of ordinary
housing with support and residential care homes, and some have
particular experience in setting up homes for disabled people. This
is considered in Part V below.

*MENCAP Homes Foundation (England)*
This charity seeks and accepts properties from any source and uses
them where appropriate to provide homes for mentally
handicapped people. Groups of homes are supervised by an Area
Management Committee and operate on a self-financing basis.

*SSMH Homes (Scotland)*
SSMH Homes was established by the Scottish Society for the
Mentally Handicapped as a separate company. It develops and
provides residential accommodation for people with profound
needs.

# PART II - HOUSING

We consider here the provision of ordinary housing for people
with a mental handicap and some legal problems that arise.

## Tenancies

Some individuals are able to live alone with supervision on a
visiting basis, and it may then be desired, both from the standpoint
of state benefits and security of tenure, for the individual to be the
tenant, but this can be difficult to establish where there is lack of
mental capacity. To maximise the number of individuals whose
tenancies are likely to be valid, enlightened landlords simplify
their tenancy agreements and write them in plain English.[16] A
parent or other concerned person may act as guarantor, become a
joint tenant, or take the tenancy and allow the individual to occupy
the home with the knowledge of the landlord, but these courses
could have undesired consequences.

*Capacity*
The legal test of capacity to enter into a tenancy is not clear, but
appears to be the general contractual test of ability to understand
the nature of the transaction. There can only be a tenancy, and the
individual can only have the status and protections of a tenant, if

---

16   *e.g.* such agreements use "we" and "you" instead of the impersonal "the
     landlord" and "the tenant".

he had sufficient contractual capacity for the contract of tenancy to be valid. When it is in the interests of the individual to take the tenancy it is to be hoped that too high a test of capacity will not be imposed. Where the tenancy is clearly in the best interests of the individual and the agreement does not contain unusual or onerous terms, the tenancy may possibly come within the special principles that apply to the purchase of necessary items. If the individual is capable of signing the landlord may be persuaded to accept this signature especially if it is witnessed by a close member of the family or a solicitor (in Scotland, as one of the two witnesses).[17]

In England, if the landlord wishes to establish an undisputed legal relationship with a tenant who is incapable by reason of mental disorder of managing his affairs, an application must be made to the Court of Protection.[18] In Scotland, either a curator bonis may be appointed or (if the only act of management required is execution of the lease) then a tutor-dative may be appointed solely for that purpose.[19] These are involved and costly processes, so it is best to find an alternative. Any documents should be worded as simply as possible to enhance the likelihood of understanding, and thus validity.

## Council tenancies

There is no legal right to a council house and waiting lists are often long, especially as the number of houses has decreased during recent years. A housing department has a discretion as to the manner in which it allocates tenancies, but is obliged to publish a summary of the rules and procedures that it adopts.[20] It may not impose a blanket condition that excludes consideration on the merits of a particular category of person, or discriminate on grounds of colour, race or sex, and reasonable preference must be given to large families or those in unsatisfactory housing conditions, but no general priority applies to disabled people. A council is likely to adopt one of the following schemes:

*date* - order of application;
*merit* - according to the views of councillors as to the merits of each application;
*points* - allocation of points according to a scale of need.[21]

The particular scheme should be examined to ensure that it has been followed. Clearly the existence of a mental handicap on the part of the proposed tenant (or perhaps a member of the family) is

---

17   A letter from a solicitor confirming that he is satisfied with the terms and has advised the tenant who has a sufficient understanding to be bound by law may satisfy a landlord who is otherwise prepared to accept the tenant.

18   Authority may be given for a Receiver appointed by the Court to enter into the tenancy, or the Court can make a short procedure Order confirming the tenancy. This topic is dealt with in Chap.10A.

19   See Chap.10B.

20   A pamphlet will usually be available from the council offices free of charge, but detailed information must be available on request, usually for a fee.

21   This has become the most popular scheme, but the factors for which points are awarded vary considerably.

likely to be relevant under the merit or points schemes, and it should be drawn to the attention of the housing officer.

*Succession*
The spouse of a deceased tenant, or another member of the family (including a cohabitee of the other sex), may be entitled to succeed to a tenancy where certain conditions are met.[22] Such successor must have occupied the dwelling as his principal or only home at the time of the tenant's death, and (except in the case of a spouse) must have lived with the deceased tenant for a period of at least 12 months prior thereto.[23] There are many cases where people with a mental handicap live with a surviving parent in tenanted accommodation until the parent dies and then wish to remain in the same accommodation, but there is no satisfactory procedure to enable them to claim succession rights if they lack capacity.[24] The situation will usually be determined by the care needs of the individual, but a relative or suitable person who wishes to move in to take the place of the deceased parent and provide continuity of care would not be entitled to take over the tenancy.

*Right to buy*
Secure tenants of public sector housing who have occupied for two or more years, have the right to buy at a notional market value discounted according to the number of years of occupation and the right to a mortgage to cover the full cost. Some tenancies are expressly excluded from this right, including those granted by charitable housing trusts or associations and housing associations which have never received public housing funds. Certain types of dwelling are automatically excluded, such as those specially designed for the physically disabled and group dwellings for persons who are mentally disordered.[25]

---

22   Housing Act 1985, s.113 (England) and Housing (Scotland) Act 1987, s.52 for public sector housing; Rent Act 1977, s.2 and Sched.1 (as amended by Housing Act 1988) for protected tenancies (England). In Scotland, only a spouse may succeed to an assured tenancy: Housing (Scotland) Act 1988, s.31. In certain circumstances another member of the family may succeed to a regulated tenancy, but then receives an assured tenancy, Rent (Scotland) Act 1984, ss.1 and 1A, Scheds. 1, 1A and 1B (as amended by Housing (Scotland) Act 1988, s.46 and Sched 6).

23   In Scotland, a child must be aged at least 16. There can be only one succession in respect of a tenancy, so if it has already passed to a spouse it cannot thereafter pass to a child - Housing Act 1988, s.17(2) for assured tenancies and Housing Act 1985, s.87 for public sector (England); Housing (Scotland) Act 1988, s.31 for assured tenancies and Housing (Scotland) Act 1987, s.52(5) for public sector.

24   The only procedure available in England is an application to the Court of Protection when a short procedure Order could be made, but this takes time and funding may not be available. In Scotland, appointment of a curator bonis or tutor-dative would be necessary. See Chaps.10A and 10B.

25   Housing Act 1985, Part V, as amended by Housing and Planning Act 1986 (England); Housing (Scotland) Act 1987, s.61. See also s.64(4).

## Homeless persons

If an individual is actually and unintentionally homeless and has a priority need, the local housing authority must provide housing.[26] Homelessness can arise in various ways and may include being threatened with homelessness. It is necessary to show a local connection with the authority to whom application is made, but the authority may meet its duty in many ways and need not necessarily provide a council house.[27] The law is complex, having generated much litigation, so only certain aspects relevant to mental handicap are mentioned, but the Government has issued guidance on how the law is to be applied.[28] Being homeless is not by itself sufficient unless the applicant can show a *priority need*. There are several categories which include, in addition to having dependent children or being pregnant, being *vulnerable* as a result of "old age, mental illness or handicap or physical disability or some other special reason". An applicant who has such a person living with him, or who might reasonably be expected to live with him, will have a priority need. In this context vulnerable means "less able to fend for oneself so that injury or detriment will result, when a less vulnerable man (or woman) will be able to cope without harmful effects". The authority must first ask whether the applicant is vulnerable, and then decide whether this is a result of one of the factors specified above, so evidence in support of the application should spell out how and why the handicap makes the applicant vulnerable. Failure to consider this would amount to a breach by the authority of its obligations.

Those who are both homeless and have a priority need are entitled to permanent accommodation, but if classed as *intentionally homeless* they may only be housed temporarily. There has been much argument about this term, but in general it means having deliberately given up accommodation which there is a right to occupy or failing to do what is necessary to keep such accommodation. An act or omission should not be seen as deliberate in certain circumstances, including where the applicant was "incapable of managing his or her affairs because of old age or mental illness or handicap". In the event of an adverse decision an appeal procedure may be offered by the council, but failing this the remedies are a complaint to the ombudsman or application for judicial review.

---

26  This duty was introduced by the Housing (Homeless Persons) Act 1977, now Housing Act 1985, Pt.III and Housing (Scotland) Act 1987, Part II. The Housing and Planning Act 1986, s.14 deals with the suitability of accommodation offered in discharge of this statutory obligation.

27  If the applicant is also in need of care and attention, the provision of residential accommodation may be sufficient, but not where there is a personal carer living with the applicant.

28  There are two separate *Codes of Guidance*, one for England and Wales and one for Scotland. Advice is available from SHAC (in London) and Shelter elsewhere, and various books are available on homeless persons.

## Licences

In many living situations, because of the need for care and an inability to enter into formal arrangements the handicapped person merely has a licence to occupy. This may be shared occupation of a house, or a room in a residential care home which may itself be shared, in which event the only exclusive facility will be a bed, wardrobe and chest of drawers. The individual's state benefits are used to finance these facilities, so a contract between the individual and the provider arises in effect by default even though one party lacks mental capacity. The usual tests of contractual capacity apply so there will only be a licence if the licensee has adequate capacity to enter it. It is accepted good practice to have a written "licence to occupy" agreement, clearly and simply structured and written in plain English, and to go through the document carefully with the licensee. Even where capacity is doubtful, every effort is made to explain the terms of licence as far as possible.

Failing to recognise this relationship is to deny the individual the occupation rights and freedoms which are generally regarded as fundamental by others, *e.g.* to a period of notice before changes are imposed, private facilities, choice of furnishings and decorations, unrestricted access, financial arrangements. One answer is for the party providing the facilities to publish standard terms in advance which deal with all usual matters and may be referred to should an issue arise. Reliance upon custom is not sufficient because people have different ideas as to what is customary, usually depending upon their standpoint in regard to the transaction.

## Owner occupation

Cases arise where a person with a mental handicap inherits money and it is desired to invest this in a home for personal occupation, possibly so as to restore entitlement to means-tested benefit. Where advance planning is possible this outcome may be achieved through a trust, but failing this an application to the Court of Protection (or, in Scotland, appointment of curator bonis or tutor-dative) is necessary unless an Enduring Power of Attorney can be executed and registered (or, in Scotland, the person has been able to execute a valid Power of Attorney) or the individual has the necessary mental capacity.[29]

*Mortgages*

If personal funds are insufficient for the purchase of a suitable home the normal solution is to borrow from a building society or similar source upon the security of the home. The person with a mental handicap may have a reliable income from state benefits and could obtain additional means-tested benefits to fund mortgage subscriptions, but may encounter discrimination when seeking a mortgage through normal sources. It helps if a guarantor can be

---

[29]    See generally Chaps.10A and 10B.

found, but it may still be necessary to satisfy the lender that the individual has the mental capacity to enter into the transaction.[30]

## Restrictive covenants

People with a mental handicap seldom live alone and, if able to live in the community, often share their home with others. Problems arise when there is joint occupation of a house subject to a restrictive covenant that it may only be occupied as a private residence, especially if the covenant also states "in the occupation of a single family".[31] It is essentially a matter of interpretation, and the authorities show that it is a question of fact and degree in each case whether the arrangements for occupation constitute a breach of the covenant. Relevant factors include the number of residents and degree of permanence of occupation, the relationship between them, whether any payment is made and its nature, whether the owner or tenant is in residence and if not whether other people supervise the residents.[32]

### Recent litigation

A High Court decision in England has caused concern in regard to the provision of ordinary houses in the community for occupation by small groups of supervised people with a mental disability.[33] The covenants were of a type often found on residential building estates, and Mr Justice Ferris held that as the residents were not related and were different from an ordinary family unit, the home was not being used as a private dwelling and the use was detrimental to the developer. It was feared that this ruling could be used by people objecting to group homes and independent living projects, and might lead to developers routinely applying restrictive covenants to houses to stop them being used for those purposes. On appeal it was accepted that this type of occupation was not use as a private dwellinghouse but it was doubted whether it comprised a trade or business and the finding of detriment to the developer was not upheld.[34] The court's reasoning is important:

> "The user covenant had two limbs: (i) not to carry on from the property any trade and (ii) not to use the dwellinghouse for any purposes other than those incidental to the enjoyment of a private dwellinghouse. ... the number of residents in each house was small, no more than four; the period of their residence was permanent or indefinite, the relationship between them was that of a group of friends or at any rate associates. They made no payment for their board and lodging. The owner did not come and could not reside there himself. He did everything in his power to make each house the home

---

30  The authors know of cases where home ownership with a mortgage has been arranged and is working reasonably smoothly.

31  In Scotland, a restrictive title condition to this effect is common, especially in tenement property.

32  *Tendler* v. *Sproule* [1947] 1 All ER 193; *Segal Securities Ltd* v. *Thoseby* [1963] 1 All ER 500;

33  *C. & G. Homes* v. *Bath District Health Authority* April 1990 (unreported). This decision is of concern in Scotland where title conditions to similar effect are common.

34  *C & G Homes Ltd* v. *Secretary of State for Health* [1991] 2 All ER 841.

of the residents, giving them so far as practicable responsibility for domestic duties and decisions, and the right to determine the composition of their group. But the owner remained under a statutory duty to care for them. He did that by means of the attendance of two staff during the day and one at night and the provision of ... services. His Lordship doubted whether the Secretary of State was carrying on a business from either of the houses. But he was using them for purposes other than those of a private dwellinghouse ... Where the owner was himself in occupation it could usually be said that he was using the house as his private dwellinghouse. Use as or for the purpose of a private dwellinghouse seemed to assume that there was at least one private individual who, whenever he chose, could occupy the house as his own, even though he might not be in actual occupation. ... no emphasis of the residents' ability to treat the house as their permanent home nor of the advanced degree of autonomy which was given them in the running of it could obscure the continuing responsibility of the Secretary of State for their care or the incidental powers vested in him. In particular he could determine a resident's licence to occupy the house and in an emergency he would have both the power and duty to do so without notice. More significant in practice was his responsibility to provide supervision and support for the residents, a responsibility which had not been diminished by the reduction in numbers of the staff who were needed to administer it. ... if a house could not fairly be described as someone's private dwellinghouse, it could not be said to be being used as such ...
With regard to the covenant 'not to cause or permit or suffer to be done in or upon the property any act or thing which might be or become a nuisance annoyance danger or detriment to the transferor or owners or occupiers for the time being of other parts of the estate', the only detriment ... was one which affected the enjoyment of some part or parts of the estate and was suffered by the plaintiff as owner of the parts which it retained for the time being. A financial loss suffered in their exploitation of the retained land, but dissociated from their enjoyment of it was outside the covenant."

The court emphasised that it was not considering the merits of the care in the community policy, but merely interpreting the covenants. The implications of this decision have not yet been fully explored, but it is of most significance to those small homes with six or fewer residents which would not need planning permission, and may also affect those with less than four which in England did not until recently need to register. If the residents had been established as joint residential tenants under appropriately drawn agreements, there may not have been a breach of the covenants, but this brings us back to the problem of how a mentally incapacitated person can enter into such an agreement.

## Homes for the disabled

A person with a mental handicap may need care and supervision rather than special facilities, but some also have some physical disability for which suitable provision must be made in the home.

### Provision

A duty is imposed on local housing authorities to consider the housing needs of their district and to have particular regard for the special needs of chronically sick and disabled people.[35] The Housing Act 1988 and the Housing (Scotland) Act 1988 changed

---

35  Chronically Sick and Disabled Persons Act 1970; also Housing Act 1985 (England) and Housing (Scotland) Act 1987.

the role of local authorities to that of strategic planner rather than direct provider and encourage housing associations to increase their use of private sector finance with a commensurate decrease in reliance on the public sector. Special grants are available from the Housing Corporation (in Scotland, Scottish Homes) for housing associations which provide houses for disabled people, but the take-up on this has been below expectations. Problems arise in obtaining private loans to fund the balance of the cost as the income of residents depends upon uncertain state benefits.

*Adaptations*

If a local authority[36] is satisfied that the home of a disabled person fails to meet special needs arising from the disability, it is under a statutory duty to ensure that those needs are met by arranging for any necessary adaptations to be made. This applies whether the home is owner-occupied or tenanted. The authority has power in its discretion to recover the cost, but cannot make the provision dependent upon prior payment though the disabled person will first wish to know the personal cost implications. The availability of grants now makes it unlikely that additional help from this source will be available, though it should be considered by those who cannot cope with the means-testing implications of a grant.[37]

*VAT*

Building alterations are subject to value added tax, but the following alterations for people with disabilities are zero-rated[38]:
- constructing ramps, widening doors or passages to enable disabled persons to enter or move within their home;
- providing a bathroom, washroom or toilet for the first time on the ground floor of a disabled person's home, or extending or adapting an existing bathroom, washroom or lavatory where this is necessary because of the disabilities;
- goods supplied in connection with any of these services;
- vertical lifts and distress alarm systems supplied to disabled persons.

## Grants

A new framework of grants for renovation, repair, improvement and adaptation of houses in England and Wales was introduced in July 1990, though in Scotland the previous grants system still exists.[39] The following help is available:
  (a) renovation grants
  (b) disabled facilities grants;

36  In England, district or borough councils. In Scotland, this duty falls on regional councils but may be administered through districts.

37  1970 Act, s.2. Any person on the Register of Disabled People can apply, but it is not essential to be on this.

38  See VAT leaflet 701/7/86, *Aids for Handicapped Persons*.

39  See Housing (Scotland) Act 1987: district councils may make improvement grants to make a house suitable for the accommodation, welfare or employment of a disabled occupant, ss.236 and 240.

(c)  minor works grants;
(d)  houses in multiple occupation grants;
(e)  common parts grants;
(f)  group repair schemes.

Although a disabled person may be eligible for any of these, we only consider the grant that is specifically intended to cover the needs of such a person.[40] It may be possible to make a combined application for a disabled facilities grant and a renovation grant, and in some circumstances there may be a choice between a disabled facilities grant and a minor works grant. Owners of properties may be able to have the whole cost of grant works paid for by the local authority, if they have a low income.[41]

*Disabled facilities grants*

Mandatory but means-tested grants are available for the following types of work which, after consultation with the social services department, are deemed necessary and appropriate to meet the needs of an occupier who is disabled[42]:

- facilitating access to and from the dwelling, or to the main family room or the disabled occupier's bedroom;
- facilitating access to or providing a room in which there is a lavatory, bath, shower or washhand basin, or facilitating the use of such facility;
- facilitating preparation/cooking of food by such occupier;
- improving any (or providing a suitable) heating system;
- facilitating the use of a source of power, light or heat by altering the position of the means of access to or control of that source or providing additional means of control.

Discretionary grants are available for any other type of work for the purpose of making a dwelling suitable for the accommodation, welfare and employment of the disabled occupant. A disability grant may also be available for works to the common parts of a building containing one or more flats if the disabled occupant has power or is under a duty to carry out the works.

The disabled person must normally live in the dwelling but, so long as the work is intended for his benefit, does not have to be the owner or tenant, though a multiple means-test may then apply in establishing the joint borrowing capacity. The grant is thus of limited value to parents looking after a handicapped son or daughter in their own home unless they are themselves of limited means. The same means-test applies as for other types of grant, and is based upon many factors so details are not set out here. There are also various other formalities to be complied with.

---

40   Joint Circular 10/90, issued by the DoE and the Department of Health, contains a useful summary of schemes, and DoE Circular 12/90 deals generally with house renovation grants.
41   Local Government and Housing Act 1989, Part VIII. Full details of the means test to be applied are set out in House Renovation Grants (Reduction of Grant) Regulations 1990.
42   DoE Circular 10/90 gives further guidance.

# PART IIIA - REGISTERED HOMES (England)

## Legislation

Registered Homes Act 1984
Registered Homes (Amendment) Act 1991
Residential Care Homes Regulations 1984
Nursing Homes and Mental Nursing Homes Regulations 1984
Residential Care Homes (Amendment) Regulations 1986 and
    1988
Nursing Homes and Mental Nursing Homes (Amendment)
    Regulations 1986 and 1988
Registered Homes Tribunals Rules 1984

## Preliminary

The growth of the private sector in the provision of residential care, most notably for the elderly, has resulted in legislation to control some of the abuses and ensure minimum standards of care and safety. Basic rules (including arrangements for supervision) are contained in legislation, but much of the detailed provision is found in codes of practice. The Registered Homes Act 1984 provides for the registration and supervision of residential care homes (Part I) and nursing homes (Part II).[43] It does not apply to Scotland or Northern Ireland. Neither the Act nor the regulations made under it contain a framework of rights for residents, or even a statement of the principle objectives, yet there may be a conflict between the welfare of the residents and the desire of the establishment to make a profit.[44] Often homes in the charitable sector do not pay their way and are subsidised from other sources.

*Registration authorities*
The appropriate registration authority depends upon the locality and type of the home. *Residential care homes* must be registered with their local social services department[45] and the registration officer should be contacted so that his requirements may be clarified. In the case of *Nursing homes* the Secretary of State has a duty to register an applicant and issue a certificate of registration, but this duty has been delegated[46] to District Health Authorities which effectively become the registration authorities.

The legislation did not apply to local authority homes and lower standards could be found in such homes than were insisted upon in the private regulated sector. This is changing, and social services

---

43  Although consolidating previous legislation it made amendments to give effect to recommendations of the Law Commission.

44  The Registered Homes Tribunal has repeatedly ruled that the legislation is to protect the frail and vulnerable and should be so interpreted. Economic and financial factors are not taken into account when considering the adequacy of standards.

45  Maintained by the non-metropolitan county councils, or the metropolitan district councils of metropolitan councils and the London Boroughs.

46  *I.e.* regulations under National Health Service Act 1977, ss.13, 14 and 17.

authorities are now required to set up "arms-length" inspection
units and to create advisory committees which meet at least twice
each year and include representatives of proprietors of residential
care homes.[47]

*Suitability for mental handicap*
The different types of home can be confusing to those seeking to
choose one that is suitable for a person with a mental handicap. As
a general guide, unless there are also medical or physical problems
which necessitate some degree of qualified nursing care, or there
is an associated mental illness which makes care or supervision by
suitably trained staff necessary, only residential care homes need
be considered. Each home is targetted at a particular clientele and
most cater for the elderly, so unless the individual also falls within
that category the search will be restricted to homes set up for the
mentally handicapped. It should not be assumed that such homes
merely comprise a number of bedrooms with communal lounge
and dining facilities; many offer considerably more than this and
some are like small village communities.

## Residential care homes

In regard to residential care homes the 1984 Act is supplemented
by regulations and by a document entitled *Home Life - A Code of
Practice for Residential Care* (1984)[48] which is often referred to
but is not legally enforceable. The Secretaries of State for Social
Services and Wales ask registration authorities to treat this
document in the same way as guidance by them. A Circular with
Guidance Notes has also been issued by DHSS.[49]

*Definition*
Registration is required in respect of:

> "any establishment which provides or is intended to provide, whether for
> reward or not, residential accommodation with both board and personal care
> for persons in need of personal care by reason of old age, disablement, past
> or present dependence on alcohol or drugs, or past or present mental
> disorder".[50]

Registration is not required for certain establishments including
hospitals, schools, most children's homes,[51] nursing homes and

---

47    See DoH booklet, *Commuinity Care in the Next Decade and Beyond -
      Policy Guidance* for suggested terms of reference. The advisory committees
      may prove to be a suitable body to deal with disputes between authorities
      (as purchasers of services) and providers.

48    Report of a Working Party sponsored by the DHSS and convened by the
      Centre for Policy on Ageing of 25 Ironmonger Row, London EC1.
      Available from Bailey Distribution Ltd., Learoyd Road, Mountfield Road
      Industrial Estate, New Romney, Kent, TN28 8XU.

49    *Registration of Residential Homes and Registered Homes Tribunals* dated
      August 31, 1984 - Circular No. LAC(84)15.

50    Registered Homes Act 1984, s.1(1).

51    Voluntary children's homes register with Department of Health, and others
      will be subject to registration and inspection under the Children's Act 1989,
      but homes for mentally handicapped children are usually within the Act.

mental nursing homes (as defined below),[52] and establishments managed or provided by a government department or local authority. Until June 1991 it was not required for homes with fewer than four residents (excluding those carrying on the home or employed there and their relatives).[53]

*Mental disorder* is defined as "mental illness, arrested or incomplete development of mind, psychopathic disorder and any other disorder or disability of mind",[54] thus adopting the same definition as used in the Mental Health Act 1983.

*Disablement* means "blind, deaf or dumb or substantially and permanently handicapped by illness injury or congenital deformity or any other disability prescribed by the Secretary of State".[55]

*Board* is generally the provision of meals, but could include the supply of food for residents to cook themselves, and *personal care* is defined as "care which includes assistance with bodily functions where such assistance is required". This may be equivalent to what is provided by a competent and caring relative able to respond to emotional as well as physical needs, and assistance with bodily functions is not necessarily required. Consultation with the registration authority is desirable because interpretations differ.

*Registration*

It is the proprietor of the home (*i.e.* the person in control or carrying on the business) who must be registered rather than the home itself. Registrations cannot be transferred and re-registration is necessary when the proprietor changes. Applications must therefore be made when:

- a new home is set up;
- an existing registered home is acquired;
- the registered person dies or leaves;
- a change in the basis of registration (*i.e.* in the number or category of residents) is required.

If the manager is not in control, whether as owner or otherwise, both he and the person in control are to be treated as carrying on the home and required to be registered.[56] Where only one person is registered and that person dies, his personal representatives or widow or any other relative may continue the home without being registered for up to four weeks or such longer period as the registration authority may allow.[57] If a limited company is registered as proprietor a change in the ownership of the company shares will not affect the registration.

Re-registration often provides an opportunity for the registration

---

52   1984 Act, s.1(5).
53   s.1(4). Registered Homes (Amendment) Act 1991 introduced registration for homes with less than four residents.
54   1984 Act, s.55.
55   s.20(1).
56   s.3. This seems to mean that the manager needs to be registered if the owner is an absentee landlord.
57   s.6. Relative is defined in s.19.

authority to seek to impose conditions which they could not otherwise force upon an existing owner. Registration can be refused, and although there is a right of appeal the new registration will not take effect until the appeal has been resolved. This can put considerable pressure on those seeking to continue the home, tempered perhaps by the fact that the act of registration is a duty imposed on the registration officer rather than a discretion. The application must be granted unless the authority is satisfied that statutory grounds for refusal exist.[58]

*Applications and procedure*
An application for registration must be made to the registration authority, contain the prescribed information and be accompanied by the registration fee.[59] Where an authority proposes to:
- grant an application subject to conditions;
- refuse an application;
- cancel a registration;
- vary any condition; or
- impose any additional condition;
it must give the applicant or registered person written notice of its proposal, with the reasons. This notice states that within 14 days of service any person on whom it is served may in writing require the registration authority to give him an opportunity to make representations to them, and this may include oral representations. The authority must not then determine the matter until the desired representations have been made, or the said period has expired without such opportunity being requested, or such opportunity has been allowed but no representations have been made within the reasonable period specified. If the authority decides to adopt the proposal it must serve notice in writing of its decision accompanied by a notice explaining the right of appeal, and the decision does not then take effect until any appeal has been determined or the time limit for an appeal has expired without an appeal being brought.[60]

*Conditions*
The number of residents cared for in the home must not exceed that specified in the Certificate, and conditions may be imposed for regulating the age, sex or category of residents in which event these must also be so specified. Only conditions of the nature specified in the Act may be made a condition of registration either by the authority or the Tribunal.[61] Unlike the situation in regard to nursing homes, no condition may be imposed on the registration of a residential care home as to the qualifications of the person in charge. The registration authority may vary these conditions from

---

58    *McSweeney* v. *Warwickshire C. C.,* (1988) Decision 64.
59    s.5(1). Residential Care Homes Regulations 1984, regs.2-5; Sched.1.
60    ss.12, 13 and 14. Notice need not be given where the applicant has proposed or agreed to the conditions, s.12(2).
61    *McSweeney* v. *Warwickshire C. C., supra.*

time to time, or impose an additional condition, either on the application of the registered person or without such application,[62] but in doing so they have a discretion and are not under an obligation (unlike the situation on registration).[63]

The classification of residential care homes by the main categories of residents that the home is intended to care for is to assist people seeking accommodation and to enable registration authorities to judge whether the facilities and services provided are appropriate to the home's objectives. It has recently been used for Income Support purposes to assist in identifying the maximum level of residential care allowance to which a resident is entitled. Categories have been laid down and a home may be registered for more than one category. This aspect of the registration should be reviewed each year.[64]

*Refusal*

Registration may be refused if the authority is satisfied[65]:

"(a) that the applicant or any other person concerned or intended to be concerned in carrying on the home is not a fit person to be concerned in carrying on a residential care home;

(b) that for reasons connected with their situation, construction, state of repair, accommodation, staffing, or equipment, the premises used or intended to be used for the purposes of the home, or any other premises used or intended to be used in connection with it, are not fit to be so used; or

(c) that the way in which it is intended to carry on the home is such as not to provide services or facilities reasonably required."

The burden of proof lies with the authority in regard to each of these reasons, so if registration is to be refused because of the employment of a particular individual in the home, the authority must show that he is not a fit person. This is quite different from the applicant having to establish that he is a fit person.

*Certificate of Registration*

Subject to these procedures, and unless the application is refused, the authority must register the applicant in respect of the specified house and issue a Certificate of Registration,[66] which must be displayed in a conspicuous place in the home. Regulations provide for the payment of an annual fee thereafter. The Register kept by the registration authority is available for inspection at all reasonable times, and any person may take copies of entries therein on payment of such reasonable fee as may be determined by the authority.[67]

---

62   s.5(3) and (4).

63   The discretion as to whether to deal with the application seems to be unfettered - *Coombes* v. *Hertfordshire C. C.*, Decision 115 - but it is suggested that if the authority actually does so their decision is capable of appeal. Where this technical difficulty is encountered a new application for registration may be made, but the full fee must then be paid.

64   See DHSS Circular No.LAC(86)6, paras.18 and 19.

65   s.9. In this context *may* probably means *must*.; Tribunal Decision No.103.

66   s.5(2).

67   s.7. The particulars to be recorded are in Sched.3 to the Regulations.

*Cancellation*

Registration may be cancelled by the authority[68]:

    (a) on any ground which would justify refusal of registration;

    (b) if the annual fee is not paid before the due date;

    (c) for non-compliance with any condition;

    (d) if the registered person has been convicted of an offence in respect of any such home;　or

    (e) if any other person has been convicted of an offence in respect of this home.

Notice of any such proposal must be given to the registered person and the procedures outlined above apply. If the registered person appeals against the proposal the home may continue to operate until the Tribunal has heard the appeal or it is withdrawn, but this may take some time[69] causing uncertainty and perhaps leaving residents in the care of an unsuitable person. Only the registration authority has power to initiate the cancellation procedure, and residents, relatives or staff who are concerned about the standards of a home may only report their misgivings to the authority in the hope that action will be taken.

*Urgent cancellation*

In urgent cases the registration authority may apply to a Justice of the Peace who may make an Order cancelling a registration, or varying a condition or imposing an additional condition, if it appears that there will be a serious risk to the life, health or well-being of the residents of the home unless the order is made.[70] Such application may be made *ex parte* but must be supported by a written statement of reasons. In practice most applications are made *ex parte*, and are invariably granted. At a later stage, perhaps at the Tribunal hearing, matters may not appear the same to persons with knowledge of the nursing home world as they did to the magistrate, whose decision on the basis of a one-sided case can cause serious injustice. There will seldom be cases where the absence of notice of the application can be justified, yet it is not insisted upon and magistrates do not get enough feed-back to alert them to this. Any Order made must be in writing, and served upon the registered person as soon as practicable with a copy of the statement of reasons. There is a right of appeal to the Tribunal but in the meanwhile the home must remain closed. When using this procedure the registration authority may also serve notice of a

---

[68]　s.10. The Act does not require cancellation of registration for breaches of the conditions imposed by the Certificate (though this is one of the options) - *Harrison* v. *Cornwall C. C., The Times*, May 15, 1991. Here again, the onus of proof of one of these grounds lies upon the authority.

[69]　Indications are that if both parties wish the matter to come on for hearing a date will be fixed within about five months and the decision should be known within about three weeks thereafter.

[70]　s.11. It is not sufficient to show that proprietor is not a fit person; a serious risk, etc., if registration is not immediately cancelled must be established, *Lyons* v. *East Sussex C. C., The Times*, July 27, 1987;　Decision 78.

proposal to cancel the registration so that the ordinary procedure may be continued without delay if an Order is not made.

## Regulations

The Secretary of State may make regulations as to the conduct of residential care homes, and in particular as to the following[71]:

    (a) the facilities and services to be provided;

    (b) the numbers and qualifications of staff to be employed;

    (c) the numbers of suitably qualified and competent staff to be on duty;

    (d) the records to be kept and notices to be given in respect of residents;

    (e) the notification of events occurring;

    (f) the giving of notice by certain persons of periods during which any person of a specified description is to be absent from the home;

    (g) the information to be supplied in such notice;

    (h) infant residents to receive appropriate religious upbringing;

    (i) the form and content of registers kept by registration authorities; and

    (j) the information to be supplied on an application for registration.

The Residential Care Homes Regulations 1984 make provision in respect of these matters and should be studied by anyone involved in the administration of such homes. In addition to the matters mentioned here, these regulations lay down detailed requirements in regard to the provision of facilities and services, and include a policy statement relating to the conduct of homes.

## Policies

The policies adopted by a home must conform to the general principle laid down in these Regulations[72]:

> "(1) The person registered shall arrange for the home to be conducted so as to make proper provision for the welfare, care and, where appropriate, treatment and supervision of all residents.
>
> (2) In reaching any decision relating to a resident the person registered shall give first consideration to the need to safeguard and promote the welfare of the resident and shall, so far as practicable, ascertain the wishes and feelings of the resident and give due consideration to them as is reasonable having regard to the resident's age and understanding.
>
> (3) Every home shall be maintained on the basis of good personal and professional relationships between the person registered and persons employed at the home and the residents."

The detailed requirements set out in the regulations should be treated as minimum standards which must be attained.

## Inspection of homes

Any authorised person[73] may at all times enter and inspect any

---

[71] s.16(1).

[72] Reg.9. There is no similar provision in the regulations for nursing homes.

[73] The authority may be given by the registration authority or by the Secretary of State - s.17(1) and (2).

premises which are used, or believed to be used, for the purpose of a residential care home, and may inspect any records required to be kept under the Act. Inspection at regular intervals is intended as well as unannounced inspections[74] and these should concentrate upon the quality of life and care of residents and standards of management. A visit would be necessary following a complaint to the authority about standards of care at the home. Inspections should not be seen as intrusive, and the discussion that takes place with the registration officer can be very constructive. Innovative and good care practice will be recognised, and advice may often be given. The registration officer must be given the opportunity of spending time alone with individual residents.

Local authorities must now set up independent inspection units which will inspect local authority run homes to the same standards as those in the independent sector, and also an advisory committee to monitor and oversee the work of the new inspection units.[75] The Government have issued to all local authorities a booklet entitled *Inspecting for Quality.*[76]

*Annual review*

Following a formal annual inspection a Report should be sent to the proprietor and manager upon the administration and state of the home, and any change of circumstances affecting the registration should be identified.

*Records and notices*

Certain records must be maintained at the home and these must be available for inspection at all times by any person authorised by the registration authority.[77]

Any notice or document under the Act may be served on a person carrying on a home by personal delivery, or by registered or recorded delivery post and usually the last known address is sufficient.[78]

*Fees*

The fees payable for registration are presently (1991)[79]:

| | |
|---|---|
| Initial registration | £770 |
| Change of owner | £770 |
| Registration of manager | £210 |
| Annual fees | £37 per registered bed. |

*Role of registration authority*

The registration authority is required to ensure that the purposes and aims of residential establishments are clearly set out and that the standards of care they offer match these. It should seek to

---

74  Reg.18(1).
75  National Health Service and Community Care Act 1990.
76  A further booklet called *Homes are for Living In* sets out how inspections should be conducted on the principles of the *Wagner Report.*
77  Reg.6. The particulars to be recorded are in Sched.2.
78  s.54.
79  Residential Care Homes (Amendment) Regulations 1991.

ensure that the best possible quality of life for residents is achieved. Members of staff appointed by registration authorities to undertake inspection, give advice to staff and be responsible for recommendations concerning registration should have sufficient experience and status to receive the respect of colleagues and staff of homes alike and be skilled in communicating with proprietors from a wide range of backgrounds.

## Small residential homes

Registration for small residential homes (*i.e.* of less than four people) was introduced in June 1991. The local authority is given the right to refuse registration if it believes the potential owner to be unfit, but does not have to charge a registration fee, although it may do so. There may be less rules attached to registration.[80]

## Nursing homes

The statutory provisions in respect of nursing homes are broadly similar to those for residential care homes, but there are some significant differences and a separate set of regulations which is more appropriate to the requirements of a nursing home.[81] Two Circulars contain guidance notes issued by DHSS,[82] and the National Association of Health Authorities has produced a handbook.[83] The powers of the Secretary of State for Social Services have been delegated to District Health Authorities which are the registration authorities for all practical purposes.[84]

*Definitions*

The definition of a nursing home is lengthy,[85] but in the present context it is sufficient to state that it includes:

"any premises used, or intended to be used, for the reception of, and the provision of nursing for, persons suffering from any sickness, injury or infirmity".

There is a special category of mental nursing home, namely[86]:

"any premises used, or intended to be used, for the reception of, and the provision of nursing or other medical treatment (including care, habilitation and rehabilitation under medical supervision) for, one or more mentally disordered patients (meaning persons suffering, or appearing to be suffering,

---

80  Registered Homes (Amendment) Act 1991. Registration authorities will be concerned with fitness of the applicant rather than the premises, services and facilities. There will be no requirement to make statutory inspections, and visits may only be made where concerns have arisen.

81  Nursing Homes and Mental Nursing Homes Regulations 1984.

82  *Health Service Management Registration and Inspection of Private Nursing Homes and Mental Nursing Homes (including Hospitals)* dated July 1981 - Circular No. HC(81)8 and dated October 1984 - Circular No. HC(84)21.

83  *Registration and Inspection of Nursing Homes: A Handbook for Health Authorities* (1985) and 1988 Supplement.

84  By regulations under National Health Service Act 1977, ss.13, 14 and 17.

85  1984 Act, s.21. Hospitals, consulting rooms, surgeries and certain other types of premises are expressly excluded.

86  s.22. Hospitals (as defined) and certain other premises are excluded. A home cannot be registered as a nursing home and a mental nursing home.

from mental disorder), whether exclusively or in common with other persons".

## Registration and conditions

Any person who carries on a nursing home or a mental nursing home must be registered, and applications are made to the Secretary of State accompanied by the prescribed fee and, in the case of mental nursing homes, must specify whether or not it is proposed to receive patients who are liable to be detained under the Mental Health Act 1983.[87] The procedure is broadly similar to that which applies to residential care homes.[88] The functions of the *registered person* and the *person in charge* are different even though they may be performed by the same person. The registered person, whose name is on the Certificate, is responsible for ensuring that the requirements of the legislation are satisfied, but need not be professionally qualified. The person in charge is responsible for day to day management of the home and the care of patients, and must be either a registered medical practitioner or a qualified nurse.[89] Both must be "fit persons" to carry out their respective functions. If the applicant for registration is a company, it will need to be registered as well as the manager, and the registration authority will wish to consider the fitness of the persons who control the company.

The conditions that may be imposed and the procedure that applies on an application for registration are similar to that in respect of residential care homes. However, in the case of nursing homes a condition may be imposed on registration as to the qualifications of the person in charge and the number of nurses to be on duty from time to time.[90]

## Refusal and cancellation

The grounds for refusal are different. The Secretary of State may refuse registration if satisfied[91]:

"(a) that the applicant, or any person employed or proposed to be employed by the applicant at the home, is not a fit person (whether by reason of age or otherwise) to carry on or be employed at a home of such a description;
(b) that, for reasons connected with situation, construction, state of repair, accommodation, staffing, or equipment, the home is not, or any premises used in connection with the home are not, fit to be used for such a home;
(c) that the home is, or any premises used in connection with the home are, used, or proposed to be used, for purposes which are in any way improper

---

87   A separate part of the Register is maintained for homes which take such patients, and special provisions apply on the death of the registered person or on cancellation - see s.36 of the 1984 Act.

88   See above, and ss.23 and 31-34 inclusive.

89   *Qualified nurse* means a nurse possessing such qualifications as may be specified in a notice served by the Secretary of State who shall have regard to the class of patients involved - s.25(2) and (4).

90   See above, and s.29 which is in wider terms than s.5. It is not clear whether staffing conditions can apply to unqualified staff.

91   s.25. The onus is upon the authority to prove unfitness if this is alleged. The Secretary of State shall have regard to the class and the number of patients involved - s.25(4).

or undesirable in the case of such a home;

(d)  that the home or any premises used in connection with the home consist of or include works executed in contravention of section 12(1) of the Health Services Act;

(e)  that the use of the home or any premises used in connection with the home is in contravention of any term contained in an authorisation under section 13 of the said Act;

(f)  that the home is not, or will not be, in the charge of a person who is either a registered medical practitioner or a qualified nurse ...;

(g)  that the following condition is not, or will not be, fulfilled namely: such number of nurses possessing such qualifications as may be specified in a notice served by the Secretary of State on the person carrying on or proposing to carry on the home are on duty in the home at such times as may be so specified."

The Secretary of State may at any time cancel the registration on grounds which are similar to those set out above in regard to residential care homes, and the urgent cancellation procedure is also available.[92]

## Regulations

The Secretary of State may make regulations as to the conduct of nursing and mental nursing homes, the absence of the person in charge, registration procedures, the keeping of records, notification of events, inspection of premises, payment of fees and certain other matters.[93]

## Inspection of mental nursing homes

Any authorised person may enter and inspect a mental nursing home and inspect the records, and may also visit and interview in private any patient residing in the home who is, or appears to be, suffering from mental disorder in order to investigate a complaint or where there is reasonable cause to believe that the patient is not receiving proper care. Regulations may be made in furtherance of these powers and offences are prescribed.[94]

## Dual registration

Registration as a residential care home does not affect any requirement to register as a nursing home, and vice versa.[95] Thus an establishment may need to register both with the local authority and with the district health authority. The distinction between a residential care home and a mental nursing home depends upon the type of care being provided. The former provides personal care which is the type of physical and emotional care normally provided by relatives and close friends, whereas the latter provides "nursing or other medical treatment" including "care under medical supervision".

---

92  ss.28 and 30 respectively.

93  ss.26 and 27. Nursing Homes and Mental Nursing Homes Regulations 1984.

94  s.35.

95  ss.1(3) and 23(2). There may be such conflict between the two registration authorities that a dual registered home is run as two separate homes.

## The applicant

The authority must consider whether the person registered or to be registered in respect of a home is a fit person but this term is not defined and interpretations differ.[96] Application forms give specified information including details of previous employment and experience, and references are required.[97] Details of criminal convictions which for other purposes would be spent may not be withheld, but these will be treated as confidential and considered only in relation to the application.[98] The authority has no power to obtain information from the police, and tribunal decisions have shown that a criminal record or association with criminals will not by itself necessarily result in an applicant not being a fit person.

### Guidance

Authorities are influenced by the guidance contained in *Home Life - A Code of Practice for Residential Care* (1984) that they should ensure that all prospective proprietors or managers possess some relevant qualifications or have experience of employment within residential care. They should have a business-like approach which will ensure that the home will be managed on a secure financial basis which will not put the future welfare of residents at risk.

### Tribunal decisions

A Tribunal seeking to identify the characteristics of a fit person used the words "trust, integrity, uprightness, honourable and truthful" and justified its refusal of the applicant by stating[99]:

> "a proprietor of a care home (has to) be such a fit person since the elderly people in their care are often frail and vulnerable and the person in control of them is in a powerful position to exploit that frailty. It is imperative that residents' well-being must be assured and that they must be protected from harm. It is a high standard that the law requires ..."

### Voluntary organisations

Where the proprietor of a home is a voluntary organisation, the chairman or secretary thereof, or someone from the management committee, will be registered along with the home's manager. Any relevant change of personnel should be notified, and the authority should identify the actual and legal division of responsibility within the organisation. The applicants may be honorary officers whose backgrounds and experience vary, and advice on aspects of home management such as staff appointments may be needed and will often be welcomed.

### Change

Once the initial Certificate of Registration has been issued, proprietors should notify the registration authority of any

---

96    The onus of proof is upon the registration authority to prove that the person in charge is not a fit person if the registration is to be refused or cancelled.

97    Residential Care Homes Regulations 1984, Sched.1, and Residential Care Homes (Amendment) Regulations 1991.

98    Rehabilitation of Offenders Act (Exceptions) Order 1975.

99    Registered Homes Tribunal Decisions, No. 76.

intended change of ownership. Registrations are not automatically transferred to new proprietors or managers, and new applications must be lodged and references taken up.

## The premises

Registration may be refused if the authority considers the premises (or any premises used in connection therewith) to be unfit. Situation, construction, state of repair, accommodation, staffing and equipment are all taken into account. The registration officer may seek to set standards, but the only binding standards are those set out in the regulations which in effect state that the facilities, services and staffing must be adequate.[100] Thus the authorities themselves do not have power to set standards, and these must always be judged objectively. DHSS has issued central guidance which seeks to set out the broad limits to local discretion.

### Location and accommodation

In respect of residential care homes it is recommended in *Home Life* that when considering new applications the authority should ensure that the location and surrounding environment is appropriate to the stated aims of the establishment, and that the home will not disrupt the balance of the neighbourhood. Accessibility of local facilities, community health services and public transport should all be taken into account.

There must be reasonable accommodation and space by day and night, including that which is required for social and occupational activities, though this will depend upon the type of resident. Where physically disabled people are to be accommodated, suitable facilities must be provided, such as ramps, lifts and wider doorways. Some architects have developed expertise in regard to particular types of homes and their services may prove of considerable value and lead to financial savings.

In respect of nursing homes it is recommended[101] that the location should be free from noise, environmental pollution, smells and heavy traffic. The building should be well lit and ideally be separate from surrounding buildings, with easy access for ambulances and other vehicles.

### Regulations

The registration authority will be concerned about fire precautions and insist on an inspection by an officer from the fire authority with all recommendations being promptly complied with. Registration may be refused or cancelled in default. The registered person is also under a duty to consult the fire authority on fire precautions in the home.[102] Care homes are not required to have

---

100  In this context *adequate* means "sufficient and suitable".

101  *Registration and Inspection of Nursing Homes: A Handbook for Health Authorities* (1985) and 1988 Supplement.

102  Residential Care Homes Regulations 1984, reg.8. *Fire authority* is defined as the authority discharging in the area in which the home is situated, the function of fire authority under the Fire Services Act 1947 - reg.1(2).

fire certificates, and fire officers usually acknowledge that their role is advisory, but in practice their recommendations become mandatory and this leads to difficulties when there is a difference of opinion between any of the parties involved.[103] In that event the proprietors should seek advice from an independent expert who may negotiate money saving modifications with the fire authority. The registration authority will also require all the standards stipulated by the environmental health services officer of the local authority to be met. An inspection is usually arranged and written confirmation that recommended work has been properly completed is required.

### Enforcement

Faced with serious breaches of these provisions by a person in charge of a registered home, the registration authority has a choice of sanctions, namely: cancellation or prosecution. The former will be dealt with before the Tribunal (though urgent cases start before the magistrates and go on appeal to the Tribunal), and the latter by the local magistrates court. Usually negotiations take place, in the knowledge that these sanctions exist, and settlement is reached. Each party will be influenced by the costs involved and the delays that occur which include the time taken for a registration authority to come to a decision and organise a hearing before its committee, and then to get an appeal hearing before the Tribunal and its decision.

### Appeals

Although there is the right to make oral representations to a committee set up by the authority, thereby overriding the registration officer, it seems that in most cases his decision is confirmed. Appeals against decisions or orders of:
  - a registration authority (residential care home);
  - the Secretary of State (nursing or mental nursing home);
  - a Justice of the Peace (urgent applications for either home)
lie to the *Registered Homes Tribunal* and are brought by giving notice in writing to the registration authority or Secretary of State (as appropriate) within 28 days after service of notice of the decision or order.[104] Many appeals relate to refusal or cancellation of registration or the imposition of conditions.

### Registered Homes Tribunal

These tribunals are constituted under Part III of the 1984 Act[105] and comprise a legally qualified chairman sitting with two experts each drawn from panels appointed by the Lord Chancellor and the

---

103  Such difficulties are quite common, not only in the setting up of a new house but also when a new fire officer inspects whose wishes may differ from those expressed by his predecessor. For this reason many homes have an annual budget for fire precautions, and this is often exceeded.

104  s.15.

105  ss.39 to 45 inclusive.

Lord President of the Council respectively. No officer of a government department may be appointed to either panel. The experts have social work, medicine, nursing or other suitable experience and sit where such experience is relevant. The Secretary of State has power to make Rules as to the practice and procedure to be followed by these tribunals.[106] The rules of natural justice apply, so that for example the Tribunal should not receive or rely upon any information or evidence that has not been put to both parties. Hearings are often arranged near to the home which is the subject of the appeal.

*Powers*

The Tribunal has power to confirm the decision or order, or to direct that it shall not have effect,[107] but it also has power to cancel, vary or impose any condition. Although section 15(6)(*c*) of the Act states: "to direct that any such condition as it thinks fit shall have effect in respect of the home", it has now been held by the High Court, contrary to the view taken by earlier Tribunals, that only conditions of the type specified in section 5(3) may in fact be imposed, *i.e.* those regulating "age, sex or categories of persons who may be received in the home".[108] On an appeal against a closure order under the urgent procedure the Tribunal may only decide the case on the same grounds as the magistrate, and does not have power to confirm the order on the basis that the appellant is not a fit person unless it also concludes that the evidence establishes serious risk to the life, health or well-being of the residents of the home.[109] The Tribunal may hear two appeals together, and this may be appropriate where in order to effect a closure the registration authority has applied the normal cancellation procedure as well as the urgent procedure (the latter would be heard first).

*Policy*

The Tribunal has had to manage without any express guidance as to the philosophy behind the Act, but one of the leading principles to emerge from its decisions is the welfare of residents. Some Tribunals have not had regard to the guidelines adopted by the registration authority, on the basis that they must not be allowed to develop into fixed rules, but others have praised efforts by the authorities to implement the standards set out in *Home Life* and to attain "the good rather than the acceptable". Although it seems that decisions of the Tribunal do not create a precedent, it is becoming clear how the Tribunal is likely to approach future cases and the principles in *Home Life* have generally been followed. Continuing breaches of the regulations over a period of time are likely to be

---

[106] Registered Homes Tribunals Rules 1984.

[107] In the case of an order of a JP it will "cease to have effect", s.15(5).

[108] *East Sussex C. C.* v. *Lyons*, *The Times,* January 2, 1988, CA; *McSweeney* v. *Warwickshire C. C.* (1988) Decision 64.

[109] *East Sussex C. C.* v. *Lyons, supra.*

viewed far more seriously than an isolated breach, and a successful prosecution has not necessarily led to cancellation.

*Burden of proof*
It has been held that the burden of proof rests on the registration authority, and that the standard of proof is on the balance of probabilities.[110]

*Costs*
The Tribunal does not have power to award costs against any party, whatever the outcome of the appeal or the circumstances. This can cause hardship to a proprietor if an authority refuses to negotiate or discuss a requirement which, on appeal, is found not to be justified.

## Offences

Part IV[111] deals with penalties for offences which have previously been created by the Act. Any person who carries on a residential care home, a nursing home or a mental nursing home without being registered is guilty of an offence.[112] It is also an offence for a registered person to fail to exhibit a Certificate of Registration in a conspicuous place in the home, or for a person with intent to deceive to describe or hold out premises as being a nursing home or a mental nursing home when registration has not been effected.[113] Further offences relate to failure to comply with conditions, breach of regulations, obstruction of inspections.[114] In certain circumstances officers of a limited company may be jointly liable for offences committed by the company.[115]

*Defences*
In the case of residential care homes it is a defence for the person charged to prove that the commission of the offence was due to a mistake or reliance on information supplied or the act or default of another person, an accident or some other cause beyond his control and that he took all reasonable precautions and exercised all due diligence to avoid the commission of such offence by himself or any person under his control. However, the act or default of, or reliance on information supplied by, another person cannot be relied on as a defence without leave of the court unless, within seven days before the hearing, the prosecutor is served with a notice in writing giving such information as is available to identify or assist in identifying that other person (s.18).

---

110  *Lyons* v. *East Sussex C. C., The Times*, July 27, 1987, Decision 78.
111  ss.46 to 53 inclusive.
112  s.2 (residential care homes); s.23(1) (nursing and mental nursing homes).
113  ss.5(6) and 23(6) respectively; s.24.
114  ss.5(5) and 29(4) respectively; ss.16(2) 26(*e*) and 27(*g*); s.17(6). Inspections are authorised under ss.17 and 35.
115  s.52. This is based upon consent, connivance or neglect.

# PART IIIB - REGISTERED ESTABLISHMENTS (Scotland)

## Preliminary

Certain residential and other establishments require to be registered with the social work authority,[116] and supervised by them, under the provisions of the Social Work (Scotland) Act 1968, ss.61-68 (as amended) and Sched.5. Nursing homes as defined in the Nursing Homes Registration (Scotland) Act 1938 require to be registered with, and supervised by, the health board under that Act.[117] If establishments come within both sets of provisions, they are jointly registrable and must comply with both. While local authorities only register and supervise the first category, they have certain obligations in relation to jointly registrable establishments. Appeals under the 1968 Act are governed by the Registration of Establishments (Appeal Tribunal) (Scotland) Rules 1983, referred to as the 1983 Rules. Strictly speaking, it is the person who carries on an establishment who is registered in respect of the establishment, but where that would be unduly cumbersome reference is made simply to registrable or registered establishments.

## REGISTRABLE ESTABLISHMENTS

The registration requirements apply to establishments if the whole or a substantial part of their function is to provide personal care[118] or support[119] within the scope of the various duties to persons in need under the 1968 Act. Establishments are included whether or not they are residential, provide board or receive payment for the services provided.

### Excluded establishments
Excluded from the definition are:
- establishments controlled or managed by a government department or local authority;
- establishments[120] which are by any other statute registrable with a government department or local authority;
- grant-aided schools and independent schools which provide personal care or support as described above (but they may register voluntarily).

### Offence
No-one may carry on an establishment within the above definition

---

116 The regional or islands council. The Secretary of State may require registration with himself rather than with the local authority - see below.

117 These are referred to as the 1968 Act and the 1938 Act.

118 Including appropriate help with physical and social needs.

119 Including counselling or other help as part of a planned programme of care.

120 Other than nursing homes within the provisions of the 1938 Act.

unless he is registered in respect of it. Contravention is an offence punishable with up to three months imprisonment, a fine, or both.

## Registration procedure

The person intending to carry on an establishment must apply in the prescribed form to the authority for the area where it is located and details of any proposed manager must be given.

### Decision and conditions

The authority may refuse registration if satisfied that:
- the applicant or anyone to be employed in the management of the establishment is not a fit person for the purpose;
- any aspect of the premises, staffing, equipment or the like makes the premises unfit for their purpose; or
- suitable services and facilities will not be provided.

At least 14 days notice of intended refusal must be given. Unless the local authority refuse registration on one of the above grounds, they must grant the application.

The maximum number and permitted categories of residents must be specified. Other conditions may be attached to the grant of registration, or subsequently imposed or varied. At least 14 days notice must be given of intended imposition of conditions at time of registration or subsequently, or of intended variation. Non-compliance with any condition is an offence on the part of the person carrying on the establishment.

A certificate of registration is issued upon registration, and must be replaced with a new certificate if there is any change in the information on it. The certificate must be conspicuously displayed in the establishment, and the register is open to public inspection at all reasonable times.

### Fees

Fees are chargeable for applications for registration, annual continuation, applications for variation of conditions, and issue of a new certificate following on change in particulars at the instance of the registered person. Children's homes and voluntarily registered establishments are exempt from payment of fees.

### Changes

A change of manager must be notified to the authority within 28 days. If the registered person dies, his executor, widow or other member of his family may carry on the establishment for up to four weeks, or longer with the permission of the authority. If for any reason the registered person ceases to be registered, the authority may permit someone else to carry on the establishment for a specified period up to 60 days.

### Termination and cancellation

The authority must be given at least 28 days notice of intention to cease carrying on the establishment. The authority may cancel registration at any time on any of the following grounds:
- any of the grounds of refusal (see above) apply;

- non-compliance with any condition of registration;
- a change of manager has not been properly notified;
- the annual fee for continuation has not been timeously paid;
- the registered person has been convicted of an offence under these provisions in relation to any establishment;
- any other person has been convicted of an offence under these provisions in relation to the establishment.

At least 14 days notice of intended cancellation must be given.

*Hearing by authority*

The notices of intended refusal or cancellation of registration, or of imposition or variation of conditions, must intimate the right to an opportunity to be heard. A hearing must be granted if requested within 14 days of receipt of the notice. After hearing the applicant, registered person, or a representative, the authority makes its decision and intimates it in writing.

## Appeal to Tribunal

Within 21 days of receipt of the notice giving the authority's decision, an appeal may be taken to the appeal tribunal.[121] Where the appeal is against conditions to be imposed on initial registration, registration does not take effect until the appeal has been determined. In appeals against intended cancellation of registration, imposition of new conditions, or variation of conditions, the decision does not take effect before determination of the appeal.

*Tribunal constitution and procedure*

If an appeal is taken, a tribunal is constituted to hear it. The Sheriff Principal in whose jurisdiction the establishment is situated is normally chairman, and the two other members are drawn from a panel. Procedure under the 1983 Rules[122] is formal, but relatively straightforward, and the chairman determines any procedural matter not specifically covered by the Rules. The parties are notified as soon as the tribunal has been constituted, the appellant has 14 days to submit written grounds, and the authority then have seven days to submit a written statement of the grounds for their decision.[123] At least 14 days notice is given of the hearing, at which parties may be legally represented,[124] and witnesses called and examined. The tribunal may inspect the establishment, and must do so if so requested by either party. The tribunal must give its decision in writing at, or within 14 days after, conclusion of the hearing.

---

[121] If there is no appeal, the decision takes effect on expiry of the 21 days.

[122] The Registration of Establishments (Appeal Tribunal) (Scotland) Rules 1983.

[123] The parties may apply for extension of time limits.

[124] The appellant may also appear in person, if a partnership by a partner, and if an incorporated or unincorporated body by an authorised director or officer. With leave of the tribunal, any other person may represent the appellant. The authority may be represented by an authorised officer.

*Tribunal's powers*
The tribunal's power to determine the appeal includes, in appeals concerning conditions, power to confirm or vary them. In a 1991 case[125] the tribunal was of opinion that it would be entitled to review the decision of the respondents only if it was satisfied either that that decision was itself unreasonable or that it had been reached in an unreasonable manner or upon unreasonable considerations. In approaching the matter in this way the tribunal was conscious of the fact that a decision taken by the respondents' Social Work Committee is essentially administrative in character, and therefore ought not to be disturbed unless there are compelling reasons for doing so. The tribunal allowed the appeal, holding that the authority had acted unreasonably in basing its decision on policy considerations which had not at that time become approved Council policy and which were at odds with earlier declared policy and with the reasonable expectations of the appellant based on her dealings with the authority. The tribunal commented that registered establishments in the independent sector could offer a better quality of life for people inappropriately housed in large institutions, and as demand for such places substantially exceeded supply, the difficulties faced by those seeking to provide such accommodation should not be unnecessarily increased, with the risk of deterring some from doing so.

## Supervision

*Removal of residents*
The local authority may remove some or all residents from an establishment which ought to be registered and is not, or when notice of intent to cancel registration has been given, even though the time for appealing has not expired or an appeal is pending. The Secretary of State has similar powers in any case of urgent necessity. Re-occupation of the premises as an establishment is an offence.

*Particulars of establishments*
The person in charge of the establishment must send prescribed particulars to the authority within three months of initial registration and by a prescribed date in each subsequent year. Non-compliance is an offence.

*Inspection and visiting*
Duly authorised officers of the local authority have rights of entry and inspection in relation to registrable establishments, and in relation to any place which the officer has reasonable cause to believe is used as a registrable establishment. Local authorities have a duty to ensure that residents in establishments are visited from time to time, in the interests of their well-being, and

---

125  *Hart* v. *Lothian Regional Council*, February 13, 1991 (unreported).

authorised persons have right of entry for this purpose. These entry powers extend outside the authority's own area to visit children under the care or supervision of the authority, and persons receiving assistance from the authority, under the 1968 Act. Obstruction of these entry powers is an offence.

### Secretary of State

The Secretary of State may direct that applications be made to him, and dealt with by him, in respect of particular establishments or classes of establishment. He then takes over the role of the local authority under the registration provisions described above in respect of such establishments, but must notify the local authority of his decisions to register and to cancel registration. He may transfer jurisdiction back to the local authority.

### Voluntary registration

Grant-aided and independent schools may register voluntarily, though exclusively educational parts of their premises are excepted from registration. The following provisions do not apply to voluntary registration:

- short-term continued operation if the registered person dies or ceases to be registered;
- removal;  and
- rights of entry to visit children outside the authority's own area.[126]

### NURSING HOMES

The registration and supervision of nursing homes is the responsibility of the health board, and the relevant provisions are described below.[127] We also consider jointly registrable establishments under this heading.[128]

### Definition and registration

The definition of registrable nursing homes includes *inter alia* "any premises used, or intended to be used, for the reception of, and the provision of nursing for, persons suffering from any sickness, injury or infirmity".[129] Excepted from the definition are NHS, government and local authority premises, private hospitals (as defined below), sanitoria at educational establishments exclusively serving them, doctors' and other surgeries, private dwellings, and others.

---

[126] Visiting rights and duties within the authority's area only apply when such schools are in fact registered.

[127] Nursing Homes Registration (Scotland) Act 1938; Nursing Homes Registration (Scotland) Regulations 1990.

[128] For jointly registrable establishments see 1968 Act, s.63B.

[129] Also included are maternity homes (for which staffing requirements differ from those described on next page); and any other premises for surgery under anaesthesia, termination of pregnancies, endoscopy or dialysis.

*Registration*

The person intending to carry on a nursing home must apply in the prescribed form to the health board and pay a fee. The board must register the applicant unless satisfied that:

- the applicant or anyone employed at the home is not a fit person for the purpose;
- the home's situation, construction, state of repair, accommodation, staffing or equipment are unsuitable (or the premises are to be used for improper or undesirable purposes);
- a doctor or qualified nurse will not be in charge; or
- board requirements as to nursing levels are not or will not be fulfilled.

The board issues a certificate of registration which specifies the permitted number of residents, and which may also limit the categories of persons who may be admitted. The certificate must be conspicuously displayed in the home, and surrendered immediately on cancellation of registration.

*Variation and cancellation*

The board may vary any conditions of registration, for a defined period or indefinitely, on application by the registered person. The board may cancel registration if:

- any of the grounds of refusal (above) applies;
- the registered person has been convicted of an offence under the 1938 Act;
- anyone else has been convicted of an offence under the Act in relation to the home; or
- there is non-compliance with any condition of registration.

*Representations and appeal*

The board must give 14 days notice of intention to refuse or cancel registration, and give an opportunity to show cause why the board should not refuse or cancel. A copy of the order refusing or cancelling registration must be sent to the applicant or registered person, who may appeal to the sheriff within 14 days of the making of the order. The sheriff's decision is final. The order does not take effect until the 14 days has expired, or any appeal has been determined or withdrawn.

## Jointly registrable establishments

Registration may be required both as a nursing home and as a registered establishment, if both sets of criteria apply. Registration as an establishment may be limited to the part of the premises qualifying for such registration, thus excepting parts used exclusively for nursing home functions. If a local authority cancel registration as an establishment of a jointly registered establishment, they must notify the cancellation, and the reasons for it, to the health board.

## Supervision

Regulations deal with conduct and inspection of homes, notification to the health board of deaths there, and the keeping, production and inspection of records.[130]

### Exemptions

Non profit-making hospitals or similar institutions may be exempted by the board from the provisions of the registration requirements, subject to conditions. Exemption is granted for a year at a time, but may be withdrawn at any time. There is a right of appeal to the Secretary of State against refusal, conditions or withdrawal.[131]

### Offences

No-one may carry on a nursing home within the above definition unless he is registered in respect of it. Contravention is an offence punishable by fine, and officials of companies are punishable unless they can show that they neither knew of the offence nor consented to it.

## Private hospitals[132]

### Definition and offences

The definition of private hospitals is limited to premises used (or intended) for detained patients, whether or not other persons are also received and treated. Excluded are hospitals vested in the Secretary of State, state hospitals, and any other premises managed by a government department or provided by a local authority. It is an offence, punishable by fine, to carry on a private hospital within this definition unless it is registered.

### Registration procedure

The person proposing to carry on a private hospital must apply in the prescribed form with a fee of £1 to the Secretary of State who has a discretion to register the premises as a private hospital, but must not do so unless satisfied as to:
- the fitness for the purpose of the premises;
- the fitness of the person proposing to carry on the hospital;
- the suitability and adequacy of the proposed arrangements for patients;  and
- the adequacy of the proposed medical and nursing staff, who should be suitably trained and qualified.

A certificate of registration is issued which specifies the maximum permitted number of patients and may regulate the permitted categories of patients. This must be conspicuously displayed in the hospital, and surrendered forthwith if registration is cancelled. Registration lasts for five years, and may then be renewed.

---

130  Nursing Homes Registration Regulations (Scotland) 1938, as amended.
131  The Secretary of State may grant exemption to Christian Science houses.
132  Mental Health (Scotland) Act 1984, ss.12-16.

*Cancellation*

The Secretary of State may at any time cancel registration on any ground on which he might have refused an application for registration, or if the person carrying on the hospital is convicted of an offence under the Mental Health (Scotland) Act 1984. Registration remains in force for up to 28 days after cancellation while any patient is liable to be detained in the hospital.

*Control*

The hospital must be kept open to inspection at all reasonable times, and prescribed registers and records must be kept, and must be open to inspection. Any conditions in the certificate of registration must be complied with. The Mental Welfare Commission must be given all necessary facilities for inspection, and for discharging their other duties. The person carrying on the hospital is guilty of an offence if these provisions are not complied with. The Secretary of State must ensure by regular inspection that the hospital is being properly carried on, and his inspectors have right to enter and inspect, on production of authorisation if asked.

# PART IV - IMPLICATIONS OF REGISTRATION

## Benefits

Registration brings certain financial benefits.

*Income Support*

Until April 1993 the residential care allowance may be claimed by those who reside in a registered home, representing a substantial increase in the weekly entitlement, though seldom sufficient to cover the full fees.[133] It may only be claimed by those residing in small homes (previously unregistered in England) if certain staffing levels are maintained.[134]

*Community Charge*

Those (other than staff) looked after in residential care homes, nursing homes and hostels providing a high level of care do not pay the charge as long as it is their only or main residence.[135]

*Uniform Business Rate*

Business rates are probably not payable in respect of nursing homes, but there may be difficulties in respect of commercial residential care homes. If they are run by charities they would in any event be entitled to 80 per cent. rating relief with further

---

133 Transitional regulations allow those already receiving the allowance on that date to continue.

134 See Chap.8, Part V. Implementation of community care policies will involve the withdrawal of this allowance and the extra cost of residential care being met by local authorities based upon an assessment of need.

135 Local Government Finance Act 1988, Abolition of Domestic Rates (Scotland) Act 1987. It seems likely that similar provisions will be applied to the council tax.

relief up to the full amount on a discretionary basis.[136] There is an exemption for property used for the disabled, but it must be used wholly for certain purposes which include:

(i) the provision of training for (or keeping suitably occupied) persons who are disabled, or who are or have been suffering from illness;

(ii) the provision of welfare services for disabled persons.

Disabled is defined so as to include persons suffering from mental disorder of any description, or permanently handicapped by illness, injury or congenital deformity.[137] The problem so far as proprietors of homes is concerned is that exemption depends upon the whole as opposed to the predominant use, so homes which seek to integrate able people with those who are classed as disabled will lose the exemption. It should not be assumed that all rating officers are sympathetic to the aims of the home in this respect.

## VAT

Building alterations are subject to value added tax, but the following alterations for people with disabilities are zero-rated[138]:

- constructing ramps and widening doors or passages for a charity to enable a disabled person to enter or move within the building;
- installation or adaptation of a bathroom, washroom or toilet in a residential home for disabled people run by a charity;
- goods supplied in connection with any of these services;
- vertical lifts and distress alarm systems supplied to a charity caring for a disabled person.

## Television Licence concession

In respect of mentally handicapped people living in one of the following types of home the usual fees do not have to be paid for television licences:

(a) a residential home whose sole or main purpose is to provide accommodation for mentally handicapped people;

(b) a registered nursing home;

(c) accommodation which forms a group of at least four dwellings, within a common and exclusive boundary, specially provided by way of erection or conversion only for disabled people and provided or run by a local authority or housing association, with a warden (who resides within the common boundary or works there for at least 30 hours per week) and a common facility for the use of all the occupants.[139]

---

[136] Certain non-profit making organisations may be eligible for discretionary relief of up to 100 per cent.

[137] Local Government Finance Act 1988, replacing from March 31, 1990 the system of rebates under the Rating (Disabled Persons) Act 1978 as amended by the Rates Act 1984.

[138] See VAT leaflet 701/7/86, *Aids for Handicapped Persons*.

[139] A common facility might comprise a lounge or diningroom, or an alarm scheme linked to a local authority control centre.

An *Accommodation for Residential Care Licence* is available at a fee of £5 for each eligible unit of accommodation and this covers all television sets used by residents in such accommodation, but not sets used communally or by the staff.[140]

*Disabled passenger vehicle taxation class*
A residential home which has a car or minibus used solely for, or for any business connected with, disabled people may be registered in the Disabled Passenger Vehicle Class, achieving a substantial saving in duty. The exemption is automatically lost if the vehicle is found to be used other than for disabled people.[141]

## Building controls

*Environmental health requirements*
These relate to houses in multiple occupation, and are designed to ensure that the amenities are provided to a reasonable standard, there are proper standards of management, and there is no overcrowding.[142] The environmental health services officer of the local authority will be involved and an inspection may be arranged following which work may be recommended. A house in multiple occupation is in England a house "occupied by persons who do not form a single household" and the following points have been given as guidance on interpreting this definition[143]:

(a) the size of the group is such that it could reasonably be regarded as a household in that area;
(b) the fluctuating character and fortuitous relationships of the group - or its durability;
(c) whether there is a permanent community, not a temporary refuge for individuals.

It seems that a small scale scheme in which permanent residents will share responsibilities for the running of the house will not come within this definition.

*Fire regulations*
Several pieces of legislation cover fire precautions.[144] In the case of a house in multiple occupation (as defined) the local authority may, in consultation with the fire authority, require adequate fire escapes to be provided and even close part of a house. Special grants may be available. Hotels and boarding houses are required

---

140 Wireless Telegraphy (Broadcast Licence Charges and Exemption) (Amendment No.2) Regulations 1988. Further information and application form from National TV Licence Records Office, Bristol BS98 1TL.
141 Further information may be obtained from The Disabled Persons Transport Advisory Committee, c/o The Disability Unit, Dept. of Transport, S10/21, 2 Marsham Street, London SW1P 3EB.
142 The relevant legislation in England has been consolidated in the Housing Act 1985 but dates from 1957. For Scotland, see Housing (Scotland) Act 1987, Pts.VII (overcrowding) and VIII (multiple occupancy), and also Public Health (Scotland) Act 1897, ss.72 and 92.
143 *Simmons* v. *Pizzey* (1976) 120 S.J. 802.
144 Housing Act 1985, Fire Precautions Act 1971, Housing and Building Control Act 1984 all relate to particular types of project.

to have a fire certificate, but few shared housing schemes will come within this regulation. The Building Regulations which apply to all new building include measures to ensure that certain basic fire safety standards are achieved.

*Planning permission*
In addition to the erection of the building, or physical alterations in an existing building, planning permission is required for a change of use. The local planning authority which is responsible for planning decisions may not be part of the same council as the registration authority but some consultation would be usual. A residential care home may in England fall within one of three *Use Classes*[145] namely:

C1  Hostels and hotels
    Use as a hostel, boarding or guest house, or hotel where, in each case, no significant element of care is provided.
C2  Residential institutions
    (a) use for the provision of residential accommodation and care to people in need of care (other than a use within C3);
    (b) use as a hospital or nursing home;
    (c) use as a residential school, college or training centre.
C3  Dwelling-houses
    Use as a dwellinghouse (whether or not as a sole or main residence):
    (a) by a single person or by people living together as a family, or
    (b) by not more than six residents living together as a single household (including a household where care is provided for residents).
Care is defined as:

"personal care for people in need of such care by reason of old age, disablement, past or present dependence on alcohol or drugs or past or present mental disorder, and in class C2 also includes the personal care of children and medical care and treatment."

In Scotland, use classes 12, 13 and 14 are similar to classes C1, C2 and C3 (respectively) quoted above.[146] Where C3(b) refers to not more than six residents, the Scottish class 14 refers to not more than five. Care is defined as personal care, including the provision of appropriate help with physical and social needs or support, and in class 13 includes medical care and treatment. English Class C3 includes not only normal family homes, but also dwelling-houses providing accommodation for not more than six residents living together as a single household including premises where care is provided for the residents. This would include a small unregistered residential care home and also (it seems) a registered home with not more than six residents including resident staff.
Planning permission is not normally required for any change of

---

145  Town and Country Planning (Use Classes) Order 1987.
146  Town and Country Planning (Use Classes) (Scotland) Order 1989.

use of premises which falls within the same Use Class, but when initially granting planning permission the local planning authority may expressly exclude this right. Applications relating to certain types of development must be advertised both by means of a press notice and a notice posted on the site, and the authority may require an application for a new residential care home to be advertised in this way. The planning authority usually notify adjoining owners and this often leads to opposition fuelled by unrealistic fears. People who support provision of this nature may be horrified when it is proposed on their own doorstep, and a good public relations campaign and interviews with neighbours is usually required to overcome this type of opposition. Once a house is occupied it seems that acceptance of the occupants often follows.

## CODES OF PRACTICE

### The Codes

*Home Life - A Code of Practice for Residential Care* (1984) sets out principles of care, and the rights of residents to fulfilment, dignity, autonomy, individuality and esteem. Self-determination and individuality are emphasised and the purpose of the home should be to enable residents to achieve their potential capacity - physical, intellectual, emotional and social. In the Foreword the Secretaries of State for Social Services and for Wales jointly recognise that voluntary and privately run residential care homes play a very important part in helping people to remain near their families and in their own communities. The Code is endorsed as an excellent guide to good practice and local authorities are asked to regard it in the same light as general guidance issued under section 7 of the Local Authority Social Services Act 1970.

The *NAHA Handbook* indicates that the objective of a nursing home is to ensure that the quality of care provided to patients is of a high standard. Patients should live in comfortable, clean and safe surroundings, and be treated with respect and sensitivity to their individual needs and abilities. The 1988 Supplement expands this by placing emphasis on privacy, consultation with patients, and access to a relative, friend, adviser or advocate.

### Quality of care

A home should be judged by the quality of the care that it provides within these policy guidelines. Relevant factors will be adequacy and attitudes of staff, the cleanliness and presentability of the residents, the activities and training available for them both inside and outside the home, the freedom that they are allowed and flexibility in arrangements. The style and layout of the building and facilities for privacy may be important factors in achieving independence and a degree of self-determination for residents, and larger homes are discouraged as being too institutionalised.

## Recommendations

We consider below the principle recommendations in *Home Life*, which is more relevant to the care of people with a mental handicap than the code for nursing homes. It is of general application to residential care homes; some later codes are more specifically targetted at mental handicap and may be applied by particular local authorities.[147] None of these are legally binding and there is always some room for discussion about care philosophies, though purely random policies are vulnerable.

*Basic rights*
The basic rights of those in care are identified as follows:

**Fulfilment:** A home should enable residents to achieve their potential capacity - physical, intellectual emotional and social.

**Dignity:** Preservation of self-respect for residents depends upon the status they are accorded. This includes privacy, the right to hold opinions (and express them or keep them private), and recognition of talents, sensitivities and beliefs. Staff should respond to residents with courtesy and respect (in particular for what is personal and private).

**Autonomy:** Residents have a right to self-determination and should not have rigid routines imposed on them, although living in a community does involve some compromises. The provision of choice is essential, as is access to external advice, representation and advocacy. Partnership between residents and staff is to be encouraged.

**Individuality:** Religious, ethnic and cultural differences should be catered for, and residents should be allowed reasonable idiosyncrasies e.g. in dress, choice of food, bedtimes and daily activities. A choice of leisure activities, both inside and outside the home, is essential.

**Esteem:** The qualities, experiences and talents of residents should be recognised so as to increase their morale.

**Quality of experience:** There should be as wide as possible a range of normal activities, including opportunities to go shopping, to cinemas, pubs, discos etc.

**Emotional needs:** Normal opportunities should be available for emotional expression, although individuals will vary in their ability to form and cope with relationships.

**Risk and choice:** Responsible risk-taking should be regarded as normal, and residents should not be discouraged from undertaking activities simply because there is an element of risk.

*Brochures*
It is recommended that a brochure is produced setting out the aims

---

[147] *e.g. Promoting an Ordinary Life*, a checklist for assessing residential care for people with learning difficulties, by Lesley Hoyes, School for Advanced Urban Studies, University of Bristol, 1990.

and objectives of the home, and indicating the type of resident catered for, the degree of care offered and any restrictions. This should also describe the facilities, accommodation and staffing, and may specify the terms on which residents are admitted.

### Admissions

Before taking up a long term place a full assessment of the individual is essential. Prospective residents should visit the home, and trial periods are encouraged for the benefit of both the resident and the home. The suitability of the placement should then be discussed by all concerned (including staff, parents and the resident), and on admission a programme of general reviews should be established. Where disagreements arise the interests and preferences of the resident are paramount. Residents should be encouraged to bring with them into the home as many personal possessions as can reasonably be accommodated, and these should be treated with care and respect and any valuable items noted.

### Agreements

Agreements between home proprietors and residents may be in many forms, and may create a tenancy or a licence, but the terms will depend on the kind of accommodation involved and the nature and extent of the services and personal care to be provided. Such agreements should be in writing, though in many cases suitable documents simply do not exist.[148] Those negotiating the contract should confirm just what they may expect for the weekly payment, and a moderately handicapped individual should be consulted and made a party to a simple agreement with an independent explanation being provided. The brochure for the home may to a large extent perform this task. Matters to be covered include:
- accommodation and facilities provided:
  - items to be provided by the resident;
  - services covered and those to be charged separately;
- amount and payment period of fees:
  - payments during temporary absences;
  - procedure for increase of fees;
- procedure for:
  - holidays and hospital stays;
  - serious illness or death;
  - termination;
  - complaints;
  - filling vacancies;
- insurance arrangements;
- terms and conditions of residence (to include general rules on matters such as keeping rooms tidy, smoking, use of drugs and medicines, visitors, pets, staying away.)

---

148 It is surprising how often elderly people are admitted to residential care homes without this basic precaution being followed! An ordinary individual is unwise to pay the substantial weekly sums involved in an arrangement of this nature without some form of contract, and there is no reason why those with a mental handicap should be treated differently.

*Respite care*
Short term care, although important, should wherever possible be provided in separate accommodation because it can be disruptive for those living in the home.

*Records*
As we have seen, certain records concerning residents must be kept under the regulations.[149] It is important to ensure that those persons to whom the records relate have access thereto and the opportunity to discuss and contribute to their own records. Counselling may be required if sensitive personal information is to be disclosed, and various safeguards will be needed in certain circumstances.[150] In exceptional cases it may be in the interests of a resident to withhold information, but such a decision should only be taken by a senior person and there is a right of appeal to the registration authority.[151] Personal details in these records must be kept in a secure place and access limited to those with overall authority for the day-to-day care of the resident. Those with access to records should be instructed in the proper handling of confidential information.

*Confidentiality*
It may be necessary to disclose confidential information about a resident, perhaps of a medical nature, to the person in charge of a residential care home. Where the resident has mental capacity a consent form may be signed, but this is not possible in the absence of capacity. Problems can then arise if confidential information is disclosed to other members of staff, perhaps through being included in the resident's file. The information may reach junior untrained staff (*e.g.* YTS trainees) and ultimately become public property, causing embarrassment to the resident and his family. Proper controls should be devised within the home, but this is easily overlooked. Such information should only be disclosed on a need to know basis, and disclosure in breach of the rules should be made a matter justifying dismissal from employment. This may be difficult in practice when many of the staff are temporary or lowly paid, perhaps without formal conditions of employment, but the privacy of residents should nevertheless be respected.

*Health care*
Residents are entitled to the same health care as other members of the community, including the right to see their own medical practitioner in private. No drugs except simple household remedies should be given without a doctor's prescription. Any drugs should be held in a safe place and a record kept of those

---

149  An indication of the records to be kept is found in Annexe 3 to *Home Life*.

150  Information about a third party should not be disclosed without that party's consent; information obtained in confidence should not be disclosed without the consent of the person giving it.

151  The need to withhold access to sensitive items should never be used to justify withholding access to other items in the records.

held and administered by the home. Medication must never be used for social control and punishment.

*Rules*

Rules relating to residents should be kept to a minimum and only used to fulfil statutory requirements, prevent disturbance to other residents or ensure reasonable standards of safety and hygiene. Residents should be involved as much as possible in making decisions as to the running of the home. Domestic routines may be necessary but should take into account individual needs and preferences, and aim at achieving normal lifestyles. Personal preferences should also be taken into account in modes of address.

*Autonomy*

It is recommended that residents have private rooms with adequate facilities in which they may keep there own possessions (including televisions) and where they may spend time during the day if they wish. Family and friends should be encouraged to visit and to maintain contact by letter and telephone, and privacy should be available to residents when they seek it, although some monitoring by staff may be necessary.

*Financial affairs*

Independent advice and assistance on financial matters should be available and encouraged. Proprietors and staff at homes should not take on the responsibility of looking after the financial affairs of residents unless it has proved impossible to find an alternative, and in the absence of relatives or friends outside the home the social services department should be referred to. It is desirable to maintain separate accounts for resident's monies where this is held, and this was made mandatory in 1988.[152]

*Staff*

Suitably qualified and competent staff must be employed, by day and night, in numbers which are adequate for the well being of residents.[153] Each home is different in its physical arrangements and make-up, so in addition to ensuring that staff have suitable formal qualifications and experience a staff training programme should be maintained. Staff should also have the right personal qualities, which include personal warmth and patience, and respect for and responsiveness to the needs of the individual. A suitable staff balance should be achieved including both male and female. Character references should always be obtained before employing new members of staff, and prospective employees in registered homes must on being asked disclose previous convictions including those which would otherwise be spent.[154]

---

[152] Residential Care Homes (Amendment) Regulations 1988 amending Sched.2, para.17 to the 1984 Regulations. See DHSS Circular No.LAC(88)15 at para.12.

[153] Regulation 10(1)(*a*). Guidance is given in *Home Life*.

[154] Rehabilitation of Offenders Act 1974, s.4(4); Rehabilitation of Offenders Act 1974 (Exceptions) Order 1975, (S.I. 1975 No.1023).

There are four main groups of staff, namely managerial and day care, night care, ancillary staff and specialist staff. The needs of the residents must be considered in regard to each of these groups and recommended staffing ratios are laid down. The balance between part-time and full-time care staff must also be carefully considered. It is important to ensure that staff are available to attend to tasks such as cooking, laundry, domestic work, gardening and general maintenance, and administration. Specialist services will usually be provided through the health authority or social services department. The person in control of the home must have sufficient training and experience, and there must be sufficient senior staff to provide adequate cover at all times. Much will depend upon the type and size of the home and the needs of the residents, but it is desirable to provide facilities for staff training and various courses may be available.

*Gifts*
Where residents can cope with money, even in small amounts, the choice about what they do with it is their own. However, because of the relationship between residents and staff there should be a clear statement about the home's attitude to personal gifts from residents. To avoid suspicion of undue influence, the proprietor should make known to all staff and residents that it is the home's practice to decline personal gifts, except for small token presents. It is wise to specify in the contract of employment with staff that a breach of this provision would justify instant dismissal.

## PART V - CONCLUSION

### RECENT DEVELOPMENTS

### Housing projects
All the above information needs to be borne in mind when setting up or running a housing project, and guidance based upon other people's experiences is increasingly being published so that the advantages and disadvantages of different schemes can be considered.[155] The starting point must be to look at the needs of the individual for whom it is hoped to make provision and to see how these needs may best be served.

*Role of Housing Associations*
Housing associations have an important part to play in the provision of ordinary housing with support and residential care homes. Some have particular experience in setting up homes for disabled people[156] and will advise on project design, development

---

155 Centre on Environment for the Handicapped of 35 Great Smith Street, London SW1P 3BJ publish booklets of this nature. Guidance is also available from MENCAP and from New Era Housing Association Ltd of 69 Old Street, London EC1V 9HX.

156 New Era Housing Association is closely linked with MENCAP, but is not

and management through the stages of getting a new project going. They are usually incorporated under the Industrial and Provident Societies Acts and registered with the Housing Corporation or Scottish Homes. A number of schemes exist which are financed in different ways, and funding may come from the Department of the Environment or the Scottish Office through local authorities, or from health authorities. Those that are registered can obtain grants and loans to cover the cost of providing a house or hostel, and a discretionary Hostel Deficit Grant may be paid annually for deficits attributable to housing costs, but grants are not generally available for projects where a high level of care is to be provided to residents. Either construction or conversion of a building may be considered, but a house not requiring renovation is less likely to gain approval because the aim is to increase the housing stock.

The advantages of linking up with a housing association include assistance towards administration and maintenance costs, access to grants and the availability of specialist skills and experience. Disadvantages include outside control, the need to satisfy additional criteria and the availability of grants on a yearly quota which may affect timing. Grants do not cover the cost of providing care, so if the weekly funding available to residents is unlikely to be sufficient assurances should be obtained from the social services department or health authority that top-up funding will be available before proceeding with a scheme.

*Mental Handicap Trusts (Consortia)*

A recent development is for a charitable trust or company to be formed by local authorities, health authorities and a housing association, perhaps with involvement of a parents group, to establish homes in the community for people with a mental handicap.[157] If these are registered as residential care homes substantial funding is available through Income Support residential care allowance for which residents are eligible.[158] This allowance, which may be supplemented by deficit grants from the health authority, is not available if the local authority itself runs the home. Capital funding can come through grants from the Housing Corporation or Scottish Homes and re-settlement monies paid by the health authority for ex-hospital patients, but the intention is

---

alone in this field. Its booklet: *Housing for People with a Mental Handicap* gives valuable information. In Scotland, Key Housing Association of Savoy Tower, 77 Renfrew Street, Glasgow likewise has links with SSMH, and other housing associations, such as Ark Housing Association fulfil a similar role.

[157] Schemes come in various forms. The formation of a Trust is considered in Chap.9, Part III and Chap.11 Part IV. There is a precedent in Appendix IV.

[158] If after August 12, 1991 the home changes its status from that of a local authority home in respect of which residential care allowance cannot be claimed to a home in respect of which the allowance could be claimed, existing residents will not be permitted to claim - Income Support (General) Regulations 1987, reg.21 as amended by Income Support (General) Amendment (No.5) Regulations 1991.

that places will also be provided for those already in the community. Once homes have been set up they will be available for future generations thereby making an important contribution to care in the community.

The position of these trusts is insecure, since after 1993 they will be dependent upon local authorities being able to make an adequate contribution towards the care costs for new residents. This in turn depends upon the level of resources transferred from the social security budget and priorities of individual authorities in the face of considerable competition for available monies. Another problem is the conflict between the desire to provide an ordinary living situation and the emphasis in legislation upon the care and safety of residents, which can result in an ordinary home adopting the trappings of an institution. Trusts represent a valuable local initiative involving close collaboration between local and health authorities and other bodies, and are perhaps a sign of things to come. However, the difficulties encountered are expressed in this extract from a Chairman's Report[159]:

> "We have also had to work within a frequently changing legislative and financial context, a situation which will no doubt continue. Even where the rules have not changed, there has often been a battle to persuade other agencies to interpret them correctly."

## Reports

There have been several recent reports upon the provision of residential care.

*The Wagner Report*[160] in its summary of recommendations stresses rights of individuals, and mentions specific circumstances such as the right to a contract, and to have a key and not to share a bedroom as a condition of residence. It recommends that a single registration and inspection system should cover all homes.

*The Firth Report*[161] considers the reasonableness of charges by homes in the independent sector and the role of consumers in determining the services to be provided.

*The Griffiths Report*[162] confirms the need for each home to publish a statement of the services that it provides and that the person in charge should have the "skills, knowledge, experience and personal qualities to be able to create the necessary environment both for residents and staff so that the home could achieve its objectives". It also recommends that there should be only one system for residential care and nursing homes.

A regular criticism is that local authorities have, through their inspection system, been able to insist upon higher standards in

---

159 Harrow Consortium for Special Needs, 1989/90 Annual Report.
160 *Residential Care: A Positive Choice*. Report of the Independent Review of Residential Care (1988).
161 *Public Support for Residential Care*. Report of a Joint Central and Local Government Working Party (1987).
162 *Community Care: Agenda for Action*. Report to the Secretary of State for Social Services by Sir Roy Griffiths (1988).

private and voluntary homes than they often attain in their own homes which are not subject to an independent inspection system. Independent inspection units, often with inspectors recruited from outside social services, have since April 1991 been set up to inspect and report upon all homes thereby applying the same criteria. The 1990 Act enables inspection by the Secretary of State.

## SUMMARY

Mentally handicapped people should have a real choice between independent living and residential care. The aim of a care home should be to provide a homely, non-institutional atmosphere suited to the needs of the residents, though this aim is often frustrated by the need to comply with the many regulations.[163] The development of small homes in the community has created new problems. Those responsible for imposing regulations may have inadequate guidelines, so some seek to protect themselves by applying existing guidelines designed for different situations which may prove to be inappropriate.[164] Those seeking to set up a home who encounter requirements that are felt to be excessive or unreasonable should ask for these to be justified. It is only by challenging inappropriate requirements that a reasonable balance is struck between the need to protect vulnerable people and the desire to enable them to live as near normal lives as possible. There seems to be no sanction against registration authorities which seek to impose their own standards or show disapproval of particular types of home, and as many homes depend upon local authority funding the future development of a wide range of homes depends upon the policies of the authorities rather than the choice of the consumer.

Figures produced by MENCAP indicate that in England alone, out of some 134,000 people with a mental handicap only about a quarter have their own supported homes in the community, and less than a fifth are now in hospitals. The rest, identified as being about 75,000, live at home with family and these are often among the most severely handicapped. The rate at which new places are being created in homes in the community may not be outstripping the rate of hospital discharges so it may be a whole generation before community care begins to have its intended meaning for the typical family struggling to cope within its own resources. Earlier statistics showed[165] that on average for every 1,000 people about three were seriously mentally handicapped, and about one-third of

---

163 The fire authority's requirements may result in the boxing off of staircases and the provision of self-closing doors and fire-extinguishers in prominent locations, even in houses for only four residents, so that an atmosphere is created which is quite unlike any ordinary home.

164 *e.g.* a fire officer inspecting a home for four persons may feel it necessary to apply the standards appropriate to a large institutional home or an hotel, thereby destroying the normal atmosphere or even making it impossible to finance the home.

165 See DHSS papers *Better Services for Mentally Handicapped* (1971) and *Mental Handicap: Progress, Problems and Priorities* (1980).

these were in hospital or some form of residential care. Of the remainder many were living with elderly parents or a single parent and only a proportion could live independently even if services were available. Thus when those at risk of losing family care are added to those who need care now or should be leaving mental hospitals, it will be seen that there is a great need for further supported housing and residential care. There is therefore considerable scope for the development of suitable homes by the private commercial, voluntary and charitable sectors with the assistance of housing associations where appropriate. There is also the need for existing registration and supervision procedures to be further refined, but this must not be to the extent of making the cost of care provision prohibitively expensive when set against the limited funding available.

*Homes for disabled people*
Despite the move towards care in the community, the number of homes provided by local authorities to appropriate standards for disabled people has declined during the last decade.[166] No disabled person capable of more independent living should have to remain in hospital or residential care simply because a suitable home cannot be made available, and the answer may be for central government to provide local authorities with specific resources to meet their statutory obligation to provide suitable accommodation. Persons with physical disabilities need accessible housing, and this refers to both external access and movement within the house. A group of voluntary organisations recommends that[167]:

(a) standards relating to accessible housing should be incorporated into building regulations and broadened to include facilities for people with sensory disabilities;

(b) a significant proportion of all new housing stock built by local authorities and housing associations should be built to the recognised standards for accessible housing;

(c) refurbishment of housing stock should include the adaptation of premises to meet access standards;

(d) the private sector should be encouraged to build accessible housing

(e) planning of housing should take into account the need for secure accessible and affordable accommodation both in the general community and in sheltered housing schemes.

*Respite care*
Good quality, reliable and flexible respite care should be seen as a right of the family and the disabled individual, with a choice between family based schemes and a residential setting rather than

---

166 DoE figures at December 1990 show 8,971 homes built in 1979 and 723 in 1990, a drop from 13 per cent to under 5 per cent in the total housing built by local authorities and housing associations. Statistics only identify wheelchair users, rather than the provision made for all groups of disabled people.

167 *An Agenda for the 1990's* published by the Disability Manifesto Group.

the local authority scheme or nothing. Although demand for residential places is increasing, indications are that these are being reduced as existing places are taken up for emergency long term admissions caused by illness or death of elderly carers. In some cases parents and concerned persons have joined together to provide local facilities but in few cases have problems of funding and staffing been satisfactorily overcome. Respite care is not viable by itself, largely because the demand is mainly at weekends and during holiday periods, yet present policies discourage this being provided by homes which have some stability because they also care for permanent residents, and though local authorities may make use of any such facility that is provided they seldom provide funding for the home as distinct from individual residents.

# CHAPTER 8    FUNDING THE INDIVIDUAL

## Introduction

Few individuals with a mental handicap become self-supporting, and parents or informal carers find that additional expenses are involved and their own ability to earn is restricted. It follows that support is needed from outside sources, both for the individual and for the parents or carers, and a system of *social welfare* has built up. This does not only come in the form of cash benefits (generally referred to as *social security*), but also includes a wide range of benefits in kind (often referred to as *social services*) of which health, education and housing are the main categories. Cash benefits are the easiest to administer and can be enforced by the claimant with an appeal process for those who are dissatisfied, but (particularly if paid to an appointee) they may not be spent for the purpose intended and do not necessarily provide the support that is required. A less obvious way of giving support or incentives is through the tax system: certain types of income (*e.g.* state benefits) are exempt from income tax, and tax allowances may be given to carers or persons with particular disabilities. In recent years there has been a move away from this towards more direct support through social security.

In this chapter we identify the sources and types of funding and then consider how a handicapped person may be financed on a day to day basis, and some problems that arise. In previous chapters we have dealt with the services and facilities that may be provided, but not all of these come free and in so far as means-testing is required we now consider the implications. The adviser will be seeking to establish a structured package of care provision and financial assistance for the individual and for the parents or carers (if appropriate).

## Sources of funding

There are many sources of funding and the following is not an exhaustive list but illustrates the means by which financial support may be available.

*Benefits Agency (formerly Department of Social Security)*
Benefits are usually in the form of a weekly benefit paid through a local office or specialised department, but may comprise a capital sum for a particular purpose, or a loan. They may depend upon National Insurance contributions or be means-tested, but some are targetted towards a particular disability group.

*Local authority*
Certain weekly income benefits related to the provision of housing are now paid by the local authority and these are means tested. In

addition, the provision of services by the local authority may be charged for to the extent that the recipient has the means to pay.

*Personal funding*
The individual may come into money and this could reduce the funding available from other sources.

*Family support*
In many cases support, both financial and otherwise, will be forthcoming from the immediate family. They will wish to ensure that this supplements the provision available from the state or local authority, especially in the case of an adult who might otherwise have been expected to be self supporting.

*Trusts*
Money may be set aside by the family, either by Will or lifetime settlement, for the support of the individual. Often trust provision gives the trustees a discretion as to the use of capital or income so that it may supplement that which is otherwise available.

*Charities*
There are many charities active in the field of mental disability, and it is likely that some help will be provided from this source.

# PART I - STATE FUNDING

## Introduction

We consider here the various state benefits that may be available. These are usually referred to as *social security benefits* though the term *welfare benefits* is commonly used for those which are means-tested. We then outline the law and procedure concerning claims, with an emphasis upon mentally disabled claimants. Their needs and circumstances can cause the adviser to press beyond the current understanding of benefits legislation and a high number of appeals relate to them, yet few lawyers have experience of such appeals. The regulations constantly change, and we do not cover all aspects, so reference should be made to other sources if further information is required. During recent years specialist welfare rights bodies have made this knowledge more readily available, and there has been publicity for welfare benefits campaigns. The inexpensive annual publications of Child Poverty Action Group[1] are invaluable, and the *Disability Rights Handbook* is essential.

*Other countries*
The same social security system covers Great Britain,[2] though there are a few differences between England and Wales on the one hand, and Scotland on the other, due to their different legal

---

[1]      Provided as part of the membership package, address in Appendix I. See also Further Reading in Appendix II.

[2]      *I.e.* England, Wales and Scotland. Northern Ireland has its own legislation, but for most practical purposes it is the same and contributions paid in one country count in another.

systems. A claimant living elsewhere in the European Community may qualify for benefit under the basic rules about going abroad or under EC rules, but these are based upon free movement of labour and involve payment of social security contributions so may not assist those with a mental disability.

## THE SOCIAL SECURITY SYSTEM

### Sources of Law

*Statutes*

The enabling provisions for all state benefits are found in:

Social Security Act 1975
Social Security Pensions Act 1975
Child Benefit Act 1975
Social Security Act 1986

These do not set out all the detailed provisions but provide for *regulations* to be made. This has led to test cases in which specific regulations have been challenged as being *ultra vires* the enabling statutory provision, sometimes resulting in confusion hastily resolved by new or amending regulations. The Social Security Contributions and Benefits Act 1992 and Social Security Administration Act 1992 will consolidate the law from July 1, 1992.

*Regulations*

Published as statutory instruments, these provide the detailed law as to entitlement and procedure, and may have been amended many times. The following apply to most benefit claims:

Social Security (Claims and Payments) Regulations 1987
Social Security (Adjudication) Regulations 1986

*Directions*

In some cases, notably in areas of particular difficulty, flexibility has been retained by reserving power to the Secretary of State to make Directions as to the manner in which particular claims shall be dealt with. These are issued to DSS offices and treated as if they were regulations, but are not widely available so a claimant cannot ascertain whether benefit is payable and there is no right of appeal from an adverse decision. Directions can also be amended from time to time with minimum formality or publicity, and whilst they may be a useful interim stage in the process of formulating all-embracing regulations, all too often they continue in force for years without being converted into regulations.

*Commissioners decisions*

Appeals against decisions of adjudication officers are dealt with by local Tribunals, but there is a further right of appeal on points of law to the Commissioners whose decisions are binding and thus become sources of law. Important decisions are published and may be quoted by the reference which indicates the type of benefit, number of the decision and year: thus *R(IS)1/91* is the first reported Income Support decision of 1991. If this were an unreported decision it might be referred to as, for example, *CIS 13/91*.[3] The different benefits are indicated as follows:

| | |
|---|---|
| R(A) | Attendance Allowance |
| R(F) | Child Benefit (formerly Family Allowance) |
| R(FIS) | Family Income Supplement |
| R(G) | Maternity Benefit, Widow's Benefit, Invalid Care Allowance, Guardian's Allowance, Child's Special Allowance |
| R(I) | Industrial Injury Benefits |
| R(IS) | Income Support |
| R(M) | Mobility Allowance |
| R(P) | Retirement Pension |
| R(S) | Sickness Benefit, Invalidity Benefit, Severe Disablement Allowance |
| R(SB) | Supplementary Benefit |
| R(SSP) | Statutory Sick Pay |
| R(U) | Unemployment Benefit |

*Courts*

Important points of law, usually on interpretation of statutes or regulations, may be dealt with on further appeal to the Court of Appeal or Court of Session, and thereafter to the House of Lords. Some cases reach the courts on judicial review.

## Classification of benefits

There are no social security benefits exclusively for people with a mental disability, but several are intended for disabled people. We deal with benefits individually but in groups according to whether or not they depend upon the payment of contributions and whether or not they are means-tested:

*Contributory benefits* - payable from the National Insurance Fund to claimants with a qualifying contributions record;

*Non-contributory benefits* - payable from general taxation as a source of income for the disabled and children, or their carers. Non-means-tested and can be claimed as of right if the qualifying conditions are satisfied;

*Welfare Benefits* - only payable if claimant satisfies a means test, and used as a top-up to other benefits and income.

Benefits may also be classified according to their purpose:
- maternity benefits;
- child benefits;
- sickness, invalidity and disability benefits;
- unemployment benefit;
- welfare benefits (means-tested);
- retirement benefits;
- death benefits.

Some provide a replacement for earnings, namely: unemployment, sickness and invalidity benefits; Severe Disablement Allowance; Invalid Care Allowance; retirement pensions.

---

3     Important decisions are dealt with by a Tribunal of Commissioners and take precedence over decision of a single Commissioner. Unpublished decisions (if they can be found) may be treated as authorities on particular points.

*Disability benefits*

Until the 1970's disabled people without resources had to live on means-tested benefits as they could not build up a contributions record and those with personal means did not receive any benefits. Various non-contributory disability benefits were then introduced to meet the gap in provision, in particular Attendance Allowance, Mobility Allowance, Severe Disablement Allowance and Invalid Care Allowance.[4]

## Administration

*Benefits Agency*

This new executive agency was launched in April 1991 to take over most of the functions of the DSS.[5] It is responsible for the administration of most benefits and its objectives include:

- an efficient customer-oriented benefit delivery service which is accessible, accurate, prompt, helpful, cost effective and does not discriminate on grounds of race, sex, religion or disability;
- comprehensive information on social security benefits so that people are informed about their entitlements and enabled to claim and receive benefits;
- clear explanations of how decisions are made, and of appeal and review rights;
- correct amounts of benefits paid on time, with safeguards against fraud and abuse.

A *Customer Charter* has been published which is intended to lead to improvements in the service given. Having to work within fixed budgets is likely to be the dominating factor, and increased use of modern technology may also result in people with disabilities being treated on a less personal basis.

*Offices*

Most benefits have been administered at local offices in larger towns each with its own territorial area based upon the claimant's place of residence. Some are administered in a special office at a single location[6] but Statutory Sick Pay is paid by employers, whilst Housing Benefit has been transferred to local authorities for administration but policy is determined by DSS. Re-organisation is taking place following creation of the executive agencies.[7]

---

4    The first two became Disability Living Allowance from April 1992.
5    Three other agencies take over other work, namely: Resettlement Agency, Information Technology Services Agency and Contribution Agency.
6    Child Benefit (Newcastle upon Tyne), Invalid Care Allowance (Preston), and Attendance Allowance and Family Credit (Blackpool).
7    In London, many functions of the inner-city offices have been taken over by Social Security Centres in Glasgow, Belfast and Wigan. Outside London, the 500 local offices are being merged together in groups to form 159 Local Management Units, with rural areas being served by mobile units or local branch offices in which Benefit Advisers will be located.

*Adjudication*
This is the process whereby decisions on entitlement are made,
usually by an *adjudication officer*, but medical issues are
determined by medical adjudicating authorities. There is an
elaborate appeal system.

*Disability Living Allowance Advisory Board*
This Board, comprising a Chairman and up to 20 members
appointed by the Secretary of State with appropriate experience,
has been set up to advise on matters relating to Disability Living
Allowance and publish an annual report. It may consult interested
parties.

*Social Security Advisory Committee (SSAC)*
The SSAC is the major UK advisory body on all social security
matters except those relating to industrial injuries, war pensions
and occupational pensions.[8] It is independent, expresses its views
in objective terms, and on occasions has strongly opposed changes
in policy.[9] Most regulations which reflect changes in benefit or
contributions policy have to be submitted to the SSAC before they
are made. It may waive reference if it does not wish to comment
on a set of regulations, but if it decides to make a report it will
consult organisations and individuals with relevant experience; an
explanatory note is circulated with draft regulations (if available),
a press release is issued and notices placed in the London,
Edinburgh and Belfast Gazettes. When the SSAC reports on
regulations, the report has to be laid before Parliament with the
regulations and a statement from the Secretary of State responding
to any recommendations, a process which assists informed debate
because regulations are usually highly technical.[10] The Secretary
of State may lay regulations before receiving a report if "after the
reference it appears to him that by reason of the urgency of the
matter it is expedient to do so".

## Contributions

Entitlement to many state benefits such as unemployment benefit,
sickness benefit and retirement pension depends upon payment of
NI contributions during the normal working life. Disabled people
may not be able to engage in normal remunerative employment, so
will not pay contributions and must rely upon the special range of
benefits intended to support them. A carer in receipt of Invalid
Care Allowance will be credited with Class I contributions.

---

8   The functions, constitution and powers of the Committee are set out in
    Social Security Act 1980, s.9 and Sched.3 (as amended).
9   *e.g.* the abandonment in 1988 of single payments under the Supplementary
    Benefit regime and the introduction of the Social Fund.
10  Under a quarantine rule those made within 12 months of commencement of
    an Act giving power to make regulations need not be referred.

## CONTRIBUTORY BENEFITS

These are benefits to which people resident in Great Britain may be entitled regardless of personal means if they have paid sufficient NI contributions. They count as income for means-tested benefits. Relatively few mentally handicapped people qualify, so only a summary is given.

### Unemployment Benefit

Provides a taxable temporary income for insured people who are involuntarily unemployed. A daily benefit based upon a six day working week and payable after three waiting days for a period of up to 312 days.[11] Claimant must satisfy the contribution conditions, be fit for work, and be available for and actively seeking employment. The day of claim must be a day of unemployment and form part of a period of interruption of employment. In certain circumstances a claimant may be disqualified for up to six months.[12]

### Sickness and Invalidity Benefits

Provides a non-taxable income for insured persons who are incapable of work because of disease or disablement, whether physical or mental. Sickness benefit is paid for the initial period of incapacity (28 weeks) and Invalidity Benefit thereafter at higher rates.[13] Claimant must either satisfy the contribution conditions or show that the incapacity is the result of an industrial accident or prescribed industrial disease. The day of claim must be a day of incapacity for work forming part of a period of interruption of employment, and the claimant must not be disqualified.[14] Limited earnings from therapeutic work are allowed.

### Industrial Injury Benefits

This package of benefits is available to an employee who, because of work, suffers a loss of faculty. A disablement benefit is paid if the degree of disablement is assessed above a specified level. Claimant must have been in employment and then suffered from a prescribed disease as a result of that employment or a personal injury caused by accident arising out of and in the course of that employment. Questions as to loss of faculty, and degree and period of disablement, are dealt with by adjudicating medical authorities and, on appeal, by Medical Appeal Tribunals.

---

11 This is one year on a six day week for those continuously unemployed.
12 If the person lost employment through misconduct, left employment without just cause or failed to take up a suitable offer of employment.
13 *Statutory sick pay* often takes the place of sickness benefit.
14 Disqualification may arise if the incapacity is due to the claimant's own misconduct or where he has failed without just cause to receive medical treatment or behaved in a way that is likely to delay recovery.

## Maternity Benefits

A group of benefits associated with birth of a child and available in the normal way to a parent of a disabled child or a disabled person who has a child. *Statutory Maternity Pay* is administered by employers and paid for a period of 18 weeks to employees who satisfy the qualifying conditions, with any disputes being resolved by an adjudication officer subject to usual rights of appeal. *Maternity Allowance* is similar to this but payable by the Benefits Agency to those not qualifying.

## Retirement Pension

Paid to men at 65 and women at 60 years who no longer need to have virtually retired from work as a condition of entitlement. Mentally disabled people may not qualify because of the need for a contributions record over a life-time of employment, although contributions of a spouse may produce an entitlement. There are four categories:

*Category A*       - a contributory benefit payable on the strength of the claimant's own contributions record:

*Category B*       - payable on the strength of a spouse's record.

*Categories C/D*    - non-contributory and payable to those over 65 and 80 years respectively on July 5, 1948.

### NON-CONTRIBUTORY BENEFITS

These are benefits to which people resident in Great Britain may be entitled whether or not they have paid any NI contributions and regardless of personal means.[15]

## Child Benefit

Child Benefit Act 1975
Child Benefit (General) Regulations 1976

A non-taxable weekly cash benefit introduced from April 1977 to replace family allowances and payable to persons responsible for one or more children living in Great Britain. Claimed as a matter of course by parents of a child being looked after at home. The claimant must be living with or contributing at least the weekly amount of the benefit towards maintenance of the child.[16] If the child is in hospital benefit continues for the first 12 weeks and thereafter if the claimant is regularly incurring expenditure in respect of the child,[17] but if taken into the care of a local authority benefit ceases after eight weeks. A child is a person under 16, or under 19 receiving full-time secondary education in a recognised educational establishment, but benefit ceases if the child is

---

15    Attendance and Mobility Allowances are included because, although replaced by Disability Living Allowance from April 1992, most of the former law has been retained and many appeals have yet to be determined.

16    A temporary absence of up to 56 days in 16 weeks is ignored.

17    Making regular visits to the hospital may be sufficient.

married, in employment for at least 24 hours per week, on the youth training scheme, in custody or in receipt of Severe Disablement Allowance. Claims are made on forms CB2 and CB3 obtained from the local Benefits Agency office, and administered from the Child Benefit Centre.[18] They may be backdated up to six months but not made before the child is born, and payment is generally made four-weekly in arrears.[19]

## One-parent benefit

A supplement available to one-parent families and payable at a weekly rate regardless of the number of children. It is not taxable but is taken into account in a claim for Income Support and may not be claimed in addition to Invalid Care Allowance for the same child. Claims are made on the form in DSS leaflet CH11.

## Attendance Allowance[20] (AA)

Social Security Act 1975, s.35
Social Security (Attendance Allowance) (No.2) Regulations 1975

A non-taxable weekly cash benefit which was paid in addition to other benefits to persons needing a lot of care, and not taken into account when claiming means-tested benefits (unless the claimant was in a residential care or nursing home). It could be claimed by a person of any age[21] who:

(a) satisfied one or both of the attendance conditions (the *day condition* and the *night condition*);
(b) had done so for a continuous period of six months immediately before the claim;
(c) satisfied a residence and presence in GB condition;
(d) was not resident in certain types of accommodation; and
(e) (for a child under 16 years) required attention or supervision substantially in excess of that normally required by a child of the same age and sex.

## Attendance conditions

The *day condition* was satisfied if the claimant was so severely disabled physically or mentally as to require throughout the day from another person:

- frequent attention in connection with bodily functions;   or
- continual supervision in order to avoid substantial danger to himself or others.

The *night condition* was satisfied if the claimant was so severely disabled physically or mentally as to require at night from another person:

- prolonged or repeated attention in connection with his bodily

---

18   PO Box 1, Newcastle upon Tyne, NE88 1AA.
19   Weekly payment is allowed to those receiving one-parent benefit, Income Support or Family Credit, or otherwise where there would be hardship.
20   Replaced by Disability Living Allowance from April 1992, but still applies if disability begins after age 65 years or claim is made after age 66 years.
21   Until 1990 it could not be claimed for a child until two years old.

functions;   or
- to be awake for a prolonged period or at frequent intervals
  for the purpose of watching over him in order to avoid
  substantial danger to himself or others.

When assessing danger it was necessary to consider whether the
existence of attendance or supervision indicated the need for it and
explained why harm or danger had been avoided in the past, and
also to decide, according to the nature of the handicap, what were
the foreseeable injurious consequences of that condition in the
setting of the claimant's daily lifestyle.[22]

### Amount and claims

There were two rates: a *higher rate* payable if both conditions
were satisfied and a *lower rate* payable if only one condition was
satisfied. The allowance could be for life or a specified shorter
period, in which event a new claim could be made at the end of the
period. There was no provision for backdating the claim, and no
appeal against the decision but a review could be asked for.
Payments in respect of an infant child were made to the adult with
whom the child was living.

In 1990 it was held[23] that the regulation preventing claims in
respect of children below two years of age was *ultra vires* because
the Social Security Act 1975, s.35 which introduced AA did not
give the Secretary of State power to limit entitlement by age.
Hence a number of claimants would have been entitled for up to
18 months before they got the allowance, and where claims had
been made for children under two and refused due to age, a late
appeal became possible.

### Qualifying conditions

Regulations provided that the allowance was not payable for any
period when the claimant was provided with accommodation in
circumstances in which the cost "is, *or may be*, borne wholly or
partly out of public or local funds" in pursuance of certain
enactments,[24] but there were exceptions "in respect of ...
accommodation in such ... case or class of case as the Secretary of
State may direct."[25] The enactments were those specified in a
Schedule.[26] The allowance would not be withdrawn during the
first 28 days (which need not be consecutive) that a claimant was

---

22  *Young* v. *DHSS* (1990), CA (Northern Ireland), see *Legal Action*, April
1991, p.21.

23  Commissioners Decision *CA/380/1990*. If it is ultimately confirmed that the
Commissioners do not have power to hold that regulations are *ultra vires*
this possibility of a late appeal may be closed - see footnote 212.

24  Social Security Act 1975, s.35(6); 1975 Regulations, reg.4(1). The
intention was that the allowance should not be paid when care was already
being provided by a public body, *e.g.* in hospital, residential school or care
home. Short stays were ignored. See Part V for a fuller explanation.

25  Reg.4(3)(*b*). This provided scope for Directions.

26  They included National Assistance Act 1948, Part III and National Health
Service Act 1977, s.21(1)(*b*) and Sched.8.

in hospital or the types of accommodation specified, but[27]:

> "2 or more distinct periods separated by an interval not exceeding 28 days, or by 2 or more such intervals, shall be treated as a continuous period equal in duration to the total of such distinct periods and ending on the last day of the later or last such period"

These regulations only applied to claims by persons over 16, but similar provisions applied in respect of a child.[28]

*Assessment*
Satisfaction of the attendance conditions was decided by the Attendance Allowance Board through a Delegated Medical Practitioner who visited and examined the claimant. He had a standard form to complete which included a checklist of activities such as dressing, washing, toiletting, eating and drinking. Parents or carers usually needed to be present for a claim by a person with a mental handicap, and it helped for them to make notes beforehand of all areas of difficulty and to emphasise the extent to which care and supervision was required. The Board published a *Handbook for Delegated Medical Practitioners* which clarified some problem areas, and though not a book of rules its directions had to be followed and provided useful arguments on a review. For example, the *Handbook* stated that when a carefully structured and limited environment had been created within which the claimant could live with an apparent degree of independence, though he could not cope with any deviation from the routine, this must be considered as providing continued supervision even though the claimant might be out of sight of the carer for short periods of time.

The Court of Appeal considered the question of continual supervision where a claimant tended to have epileptic fits during the night and concluded that supervision might be precautionary and anticipatory and there was no justification for drawing hard and fast distinction as to the position between and during attacks. A person who was standing by to intervene in the event of an attack might be exercising supervision between attacks; it was a question of fact and degree in each case. The frequency of attacks was immaterial to the question whether supervision was continual so long as the risk of substantial danger was not so remote a possibility that it ought reasonably to be disregarded.[29]

## Mobility Allowance[30] (MA)

Social Security Act 1975, s.37A
Social Security (Mobility Allowance) Regulations 1975

This non-taxable weekly cash benefit was paid to persons resident

---

[27] Reg.5(2)(*a*). The exceptions are found in reg.5(1).
[28] Reg.7. A child was defined in reg.1(2) as a person under 16 years.
[29] *Moran* v. *Secretary of State for Social Services*, Appendix to R(A) 1/88. Latterly this only applied to the day condition, since the night condition was changed to avoid the consequence of this decision.
[30] Replaced by Disability Living Allowance from April 1992, see below.

in Great Britain in addition to earnings or other state benefits and designed to help severely physically disabled people become more mobile. It operated as a passport to several other benefits and privileges.[31] It could be claimed for the first time by a person between the ages of five and 66 years, and once established could continue to 80 years. There were stringent qualifying conditions based upon inability (or virtual inability) to walk and mental handicap by itself was not sufficient.[32] The following medical questions had to be answered[33]:

> "A person shall be treated .. as suffering from physical disablement such that he is either unable to walk or virtually unable to do so only if
> (a)  his physical condition as a whole is such that, without having regard to circumstances peculiar to that person as to the place of residence or as to the place of, or nature of, employment
>      (i) he is unable to walk; or
>      (ii) his ability to walk out of doors is so limited, as regards the distance over which or the speed at which or the length of time for which or the manner in which he can make progress on foot without severe discomfort, that he is virtually unable to walk;  or
>      (iii) the exertion required to walk would constitute a danger to his life or would be likely to lead to a serious deterioration in his health, or ...."

The difficulty in walking must have a physical cause, such as brain damage, and this proved an obstacle in cases of mental handicap.[34] It was held that someone who needed occasional supervision because of some condition unrelated to walking, or who needed assistance so as to go in the right direction,[35] was able to walk for the purposes of this test. In the case of behavioural problems, hyperactive and controlled movements must be distinguished from temporary paralysis (as far as walking is concerned); only the latter would qualify and it was necessary to consider the degree and frequency of such paralysis.[36]

Most decisions in regard to such claims were dealt with by adjudication officers with the usual rights of appeal, but the medical questions were dealt with by medical boards with an appeal to the Medical Appeal Tribunal. The circumstances in which claims could be backdated were severely limited.

## Disability Living Allowance (DLA)

> Disability Living Allowance and Disability Working Allowance Act 1991
> Social Security (Disability Living Allowance) Regulations 1991

---

31   *e.g.* Severe Disablement Allowance, disability premium, exemption from road tax, provisional driving licence at age 16, car parking privileges.

32   Since April 1990 those who are deaf and blind have been deemed to be virtually unable to walk.

33   Social Security (Mobility Allowance) Regulations 1975, reg.3(1).

34   Nevertheless, Down's Syndrome has been held to be a physical disorder because it is due to faulty genetic inheritance - R(M) 2/78.

35   *Lees* v. *Secretary of State for Social Services* [1985] 2 All ER 203, HL. If someone must be accompanied at all times because they are not aware of dangers or unable to find their way to a destination, this was unlikely to qualify them, but see the new Disability Living Allowance.

36   R(M) 3/86.

From April 6, 1992 this non-means-tested allowance replaces AA and MA for new claimants whose disability begins before age 65,[37] though once awarded it may be paid irrespective of age provided that the criteria continue to be met. It also extends help to less severely disabled people.[38]

*Components and levels*
There are two separate components:
   a *care component* at three levels;
   a *mobility component* at two levels.
Claimants can qualify for either or both components, and the lowest level of each is available to those who did not qualify under the previous rules. The criteria for the higher and middle care levels are virtually the same as those for higher and lower AA and for the higher mobility level as that for MA. Thus in effect a third rate for AA and a second rate for MA are introduced.

The third care level is available for those who need help with self care, but less frequently than those who qualified for AA. A claimant who does not qualify for one or both of the higher levels may qualify for the lower rate if he[39]:

> (a) requires in connection with his bodily functions attention from another person for a significant portion of the day (whether during a single period or a number of periods); or
> (b) cannot prepare a cooked main meal for himself if he has the ingredients.

The higher mobility level has been opened up to those who are severely mentally impaired, display severe behavioural problems *and* are eligible for both day and night care components.[40] The lower level is paid to one who does not otherwise qualify and:

> "... is able to walk but is so severely disabled physically or mentally that, disregarding any ability he may have to use routes which are familiar to him on his own, he cannot take advantage of the faculty out-of-doors without guidance or supervision from another person most of the time."

Although it may be paid to people who are independently mobile, those with behaviour problems who require physical control to reach any intended destination outdoors may still not be entitled. The mobility components may only be claimed for the first time by people between ages five and 66 years.

*Children*
An extra condition must be satisfied by those under 16. They must have "substantial requirements .. which younger persons in normal

---

37   Claimants getting either allowance should simply transfer over to the appropriate level of the new allowance. AA continues for those whose disability begins after 65.

38   This followed the White Paper: *The Way Ahead: Benefits for Disabled People*, HMSO (CM917 of 1990). The Act inserts five new sections in the Social Security Act 1975, ss.37ZA-ZE.

39   Significant means at least 40 minutes. The cooking test will take account of functional, physical and mental factors.

40   A further 9,000 people may qualify under this new rule, but it seems illogical that a claimant's sleep pattern will affect the mobility entitlement.

physical and mental health may also have but which persons of (their) age and in normal physical and mental health would not have". This means that children should not be denied benefit merely because they have major care needs which may be shared by younger children without disabilities. Children qualify for the lowest care level only if they need attention with their bodily functions for a significant portion of the day, and the cooking test is inappropriate. In order to qualify for the lower mobility level, children under 16 must require more guidance or supervision than other children of the same age.

*Qualifying*

There is a common three months qualifying period and six months forward test (unless terminally ill) for both care and mobility components thus removing the need for separate medical assessments.[41] The allowance is awarded either for a fixed period or for life, but where a claimant is entitled to both components they cannot be awarded for different fixed periods and the shorter of the two will be adopted though there may be repeat claims. Most awards to mentally handicapped persons will be for life, though the care component may be awarded for life and the mobility component only for a fixed period. Only a single claim need be made, and there is a new adjudication and appeals structure. The claim pack includes a long self-assessment questionnaire with the option to request a medical examination, and the initial determination is made by an adjudication officer who may refer to a doctor for an examination and report.

DLA is disregarded for means-tested benefits,[42] and is a passport to the disability and disabled child premiums for Income Support and Housing Benefit. This applies to all levels of the new benefit, thus including people who would not have qualified before. The lower care level will not be a passport to severe disability premium, or for a carer to claim Invalid Care Allowance.

## Severe Disablement Allowance (SDA)

Social Security Act 1975, s.36
Social Security (Severe Disablement Allowance) Regulations 1984

A non-taxable weekly cash benefit with additions for dependants payable in addition to other benefits to persons who satisfy a residence condition and whose medical condition makes them unfit for work on a long term or permanent basis and who have an incomplete contribution record.[43] It cannot be claimed in addition to another income replacement benefit,[44] and counts in full as an

---

41   There was no qualifying period but a 12 month forward test for MA; a six months qualifying period but no forward test for AA.

42   Except the care component (previously Attendance Allowance) for those in residential care, see Part V of this chapter.

43   The allowance replaces the former "Non-Contributory Invalidity Pension".

44   *I.e.* Sickness or Invalidity Benefit, Maternity Allowance, widow's benefit, Retirement Pension, Invalid Care Allowance or a training allowance.

income resource for Income Support though it qualifies the claimant for a disability premium. There are age related additions for those who became incapable of work before their 60th birthday, the amount depending on how old the claimant was on the first day of incapacity for work in the qualifying period for the allowance. Claimants receiving Income Support gain nothing because the additions are means-tested, but those getting housing benefit keep 35 per cent.

*Entitlement*
A claimant must be at least 16 and those over pensionable age may not apply for the first time, but the allowance continues after that age if already in payment. Those aged between 16 and 19 in full time education[45] will not qualify unless they are receiving special education designed for persons with a physical or mental disability; thus people with a mental handicap will usually be eligible to claim at 16 even if they remain in a special school. The claimant must be incapable of work and have been so incapable for at least the previous 196 consecutive days (including Sundays), and either:
- have been under 20 years of age when incapacity began[46]; or
- suffer from disablement assessed at 80 per cent. or more.[47]

In the case of persons with a severe mental handicap the incapacity will have existed from birth so the only question is whether they are as a result incapable of work.[48] Disqualification may arise on grounds similar to those for sickness benefit (*e.g.* failure to follow advice or undertake treatment).

*Application*
Claims are made on form SDA 1 supplied with leaflet NI 252 and sent to the local Benefits Agency office, but the allowance may be awarded where the original claim was for certain other benefits.[49] A first claim may be backdated for one month, or up to a year if good cause for the late claim can be shown and this will often be possible in the case of a person with a mental handicap because the test of good cause applies to the claimant. The 80 per cent. disablement test is referred to the medical authorities, but questions of incapacity for work are determined by adjudication officers with an appeal to the Social Security Appeal Tribunal.

---

45    This means more than 21 hours per week at a university, college, school or comparable institution.
46    The claim does not need to be made before the age of 20; the claim may be made much later but it is necessary to show that the incapacity for work began before that age and has been continuous since.
47    This may be passported from another benefit, *e.g.* AA or MA, or Vaccine Damage Payment.
48    Problems arise where a claimant is offered a trial period in a job, because if this does not continue the individual may no longer be classed as incapable of work (even though unable to get another job) and so lose the allowance. There are provisions dealing with therapeutic work.
49    Sickness or Unemployment Benefit, Invalidity Pension, Maternity Allowance.

### Invalid Care Allowance (ICA)

Social Security Act 1975, s.37
Social Security (Invalid Care Allowance) Regulations 1976

A taxable weekly cash benefit with additions for dependants[50] paid
to those who satisfy residence conditions and provide care for a
person who is so severely disabled as to be in receipt of the higher
levels of the care component of DLA. It is claimed by and paid to
the carer as an earnings substitute and class I NI contributions are
credited to the recipient. It overlaps with several other benefits[51]
so the claimant cannot receive both (but it may be worth applying
so as to receive NI credits), and counts as an income resource for
Income Support, but recipients are not required to be available for
employment. Although the allowance is not means-tested the
claimant must not be gainfully employed[52] or in receipt of full
time education.

*Entitlement*

It can only be claimed by persons between the ages of 16 and 65[53]
who are "regularly and substantially" engaged in caring for a
person in receipt of DLA. This means caring for more than 35
hours in a week, but holidays of up to four weeks in any six month
period are allowed.[54] "Caring" is not defined, but personal
supervision or even keeping the person company will be sufficient.
Only one allowance may be claimed for each person in receipt of
AA, and a claimant will only be entitled to one allowance no
matter how many persons are cared for. As a result of a 1986 test
case to the European Court of Justice, married women may now
claim ICA even if they would not otherwise have worked, and the
different pensionable age for women has also led to the rules being
challenged so women aged over 60 who wish to claim for the first
time should make further enquiries.

*Application*

Leaflet NI 212 should be obtained from the local Benefits Agency
office and the claim form at the back completed by the carer and
submitted to the ICA Unit.[55] Claims may only be backdated up to
12 months, but a claim for Income Support or unemployment
benefit may be treated as a claim for ICA if the Secretary of State

---

50   An increase in respect of dependant children is not taxable.
51   *I.e.* Sickness or Invalidity Benefit, Maternity Allowance, widow's benefit,
     Retirement Pension, Unemployment Benefit, SDA.
52   This simply means earning more than a specified weekly amount (£40 in
     1992). Earnings mean gross wages or salary, and include overtime,
     bonuses, tips and commission and any other payment in cash or kind from
     employment or self-employment. The carer may earn more than the limit in
     weeks when he or she is not caring.
53   The allowance may continue beyond the retirement age if previously being
     paid, though it may not be paid in addition to retirement pension.
54   Up to 12 weeks is allowed if the claimant or person cared for is in hospital,
     though after four weeks the latter will lose AA so ICA ceases.
55   Palatine House, Lancaster Road, Preston, Lancashire PR1 1HB.

so allows.

*Home Responsibilities Protection scheme*
A person who does not qualify for ICA but looks after someone who gets DLA should consider applying under this scheme which may help to protect basic Retirement Pension rights. Leaflet CF 411 is available.

## Vaccine Damage Payments[56]

Vaccine Damage Payments Act 1979

A tax-free lump sum of £30,000[57] can be awarded to a person who has suffered as a result of a routine vaccination against certain diseases.[58] As a result of extensive public pressure particularly from parents who considered that their children had suffered disablement as a result of vaccination, an extra statutory scheme was set up in May 1978 and this was followed by legislation.[59]

*Entitlement*
The claimant has to satisfy several non-medical conditions:
   (a) the vaccination must have been carried out in the UK[60] and (except for rubella and poliomyelitis) either when the claimant was under 18 or at a time of an outbreak of the qualifying disease within the UK;
   (b) the claimant must be over two on the date of claim;
   (c) the claim is made within six years of the vaccination[61];
   (d) the claimant must normally live in the UK or the Isle of Man and have been present there for a continuous period of six months at the time of the claim;
and two medical conditions:
   (e) the disablement must be severe[62] and
   (f) it must be caused by the vaccination.

*Application*
Claims are made to the Vaccine Damage Payments Unit,[63] and

---

56   This material is based upon an article by Rodney Huggins, Regional Chairman of the London South SSATs published in the OPSSAT News.
57   Vaccine Damage Payments Act 1979 Statutory Sum Order 1991. Previously £20,000 for claims made before April 15, 1991, and £10,000 for claims made before June 18, 1985.
58   Set out in s.1(2) and include diphtheria, rubella, smallpox, tuberculosis, whooping cough, poliomyelitis, tetanus and measles. Those damaged before birth as a result of vaccinations given to their mothers are also included in the scheme.
59   The Association of Parents of Vaccine Damaged Children (address in Appendix I) is still pressing for a proper compensation scheme.
60   Or the Isle of Man. This restriction does not apply to serving members of the forces and their families.
61   If the claimant was under two at the time, within six years of his second birthday.
62   At least 80 per cent. measured in accordance with criteria for determining the extent of disablement for the purposes of Industrial Disablement Benefit.
63   DSS North Fylde Central Office, Norcross, Blackpool FY5 3TA. Obtain leaflet HB3 "Payment for people severely disabled by vaccine".

determined by reference to the information put forward by or on behalf of the claimant on a claim form together with any medical evidence then supplied or obtained (with the consent of the claimant) by the Unit. The Secretary of State must give notice in writing to the claimant of his decision and the grounds for a refusal, and can reconsider a refusal within six years if it was made in ignorance of, or based on a mistake as to, a material fact or there has been a material change of circumstances.[64] Where the claim is rejected only on one of the medical conditions the claimant is notified of the right to seek a review by a Vaccine Damage Tribunal.

## Causation

The High Court examined vaccine damage and its causation in a civil claim in 1988[65] involving a girl whose parents alleged that she had suffered brain damage following the administration of the DTP (Diptheria, Tetanus, Pertussis[66]) vaccine. It was held on the balance of probabilities on the facts of that case that the vaccine could not cause brain damage, and although this finding is not binding in regard to vaccine damage claims under the statutory scheme, it has a bearing on attitudes at the present time especially with many whooping cough claims outstanding. Decisions in other countries are awaited with interest. Whooping cough surges every four years and the question of whether to vaccinate a child then becomes of importance to parents. Compensation will only be payable for apparent damage if the parents can establish that the onset of the child's condition resulted from the vaccination rather than being simply coincidental with it in point of time.

## Trust Fund

Inevitably, the lump sum award is held in trust and there is a special form available. The parents will usually be the trustees in which event payment is made to them in that capacity. Such a trust for a dependent child is ignored for most means-tested benefits and makes no difference to other benefit claims, and once the child claims a means-tested benefit as an adult in his own right, the value of the trust fund is still ignored.[67] Until October 1990 it was only ignored for two years from the date of that claim and longer if that was "reasonable in the circumstances".[68] Payments made by the trust are treated as income or capital depending on the nature of the payment. The fund forms part of the person's estate on death, so the trustees cannot determine its destination.

---

64  He can reconsider at any time if he has reason to believe that there was a deliberate misrepresentation or non-disclosure of information.

65  *Loveday* v. *Renton,* March 1988,  Stuart-Smith J, (unreported).

66  *I.e.* whooping cough.

67  Income Support (General) Regulations 1987, Sched.10, para.12;  Family Credit (General) Regulations 1987, Sched.3, para.13. (as amended).

68  There was no guidance as to what was reasonable, and adjudication officers or SSAT's came to different conclusions on the same set of facts. This put unreasonable pressure upon trustees to spend the capital.

## Welfare Benefits

Finally, we consider the state benefits to which persons resident in Great Britain may be entitled, whether or not they have paid NI contributions, if their personal means fall below specified levels.

### Income Support

Social Security Act 1986, s.20-27
Income Support (General) Regulations 1987

A weekly income supplement for those not in full-time work, intended to bring resources up to needs (as defined) and normally paid at the same intervals as the appropriate social security benefit.[69] Based upon a *personal allowance* which depends upon age and marital status with *premiums* which include disability and severe disability. The rules are complicated and we only consider aspects relevant to persons with a mental handicap and carers. It is a passport to other benefits.

### *Entitlement*

A claimant must generally (subject to certain exceptions):
- be at least 18 and not in full time secondary education;
- be available for and actively seeking full time work;
- not be (nor have a partner) in remunerative work[70]; and
- pass a means-test as regards both income and capital.

The requirement to be available for and actively seeking work does not apply to several categories, including those who are too disabled to work[71] or staying at home to look after a severely disabled person, or getting ICA. People with a serious mental disability may qualify when they attain 16 even if still at school, provided they satisfy the other qualifying conditions.[72]

Either a man or woman can claim but entitlement covers the claimant and any members of his or her family, and only one person at a time can claim for the family. *Family* includes married couples living as members of the same household and unmarried couples living together as husband and wife, plus children (under 16) or young persons (16-19 in full-time secondary education) in the household for whom the claimant or partner is responsible.[73]

---

69   Thus unemployed people are paid fortnightly in arrear whilst pensioners and most widows are paid in advance. Entitlement qualifies the claimant and family members to help with NHS costs such as free prescriptions, dental treatment and eye tests.

70   This generally means working for 16 hours per week or more unless, because of physical or mental disability, earning 75 per cent. or less of what would be normal for a fit person or, since Oct. 1991, in residential care (*i.e.* can still work full time if in such care and claim Income Support).

71   Or if because of mental or physical disability they would be able to earn only 75 per cent. or less of what they would expect to earn if fully fit. They are treated as being so incapable if in receipt of SDA.

72   See Part IV below under the heading "Child or Adult?"

73   Social Security Act 1986, s.20(11).

## Applicable amount

Both entitlement and the amount are determined by setting the claimant's income against his *applicable amount*: if income equals or exceeds this there is no entitlement; if less, the difference is the amount of benefit. The applicable amount comprises the total of:

    (a) a *personal allowance* for each member of the family;

    (b) the *premiums* for which the claimant is eligible;   and

    (c) any *housing costs*.

### Personal allowance

Rates are stipulated annually for claimants according to age and whether single or a couple, with additional sums for each child of the family again depending on age. Until April 1993 (when the full community care policies are implemented) *residential care allowances* are available to those in residential care or nursing homes, but because of an explosion in the cost during the 1980's, limits have been placed upon the weekly amounts depending upon the category of care provided.

### Premiums

These additional sums may be added to the claimant's personal allowance, qualification being based on membership of categories which sometimes depend upon entitlement to other benefits. The amounts, unrelated to individual needs, are fixed annually.

| | |
|---|---|
| *Family* | a single sum in addition to any other premiums where a member of the family is a child or young person. |
| *Lone parent* | a single sum where the claimant has a child or young person in the family but no partner. |
| *Pensioner* | various sums for those of retirement age, including *higher pensioner premium* for those who are sick or disabled. |
| *Disabled child* | payable for each disabled child[74] in addition to other premiums. |
| *Disability* | for an adult under 60 treated as disabled.[75] |
| *Severe disability* | for severely disabled people needing care.[76] |
| *Carer's* | for those getting ICA (or eligible but getting another benefit at a higher rate).[77] |

In some cases where there is entitlement to more than one premium only the higher one is allowed.[78]

---

[74]   *I.e.* receiving the upper levels of DLA.

[75]   *e.g.* in receipt of SDA or the relevant level of DLA.

[76]   This has proved highly contentious, see Part IV, p.445.

[77]   A carer who ceases to get (or be treated as getting) ICA will still qualify for the premium for a further eight weeks.

[78]   Lone parent, disability and pensioner premiums are alternatives. Family, disabled child and carers premiums are paid in addition to other premiums. Severe disability premium may be paid on top of disability or higher pensioner premium.

*Housing costs*
The sum allowed relates to the claimant's home and covers interest on mortgages and on loans for improvements and repairs,[79] and certain other housing costs. It is reduced if there are non-dependants living in the home. Water rates are not included and must be met from the personal allowance; rent is covered by Housing Benefit and a separate claim must be made to the local authority.

*Transitional protection*
For some claimants from April 1988 their entitlement to Income Support was less than it had been under Supplementary Benefit. Transitional rules ensured that they did not suffer a reduction but continued to receive their existing level until their new entitlement resulted in an increase. There have been problems where an individual has for some reason ceased for a short period to be entitled to Income Support and has thereby lost this transitional protection.

## Assessment of resources
Having worked out the applicable amount, the income and capital resources of the claimant must be calculated according to special rules and the income shortfall will represent the Income Support entitlement provided that capital is below certain levels.

*Income*
The income of all members of the family is added together (with some exceptions for children) and most kinds of income are taken into account, including social security benefits. This may include a *tariff* income from capital, but certain types of income (or a proportion) are disregarded.[80] Charitable or voluntary payments made regularly are ignored if intended and used for certain purposes, and those made on an irregular basis are treated as capital. Topping-up by other persons is allowed where residential home fees exceed residential care allowance.[81]

*Capital*
There is a *capital cut-off limit* which means that if the claimant's capital exceeds the specified sum (presently £8,000) there can be no entitlement. If the capital exceeds a lower sum (presently £3,000), for every £250 or part thereof above this a weekly income of £1 is assumed (an effective capital levy of over 20% per annum). The capital of the claimant's partner is included, but not that of any children in the family, though if a child has more than the lower sum there will be no personal allowance for that child.

---

79  Only 50 per cent. for the first 16 weeks of a claim if under 60.
80  These are set out in Sched.9 to the 1987 Regs., and include the first £5 of earnings (£15 for the disabled, couples and lone parents), voluntary or charitable income payments (*i.e.* at regular intervals) of up to £10 per week and the actual income from most forms of capital.
81  Sched.9, para.30(d).

Anything which has a market value can be a capital asset, and the general law is applied to determine when a person has an interest in an asset which is capable of being sold. The current market value applies. Certain forms of capital are disregarded,[82] the most important being the value of the claimant's home and possessions.

*Notional resources*
The claimant may be treated as possessing capital or income which he or she does not actually possess.[83] Discretionary payments by trustees are taken into account as income or capital depending upon how made but, unlike the old Supplementary Benefit rules, discretionary trusts under which the claimant may benefit are no longer assessed according to the real possibilities under the trust. Payments by others to third parties for the benefit of the claimant are only treated as notional income or capital to the extent that they are used for items deemed to be covered by Income Support (*e.g.* food, fuel, clothing and housing). This enables family and carers to buy extras for a mentally handicapped person who is dependent on Income Support, but there remains doubt as to whether this applies to expenditure by a discretionary trust as distinct from an individual, though this may depend upon the specific terms of the trust.[84]

## Family Credit

Social Security Act 1986, s.20-22
Family Credit (General) Regulations 1987

A weekly means-tested tax-free top-up benefit for low income working couples or single parents with an infant child or children, paid weekly in arrears by order book or direct bank credit. The amount depends upon the income of the family and number and ages of the children, and the calculation is complex. Once credit has been awarded it continues for a six month period before re-assessment, regardless of any changes of income in the meanwhile. Entitlement qualifies the claimant and family members to help with NHS costs.

*Entitlement*
Either the claimant or partner must be in remunerative full-time work, which means normally working on average for 16 hours or more per week, but this may be for an employer or on a self-employed basis.[85] They must not have capital of more than £8,000,

---

82  These are set out in Sched.10.
83  Reg.42 deals with notional income and reg.51 with notional capital.
84  There may be a difference between a discretionary power to purchase an item for the beneficiary, and a discretionary power to pay money to or for the benefit of the beneficiary which is exercised in the purchase of an item. The safest course may be to purchase the item as a trust investment and allow the beneficiary to use it.
85  This was reduced from 24 hours in April 1992, thus moving more people from Income Support to Family Credit, though some will not be eligible for the latter, *e.g.* those without families. There is also a loss of mortgage

which means all savings and property except certain disregarded items, and capital in excess of £3,000 produces a tariff income. There is a means-test as to income, with provisions for notional income, but child benefit and benefits connected with disabilities are disregarded.[86] Capital and income of a child is not taken into account save that credit is not payable for a child with capital or income in excess of the specified amounts.

The claimant or partner must be responsible for a child or young person who is a member of the same household.[87] A child for this purpose is under 16 and a young person over that age but under 19 and receiving full time education (as defined). Both married and unmarried couples qualify, but the latter must be living together as husband and wife.

## Disability Working Allowance (DWA)

Disability Living Allowance and Disability Working Allowance Act 1991
Disability Working Allowance (General) Regulations 1991

This entirely new allowance introduced in April 1992 is targetted on people who are partially rather than wholly incapable of work, and is intended to encourage them to take up work by topping-up low earnings thus providing more opportunity for integration with non-disabled people. It is a weekly means-tested benefit payable to people aged 16 or over in low paid work for at least 16 hours per week who were previously getting a qualifying benefit.[88] A claimant must also have "a physical or mental disability which puts him at a disadvantage in getting a job". It is similar to Family Credit, being awarded for six month periods with a tapered withdrawal of benefit as income rises, but does not act as a passport to exemption from health service charges, though NI class 1 credits may be awarded. It is available to disabled people, either single or living as a couple, without children.[89]

Receipt of DWA may be one of the passports to other disablement benefits and those receiving SDA or Invalidity Benefit before starting work should, if they again become incapable of work within two years, move straight back onto those benefits thus avoiding the penalty hitherto associated with an unsuccessful attempt at work. Those who can only work part time (at least 16 hours a week) or to a limited capacity will be able to rely upon DWA for support rather than having to push themselves beyond their capacity or give up all work and rely totally on disability benefits. For the first time the benefit system will support disabled

---

interest relief and passported benefits, but there is some transitional protection.

86 But not Disability Working Allowance.

87 A child who has been in hospital or residential accommodation due to mental handicap for a period of 12 weeks before the claim and is not in regular contact with a member of the household, will not count.

88 Invalidity Benefit, SDA, Income Support disability premium, or DLA.

89 The capital limit is £16,000 as distinct from £8,000 for Family Credit, but it may not be awarded to a family at the same time as Family Credit.

people in work rather than only when they are unable to work, but short term experimentation with increased hours at a higher wage could carry the risk of being left without a job and benefit.

## The Social Fund

Social Security Act 1986, Part III, ss.32-35

The Social Fund was established in April 1988[90] to meet needs "in accordance with directions given or guidance issued by the Secretary of State". These are found in the *Social Fund Manual*; directions must be followed but the guidance is persuasive.[91] Either loans or grants may be made and the terminology used is *applicant* rather than claimant. The applicant may, according to circumstances, be either the handicapped person or the parents or carers of such person.

### Procedure

Application Form SF 300 *Help for people with exceptional expenses* should be completed by the applicant or someone acting on his behalf, save that for crisis loans contact is made direct with the local office. Decisions are made by *Social Fund Officers* (SFO's) appointed by the Secretary of State, and although there is an internal review procedure, there is no independent right of appeal. They should be made within 28 days or, for crisis loans, without delay.

Although the applicant may not automatically be given the reason for a refusal, this should be stated if it is queried. Within 28 days of the determination the applicant may request a review and if this is not favourable should be invited to an interview where he may be accompanied by a friend or adviser. The SFO must give an explanation of the reasons for the decision and the opportunity to make representations. A written record should be made and agreed with the applicant, and this is then passed to a higher executive officer for a final decision unless the SFO has at that stage granted the application. A further review can be requested by the applicant in writing (stating the grounds for the request and signed) within 28 days of notification of this decision, or longer if there are special reasons, and this will be carried out by a *Social Fund Inspector* at a regional office.

### Budget

Unlike other benefits which are demand led, payments from the Social Fund are subject to budget constraints on an annual basis.[92] The Secretary of State pays into the Fund each year separate amounts for loans and grants, and each office receives an

---

[90] On the change from Supplementary Benefit to Income Support with the consequent withdrawal of single payments.

[91] s.33(10A).

[92] The intention was to reduce previous levels of expenditure and keep them under control, whilst being more flexible and targetting those in greatest need. Take-up campaigns became necessary, but the Fund has proved to be the most expensive social security benefit to administer.

allocation similarly divided (funds cannot be moved between the two categories). The SFO must assess the relative priority of every application and have regard to the budget allocation when determining whether to make an award and how much it shall be. The budget is divided into monthly spending profiles and any deficit or excess in expenditure is spread throughout the rest of the year. Waiting lists are not allowed, but borderline applications may be held back and repeat applications may not be made within 26 weeks unless there has been a change in circumstances.

*General considerations*
An SFO must have regard to the following factors when deciding whether to make a loan or a grant and how much to award[93]:
- the nature, extent and urgency of the need;
- the existence of resources from which the need may be met;
- the possibility that some other person or body may meet the need, wholly or in part;
- where the payment is repayable, the likelihood of repayment and the time within which this is likely;   and
- the budget allocation.

The *Manual* sets out general exclusions for grants and loans.[94]

*Community care grants*
These non-repayable grants are designed to promote community care and complement the role of the local authority by[95]:
- helping re-establish a person in the community following a stay in residential or institutional care[96];
- helping a person remain in the community rather than enter residential or institutional care;
- easing exceptional pressures on that person and the family;
- assisting with certain travel expenses within the UK.

The first two categories have priority, and within each of these four categories the Manual identifies *priority situations*, with priority groups and priority items, but this is merely guidance and the SFO is left with discretion to identify further priorities. Vulnerable groups are identified who should be given priority and one such group is mentally handicapped people. Specific priority situations of relevance here include:
- moving house to look after someone who is moving from residential or institutional care;
- moving to more suitable accommodation;
- moving house to be nearer, or to live with, a mentally

---

93   s.33(9). See also paras.6008-6009 of the *Manual*.
94   Directions 12 and 29. These include education or training needs, domestic assistance and respite care, a medical item or service.
95   Direction 4. SFO's are expected to liaise closely with local social services authorities, see paras. 6001-6006 of the *Manual*.
96   Hostel type accommodation is not treated as community rather than residential care even for those who have left hospital to live there. This disadvantages mentally handicapped people for whom the hostel offers the best opportunity for independence.

handicapped person;
- living in the community but moving in order to set up an independent home for the first time;
- staying in the community, rather than entering residential or institutional care, and improving living conditions.

Typical awards relate to start-up grants, clothing, removal expenses, fares when moving, connection of appliances, laundry costs for a disabled child and, in some situations, essential furniture and household appliances. Certain expenses cannot be covered, including those which a local authority has a statutory duty to meet and fuel and housing costs, and there are suggested maximum and minimum payments. Travelling expenses may be payable for visiting a mentally handicapped person who is a close relative, or a member of the household who is a patient in a hospital or nursing home, or in a residential care home or Part III (Scotland, Part IV) accommodation or staff-intensive housing which provides a major level of personal care.[97]

The applicant must be receiving Income Support unless to be discharged from residential or institutional care within the next six weeks and then likely to receive it. Capital is assessed as for Income Support and any capital over £500 will reduce the amount of the grant.

## Loans

### Budgeting

These loans are to assist a person to meet important intermittent expenses for which it might be difficult to budget.[98] The applicant must have been receiving Income Support for the past 26 weeks, though there could be a gap of up to 14 days. Any capital over £500 will reduce the amount. There are maximum and minimum amounts, and the maximum takes into account any outstanding balance of previous loans.[99] The loan may not exceed that which the applicant can afford to repay. In general, housing and fuel costs are excluded (though rent in advance may be covered) and there is a list of items divided into high, medium and low priority, though the applicant's circumstances may give an item a higher priority. In all cases high priority must be given where refusal could cause hardship, or damage or risk to the health of the applicant or family.

### Crisis

These loans are to assist a person in an emergency or following a disaster where either[100]:

- such payment is the only means by which serious damage or serious risk to the health or safety of that person or a member of his family may be prevented;  or

---

97   See Direction 4 and paras.6551-6554 of the *Manual*.
98   Direction 2.
99   The minimum is presently £30 and the maximum £1,000.
100   Direction 3.

- the payment is for rent in advance to a landlord (other than a local authority) and the person has received a community care grant by virtue of leaving residential or institutional care.

The applicant must be 16 or over without sufficient resources to meet his immediate short-term needs, and various people are excluded, including those in Part III accommodation, nursing home or hospital, and those in full-time secondary education (unless receiving Income Support). Any resources actually available to the applicant will be taken into account, including credit facilities, though those on Income Support are not expected to use credit. SFO's have a discretion to disregard resources which they consider it reasonable to disregard, such as the value of a home. There is no minimum loan but the maximum for immediate living expenses is 75 per cent. of the appropriate Income Support personal allowance plus the under-11 rate for each child, and in other cases the total Social Fund debt must not exceed £1,000.

Crisis loans tend to have highest priority, but there are certain excluded items and also situations that are generally recognised.

*Repayment*

Loans are interest free. An officer acting in the name of the Secretary of State rather than an SFO decides how the loan is to be recovered, including the period and rate of repayment. Recovery is normally by deduction from subsequent Income Support or from some other benefits of the applicant or a partner, but payment may be made direct.[101] There is a basis on which deductions from benefit should be calculated, and repayment may also be re-scheduled if there is a change in circumstances. There can be no review but there is a complaints procedure, though written complaint about repayments before the loan is made may cause the original decision to be re-examined. A complaint after acceptance is treated as a request to re-schedule the repayments.

## PROCEDURE

Social Security Acts 1975, 1986 and 1990
Social Security (Adjudication) Regulations 1986
Social Security (Claims and Payments) Regulations 1987
Social Security (Payments on account, Overpayments and Recovery)
   Regulations 1988

## Claims

It is necessary for the claimant or appointee[102] to make a claim to the appropriate Benefits Agency office before any benefit will be paid. Although the application must be made on the official form the claim may be treated as having been made on the date of receipt of a letter asking about the benefit if the official form that is sent out in response is returned to the office within a few days (or six weeks in the case of DLA). If the form is not properly

---

101  s.33(7). Deduction may not be made from Child Benefit, or DLA.
102  See below and Chaps.10A and 10B for the appointee procedure.

completed it may be sent back to the claimant but if it is then returned duly completed within a month the claim will be treated as having been made when the form was first submitted.[103]

*Time limits and back-dating*
Most state benefits can only be paid from the date of claim[104] but there are time limits from the date that entitlement arose for claiming other benefits[105] which means that payment may be automatically backdated for the specified period.[106] Arrears for an earlier period of up to 12 months can in general only be recovered if there is continuous good cause for a late claim,[107] but it may be possible to make a late appeal against an earlier decision (with leave of a Tribunal Chairperson for special reasons) or to treat a claim for one benefit as a claim for another. It is important to apply for backdating when the initial claim is made and good cause may be found in[108]:

> "some fact which, having regard to all the circumstances (including the claimant's state of health and the information which he had received and that which he might have obtained), would probably have caused a reasonable person of his age and experience to act (or fail to act) as the claimant did."

Thus, ignorance of benefit entitlement is not by itself sufficient, but ill-health or being misinformed after making appropriate enquiries may be. A mentally handicapped person will always have good cause for not having applied earlier, though once someone is appointed to act for him the good cause test will apply to the appointee not only for the particular benefit that the appointee has claimed but also for the full range of benefits. This can cause prejudice if the appointee does not at an early stage become aware of all potential benefits. The appointee will often be a parent, so the stress of coping (not only with the handicapped child but also the claims procedures) and complexity of the benefits regulations may be good cause for failure to claim. Sometimes it is suggested by the department that a decision was made not to claim, but this may be countered by the argument that the parent simply did not make a decision and was not in a fit state to do so.[109]

## Decisions

Every claim is considered in the first instance by an *adjudication officer* on the staff of the Benefits Agency office,[110] who may

---

103  1987 Regulations, reg.4.
104  *e.g.* Income Support.
105  *e.g.* for ICA it is 12 months.
106  Most time limits are set out in the 1987 Regs., Sched.4; see also reg.19(6).
107  Reg.19(2). To establish *continuous* good cause it is necessary to work backwards from the date of claim, and any gaps cannot be abridged. Claims for DLA cannot be backdated,
108  Approved by a Tribunal of Commissioners in *R(S) 2/63*.
109  It is worth appealing in these cases because SSATs are usually sympathetic and will respond to a well argued case.
110  The Department of Employment for unemployment benefit. Claims for DLA are dealt with at a disability benefits centre.

determine the claim or refer it for decision by a Tribunal, but certain decisions are taken by the Secretary of State.[111] Whilst a decision should be taken within 14 days of the application there is no sanction to enforce this (other than possible judicial review).

*Reviews*

A decision affecting entitlement to benefit may be reviewed by:

(i) an *adjudication officer* if:
- given in ignorance of, or based on a mistake as to, a material fact; or
- there has been a relevant change of circumstances; or
- it must take into account a new decision of the Secretary of State or the adjudicating medical authorities; or
- made by an adjudication officer and wrong in law.

(ii) the *Secretary of State* at any time if the original decision was made by him; or

(iii) a *medical board* if the decision was made by an adjudicating medical practitioner, a medical board or a tribunal and:
- given in ignorance of, or based on a mistake as to, a material fact (but there must be fresh evidence); or
- (in a decision concerning the disablement question for a severe disablement allowance or disablement benefit claim), there has been unforeseen aggravation of the disability.

Claimants can ask for a review at any time by writing to the relevant office, or an adjudication officer may review a decision of his own initiative. A review may be preferable to an appeal because it is simpler and quicker, and if it is refused the right of appeal remains. However, the review may only operate from the date thereof, and there are restrictions on review in certain cases, whereas a successful appeal will change the original decision thus causing arrears to be paid. Usually a review can only go back 12 months, but this does not apply if the decision was[112]:

(a) erroneous because of a mistake by or something done or omitted to be done by the Department for which the claimant was not responsible;

(b) given in ignorance of or based on a mistake as to a material fact, as established by new evidence which could not reasonably have been produced at the time and has been produced as soon as reasonably practicable.

Where the review is because of a new interpretation of the law by a Commissioner or court (a test case) arrears may not be backdated prior to such test case.[113]

## Payment

Benefits are usually paid by order book or girocheques which are cashed at nominated post offices, but the payment period can be confusing because some benefits are payable weekly in arrears whereas others are paid in advance. Some benefits can be paid by

---

[111] Often by his authorised representative in the local DSS office in accordance with Directions or set guidelines, but with no right of appeal.

[112] 1986 Regulations, reg.72(1).

[113] 1975 Act, s.104(7) and (8) as inserted by 1990 Act from July 13, 1990.

direct credit to a bank or building society account either four-weekly or quarterly in arrears. The Secretary of State has power in respect of all benefits to make payment by such means as appear appropriate, and to pay direct into the account of the claimant, or the spouse or other person acting on behalf of the claimant,[114] and this may be helpful to disabled people, but direct credit transfers are presently only available for some computerised benefits.[115]

### Agency and appointees

A claimant may nominate an agent to collect benefits from the post office. This is not provided for in the regulations but is a standard procedure, the form of authority usually being printed on the allowance order slip. In the case of a claimant who is unable to act personally, perhaps through mental disability, another person may be appointed to receive the benefit and deal with claims.[116]

### Overpayments

The Secretary of State is entitled to recover an overpayment of benefit where any person whether fraudulently or otherwise misrepresents, or fails to disclose, any material fact and this results in an overpayment of benefit.[117] A material fact is some fact which if known to the adjudication officer would have affected the benefit. Recovery is from the person misrepresenting or failing to disclose the material fact, but the original decision must first be changed on review or appeal.[118] A misrepresentation can be wholly innocent, and a failure to disclose may be the result of forgetfulness but knowledge of the material fact by the person who fails to disclose it must be established. Disclosure need not be in writing but it must be made in such a manner that it is brought to the attention of the adjudication officer handling the claim and it is sufficient if made by someone delegated to act on behalf of the claimant.[119] The claimant is expected to have read the information in the back of the order book or on any leaflets forwarded with payment, and these may indicate the changes of circumstances which affect the benefit and which it is necessary to disclose. Overpayment calculations tend to be complicated because of the need to take into account the claimant's position as it would have been if the overpayment had not been made.[120]

---

114   1987 Regulations, regs.20 and 21(1).
115   DLA, pensions and Family Credit, but not Income Support.
116   1987 Regulations, reg.33. See Chap.10A, Part III and 10B.
117   1986 Act, s.53, and 1988 Regulations. The rules were different for certain benefits before April 1987 and there has been litigation as to the extent to which the new rules are retro-spective.
118   It is unusual for recovery to be sought other than from the claimant, his (or her) spouse or the estate of either of them.
119   Problems arise where disclosure is made to a different benefit office than that dealing with the relevant claim. There may be a continuing obligation to disclose where an initial disclosure has clearly not been acted upon.
120   The "diminishing capital rule", which may only apply to cases of undisclosed capital.

*Underpayments*

There is a non-statutory scheme which has received little publicity whereby claimants who have been underpaid benefit may receive compensation payments. There is no leaflet or claim form, but the DSS administrative code instructs local offices to consider such a payment automatically when arrears of benefit are paid late due to DSS error. Claimants are entitled to compensation if they are underpaid benefit of £50 or more resulting from clear and unambiguous error by the DSS and the delay in payment was more than 12 months. Normal delays in the adjudication process do not count towards the 12 month period. Calculation of compensation is based on interest rates supplied by the Treasury.[121] The onus is on the claimant to raise the issue and requests for compensation should be sent to the office dealing with the claim. Those who are refused may pursue this via their MP or the Ombudsman.

## Overlapping benefits

There are special rules to prevent a claimant from receiving two overlapping benefits, and in particular two or more earnings replacement benefits.[122] Thus ICA cannot be paid to a claimant at the same time as unemployment benefit, sickness benefit, SDA or a state pension; instead the claimant receives the benefit with the highest rate. The following appeal to the European Court of Justice, in which the principle was challenged on grounds of sex discrimination, illustrates the point[123]:

> A widow claimed Invalid Care Allowance for the care of her daughter. She was eligible but also received a widow's pension which was greater, so no part of the allowance was paid. She claimed that this was unlawful sex discrimination as it was the widow's pension which rendered her unable to receive the care allowance thus causing her to be treated less favourably than a male. It was held that this was not caused by discrimination but resulted from the fact that she started from a different situation from that of any man, who may not receive a widow's pension.

Benefits which are intended to provide for different purposes can be claimed simultaneously, thus an individual with a mental handicap may be in receipt of both DLA and SDA whilst the carer may be able to claim ICA.

*Christmas bonus*

A special non-taxable bonus (£10 in 1991) is automatically paid to those receiving one or more qualifying benefits[124] during the week beginning with the first Monday in December but each claimant is only entitled to one such bonus. Where ICA and DLA are being claimed the carer receives the bonus as well as the person cared for because each are claimants in their own right.

---

[121] *e.g.* underpayment over a 10-year period of approximately £5,500 should involve compensation of £1,400.

[122] Social Security (Overlapping Benefits) Regulations 1979.

[123] [1990] 2 CMLR 399.

[124] These include Invalidity Benefit, SDA, ICA, DLA and Income Support.

## APPEALS

Social Security Acts 1975 and 1986
Social Security (Adjudication) Regulations 1986

Appeals against a refusal of benefit or the amount awarded are dealt with by local tribunals with a further right of appeal to the Social Security Commissioners on a point of law only. The procedure is relatively slow, so before insisting upon an appeal it may be worthwhile considering whether there are circumstances which justify a review of the previous decision by the adjudication officer, as this may produce a quicker result (though the decision should be reviewed in any event if an appeal is lodged).

*Legal Aid*
Legal Aid is not available for representation before tribunals or for appeals to the Commissioners, but assistance and advice may be given under the Green Form scheme.[125]

### Independent Tribunal Service

Responsibility for the organisation and administration of tribunals is vested in the *Independent Tribunal Service*[126] (ITS) appointed by the Lord Chancellor and independent from the administration of the DSS. Tribunals are organised in regions under a Regional Chairman and there are five types[127]:
  - Social Security Appeal Tribunal (SSAT);
  - Medical Appeal Tribunal (MAT);
  - Disability Appeal Tribunal (DAT);
  - Child Support Tribunal (CST);
  - Vaccine Damage Tribunal.

### Social Security Appeal Tribunals

SSATs hear appeals against decisions of adjudication officers and comprise a legally qualified chairperson with two lay members and at least one of such persons should be of the same sex as the appellant. The chairperson must always be present but if there is only one lay member the hearing may continue with the consent of the appellant in which event the chairperson will have a casting vote. Tribunals sit in public unless the appellant requests a private hearing, and are attended by a clerk who is a full time employee but does not play any part in the decision making process.

*Notice of appeal*
An appeal is made in writing to the Benefits Agency office within three months of notification of the decision. A form is available

---

125 In Scotland, legal advice and assistance.
126 Clements House, Gresham Street, London EC2V 7DN. tel: 071-606-2106. Until 1991 known as *Office of the President of the Social Security Appeal Tribunals* (OPSSAT).
127 The CST commences April 1993. SSATs were preceded by *Supplementary Benefit Appeal Tribunals* (SBATs) and *National Insurance Local Tribunals* (NILTs) administered by DHSS.

but a letter will be sufficient. The grounds of appeal should be stated, because these will then be included in the papers sent to the members prior to the hearing giving them an opportunity to read up the relevant law which may not otherwise be covered in the submissions of the adjudication officer. Whilst the appellant is not restricted to such grounds, an adjournment of the hearing may be necessary if arguments are then introduced for the first time.

## Late appeals

A chairperson may give leave to appeal out of time for *special reasons*.[128] Application is by letter to the Benefits Agency office that made the decision, but care should be taken to include all circumstances that may justify leave being granted because the chairperson will deal with the application on reading the letter and there may be no further opportunity to make representations, although further information may be requested before the decision is made. Many applicants request an oral hearing in the event that the chairperson is not prepared to grant the late appeal and whilst this is not provided for in the regulations there is nothing to prevent it. Even if the chairperson would not consider a hearing, the request emphasises that this is not simply a casual application and that there are arguable grounds.

There is no guidance as to what constitutes special reasons but they need not relate to the delay as such and can be found in the surrounding circumstances. The fact that the claimant has a mental handicap should always be mentioned as it may favourably influence the decision. It has been held that a family crisis can amount to special reasons, so it could be argued that where the claimant was coping alone with a severely mentally handicapped child this in itself amounted to a permanent family crisis making it impossible to concentrate upon ongoing benefit claims. Other examples of special reasons include:
- DSS did not fully investigate the claim (*e.g.* in the light of a subsequent Commissioner's decision which clarified the law);
- publicity material was wrong (*e.g.* for the above reason);
- this was an extremely complicated area of the law, perhaps only recently clarified by a Commissioner's decision;
- a considerable amount of benefit is at stake.

## Notice of hearing

A few weeks (or months) later the appellant receives from the Regional Office notification of the date, time and place of the hearing. At least 10 days notice should be given and if the date is not convenient a letter may be sent asking for a postponement to a later date, which will usually be granted if sufficient reason is given. Cases are normally listed in 20 minute slots either in a morning or afternoon list, so that if the case is listed in the morning it is unlikely to be heard in the afternoon and vice versa, though delays can occur when cases overrun. Complex cases are

---

128  1986 Regulations, reg.3(3).

likely to be adjourned for a full hearing at a later date when adequate time is allowed, so if a case is considered to be complex the Regional Office should be notified and special arrangements for the hearing may be made.

With such notification will be a full statement prepared by the adjudication officer on form AT2, setting out the facts taken into account, the regulations applied and the reasons for the decision, with copies of all relevant documents annexed. This statement is helpful and may be the first full explanation of the decision that the appellant has received. It will at the same time be sent to the members of the tribunal so that they may have an opportunity to study it before the hearing. The appellant should be prepared to challenge the statement where necessary.

*Hearing*

The hearing takes place before the SSAT sitting in the area in which the appellant resides, which may not be the area in which the original decision was made if the appellant has since moved. Travelling expenses may be paid for attending together with a contribution to loss of earnings. The hearing is relatively informal and should be attended by the appellant in person wherever possible. The procedure is within the discretion of the chairperson (though the rules of natural justice apply) and the appellant or representative should not hesitate to enquire at the commencement of the hearing as to the procedure being adopted (if this is not explained by the chairperson in his introduction) or to request a particular procedure if that is desired, though this may not necessarily be granted. The appellant may prepare a written submission, which is useful in complicated cases, and it is helpful to hand five copies to the clerk before the hearing commences,[129] and to notify the clerk of any Commissioner's Decisions which are to be referred to other than those on the AT2.

*Decision*

The decision is by a majority if the members cannot agree[130] and may be notified verbally by the chairperson after the conclusion of the hearing, but in any event a full written decision is sent out approximately two weeks thereafter. This will set out the evidence before the Tribunal, the findings of fact, the decision and the reasons for the decision.[131]

*Setting aside, correction and review*

The Tribunal may correct an accidental error in its decision but may not change the decision once it has been made, though the same or a different Tribunal may set the decision aside if due notice of the hearing was not given, or a party was not present or

---

129  One for each member of the tribunal, one for the adjudication officer and one for the official file in respect of the hearing.

130  The lay members can outvote the chairperson, who will only have a casting vote when there are only two members and they do not agree.

131  Also the reasons of the dissenting member if the decision is by a majority.

represented at the hearing, or the interests of justice so require and (in all cases) it appears just to do so.[132] Application to set aside may be made in writing within three months of notification of the decision,[133] and there will be a hearing which the applicant can attend. In appropriate cases it may be preferable to make such application rather than to appeal to the Commissioners.

Where new evidence comes to light which was not considered by the Tribunal or which shows that the Tribunal made an incorrect finding of fact which influenced the decision, the adjudication officer has power to review the decision. A review should be asked for in these circumstances and a refusal to review is a new decision which carries a further right of appeal.

## Disability Appeal Tribunals

These new Tribunals hear appeals in respect of disability questions arising under the new Disability Allowances, and consist of a legally qualified chairperson plus a general medical practitioner and a person who is either disabled or deals with disabled persons. Unlike SSATs, all three members must be present at the hearing. Medical examinations will not be conducted and if medical information is required a special examination and report will be arranged. Further appeals are to the Commissioners.

## Medical Appeal Tribunals

These Tribunals hear appeals against the decisions of adjudicating medical authorities and comprise a legally qualified chairman sitting with a surgeon and a consultant physician who is likely to be a specialist in the relevant field of medicine. The medical members will usually carry out an examination of the appellant in private.

## Vaccine Damage Tribunals[134]

This Tribunal deals with reviews of decisions on vaccine damage claims and its role is limited to questions of extent of disablement and its causation, the latter being determined on facts found on the balance of probabilities. The Tribunal comprises a legally qualified chairman and two medically qualified members, similar to that of MAT except that normally one member is a paediatrician. Hearings are in public (unless the chairman otherwise directs) and all three members must be present. Both the claimant and the Secretary of State have the right to be heard and may be represented by any person, call witnesses and address the Tribunal. The hearing is informal and in practice only the disabled claimant and the parents normally attend. Strict rules of evidence

---

132 1986 Regulations, reg.11. Only procedural irregularities may be relied upon, and where a mistake of law is alleged the correct course is to appeal to the Commissioners; *R(SB) 4/90.*

133 A late application may be accepted for special reasons.

134 This material is based upon an article by Rodney Huggins, Regional Chairman of the London South SSATs published in the OPSSAT News.

do not apply, and there are facilities for medical examination though this is seldom required.

## Causation

The most difficult question is that of causation, so evidence as to events at the time of and immediately following the administration of the vaccine is important. The Tribunal will seek evidence as to the disabled person's condition just before the vaccination and of any change immediately thereafter, especially sudden increase in temperature and screaming fits. Occasionally precise clinical symptoms are recorded in medical records, but often the only evidence available is the recollection of members of the family.

## Decision

The members are entitled to rely on their clinical assessment and are not bound to determine the issue only on the basis of the evidence, but they must give proper reasons in writing for their decision which will be conclusive on any finding of medical fact. There is no right of appeal from the decision, which may only be challenged by an application to the High Court or Court of Session for judicial review.

## Tribunals compared

SSATs and MATs deal with complementary aspects of social security adjudication. MATs deal with appeals from adjudicating medical authorities which determine medical questions (*e.g.* for SDA and disablement benefits) whilst SSATs deal with appeals from adjudication officers who determine the non-medical conditions of entitlement. SSATs alone deal with benefits which have no significant medical component, and they also deal with questions of incapacity for work which are based upon medical determinations but also involve questions of ability to undertake tasks. DATs deal with appeals relating to disability questions under the new disability benefits. The jurisdiction of Vaccine Damage Tribunals is limited to deciding whether vaccination is the cause of a disability and whether or not disablement is severe.

## Social Security Commissioners

The Commissioners hear appeals, on points of law only, from the SSAT, MAT and DAT and have the status of judges. Such appeals may be possible where the previous decision:
- was based on a mistake as to the relevant law;
- does not record reasons and findings of fact adequately;
- is not supported by any evidence;
- could not be supported by the findings of fact; or
- was in breach of the rules of natural justice.

## Leave to appeal

The appellant must first obtain leave to appeal from a Tribunal chairperson on a written application made within three months of receipt of the decision, but if this is refused an application for leave may be made direct to the Commissioner within six weeks thereafter. A claimant who fails to apply within the three months period may make an application direct to a Commissioner who may grant leave only for special reasons and if this is granted a further six weeks is allowed within which to send in the notice of appeal which should be on the form provided.

## Hearing

The appellant can ask for an oral hearing but this is not always granted and most appeals are dealt with on written representations. A Commissioner has power to expedite proceedings in such manner as he thinks fit, and this should be applied for if hardship will be caused by delay. Bundles of documents with submissions from each party are sent out before the hearing and there is the right to reply to any such submissions. The case will only be determined when both sides have made all their submissions and the process takes months (and can take years). Where the Chief Commissioner considers that an appeal involves a question of law of special difficulty, he may direct that it be dealt with by a *Tribunal of Commissioners* (on a majority decision if necessary).

## Decision

The decision is ultimately sent to the parties in writing and is similar to a court judgment. If the previous Tribunal decision was found to be wrong in law or it did not determine material facts which are in dispute, the case is usually sent back to another Tribunal with directions as to how it should be dealt with, but if the decision contains all material facts the Commissioner may make the final decision. All decisions of the Commissioners are treated as precedents binding in law, and the most important ones are reported[135] and may be cited in subsequent appeals; unreported decisions may be cited, if they are known or can be ascertained.

# Courts

## Appeal from Commissioners

A decision of a Commissioner may be appealed to the Court of Appeal or Court of Session on a question of law, but leave to appeal must first be obtained either from the Commissioner within three months[136] or, if refused, from the court. Legal aid is available for the first time in the appeal process at this stage.

## Judicial review

An application to the High Court or Court of Session for judicial review may be made in certain circumstances, but this is discretionary and will usually be refused if another remedy is available. In the case of state benefits the normal appeal procedure through the Tribunal and the Commissioners and thence to the

---

135 The general basis for the reporting of decisions, etc is set out in a Practice Memorandum issued by the Chief Commissioner on March 31, 1987. Individual reported decisions may be purchased from HMSO, and bound volumes are issued every couple of years.

136 This period may be extended for special reasons.

Court of Appeal or the Inner House of the Court of Session should be followed,[137] even though an issue of law of national importance is involved and these procedures are slow, but DSS have been known to consent to judicial review when it was anxious for a speedy final decision as to the validity of the regulations.[138] Some decisions are taken by the Secretary of State without a right of appeal and there is scope for judicial review if he exercises his powers improperly and also where there is excessive delay by DSS in carrying out its statutory duties. Although the DSS has argued that judicial review is the appropriate course where a claimant contends that regulations are *ultra vires*, the Commissioners have held that the Tribunals have jurisdiction to determine such issues and must do so in order to be able to come to a decision.[139] Most Social Fund decisions are outside the appeal process, and there is little scope for judicial review because decisions are discretionary, but there is an internal system of appeal.

Refusal of leave to appeal can usually be dealt with by an application to the intended appeal court, but judicial review may be available in respect of refusal by the Commissioners to give leave to appeal to themselves on the basis that the reasons given are wrong in law or no reasons have been given. It is also necessary to show that the original decision gives rise to an arguable point of law and that there are no other good grounds for refusing leave.

*European Court of Justice*
As the ultimate appeal court on matters relating to the Treaty of the European Community, any issue of European Community law arising before a national court concerning questions of interpretation or validity can be referred to this Court for a preliminary ruling.[140] In social security matters, a reference can be made by an SSAT, a Commissioner or the courts, and it is becoming increasingly common for the Commissioners to make a reference. There are no specific time limits.

---

137　*R* v. *Adjudication Officer ex p.Bland, The Times,* February 6, 1985.
138　*R* v. *Secretary of State for Social Services ex p. Cotton, The Times* December 14, 1985, a decision about the validity of the old Supplementary Benefit board and lodging regulations.
139　*R(SB) 10/88* and *CSB/886/1988*. The Court of Appeal disagreed in *Chief Adjudication Officer and Secretary of State for Social Security* v. *Foster* in February 1991 and clarification from the House of Lords is awaited.
140　Article 177 of the Treaty of Rome.

# PART II - LOCAL AUTHORITY FUNDING

## Introduction

Changes are taking place in the extent to which local authorities fund the care needs of disabled people and in the manner in which they are required to contribute. Part III Accommodation funding in England (Part IV in Scotland), and Income Support residential care allowance, will in April 1993 be replaced by community care provision. We consider here the powers and procedures that have developed over the years and the implications of these changes.

## BENEFITS

### Community Charge Benefit

This relief from the Community Charge (poll tax) is administered by local authorities. It is not considered here because many people with a mental handicap will be exempt,[141] and it will cease to be relevant when the charge is itself abolished in April 1993.

### Housing Benefit

Social Security Act 1986
Housing Benefit (General) Regulations 1987

This benefit helps people on low incomes to pay rent in respect of a dwelling which they occupy as their home, which includes any residential accommodation in Great Britain whether furnished or unfurnished and hostels or lodgings in the public or private sector. It replaced Income Support board and lodging allowance from April 1989. Entitlement is not dependent on NI contributions and may be claimed by people in full-time work or self-employed. The amount depends upon rent paid, income, number of people in the family and the age or disability of claimant, partner or child. Up to 100 per cent. of the eligible rent can be allowed, and claimants on Income Support receive maximum benefit but others only a proportion according to their income.

### Assessment

Income is compared with the statutory sum needed to live on, calculated as for Income Support, *i.e.* personal allowance plus premiums,[142] and people with disabilities get more because of the premiums. The maximum benefit is reduced by any excess income and a deduction is made for most non-dependants living with the claimant.[143] Both earned and unearned income are taken into account, and earnings include both wages and profits from self-employment but only the net amount is counted so tax and NI contributions (and one-half of pension contributions) are deducted

---

141 See Chap.2, Part II at p.53.
142 The lone parent premium is higher for Housing Benefit.
143 Unless the claimant or partner is in receipt of Disability Living Allowance.

and at least the first £5 per week of earnings is disregarded.[144] Most social security benefits will be taken into account as unearned income, but not Disability Living Allowance. A claimant may have up to £16,000 in capital and the first £3,000 is disregarded, but capital above that figure is deemed to generate £1 per week for every £250 or part thereof. Capital is defined as for Income Support, including notional capital.[145]

### Eligible rent

The rent sometimes includes an element (*e.g.* a service charge) which may or may not be eligible for Housing Benefit. *Eligible* charges include wardens and caretakers, removal of refuse, lifts, portering, gardening and general management charges. *Ineligible* charges include water and sewerage charges, meals, fuel,[146] laundry, leisure items, cleaning of personal rooms,[147] transport, medical expenses, nursing or personal care, counselling or support services, and any other services not connected with the provision of accommodation. Ineligible services must be identified and the cost deducted from the charges made so as to identify the true rent. Where fuel or meals are included a specific amount is deducted regardless of the actual charge, but in the case of fuel charges which are readily identifiable the actual charge will be deducted. No deduction is made for support services provided by volunteers or by staff who spend more than half of their time providing eligible services.[148]

### Rent stops

Eligible rent cannot exceed any fair or reasonable rent registered by a rent officer (or rent assessment committee or rent tribunal), and apart from this the local authority may reduce the eligible rent in certain circumstances by such amount as it considers appropriate having regard in particular to the cost of suitable alternative accommodation elsewhere. No deduction may be made if the claimant or a member of the family is over 60, under 19 or incapable of work, unless suitable cheaper alternative accommodation is available and it is reasonable to expect the claimant to move.[149]

### Hostels

Before October 1989 the extra cost of hostel accommodation could be claimed through Income Support, but since that date only normal allowances and premiums can be claimed and the rent element must be claimed as Housing Benefit (unless the hostel is

---

[144] Other disregards are broadly similar to Income Support.

[145] A dependant child's capital is not taken into account, but results in the child not being treated as a dependant if it exceeds £3,000.

[146] *I.e.* heating, lighting, cooking and hot water, but not that used for communal areas or rooms in common use.

[147] Except where residents cannot do this themselves.

[148] This has been extended to workers whose salaries are paid by grant aid.

[149] 1987 Regulations, reg.11(2) and (3).

registered as a residential care home). This resulted in many cases in an overall reduction in benefits which was temporarily relieved by transitional provisions. Local authorities may restrict the rent that is allowed for hostels, but in the case of many residents they must before doing so show that it is reasonable to expect the resident to move.[150] The calculation of eligible rent is important in the case of hostels.

### Liability for rent
The claimant must be the person who is legally liable to pay the rent, but a person is treated as liable who[151]:
- is the partner of the person liable;
- has to make the payment to continue to live in the home because the liable person has failed to do so; and
- has actually met the liability before claiming.

In order to prevent abuse it is provided that claimants are to be treated as not liable and cannot claim where[152]:
- living with the person to whom the rent is paid, where that person is a close relative or the agreement is not on a commercial basis;
- liability has been created to take advantage of the benefit (but not if in the previous eight weeks the claimant was genuinely liable); or
- in the eight weeks before the creation of a joint tenancy the claimant was a non-dependant of one of the other joint-tenants (unless the tenancy was not created to take advantage of the benefit).

### Claims
Those in receipt of Income Support will include a claim for Housing Benefit on that claim form (this is a passported claim), but others should complete a claim form which is obtained from and returned to the local district council (or other housing authority). The claim may only be backdated if there is good cause for a late claim,[153] but may be made up to 13 weeks before entitlement is likely to arise. Couples make a single claim, but either partner may claim. People who are away from their home for a substantial period of time can still get Housing Benefit if they intend to return and do so within 52 weeks.

### Payment
Claimants who pay rent to a private landlord receive their Housing Benefit by cheque or by direct credit to a bank or building society account, but it must be paid direct to the landlord in certain circumstances where there are arrears. The authority also has a discretion to pay direct where the claimant requests or consents to

---

[150] Reg.11. The common practice of applying rent officer's ceilings regardless of reg.11 should be appealed.

[151] Reg.6.

[152] Reg.7.

[153] See the rules that apply for Income Support above, at p.412.

this, or it is in the interest of the claimant and his family. Where the rent is payable direct to the council it will simply be reduced by the amount of the benefit.

*Appeal*
Claimants may ask for a written statement as to how their claim has been worked out and this should be supplied within six weeks. There is no proper right of appeal but merely an administrative review followed by a *Housing Benefit Review Board* composed of three local councillors who have no training in this complex area of law. Accordingly decisions that are wrong in law may be made, but there is no further right of appeal. An application for judicial review may be made if the Board has failed to record its findings of fact and reasons for the decision, has interpreted the regulations incorrectly, or there is a breach of the rules of natural justice.

*Implications to mental handicap*
Housing Benefit is likely to be of increasing importance to persons with a mental handicap under community care policies, because they are encouraged to live more independently. There are difficulties in establishing a legal tenancy for such persons, and there is no appointee procedure similar to that for state benefits. Local authorities differ in their approach, and the absence of a formal appeal procedure means that there is little case law on the regulations. Practice and policy tend to become more significant than interpretation of the regulations.

## RESIDENTIAL ACCOMMODATION

An English local authority has a general duty under the National Assistance Act 1948, Part III to make arrangements for providing residential accommodation "for persons who by reason of age, [illness, disability] and any other circumstances, are in need of care and attention which is not otherwise available to them".[154] Hence this type of provision is known as Part III accommodation. In Scotland, this is known as Part IV accommodation because the duty arises under Part IV of the Social Work (Scotland) Act 1968.[155] Under this heading we consider the basis of funding that has applied in recent years and will continue to apply until the full implementation of community care policies. The whole basis of funding then changes, but transitional provisions may make the old rules relevant for some time.

### Charges and contributions

People who are provided with accommodation must pay for it.[156] Although charges are discretionary, each authority must fix a

---

[154]  s.21(1)(*a*). The 1990 Act substituted "illness, disability" for "infirmity", see generally Chap.5, Part II.

[155]  s.59(1), see also s.13A.

[156]  National Assistance Act 1948, s.22 which by s.65(f) applies both to Part III accommodation in England and Part IV accommodation in Scotland.

standard weekly charge for its homes which should represent the true economic cost of providing the accommodation. Residents are generally required to contribute in accordance with their resources up to this charge, but no-one will be required to pay more regardless of personal resources. An authority's rules for the conduct of its homes may provide for the waiving of part of the charges for a resident who assists in the running of the home.[157] This would not constitute employment under a contract of service or affect means-tested benefits.

*Financial contributions*
If a resident cannot afford the standard charge an assessment is made of ability to pay taking into account capital and income,[158] and the local authority meets the rest of the cost. Assessments tend to be reviewed annually, but a resident may ask for re-assessment if this would be beneficial. There is a minimum charge payable by all residents, and the assessment determines what should be paid above this leaving a personal allowance. Most residents hand over their allowance books to the manager and are (or should be) handed their personal allowance each week.[159] Unless the resident's own income exceeds the cost of the residential care, it will be of no personal benefit because it must be paid over as a contribution towards the fees. The minimum charge and personal allowance are usually covered by state benefits, but the amount will be made up by Income Support for those who do not otherwise have a sufficient income.[160] The official explanation is that the personal allowance is intended to be used by the resident for incidental expenditure of personal choice, such as stationery, personal toiletries, treats and small presents for relatives or close friends. In practice it may be spent on sweets, drinks, cigarettes, music or video cassettes and other such items which may well be regarded as treats. Residents should not be expected to use the allowance for normal replacement of clothing and shoes as these items are provided by the home, but they may choose to do so. Practice varies between direct provision of such items and cash allowances for their purchase, but any arrangement should be

---

[157] s.23(3), which does not apply to Scotland. More use of this provision could perhaps be made in the case of residents with a moderate mental handicap, though few of them will be subject to a personal means assessment. In Scotland, the Secretary of State has a general power to provide by regulations for the waiving of payments in whole or part "in such circumstances as may be specified" - 1968 Act, s.87(5).

[158] The local authority works out how much the resident can afford to pay according to the rules laid down in Supplementary Benefits Act 1976, Sched.1, Part III which have been kept in force solely for this purpose pending the introduction of new arrangements.

[159] In practice this money may be spent collectively upon residents with a mental handicap, though they should each have their own spending power.

[160] The minimum charge is fixed by the Regulations. In 1991 it was £41.60 per week and the personal allowance £10.40. These add up to the basic state retirement pension and are changed yearly with pension increases.

designed to respect the personal wishes of individual residents.

The personal allowance may be increased where it would assist a handicapped resident working outside the home to enjoy a fuller life, but only to the extent that the resident is already paying more than the minimum charge. Effectively the authority would be exercising its discretion over the assessment. In some cases it will be desirable not to hand to a resident the full weekly sum, perhaps because of an inability to cope with this. Such decision should only be taken after appropriate consultation, and not in an arbitrary manner or as a punishment. The money withheld should be deposited in an interest earning account in the resident's name and expended on his personal needs with any unspent balance forming part of the his estate.

### Income assessment

There is a list of sources of income disregarded in whole or in part and of relevance to persons with a mental handicap are:
  - up to £4.00 per week of regular charitable or voluntary payments for unspecified purposes;
  - charitable or voluntary sums for a specific purpose not provided by the home (*e.g.* television rental and lump sum payments for holidays, room decoration or furnishings).

Actual income from investments and savings is not counted in view of the rules for capital assessment. Apart from these exceptions, all weekly benefits and other income are taken into account. Any entitlement to a tax refund should be aggregated with the net taxed income.

### Capital assessment

A separate assessment of capital resources is also made. Capital of less than £1,250 is ignored but each complete £50 over £1,200 is deemed to produce an income of 25p per week which is included in the income assessment.[161] Shares and marketable securities are valued at current market selling price, but special tables are used to determine the value of National Savings Certificates. Where assets are held in joint names each party will be treated as entitled to an equal share unless there is evidence that the interests are not equal or there is a trust. The value of a home no longer occupied by the resident is normally included as a capital resource, but not during periods of respite care or trial periods where the resident may still return there.[162] The market value is taken less any loans

---

161  Supplementary Benefits Act 1976, Sched.1, Part III, paras.19 and 20. This is effectively a capital levy of 26 per cent. per annum, which may soon result in the capital being exhausted even after taking into account the income actually derived from it. In *Caring for People* the Government undertook to put these assessments on the same footing as those for Income Support - see Chap.5, Part II.

162  The question is whether the individual has become a permanent resident; if not he is still treated as being in residence in his own dwelling. Persons admitted to a care home on a permanent basis will normally be assumed to have given up residence in their former dwelling.

secured on the property and a 10 per cent. deduction for selling expenses. This causes complications where a family home has been placed in joint names with a mentally handicapped son or daughter at an earlier stage perhaps to avoid means testing of money inherited by the son or daughter.[163] The authority cannot force a sale, but can invite other occupiers to pay the charges or accept a Legal Charge or Standard Security to cover all accrued charges so that these may be recovered when the dwelling is ultimately sold, up to a maximum of the resident's beneficial interest therein.[164]

There are rules for assessing *notional capital*, being capital which the resident is deemed to possess. This could be capital which the resident has given away with the intention of securing additional benefits, or would possess if some step had been taken to claim it, or potentially has.[165] There is a provision whereby an authority may recover payment from any person to whom a resident has transferred assets not more than six months before moving into a home, or whilst residing there, if this was done knowingly and with the intention of avoiding charges for the accommodation.[166] A *Memorandum of Guidance* issued to local authorities[167] states that where the resident has an interest in a discretionary trust the local authority should ascertain from the Trust Deed the extent of the trustees' discretion. If there is a discretion to release capital, or capital and income, for the benefit of the resident, it is reasonable to treat the capital value of the trust fund as part of the resident's capital resources, and the income released is then ignored. If there is a discretion to release only income for the benefit of the resident, the total income available for release under the terms of the trust is taken into account as income subject to the disregard of £4 per week, and the capital value of the trust is ignored.

*Implications*
The assessment rules were created for Supplementary Benefit and though long since replaced in that context have been kept in force solely for the purpose of Part III (and in Scotland Part IV) accommodation.[168] The whole body of case law on these complex and out of date provisions must therefore be referred to in the event of any dispute with a local authority over the assessment of

---

163  Authorities have a discretion in such cases and negotiation will be required, see Circular LAC (85)2.

164  Questions arise as to whether interest should be added to the accruing charges, and whether the property should be re-valued from time to time.

165  Supplementary Benefits Act 1976, Sched.1, Part III, para.28. These are far more stringent than those for Income Support, see Part I of this chapter.

166  Health and Social Services and Social Security Act 1983. This provision was not in force as at May 1992.

167  *Residential Homes under Part III of the National Assistance Act: Charging and Assessment Procedures* issued by DHSS and Welsh Office (1978). This does not apply to Scotland where there seems to be no standard policy.

168  In its Report in July 1987 a joint central and local government working party on *Public Support for Residential Care* recommended that these assessments should be brought into line with those for Income Support.

contributions. Few authorities understand the law and there is no independent appeal procedure, so there is a reluctance to apply the rules rigidly and most cases are dealt with by negotiation.[169]

## Sponsorship

We deal here with financial support given by local authorities to residents of private or charitable residential care homes (*i.e.* homes not run by the local authority). The fees may be financed wholly or in part by Income Support residential care allowance, which is subject to maxima depending upon the category of care being provided.[170]

### Top-up

In England and Wales an authority may fulfil its statutory duty by placing people in its own homes or sponsoring them in residential care homes run by others (paying the fees or topping-up the Income Support limit).[171] In such case the weekly charge is agreed between the authority and the home and paid by the authority; the resident's ability to pay is assessed in the same way as for a local authority home, and the authority recovers the residential care allowance from the resident. These top-up powers do not extend to elderly residents unless they have first qualified by reason of mental disorder. Scottish authorities are able to give similar assistance.[172]

### Dual assessment

The difference between the two systems of financial assessment is most noticeable for a resident in receipt of Income Support with top-up from the local authority, because both then apply simultaneously and any capital resources will be under greater threat from the local authority. It is not clear how the two methods of means-testing inter-react. In these cases the authority cannot waive part of the charges for a resident who assists in the running of the home, but the manager of the home can come to an arrangement with individual residents for payment in cash or kind for such assistance though regular cash payments may be means-tested subject to the usual disregards.

### Homes of other authorities

A local authority may support a resident in the home of another authority outside its own area. The terms in such cases are agreed between the two authorities. The authority managing the home

---

169 The Memorandum of Guidance suggests that the local Supplementary Benefits Commission will advise, but that function has been taken over by the Income Support Section of the DSS, and there remain few members of staff with a working knowledge of the former regime.

170 Residents in local authority homes cannot claim this allowance so the entire cost falls upon the authority.

171 National Assistance Act 1948, s.26 as amended by Health Services and Public Health Act 1968, s.44. National Health Service Act 1977, Sched.8.

172 Social Work (Scotland) Act 1968, s.12 (and also s.87 which applies, with modifications, National Assistance Act 1948, s.26(2)-(4)).

should assess the resident's ability to pay in the usual way and collect the assessed contribution, accounting for this to the authority supporting the resident.[173]

## COMMUNITY CARE

We have seen in Chapter 5, Part II how, under the new policies of community care, local authorities will be responsible for securing and funding services needed by persons with a mental handicap. Authorities already have power to make whatever charges they think reasonable for non-residential services,[174] but do not have to do so and cannot charge more than is reasonably practicable for the client to pay. This allows the authority to charge for such things as home help, meals on wheels and day care, but the government accepts that it would not be appropriate to charge for social work support, occupational therapy, advice and assessments of need. The authority may only charge the person receiving the services and not other persons (*e.g.* carers) and whilst such persons may wish to pay for "extras" the definition of these should not be enlarged so as to secure a contribution.

## Children

Although financial help for young children and families is not generally the responsibility of social services departments there are certain statutory powers under which this can be given. Authorities have a general duty to safeguard and promote the welfare of children who are in need, including disabled children, and in exercising this duty they may give assistance in kind or, in exceptional circumstances, in cash.[175]

### Means testing

In England, most services for young children are provided under the Children Act 1989 rather than under other legislation which now relates only to adults. Where any services (except advice and counselling) are provided by a local authority under the Act it may recover from specified persons such charge as it considers reasonable.[176] Such persons are:

- the parents, in the case of a child under 16;
- the child, on reaching 16; and

---

173 National Assistance Act 1948, ss.22(8), 21(4) and 32. Under Social Work (Scotland) Act 1968, s.86 an authority providing accommodation can recover costs from the area where the person is "ordinarily resident".

174 Health & Social Services & Social Security Adjudications Act 1983, s.17 (England); Social Work (Scotland) Act 1968, s.87(1) and (1A).

175 Children Act 1989, Part III, s.17 and Sched.2, Part I (England); Social Work (Scotland) Act 1968, s.12.

176 s.29. Charging is not mandatory and the charge may not be more than the person can reasonably be expected to pay. Families on Income Support or Family Credit are not liable to pay any charge. In Scotland, contributions in respect of children in care may be recovered under Social Work (Scotland) Act 1968, ss.78 and 78A, and otherwise charges for services may be made under s.87.

- the member of the family for whom the service is provided.
DoH Guidance and Regulations give local authorities a discretion
to decide whether to impose reasonable charges for services,
assistance in kind or cash provided under the Act and suggest that
in some cases parents may accept the provision of services more
readily if they are given the opportunity to contribute to the cost.
Any charge may be recovered as a civil debt. There are also
provisions relating to contributions towards the maintenance of
children who are being looked after by local authorities and one
authority may recover expenses incurred from another on the
basis that the financial responsibility lies with the authority in
whose area the child is ordinarily resident rather than with the one
that actually provides the service.

### Implications to mental handicap

It may seem inappropriate to charge the parents of a mentally
handicapped infant child for services that are essential by reason
of that handicap, especially as hospitals do not charge for their
services in respect of a physically disabled child. Yet where poor
or disadvantaged children enter care, sometimes against the wishes
of the parents, it has long been the policy to make the parents
contribute towards the cost if they have the means to do so. Should
a distinction be made between inadequacies of the parents and of
their child? Some parents can cope with demands which would be
too much for others, but is a parent who cannot cope inadequate if
the average parent would not be able to cope in that situation?

## Education

Education in schools is provided without charge or means-testing
and this includes the special education needed by children with
learning difficulties. The Education Reform Act 1988 (which does
not apply to Scotland) allows for some charges to be made, in
particular for education provided out of school hours, but
provides that in general no charge shall be made for:
  (a) activities that occur during school hours;
  (b) activities partly outside school hours where more than half,
      including travel, are in school hours;
  (c) activities wholly or partly outside school hours which are
      part of the national curriculum or of the exam. syllabus.
In Scotland, education authorities may charge for school trips and
special courses, additional tuition out of school time (provided it is
not a substitute for ordinary lessons), articles made in school
lessons which pupils wish to keep, and social, cultural and
recreational activities.[177]
Education authorities may charge fees if they provide board and
lodging but not where this is because education suitable to the
pupil's ability, age and aptitude cannot be otherwise provided.
This situation is likely to arise in the case of children with very

---

[177] Education (Scotland) Act 1980, ss.3 and 11.

special needs or disabilities which can only be provided for in a residential environment, or children who can only be educated suitably (or at all) some distance from their home. In England, authorities may charge reasonable fees for non-advanced further education and some now do, but fees should not differ substantially from the corresponding fees charged for similar courses in neighbouring authorities.[178] In Scotland, Boards of further education colleges will be empowered to charge fees.[179]

### Travelling and school meals

Where authorities are required to make arrangements for the provision of transport for school pupils they must do so without charge. The availability of free school meals depends upon the parents claiming Income Support (or Family Credit), but where the child claims Income Support in his own right (*e.g.* a mentally handicapped student on attaining 16) it may be the child rather than the parents that should be assessed. Not all authorities recognise this, and the situation is worth exploring.

### Disabled students allowance

Education grants, either mandatory or discretionary, and student loans are available in respect of further or higher education. In England, local education authorities are generally responsible for this. In Scotland, the Scottish Education Department is responsible in relation to degree and equivalent courses, and local authorities for further education. Disabled students awarded a mandatory grant can claim a special allowance for additional non-travel costs incurred because of the disability and as a result of going on the course.[180] Some authorities are more generous than others, and some pay the allowance with a discretionary grant. Extra travel costs must be met above the travel element in the basic grant.

## Day care

There has been a tendency during recent years for local authorities to seek contributions towards the cost of day care and incidental expenses such as travelling, meals and admission to other facilities where a charge is normally made. A survey of London Boroughs in May 1991 revealed that two were charging for day services, whilst thirty did not, but three were considering the option. However, twenty-six paid users either attendance or earnings allowances (including those that charged for services) whilst only six made no such payment at all. It is an open question whether it is reasonably practicable for an individual who is dependent on Income Support to pay for day services, and those in receipt of Disability Living Allowance have been assessed as needing this supplement so it is suggested that it should not be reduced by a

---

178  Education (Schools and Further Education) Regulations 1981, reg.17(2).
179  Further and Higher Education (Scotland) Act 1992, s.12(2)(*b*).
180  This may include up to £3,000 for specialist equipment and up to £4,000 for non-medical helpers.

charge for day services which fulfil a different need. Any mobility component may be taken into account in regard to travelling expenses, and any charge for meals should be within the Income Support mid-day meal allowance.

# PART III - MISCELLANEOUS FUNDING

Financial assistance or support may be received in a variety of ways from other sources. Income Support is a passport to other benefits, so it is wise to establish entitlement even if the top-up that it provides is only small.

## NATIONAL HEALTH SERVICE

We consider here the financial implications of receiving services under the NHS. Some people qualify for free services, and no charge is made for most hospital services, whether or not as an in-patient, but social security benefits may be affected. Admission to hospital is no longer appropriate by reason of mental handicap alone, and a patient with a mental handicap is generally in the same position as any other patient. The funding of provision in private nursing homes and residential care homes is dealt with in Part V below.

### Hospital provision

*Effect on benefits*
If anyone in a family receiving Income Support or Housing Benefit goes into hospital the amount thereof will be progressively reduced to reflect the fact that part of the patient's needs is being provided for.[181] Other state benefits are reduced from the appropriate pay day after the claimant has been in hospital for a specified period, with linking provisions for successive periods in hospital. Usually there is no change for the first four weeks, but thereafter Invalid Care Allowance will stop and after six weeks Severe Disablement Allowance and certain other benefits are reduced. A carer will lose Invalid Care Allowance after being in hospital for 12 weeks (if not earlier). Family Credit is not affected until the end of the six month award, and then it is re-assessed. The mobility component of Disability Living Allowance is the only benefit that will survive a long period in hospital.

*Benefits after one year*
The amount of benefit paid to a patient after one year in hospital is reduced to a weekly sum fixed annually, although further benefits may be paid to any dependants. A patient can no longer be treated as occupying a home after this period so any Housing Benefit or Income Support housing costs will depend upon the existence of other occupiers. The right of dependants to claim benefits after the

---

181 The rules are complex and reference should be made to the current edition of *Disability Rights Handbook*.

12 months depends upon their own circumstances. People who have been in hospital for many years may receive *Resettlement Benefit* on discharge (unless to a local authority home) but this has been abolished for those who entered hospital after April 1987.

### Leaving hospital

Benefits should be re-instated during temporary absences from hospital (*e.g.* days spent at home for trial periods) and the leaving and returning days count as days away from hospital. Regular absences (*e.g.* each weekend) could result in a carer being entitled to the full Invalid Care Allowance because this is a weekly rather than a daily benefit. Most weekly benefits can be adjusted on a daily basis if the claimant is expected to return to hospital within 28 days. If this is not the case or the claimant is finally discharged, full benefits resume from the next pay day, but this could mean waiting so the date of discharge can be significant.

## Financial assistance

Some people qualify automatically for free services from the NHS because of their age or personal circumstances, and means testing does not then apply. Others may be passported to help because they receive certain state benefits, but it is also possible to qualify on low income grounds. Claim Form AG1 should be submitted to the Agency Benefits Unit and Certificate AG2 may be issued which lasts for six months.[182] Those who do not qualify on income grounds may be entitled to Certificate AG3 which provides partial help with NHS charges and travel expenses. There is no specific category of persons with a mental handicap, but in practice they will usually qualify by reason of their limited means.

### Prescription charges

Certain groups get free prescriptions, including persons under 16 (19 if still in full time education) or over normal retirement age, expectant mothers and those in receipt of Income Support or Family Credit and their families. There are also certain medical grounds on which a person may qualify,[183] but these do not include mental handicap as such.

### Dental treatment and spectacles

The rules for free dental treatment and spectacles are basically similar to those for prescriptions, and anyone entitled to free treatment or provision is entitled to a free check-up or sight test.

### Travel costs

Help with fares or other travel expenses to hospital for treatment is available and Income Support and Family Credit are passports for this. Only the cost of travelling by the cheapest form of

---

182  DHSS (Agency Benefits Unit), Newcastle upon Tyne, NE98 1YX. Assessments are dealt with by the *Health Benefits Unit* and are broadly similar to those for Income Support.

183  *e.g.* a continuing physical disability which prevents the individual from leaving home except with the help of another person.

transport available is covered, but a companion's travelling expenses may also be paid where this is medically necessary. Enquiry should be made of the hospital receptionist.

## SPECIAL FUNDS

### The Family Fund

This Fund[184] exists to help families caring for a child up to the age of 16 who is handicapped by a very severe disability.[185] Families with such a child who normally lives at home may be eligible even though the child has to spend periods in hospital or is at school during term-time.[186] Help may take the form of goods, services or a grant of money for some definite purpose related to the care of the child. This will usually be for items or services not covered by statutory schemes, and any grant will not affect means-tested benefits. The emphasis is upon items or services which relieve stress in the family. The Fund is not cash limited and operates on a discretionary basis, so the financial circumstances of the family are taken into account. Funding is from the government but the Joseph Rowntree Memorial Trust administers the scheme. When the government set up the Fund in 1973 the Secretary of State for Social Services acknowledged that in many cases parents need more help in shouldering the various burdens which caring for a disabled child entails. It was not intended that this money should be by way of compensation for being disabled, but rather that it should serve to complement the services already being provided by statutory and voluntary bodies to help the families concerned.

### Independent Living Fund

This Fund is a charitable trust set up by DSS in co-operation with the Disablement Income Group[187] to give more help to very severely disabled people choosing between residential care and an independent life in their own home. It is funded by the government but administered by a board of independent trustees, and helps such people who need to pay for help with domestic duties or personal care to live independently in the community.[188] It was a flexible solution to the problem caused by the withdrawal of such support on the change from supplementary benefit to Income Support in April 1988. The Fund is to be replaced by a successor body in 1993, but people already receiving payments

---

184 Address in Appendix I.

185 This may include severe mental retardation and some multiple handicaps. The age limit may be extended in certain circumstances.

186 They will not be eligible if the child lives permanently in a residential home or hospital, apart from limited and specific provision for visiting expenses.

187 In addition, the DIG (Scotland).

188 The budget of £24 million for 1990/91 was committed before the financial year even began so the Fund had to be suspended for a while. When it re-opened in October 1990 claims were restricted to persons aged between 16 and 74 receiving higher rate Attendance Allowance.

will continue to be paid by the new body. Thereafter, applications will be made to the local social services department who will be designing and providing packages of care under the new community care arrangements.

*Eligibility*
The Fund is open to any disabled person living in the UK who satisfies the following criteria, but there are no age limits:
- living alone or with another person who is unable to provide all the care that is needed;
- unable to pay for the care that is needed[189];
- receiving (or would satisfy the conditions for) DLA;
- needs to employ someone to carry out domestic duties or personal care tasks.

*Application*
Application is initially by letter[190] indicating whether the claim is made on behalf of a person over 16 or the parent of a disabled child under that age. The appropriate form is then sent with an explanatory leaflet.[191] The procedure is quite simple, so those who are not sure if they will be entitled are encouraged to apply and a home visit will be arranged if they appear to need help on the basis of the application form.[192]

*Financial support*
Applicants may get financial help from the Fund to continue living in their own homes or to move out of hospital or residential care. Regular payments are usual, but a lump sum award may be made where this would reduce the need for paid care.[193] For example, applicants may get help to pay for someone to look after them or help with things like housework, or to buy some item so that they can manage with less help. Awards are reviewed by post, usually on a 12 monthly basis.

*Means testing*
In order to determine the amount of help that the Fund should give, the total cost of the care required is calculated and from this is deducted any income which the applicant has to help pay for it. Most sources of income other than Income Support are taken into account, but the rules are not inflexible. The Fund is primarily intended to help people in receipt of Income Support but applications from other needy claimants may also be considered. Any financial help given is neither taxable nor taken into account when calculating means tested benefits.

---

189  This generally, but not necessarily, means eligible for Income Support.
190  Address in Appendix I.
191  Form ILF 100 for an adult and Form ILF 200 for a child.
192  The Fund has over 100 Visiting Social Workers throughout Great Britain.
193  Payment is made four-weekly in arrear by bank transfer. There is no limit on the amount, but payments of more than £200 per week are exceptional.

## OTHER SOURCES

### Family

Support is likely to be given to the individual by parents and other members of the family even after he has reached the age when an independent way of life is normally established. Carers should not neglect to claim all financial benefits that are available as of right either for themselves or the individual cared for. In so far as financial support is given, this will normally be on an informal basis without any legal commitment, and care should be taken to ensure that such support does not result in the reduction or loss of means-tested funding.[194]

A parent is not under a legal obligation to maintain an adult son or daughter however severely that child may be disabled (but for those aged 18-25 in Scotland see page 152). In England, there may be an obligation to make reasonable financial provision following death. In Scotland, legal rights entitlements are not affected by disability.[195]

#### Court Orders

An obligation to make periodic payments for the maintenance of a child may arise under a court order in several situations, the most obvious being following a divorce or separation.[196] The Child Support Act 1991 creates a *Child Support Agency* responsible for collecting maintenance from an absent parent, and a standard formula is introduced to be used in calculating the amount of maintenance which a child should receive. During the passage of the Act attempts were made to build into this formula some provision for the extra costs involved in bringing up a child with a mental handicap. Of course, factors such as unemployment, low pay and single parenthood can be taken into account by the court when dealing with a maintenance application in the context of a divorce, but it is necessary to draw them to the attention of the court when the level of maintenance is being determined.

### Charities

Many charities,[197] national and local, exist for the purpose of giving support to disabled people and steps should be taken to make and maintain contact with those which are relevant to the individual.

---

[194] It may be better to buy useful items and give these rather than to make gifts of money. Presents such as those given at Christmas and birthdays are unlikely to affect state funding and may be of great value to the individual.

[195] These topics are considered in Chap.9, Parts IVA and IVB respectively.

[196] This topic is considered in Chap.3, Part III.

[197] See Appendix I.

# PART IV - WEEKLY FUNDING

## Introduction

Having outlined the various state and other benefits that may be available to or for the benefit of a mentally handicapped person or the parents (or carers), we now consider when these benefits may be claimed in practice and some problems that arise. We assume here disability of a degree that makes it unlikely that the individual will ever become financially self-supporting and that the parents and child reside in Great Britain. It may be thought that any state benefit specifically intended to assist disabled persons would anticipate and deal with the situations in which they find themselves, but this is often not the case and claimants find that ordinary arrangements create problems in the interpretation of the Regulations. Considerable delay in obtaining payment may result without any compensation, and there is seldom funding available to pursue appeals. It is always wise to ascertain what benefits are actually being paid to or for the benefit of the handicapped person or carers and then to check that the amounts are correct and that no further benefits could be claimed.

### Implications of state benefits

A survey of households in which there was a dependant with a mental handicap showed that the main source of income was earnings and state benefits.[198] One in three of the working fathers found that his earnings were reduced because of the caring role, and mothers had difficulty finding a substitute carer or a job with convenient hours thereby reducing their earning potential even if they could cope with a job. The sample households received on average three different social security benefits out of a range of 14, and had experienced difficulty in finding out and obtaining those benefits to which they were entitled.

## FUNDING A CHILD

Parents normally expect to be responsible for maintaining their mentally handicapped child up to a certain age. It could be some time before they realise that they may be eligible for certain special benefits.

### State benefits

The benefits that may be payable are as follows:

### Child Benefit

This weekly benefit (and also *one-parent benefit* if appropriate) is paid from the birth of the child until he becomes an adult. This is normally on leaving school, but in the case of a mentally

---

198 *Mental Handicap Costs More* by Judith Buckle published in 1984 by Disablement Income Group Charitable Trust of Attlee House, 28 Commercial Road, London E1 6LR.

handicapped child it may be beneficial to cease claiming child
benefit at 16 even though the child remains at school (see below).

### Disability Living Allowance (DLA)

This is the first additional benefit and the *care component*, at
whichever level is appropriate, may be claimed when the child
attains six months. It replaces Attendance Allowance with which
most parents would be familiar. Special rules relate to entitlement
for a child whilst in residential care (including respite care) and
these are considered later. When the child is five years old a claim
for the *mobility component* should be made, especially if there is
severe physical as well as mental handicap. This replaces the
previous claim for Mobility Allowance.

### Invalid Care Allowance (ICA)

This is the next state benefit for the parents to consider if either of
them is not working or wishes to give up work in order to look
after their child. It may be claimed by the father or mother if
spending at least 35 hours a week caring for a child who is in
receipt of the relevant level of DLA. It is taxable but in practice
there may be no liability because it can be set against the wife's
earnings allowance.

### Income Support

A *disabled child premium* can be claimed by parents, or a single
parent, in receipt of Income Support. This is a weekly supplement
for a disabled child in addition to the basic allowance for the child.
A *carer premium* is available on top of any other premium for
Income Support or Housing Benefit claimants who get ICA (or
would do but for the overlapping benefit provisions). Some
couples, where each partner is caring for a different disabled
person, can qualify for a double premium.

The availability of these premiums could result in an individual
qualifying for Income Support who would not otherwise be
eligible.

## Conclusion

Parents who take the trouble to claim these various benefits have a
substantial supplement to their income whilst looking after their
mentally handicapped child, and unless they are themselves in
receipt of Income Support no amount of financial support given
by them or others for the infant child will affect these benefits.
Because the care components of DLA operate as a passport to
other benefits, it is important for parents or carers to ensure that
application is made for this at the earliest possible date and to take
great care in the application.

## Example

The following example shows the benefits entitlement of a family
with a mentally handicapped child in 1991:

*Mr and Mrs Brown are council tenants with three children aged 16, 13 and 9 all still at school. The youngest child is mentally handicapped and Mrs Brown receives Attendance Allowance for him and also claims Invalid Care Allowance. Mr. Brown has been made redundant and receives Unemployment Benefit. They have no savings or assets.*

|  | £ p | £ p | £ p | £ p |
|---|---|---|---|---|
| **Unemployment Benefit** |  |  |  | 66.95 |
| **Child Benefit** |  |  |  | 22.75 |
| **Attendance Allowance** (lower rate) |  |  |  | 27.80 |
| **Invalid Care Allowance** |  |  |  | 31.25 |
| **Income Support** |  |  |  |  |
| Applicable amount |  |  |  |  |
| Personal allowances |  |  |  |  |
|    couple | 62.25 |  |  |  |
|    child under 11 | 13.35 |  |  |  |
|    child 11-15 | 19.75 |  |  |  |
|    child 16-17 | 23.65 |  |  |  |
|  | ------- | 119.00 |  |  |
| Premiums |  |  |  |  |
|    family | 7.95 |  |  |  |
|    disabled child | 16.65 |  |  |  |
|    carers | 10.80 |  |  |  |
|  | ------- | 35.40 |  |  |
|  |  | ------- | 154.40 |  |
| less: Income |  |  |  |  |
| Unemployment Benefit | 66.95 |  |  |  |
| Child Benefit | 22.75 |  |  |  |
| Invalid Care Allowance | 31.25 |  |  |  |
|  | ------- | 120.95 |  |  |
|  |  | ------- | 33.45 |  |
|  |  |  | -------- |  |
| **Total Income** |  |  |  | 182.20 |

**Plus** Housing Benefit for rent and 80% of Personal Community Charge for both Mr and Mrs Brown.

## FUNDING AN ADULT

On becoming treated as an adult, a child though in theory independent of parents is unlikely to be self-supporting so depends on non-means-tested state benefits topped up with a means-tested benefit and/or any financial support that parents or others may give. It is desirable to ensure that any such support is provided in a way that does not result in withdrawal of or equivalent reduction in means-tested benefits.

### Changes in state benefits

Parents no longer claim Child Benefit at this stage, but ICA is still available if they continue to provide care. DLA (if awarded) continues but is henceforth claimed by the child if capable, or by the parent as appointee. The following new benefits arise:

*Severe Disablement Allowance* (SDA)
This is a significant weekly benefit for which the individual will usually qualify on being treated as an adult.

*Income Support*
The individual may now be entitled to this means-tested benefit in his own right, and the parent or some other appropriate person can claim as appointee. A disability premium is available in most cases, and also the higher personal allowance (even though under 18 if treated as an adult). Regular funding by parents or others may affect entitlement, which may not be significant whilst the claimant is looked after by parents, but could make such funding pointless if in receipt of a substantial top-up.

*Claiming benefit*
It is usually best to claim all non-means-tested benefits to which there is entitlement and then rely upon means-tested benefits as a top-up. If the means-tested benefit is later withdrawn because of a change of circumstances it does not then become necessary to claim entitlement to non-means-tested benefit for the first time which could result in delay and cash flow problems.

*Medical certificates*
When new benefits were introduced in April 1988 some claimants encountered problems proving incapacity for work. It was then established that DSS will accept a GP's certificate as evidence of permanent incapacity, or in some cases yearly certificates (as distinct from the usual maximum of 13 weeks) where there is mental disability. No charge may be made for these certificates, which must be provided as part of the GP's terms of service.

**A typical weekly calculation**

In respect of a severely mentally and physically handicapped adult aged 25 or over cared for by a non-working mother whose husband is in employment, the total weekly income from state benefits coming into the household in 1991 could have been:

|  |  | £ p |
|---|---:|---:|
| Attendance Allowance - higher rate |  | 41.65 |
| Mobility Allowance |  | 29.10 |
| Severe Disablement Allowance |  | 31.25 |
| Income Support |  |  |
|   - personal allowance | 39.65 |  |
|   - disability premium | 16.65 |  |
|  | ------ |  |
|  | 56.30 |  |
| *less* severe disablement allowance | 31.25 |  |
|  | ------ | 25.05 |
|  |  | ------- |
| Income (disabled adult) |  | 127.05 |
| Invalid Care Allowance (mother) |  | 31.25 |
|  |  | -------- |
| Total Income | £ | 158.30 |

## BENEFIT PLANNING

Care must be taken to see which claims will maximise benefit. The regulations change constantly and the following examples merely illustrate the type of problems that arise.

### Child or adult?

The normal rules as to when a child becomes an adult for the purpose of state benefits do not apply to one who has a serious mental disability. The change does not happen automatically and it is for the parents or carers to ensure that claims are made at the relevant time if it is advantageous to do so.[199]

*The Regulations*

A mentally handicapped person may claim SDA from his 16th birthday even if staying at school. The Regulations say that you can claim if you are either:

    (a) incapable of work and attending classes for less than 21 hours per week; or

    (b) attending classes for more than 21 hours per week which would not be suitable for a non-disabled person of the same age and sex.

If the claim is made Child Benefit is no longer paid to the parents. Income Support can be claimed by (or in the name of) the child for the first time at this age as he will not have to sign on for work, being a disabled student who would be unlikely to get a job within a reasonable period compared to other students because of the disability. The higher rate personal allowance may apply.

*A typical comparison*

It will usually be found that this new package of benefits produces a greater weekly income, and receipt of Income Support is a passport to other benefits (*e.g.* an Education Maintenance Allowance from the local authority as well as free school meals). For a child aged 16 staying on at school and living at home, a comparison of weekly benefits in 1991 would have been as shown in the following calculation. Assuming that the child did not have assets or a personal income sufficient to affect means-tested Income Support, the family would be £39.55 better off overall by making the switch to the adult basis of benefit notwithstanding that their child remained at school. However, it is important, if all members of the household agree, to look at the overall income coming into the family because other members may lose Income Support if the disabled person ceases to be a dependant.

Sometimes a child will not be entitled to Income Support at age 16 because other sources of income are too high, but the claim should be repeated at yearly intervals (more often if other circumstances

---

199 Recipients of DLA in respect of a child receive a helpful letter from the Benefits Agency with a continuation claim form and leaflets and application forms relating to other relevant benefits some time before the 16th birthday.

change) because the personal allowance increases up to age 25 and also changes in benefit rates may result in entitlement.

| | Child/young person £ p | | Adult £ p |
|---|---|---|---|
| Attendance Allowance | | | |
| - lower rate | 27.80 | | 27.80 |
| Child Benefit | 8.25 | | nil |
| Severe Disablement | | | |
| Allowance | nil | | 31.25 |
| Income Support (top-up) | | | |
| - personal allowance (higher) | nil | 31.15 | |
| - disability premium | nil | 16.65 | |
| | | ------ | |
| | | 47.80 | |
| less income (SDA) | | 31.25 | |
| | nil | ------ | 16.55 |
| Invalid Care Allowance (mother) | 31.25 | | 31.25 |
| | ------- | | ------- |
| | £ 67.30 | | £ 106.85 |
| | ------- | | ------- |

*Best of both worlds?*
A young person (aged 16-19) doing 12 hours or less a week in ordinary education does not count as in full time education and therefore is not a dependant for Income Support purposes. A young person doing more than 12 hours, depending on the hours and the nature of the education, may be able to choose whether or not to claim SDA plus Income Support in his own right, or whether to remain a dependant. Both SDA and Child Benefit cannot be claimed. To qualify for SDA the young person must not be studying for more than 21 hours a week, unless the additional hours are accounted for by classes that are not "suitable for persons of the same age and sex who do not have a disability". It is arguable that the young person can get SDA whilst the parents continue to get Income Support for him as a dependant child, although in practice DSS automatically treat a person who claims SDA as no longer a dependant for Income Support purposes.

## Disability premium

People who are fit for full-time work have to sign on regularly to prove that they are available for and actively seeking work, but those who are not fit because of mental or physical disability should get medical certificates instead so that they qualify for a disability premium after 28 weeks. If because of mental handicap they have not understood this and have been signing on, it is sometimes possible to get their incapacity backdated.

## Severe disability premium

According to pamphlets originally issued by DSS this premium for Income Support or Housing Benefit was intended to help disabled people who live alone, but this interpretation has proved to be inconsistent with the regulations.[200]

### Entitlement

The conditions of entitlement for a single claimant were:

    (a) receipt of Attendance Allowance[201];

    (b) no-one receiving ICA for the claimant; and

    (c) no *non-dependant* age 18 or over residing with claimant.

A non-dependant was, until October 1989, defined as any person "who normally resides with a claimant" but this was subject to five exceptions one of which was "a person who jointly occupies the claimant's dwelling".[202] Thus an adult who resides with the claimant in a dwelling but does not jointly occupy the dwelling is a non-dependant, whereas if that adult jointly occupies the dwelling with the claimant he or she will not be a non-dependant. What does jointly occupies mean?

### Joint occupiers

In May 1989 an SSAT held that the parents of an adult mentally handicapped claimant who resided with him were persons who jointly occupied his dwelling so he qualified for the premium. This showed up the contradiction in the regulations, because many other handicapped individuals still living with their parents could be treated as joint occupiers. Other appeals followed, and eventually two reached the Commissioners[203] who formulated tests of joint occupation on the basis of "live together on an unrestricted and equal basis" and "jointly occupy the premises in the sense of equality of access and use". There followed claims by thousands of disabled people still living with their families.

### Change of Regulation

By the time this received publicity the government had changed the rules. From October 9, 1989 the words in square brackets below were added to the joint occupier exception[204]:

> "a person who jointly occupies the claimant's dwelling [and either is a co-owner of that dwelling with the claimant or his partner (whether or not there are other co-owners) or is liable with the claimant or his partner to make payments in respect of his occupation of that dwelling]".

These words were considered by Commissioner Sanders who was not sure that they were actually capable of producing any result, but felt obliged to give them some meaning and stated that their

---

200  Income Support (General) Regulations 1987, Sched.2, para.13.

201  Now the higher two levels of the care component of DLA.

202  Reg.3(2)(c).

203  *CIS 144/89* (the Simon Crompton case) and *CIS 180/89*.

204  Income Support (General) Amendment No.3 Regulations 1989, reg.3.

effect is[205]:

> "that the claimant does not satisfy the condition unless he or she and the other person are jointly liable to make payments as co-owners or co-tenants or perhaps co-licensees".

Some parents put their handicapped child's name on the rent book, or made the child jointly liable for services, in order to maintain or create entitlement to the premium. Doubt has also been expressed as to whether the amendment takes away accrued rights for those already receiving the premium.[206]

### Reviews

Arguments then followed as to whether on a review the restriction to 12 months arrears applied in these cases or not,[207] depending perhaps upon whether the ground for review was the test case decision (which it surely could not be if the review was requested before that decision!). Later appeals have dealt with reviews at different dates in relation to the Simon Crompton case.[208]

Further changes in the Social Security Act 1990,[209] which came into force on July 13, 1990, purported to prevent the payment of benefit arrears prior to a test case decision of the Commissioners when those arrears were the result of a new interpretation of the law in that decision. This provision is very difficult to interpret, and is in itself resulting in many appeals, but its relevance to severe disability premium is as follows.

### Backdating

Problems of backdating arose as a result of the interpretation of joint occupier in the Simon Crompton case. Those who, in reliance upon the new interpretation, prior to July 13, 1990, requested a review of the earlier decision not to pay the premium received considerable arrears up to October 9, 1989, whereupon entitlement usually ceased because of the amended regulation. Many social services departments and adult training centres, and some voluntary organisations, notified parents of the possible claim and deadline for requesting a review. Those who for some reason did not claim by that date were caught by the 1990 Act and could receive nothing on a review because the Simon Crompton case was after October 9, 1989, when the amended regulation took

---

205  *CIS/299/90.*

206  Interpretation Act 1978, s.16; presumption against retrospective legislation.

207  Arrears are only allowed for up to 12 months prior to an application for review under Social Security (Adjudication) Regulations 1986, reg.69. The exceptions under reg.72 may not apply because of reg.72(2), but this interpretation is being challenged.

208  *e.g. CIS/11/1991* (which is to be a reported decision) where review was requested before the test case but not determined until thereafter. *CIS/111/1990* where the review decision and the Tribunal appeal were both concluded before the test case. In both appeals it was held that the 12 month restriction did not apply and it seems to be the date of the request for review that is relevant.

209  Social Security Act 1975, s.104(7) and (8) and s.165D as added by the 1990 Act, Sched.6, para.7.

effect (presumably to prevent the premium being paid in such cases). Their only remedy was a late appeal.

## Outstanding appeals

Further problems arose over the many appeals against refusal to review which had been held back or adjourned pending the decision in the Simon Crompton case and by then (June 1990) such appeals were caught by the new provisions of the 1990 Act. Rights given by the Commissioners' decision were effectively being taken away by the retrospective effect of that legislation so appropriate *ex gratia* payments were made in those cases.

## Late appeals

A late appeal (*i.e.* after the three month time limit) against an earlier decision does not appear to be caught by the 1990 Act which only applies to reviews, but leave of a Tribunal chairman is required for special reasons.[210] The system was inundated with requests for late appeals such as the following:

> David, who has a mental handicap and receives Attendance Allowance and Income Support, lived with his divorced mother in her home. She was not entitled to Invalid Care Allowance because she claimed the higher Invalidity Pension. He was handed at his Adult Training Centre an envelope containing a claim form for severe disability premium and a letter explaining that this should be submitted before July 13, 1990 but he hid this (as was his tendency) and his mother did not find it till after that date. Her claim was disallowed in consequence. Leave to appeal out of time was sought against the original decision awarding Income Support in April 1988 which should, on the basis of a correct interpretation of the law, have included severe disability premium. It was contended that there were special reasons in the fact that the mother (who was the appointee) was coping alone with her mentally handicapped son and could not be expected to cope with the complexity of the rules regarding entitlement to the premium on the introduction of Income Support, especially as leaflet IS1 incorrectly stated that only people living alone could qualify. A domestic crisis can amount to special reasons, and for this mother coping in those circumstances represented a permanent domestic crisis. A late appeal was admitted.

Many mentally handicapped claimants put forward similar, or additional, reasons for a late appeal thereby circumventing the restrictions upon reviews (if indeed those restrictions are valid) and the financial incentives for them to do so were considerable. Initially the requests were dealt with by part-time chairmen, with the result that a consistent approach was not adopted and it became something of a lottery whether they were admitted, but in at least one Region the full-time chairman then took all decisions himself and those relating to mentally handicapped claimants were almost all granted.

The effect of a late appeal against a decision on a claim is that the earlier decision is looked at again, in the light of subsequent interpretations of the law, and the restrictions upon backdating following a review do not apply. Sometimes a review had already resulted in the premium being paid, but this could only go back 12

---

210 Social Security (Adjudication) Regulations 1986, reg.3(3). There is no right of appeal against a refusal.

months and the late appeal would then grant the premium for the earlier period back to April 1988.

*Validity of the Regulations*

Further confusion arose when in late 1990 a Commissioner held that the Social Security Secretary had no power "to withhold the premium from a severely disabled person by requiring that person to satisfy extraneous conditions" and that the conditions regarding ICA and non-dependants in the regulations were *ultra vires*.[211] The decision effectively opened up the severe disability premium to anyone receiving Attendance Allowance, but DSS put an embargo on claims pending a reference to the Court of Appeal which reversed the decision.[212] Among the matters decided was that the Commissioners did not have power to decide that the regulations were *ultra vires* the enabling statute. At the time of writing a decision from the House of Lords is awaited, but if this does not produce the desired result further amending legislation, possibly of a retrospective nature, seems inevitable. In the meantime, most tribunals dealing with late appeals adjourned consideration of the period after the benefit week of October 9, 1989 pending clarification of the law by the House of Lords.

*Further arguments*

From April 1989 another exception to the definition of non-dependant was introduced[213]:

> "any person who is liable to make payments to the claimant or the claimant's partner or to whom or to whose partner the claimant or the claimant's partner is liable to make payments, in respect of his occupation of the dwelling".

A mentally handicapped adult living with his parents could be within this provision and therefore entitled to severe disability premium. The regulation was amended again from October 1, 1990, perhaps to avoid such conclusion, so as to read[214]:

> "any person to whom or to whose partner the claimant or the claimant's partner is liable to make payments *on a commercial basis* in respect of *the* occupation of the dwelling"

but nevertheless at least one Tribunal was prepared to accept that an adult could enter into an arrangement on a commercial basis with a close member of his family. Perhaps this was realised, because with effect from November 11, 1991 yet further amendments were introduced which appear to address the question of close relatives of the claimant. This may finally deprive mentally handicapped adults living with parents of the severe disability premium from that date.

---

211 *CIS/372/1990*, December 5, 1990.
212 *Chief Adjudication Officer and Secretary of State for Social Security* v. *Foster,* CA, February 21, 1991.
213 Reg.3(2)(*d*) added by Income Support (General) Amendment Regulations 1989, reg.2.
214 Reg.3(2)(*da*) amended by Income Support (General) Amendment No.3 Regulations 1990, reg.3.

*Difference in Scotland?*
It has been suggested that the regulations would give a different result in Scotland, because there a person not contractually liable could nevertheless be liable quasi-contractually under the principles of recompense or negotiorum gestio. This argument has been disputed as probably stretching those principles too far.[215]

## Invalid Care Allowance[216]

Before October 1990 ICA may not have been claimed by those on Income Support because (unlike under Supplementary Benefit) they would not be any better off, the allowance being taken into account as a resource. Also, those whose partners were receiving a dependant's increase for invalidity benefit or retirement pension would lose this increase if the allowance was claimed, and it could not be claimed as well as certain other benefits (widow's benefit).

*Carer premium*
Since October 1990 a carer premium has been introduced for persons receiving Income Support or Housing Benefit who are entitled or treated as entitled to ICA. Carers who were claiming the allowance should automatically have received the premium, but so should those who had not bothered to claim. People already over pensionable age are not eligible for ICA so may not receive the premium, but women between 60 and 65 years should claim because the discriminatory effect upon such women is being challenged. People who have been just over the limit for Income Support or Housing Benefit may become entitled by reason of the premium. Providing the carer satisfied all the conditions of entitlement, a claim for ICA may be backdated for up to 52 weeks without having to show good cause for a late claim, and a claim for Income Support may be treated in the alternative as a claim for ICA thereby extending the backdating limit. However the full implications of backdating should first be worked out.

*Severe disability premium*
It is possible that the person cared for is receiving Income Support with severe disability premium, and the amount of this premium is the same as ICA. Both amounts cannot be claimed at the same time by or in respect of the same person. A carer who satisfies the conditions for ICA but receives another benefit that overlaps with it (*e.g.* Invalidity Pension) can safely claim ICA and be refused, thereby getting the carer's premium notwithstanding that the person cared for gets severe disability premium.

*Maximum benefit*
To ensure that maximum benefit is paid the following factors should be taken into account before a claim is made for ICA:
   - the person cared for will lose severe disability premium if

---

[215] See *Scolag* 1991, pp.168 and 181.
[216] See Article by Janet Barlow and Penny Lamb, *Legal Action* Dec. 9, 1990).

the carer claims ICA;
- the only gain to a claimant receiving Income Support or Housing Benefit is the amount of the carer premium;
- if neither ICA nor severe disability premium are being paid, but either could be claimed, a calculation is necessary to see which would maximise benefit.

The following example illustrate these points based on 1991 rates.

---

*Carers are a married couple claiming Income Support and supervising their mentally handicapped son.aged 30 who lives alone:-*

| Son | | £ p |
|---|---:|---:|
| Attendance Allowance - lower rate | | 27.80 |
| Severe Disablement Allowance | | 31.25 |
| Income Support - personal allowance | 39.65 | |
|     - disability premium | 16.65 | |
|     - severe disability premium | 31.25 | |
| | ------- | |
| | 87.55 | |
| *less* Severe Disablement Allowance | 31.25 | |
| | ------- | 56.30 |
| | | --------- |
| Son's income | | 115.35 |
| Carers | | |
| Income Support - couple | | 62.25 |
| | | --------- |
| Total Income | | £  177.60 |
| | | --------- |

---

*Mother increases the hours that she looks after her son so qualifies for Invalid Care Allowance with consequent entitlement to carer premium but if she claims her son will lose his severe disability premium:-*

| Son | | £ p |
|---|---:|---:|
| Attendance Allowance - lower rate | | 27.80 |
| Severe Disablement Allowance | | 31.25 |
| Income Support - personal allowance | 39.65 | |
|     - disability premium | 16.65 | |
| | ------- | |
| | 56.30 | |
| *less* Severe Disablement Allowance | 31.25 | |
| | ------- | 25.05 |
| | | --------- |
| Son's income | | 84.10 |
| Carers | | |
| Invalid Care Allowance - mother | | 31.25 |
| Income Support - couple | 62.25 | |
|     - carer premium | 10.80 | |
| | ------ | |
| | 73.05 | |
| *less* Invalid Care Allowance | 31.25 | |
| | ------ | 41.80 |
| | | --------- |
| Total Income | | £  157.15 |
| | | --------- |

---

**Conclusion:** *The family will be £20.45 worse off if the claim is made.*

## Compensation for personal injury

Where the funds of a trust are derived from a payment made in consequence of any personal injury to the claimant, the value of the trust fund and of the right to receive any payment under that trust are disregarded for the purpose of Income Support.[217] Until October 1, 1990 such value was only disregarded for a period of two years or such longer period as was reasonable in the circumstances, and this provision created a perverse incentive to spend the money[218] and resulted in many appeals. It has been held that "personal injury" must be given its ordinary meaning and may include a disease and injuries suffered as a result of a disease (*e.g.* amputation of a leg due to septicaemia).[219]

## Arrears of benefit

In a number of cases appeal tribunals have awarded arrears of Supplementary Benefit additional requirements going back many years. The argument is that where DHSS (as it then was) had information as to serious mental handicap it should have informed the claimant when originally assessed of the whole range of allowances he was entitled to and it was this failure that led to underclaiming.[220] This was a broad view of the regulations,[221] which allowed for payment of unlimited arrears of benefit in the case of an official error or where new evidence was produced in certain circumstances. Until these appeals were brought it had been assumed that appointees who failed to claim their full entitlement through ignorance could not rely upon the inability of the person with a mental handicap to act in his own best interests or on any obligation on the part of the DHSS local office to explain the full possible entitlement.

The success of these cases led to a hasty change in the regulations, aimed at stemming the flood of benefit review applications which were being organised by advice agencies.[222] Unlimited backdating on a review is now only possible, as regards all social security benefits, in circumstances where:

- at the time of making the decision under review, the adjudication authority had before it specific evidence relevant to a claim, but failed to take it into account; or
- a member of staff of the department failed to submit a document or record containing evidence to the adjudicating authority which determined the question; or

---

217 Income Support (General) Regulations 1987, Sched.10, para.12.
218 Or invest it in a dwelling-house for personal occupation which would also be disregarded.
219 *R(SB) 2/89.*
220 This included eligibility to such items as discretionary grants for baths, diet, clothing, heating and bedding under the old rules.
221 Social Security (Adjudication) Regulations 1986, reg.72.
222 Reg.72 is replaced by a new reg.64A with effect from August 31, 1991; Social Security (Adjudication) Amendment (No.2) Regulations 1991.

- the evidence now relied upon did not exist and could not have been obtained at the time of the original decision, but was produced to the department as soon as reasonably practicable after it became available to the claimant;  or
- an adjudication officer has overlooked or misconstrued a provision in legislation or caselaw.

It was stated that this accords with the government's original policy intention of paying unlimited arrears of benefit in cases of official error without the need to resort to the onerous procedure of late appeal. A similar approach was adopted to the payment of unlimited arrears where fresh evidence was adduced which could not have been produced before, but which was produced as soon as reasonably practicable (DSS press release, August 21, 1991). It remains to be seen just how far this change has restricted the right of claimants to unlimited arrears. In cases involving mental handicap it may be possible to show that there was information in the department's files which amounted to specific evidence within the above criteria.

# PART V - RESIDENTIAL CARE FUNDING

**Note:** the whole basis of funding for residential care will change when the full community care policies are introduced in April 1993. Most of the material in this Part relates to the funding system that has evolved over the years and applies until then, but this Part concludes with an indication of what to expect under community care.

## Introduction

Many mentally disabled people who are no longer cared for in a family environment now live in residential care homes. These may comprise ordinary houses or large buildings housing many people, but in both cases care and accommodation is provided on a fee paying basis. The proprietor may be a local authority charging according to ability to pay, or an individual, company or charity charging fees on a commercial basis. The circumstances in which such homes need to be registered are considered in Chapter 7, Part III, and we have already considered the legal basis for funding. We now ascertain how the fees are funded in practice and examine the special rules for small unregistered homes and problems which have arisen with Attendance Allowance and which have yet to be resolved with the care component of Disability Living Allowance. We also look at ways in which respite care may be funded, and the different basis that applies to hospital care.

*Moving to residential care*
An individual may need to move into a residential care home in any of the following circumstances:
- parents cannot cope with their young handicapped child at home so it is necessary for arrangements to be made for some form of residential care (or schooling);
- parents who cope whilst their child is at school wish (or

need) to arrange for the child to live in a residential care home thereafter;
- the family home breaks up, perhaps on divorce, and there is no continuing provision for the child;
- parents continue to look after their child for as long as they can but ultimately by reason of age or infirmity must let go;
- parents die.

The move from home will be a traumatic time for the individual and also for the parents, but even if they overcome this barrier there is no certainty that the necessary funding will be available, having in mind that weekly fees are substantial and beyond the means of the average parent.

## Income Support

Until the new community care arrangements take effect in April 1993 a special allowance is available to claimants in certain types of residential care.

### Residential care allowance
Only claimants living in registered residential care or nursing homes and small homes that fulfil certain stringent staffing requirements (or continue to qualify under transitional provisions) qualify for this allowance. It is subject to financial limits laid down in the Regulations which depend upon the type of home and the nature of the disablement or care provided.[223] In addition, the claimant is paid a weekly sum for personal expenses.

### Categories of care
The categories of care identified for the purpose of the different financial limits include:
- mental handicap;
- mental disorder other than mental handicap;
- physical disablement below pension age;
- elderly.

For each category separate limits are specified for nursing homes and residential care homes. The regulations make provision as to the maximum payable as follows[224]:

(a) where the personal care that the claimant is receiving corresponds with a category of care for which the home is registered, the amount is determined in accordance with that category;

(b) where the personal care does not so correspond, the amount is determined according to the lower or least of the claimant's own category and the categories for which the home is registered;

(c) in any other case the amount is determined in accordance with the category most consistent with the personal care being received.

---

223  Income Support (General) Regulations 1987, reg. 19 and Sched.4.
224  Sched.4, paras.6, 7 and 10.

### Attendance Allowance

This allowance was usually withdrawn during periods of residential care. Regulations provided that payment ceased after the claimant had been living for four weeks in a hospital or "accommodation provided ... in circumstances in which the cost ... is being *or may be* borne wholly or partly out of public or local funds in pursuance of a Scheduled enactment".[225] The Scheduled enactments included:

> National Assistance Act 1948, Part III
> National Health Service Act 1977, ss.21(1)(*b*) and Sched.8, para.2
> National Health Service (Scotland) Act 1978, s.37
> Education Act 1944, ss.9(1), 33(2), 34(4), 41, 42 and 50
> Children and Young Persons Act 1933, s.53
> Children and Young Persons Act 1969, ss.23 and 28
> Child Care Act 1980, ss.2 and 21(part)
> Social Work (Scotland) Act 1968, (various sections)
> Education (Scotland) Act 1980, ss.1 and 2.

Problems have arisen since the Commissioners held that *may* means *may*, and that the allowance was not payable if the claimant was being provided with accommodation and the cost was being, or could be, met either wholly or in part out of public funds.[226]

*Directions*
It is difficult to think of any case in which the local authority did not have power to pay for residential accommodation for a person eligible for Attendance Allowance and in consequence a new regulation was introduced which gave power to depart from the Regulations in such case or class of case as the Secretary of State may direct.[227] In practice the decision was still made by a Benefits Agency officer but in accordance with Directions issued by the Secretary of State which are not published so it was seldom possible to determine in advance if the allowance was payable.

*Respite care*
The Regulations also provided that two or more distinct periods separated by an interval not exceeding 28 days, or by two or more such intervals, should be treated as a continuous period equal in duration to the total of such distinct periods and ending on the last day of the later or last such period. The effect of this rule was that if an individual returned to respite care within 28 days of a previous period of such care, the linking rule applied so as to add together those periods and any earlier linked periods. Once the total reached 28 days no further allowance would be paid during periods of respite care until the individual had spent at least 29 consecutive days at home, then the linking was broken and the sequence started again. Thus it became common practice to advise parents of a handicapped child to establish a pattern of respite care

---

[225] Social Security (Attendance Allowance)(No.2) Regulations 1975, reg.4(1).
[226] *R(A) 3/83* affirmed by the Court of Appeal in *Jones* v. *The Insurance Officer* (published as an appendix to *R(A) 3/83*).
[227] Reg.4(3)(*b*).

which broke the link after every 28 days of respite care by having a continuous period of at least 29 days at home.[228] If parents were able to adopt this pattern they retained the allowance even though the respite care was paid for in full by the local authority.

### Interaction with Income Support

Attendance Allowance was not disregarded as a resource for the purpose of Income Support in the case of a person living in a residential care home so would not be available over and above the maxima applicable for Income Support. In the unlikely event of a mentally handicapped person paying for residential care out of his own resources and not relying upon any local authority funding, Attendance Allowance could still be claimed in view of the manner in which the Directions were applied. This was the situation for elderly persons living in fee-paying nursing or retirement homes.

### Disability Living Allowance

The provisions referred to above in respect of Attendance Allowance have been included in the Social Security (Disability Living Allowance) Regulations 1991, regulations 8, 9 and 10[229] which also appear to incorporate the former Directions. However, the previous reference to the Scheduled enactments has been extended so as to include "any other enactment relating to persons under disability or to young persons or to education or training" thereby closing some of the potential loopholes. The opportunity does not appear to have been taken to cover the situation of parents paying for most, but not all, of the care provision and further problems in this area may be anticipated.

## RESIDENTIAL CARE HOMES

### Funding a child

There are no additional state benefits available to pay the high cost of residential care for a child under the age of 16 and if this is needed it will be a matter for arrangement with the local authority who, through its social services department, should be concerned as to the welfare of the child and of the family. In appropriate cases the authority will arrange and/or pay for residential care, though financial contribution from parents may be appropriate. After an initial period (usually 28 days) the parents may cease to be entitled to all state benefits in respect of their child for those periods when the child is not in their care and is being funded in whole or in part by the local authority. The position becomes more complex if the parents themselves meet all the cost of the residential care (see below under Respite Care).

---

228 It does not matter whether the respite care is 28 consecutive or separate days. Days returning to and leaving home are not counted, so a one night stay does not count, and alternate nights in respite care over a long period should not be taken into account even if days are all spent in such care.

229 As amended by the Social Security (Disability Living Allowance) Amendment Regulations 1992

## Funding an adult.

Even if a suitable home can be found with a vacancy for the adult, there is no certainty that arrangements can be made for payment of the fees which will usually exceed the limits imposed on Income Support. Whilst the parents may be willing to meet the balance of the fees during their lifetime (and this is allowed under the regulations) few parents can afford to make adequate provision following their death to cover the full fees or shortfall for the rest of their child's life especially after taking inflation into account. In any event, top-up is difficult to arrange after death because income left to the child in trust reduces state benefits. Most care homes considering taking a resident, possibly for life, require local authority sponsorship before acceptance in case any parental funding ceases (*e.g.* on death or retirement).

*Topping-up by local authorities*
In so far as fees exceed the Income Support residential care allowance maxima, topping-up is required and it will usually be for the local authority to provide this, but there is no legal entitlement. Parents of a mentally handicapped adult are thus not in a position to arrange residential care, and there are many instances where despite encouragement from a social worker to let go and a suitable vacancy having arisen after a wait of many years, the authority declines to sponsor due to financial constraints. In this situation parents must resort to non-legal remedies, but a lawyer can still assist with the writing of letters and by articulating the reasons why such provision is appropriate.

*Periods away from the home*
It is not clear how much time an individual may spend with family without suffering a reduction in the residential care allowance but much will probably depend upon the extent to which the home continues to charge fees during periods of absence. An individual who uses the allowance to fund accommodation in a residential care or nursing home may need to spend periods away from the home, *e.g.* whilst on holiday or in hospital for treatment. The allowance may continue during a temporary absence, but at 80 per cent. of the normal rate, for up to four weeks or in the case of temporary admission to hospital for up to 12 months.[230] The problem is that there will be no additional funds to cover the extra costs of the absence (*e.g.* a holiday) apart from the usual personal allowance, and if the absence is long there will be no income to cover any continuing charges of the home.

## General

*Role of charities*
Some charities provide top-up for fees, often in their own homes. However, this masks the true cost of residential care and once a

---

[230] Income Support (General) Regulations 1987, Sched.7, para.16.

charity tops-up the fees of an individual it may become trapped into continuing to do so. It should first be ensured that the resident is receiving maximum social security benefits according to the circumstances, and some charities impose their own topping-up limits. The Charity Commission has stated that top-up may be a legitimate charitable activity, and that a charity may admit people not covered by its charitable aims and objectives, if these people pay the full costs of care and are not preventing people within the charitable aims from taking up places.

Charities which run homes, and also homes in the commercial sector, may charge differential fees, which means to some extent loading the fees of those who can afford them to cover the shortfall from those on state benefits. Sometimes a charity is obliged to raise funds from the public to meet the annual trading deficit when such efforts would be better employed for capital funding to improve the facilities. This may result in closure of homes, poor staff wages and resentment over the cost of complying with the requirements of the registration officer.

*Employment*

Disincentives apply if a resident could contemplate some form of employment, as the following case history shows:

> Reginald never had an education because he was well over school age by the time of the Education Act 1970 and deemed to be ineducable under the old system. He stayed at home, but after his parents died moved into a MENCAP Homes Foundation house which was funded as a residential care home. He then started to attend a day-centre and was soon found to be a competent worker so joined a pre-work group. The local Pathway Officer felt that he could find Reginald a job, but not at a wage equivalent to the state benefits which funded his place in the care home. Reginald could not afford to work because he would lose his home, but also faced the prospect of losing his place at the day-centre as he was genuinely able to work.

New provisions from October 7, 1991 allow residents who are in employment to be treated as not being in full-time work and to be exempted from signing on.[231]

*Categories of care*

A home may be registered for more than one category of care, (*e.g.* both mentally and physically handicapped persons), but the amount of residential care allowance differs according to the category. In cases of doubt a questionnaire is completed by the home describing the kind of care that the claimant receives. It is important to check that the appropriate limit is being applied because a resident with a mental handicap may have profound physical disabilities which would justify a higher weekly payment, and in that event the home should ensure that it is registered for both categories. Problems arise when a person with a mental handicap is placed in a residential care home which is not registered for that category. This might be an elderly mentally handicapped person who is placed in a home registered only for

---

[231] Income Support (General) Amendment (No.4) Regulations 1991.

the elderly. A 1991 Tribunal decision illustrates how illogical the result can be:

> At the age of 75 years Albert, who is severely mentally handicapped, moved on the recommendation of social services from a mental hospital into a private residential care home registered for the elderly and the physically disabled. The home wished to charge the weekly rate appropriate for mental handicap (£195) but Albert was only allowed the lower rate for the elderly (£160). He did not qualify as physically disabled (£230), and the home could not re-register to include mental handicap because it was no longer the policy of the registration officer to allow registration for more than one category. There was some consolation, because the Tribunal discovered that Albert had been certified as being eligible for Attendance Allowance at the higher rate but that this was not in payment. Nevertheless, this entitled him to the higher rate for the very dependent elderly (£185). In addition he received the allowance for personal expenses (£11.40 per week).

## Unregistered homes

Problems have arisen following a change in the regulations affecting small unregistered care homes.

### England

In England, a residential care home with less than four residents does not need to be fully registered[232] but the residents can claim residential care allowance to meet the fees up to the maxima if certain stringent conditions are satisfied.[233] Since April 1988 an establishment providing residential accommodation with both board and personal care for fewer than four persons with a mental handicap, excluding those carrying on the home or employed there and their relatives, has qualified if:

- at least two employed or self-employed persons ("responsible persons") are each engaged in providing personal care to residents of the establishment for a minimum of 35 hours a week and those persons are not engaged in any other remunerative work;
- each of those responsible persons has at least one year's relevant experience in caring for people with a mental handicap;
- at least one responsible person is available throughout the day, and on call throughout the night, to care for the residents; and
- all residents have free access to the premises at all times.

These stringent conditions were introduced to prevent homes that did not deserve to be treated as residential care homes from charging high fees. The problems that arise over the interpretation of these conditions are resolved by SSATs.

### Scotland

There is no equivalent minimum number of residents for

---

232  Registered Homes Act 1984, s.1(4). The Registered Homes (Amendment) Act 1991 introduces a limited form of registration for such homes.

233  Income Support (General) Regulations 1987, reg.19 (as amended).

registration as an establishment in Scotland[234] and an establishment registered under the Scottish provisions is included in the Income Support definition of a residential care home.[235]

*Adult placement schemes*

In many areas social services departments set up schemes under the Supplementary Benefits regime whereby mentally handicapped adults could live and be cared for in ordinary households for fees that were met out of the resident's residential care allowance. Some of these households do not satisfy the present day conditions for treatment as a residential care home, but if there has been continuity in the arrangements since before July 27, 1987, the allowance is still paid because the new regulations provided that in circumstances such as this the weekly applicable amount should be calculated[236.]

> "as if the home was a residential care home within the meaning of this regulation if, and for so long as, the claimant remains resident in the same home apart from any temporary absence, and the home continues to provide accommodation with board and personal care for the claimant by reason of his old age, disablement, past or present dependence on alcohol or drugs or past or present mental disorder."

A question that arises is whether this continuity is broken if the household moves to different accommodation, and this was dealt with by the English writer in a recent case:

> In 1986 Mrs D. was looking after Adrian, a 20 year old man who was not related to her but was severely mentally handicapped. She initially claimed Invalid Care Allowance, but intended to provide respite care for other handicapped persons, and from March 1987 the social services department arranged for her to be treated as an unregistered residential care home. She then charged weekly fees for providing care, which involved her in keeping accounts and paying income tax on the annual profit, but her household income was increased because Adrian claimed residential care allowance to meet the fees. On the change to Income Support Mrs D. no longer qualified as a residential care home, but the allowance continued for Adrian because there was continuity in the arrangements.
>
> In 1990 Mrs. D. moved to a house in another town and took Adrian with her. The allowance was withdrawn and she was given the choice of charging the considerably lower board and lodging rate (which would be covered by Adrian claiming housing benefit), or claiming Invalid Care Allowance. Either way she faced the prospect of ceasing to be able to care for Adrian so an appeal was lodged with a request for an immediate review of the decision because Mrs D. could not have survived the delays of the appeal process. As the review would depend upon a specific interpretation of the regulations the local DSS office was asked to refer the matter to the Chief Adjudication Officer for a definitive view.
>
> The continuing claim depended upon whether Adrian remained resident in the same home despite the move. It was submitted that in this context *home* refers to residential care home and this expression is specifically defined in the regulations as meaning "an establishment ..." for which the Oxford dictionary gives the closest meaning as "household". Regulations define

---

234  Social Work (Scotland) Act 1968, s.61.

235  Reg.19: the definition covers a registered establishment under the 1968 Act or an establishment provided by a registered housing association which provides care equivalent to that given in residential accommodation provided under Part IV of the 1968 Act.

*nursing home* by reference to *premises* and previously defined *hostel* as meaning a building[237], a quite different concept from a household which tends to refer to the persons living in a building. The regulations could have used the word premises or building when defining a residential care home, but did not, so it might be assumed that a distinction was intended.

As the claimant had moved with the proprietor of the home and all the household furnishings and their personal possessions to another house, it was submitted that they remained in the same household and hence in the same home for the purpose of the regulation. This interpretation was accepted by the Chief Adjudication Officer on the basis of an unreported Commissioner's Decision,[238] and the decision was revised without an appeal being necessary. Benefit arrears in excess of £2,000 were promptly paid and the residential care allowance re-instated.[239]

### Category of care

In the case of a small home no category of care will have been registered, so it is necessary to ascertain, having regard to the types of personal care that the home provides, which category is most consistent with the personal care being received by the claimant in that accommodation.[240] If there is physical disability as well as mental handicap the higher rate applicable to the former may be claimed.

### Conclusions

It may now be possible for those who maintain small unregistered residential care homes which would no longer qualify under the new regulations to move house without residential care allowances being withdrawn from the residents. It seems to be accepted that where such an establishment moves to new premises, any resident who has been living there since before July 27, 1987, and claiming the allowance, may continue to do so. Even with the change to community care, transitional provisions will ensure that those receiving residential care allowance in April 1993 continue to do so. There may also be persons who have had the allowance withdrawn in these circumstances, and they should ask for a review of the decision and apply for leave to appeal out of time, but unfortunately they are likely to have ceased providing this care because of the withdrawal of funding, and it may be too late now to re-establish the same small residential care home.

## Implications for mental handicap

Enquiries of charities with established homes reveal many uncertainties and inconsistencies in regard to funding. There is no national standard, and the response of local authorities varies from one area to another. They will rarely provide sponsorship if there

---

236  Reg.19(2).
237  Reg.20, repealed (October 1989) by Income Support (General) Amendment Regulations 1989 when hostel-dwellers were transferred to housing benefit.
238  *CSB/1348/1988* by Commissioner Sanders on July 23, 1990.
239  This decision will not apply in respect of any additional respite care which Mrs D. provides in the future, but she may then employ additional staff on such a basis that she qualifies under the new regulations.
240  Income Support (General) Regulations 1987, Sched.4, para.10(4).

is within their own provision a place for which the applicant might be deemed suitable. The only likelihood in such a case is if the parents have been a thorough nuisance to them over the years and a trial placement of their child has broken down. A charity with several homes was, in 1984/85, dealing with six DHSS offices each of which adopted a different interpretation, and up to 60 local authorities all of whom had different views. The emphasis appeared to be on financial buck-passing.

*Background*
Until 1985 social security benefits largely met the full costs of residential care and residents were admitted on this basis, but as a result of an explosion in this type of care (particularly for the elderly) due to benefits being available without restriction, limits were then progressively placed upon the amounts payable which no longer cover economic costs. This results in a funding deficit for many such residents which is still having to be absorbed by the homes.[241] These limits are not inadequate in all cases; much depends upon the care provided. Local authorities have used many excuses to avoid topping-up the funding of these existing residents, including arguments as to which authority is responsible, yet the homes have not wished to turn them out.[242] At the same time some authorities continued to fund residents in private homes not realising that, unlike their own homes, state benefits could be claimed and only funding for top-up was required.

*Top-up*
Where the need for residential care arises by reason of mental handicap top-up has usually been necessary because few homes can provide the care needed within Income Support financial limits.[243] This is especially so if the home is providing day-time activities, because the residential care allowance was not intended to extend to this, yet many residents in homes for the mentally handicapped are not provided with places in day care centres. In practice the amount of Income Support will not be affected by whether the claimant attends day care facilities or not, but a local authority which provides a place at an Adult Training Centre may be less willing to provide top-up for residential care. Conversely, where the residential care home provides full day care, there is little excuse for the local authority to decline top-up, because the weekly amount thereof may well be less than the cost of providing a place in a day centre and this could leave the valuable day centre place available for someone else. Furthermore, unless the local

---

241  Homes for the elderly cope with this by mixing fee paying residents with state funded residents and charging higher fees to the former. Homes for mentally handicapped persons cannot do this.

242  The local authority in whose area the resident previously lived would remain responsible, but state benefits would be dealt with by the office for the area of the residential care home.

243  The English writer is involved with a home run by a small charitable society which survives on residential care allowance, but this is the exception.

authority takes advantage of residential care allowance under the present system while it has the chance, it could find itself meeting the full cost of both day and residential care. Such reasoning may not assist, because authorities tend to be more concerned with the particular fund out of which the payment is to be made than the overall cost to them, and there is a preference for seeing funds expended on local authority services rather than paid to outside agencies. This type of perverse reasoning may change under the new community care policies, and service users should be encouraged to ask searching questions to ensure that it does.

*Action to be taken*
There have been many cases where lifetime places in a suitable residential care home have been offered, perhaps after a wait of many years, only to be abandoned because of lack of sponsorship from the local authority which may previously have expressed support for this type of care for the individual. Experience tends to show that in such cases it is preferable to build up a compelling case through councillors and other local authority contacts rather than to involve the Member of Parliament.

Many homes run by charitable organisations have very long waiting lists, and some decline to consider persons over 45 because by the time a place has become available for them they no longer have the prospect of spending many years in the home. Yet the problem of providing suitable care often arises at about that age when the parents have died or are no longer able to cope. The conclusion must be that parents should plan early, and it is often the more articulate ones who overcome all the obstacles, rather than the less able ones.

*Financial negotiations*
Conflict may arise where money is held in a discretionary trust whilst the local authority is asked to provide top-up. A third party, including a local authority, cannot force trustees to exercise their discretion in a particular way despite the means-testing rules,[244] but the local authority may refuse to exercise its own discretion to provide top-up. The deadlock is best resolved by negotiation, because if the trustees make available a reasonable sum by way of income from the trust the authority will usually accept this as a contribution and not seek to assess the capital or a deemed income.

## RESPITE CARE

Whilst looking after their mentally handicapped son or daughter parents may desire periods of respite care either to give themselves a much needed break or to provide a welcome change of environment for the individual. We now consider how such respite care can be financed for children and for adults.

---

[244] *Gisborne* v. *Gisborne* (1877) 2 App.Cas.300.

## Funding a child

In the case of a child, unless parents have relatives who can cope for periods or they can afford to pay for respite care themselves, they must look to their local authority social services department to provide care or financial help.

### Local Authority support

No matter how great the need for relief, the parents have no right to respite care and are dependent upon the willingness of the local authority to provide or finance this in such manner and to such extent as it thinks fit. A minimum of three weeks in each year may be allowed as holiday relief without taking into account the means of the parents. There is no legal right of appeal on the part of parents who consider that insufficient support is being provided or find the arrangements made far from satisfactory. A supportive social worker is needed, but ultimately what can be arranged will depend upon the funds allocated by the authority for this type of provision and the calls upon those funds. In most areas such funding is inadequate. The authority may have developed a fostering scheme which costs less than residential care and offer this provision to the parents with no choice, but some parents prefer residential care, and an enlightened authority will discuss a care scheme with them possibly on the basis that a certain amount of money is available for respite care and they may utilise this how they want. Advance planning is desirable to assist the authority with its budgeting.

### Attendance Allowance

We have seen how this allowance may be withdrawn during periods of respite care. A case where parents could not cope for 29 days without a break[245] highlights the difficulties encountered in practice:

> The parents of a severely mentally handicapped child needed regular respite care and arranged this with a local home run by a charity. Their local authority would only pay for 2 weeks annual holiday relief so they paid the rest of the fees themselves using state benefits as a contribution. Under the Regulations they ceased to be entitled to Attendance Allowance (and Invalid Care Allowance which is dependent thereon) because the local authority had power to pay the fees (and did pay the 2 weeks) yet other parents who were having similar respite care paid for in full by their local authority were retaining these allowances because they could comply with the 28 day cycle. After protracted correspondence DHSS ultimately acknowledged that *'it was never the intention of Ministers that people ... who have undertaken the cost of respite care at their own expense should be penalised'* and indicated that the Directions would be amended to cover this situation.

Parents who have had their allowances withdrawn in this situation without any right of appeal should seek retrospective payment. In all cases parents who use respite care should keep records of all dates and arrangements, and inform the Benefits Agency in advance of what is happening. Similar problems may arise with

---

245 For the relevance of this, see p.394.

the care component of Disability Living Allowance unless parents pay the whole of the cost themselves.[246]

## Funding an adult

During periods of respite care in a registered residential care or nursing home, Income Support residential care allowance can be claimed by an adult to top-up the income received from other state benefits to the limit allowed. Payment is usually calculated on a weekly basis, but if respite care is arranged for eight weeks or less the allowance will be available from the day of admission whatever day of the week this is,[247] and if a full week's charge has to be paid even for a few days it may be allowed in full.[248]

### Top-up

Although it is unlikely that a home providing respite care can be found whose charges are within the limits, the regulations permit the balance of fees to be paid on a voluntary basis by other persons without affecting means-testing. Thus the problem is restricted to finding the difference between the fees and the Income Support limit, though the care component of Disability Living Allowance (formerly Attendance Allowance) will not be paid in addition as it is taken into account in the Income Support assessment during periods of residential care. If parents are unable or unwilling to find this difference they may approach the local authority who should provide some support on a structured basis. Some local authorities have continued to pay the entire fees and failed to take advantage of Income Support, so in such circumstances it is desirable to draw attention to the state subsidy and negotiate for a larger number of weeks at less cost to the authority.

### Family based care

Until April 1989 handicapped people receiving Income Support could claim board and lodging allowance, with a top-up for the extra care and attention required, in respect of any time spent with another family for respite care. Several family based care schemes relied upon this funding being available for the family providing the respite care. When these allowances were abolished (except for residential care and nursing homes) this additional funding ceased to be available because the new Housing Benefit administered by the local authority could only relate to the person's home address.[249] The shortfall, which could not be made up in all cases, discouraged the provision of such respite care and discriminated against families who were not so well off. This type of care in the community may cease to be a viable proposition as a result.

---

246 Accepting payment from the local authority for even an odd week could result in the withdrawal of benefit for all other weeks; see Social Security (Disability Living Allowance) Regulations 1991, reg.9.

247 Social Security (Claims and Payments) Regulations 1987, Sched.7.

248 Income Support (General) Regulations 1987, reg.73(2)-(5).

249 Before April 1989 it was possible to claim £67.50 per week, but thereafter this was reduced to £34.65 in a comparable situation.

*Private dwellings*

The Secretary of State for Social Security confirmed that if a respite care scheme provided accommodation in a private dwelling,[250] Attendance Allowance should not be stopped for those under 18. This concession was restricted to those circumstances and would not apply over that age or in a residential care home. It is assumed that the concession will apply to the care component of Disability Living Allowance.

## Health Authority homes

There has recently been a trend for health authorities to move patients out of hospitals into staffed homes in the community which they themselves provide and fund, though the patients must contribute towards the cost of food and heating from their state benefits. It seems that this category of home was not anticipated when some of the benefit regulations were enacted, and problems of interpretation have arisen.

*Scheduled accommodation*

We have seen that a claimant otherwise entitled to Attendance Allowance, having satisfied the medical criteria, was not paid the allowance if he was living in accommodation in respect of which the cost was being, or might be, met from public funds pursuant to a Scheduled enactment. Those enactments appear to contemplate care provision by local authorities and not health authorities, so it has been argued that the allowance continues to be paid if the accommodation is provided by the health authority[251]:

William was moved out of a mental hospital with other patients into a staffed house provided and supervised by the health authority. No rent was charged (it appeared that the authority did not have power to charge rent) but each resident paid £25 per week as a contribution towards the cost of food and heating. He applied for Attendance Allowance and was found on a medical assessment to be entitled at the lower rate, but payment was refused on the ground that he was living in accommodation *provided for him in circumstances in which the cost is being, or may be, borne wholly or partly out of public or local funds in pursuance of a Scheduled enactment*. The Secretary of State did not make a Direction. The Tribunal took the view that the onus was upon the Department to prove that this particular accommodation was being or could be funded *pursuant to a Scheduled enactment* . The presenting officer was unable to point to any provision in any of the Scheduled enactments authorising this type of funding by a health authority, and did not suggest that this was a hospital. Accordingly, payment of the allowance was ordered, but the Chief Adjudication Officer has appealed to the Commissioners and the outcome is awaited.

## RESIDENTIAL SCHOOLS

In some cases a child of school age is sent by the local education authority to a special residential school, in which event there is power in England for fees to be paid by that education

---

250 *e.g.* with a family under National Health Service Act 1977, s. 21(1)(*b*) and Sched.8, para. 2.

251 Based upon a recent decision of a Tribunal chaired by the English author.

authority.[252] In Scotland, the education authority must meet the cost of board and lodging (in a school, hostel or elsewhere) if arranged, after consultation with the parents, in cases where in the authority's opinion suitable education can best be provided at a particular school, or where the pupil will only thus receive the full benefit of school education owing to the remoteness of his home, the conditions under which he is living, "or other exceptional circumstances".[253] In such cases parents will be concerned to know what happens to state benefits for and in respect of the child both during term time and holidays. The regulations covering social security benefits in this situation are complex. The child may be under 16, or aged 16-17 (with the option of being treated as a dependant or not) or 18 and over, but it is the treatment for benefit purposes rather than the actual age that is relevant.

## Income Support

### Parent's claim

If a child is maintained at a residential school by a local education authority the parents do not receive Income Support for that child on any day when he is away at school. Nevertheless, they will feel obliged to see that their child is adequately kitted out during the holidays so as to return to school at the beginning of each term with all the clothes and personal items that are needed, even though the school must in default pay for any items needed during term time. This is difficult to finance if the parents only receive an allowance for the child during holidays. Normally parents receive an applicable amount for each dependent child in the calculation of their Income Support, but a child "who is residing at an educational establishment at which he is receiving relevant education" is treated as having an income during periods at the school equal to payments made by someone outside the family to the school in respect of his maintenance. Benefit during periods at home is unaffected by those payments to the school. The maximum income attributable to the child is equal to the applicable amounts directly attributable to the child (*i.e.* personal allowance and disabled child premium).[254] The question that arises is whether a child in these circumstances *resides* at the school, because if not this provision will not apply.

It may be argued that a child still resides at home during periods spent at boarding school, but the correct interpretation appears to be that a child may be residing at school at the same time as being a member of his parents' household. That is because a child is someone under the age of 16 and no child under that age can claim benefit himself.[255] Therefore, the provision can only apply to a child who is a member of a family, which means that he must be a

---

252  Education (Miscellaneous Provisions) Act 1953, s.6.
253  Education (Scotland) Act 1980, ss.50 and 52.
254  Income Support (General) Regulations 1987, reg.44.
255  Social Security Act 1986, s.20(11) and (3).

member of his parents' household if they are to claim at all, and it is difficult to argue that a person remains a member of a household while absent from it unless it can be said that he resides with the other members of the household. Thus the child is still residing at home during term-time but, if that be so, the draftsman in using the term residing, must have intended that word to be understood as applying to a child's attendance at boarding school, *i.e.* that the child could be residing at an educational establishment at the same time as with the claimant. This is consistent with other fields of law where it has been held that a person may be resident in more than one place at a time.

Thus as the child may be resident during term time both at home and at school the provision applies so as to eliminate the applicable amounts for the child in the parents' benefit claim. They will have to fund all clothing and other personal items for their child out of the allowance for the child which merely covers the holiday periods unless they wish the child to return to school with inadequate clothing in which event the school will have provide what is lacking to the embarrassment of the child and the parents.

### Student's own claim

We have seen how a mentally disabled person may have the option of claiming Income Support on attaining 16 even if still at school. It seems that payments made by an education authority to cover the cost of boarding (and perhaps tuition) at a residential school will be taken into account as a notional income resource and are not disregarded.[256] The weekly cost inevitably exceeds the claimant's applicable amount, so Income Support is not payable during periods at school, though it will revive during holidays.

### Further education colleges

Not all boarding establishments are set up as schools, and some which only admit persons with a mental handicap who have attained 16, are registered as residential care homes even though they concentrate on providing training courses. The basis of funding outlined above for such homes applies, and residents claim Income Support residential care allowance with a top up of fees usually coming from the local education authority as part of its provision of special educational needs though there is scope for social services involvement in the funding.[257] Joint assessments and placements by both authorities are needed and will become necessary under the new community care policies.

## Other state benefits

Where the student is claiming Income Support in his own right, any other benefits are usually taken into account as a resource so will not increase the overall amount.

---

256  Income Support (General) Regulations 1987, reg.42(4)(*a*)(ii).

257  Where the young person resides at the establishment throughout the year, the education authority may only pay for four-fifth of the year (the normal school terms), leaving social services (or the parents) to pay the balance.

*Disability Living Allowance* (DLA)
The special rules outlined above meant that Attendance Allowance
was payable for the first 28 days at residential school, and
thereafter only for days when the child came home. The days
when the child left and returned to the school were counted as
days at home. It was possible for the allowance to be payable for
further such periods if the child spent at least 29 days at home
after the last day at school and this could arise on return after the
long summer vacation. Payment of Mobility Allowance was not
usually affected as long as the child was able to make use of the
allowance to get about, but questions arose as to whether the
amount should be retained by the parents within the home or to
some extent made available for extra facilities whilst at the school.
Reference must now be made to DLA which replaces these two
allowances.

*Invalid Care Allowance* (ICA)
Usually when Attendance Allowance stopped this allowance
claimed by the carer also ceased, though in certain circumstances
it could be withdrawn earlier. It is now linked to DLA.

*Child Benefit*
If still being claimed by the parents, this continues whilst the child
is at a residential school.

*Housing Benefit*
The parents' claim will not usually be affected whilst their child is
away at school provided that they still have primary responsibility
for the child. It may increase (or arise for the first time) where
there has been a withdrawal of ICA.

*Family Credit*
The parents' claim will not usually be affected whilst their child is
away at school, save that it may increase where there has been a
withdrawal of ICA though not during the current period.

*Fares to school*
The local education authority should pay the fares of parents who
escort their child to and from a residential school at recognised
holiday times. The fares for the child are also paid.

## HOSPITAL CARE

### State benefits

There is no charge for treatment or accommodation provided
under the NHS but as we have seen, most state benefits are affected
after an initial period in hospital and there are provisions for
linking together separate periods.[258] In some cases, members of

---

258 Attendance Allowance was withdrawn after four weeks and any ICA stops
with this, though if the carer is in hospital it continues for 12 weeks. After
six weeks Sickness Benefit, Invalidity or Retirement Pension, or Severe
Disablement Allowance are reduced but Mobility Allowance was unaffected.

the family are expected to assist, perhaps by doing the patient's washing, and this can result in financial hardship where they themselves depend on means-tested benefits and there is no additional allowance to cover the costs involved. Cases are known of severely handicapped people who spend part of their time in long-stay hospitals and part at home, but continue to be treated throughout as hospital in-patients so that they receive reduced Severe Disablement Allowance and no Income Support.

*Accumulation of income*
A small amount of benefit is retained by the patient for personal expenses and this is collected by the hospital authorities and held in a special account. Although it is intended that this money shall be for the personal benefit of the patient, there is a danger that it simply accumulates because nursing staff are too busy to find ways of spending it on the patient. Mobility Allowance continued to be paid notwithstanding that there are few opportunities to spend it for a person resident in hospital, and this could accumulate quite rapidly; this problem may still arise with the mobility component of Disability Living Allowance.[259]

## Care provision

It is no longer the policy for people with a mental handicap to be cared for by the Health Authority in hospitals unless they need the kind of nursing that only a hospital can provide, and those who have been in hospital for many years are progressively being moved out into the community. Care packages must be arranged for them by social services or social work departments, and the usual state benefits outlined in this chapter should then be claimed. An individual who has been in hospital for many years may have accumulated a substantial sum of money which simply could not be spent, so means-testing will result in this being expended on future care provision. In some cases parents may make little or no provision by Will for a child who has been living and expected to remain in a mental hospital, and in England claims may then arise under the Inheritance (Provision for Family and Dependants) Act 1975, or in Scotland legal rights may be claimed.[260]

## COMMUNITY CARE

In Chapter 5, Part II we identified the sources of funding for local authorities responsible for implementing the new community care policies. We now consider how residential care for an individual may be funded in the future and the extent to which he may be required to contribute.

*Background*
The residential care allowance has hitherto provided a financial

---

259 Guidance on good practice in Scotland is given in *Report of the Working Party on Incapax Patients' Funds*, SHHD (the "Crosby Report").
260 See Chap.9, Parts IVA and IVB.

incentive for authorities to rely upon private or charitable homes rather than run their own and to some extent this accounts for the recent growth of such homes. This trend will continue under community care because authorities are encouraged to adopt an enabling rather than a providing role, but it may be offset by the move away from large residential care homes to small homes in the community with care support. In order to benefit from the residential care allowance, some authorities have promoted independent charitable trusts to run homes in which they retain influence as co-trustees.

For some years the transitional provisions for those already receiving residential care allowance will continue to benefit such homes, but not homes run directly by the authority. There has during recent years been a shortfall in the amount available to meet the costs of residential care, resulting in many people with a mental handicap who undoubtedly needed this type of care having to remain with their families. There are no plans to cope with this shortfall and, as we have seen, the existing residential care funding being transferred from DSS to local authorities is not being earmarked for that purpose so some may be diverted elsewhere.[261]

### Proposals for change

A Report in 1987[262] concluded that a system in which local government provides public support for people in residential care homes offered the best way forward. Several options were set out whereby this might be achieved and the need for transitional arrangements for those already in such care was identified. In regard to respite care it was recognised that the funding system needs to be flexible, to permit decisions to be made quickly and to allow respite care to be provided as part of a package of care. This was followed by the recommendations in the Griffiths Report which formed the basis for the new community care policies.

### Changes

Although under the new system residents were to be eligible for Income Support for normal expenses and Housing Benefit for board and lodging costs, they were to rely upon local authority funding for the care element. The Government sought to keep things simple by devising a system whereby local authorities meet the full costs of residential care and receive transfers of notional Income Support and Housing Benefit. In March 1992 it concluded that this would be too complicated and result in anomalies, so instead a Residential Allowance is proposed as part of Income Support for those entering residential care from April 1993. This is to be related to rents for those in sheltered housing. At the time

---

[261] In its Second Report, Session 1989-90, *Community Care: Future Funding of Private and Voluntary Residential Care*, the Social Services Committee made some strong recommendations about this.

[262] *Public Support for Residential Care* - Report of a joint central and local government working party, DHSS July 1987.

of writing, this proposal is still being developed.

Charges may be made to residents based upon their ability to pay,[263] and hostel accommodation will come within the same system.[264] It does not matter whether the authority provides or buys in the accommodation. Local authorities are also being given power to place and fund people in private nursing homes, so that there will be more flexibility and the same charging system may apply to both forms of residential care.[265] Unlike local authorities, health authorities cannot charge for their services. Local authorities will carry out a benefits check as part of the assessment procedure, because they have an incentive to ensure that people going into residential care or nursing homes are receiving all the state benefits to which they are entitled. In most cases the authority will enter into an agreement with the home under which it is obliged to pay the fees, and claim back from the resident as much as he can afford, leaving him with a sum for personal expenses.

These changes in the funding of residential care are fundamental to the new community care policies, because they are linked to assessments of need. There will no longer be a right, subject to means testing, to funding for such care simply because it is chosen and there will no longer be an incentive to provide residential care rather than other forms of care. It is said that this has provided a perverse incentive to move into residential care homes in the private sector and fuelled the growth in such homes during recent years. That may well be so for the elderly, but in regard to persons with a mental handicap indications are that many are denied a place in such homes through lack of top-up funding, and the growth of places has been less than the numbers discharged from mental handicap hospitals. If the provision of residential care is to be so dependent upon the willingness of the hard pressed local authority to fund the place, what choice will the individual or the family have in regard to the actual home? One of the objectives of community care is partnership, but the funding and means-testing arrangements provide little scope for this unless local authorities are willing to adopt an imaginative and flexible approach in their negotiations with families.

*Respite care*

There is some concern that Housing Benefit cannot be claimed for respite care, whereas it has hitherto been possible for a recipient of Income Support to claim residential care allowance as a substantial contribution towards the cost of respite care. This could create a disincentive for local authorities to provide respite care, because they would be obliged to meet much of the cost. It is

---

263 Health and Social Services and Social Security Act 1983.

264 1990 Act, s.44(7). This is provided under s.29 of the 1948 Act. (Not applicable to Scotland).

265 National Assistance Act 1948, ss. 26(1)(A-C) inserted by National Health Service and Community Care Act 1990, s.42(2). (Not applicable to Scotland).

not clear to what extent the proposed new Residential Allowance will be available to assist with respite care for those on Income Support.

*Transitional provisions*
Those in residential care homes when community care is fully implemented will have their right to Income Support funding preserved as at present, and it will be necessary for the maximum allowances to be reviewed annually to allow for increases in costs. It will still be necessary for local authorities to provide top-up, and they will be allowed to do so for mentally handicapped persons though probably not for the elderly (unless they previously qualified as mentally handicapped).

# PART VI - CONCLUSION

## Summary

Most mentally disabled people depend on state benefits, but in the view of many voluntary organisations the social security system is often discriminatory, complicated or inadequate. Entitlement can be determined by age, type or origin of disability, or National Insurance contributions paid, but there are no benefits to meet the majority of disability-related extra costs. The gap in benefit income of two equally severely disabled people can be substantial, and different types of benefit and assessment, adjudication and appeals procedures result in complexity and confusion. In addition to coping with their handicapped child, parents must learn to cope with a system which puts them in the middle of a conflict between national and local government funding. If their child remains at home they are subsidised to an extent that may discourage them from letting go, notwithstanding that this may be in the child's best long term interests. Yet if they seek to arrange for the child to leave home they may not only be denied the additional financial support necessary but also have the basic subsidy withdrawn.

Underlying all this is a shortage of funding. No matter how worthy the objectives and how good the administration, if sufficient funds are not made available there cannot be adequate provision. Community care policies will result in greater expense, yet there are no signs of more funding being made available and that which is to be transferred to local authorities may be diverted to other more politically satisfying purposes. Assessment of need must now come before the making of provision, and this may stem the flow of money for residential care to those who do not need this type of expensive provision, but the danger is that resource-led assessments will be made. Authorities may then state that they provide everyone with everything that they need. Far better to carry out genuine assessments in the knowledge that everything cannot be provided because of financial constraints, because then the overall deficit in funding can be identified and pressure brought to bear for more money to be made available.

Moving mentally handicapped people out of special hospitals has coincided with the closure of geriatric hospitals. Policies tend to be dominated by the needs of the elderly who make ever increasing demands upon limited resources as improved health care and medical advances result in a growing elderly population. Yet the mentally handicapped need a lifetime of support of which residential care is only one aspect for those who are more dependant and need greater supervision. Until they are treated as a class by themselves with separate funding implications, their needs will not be adequately provided for.

## LAW REFORM

### Claims for state benefits

*Procedure*

The types of state benefits that may be claimed are constantly changing, as are the rules relating to particular benefits. There are also many different benefits to which a handicapped person or the carers may be entitled, mostly dealt with by different authorities or departments. Thus an official responsible for the award of one benefit may be unable to advise as to the existence of or eligibility for another relevant benefit. It is not therefore surprising that many benefits go unclaimed. One solution would be to have officers with suitable training in each Benefits Agency office with specific responsibility for overseeing the claims made by or on behalf of a disabled person. Another more comprehensive solution would be to create a new non-means tested disablement benefit with different components or allowances dealing with the several aspects now covered by completely different benefits.[266]

*Payment*

It is unfortunate that many benefits, especially those available to disabled people, may not at present be paid by direct credit to a bank or building society account. This facility would benefit many recipients, either by reducing reliance upon others and thereby promoting independence, or by enabling another person more conveniently to assist the disabled claimant.

### Disability Manifesto

A group of voluntary organisations considers that disabled people have the right to benefits that meet the full costs of disability and recommends a disability income scheme which would include[267]:

(i)  Disablement Costs Allowance - a tax free non-means-tested benefit to cover the extra costs of disability. Based only on severity of disability (not cause, type or origin) and paid regardless of age, sex, and marital or employment status, it should not be included as income for means-tested

---

266  The Disablement Income Group recommends the introduction of a *national disability income* consisting of an income maintenance element, to help offset the loss of earning capacity arising from disability, and a disablement costs allowance to help with higher living costs incurred by disabled people.

267  *An Agenda for the 1990's* published by the Disability Manifesto Group.

benefits assessment.

(ii)  Disablement Pension - a non-contributory and non-means-tested benefit payable to persons of working age unable to work because of long-term sickness or disability. Paid at a high enough level to avoid dependence on means-tested benefit.

(iii) Partial Capacity Benefit - a flexible provision for people who, though able to work, have a reduced work capacity because of their disability.

(iv) Provision for Carers - Both the disabled person and any carer should have their own independent incomes without recourse to means-tested benefits.

# CHAPTER 9   FINANCIAL PROVISION FOR THE INDIVIDUAL

## Introduction

A testator who wishes to make financial provision for a person incapable of providing for himself by reason of mental or physical disability faces special problems. There is no simple solution and each case must be dealt with according to the circumstances, but in this chapter an attempt is made to explain the problems and indicate various options available. The answer may be to adopt a combination of these tailor-made for the particular circumstances. It is difficult enough to make a suitable Will when it is known what the dependent beneficiary's future circumstances will be, but it is almost impossible when this is a matter of speculation. Nevertheless, in many cases (especially that of a young child) it is necessary to prepare a Will for a testator who has no idea what the future holds. A further difficulty is that like tax-planning the rules keep changing and what is sensible today may be unwise tomorrow. We can only advise on the basis of the law as it stands and endeavour to anticipate adverse changes, but the testator should review the Will at frequent intervals and in particular if there is any substantial change in the funding of persons who are dependent upon state provision.

*Scope of this chapter*
This chapter is written on the basis of parents seeking to make financial provision for a mentally handicapped son or daughter, but the principles involved are not restricted either to parents or to mental handicap, and may be applied to anyone wishing to make financial provision for someone suffering from a disability. The emphasis is upon the loss of substantial state or local authority funding that could result from even moderate financial provision and the strategies that are available to avoid this. A trust fund will be needed in any event if the beneficiary is unable to handle financial affairs other than at a basic level, but even if this is not so, the potential loss of funding is a factor that may dictate the creation of a trust. References to a child in this chapter may include an adult son or daughter.

## PART I - THE PROBLEM

### Preliminary

It is expensive to keep an elderly or infirm person in a retirement or nursing home but where necessary the state either provides the home or assists with payment of the fees subject to a contribution from any personal resources that are available. Members of the family may assist but usually only to the extent that sufficient funding is not already available, and then by way of gift as and when the need arises. In the case of a person with a mental handicap a whole lifetime of dependency is involved, and the persons wishing to make financial provision are usually the older generation who can only do so by Will or lifetime settlement rather than the younger generation who can make flexible voluntary provision. The cost of keeping a seriously mentally (and possibly also physically) handicapped person in a residential care home may be comparable with providing nursing home care for a terminally ill patient, but though there is no prospect of recovery there may be a normal life expectancy.

The trend is towards community care which experience shows is not a cheap option, and although funding is being transferred from health services and social security to local authorities, there will not be enough to achieve the worthwhile objectives. Local authorities increasingly look for contributions towards the cost of providing for those for whom they are made responsible. Few parents can hope to provide an adequate index-linked annuity to support their child for life especially if they have other children to share their estate, so reliance upon means-tested state benefits and local authority provision becomes inevitable.

*Loss of state benefits*

The type of beneficiary envisaged in this chapter will be in receipt of one or more state benefits and may be totally dependent thereon. Some, but not all, of these benefits are means-tested. Local authority services or funding will also be provided and these may also be means-tested. In these circumstances any financial provision that is made for the beneficiary could result in the reduction or withdrawal of a significant source of income, or a charge for services that are provided.

Financial provision of an income nature may result in the loss of an equivalent amount of weekly state benefits, or charges for local authority services, with the result that no additional benefit is enjoyed by the beneficiary. Financial provision of a capital nature may result in the withdrawal of weekly state benefits or a levy on the capital in excess of the income it produces, with the result that the capital is ultimately exhausted thereby frustrating the intention of providing a real long term benefit. Few parents wish to make financial provision for a disabled child on this basis, so some method must be found of making provision which supplements state and local authority benefits and provision rather than jeopardising them or, if this cannot be done effectively, of creating a financial lifeboat so as to be reassured that the child is provided for as best possible.

## THE CIRCUMSTANCES

### Care provision

The first step is to ascertain by whom and on what basis the child will be looked after following the death of the parents.

## Future arrangements

In the ideal case the parents will already have made arrangements for the future. If their child is living independently of them, even though dependent on others, no change in circumstances or (probably) in funding arrangements will arise on their deaths so a strategy for their Wills can be devised based upon known factors. If the child is still being cared for by the parents in their home but they have made arrangements for future care when they are no longer able to provide this, those arrangements may be taken into account though with some degree of caution lest they do not work out as planned. It is more likely, especially where the child is young, that the parents will have made no plans and simply do not know what would happen to their child if they died prematurely. They will in these circumstances look to the solicitor to provide the solution by Will to the problem that has not been faced and this cannot be done. At best the Will can provide a financial structure appropriate to the personal circumstances and if these are not correctly anticipated the results may be disastrous. The solicitor must advise as tactfully as possible that in the child's best interests the parents must seek to make adequate arrangements during their own lifetimes for when they are unable by reason of death or infirmity to continue to look after their child.

## Uncertainty

In those cases where it cannot be known what the future holds it is necessary to assess the needs and degree of dependence of the child so as to form the most realistic view possible as to the future care that will be provided. Knowledge is thus required of the types of care provision available and how they are financed, hence the significance of the earlier chapters in this book. In all cases there will be uncertainty as to funding arrangements, and even if these are at present known they are vulnerable to change both as to availability of funding from a particular source and as to the means-testing provisions that apply.

## Personal circumstances

After the death of the parents the personal circumstances of their child depend upon the following factors, none of which should be considered in isolation:

    (a) the nature and degree of the disability;
    (b) the availability of personal carers or care provision;
    (c) the funding available, whether in the form of private provision, state benefits or local authority support.

## Categories of care

Depending upon the above factors, the circumstances of the child are likely to fall within one of the following categories:

- continue to live with and be cared for by another member of the family or a friend, in their own home;
- live in his own home with some degree of supervision by social services or members of the family;

- provided with a basic income and left to cope as best possible with no, or only limited, supervision;
- live in an ordinary house set up for and shared with other disabled people supervised by social services (social work);
- live in a hostel administered by social services (social work);
- looked after in a local authority residential care home;
- looked after in a residential care home run by a charity but charging fees on a regular basis;
- looked after in a private residential care home charging fees on a commercial basis;
- in need of full time nursing care in hospital.

## Changes in circumstances

No matter how firm the future intentions or arrangements may be, caution must still be exercised, and in appropriate cases some flexibility built in to the financial provision, because the child's circumstances may change. If the providing parent dies while the child is still young (and many mentally handicapped children are born to older parents) the trusts set up under a Will may last for 60 or more years.

### Local authority care

If the child is already living in a local authority funded home, it may not be assumed that this will continue for the child's life, because funding arrangements may change or social policy may result in the child being moved into the community - a change which may in the particular circumstances be for the better or for the worse but will inevitably affect funding arrangements.

### Family care

The testator (being the providing parent) may be adamant that a member of the family will continue to look after the child after the parent's death and may wish to make financial provision on this basis. There is no certainty that a member of the family will always be available to provide a home and care, and should this arrangement fail or cease a different type of financial provision would then be appropriate.

## Financial arrangements

When considering what income will be available all potential sources must be taken into account though these may change from time to time. Whatever the circumstances the child is unlikely to make sufficient money to live independently without some supplement, and this will be provided in the form of state benefits and local authority provision perhaps topped up by private funding from the family (if any).[1] The problem is balancing the forms of supplement and trying to ensure that any private funding does not result in an equivalent reduction in state benefits or contribution towards the cost of local authority provision.

---

1    The state and local authority benefits available are considered in Chap.8.

*Trust provision*
The child will probably be unable to handle money other than in small amounts, so some form of trust will be required in respect of provision made following the death of the parents and if by default or error (*e.g.* under the Will of a relative) capital is left to the child absolutely it will be necessary in England and Wales for a Receiver to be appointed and supervised by the Court of Protection, and in Scotland for a curator bonis to be appointed. Both of these procedures entail a complication and an expense that may be best avoided, although there are contrary views on this.[2]

## THE MEANS TESTS

The rules in relation to means-testing change at frequent intervals, yet a Will operates from a future date and any trust provision is likely to be in existence for many years. It is therefore necessary to make such provision taking into account general principles of means-testing, both past and present, lest there be a return to former approaches.

### The past regime

Until the introduction of Income Support additional state funding was provided either by Supplementary Benefit or by the local authority. The means tests that applied were as follows:

*Supplementary Benefit*
- Income resources (including the right to receive income from a trust) were taken into account in full and reduced by an equivalent amount the benefit otherwise payable.
- If capital resources exceeded a cut-off limit (excluding a home and personal possessions) benefit was not payable so capital had to be resorted to until reduced below that limit.

The problem for parents of a mentally handicapped child was that Commissioners Decisions held that:

- any person who may receive benefits under a trust, even under a power, was treated as having an appropriate share in the trust capital according to the purpose as well as the terms of the trust - a *notional* capital resource. A discretionary beneficiary was thus treated as entitled to a substantial part of the Trust Fund "having regard to the real probabilities" under the trust even if there were other beneficiaries[3];

- a life tenant had a capital resource (the value of the right to future income, though this was disregarded) as well as an income resource (the income itself) but a protective life interest without a discretionary power to advance capital[4] was valueless so only treated as an income resource.

Thus whilst a life interest was not treated as a capital resource, and

---

2   See Chap.10A (England and Wales) and Chap.10B (Scotland).
3   *R(SB)25/83*.
4   Or a life interest subject to an overriding power to advance capital only to other beneficiaries. In Scotland, the liferenter under an alimentary liferent was in the same position, for this purpose, as an English life tenant under a protective life interest.

a protective life interest was safe in that respect, any power to advance capital to or for the benefit of the beneficiary could result in the loss of benefit.

*Part III (Scotland, Part IV) Accommodation*
We have already considered the basis upon which local authorities could assess individuals provided with residential care.[5] Few authorities applied the guidelines rigidly but they posed a threat because they allowed for assessments based upon *notional* capital as explained above.

## The present regime.

From April 1988 Supplementary Benefit was replaced by Income Support but other sources of funding remained largely unchanged.

*Income Support*
The Income Support (General) Regulations 1987 deal with the eligibility of claimants to this new means-tested welfare benefit and define the extent to which resources are taken into account. The capital cut-off limit was initially £6,000 and has since been increased to £8,000 but for every £250 of capital above £3,000 a weekly income of £1 is assumed (an effective capital levy of over 20 per cent. per annum which is best avoided).

There are definitions of *notional income* and *notional capital* [6] but these are far less all-embracing than before. In particular there is an express exclusion of "discretionary trusts" and although this expression is not defined, the Minister of State for Social Security and the Disabled confirmed by letter that account will only be had of income or capital actually received from a discretionary trust.[7] Payments of a voluntary nature by other persons to third parties (*e.g.* a shop) will only be treated as notional income or capital if in payment of an expense which the benefit is normally meant to cover (specifically food, fuel, clothing and housing costs). There is a disregard of £10 per week on payments of income (*i.e.* at regular intervals) from a charitable or voluntary source and any payments not at regular intervals from such a source are treated as capital and taken into account accordingly. Payments made by trustees in the exercise of a discretionary power do not come within these provisions but are taken into account as income or capital depending upon how they are made. Topping-up is allowed where the fees charged by a residential or nursing home exceed the maxima set out in the Regulations[8] but this would only appear to apply to voluntary payments made specifically for that purpose

---

5     See Chap.8, Part II. The last but one set of Supplementary Benefit regulations was retained for local authority assessments, hence the capital cut off limit remained at £1,250 for local authority assessments when it was higher for state benefits.

6     Regs.42 and 51 respectively.

7     There has been discussion amongst lawyers as to whether a "discretionary trust" includes a mere discretionary power.

8     Sched.9, para.30(*d*).

and not to payments from a discretionary trust which, if made, become the taxable income of ~~the beneficiary and~~ may be assessed as such for Income Support.

*Part III (Scotland, Part IV) Accommodation*
There was no change in financial assessments by local authorities for residential care, so these in theory continue on the basis of the earlier Supplementary Benefit regulations. If discretionary trustees pay a reasonable sum to a dependent beneficiary out of income the local authority may accept this and not seek to assess the trust capital. The appeal procedure for Income Support claims is not available for local authority assessments and there is a danger that withholding services may be used as the ultimate sanction to secure contributions towards the cost whether or not such contributions are legally enforceable.

## The future regime.

Under Community Care policies from April 1983 the extra cost of residential care or care in the community, above an income level to which all severely disabled people will be entitled from state benefits, is to be funded by local authorities. There will be an assessment of the care needs of the individual and, independently of this, the authority should assess ability to pay for or contribute towards the cost of the services needed. A new basis of means assessment will be introduced and it has been recommended that this be the same as for Income Support, but there may not be an independent appeal procedure. Of course, the Income Support rules may themselves change, either at that stage or in the future, to incorporate notional capital or notional income provisions.

## Hospital care

Where a person is looked after in hospital under the NHS all basic needs are provided for and there may be little opportunity to spend even small amounts of pocket money. No means-testing applies, though most state benefits cease to be payable after an initial period. Financial provision should be discretionary in these circumstances otherwise there is a danger of a substantial fund of unspent income building up in the hands of the individual which may make it necessary to apply for the appointment of a Receiver or curator bonis, and also affect entitlement to means-tested funding or support in the event of discharge from hospital.

## CONCLUSIONS

Parents wishing to make financial provision for their disabled child are discouraged from making provision for fear that this will be of no long term benefit to their child and simply result in the withholding of benefits or charges for services. It remains desirable in many cases to avoid giving the child a legal entitlement to income, but the risk that any power to advance capital could result in a part of the trust fund being treated as a notional capital resource may no longer be a problem with Income Support. The obvious solution of a discretionary trust of income and capital may again be a reality, but caution should be exercised because:

(a) capital assessment still applies for persons looked after in local authority homes and there could be a tightening up in the operation of the rules relating to notional capital;

(b) the change to local authority funding of persons in private residential care homes with uncertain means-testing implications must be taken into account;

(c) even if residential care is not required, care in the community is not a cheap option and local authorities which are responsible for providing most of the services are increasingly imposing charges;

(d) it cannot be anticipated how Community Care will operate in practice and regulations will be amended from time to time to cover deficiencies identified by the government of the day. Further means-tests or financial assessments may be introduced, including the rules for notional resources.

## Objectives

The child will usually be dependent to a greater or lesser extent upon the provision of services by the local authority whether these be in the form of residential care, day care, regular supervision or other means of support. The care package should be on the basis of an assessment of needs carried out independently of funding, but the danger is that it will be influenced by both the ability of the authority to fund the services and of the individual (or family) to contribute towards the cost. In consequence when parents seek to make financial provision following their death, two potentially conflicting objectives may need to be achieved:

(i) they will not wish to make monies available to their child if this will merely result in the loss of or a substantial reduction in other funding;

(ii) they will be concerned about future standards of care provision and wish to give their trustees power to fill gaps.

It may be desirable for parents to include in any trust provision some power whereby the trustees may do a deal with the local authority or other care providers when this would be in the best interests of their child. Any such power may of itself make the trust fund vulnerable to means-testing, so where substantial funds are available the power should not relate to the entire fund and it may be wise to set up more than one trust fund, each on a different basis. Whilst parents will be reluctant to leave the child's future entirely in the hands of the local authority, they will be equally reluctant to make their own financial provision dependent upon the exercise of discretion by the trustees. But where there is likely to be heavy reliance upon state or local authority funding or support all income or capital to which the child is legally entitled will be taken into account in any system of means-testing. It is necessary to ascertain the relative priority to the parents of these conflicting objectives before their Wills can be prepared, as it will not usually be possible to achieve them all.

# PART II - STATE OR TAX BENEFITS?

*Preliminary*

When preparing a Trust (whether by Will or lifetime settlement) it is appropriate to consider principles of tax planning. Lawyers experienced in this field will devise their own trusts which take into account the desire to preserve state and local authority funding whilst at the same time being tax effective. Tax planning is beyond the scope of a book, but there are two statutory tax concessions intended to be for the benefit of disabled persons so it is necessary to consider these. There is a danger that when drafting a trust practitioners may be so concerned to achieve the benefit of these tax concessions that they overlook the state benefits implications. We now consider whether it is possible to take advantage of the tax concessions for trusts for the disabled and still avoid the loss of state benefits.

## TAX CONCESSIONS

### Inheritance Tax

There are provisions whereby trusts may be created for disabled persons which have in regard to Inheritance Tax, to a large extent, the flexibility of discretionary trusts but the tax consequences of life interest trusts.[9] A lifetime transfer into such a trust will be a potentially exempt one and in all cases the disabled person will be treated as having an interest in possession, so that there are no ten yearly charges though there will be a charge on the death of the disabled person. These provisions apply in relation to property held on trusts:

(a) under which, during the life of a disabled person, no interest in possession in the settled property subsists, and
(b) which secure that not less than half of the settled property which is applied during his life is applied for his benefit.

Thus restrictions are imposed on the potential use of the settled property (which is believed to mean the capital and not the income), but there are none on the use of income. Although the trust must provide that half of the capital that is applied during the life of the disabled person must be for his benefit, there is no requirement that any capital must actually be applied. It is specifically provided that the existence of the powers conferred on the trustees in England by Trustee Act 1925, section 32 do not take a trust outside the dispensation.[10]

---

9 Inheritance Tax Act 1984, ss.3A(1)(3) and 89.
10 It is not clear whether these powers may be widened in the usual way. In Scotland, a liferenter with an alimentary liferent has no interest in possession.

*Disabled persons*

A disabled person is defined as a person who, when the property was transferred into the settlement (the date of death in the case of a Will), was:

(a) incapable, by reason of mental disorder within the meaning of the Mental Health Act 1983 (in Scotland, the Mental Health (Scotland) Act 1984), of administering his property or managing his affairs;

(b) in receipt of an attendance allowance under Social Security Act 1975, s.35; or

(c) in receipt of a disability living allowance under Social Security Act 1975, s.37ZA by virtue of entitlement to the care component at the highest or middle rate.

Most mentally disabled beneficiaries would qualify through entitlement to Disability Living Allowance, but this is usually withdrawn from persons in residential care homes so they must qualify (and usually will) as a mentally disordered person.

## Capital Gains Tax

Further provisions allow certain trusts for the disabled to enjoy in relation to CGT the full annual exemption available to individuals instead of the reduced exemption normally available to trustees (and without loss of the disabled person's own allowance, which is still available for any property which he may have).[11] These provisions apply in any year of assessment:

"during the whole or part of which settled property is held on trusts which secure that, during the lifetime of a mentally disabled person or a person in receipt of attendance allowance or of a disability living allowance by virtue of entitlement to the care component at the highest or middle rate -
(a) not less than half of the property which is applied is applied for the benefit of that person, and
(b) that person is entitled to not less than half of the income arising from the property, or no such income may be applied for .... any other person."

Trusts are not disqualified by the existence of the statutory power of advancement[12] or the use of protective trusts.[13] It appears that the alternatives in (b) above are interchangeable, so that a trust will be eligible if it requires the income to be either used for the disabled person or accumulated during the first 21 years, and thereafter used as to half at least for the disabled person and as to the rest for other people.

The definition of disabled person is the same as for Inheritance Tax but it appears that this definition must be fulfilled during the whole or part of the year of assessment so the concession could conceivably be lost during the subsistence of the trust.[14]

---

11 Taxation of Chargeable Gains Act 1992, Sched.1, para.1 (formerly Capital Gains Tax Act 1979, s.5 and Sched.1, para.5).

12 Trustee Act 1925, s.32. It is not clear whether this power may be widened.

13 Trustee Act 1925, s.33. The conditions must then be fulfilled not "during the person's lifetime", but "for the period during which the income is held on trust for the person". In Scotland, reference to alimentary liferent.

14 Unlike the position for Inheritance Tax where it is sufficient if the beneficiary qualifies when the trust is created.

## Comparing the concessions

The Capital Gains Tax concession requires the disabled person to have an interest in possession in at least half of the trust fund whereas the existence of such an interest breaches the Inheritance Tax requirements, so it seems that no trust can be eligible for both concessions! It is true that income could be accumulated for up to 21 years under the former concession, but an interest in possession would have to arise (in at least half the trust property) after that, and the prospect of this means that the trust would not be one "under which, during the lifetime of a disabled person, no interest in possession ... subsists".

## CONCLUSIONS

Neither of the tax concessions will be available unless the disabled person has some minimum entitlement to capital compared with the other beneficiaries; he must receive at least half of any capital that is applied. This conflicts with the general principle in regard to the preservation of welfare benefits that a power to advance capital is best avoided. Previously published precedents for Wills providing for a disabled beneficiary have concentrated on achieving these tax concessions and must have misled unwary solicitors into the trap of depriving the beneficiary of valuable state benefits.

### Alternatives

In the case of trusts under a Will the effect of the Inheritance Tax concession is to avoid the 10 yearly charge which would apply to a discretionary trust whilst retaining some control over capital and income, but the same result may be achieved by giving the beneficiary a life interest with an overriding power to apply capital in various ways. If half of any capital applied must be applied for this beneficiary the Capital Gains Tax concession will also apply, but this benefit may be outweighed by the welfare benefit risks. There would also be the advantage of avoiding the additional rate tax on income and capital gains. However, because the beneficiary would have an income entitlement this type of trust would only be suitable for a beneficiary who was, and was likely to remain, self-reliant.

### Summary

It may be that the inclusion of a discretionary power to advance capital will not affect a claim to Income Support at present, but the extent to which such power can or will be taken into account by local authorities is not known. Any actual advancement of capital will in many cases affect state funding and may create assets that the beneficiary cannot cope with. Any income received from the trust will be treated as a resource and result in an equivalent reduction in state funding. This may be alleviated initially by accumulating the income and later by investing for capital appreciation, and if the Income Support top-up is small and no local authority funding is involved (the situation of the self-reliant beneficiary) the trust income may exceed that which the beneficiary would otherwise have received thereby producing a real benefit. The conclusion must be that, except in the case of the self-reliant beneficiary not heavily dependent on state funding, the benefit of the tax concessions is outweighed by the burdens and it is still a question of state benefits **or** tax benefits.

# PART III - A STRATEGY

*Preliminary*

We have considered the pitfalls involved in making financial provision for a mentally handicapped beneficiary, and indicated the extent to which the desire to achieve tax planning may conflict with the need to avoid the loss of means-tested state funding. We now set out a strategy for making a Will, but it should be explained to the testator that there is no guaranteed solution to the problem and that provision can only be made on the basis of the best assessment as to what may happen in the future.

## INSTRUCTIONS

### Information required

When a Testator desires to make financial provision for a mentally handicapped child it is necessary to ascertain, in addition to the usual information about the testator, the estate and other members of the family, the following specific information about such child:
- name and date of birth;
- nature and degree of handicap, prognosis and likely life expectancy;
- present residence and arrangements for care, training and occupation, and any change that may arise in the foreseeable future or on the death of the testator;
- present funding arrangements and any alteration that may arise, *e.g.* when parents or other carers are no longer able to provide personal care;
- present capital and income of child and any other financial provision made or likely to be made;
- has a receiver or curator bonis been appointed, or is there (in England) a registered Enduring Power of Attorney or (in Scotland) a Power of Attorney executed after December 31, 1990, which will continue in force regardless of capacity;
- the guardian, if still an infant (in Scotland, under 16);
- any help likely to be provided by charitable organisations.

*Funds Available*

It is essential to know the potential size of the testator's estate so as to assess the amount that could be available for the benefit of the handicapped child. Even though the testator may have little money to spend during lifetime the estate could exceed £50,000 if a house is included or there are life assurance policies or entitlements under a pension fund. In the absence of other children the entire amount is likely to be available for the child.

*Other provision*

Any resources already available to the child and any provision likely to be made by others should be taken into account. There is always the danger that another relative may inadvertently leave money directly to the child thereby creating the problems that the parent is seeking to avoid. A testator should be advised to mention to relatives who might otherwise include the child in their Will that there are special problems. It is common for grandparents and aunts and uncles without children to provide that any money left to a parent who predeceases shall pass to the issue, and the solicitor would not then be aware of the mental handicap. One hesitates to suggest that other relatives should make a Will of the type being considered in this chapter, so it may be desirable for the parent to create a lifetime settlement on similar lines in which event other testators could leave money intended for the child to the trustees of that settlement upon the trusts thereof.

## Trustees

The executors are usually destined to be the first trustees of any trust fund created under a Will, although it is possible to appoint different trustees. It is prudent to ascertain that the persons being appointed are willing to act. A trustee must have attained legal majority at the time of appointment, which in the case of a Will is the date of death.[15] A parent need not be discouraged from appointing a child who has not at the time attained the age of 18 but will do so shortly and is expected to have sufficient maturity to cope with the responsibilities involved.

There should be at least two trustees, though two (or three) may be the optimum number, and in England and Wales there may not be more than four. Usually the present trustees will have power to appoint new or additional trustees and thereby to appoint their successors,[16] but the testator may nominate a person in the Will to have this power.

*Choice*

An enduring trust will usually be required so care should be taken over the choice of trustees. Collectively they should be in close contact with the persons caring for the child so as to be aware of any special needs but also have the ability to administer the trust and cope with the investment and tax implications. A solicitor or accountant may be a suitable trustee jointly with a concerned

---

15 In Scotland it is technically possible, but inadvisable, to appoint a 16 or 17-year old, but not a person under 16. For a summary of the disadvantages of appointing a minor, see *Stair Memorial Encyclopaedia*, Volume 24, pp.86 and 87.

16 This is the statutory power under Trustee Act 1925, s.36.

member of the family.[17] Older testators should appoint (or at least
include) executors and trustees who are younger than them and
therefore more likely to survive.

*Corporate trustees*
Banks and some other bodies accept appointment on their
published terms, but they charge fees which are based upon a
percentage of the value of the estate and these are usually more
than a solicitor or accountant would charge. Many people consider
that corporate trustees are inflexible and lack the personal touch
that is so important in dealing with beneficiaries who have special
needs. An understanding solicitor who knows the family may be
more suitable, but to fill the vacuum that so often exists for
parents in this situation MENCAP offers in England and Wales a
service through National Trustees for the Mentally Handicapped
Limited, and the Scottish Society for the Mentally Handicapped
offers the SSMH Trustee Service.

## Guardians

Where the child or any other children are infants (in Scotland,
under 16) the Will should include the appointment of guardians on
the death of the surviving parent[18] if a suitable person or persons
can be nominated at that stage. The willingness of the proposed
guardian to take on this responsibility should first be ascertained.
English law does not permit the appointment of guardians in
respect of an adult, but there are proposals for adult guardianship
in the case of persons who are incapable of making informed
decisions so it would do no harm to appoint persons to act as
guardians of a mentally handicapped adult child "in so far as the
law allows". In Scotland, one or more tutors-dative may be
appointed to act as personal guardians, and it may be wise to
include in the appointment a younger person who would continue
to act after the deaths of the parents.

## The beneficiary

The terms of the trust will depend upon whether the child is, or is
likely to be, largely self-reliant or utterly dependent upon the care
of others, though many potential beneficiaries tend to fall between
these extremes. It must be remembered that there are varying
degrees of handicap and the child's future is dictated as much by
his own abilities (or lack of them) as by the availability of
relatives or friends able and willing to assume the responsibilities
of caring.

---

17   There may be advantages in appointing a solicitor trustee, because any fees
     charged can be challenged (by means of a remuneration certificate in
     England) whereas this procedure is not available in the case of other
     professionals.
18   Or immediately on the death of the testator if the parents are in dispute. In
     England the provisions of the Children Act 1989 in regard to parental
     responsibility should be taken into account.

*The self-reliant beneficiary*

If the child is able to live in an ordinary household (even though some degree of supervision may be required) the entitlement to means-tested social security benefits may be small so provision of a capital nature and a private income may be beneficial. The child may be better off financially and more independent by being a beneficiary under a Trust Fund. A mentally handicapped person living with parents or another member of the family would normally come within this category because no exceptional regular expense is involved, but caution must be exercised because there may be a charge for community care facilities.

> *Conclusion*:  if the child is likely to remain self-reliant for a lifetime there is no reason why the parents should not set up a Trust Fund specifically for the benefit of the child with power to apply capital for the child's benefit. A protective trust (alimentary liferent in Scotland) is favoured, with power to re-settle in case of a change of circumstances.

*The dependent beneficiary*

Many mentally handicapped people live in residential care homes because this is the most suitable environment or they cannot live with family and are not capable of living in their own home with limited supervision. The fees are considerably in excess of normal entitlement to non-means-tested benefits and any personal capital resources must be exhausted before the deficiency in income resources is made up by Income Support or the Local Authority.

> *Conclusion*: if the child is or is likely to become within this category great care must be taken as to the financial provision that is made.

## OPTIONS

### Interest of spouse

Where both parents are still alive they will usually wish to make mirror-image Wills whereby the residue of the estate is left to the other of them and on the death of the survivor the combined estate passes to the children.[19] It is at this stage that special trusts will arise. There are Inheritance Tax advantages in leaving monies to the children on the first death (thereby taking advantage of the nil rate band) if the combined estates are likely to be over the exempt limit, but not all parents wish to do this. The spouse's inheritance may be made dependent on survivorship by 28 days to cover death in a common accident. In view of the high incidence of divorce amongst parents of a disabled child, in England care may be needed in drafting their Wills to deal with the implications of Wills Act 1837, section 18A.[20] This provides that where a married

---

19  In Scotland this raises the issue of the children's legal rights, see Part IVB.

20  This section was added by Administration of Justice Act 1982, s.18(2). This is not the position in Scotland, though the Scottish Law Commission has recommended change.

testator has made a Will and subsequently the marriage is dissolved, the Will is to take effect (unless a contrary intention appears therein) as if any appointment of the former spouse as an executor or trustee had been omitted and "any devise or bequest to the former spouse shall lapse". It has been held[21] that this shall not be equated with lapse by reason of prior death, so the alternative provisions in the event of the spouse predeceasing may not take effect unless the wording thereof is extended, and an intestacy could result which in the present context would be disastrous. The alternative provisions, which will usually include a trust, should be expressed so as to operate following a divorce.

## Basic options

We are concerned here with the stage at which a parent chooses to leave money to a child or children and the manner in which this may be done where there is a disabled child. The following options are available and should be considered, although the most suitable provision will usually be a combination of these tailor-made to suit the best assessment that can be made of the child's future needs:

- leave the estate, or desired share, to the child absolutely and let the law take its course - this is highly undesirable but would be the effect of not making a Will at all or of making a Will without appropriate advice;
- leave everything to the other child or children in the hope that they will support as necessary the disabled child. Whilst this strategy has in the past been adopted by many parents, there are serious risks, not least being inheritance claims[22] and financial collapse, divorce or death of the other child;
- leave the child a life interest (liferent) in an appropriate share of the estate - *see below*;
- create a discretionary trust of income and/or capital - *see below*;
- create a charitable trust of capital and income, limited to charities with specific objectives - *see below*;
- leave a sum to charity on one of the special schemes that are available - *see below*.

## Balancing the children

Parents must decide the amount of money, or the share of the estate, that is to be allocated for the disabled child whether this is to be retained in trust or otherwise disposed of. In many cases parents consider that the only fair course is to divide the estate

---

21   *Re Sinclair, Lloyds Bank Plc* v. *Imperial Cancer Research Fund* [1985] 1 All ER 1066, CA.

22   In England and Wales, claims under Inheritance (Provision for Family and Dependants) Act 1975 (see Part IVA) and in Scotland, a legal rights claim (see Part IVB). If a Will is made on this basis the solicitor should explain the risks and keep a record that he has done so, because failing this he may be open to criticism if substantial costs are incurred in such a claim.

into as many shares as there are children, having in mind that the disability must be taken into account in deciding how best to dispose of the equal share to which the disabled child would otherwise be absolutely entitled. Some parents will express the view that the needs of the disabled child are greater than those of the other children who are well able to provide for themselves, and it may be desirable to remind them of the limitations upon their ability to make meaningful provision for that child. Other parents will state that their normal children have been deprived of so much by reason of the need to satisfy the demands of the disabled child that they should be compensated by receiving a greater share of the estate. Clearly the wishes of the parents will decide the matter, but they are entitled to receive comprehensive advice before they give final instructions.

## TRUST PROVISION

In most cases provision by way of a trust will be assumed, and whether this be a discretionary trust or a life interest will largely depend upon the extent to which the beneficiary is and is likely to remain self-reliant. We now consider the different trust options.

## Life interest *(liferent)*

The simplest form of trust provision is a life interest (in Scotland, a liferent) whereby the disabled beneficiary is entitled to receive the income from the trust investments for life with capital passing to other beneficiaries thereafter. We have already seen why it may not be wise to give such beneficiary an entitlement to income, though one way round this may be to invest the capital so that it does not produce an income or only produces a very small income.[23] It is the duty of trustees when adopting an investment policy to balance the interests of life tenant and those ultimately entitled to capital, so it may be desirable to expressly exclude this duty and give the trustees a complete discretion in this respect.

### *Protective trust (alimentary liferent)*
This is a variation of a life interest which in its simplest form is in England recognised by statute.[24] It was intended to be used in the case of an improvident beneficiary who is given a life interest but prevented from disposing of the capital value of the future right to receive the income.[25] A discretionary trust is substituted for the life interest if any situation arises whereby the beneficiary may be deprived of the future right to receive the income. It is attractive in the case of a disabled beneficiary who is unlikely to be dependent on substantial means-tested funding.

---

[23] This strategy will not work if a capital assessment can be made.
[24] Trustee Act 1925, s.33.
[25] In Scotland, a similar effect is achieved by creating an alimentary liferent: where trustees are directed to pay income to the beneficiary for life as a strictly alimentary provision, the liferent is neither assignable nor liable to the diligence of creditors.

*Power to advance capital*
Power is sometimes given to the trustees to advance capital to the income beneficiary and this may be general in its terms or restricted to particular circumstances. We have already seen how such a power may make the capital of the trust fund vulnerable to means-testing, and it should be considered whether it would really be necessary or desirable to exercise the power in favour of a severely disabled beneficiary having in mind that the same result may be achieved by other means[26] and the ownership of a capital asset by the beneficiary may create further problems.[27] Consideration may be given to the inclusion of power to advance capital to the beneficiary in certain restricted circumstances only.

*Accumulation of income*
Rather than pay all the income to the beneficiaries, an overriding power may be included for the trustees in their discretion to accumulate income and either add it to the capital or treat it as income in a later year. Any such power must by law be limited to a maximum period of 21 years, and additional income tax liabilities arise which are mentioned in Part V below.

*Payment of income to others*
There is a further variation whereby the trustees instead of paying the whole income to the person with a life interest, may be given power to pay some or all of it to other persons. This presents a trap for the unwary, because the revenue treat such trust as one under which there is no life interest in possession, so it will have all the tax disadvantages of a discretionary trust. Although a flexible life interest of this nature may appear attractive to parents because it directs attention to the disabled child, this may not be desirable from the point of view of means-testing and the ordinary form of discretionary trust is to be preferred. On the other hand, it may reduce the risk of an inheritance or legal rights claim.[28]

*Termination*
In order to retain flexibility in case there is a change of circumstances or things go wrong, power may be given to the trustees to terminate the trust by advancing the capital to other persons or re-settling upon different trusts.

## Discretionary trust

In those cases where the disabled beneficiary is, or is likely to be, heavily dependent upon means-tested funding or support a discretionary trust is more likely to be appropriate. The tax disadvantages of this type of trust in which there is no interest in

---

26  A house or chattel may be acquired as a trust asset and made available to the beneficiary.

27  It may make it necessary to apply to the Court of Protection for the appointment of a Receiver (Chap.10A) or in Scotland to apply to the appropriate court for appointment of a curator bonis (Chap.10B).

28  See Part IVA for a consideration of this topic.

possession are summarised in Part V of this chapter.

*Period*
It will be desired to create a trust which will last for the life of the disabled beneficiary and the parent may wish to express the trust by reference to that life. As this draws attention to the discretionary fund as being intended for the benefit of that person it may be desirable to make the trust continue for some other period which is likely to exceed the life of the beneficiary.[29] This may be counter-productive in the event of an inheritance claim.

*Income*
An unfettered discretion to distribute the income between a wide class of beneficiaries which includes the disabled child will usually be given to the trustees, coupled with power to accumulate income for as long as the law allows. The class of potential beneficiaries should be as wide as possible, and where there are few living members of the family or other persons whom the testator wishes to include, it may be widened by adding charities (perhaps limited to those concerned with mental handicap). The testator may express wishes as to how the discretion should be exercised in a letter addressed to the trustees which they will refer to for guidance but need not disclose to others.[30]

*Capital*
There may also be discretionary powers for the trustees to pay capital from time to time to members of the class of income beneficiaries or a different class, but it will often be wise to exclude the disabled beneficiary from any such power for the reasons already indicated.

*Tax concessions*
Some of the tax disadvantages of this type of trust may be avoided if the disabled beneficiary is given a minimum entitlement to capital or income as outlined in Part II of this chapter. The price to pay may be vulnerability to loss of means-tested funding.

*Charities*
Although in the absence of other persons it may be necessary to include charities as potential beneficiaries under a discretionary trust, and there may be other advantages in doing so, the tax exemption for money left to charity will not be available. Where there is sufficient money to justify separate funds, consideration should be given to an exclusively charitable trust.

---

29  Any fixed period may not exceed 80 years, though this will be sufficient unless the child is young. The Settlement adopted by MENCAP uses the device of making the discretionary trust continue until the expiration of 20 years after the death of the last survivor of the issue born before the date of the settlement of His Late Majesty King George V, but this confuses testators and a simpler formula may be preferred.

30  An example of such a letter is included in Appendix IIIA.

### The "wait and see" option

This is a variation which will not suit the parent who desires the appearance of certainty as to what will happen to the money but which is very useful in cases where it is not known what will happen to the disabled beneficiary (*e.g.* a young child). There are two possibilities:

(i)   separate Trust Funds are set up for the benefit of the child and charities, the trustees having power (within two years of death and subject to defined limits) to allocate the child's share between such Funds in the proportions they think fit with specified allocation in default of exercise of that power;

*Advantages:* a once and for all flexibility after death.

(ii)  the trustees are given power within defined limits to settle the child's share on such trusts as they deem appropriate. Income may be accumulated or paid to the child (or other children) in the meanwhile and a power to advance capital may be included;

*Advantages:* the circumstances of the child and effect on state benefits or local authority funding may be taken into account when the trustees exercise their discretion; the tax exemption may be available for money allocated to a charitable trust within two years (though not initially).[31]

### *Tax planning*

Since 1975 a change in the distribution of an estate within two years of death by the exercise of powers given to the executors or under a family arrangement may, in certain circumstances, be treated as having been included in the original Will for Inheritance Tax and Capital Gains Tax purposes. "Two-year" discretionary trusts have become a popular option. If such a trust is established by Will, any distributions or appointments from the trust within two years of death will be treated for tax purposes as a disposition under the Will of the testator occurring on death though full tax (except on instalment option property) will have been payable initially unless the executors exercise their powers before applying for probate or confirmation.[32]

Another form of post-death tax planning is a family arrangement whereby within two years of death all beneficiaries agree to vary the terms of the Will and redistribute the estate, or part of it. The changed distribution will be treated as having been made on the death by the Will if the executors and beneficiaries so elect.[33] The government initially sought to revoke this provision in the Finance

---

31   Doubt has been expressed as to whether exemption can be claimed on any money allocated to a charity, because the provision only effectively back-dates the transfer where the distribution would have been chargeable to inheritance tax, and a distribution to a charity would be exempt.

32   The provision is now found in Inheritance Tax Act 1984, s.144(1).

33   Inheritance Tax Act 1984, s.142. A separate election is required for Capital Gains Tax purposes.

Bill 1989, and has indicated an intention to examine the position more closely in the future. In any event, this provision may not be available where there is an infant, unborn or mentally incapacitated beneficiary who cannot enter into the Deed of Family Arrangement.[34]

## A "Personal Fund"

Whilst the state may of necessity provide for the essential needs of a disabled child following the death of the parents there will be little money available for those extras which parents would normally provide as a matter of course by way of gift (*e.g.* a modern wheelchair, personal radio, television, better clothes). It may be hoped that brothers or sisters would be attentive to such needs especially if left an enhanced share in the estate with that wish being expressed, but there is no certainty of this and parents with only the one disabled child do not have this option. Normally these needs would be dealt with by applying a power to advance capital, but the inclusion of such a power could result in the withdrawal of means-tested funding. Thus it may be desirable to include in the Will a legacy to the child of such amount as will not cause the child's resources to exceed the relevant capital limit (presently £3,000 if only Income Support is payable but £1,250 if a local authority home or sponsorship is involved).

### Small Trust Fund

As the child would not be able to cope with this money it will be necessary to leave the sum to trustees, who need not be the general trustees of the Will, but unlike other provision this may be on the widest possible trusts for the benefit of the child. The trustees may then hand over cash (either capital or income) in such amounts as the child can cope with, or expend the fund from time to time on items needed by or for the benefit of the child.

## Charitable trusts

It may be worthwhile to create a private wholly charitable trust if the child is being (or is likely to be) cared for in a residential care home administered by a charity or otherwise supported or helped by charities. It is tempting simply to include charities in the general class of beneficiaries under a discretionary trust, and this may be done as well especially when there are few potential beneficiaries in the family, but exemption from Inheritance Tax will not then be available so the creation initially of separate Trust Funds is preferable (perhaps using the "wait and see" option described above to decide how much is allocated to each fund).

### Advantages:
(a) freedom from capital and income taxation;
(b) ability to benefit any charity for the time being supporting

---

34  In England, a receiver could be appointed to enter into the deed on behalf of a mentally incapacitated adult, and in Scotland a tutor-dative can be appointed with authority to execute such a Deed, *Queen*, 1992 (unreported).

the child;
(c) no loss of state or local authority funding;
(d) the existence of the Fund may be a factor in obtaining a place for the child in a home run by a charity[35];
(e) the ability of the trustees when winding up the trust to benefit those charities which have done most for the child.

*Disadvantages:*
(a) trust money cannot be used for the direct benefit of the child;
(b) the local authority may disapprove of this strategy and refrain from providing adequate support for the child.[36]

### Tax planning

If the entire estate is left to charity there will be no liability to Inheritance Tax. If only part of the estate is left to charity there will be no tax on that part, and the tax exemption must accrue for the benefit of the charity and not for the other beneficiaries.[37] Thus where an estate of £400,000 is left equally to charity and relatives, tax will only be charged on one-half of the estate and this should be deducted from the relatives share leaving the charity with the full £200,000; the net estate is not divided equally.

### Charities Aid Foundation (CAF)

Interesting possibilities arise in regard to the use of Personal Charitable Trusts which are available through CAF, and these are considered below under the heading Settlements.

## Schemes by charities

Several charities have devised special schemes and parents may wish to consider those available from charities with whom they are in contact. This may be a charity concerned with a particular type of handicap, or one that runs a residential care home. A parent whose child is already living in such a care home may contemplate leaving money to that home especially if this provides added security for the child or there is the prospect of some indirect benefit to the child, but the home may close, or cease to be suitable, so rather than make an outright gift it may be preferred to create a charitable trust of the type proposed above. A more recent development is a Charitable Support Trust of the type mentioned below.

### MENCAP Visitors Service

One of the concerns of parents is who will monitor the care and welfare of their child, and to meet this need MENCAP established

---

35  It is still necessary to ensure that state funding is available (with local authority sponsorship) but the charity has the prospect of receiving fees and also donations.
36  It may then be useful if there is a separate Trust Fund which can be used for the benefit of the child thereby enabling the trustees to do a deal with the authority (*i.e.* give capital in return for sponsorship).
37  Inheritance Tax Act 1984, s.41.

the Visitors Service in 1963. It provides for the appointment of a personal visitor to the handicapped person (the beneficiary) on the death of both parents. The visitor visits the beneficiary at regular intervals, seeks to become a friend, remembers birthdays and perhaps organises outings and generally monitors his welfare. A report is made to MENCAP after each visit and if there are any problems the Trustees may authorise appropriate action to be taken. The Service is financed by contributions made by parents and others who are invited to nominate a handicapped person whom they would like to benefit. Contributions can be by life-time gift or under a Will.

## ADCARE Foundation

Adcare is a registered charity administered by MENCAP that provides funds for the care of people with a mental handicap. It holds a charitable fund available at the discretion of the Trustees for any person with a mental handicap who is in need of financial support. People who make donations are invited to name a potential beneficiary if they so wish, but must rely on the Trustees' integrity in fulfilling their moral obligations to potential beneficiaries, as no legally binding undertaking can be given. To do so would jeopardise charitable status and the beneficiary's position with regard to state benefits.

## Homes Foundation

This department of MENCAP aims to provide small, family-sized homes in ordinary houses in the community, where mentally handicapped adults can live as independently as possible. Parents who have continued to look after their child often wish to make an arrangement whereby the child may continue to live in the family home after their death, and in suitable circumstances they may leave their home to the Foundation to this intent. Not all homes are suitable, and arrangements must be made well in advance with a local management committee being formed. It is usually more realistic for parents to participate in a local scheme and arrange for their child to be accommodated in a home during their lifetime, leaving money or the value of their house to MENCAP by their Will in order to support the scheme. There can be no binding agreement that the child will be provided with a home for life in consideration of the gift.

## SSMH Homes

In Scotland, similar provision is made for persons who are severely and profoundly handicapped, but this does not include arrangements with families to bequeath homes.

## DRAFTING THE TRUST.

### Terminology

Care should be taken not to identify any trust fund too closely with the disabled child. In particular the temptation to define the Trust by reference to the child (e.g. "John's Trust Fund") should be avoided and it is preferable to set aside a specified share in the estate rather than "the share to which my handicapped child would have been entitled ...." The difference may be cosmetic from a legal stand-point but under the former Supplementary Benefit regulations it was necessary to *have regard to the real probabilities under the Trust* and the Will was likely to be read by a DSS adjudication officer and a Tribunal on appeal, and it may still be studied by the local authority. The Trust may be capable of being used entirely for the benefit of persons other than the disabled child and it may be necessary to emphasise this, but it is not so easy to do so if it is "John's Trust Fund".

## Trustees Powers.

It is important to include adequate discretionary powers for the trustees although it may be desirable to provide that some of the wider powers are not exercisable by a sole trustee. Under no circumstances should powers aimed at directly helping the disabled child extend to charitable trusts or they may lose charitable status.

### Advancement of capital

A controversial question is whether the trustees should be given power, with or without restrictions, to advance or appoint capital to the disabled beneficiary. The possibility of other funding being withheld because of the existence of such power has been explained above. There is a difference here between the person who is largely self-reliant but needs protecting against personal financial mismanagement and the more severely handicapped individual who will never be self-reliant. Large advancements of capital must be avoided in the case of the latter because the beneficiary would not be able to cope with the money or ownership of any asset purchased, and the advancement will of itself affect means-tested funding.

Regular payments of capital may enable the beneficiary to be provided initially with care which would not otherwise be available,[38] but the full cost then falls on the trust and there is no certainty that the local authority will continue to finance such care when the trust provision is exhausted. Nevertheless there will be some testators who feel that making their own money fully available is the only way of satisfying themselves that they have done the best that they can for their child, regardless of means-testing, and their wishes must be respected as long as they know the implications of what they are doing.

It may be helpful to ask in what circumstances the power would be likely to be exercised. If the child is in residential care, capital funding is only likely to be needed to provide extra items or facilities which the parents might have funded as a gift during their lifetime. If the trustees have suitably wide powers of

---

38   This should not be assumed because residential care homes will usually require local authority funding for fear that private funding runs out while they are still looking after the individual.

investment, and are relieved from personal liability for any loss in the event that they permit a beneficiary to have the use of an investment, the same objective can be achieved in other ways. Thus without any risk of means-testing they can purchase a colour television, personal stereo or wheelchair as a trust asset and let the beneficiary use this. The same approach may apply to a house, or a share in a house, which remains a trust asset ultimately passing to the residuary beneficiaries. Alternatively the trustees could exercise their discretion in favour of other beneficiaries who have provided items for the disabled beneficiary by way of gift.

### Limited power to advance capital

There may be scope for a limited power to advance capital to the disabled beneficiary. If the power can only be exercised in certain circumstances (*e.g.* if not in receipt of means-tested benefits) or for particular purposes (*e.g.* in respect of expenses not otherwise covered by public funding) it may not create vulnerability to trust capital being means-tested. Another possibility is to restrict the exercise of the power to part of the trust fund (*e.g.* accumulations of income, the amount of which can be controlled) or particular amounts (*e.g.* such sum as shall not for the time being cause a loss to the beneficiary of state or local authority funding). The trustees should have power to release or restrict the power.

### Special powers

It may be valuable to give the trustees discretionary power to[39]:

(a) pay capital to a charity (or other body) in pursuance of any scheme or plan which in the opinion of the trustees may provide a sufficient degree of security and protection for the child[40];

(b) invest in chattels (corporeal moveables);

(c) appropriate assets without consent;

(d) permit the child to have the use and enjoyment of a chattel without being liable to account for consequent loss;

(e) permit the child to occupy any house or flat held as a trust investment on any terms that they think fit whether alone or jointly with any other person;

(f) lend trust monies on any terms that they think fit;

(g) apply trust monies in or towards the cost of expenses which may be for the benefit of the child;

(h) claim and administer tax refunds in respect of trust income on behalf of the disabled beneficiary[41];

(i) transfer funds from one trust to another.

---

[39]  See the Precedents or Styles in Appendix IIIA or B for suggested wording.

[40]  The scope of this provision has not been fully explored, but it may perhaps be used by trustees to "do a deal" with a local authority to secure sponsorship in a residential care home, or compromise an inheritance claim.

[41]  Strictly speaking the Will cannot give this power, but if it states that in the absence of a receiver or attorney (curator bonis in Scotland) the beneficiary is "deemed to have authorised" the trustees to do this by accepting the income, the tax office may accept a repayment claim by a trustee.

## Personal interest

A family trustee may be personally affected by the manner in which the trustees exercise their discretionary powers, and special provision can be made to cover this. The trustee may be expressly authorised to join in the exercise of powers notwithstanding any personal interest,[42] and whilst it may be provided that there must be at least one other trustee who is not so involved this will not be practicable where all the trustees are members of the family. An alternative is to permit the trustee to leave the exercise of a power to the other trustees.

## Charging clause

In addition to the usual professional charging clause, the trustees should be authorised to reimburse themselves out of the trust in respect of the cost of periodically visiting and making enquiries as to the welfare of the disabled beneficiary, or of employing some suitable person to do so.

## Legacy to trustees

It can be an onerous task to be a trustee, especially where there is a dependent beneficiary. Professional trustees will be given an express power to charge for their services otherwise they would not accept the appointment, but it is considerate to leave a suitable legacy to any trustee who would not otherwise charge or be a beneficiary. In England and Wales, this may be expressed to be conditional upon proving the Will; in Scotland, upon the trustee accepting office.

## Funeral expenses

Parents are concerned to ensure that there is ultimately a sufficient sum available to provide a proper funeral and memorial for their disabled child without relying upon the goodwill of others, especially as state benefits would only cover basic costs. Any discretionary provision may cease on the child's death so the trustees' powers should be expressly extended to cover this expense, or the trust period extended for the purpose.

## A "side letter"

Testators should prepare and sign a suitable letter addressed to the trustees setting out their wishes and intentions in regard to any particular Trust Fund. Whilst this cannot be legally binding on the trustees it will be of great assistance to them when they consider exercising their powers especially if the original trustees have died and successors have been appointed who may not have known the parents. The existence of such a letter will also be of comfort to the parents, and may be of assistance if the Will setting up the trust is challenged under the Inheritance (Provision for Family and Dependants) Act 1975 or if a legal rights claim is contemplated.

---

42   This is not strictly necessary because there is nothing in general trust law to prevent a trustee from exercising a power in his own favour provided that the power is exercised in a fiduciary manner.

*Trust for the Child*
The letter in this case will:
- explain the reasons why the parent has chosen to restrict the extent to which the child may receive benefits;  and
- express the parent's hopes and wishes as to the future of the child and the manner in which the trust may assist or protect the child (and perhaps in default be used for the benefit of other children).

*Charitable Trust*
This letter will:
- indicate why the trust has been created;  and
- request the trustees to have regard when exercising their discretionary powers to any charities that have supported or helped their child, or may do so.

Suggested letters are included in Appendix IIIA which should be adapted to reflect the views of the parents and the circumstances of their child.

## SETTLEMENTS

### Uses

In suitable circumstances the creation of a lifetime settlement should be seriously considered. This would set up the desired trusts for the benefit of the disabled child and/or charities. Only a small amount of money need initially be invested in the settlement, with the option to credit further monies as and when appropriate.

*Advantages*
- the parent's Will may be kept simple (the share of the estate allocated to the disabled child being simply left to the trustees of the settlement upon the trusts thereof);
- other people (*e.g.* grandparents) wishing to support the child may be encouraged to leave money to the settlement rather than setting out trusts in their own Will;
- death in service benefits of a pension scheme, or other life assurance monies, may be paid into the settlement, thereby being held upon the desired trusts without passing directly to the child. These monies will then be immediately available, perhaps at a time of great need, without waiting for probate or confirmation;
- more than one lifetime settlement can be created if appropriate (*e.g.* a private wholly charitable trust and a separate trust containing funds which can be available to the child) and subsequent Wills can specify the proportion of the estate to go to each according to prevailing circumstances;
- an exclusively charitable settlement will benefit from tax exemptions (including exemption from Inheritance Tax on monies bequeathed or transferred thereto) and also provide the advantages outlined in this chapter.

*Disadvantages*
- additional cost of creating the settlement;
- further administration costs on an annual basis;
- loss of flexibility and difficulty of getting it right.[43]
- if successive sums of capital are paid into a discretionary settlement without regard to the timing (as could happen in the case of monies left by Will) an unexpected liability to inheritance tax could arise by reason of the 10 yearly charge.

## Special settlements

*MENCAP (England and Wales)*
A standard settlement is offered which may be used by parents who have no-one else suitable to administer their financial affairs following death. National Trustees for the Mentally Handicapped Limited (NTMH), a wholly-owned subsidiary of MENCAP, acts as trustee to administer the trust fund on behalf of the mentally handicapped beneficiary. Parents or other benefactors are invited to register with NTMH by providing details of the beneficiary, completing the standard form of Trust Deed and settling a nominal sum of £5. They may then bequeath a sum or share of the estate to NTMH to hold upon the trusts declared in the Deed. Thus, all formalities are dealt with in advance and when the estate of the deceased parent or other settler is distributed the trust fund will be activated. The Trust Deed provides for a discretionary trust with power for the trustees to pay the whole or any part thereof to any charity or foundation (including the Adcare Foundation) whose objects extend to assisting persons with a mental handicap. The aim is to provide the trustees with maximum flexibility in the face of changes to state funding and to enable the trustees to negotiate with a funding authority who may wish to seek contributions from the fund towards the cost of care and accommodation (which might otherwise jeopardise the future of the fund).

*SSMH Trustee Service (Scotland)*
SSMH Trustee Service is a company limited by guarantee, set up by the Scottish Society for the Mentally Handicapped (SSMH) to act as a trustee for individual trusts created for the benefit of one or more people with a mental handicap. Parents or others interested in establishing a trust using the SSMH Trustee Service are recommended to consult their own solicitor, who normally draws up the Trust Deed in consultation with the Service's legal adviser. The Trustee Service is appointed trustee solely, or jointly with individual trustees selected by the testator. Once the Trust Deed has been executed, a copy is lodged with the Trustee Service

---

43   The child's circumstances and the rules for state funding will inevitably change and the terms of the settlement may become out of date by the time it is really needed. This can possibly be overcome by giving the trustees power to re-settle the funds but such power would need to be fairly wide and could cause the very problems that the trust is intended to avoid. A charitable trust is unlikely to have this disadvantage.

and a small administrative fee paid. The Service has a general knowledge of the lifestyles and aspirations of people with a mental handicap, and through its connection with SSMH is in a position to take a general interest in the welfare of the beneficiary. When the trust is activated, the Service identifies the beneficiary's needs and thereafter employs its specialist skills in administering the trust.

## Personal Charitable Trusts

Setting up a charitable trust can be costly and time consuming, but may be seen as a necessary step where there is a mentally handicapped member of the family. The *Charities Aid Foundation* (CAF) offers a viable alternative, though this may not provide all the flexibility of the private charitable trust.[44] CAF has its own Trust Deed containing power to create or hold sub-trusts which, for most practicable purposes, provide the facilities associated with an independently constituted charitable trust. A trust account can be set up by a simple Letter of Intent and the income and/or capital distributed to charitable institutions by a named person (or persons).[45] There is power to make interest free loans to charities, so this useful device may still be available to the named person. The normal minimum initial investment is £10,000, but in practice this is £7,500 as funding arrangements are made under the current Gift Aid legislation. Special arrangements can be made where it is intended to introduce the bulk of the money by Will and there is a mentally handicapped beneficiary involved; a Gift Aid contribution of £750 will be sufficient (making a total of £1,000 under present rates of tax) and the trust account is then available to receive further monies under the Will. If the child predeceases the parents the trust account would be terminated and the initial amount distributed to charities selected by the named person. Certain conditions attach to trust accounts, but these are not onerous and there is no need to worry about continuity of trustees as CAF manages the trust and deals with all tax repayments, normally charging 1 per cent. per annum of the capital value as a contribution to its overheads. CAF normally utilises its powers to invest in its own common investment funds which are managed by Cazenove and Co., an independent firm of stockbrokers.

Thus CAF is able to set up without undue formalities, a charitable trust account which is independently invested and can be used to distribute income or capital in accordance with the directions of a named person and which will be terminated at such time as is determined by the donor. The account may be given a name of choice, or may be anonymous, and it is possible to provide that the account shall only support a particular class of charities (*e.g.* those concerned with mental handicap). It may be commenced during the lifetime of the parent in a tax efficient manner by covenant or gift aid and then increased by legacies or gifts by the parents or

---

44   Address in Appendix I.
45   A typical Letter of Intent will be found in Appendix IIIA.

others which are free of inheritance tax. It is necessary to select nominated persons who would take the trouble to check upon the welfare of the child and accept responsibility for distributing the account to appropriate charities, and also to ensure that they are young enough to survive the child or have power to appoint successors who would do so, but these may be the persons who would otherwise be trustees of the Will.

### Charitable support trusts

Interesting possibilities exist for a group of parents with children in a residential home run by a charitable organisation to set up a support trust. Such parents may be reluctant to leave money directly to the charity in case their child ceases to be cared for in the home, but may wish to give financial support to the charity for the benefit of the home (and thereby indirectly for the child) as long as the child remains there. A charitable Trust Fund may be set up for the benefit of the specific charity and of any persons who are or have been resident at the home, and any other charity maintaining a home at which any such person may for the time being reside. Care must be taken to ensure that the Trust may be registered with the Charity Commissioners, or be recognised as a charity in Scotland once Part I of the Law Reform (Miscellaneous Provisions)(Scotland) Act 1990 comes into force. (The anticipated date for the main provisions is July 27, 1992). Once established it may receive legacies and lifetime gifts, and the trustees can use the fund primarily for the benefit of the charitable home that it was set up to support whilst still being able to help any resident who moves elsewhere. A trust of this nature may prove attractive to parents of residents in a charitably run residential care home, and the support of such a trust could be invaluable to the future of the home.

## PART IVA - INHERITANCE OR STATE PROVISION?
### (ENGLAND AND WALES)

### Preliminary

Most legal systems seek to protect close relatives from being disinherited unfairly and unreasonably, and the methods employed fall into two categories:
  (a) confer upon the courts a discretion to make suitable provision for the relative from the estate;
  (b) give specified relatives a share in the estate calculated by fixed formulae, regardless of need.

English law adopts the first method, but we shall later see how Scots law employs the second. The regimes in the two systems are thus fundamentally different and both give rise to significant problems in relation to people with a mental handicap; yet while the problems are quite different, the practical consequences are remarkably similar. So whilst we describe English law and Scots law separately in Parts IVA and IVB, the conclusions reached in both cases are similar.

Problems may arise when a surviving parent does not make any specific or substantial financial provision by Will for a severely mentally disabled child even though this may be because such provision would merely result in the loss of state or local authority funding (or charges for services) without any real benefit to the child. Although the general principle of English law is that a person can dispose of his estate by Will as he wishes, under the Inheritance (Provision for Family and Dependants) Act 1975 a child, whether or not a dependant, may apply to the court for financial provision out of the estate of a deceased parent who died domiciled in England and Wales on the ground that the disposition of the estate by Will and/or intestacy does not make reasonable financial provision for him. In deciding whether to make an Order the court takes into account all the circumstances.

## Applicants

Only certain categories of person may bring a claim. In addition to a spouse or former spouse (in respect of whom different rules apply), the following may make a claim against a deceased's estate:

(a) a child of the deceased;

(b) a person who was treated by the deceased as a child of a marriage to which the deceased was a party;

(c) any other person who immediately before the death was being maintained by the deceased, either wholly or partly.

As regards the third category, the deceased must up to the time of death have been making a substantial contribution in money or money's worth towards the reasonable needs of the applicant otherwise than for full valuable consideration, and if this had ceased before death, even for a short period, the claim will fail.

## BASIS OF THE APPLICATION.

### General

The application is made on the basis that the disposition of the deceased's estate effected by his Will or the law relating to intestacy, or a combination of both, is not such as to make reasonable financial provision for the applicant. For an applicant other than a spouse this means "such financial provision as it would be reasonable in all the circumstances of the case for the applicant to receive for his maintenance".[46] Maintenance includes payments which directly or indirectly enable the applicant in the future to discharge the cost of living, and has been stated to refer to "no more and no less than the applicant's way of life and well-being, his health financial security and allied matters". However[47]:

"What is proper maintenance must in all cases depend upon all the facts and

---

46   1975 Act, s.1(2)(b).

47   Re Coventry (dec'd) [1979] 3 All ER 815, per Goff LJ.

circumstances of the particular case being considered at the time, but I think it is clear on the one hand that one must not put too limited a meaning on it; it does not mean just enough to enable a person to get by; on the other hand, it does not mean anything which may be regarded as reasonably desirable for his general benefit or welfare."

### Relevant matters

When determining whether reasonable financial provision has been made the court must have regard to the following matters[48]:

    (a)  the financial resources and financial needs which
        (i) the applicant has or is likely to have in the foreseeable future;
        (ii) any other applicant has or is likely to have;
        (iii) any beneficiary of the estate has or is likely to have;
    (b)  any obligation and responsibilities which the deceased had towards the applicant (or any other beneficiary);
    (c)  the size and nature of the net estate;
    (d)  any physical or mental disability of any applicant or beneficiary;
    (e)  any other matter, including the conduct of the applicant or any other person, which in the circumstances of the case the court may consider relevant.

In particular, if the applicant was a child or treated as a child of the deceased the court must have regard to the manner in which the applicant was being (or might be expected to be) educated or trained and, if treated as a child, also to the extent to which the deceased had assumed responsibility for maintenance and whether any other person was liable. Otherwise the court must have regard to the extent to which, and the basis upon which, the deceased assumed responsibility for the maintenance of the applicant, and the length of time for which the deceased discharged that responsibility. In any case the court may have regard to the standard of living enjoyed by the applicant during the lifetime of the deceased and the extent to which the deceased contributed to that standard.[49] The court is required to take into account the facts as known to the court at the date of the hearing. In considering financial resources the court takes into account earning capacity, and in considering financial needs the court takes into account financial obligations and responsibilities.[50]

### State benefits

The question arises whether the financial resources of the applicant should include any means-tested state benefits that could be received. The case of *Re Watkins, Hayward* v. *Chatterton* is relevant[51]:

> The plaintiff, who was the testator's daughter, was detained in a mental hospital with no hope of her recovery. There was evidence that the testator took the view that since the duties of the Minister under the National Health Service Act 1946 would require the Minister to maintain the daughter in a mental hospital free of charge, there was no duty on the deceased to make provision for her out of his comparatively large estate. Roxburgh J. thought

---

48   Set out in s.3. Also certain further matters if the claim is made by a spouse.
49   s.3(3) and (4). see *Harrington* v. *Gill* (1983) 4 FLR 265, CA.
50   s.5(5) and 5(6).
51   [1949] 1 All ER 695, Roxburgh J.

that the testator was entitled, if he was so minded, to distribute his estate on the footing that his daughter could take advantage of the provisions of that Act, and that in doing so he acted reasonably.

In *Re E. (deceased)*[52] it was held that where the deceased's estate is so small that the only effect of making provision for the claimant would be *pro tanto* to relieve the national assistance fund, it would not be unreasonable for the deceased to make no provision for the claimant. Referring to *Re Watkins* the Judge commented that:

> Although with experience of the needs, by way of comforts, of patients in NHS hospitals, one might perhaps think that something might have been provided for comforts, this decision seemed logical and sensible; for a man could not be said to be acting unreasonably in not providing for something for which the state would provide and the provision for which by him would only operate to relieve, not the defendant, but the state.

He would take the principle no further and held that the fact that people who are badly off can obtain national assistance does not justify a deceased in making no provision for a claimant out of a large estate, adding:

> "The purpose of the (Act) is not to require a deceased to keep the dependants .. above the breadline but to ensure that reasonable provision is made for them having regard to all the circumstances of the case.   ... if (the claimant) ... was, at the death of the deceased, in a position to obtain national assistance, or was likely to be in that position, that would ... be an additional reason for regarding the deceased as not having failed to make reasonable provision for her".

Thus the receipt, or potential receipt, of means tested state benefits was a factor to be taken into account. In the recent case of *Re Collins (deceased)*[53] it was submitted that there could not be said to be a failure to provide reasonable provision where the applicant was in receipt of support from the DSS, but Hollins J. stated[54]:

> "I do not consider that the fact of support from the DSS precludes consideration of whether the intestacy has or has not made reasonable financial provision for her".

It should be noted firstly that this statement only purports to deal with social security benefits and not local authority funding or provision, and secondly that it does not distinguish between means-tested and non-means-tested benefit although only the former would be affected by any testamentary provision.

The Judge then considered the previous authorities, including *Re E (deceased)* in which Stamp J. had held that receiving national assistance was "a totally different consideration from the ability to rely on the national health service", and continued:

> "Likewise, in matrimonial cases, it is well established that a person, otherwise liable to maintain a child, for instance, or a wife, or ex-wife, unless he or she is also in receipt of DSS payments, cannot excuse himself or herself from liability to pay maintenance on the ground that the claimant is

---

52   [1966] 2 All ER 44, Stamp J.
53   [1990] 2 All ER 47.
54   The headnote to the All England Law Report should not be relied upon because it goes beyond the terms of the judgment in suggesting that the financial resources of the applicant do not include social security benefits.

in receipt of DSS payments. And so in this case I have to look at the situation
as it is today in the case of this young lady ... and the question is: what if
anything does she need for her maintenance, bearing in mind the matters set
out in s.3 of the 1975 Act, which are relevant and material to this case?"

On the facts a lump sum was awarded to the claimant who was a
19 year old, unemployed, illegitimate child of the deceased, but
there was no question of mental handicap. The deceased died
intestate and her estate would have gone to her husband (stepfather of the claimant) who was a violent man from whom she was
separated after a marriage lasting only three months. A decree nisi
of divorce had been obtained, but this had not been made absolute.
There were therefore compelling reasons for the Judge to make
some provision for the child, thereby to such extent stopping the
money going to the non-deserving husband, and the fact that the
child was able to claim state benefits was something of a side issue.
This is different from the situation of a mentally
handicapped child who has made careful trust provision so as to
avoid the withdrawal of substantial means-tested funding. It is
submitted that the existence of means-tested support remains one
of the factors to be taken into account notwithstanding the decision
in *Re Collins (deceased)*. In considering whether a father with
limited means should be required to maintain his children
following a divorce the Court of Appeal has held that regard
should be had to the availability of social security benefits for the
mother.[55]

### Date for consideration

There was a younger child in *Re Collins* who had been adopted by
the date of claim, and the Judge's remarks in regard to that child
are also relevant. Having held that there was no jurisdiction to
make an order, he stated:

"... if I had felt empowered to make an award in his case, I would have
found it difficult to say that there had been a failure to make reasonable
provision for him, in light of the fact that I have to take into account his
circumstances as they are today, as is provided by the 1975 Act. Fortunately,
in his case, he is in the care of loving parents, supported by a father (as he
now is) ... who is in good employment at a good salary ... in (his) case there
will be no deprivation."

Thus the claimant's circumstances at the date of the hearing were
relevant, rather than those at the date of the Will, and the Judge
would not have relieved the adoptive parents of the cost of caring
by making an award out of the estate of the natural parent.

### Deceased's reasons

The previous Act[56] expressly required the court to consider the
testator's reasons "so far as ascertainable" for making no, or
limited, testamentary provision for the applicant. The court would
take into account documentary and even oral evidence of the
deceased's reasons but would not always follow them or comply

---

55    *Delaney* v. *Delaney* [1990] *The Times*, June 4, 1990.
56    Inheritance (Family Provision) Act 1938, s.1(7).

with the deceased's wishes. The 1975 Act does not expressly provide that the deceased's reasons are to be considered by the court when dealing with an application, but such reasons may come within "any other matter ... which in the circumstances of the case the court may consider relevant". Thus the previous decisions of the courts are still relevant[57] but the deceased's reasons and wishes comprise only part of the circumstances of the case and may be outweighed by other factors. A statement made by the deceased, whether or not in writing or signed, is admissible as evidence of any fact stated therein.[58]

The importance of the deceased's reasons must be qualified by the following interpretation of the test to be applied[59]:

"... any view expressed by a deceased person that he wishes a particular person to benefit will generally be of little significance because the question is not subjective but objective. Any express reason for rejecting the applicant is a different matter and may be very relevant to the problem".

## Objective test

The courts have made it clear that the question is whether, in all the circumstances, the disposition of the deceased's estate makes reasonable financial provision for the applicant. This is an objective test, and the financial resources and needs of the applicant, actual and anticipated, must be taken into account in all cases, but the court will not interfere merely because the applicant is in need of assistance. An early view was expressed as follows[60]:

"... the court has to find that it was unreasonable on the part of the testatrix or the testator to make no provision for the person in question, or that it was unreasonable not to make a larger provision."

But this approach was not followed in a decision by Megarry J.[61]:

"The question is simply whether the will or the disposition has made reasonable provision, and not whether it was unreasonable on the part of the deceased to have made no provision, or no larger provision, for the dependant."

Lord Denning MR approved this in a later case when he added[62]:

"It is not a question whether she was acting reasonably or not. It is whether the will made reasonable provision in circumstances as they in fact existed, and not as she may have thought they existed ..."

## Trust provision

A decision of the Court of Appeal in the context of maintenance for children may be worth mentioning[63]:

The mother had died leaving the children a discretionary interest in her estate

---

57    In *Re Collins (deceased)* it appears to have been held that the court may take into account any wish of the deceased expressed before death.

58    Civil Evidence Act 1968, s.2.

59    *Re Coventry (dec'd)* [1979] 3 All ER 815, *per* Goff LJ.

60    *Re Styler* [1942] Ch 387, *per* Morton J.

61    *Re Goodwin* [1968] 3 All ER 12.

62    *Millward* v. *Shenton* [1972] 2 All ER 1025.

63    *Jones* v. *Jones and Croall* reported in *The Daily Telegraph*, February 2, 1989.

until such time as they attained their legal majority whereupon they inherited the capital. To what extent should this be taken into account in determining the father's liability to maintain the children? Booth J. held that the court must have regard to the children's interest under the mother's Will. It became necessary for some assessment to be made of the realities of the situation and what each child might reasonably expect to receive until he or she reached 18. The court had to perform a careful balancing exercise to ensure that the children's needs were met without requiring the father to pay more than he could properly afford. At the same time, improper pressure should not be placed upon the trustees in the exercise of their discretion,

One could imagine a similar approach being applied to an inheritance claim although the principles may be different.

### Moral obligation

The deceased's moral obligation, if any, may be a relevant factor, though again this must be balanced against all the other factors[64]:

"It cannot be enough to say, 'Here is a son of the deceased; he is in necessitous circumstances; there is property of the deceased which could be available to assist him, but which is not available if the deceased's dispositions stand: therefore those dispositions do not make reasonable provision for the applicant'. There must it seems to me, be established some sort of moral claim by the applicant to be maintained by the deceased, or at the expense of his estate, beyond the mere fact of a blood relationship, some reason why it can be said that, in the circumstances, it is unreasonable that no or no greater provision was in fact made".

## COURT'S POWERS

### Orders

Once the court is satisfied that the disposition of the estate does not make reasonable financial provision for the applicant, it must decide whether, and if so in what manner, to exercise its powers. The court may make an order in favour of the applicant for:

    (a) periodical payments;
    (b) a lump sum;
    (c) transfer of property;
    (d) acquisition and transfer or settlement of property.

Sometimes interim orders are made, but in all cases the order may only be made out of the net estate (as defined). An application may be adjourned if an immediate order is not required but provision may be required in the future.

### Periodical payments

This order will specify the period that the payments will be made, and such payments may be:

    (a) a specified amount;
    (b) the income on part of the estate set aside for the purpose;
    (c) a proportion of the income on the entire estate; or
    (d) as the court thinks fit.

However, the court must not set aside, in anticipation of future needs, more than is sufficient to meet, by the income thereof, the

---

[64] *Re Coventry* [1979] 3 All ER 815, *per* Oliver J.

amount initially ordered to be paid.[65]

### Trust provision

Where a parent has misguidedly made no provision for a disabled child, an imaginative approach to the above powers may entitle the court to make trust provision of the type proposed in this chapter and this might be suggested by members of the family concerned at lack of provision, even though they be beneficiaries in default. Where agreement is reached between all parties, a *Tomlin Order* may be appropriate.[66]

### Backdating

There is power to backdate the order, but this is discretionary and though this may not be appropriate where the applicant has been in receipt of means-tested state benefits which would have to be reimbursed it was ordered in one case when Marshall J. stated[67]:

> "The former wife, who has no financial resources, has been in receipt of national assistance, and the only matter that would be proper for me to consider is whether or not the fact that she has received by way of national assistance weekly payments is a matter which should in any way modify the date on which payments should begin. ... if I took into consideration the question of payment of national assistance, the effect would be that the estate might well benefit from the fact that the payments have been made. The payments ... are less than the payments that she would have been entitled to receive, had the former husband continued to live, under the order for maintenance made in her favour. I have considered ... whether, because the national assistance payments have been made, I should delay the commencement of my order to a date later than the date of death. ..." (The Judge declined to delay the order in these circumstances.)

### Variation

The court may vary, discharge, suspend or revive orders.[68]

### Joint property

For the purpose of facilitating the making of financial provision the court may treat a joint tenancy in any property as severed and the deceased's beneficial share as part of the net estate to such extent as appears just in all the circumstances.[69]

### Setting aside dispositions

There are also powers whereby the court may set aside dispositions made by the deceased within six years prior to the death with the intention of defeating an application for financial provision.[70]

### Tax implications

Where an Order is made in relation to any property forming part of the net estate of a deceased person, then that property will be

---

65   s.2(2) and (3).
66   Proceedings are stayed upon the terms set out in the Schedule to the Order.
67   *Lusternick* v. *Lusternick* [1972] 1 All ER 592 - a case involving a claim by a former wife. A similar conclusion was reached in *Re Goodwin*.
68   s.6.
69   s.9.
70   s.10. It is necessary to establish such intention if the claim is to succeed.

treated for Inheritance Tax purposes as if it had on the death devolved subject to the provisions of the Order. This applies also to the provisions of a *Tomlin Order* to the extent that they could have been included in an order made by the Court.[71] There is uncertainty as to liability for income tax on the intermediate income so this should be anticipated in the terms of the Order.

*Costs*

The court has a discretion as to costs on any application and may make no order, or may order costs to be paid out of the estate, by any party to the proceedings (or their solicitors), or out of the legal aid fund. As there is a prospect of the costs of all parties being awarded out of the estate most claims are settled.

## PROCEDURE

Applications may be made in the county court for the district in which the deceased resided at the date of death and there are criteria for determining whether a case should be moved up to the High Court (Chancery Division or Family Division).[72] Rules and Practice Directions set out the detailed procedure to be followed.

*Parties*

The rules provide who shall or may be parties, and usually the personal representatives and beneficiaries under the Will or intestacy are defendants. The court has power to appoint someone to represent any person or class of persons who may be interested in, or affected by, the proceedings when such person or class cannot be ascertained or found or it appears to the court expedient for the purpose of saving expense. This may not be wide enough to enable the court to appoint someone acting on behalf of a mentally disabled person to bring the application in the first place so the usual procedure for the appointment of a next friend would be appropriate. When an application is first made the executors are under a duty to file an affidavit giving particulars of the estate and they should mention any mental disability on the part of a child, so directions may then be made for representation of such child.

## Time Limit

An application under the 1975 Act must be made within six months from the date of the Grant of Representation to the estate, unless the court in its discretion gives leave to extend time.[73]

---

[71] Inheritance Tax Act 1984, s.146. A compromise recorded in a *Tomlin Order* may extend to persons who could not have brought a claim, and they will not be within this tax provision, though it may be possible to achieve the same result by treating the settlement as a Deed of Family Arrangement if within two years of death.

[72] Courts and Legal Services Act 1990. The former limit of £30,000 on the County Court jurisdiction has been removed.

[73] s.4.

*Application for leave to extend*

Leave must be expressly asked for in the originating process and the grounds set out in an affidavit in support. This application will be considered as a separate issue before the hearing of the substantive issue. The Act does not lay down any principles upon which the discretion may be exercised so it is necessary to consider case law. The court will look at all the circumstances and consider whether "it is reasonably clear that the extension of time is required in the interests of justice".[74] Whilst the discretion is unfettered, it must be exercised judicially and the onus lies on the claimant to make out a case for it being just and proper for the court to exercise its discretion. All the circumstances must be looked at, including the reasons for the delay and how promptly notice of the proposed application was given and whether the estate has been distributed.[75] It seems that the circumstances at the date of the application rather than at the date of death may be taken into account, though there must surely be some limit upon this otherwise claims could be brought many years later.

The following is an example of a late application being allowed in consequence of a change of circumstances which arose more than nine months after the death[76]:

> The deceased died intestate in April 1980 leaving an estate of £26,737 derived from her side of the family and was survived by a severely mentally handicapped child and a husband (who was the stepfather of the child). The husband inherited £25,000 and the child the balance of £1,737 (subject to the husband's life interest in one-half). The husband died in January 1981 leaving his entire estate to his own son. The time limit for an application to be brought on behalf of the child was waived.

*Handicapped beneficiary*

Where an application is made on behalf of a mentally disabled person it may be possible to give good reasons for a delay and establish that it is just and proper for the court to exercise its discretion to allow an application after a moderate delay, especially if a Receiver had not been appointed for the claimant at the time when the application should have been made and part of the capital of the estate has not been distributed but is still available in a continuing trust fund.[77]

## IMPLICATIONS FOR MENTAL HANDICAP

### Obligations of parents

A parent is under no obligation to maintain any adult child, handicapped or not, but if the parent makes no provision by Will despite leaving a substantial estate, a local authority with a heavy

---

74   *Re Ruttie* [1969] 3 All ER 1633.
75   Sir Robert Megarry VC in *Re Salmon* [1980] 3 All ER 532.
76   *Re Wood (dec'd) Law Society's Gazette*, June 16, 1982, p.774.
77   The decision in *Re Wood* (above) may also have been influenced by the delay caused by the need to obtain the approval of the Court of Protection.

financial burden is likely to examine the position especially if such burden commences at that time. There are two extremes, though many cases will fall between these:

(a) Where the child is an adult and receiving a package of care provided or paid for by the local authority or DSS to which the parent does not contribute. There may be no benefit to the child from any further income provision and there will seldom be sufficient monies available in the parent's estate to avoid the need for some state or local authority funding other than for a limited period.

(b) When the parent has actually been supporting the child up to the date of death. The argument for continuing provision then becomes stronger, and if the child is still an infant there is an obligation to maintain the child during minority which may be made to continue thereafter.

In both these situations there is little the parent can do to materially improve the long term circumstances of the child, and if means-testing is taken into account as one of the relevant factors it may be argued that testamentary provision of the nature proposed in this chapter amounts to reasonable provision. Failure to leave anything to or for the benefit of the child is unlikely to be acceptable to any court. The crucial question is therefore whether means-tested funding or provision should be taken into account and it is submitted that this point remains open. It may be argued that a claim under the Act is for the benefit of the applicant and not the state, and consideration should be given to whether there is sufficient money available in the estate to remove the applicant from dependence upon state funding, not just for a short period, but for a realistically long time.[78]

*The test*
If the parent was not maintaining the child prior to death, the application could only be made on the grounds of the relationship, but if maintenance was being provided there would be the additional ground that this has ceased. In either event the question to be answered is the same, namely: "Has reasonable financial provision been made where parents, knowing that their child needs expensive lifetime financial support in excess of what they could provide and that any provision made by them would merely result in an equivalent reduction in state support with no long term benefit to the child, refrain from making such provision?"

This begs the question of what is reasonable. Should parents, who may have made great sacrifices during their lives, be expected to provide financially for a disabled child after death to the extent of their estates, thereby relieving the state (or local authority) from

---

78   Support can be found for the principle that claims under the Act are for the benefit of the applicant rather than the state in *Re E.* [1966] 2 All ER 44 - a small estate where there was a competing claim; *Re Watkins* (1949) 1 All ER 695 - daughter would go into a mental hospital so her needs were small, but there would have been no question of a contribution to hospital costs.

some of the financial burden that it would otherwise have to bear? Views on this will vary according to the attitudes (and perhaps the political persuasion) of the individual, but this represents a real problem for parents and it has yet to be resolved. There is little guidance from the courts, but it must be remembered that the test is not has the parent acted reasonably, but has reasonable financial provision been made.

*Reported cases*

There are no reported decisions directly on the point but some of the principles that may be involved have been considered in the following cases:

> A mother left her estate to charities and it was found, on an application for provision by her daughter who was an epileptic living on supplementary benefit, that there was some moral obligation on the part of the mother to help the daughter notwithstanding that the mother had never shown any interest in her and had no legal obligation. The small legacy contained in the will was not considered to be reasonable financial provision and an annual sum was awarded out of the estate. The judge specifically referred to the applicant as having been on subsistence level, and this was a substantial estate. However, the judge declined to backdate the order for periodical payments because this would cause problems with social security benefits.[79]

> A mother left her entire estate to charity in the incorrect belief that all her children were adequately provided for, but her son who had been an invalid for some years was entirely dependant on state benefits. The Court of Appeal awarded him a lump sum of 11/12th of the estate. Lord Denning MR made it clear that the test is not whether the deceased had acted reasonably but whether reasonable provision had been made.[80]

In both these cases, although the applicants would cease to be entitled to supplementary benefit, the provision ordered by the court would make them considerably better off and this may be a material point. In another case involving a severely mentally handicapped child the question of means-tested state funding was not considered, presumably because it was not relevant[81]:

> A mother died intestate leaving an only child described as severely mentally subnormal, incapable of speech, and having an understanding of only the simplest and most basic matters, but with a normal life expectancy and capable of appreciating extra comforts and clothing. There was no prospect of recovery. In the circumstances as they existed at the time of the hearing almost the entire estate would pass to a stepson of the deceased who was adequately provided for, and no other person was concerned in the application. The child had some capital, and a tax free income from invalidity pension and mobility allowance, but was not in receipt of means-tested benefit (presumably because she lived in a hospital). Whilst it was difficult to see what her financial needs were, there was evidence that certain sums could usefully be put to making her life better (*e.g.* better clothing, holidays and an electric wheelchair).
> It was held that this was a case where a lump sum order must be made in favour of the child as 'maintenance' did not relate merely to 'subsistence' but must be given a more generous construction. Under s.3(1)(*d*), the deceased had a compelling obligation towards the child, and more so since her father

---

79   *Re Debenham (deceased)* [1986] 1 FLR 404 Ewbank J.
80   *Millward* v. *Shenton* [1972] 2 All ER 1025.
81   *Re Wood (dec'd) Law Society's Gazette*, June 16, 1982, p.774.

was without resources from which he could be expected to make provision for her. As to s.3(1)(g) it should be borne in mind that the deceased's estate was derived from her side of the family and not from her husband's side (the child's stepfather) and unless an order was made the bulk of this would pass to the husband's son leaving virtually nothing for the child.

In none of these cases was the court asked to consider provision by means of a trust targetted at the disabled applicant and structured so as to insulate the fund from means-testing. Nor were any of these cases apparently brought for the benefit of the local authority as distinct from the disabled person.

## Procedural matters

In cases of mental handicap, a next friend would have to be appointed to bring a claim under the Act, but a Receiver may already have been appointed by the Court of Protection (or such an application may be made as a tactic to involve that Court) and he would then normally be the next friend. In any event a Receiver would have to be appointed if the Will was varied so as to provide financial benefits for the individual unless those benefits were in the form of trust provision.

### Local authority claims

Where there is a Will of the nature proposed in this chapter, the family are likely to resist the bringing of any claim, if only because they would otherwise be beneficiaries, whereas a local authority bearing a heavy financial burden for the testator's child may seek to bring such claim and have it dealt with on the merits. The local authority will seek to have its nominee appointed as next friend of the handicapped child and members of the family will wish to make representations at that stage. Any such conflict may be resolved by appointing the Official Solicitor to represent the mentally handicapped child.[82]

If a Receiver has already been appointed this is likely to be a member of the family who approves of the Will of the deceased parent. There may thus be a conflict between the Receiver and the local authority as to whether a next friend should be appointed to bring the inheritance claim and who that should be. The Court of Protection will usually consider that it is in the best interests of the individual to have money if this can be available, notwithstanding the effect upon means-tested benefits, so the Receiver may be directed to bring the application for inheritance provision and could be replaced if he refused to do so. Alternatively the Court of Protection could authorise someone other than the Receiver to be appointed next friend and thereupon the court dealing with the inheritance claim would be free to make such appointment.

### A positive approach

#### Consent Orders

It should not be assumed that only a local authority will instigate a

---

82   In *Re Wood* (see above) the application was made by the Official Solicitor as next friend with the approval of the Court of Protection.

claim under the Act. An example of a claim in other circumstances is now given:

> A parent refrained from making any financial provision for an adult mentally handicapped daughter who had been in a mental hospital for many years because of the mistaken belief that she would have no needs. Instead the entire estate was left to ten nephews and nieces, none of whom had any moral claim to the money and some of whom were concerned as to the lack of support for the daughter. There were no other relatives, but one of the nephews was appointed next friend of the daughter for the purpose of bringing a claim under the Act. By this time, contrary to the position when the Will was made, there was the prospect of the daughter leaving the hospital and being cared for in the community, so financial support was likely to make a material difference to her circumstances. The High Court was asked to make a consent Order varying the terms of the Will by creating a discretionary trust of income of the nature proposed in this chapter (*i.e.* with power to use capital in a supportive manner) in respect of the bulk of the estate, with the ultimate capital beneficiaries being the nephews and nieces. A Tomlin Order was made.

### Trust provision

In the above example the court's powers were being used to support the daughter whilst at the same time protect the estate from the effects of means-testing. Whether the court would adopt this approach other than in the context of a consent order is a matter of doubt, but it is submitted that the court does have the power. Section 2(1)(*d*) of the 1975 Act enables the court to make "an order for the settlement for the benefit of the applicant of such property comprised in that estate as may be so specified" and section 2(4) provides that an order:

> "may contain such consequential and supplemental provisions as the court thinks necessary or expedient for the purpose of giving effect to the order or for the purpose of securing that the order operates fairly as between one beneficiary of the estate of the deceased and another and may, in particular, but without prejudice to the generality of this sub-section ...
> (c) confer on the trustees of any property which is the subject of an order under this section such powers as appear to the court to be necessary or expedient."

If the court can be persuaded to approach the matter in this way and create a suitable trust, a subsequent application to the Court of Protection may be avoided, and there is some indication that that Court will approve this course if approached in advance.

## PART IVB - INHERITANCE OR STATE PROVISION?
### (SCOTLAND)

### Preliminary

Most legal systems seek to protect close relatives from being disinherited unfairly and unreasonably. The methods employed fall into two categories:
- (a) confer upon the courts a discretion to make suitable provision for the relative from the estate;
- (b) give specified relatives a share in the estate calculated by fixed formulae, regardless of need.

We have seen in Part IVA that English law adopts the first

method, but Scots law employs the second. The regimes in the two systems are thus fundamentally different. They both give rise to significant problems in relation to people with a mental handicap, yet while the problems are quite different, the practical consequences and conclusions reached in both cases are remarkably similar. The regime which applies is the law of the deceased's domicile at time of death.[83] Thus Scots law determines the entitlement of a person resident in England or elsewhere in the estate of a person who dies domiciled in Scotland, and vice versa.

## LEGAL RIGHTS

### Introduction
Scots law confers fixed rights, known as *legal rights*, upon the spouse and children of the deceased, and upon issue of any predeceasing child. These are common law rights of ancient origin, but in present form have been modified by the Succession (Scotland) Act 1964. Legal rights arise automatically on death, whether the deceased died testate or intestate, but the relative may discharge legal rights before death and upon death may renounce them. When there is a Will, the relative may elect to accept the provisions of the Will or to claim legal rights, but cannot have both, unless the Will expressly says so. A relative with capacity to do so can - and should - be put to this election, but difficulties arise when a relative with a mental handicap lacks the capacity to elect, or to discharge or renounce the legal rights claim.

### Time limit and interest

Legal rights may be claimed at any time within twenty years of date of death, with interest from that date until payment.[84] If twenty years elapse, the right to claim will be irrevocably lost. For Inheritance Tax purposes, legal rights are presumed to have been claimed unless discharged or renounced within two years of death. This presumption sits uneasily with the general law. A person with a mental handicap lacking capacity to elect, but without a curator, may be presumed for those purposes to have claimed legal rights, yet no such claim may in fact ever be made.

### Calculation of legal rights

*Exigible from moveable estate only*
Legal rights are exigible only from moveable estate, not from heritable estate.[85] In calculating legal rights, heritable assets and their value are disregarded, as is the question of who will inherit them, so a person may reduce the value of potential legal rights claims by increasing heritable estate and reducing moveable estate. If however a Will directs the executors to sell heritage, the

---

83    "Domicile" is a complex concept and we do not seek to explain it here.
84    There is no prescribed rate of interest for this purpose, and in the absence of agreement the interest rate is fixed by the court.
85    Houses and other buildings, land and fixtures on them are all heritable.

proceeds are treated as part of the moveable estate (unless the beneficiary entitled to the proceeds overrides the instruction and chooses to take a conveyance of the heritage). If the Will confers only a discretion to sell, but the provisions of the Will cannot be implemented without selling, then the consequence is the same as an outright direction to sell, and the proceeds of sale are again treated as part of the moveable estate.[86]

## Testacy and intestacy

When the deceased dies testate, legal rights are calculated as a proportion of the entire net moveable estate.[87] When the deceased dies intestate survived by his or her spouse, the *prior rights* of the surviving spouse (see below) are deducted first, and legal rights are calculated upon the remaining moveable estate, in the same proportions as apply to the entire net moveable estate when there is a Will. The legal rights entitlement of children will thus be less in an intestate estate than in a testate estate of the same size, where there is a surviving spouse. Moreover, depending upon the size of estate, the entitlement of the children upon intestacy may be less than their legal rights claim where there is a Will. Accordingly, a married person wishing to minimise children's entitlement may in some circumstances opt for intestacy - an exception to the normal advice that it is better to make a Will than risk dying intestate.

## Proportions

The proportions, whether of net moveable estate where there is a Will, or of net moveable estate after deduction of spouse's prior rights upon intestacy, are as follows:

(a) A surviving spouse's legal rights amount to one-third when the deceased left children or other issue, and one-half when there are no issue;

(b) The legal rights of children or other issue amount in total to one-third when there is a surviving spouse, and one-half when there is no surviving spouse.

If a relative has discharged legal rights prior to death, that relative is left out of the computation as if he or she had predeceased. Accordingly, when a surviving spouse has discharged legal rights, the total fund for the children will be one-half, not one-third.

## The legitim fund

The total legal rights fund for children is termed the *legitim fund*. It is divided into a number of equal shares, one share for each child who survives or has predeceased leaving issue who survive. This equal division is subject to *collation* (see below). Children

---

86   The law is stated thus in several texts, but without authority, and doubts have been suggested to the Scottish author.

87   This means the realised value of moveable estate less (a) the deceased's debts, other than those exigible from heritable estate, (b) deathbed and funeral expenses, (c) expenses of obtaining confirmation to, and realising, the moveable estate and (d) inheritance tax upon the estate which forms the fund for legal rights.

who have discharged legal rights prior to death, or predeceased without leaving issue who survive, are left out of the reckoning. Spouses of children have no claim on the legitim fund.

The legitim fund is divided equally *per capita* at the level of the nearest surviving relatives, so that if the deceased leaves grandchildren but no surviving children, the division is made equally among them, regardless of how they may be grouped in the families of their parents. A child or other descendant who was *in utero* when the deceased died, and who is subsequently born alive, has the same rights in succession, including in relation to legal rights, as if he or she had been born before the deceased died. There is no differentiation among children or other descendants of different marriages, or who are illegitimate.[88] It may be helpful to provide a practical example of the working of these rules.

> A man dies intestate survived by a widow, three children, and two grandchildren through a fourth child who predeceased. None of these relatives discharged legal rights prior to death. The legal rights entitlement of each is as follows - the widow's legal rights amount to one-third of the deceased's net moveable estate, each of the three children is entitled to one-twelfth, and each of the two grandchildren is entitled to one-twenty fourth. Grandchildren through any of the surviving children have no claim.
>
> The entitlement of each of these relatives is the same regardless of that relative's circumstances, and regardless of the extent, if any, to which that relative was financially dependent on the deceased. Each, quite independently of the others, may choose to claim or renounce his or her legal rights, and may elect between legal rights and any provision under the Will. The entitlement of each remains the same whatever decisions others may make. So if one child is the only claimant, that child's entitlement is still one-twelfth.

## Collation

The principle of collation takes account of gifts from moveable estate made prior to death by the deceased to any child or issue of children. The amount or value of the gift, without interest, is added to the legitim fund, then deducted from the share of the recipient. Issue of children must collate their share of advances to the person from whom they derive entitlement, as well as the amount of advances to themselves. The sole purpose of collation is to ensure fairness in dividing the legitim fund, and it applies only among those children, or issue of children, who actually claim legal rights. Thus collation does not apply if only one person makes a claim on the legitim fund; and there is no collation between legitim claims on the one hand and the legal rights of a surviving spouse on the other.

Not all sums received from the deceased prior to death require to be collated. Maintenance payments do not, neither do loans though they may require to be repaid. Marriage gifts and gifts of a capital nature do require to be collated. Where one child has received

---

88    Succession (Scotland) Act 1964, s.10A, which takes effect in relation to deaths after November 25, 1968.

substantial gifts, that child's position on death may vary considerably depending upon whether there are any other claims on the legitim fund. An example follows:

> The deceased left four children, having made gifts totalling £6,000 to one child (Mary) and none to the other three, and no provision in favour of Mary in his Will. The legitim fund amounts to £16,000. If only Mary claims, she will receive £4,000. If there is another claimant, Mary must collate the £6,000 which she has received. To calculate each child's share, Mary's £6,000 is added to the fund of £16,000, so that each share now amounts to £5,500. However, Mary's £6,000 is deducted from her share, and she receives nothing.

## Effect of prior rights

Legal rights arise upon both testacy and intestacy, whereas the prior rights of a surviving spouse arise only upon intestacy. They are a first charge on the estate, and comprise three elements, the values of each being as fixed from time to time by the Secretary of State.[89] The three elements are:

(i) *Dwellinghouse*

Rights in the dwellinghouse where the surviving spouse was ordinarily resident, currently set at £65,000. Where the value of the deceased's interest in the house does not exceed that figure, the surviving spouse receives the house. If the deceased's interest in the house is worth more, the surviving spouse receives a payment of £65,000.

(ii) *Furniture and plenishings*

Rights in the furniture and plenishings of the house referred to above. The spouse receives furniture and plenishings up to the value of £12,000, or the deceased's whole interest in furniture and plenishings if worth no more than that sum.

(iii) *Financial right*

A right to financial provision, currently set at £21,000 if the deceased leaves children or other issue, however remote, and £35,000 if the deceased leaves no children or other issue. The financial right is paid from heritable and moveable estate pro rata to the value of each.[90]

*Testacy or intestacy*

If the deceased is survived by spouse and children, and the entire estate falls within the prior rights of the surviving spouse, then if the deceased dies intestate the spouse will receive the entire estate. If, however, the deceased leaves a Will leaving the whole estate to the spouse, the children will have legal rights claims upon one-third of the net moveable estate.

---

89  The current values are given as at May 1992.

90  The surviving spouse is entitled to interest upon the financial prior right from date of death to date of payment at a prescribed rate, currently 7 per cent.

*Partial intestacy*

Prior rights also apply on partial intestacy. Thus, if the deceased leaves only an interest in the house to a value exceeding the total of prior rights in the dwellinghouse and the financial right, and an interest in furniture and plenishings not exceeding the prior rights limit for those items, then the deceased may make a Will leaving the interest in the house to the spouse, but making no provision about moveable estate. The house will pass to the spouse under the Will, as there is no legal rights claim upon heritage; the moveable estate falls into intestacy, and the spouse will be entitled under prior rights to the furniture and plenishings.

*Comparisons*

Upon intestacy, after prior rights and legal rights have been satisfied, all of the remaining estate passes to the children. This creates a marginal band within which the surviving spouse will still be better off under intestacy than under a Will wholly in favour of the surviving spouse, if the children claim their legal rights. The simple case is where there is no excess value above prior rights in respect of house or furniture and plenishings, but other moveable estate does exceed the prior right to financial provision. Upon intestacy, the children will receive two-thirds of this excess.

If there is a Will in favour of the surviving spouse, the legitim fund comprises one-third of the whole net moveable estate (including the value of the deceased's interest in furniture and plenishings) and there is a break-even point when the whole net moveable estate is twice the total current prior rights figures for furniture and plenishings and financial right, *i.e.* on present figures a total of £66,000 provided that furniture and plenishings are worth at least £12,000 and other net moveable estate at least £21,000. With less moveable estate, the surviving spouse would be better off upon intestacy. With greater moveable estate, the surviving spouse would be better off with a Will wholly in his or her favour.[91]

## MENTALLY HANDICAPPED PERSONS

### Persons with a Curator Bonis

Where a mentally handicapped person with a potential claim to legal rights has a curator bonis,[92] any decision to elect rests with the curator bonis. If the curator bonis proposes to make the choice which is clearly more advantageous to the estate of the mentally handicapped person, he may make the decision on his own authority, but in any other case he must apply to the court. This would apply, for example, where the curator bonis proposed to elect to accept a relatively insubstantial provision in the Will,

---

91  These examples disregard the effect of income received by the estate, and interest payable.

92  See Chap.10B.

rather than claim legal rights.

*Application to court*

The curator bonis applies to the court for special powers to elect, and may ask the court to decide how the election should be made.[93] The court will only grant special powers to elect if it is necessary that a decision be made.[94] The executors may insist that the curator bonis elects, if necessary by seeking special powers to do so, if delay would be prejudicial to other beneficiaries, and such prejudice would arise if, for example, a decision was required to enable the estate to be distributed.

The reluctance of the courts to authorise election unless necessary derives from the older view that the curator bonis should preserve the estate pending recovery or death of the ward. Thus the decision should if possible be left for the ward to make upon recovery, or for the ward's executors to make upon the ward's death. The decision remains open even if the curator bonis has in fact received payment in terms of the provisions of the Will, provided that the curator bonis has not formally elected.

*The position in practice*

From the point of view of a parent of a mentally handicapped person making a Will, it is relatively unlikely that the child's potential claim to legal rights will pose a problem where the child already has a curator bonis. Firstly, the motive of avoiding the problems of a curatory will not apply, for the child already has a curator. Secondly, the motive of preserving means-tested state or local authority funding is unlikely to apply, because - particularly in modern practice - a curator will only have been appointed if the child already has significant capital, and is thus probably already disqualified. Accordingly, the usual motives for making no provision, or provision less than legal rights entitlement, are unlikely to apply to a parent whose mentally handicapped child already has a curator bonis.

*Arguments*

However, if a parent has made testamentary provision less than legal rights entitlement for a mentally handicapped child, the court can be expected to authorise the curator to elect to accept the testamentary provision if it can be shown that this would probably have been the wish of the ward, had the ward been capable of deciding. If the larger legal rights provision would be of no real benefit to the ward, or would be absorbed in lost state or local authority funding, it would be reasonable to argue that the ward, if capable, would be likely to have opted for the more modest provisions of the Will, thus preserving a scheme devised by the parent with due regard to the ward's best interests and to the

---

93  *Skinner's Curator Bonis* (1903) 5F 914; *Burns' Curator Bonis* v. *Burns' Trustees* (1961) SLT 166.

94  In *Mitchell* 1939 SLT 91 an application was refused on the grounds that there was no necessity to elect.

circumstances of the family as a whole. There appears to be no reported authority on this issue.[95]

The English Court of Protection apparently takes the view that it is in the best interests of an individual to have money if it can be available, notwithstanding the effect upon means-tested benefits. One trusts that the Scottish courts would not follow the view that state benefits should be disregarded, when in reality they represent the dominant element of financial provision and planning for the vast majority of people with a mental handicap.

*Discharge or renunciation by curator*

There appears to be no specific authority on the question of discharge or renunciation of legal rights by a curator bonis. Similar principles would probably apply to those concerning election. If the curator bonis proposed to discharge or renounce legal rights, he would require to seek special powers from the court, which would not entertain the application unless it could be shown that it was necessary for the curator to make such a decision. The court would be likely to apply the same test of what the ward would probably have wished, if capable. It would be reasonable to ask the court to sanction discharge or renunciation in order to permit an arrangement, or preserve the scheme of a Will, carefully devised with regard *inter alia* to the best interests of the mentally handicapped ward, and in practical terms conferring advantage, or at least no disadvantage, upon the ward.

## Persons with no Curator Bonis

Where a mentally handicapped person lacks capacity and has no curator bonis, no decision to discharge or renounce legal rights, and no election, can validly be made by or on behalf of that person. In relation to election, three things may happen:

1. Legal rights may not be claimed within twenty years of the parent's death and the right to claim will then be lost.
2. The person may die within twenty years and his executor will then be able to elect. In doing so, the executor will have regard to the interests of those entitled to his estate. If they are relatives who have already benefited under the parent's Will, an election to claim the legal rights of the mentally handicapped, and now deceased, child will probably be considered pointless or inappropriate. If the child's executor does elect to claim, the executors of the deceased parent must pay out the legal rights, with interest.
3. Any curator bonis subsequently appointed may seek to claim legal rights. Again, any such claim within twenty years of the parent's death must be paid out by the executors, with interest. Even if no relative or other person sought appointment of a curator bonis in order to make a claim for legal rights, the regional council as social work authority

---

[95] Some assistance may be provided by the English cases quoted in Part IVA.

might do so. That authority has a duty to apply for appointment of a curator bonis if satisfied that the person is incapax, that a curator bonis ought to be appointed, and that no-one is arranging this.[96] It might interpret this duty as applying when the handicapped person received no benefit, or less than legal rights entitlement, from a parent's estate.[97]

*Strategy for parents*

Any parent making a Will and proposing to leave nothing, or less than legal rights entitlement, to a mentally handicapped son or daughter must have regard to the second and third of the above possibilities. The second is only likely to arise if the child's disability is such that he is unable to make a valid Will, so it should be relatively straightforward to ascertain who would be the child's beneficiaries under the rules of intestate succession, and to consider whether they would be likely to decide that the child's legal rights should be claimed. More difficult is the problem of possible subsequent appointment of a curator bonis and one should consider whether such future appointment is likely for any other reason. Even if it is not, there remains the possibility that the local authority may apply.

*Should a curator bonis be appointed?*

There is no case law as to the criteria for determining when a curator bonis ought to be appointed. There would be a *prima facie* case for a local authority seeking such appointment if the legal rights claim of the mentally handicapped person, if made and paid, would be of significant value, and clearly in excess of any testamentary provision. However, if the legal rights matter was the only reason for contemplating such appointment, then there would arise the issues already discussed in the context of election, as to whether it was truly in the ward's best interests to destroy the scheme of a Will which took careful account of the ward's circumstances and best interests. There would be the further issue of whether in the circumstances it would be in the ward's best interests to impose the disadvantages of a curatory.[98] It is difficult to see how it could be a proper exercise by a local authority of its powers to do so with the motive of reducing expenditure from its own or other public resources, rather than for the benefit and in the best interests of the mentally handicapped person.

## Techniques

The question of legal rights should not be a problem when a parent proposes to leave by Will for the benefit of the mentally handicapped person a fund greater than or equal to that person's legal rights claim. This should be so even if, as will often be the

---

[96]  Mental Health (Scotland) Act 1984, s.92(1)
[97]  Possible grounds for opposing appointment of a curator bonis to claim legal rights are considered below.
[98]  See Chap.10B.

case, the provision is left in trust rather than outright, provided
that the trust has clearly been designed to achieve appropriate
management having regard to the circumstances, abilities and best
interests of that beneficiary. Problems arise if parents consider it
appropriate to make lesser provision, having regard to the
circumstances and needs of the beneficiary.[99] Techniques which
might assist include the following:

1. Leave in trust for the benefit of the person a fund defined as
   at least equal to the child's legal rights claim. If husband and
   wife leave their estates in the first instance outright to each
   other, then the trust fund established upon the death of the
   survivor will at least equal legal rights in the first estate,
   interest thereon, and legal rights in the second.

2. Ensure that the executors are the same persons as the
   residuary beneficiaries. They may then decide whether to
   set aside a contingency fund, or simply to bear in mind the
   contingency of a subsequent legal rights claim. Unless all the
   executors are also the beneficiaries from whom any legal
   rights claim would have to be retrieved, they would be
   likely to be advised to set aside a contingency fund, rather
   than risk having to pay out legal rights, with interest, from
   their personal funds, then attempt to reclaim from the
   beneficiaries.

3. Techniques for minimising the legitim fund have already
   been identified. During lifetime, moveable estate can be
   reduced, either by divesting or by converting to heritage. A
   direction to executors to sell heritage should be avoided, as
   should a discretion to sell if the purposes of the Will cannot
   be implemented without exercising the discretion. A
   married person may opt for intestacy, if the estate is such
   that children's entitlement would be less upon intestacy than
   their legal rights if there was a Will in favour of the spouse.

4. Techniques have also been identified to minimise the
   mentally handicapped child's share of the legitim fund,
   when there are other children. None of the other children
   should discharge legal rights before death, and if there have
   been advances which should be collated, these should be
   recorded. Moreover, as collation only applies if more than
   one child claims legal rights, the Will should specifically
   permit the other children to claim legal rights without
   forfeiting any testamentary provisions in their favour.

5. Maintenance payments and loans are not collatable, but it
   may be appropriate to treat maintenance and other payments
   during adulthood as loans repayable on demand, with a
   direction in the Will to the executors to demand repayment
   up to the amount of legal rights entitlement, and to waive
   any excess.

---

99  Circumstances in which parents might consider it reasonable to do this are
    discussed in Part IVA at p.513.

# PART V - ADMINISTERING A TRUST

## Preliminary

It is almost inevitable that some continuing trust provision will be required both in an attempt to preserve means-tested state or local authority funding and to enable the capital and income to be looked after and, to the extent required, expended for the benefit of the handicapped beneficiary. The general law relating to the administration of trusts will apply in the normal way, but we now consider some specific matters that may arise.

### Will or settlement

Once trust provision has been made it is unlikely to make any difference whether this was initially by Will or lifetime settlement. The result is the same, namely a fund held upon trusts for certain persons or charities, with the trustees having defined powers which they may exercise if they think fit. Whilst they are obliged to carry out the overriding trusts, in England and Wales they may only exercise their powers if they all agree and as a precautionary measure the powers may have been expressed to be exercisable "by my Trustees *being at least two in number* ". In Scotland, by contrast, decisions may normally be made by a majority, and a majority normally forms a quorum, but the trust deed may make express provision as to such matters.

## BENEFICIARY'S NEEDS

The first step is for trustees to ascertain the circumstances and needs of the disabled beneficiary. The terms of the trust may make it clear that he is to be treated as the principal beneficiary, or out of caution a testator may have simply included him in a wider class but written a letter to the trustees indicating this intention. In either event the trustees will wish to carry out the wishes of the testator (or settlor) known to them.

## The circumstances

Ideally the trustees will already know the kind of care package that is being provided for the beneficiary and the basis on which this is funded. However, in some cases this will change as a result of the testator's death, and the care and housing then to be provided may depend upon the manner in which the trustees exercise their powers. There are advantages if one of the trustees is already involved in providing or arranging care, and the trust document may make it clear that such trustee may join in exercising powers notwithstanding that he may benefit thereby, though this is not strictly necessary.[100] The trustees should consider the future plans and the extent to which the trust may be instrumental in carrying

---

[100] There is nothing in general trust law that prevents a trustee from exercising a power in his own favour if he is acting within the scope of the power.

them into effect, and investment decisions will be made on the basis thereof.

In other cases, though a concerned member of the family may be a trustee, there may be uncertainty as to future care arrangements. This is likely to arise where a parent has looked after the handicapped child and died without making any arrangements. The family trustee will probably take a lead role in planning future care, in co-operation with a social worker. Any professional co-trustee will concentrate upon the business side of the trust and advising as to the extent to which financial assistance may be forthcoming, whilst giving encouragement as to arrangements being made. The existence of such professional trustee may prove invaluable because he can discourage any tendency to assume that the trust rather than the local authority will carry the financial burden and will not be vulnerable to the emotional blackmail that might otherwise be applied to a family trustee.

There are cases where a parent has appointed only professional trustees, perhaps because there is no concerned member of the family. The beneficiary may already be living independently, perhaps in residential care, but in some instances no provision will have been made and a period of uncertainty arises. The trustees will wish to be supportive, but their legal duties are confined to financial arrangements and in the absence of other carers the welfare of the beneficiary will be a matter for the social services department. Professional persons should not be deterred from accepting appointment as trustees by reason only of the fear that they will become responsible for the care and welfare of the disabled beneficiary.

## Enquiries

If the trustees do not have an involvement in the care provision they will have to make enquiries, directed as to the existing needs of the beneficiary and any improvements that may be made in care provision by reason of the availability of the trust fund to the extent that this may be spent on or for the benefit of the beneficiary. Accurate information should be obtained as to the manner in which the beneficiary is being funded, drawing a distinction between means-tested and non means-tested benefits and provision. Unless the trustees already have a clear picture, they may wish to arrange for one or more of their number to visit the beneficiary and ascertain at first hand the adequacy of the housing or care provision. Enquiry should be made as to additional needs, having in mind that even small expenditure may result in enormous improvement in life style.

### Local authority involvement

Where the trustees have little knowledge of the beneficiary and are reluctant to make their own assessment, an approach to the social worker or care manager may be necessary, indicating that there are funds which do not belong to the individual but could be used for his benefit in certain circumstances. It is likely, in view of budget pressures upon local authorities that an attempt will be made to extract income funding and this should be resisted because it will merely relieve the authority of some of its existing financial commitment without producing any change or improvement in the quality of life of the beneficiary. The discussions must be widened, although the extent to which changes may be negotiated depends upon the amount of money at the disposal of the trustees.

### Charity provision

If there are some charitably funded homes in the area it may be possible to interest them in taking on the care of the beneficiary especially if capital is available to make a loan or gift, *e.g.* to help finance an additional house or an extension.[101] Income provision may not then be affected, and the trustees will have achieved the objective of improving the life-style of the beneficiary whilst at the same time providing additional long term facilities for other persons with a handicap. Even if only limited funds are available an offer can be made to decorate the beneficiary's room or pay for furnishings.

## INCOME TAX

Trustees must complete and submit annual Tax Returns on special forms in respect of the trust, and are liable to pay tax on all trust income. When they distribute income they hand to the beneficiary, usually on an annual basis, a certificate of deduction of tax[102] and the beneficiary may be able to claim repayment of that tax to the extent that all personal tax allowances have not been utilised.[103] Tax is usually paid by trustees at the basic rate but for certain types of trust there is an additional rate of tax.

## Type of trust

There are two basic types of trust which must be identified.

### Life interest

Where the beneficiary has a vested interest in the trust income, it will be taxed only at the basic rate in the hands of the trustees. This will be the case where the beneficiary has a life interest, or is a child absolutely entitled to the capital but unable to receive it until attaining legal majority.

### Discretionary or accumulation

Where there is no beneficiary who is entitled to the trust income, the trustees will be liable to an additional rate of tax.[104] This will

---

101 The "bargain bounty rule" may prevent a charity from entering into a legally binding obligation to provide care in return for a gift.

102 Form R185E.

103 If the beneficiary pays tax at higher rates he will have a credit to the extent of the tax paid by the trustees.

104 Income and Corporation Taxes Act 1988, ss.686-687. The rate is presently 10 per cent. but it has been as high as 18 per cent.

be the case where there is a discretionary or accumulation trust or the beneficiary is an infant entitled conditionally on attaining legal majority.[105] The trust income must be grossed up for the purpose of calculating the additional rate tax, but will not include income used for management expenses.[106] Any income paid to a beneficiary by the trustees in the exercise of their discretion will be treated as a net amount from which tax at the aggregate of the basic and additional rates has been deducted.

In general, payments made out of accumulated income are not to be regarded as the income of a beneficiary, irrespective of the purpose for which they are made. Once the trustees have decided to accumulate income, it is added to the capital and becomes capitalised. A payment out then becomes a payment of capital not income in the hands of the beneficiary, and the tax borne on this accumulated income may not then be reclaimed by the beneficiary when it is distributed. However, the Trustees are not obliged to pay out all of the income annually, so any income retained pending the Trustees' decision as to what to do with it can still be regarded as income in the following year, but if the Trustees decide to pay part of the income out and accumulate the remainder then the income accumulated becomes capital.

Thus whilst there may be some scope to distribute accumulations of income from a previous year as if they were income of the current year, in general once income is retained beyond a tax year end it will be treated as having been accumulated and become part of the capital. A payment out then becomes a payment of capital not income in the hands of the beneficiary.

### Implications

As we have seen, the disabled beneficiary will seldom be given a life or absolute interest, so for tax purposes a discretionary or accumulation settlement will be created. This may have income tax disadvantages, especially as regards the charge to additional rate tax which will only be recoverable to the extent that the income is actually distributed to a beneficiary. If the income is paid to or for the benefit of the disabled beneficiary it may be possible for him to reclaim all or part of the tax, but the amount of the income and the tax repayment may then be taken into account in regard to any means-tested funding.[107] It may therefore be preferable for the trustees to retain the income and pay the tax.

### POLICY

There are special policy considerations that the trustees will wish to take into account when dealing with disabled beneficiaries.

---

[105] Trusts established for charitable purposes only are not liable to this tax.

[106] These expenses may not be deducted before calculating basic rate liability.

[107] It is arguable that if discretionary powers to expend trust income are used for the benefit of the disabled person, the income is treated as his for tax purposes but not for means-testing, so achieving the best of both worlds.

## Investments

*Powers*

Usually the investment powers given to the trustees will be as wide as possible and equivalent to those of a beneficial owner.[108] The trustees may also be released from the general duty to adopt an investment strategy which is fair to both the beneficiaries entitled to income and those ultimately entitled to capital.

*Policy*

Where the disabled beneficiary is entitled to trust income but this is of no real benefit because it merely results in an equivalent reduction in means-tested funding, the trustees will wish to reduce the income and look for capital growth. In some circumstances they may acquire a house or flat for occupation by the beneficiary (possibly with other handicapped persons) and this will be exempt from means-testing whilst preserving the capital. Where the beneficiary is not capable of benefiting from the provision of a home, it may still be possible to invest in assets that can be made available for his use and benefit such as a television or wheelchair.

## Application of income

*Discretionary trust*

Obviously income will not be paid to the beneficiary under a discretionary power if and to the extent that this merely results in an equivalent reduction in state or local authority funding, but this is not the only problem that may arise. Any income distributed will have suffered tax at both the standard rate and the additional rate, so there will be a recoverable overpayment even if the beneficiary has used up all his or her personal allowances. Only if the repayment is sufficiently large or on a regular basis will it be practical to set up a procedure for tax repayment claims. Of more concern is the prospect of income, and perhaps tax repayments, accumulating in the hands of the beneficiary to the extent that it becomes necessary in England and Wales for a Receiver (or in Scotland, a curator bonis) to be appointed. Not all mentally handicapped adults are able to spend income, and where hospital care is provided under the NHS income can prove an embarrassment because there is often no way of spending it for the benefit of the individual who is already being provided with as much as may be needed. Accumulations of unspent income may also result in sufficient savings to exclude the beneficiary at a later date from means-tested benefit.

Thus although accumulations of income in a trust result in liability to additional rate tax, the payment of income to the beneficiary may create even bigger problems if it cannot be spent, and it may

---

108 The trust deed will normally confer wider powers of investment than are contained in the Trustee Investments Act 1961. In Scotland, such wider powers are strictly construed, see *Henderson* v. *Henderson's Trustees* (1900) 2F 1295, 8 SLT 222.

be preferable to retain the income in the trust for as long as possible notwithstanding the tax liability.

*Life interest (liferent)*
These problems are more significant in the case of a life interest (liferent), but may be avoided by including an overriding power to accumulate income, although this may not exceed a period of 21 years. For this reason it may be wise to use a discretionary trust in most cases even though other factors, such as the personal independence it gives to the beneficiary, may point towards a life interest. Where there is a life interest with the trustees having a discretionary power to pay income to others or accumulate, the tax disadvantages of a full discretionary trust apply.

## Application of capital

We have seen why it is usually unwise, and may be unnecessary, to include a power to advance capital to the disabled beneficiary. Where this power is included there are policy considerations that the trustees will wish to take into account.

*Management and taxation*
Will the beneficiary be able to manage the capital? Once the money leaves the trustees they will have no further legal control over it, and it would be unfortunate if the exercise of their discretion made it necessary for a Receiver or curator bonis to be appointed to administer the financial affairs of the beneficiary.[109] The trustees may be tempted to use capital as a supplement to the beneficiary's income, but if they do so on a regular basis, perhaps by making up the income to a fixed amount each year, the payment may be treated as income in the hands of the beneficiary and taxed as such even though partly derived from capital.[110]

*Means-testing*
Of more significance may be the effect of a capital advancement upon means-testing. If the extra capital brings the beneficiary's total capital resources above the relevant cut-off point, means-tested funding may be withdrawn until sufficient capital has been expended. Receipt of capital may also cause those responsible for funding the beneficiary to enquire as to the source of this windfall and attempt to assess the trust capital as if it belonged to the beneficiary or even withhold further support in the hope of forcing the trustees to exercise their discretionary powers. Until then the existence of a discretion may not have been known.

## Charitable trusts - capital taxes

A gain is not liable to capital gains tax if it accrues to a charity and is applicable and applied for charitable purposes.[111] Thus where

---

[109] See Chap.10A for England and Wales; Chap.10B for Scotland.
[110] *Brodie's Will Trustees* v. *IRC* (1933) 17 TC 432;  but see also *Stevenson* v. *Wishart* [1987] 2 All ER 428.
[111] Capital Gains Tax Act 1979, s.145.

during the administration of the estate an asset is to be sold which has significantly increased in value since death it should be allocated to the charitable trust prior to sale.

Where inheritance tax has been paid on an estate and there is power to pay capital to a charity, consideration should be given to the exercise of this power within two years of the date of death in order to benefit from the tax exemption on money left to charity. Whilst a proportion of such tax may be reclaimed for the benefit of the charity within that period this will not be possible thereafter.

## Practical planning

Despite the restrictions imposed by both practical considerations and means-testing, there are several courses that trustees may wish to consider. The following example illustrates some of these:

> Adrian lives in a residential care home run by a charity charging weekly fees. He is funded by state benefits (including Income Support residential care allowance) topped up by the local authority. His parents have died leaving a discretionary trust fund (for the family and charities) and a separate charitable trust. His brother and sister visit on occasions, and the sister and a solicitor are the trustees. The trustees find that he could cope with a television for his own room, so they buy this as a trust investment. They notice that his clothes are wearing out and his funding does not permit adequate replacement , but they do not consider that they could hold personal clothes as a trust investment. They are aware that if they pay income to Adrian for the purchase of clothes it may be means-tested, so the sister volunteers to provide suitable clothes as a gift. Subsequently the trustees recognise such support by allocating income to the sister. (As the brother is not a trustee it might be better for him to fulfil this supportive role).
>
> The charity relies on donations and legacies, so the trustees resolve to give the charity a tax free income from the charitable trust, thereby supporting its work (and indirectly Adrian). An alternative is to pay such income from the discretionary fund because the charity can recover the tax paid. Another organisation proposes to take a group of handicapped people on holiday and Adrian is offered a place. The trustees contribute towards the cost from the capital of the discretionary fund using the special powers given to them, and provide financial assistance for the care worker allocated to Adrian.
>
> Plans are proposed by the charity to provide self-contained flats for more independent living and Adrian could benefit from sharing one of these. The trustees lend to the charity a substantial capital sum from the charitable trust so that an additional flat can be built. No interest is charged on the loan, and the trustees write off the capital sum at intervals or determine not to seek repayment if Adrian is cared for by the charity for the rest of his life.

# PART VI - CONCLUSION

The treatment of discretionary trusts under the Income Support regime may be less severe than that for supplementary benefit, but it is premature to relax the restraints hitherto imposed in both England and Scotland upon the making of financial provision for a person with a mental handicap. As we move towards Community Care, local authorities which are short of money will increasingly look to the individual, and perhaps the family, for a contribution towards the cost of services whenever funds are or may be available. In addition to charges for residential care they have power to charge for personal social services (*e.g.* day care) but must reduce the charge to such amount (if any) as appears reasonable to them if the individual does not have adequate funds. A mentally handicapped adult is unlikely to have any financial resources unless these are left under a Will, and in those cases where expensive care or services are or may become necessary, parents are discouraged from making specific financial provision for their son or daughter because means-testing would have the effect of exhausting such provision without any long-term benefit. Most parents in those circumstances choose, with misgivings, to deal with their money in other ways thereby withholding substantial sums from the funds potentially available to assist with caring and allowing the full financial burden to fall on the state. This is not what the parents really want but the cost of lifetime care exceeds that which they can provide and they do not have the option of working in partnership with the body that becomes responsible for their child's welfare.

In England, if a surviving parent makes no financial provision for a mentally handicapped son or daughter, the local authority could cause an application to be brought for reasonable provision out of the estate. In Scotland, it remains to be seen whether a local authority could successfully apply for appointment of a curator bonis, or whether a curator bonis would be authorised to make a claim, where either parent had made no financial provision for a mentally handicapped child, or had made a lesser provision than the child's legal rights entitlement. In both countries, some clearly thought out testamentary provision is clearly better than no provision at all, and the parent should consider leaving a signed statement explaining the manner in which the question of maintaining this child has been approached and why only limited provision has been made. A parent who has made trust provision in the manner suggested in this chapter will have demonstrated a desire to support the child in the most effective way possible, and the underlying submission will be that the implications of means-testing upon any monies awarded directly to the child are a factor to be considered and that the matter should be determined on the basis of the best long-term interests of the applicant (or claimant) *i.e.* the child. If in England an application is brought against the parent's estate, it may be argued that the court can and should create a trust of the nature proposed in this chapter and in a form to suit the circumstances.

## LAW REFORM

With the change to Community Care the opportunity should not be missed of enabling a true partnership between the state and parents in regard to financial provision for their child. The White Paper *Caring for People - Community Care in the Next Decade and Beyond* (1989) places the duty of funding the extra cost of residential care upon local authorities and emphasises the need for partnership between such authorities and carers and the private sector. It retains the Income Support basis of means-testing which is also to be applied to some local authority funding thereby removing the anomaly of the far stricter means-testing that presently applies to local authority funding. The Income Support regulations presently provide more scope for the use of discretionary trusts than was possible under the former supplementary benefit regime or permitted with local authority funding, but parents when making their Wills must look ahead for many years and have no assurance that the former strict means-testing rules will not be re-introduced.

What is needed is a reliable and state approved system which encourages parents to dispose of their money on death in a way which will materially improve the life of their handicapped child, and perhaps also other such persons (*e.g.* by the provision of shared homes and facilities) whilst at the same time easing the financial burden of the state. If a way can be found of enabling them to do so the presently untapped millions will in the course of time become added to the pool of monies available for the next generation of persons suffering from a handicap. A simple solution would be to extend the disregard for Income Support of trust funds derived from a payment made in consequence of any personal injury to funds provided by parents and others. The income from the trust would then be assessed but not the capital, but a similar basis of assessment would have to apply to local authority provision.

The Scottish Law Commission *Report on Succession* (Report No. 124) recommends changes which would alter some of the details, but not the general principles, of the issues discussed above. The most helpful proposal, in the present context, is that the period for claiming legal rights be shortened from twenty years to two. It is proposed that issue of a deceased person should still be entitled, as of right, to a fixed share, but that this "legal share" should be exigible from the whole net estate, with no distinction between heritable and moveable property. A sliding scale is proposed (15 per cent. of the first £200,000 of net estate and 5 per cent. of the remainder where there is a surviving spouse, and twice these figures where there is not). The Commission also recommended that measures to counteract lifetime transactions designed to avoid or minimise legal share should not be introduced.

## The role of charities

One answer to the problem of enabling parents to make financial provision in partnership with the statutory authorities may be the development and wider use of Mental Handicap Trusts. The nature and purpose of these trusts is considered in Chapter 11 with a precedent in Appendix IV.

Another option for groups of parents seeking self-help is the development of Charitable Support Trusts of the type described earlier in this chapter (see the precedent in Appendix IV).

# CHAPTER 10A DELEGATION OF FINANCIAL POWERS
## (ENGLAND AND WALES)

## Introduction

People with a mental handicap are likely to be unable to manage their own financial affairs so ways have to be found to do so on their behalf. In the majority of cases the individual has limited resources, so parents or carers find informal ways of dealing with financial matters as they arise; the methods adopted may be of doubtful legal validity but are unlikely to be questioned and those involved are only concerned with whether they work. Many small transactions take place on this basis as a practical response to the failure of the law to provide a simple and inexpensive procedure, but the limitations of this approach should be borne in mind. The management of other people's money is fraught with difficulties and widely varying practises are followed even by professionals Confusion surrounds what can and cannot lawfully be done, but if there is more than a small amount of money involved or there is a dispute of any kind, it is necessary to use the procedures available.

In this chapter we consider first the circumstances in which a person with a mental handicap may delegate financial powers and second the manner in which powers may be exercised or delegated by the Court.[1] We then identify circumstances in which specific financial powers may be delegated without the involvement of a court and proceed to consider the manner in which a Will may be made for a person who does not have testamentary capacity. In most of these instances the Court of Protection will be involved.

## The Court of Protection

This Court is an office of the Supreme Court of Judicature under the direction of a Master, and is governed by the Mental Health Act 1983, Part VII. Its operation is financed by those who use it,[2] and unlike other courts, much of its work is done by senior officials and is carried out by correspondence.

### Jurisdiction

The Court has authority to make orders and give directions in relation to the estates of persons who, by reason of mental disorder, are incapable of managing and administering their property and affairs (known as *patients*).[3] This includes elderly

---

1    This will only be necessary if such person has or acquires any money or assets, and in many cases this can be avoided, *e.g.* by ensuring that any financial provision is made by a trust.

2    Fee income for 1990/91 was £7,750,423 and the number of patients whose affairs were being administered at April 30, 1991 was 30,842.

3    1983 Act, s.94(2). *Mental disorder* is defined in s.1(2), see Chap.4.

persons who have become senile, those who suffer brain damage or have a nervous breakdown, and persons who have a severe mental handicap. There are two main areas where the court will become involved in supervising their financial affairs, namely registering Enduring Powers of Attorney and appointing and supervising Receivers. We look at these in turn, but it must be emphasised that the Court only has power over financial affairs and cannot control the individual, *e.g.* where or with whom he or she shall live. By contrast, in Scotland the court may not only appoint a *curator bonis* to manage the financial affairs of an incapacitated person, but also in exceptional circumstances give the curator powers of custody and control over the person, though these powers do not appear to be generally exercised in practice.

### The Public Trustee
The Public Trustee, operating from the Public Trust Office, has carried out administrative functions on behalf of the Court of Protection since January 1987 following the changes made by the Public Trustee and Administration of Funds Act 1986.

### Information
The Public Trust Office has produced booklets entitled *Handbook for Receivers* and *Enduring Powers of Attorney* and issues leaflets on specific topics. The Supreme Court Practice (*The White Book*) in Part 9 contains comprehensive information on matters concerning the Court of Protection and its jurisdiction and sets out the relevant statutes and rules.

# PART I - POWERS OF ATTORNEY

## Preliminary

A power of attorney is a document whereby a person (the *donor*) gives another person (the *attorney*) power to act on his behalf in his name in regard to his financial affairs. It must be executed as a deed[4] and the power granted may be in general terms or limited to specific acts or circumstances. The attorney is thus able to produce a document defining the extent of that power, but in practice it may be some time after production before a body (*e.g.* a bank) accepts its validity and allows the attorney to conduct the donor's affairs. Only a competent person can appoint an attorney, *i.e.* the donor must have attained 18 and understand what he is doing and what the effects will be.

### Production of powers
There is a procedure for producing certified copies of a power instead of the original which may thus be retained in safekeeping. A copy which meets the following requirements must be accepted

---

4    Until July 31, 1990, it had to be "signed sealed and delivered" but the Law of Property (Miscellaneous Provisions) Act 1989 relaxed this requirement from that date and now it need merely be "signed as a deed".

as proof of the contents of the original[5]:
- it must be a photocopy;
- it must bear a certificate at the end (of each page) that the copy is a true and complete copy of the original; and
- the certificate must be signed by a solicitor.

A certified copy of a certified copy must be accepted if satisfying the above requirements. In the case of an Enduring Power of Attorney which has been registered, an office copy is evidence of the contents and this will be the more satisfactory course.[6]

*Limitations of ordinary powers*
Clearly such a power, especially if unrestricted, is most valuable if the donor becomes ill or has difficulty in conducting his affairs, but once the donor becomes "incapable by reason of mental disorder of managing and administering his property and affairs" an attorney under an ordinary power can no longer act. Thus it becomes invalid in the very situation in which it is most needed.

*Solicitor's duty*
A solicitor will normally prepare a power of attorney but, though instructions may come from the intended attorney, the solicitor is acting for the donor and this will usually mean that he should see the donor personally. Unless the solicitor knows the family well, he should take instructions from the donor in the absence of the intended attorney so that independent advice may be given and in order to be satisfied of the true intentions and wishes of the donor. When acting on the instructions of the attorney a solicitor should remember that his client is the donor whose best interests should be safeguarded, even if this results in conflict with the attorney.

## Legislation

> Powers of Attorney Act 1971
> Enduring Powers of Attorney Act 1985
> Enduring Powers of Attorney (Prescribed Form) Regulations 1990
> Court of Protection (Enduring Powers of Attorney) Rules 1986
> *ditto* (Amendment) Rules 1990

## ENDURING POWER OF ATTORNEY

To overcome the problem of a donor's subsequent loss of capacity and provide a practical, inexpensive way in which the elderly and infirm may anticipate incapacity, the Enduring Powers of Attorney Act 1985 was passed. This creates a new document known as an *Enduring Power of Attorney* (EPA). Ordinary powers and the procedure for appointing a Receiver remain

---

5    Powers of Attorney Act 1971.
6    The requirement that each page must be certified was not initially a problem because most powers consisted of only one page, but the new form of Enduring Power of Attorney is at least four pages and it is inconvenient to certify each page (especially if the entire document is photocopied onto a single sheet), but that is the result of the 1971 Act.

unaffected, but a power which is an enduring power within the meaning of the Act is not revoked by subsequent mental incapacity of the donor.[7]

## Requirements

### Form

An enduring power is one executed in the manner and form prescribed in regulations.[8] The Enduring Powers of Attorney (Prescribed Form) Regulations 1990 provide that an EPA must be in the exact form prescribed by those regulations.[9] This states that the donor intends the power to continue after he becomes mentally incapable and is indorsed with certain explanatory information intended to tell the donor what the effect of executing the power will be. The marginal notes are part of the prescribed form and must not be omitted, even though this may cause problems to those using word processors. The standard form is made up of pairs of alternatives with space for the inclusion of additional wording so that it may be adapted to the particular wishes of the donor by limiting the authority of the attorney or restricting the manner in which such authority may be exercised.

### Execution.

The donor signs first and each attorney then executes the form to signify acceptance of appointment and acknowledge his statutory duty to register the power in certain circumstances. Deletions or additions need not be initialled as they will be presumed to have been made before execution of the form. The signatures of donor and attorney(s) should be witnessed by an independent person or persons (*i.e.* they cannot witness each other's signatures and a spouse should not be asked to witness). They do not need to be together and can each sign on separate occasions. The witness does not need to know the contents of the document. If the donor does not have a signature or is not able to sign it is sufficient for him to make a mark and the attestation clause should be amended to explain this and that the power and explanatory information were read over to the donor who appeared fully to understand it. The latest regulations even permit an authorised person to sign on behalf of the donor or an attorney in certain circumstances but two witnesses are then needed.[10]

## Restrictions

### Voluntary

An EPA may be general in its terms or for specific purposes only,

---

7   1985 Act, s.1(1)(*a*).

8   s.2(1).

9   Replacing the previous 1986 and 1987 Regulations. Forms can be purchased from law stationers (some produce a short version) and it is usually best to use the printed form.

10  Previously the power could not validly be signed by someone else on the donor's behalf and under his or her direction, but ways could usually be found of enabling a donor to make a personal mark, *e.g.* a thumb print.

and the donor may also place restrictions or conditions on the power. For example, it may be expressed to be only for the sale of specific property and investment of the proceeds, or exercisable only if the donor ceases to have mental capacity. In deciding what the terms should be, it is important to consider the circumstances of the particular donor and to tailor the form to meet these.

*Statutory*

There are restrictions on what an attorney under an EPA can do after the power has been registered.[11] He may not benefit himself or persons other than the donor except to the extent that the donor might have been expected to provide for his or their needs. He may not make gifts except for presents of reasonable value at Christmas, birthdays, weddings and such like to persons related to or connected with the donor or charitable gifts which the donor might have been expected to make. The value of such gifts must not be unreasonable having regard to all the circumstances and in particular the size of the donor's estate.

## Registration

The attorney is under a duty to apply to the Court for registration of the EPA as soon as practicable after he has reason to believe that the donor is *or is becoming* mentally incapable, which means "incapable by reason of mental disorder of managing and administering his property and affairs".[12] Once this situation arises the attorney cannot (subject to narrow exceptions) validly exercise the power until it has been registered, and it is suspended (save for essential action) until submission of an application for registration whereupon certain limited authority is automatically restored. Once the power has been registered the attorney can again exercise all his functions under it.

*Notice.*

Notice must first be given to the donor and to the donor's closest relatives in the prescribed form (EP1), which states that the attorney proposes to apply for registration of the EPA and that the recipient may object to this within four weeks on any ground therein specified. A covering letter may be helpful, but any explanation given must not prejudice the statutory requirements. Such relatives must be taken in order of priority, class by class, the order being:

> spouse; children; parents; brothers and sisters (whole or half blood); widow or widower of a child; grandchildren; children of brothers and sisters of the whole blood; children of brothers and sisters of the half blood; uncles and aunts of the whole blood; children of uncles and aunts of the whole blood.

---

11   s.3.
12   See s.4 and s.13(1). *Mental disorder* has the Mental Health Act meaning. The size and nature of the donor's affairs will be relevant in deciding whether he has capacity to manage those affairs.

At least three relatives must be served,[13] and if anyone from a class has to be served then all of that class must likewise be served save that the attorney need not give notice to anyone if:
  (a) his or her name and address are not known to the attorney and cannot be reasonably ascertained;
  (b) such person has not attained the age of 18 years;
  (c) such person is mentally incapable.

Application can be made to dispense with the requirement to give notice to a particular person for special reasons (Form EP3).[14] If there are less than three living relatives, only they need be given notice and this is stated on the application to register. If the attorney(s) are also notifiable relatives they can count themselves as having been notified. If there are joint attorneys then they must jointly apply for registration, but if they are joint and several then one may apply alone but notice must be given to the other(s).

*Service and objections*

The attorney must give notice to the donor by handing Form EP1 to him, but in the case of relatives service may be by first class post. The court has power to dispense with these requirements but as regards donors rarely does so. The persons to whom notice is given have an opportunity to object to registration on several grounds which include[15]:
  - the power was not validly created;
  - the power no longer subsists;
  - the application is premature;
  - fraud or undue pressure was used to induce the donor to create the power; and
  - having regard to all the circumstances and in particular the attorney's relationship to or connection with the donor the attorney is unsuitable to be the donor's attorney.

A copy of any objection is supplied to the attorney or his solicitor, (if any) and if the parties cannot resolve this between themselves the court may fix a date, time and place to hear the objection and will give such directions as it thinks fit.[16] When an application is opposed, it is usually because someone in the donor's family does not know the attorney or does not trust him, and the underlying reason may be a struggle for influence over the donor.[17]

---

13    The attorney, if a relative entitled to notice, does not need to give notice to himself but may nevertheless be included in the three. Notice need also not be given to a co-attorney who is joining in the application to register.

14    s.12 enables the Lord Chancellor to make an Order exempting attorneys of specified descriptions (*e.g.* a solicitor or chartered accountant) from the duty to give notice, but no such Order has yet been made.

15    s.3.

16    *e.g.* how any further information or evidence is to be put before the court, and who is to be given notice of the hearing.

17    Research carried out by Bristol University shows that only about 5 per cent. of applications are contested, and very few of these result in a full hearing.

*Application*

After all necessary notices have been served the attorney(s) must send the application to the Public Trust Office within three days of service of the last relevant notice. This will comprise:

(a) Form EP2 duly completed;
(b) the original EPA;
(c) a registration fee of £50.[18]

If the application is in order, the papers are held for 35 days and if no objections are received the power is registered. The original is then returned to the attorney(s), but will have been stamped as registered and carry the seal of the court.

*Effect of Registration*

Once an EPA is registered the attorney(s) can again operate under its authority, but registration does not amount to certification that it is valid. The Court has only the word of the attorney that the donor was capable of creating the power so registration has no validating effect but creates an opportunity for it to be challenged. Even if the EPA did not impose any restrictions or conditions, the attorney must act reasonably and have regard to the limits imposed by the 1985 Act. The attorney will have no power over the donor so cannot dictate where he shall live, though the person having control of the money inevitably has considerable influence over such matters. The attorney should keep accounts but only needs to produce these to the Court if so directed which is unlikely unless there is a challenge from a relative or another concerned person.

## Supervision

The attorney is generally expected to manage the donor's affairs in accordance with the terms of the EPA and without recourse to the Court, taking advice from a solicitor where necessary. If in doubt about a particular course or there is a dispute, the attorney may seek the guidance of the Court which has wide supervisory powers in the case of a registered power and may[19]:

(a) give directions as to the management or disposal by the attorney of the donor's property and affairs;
(b) direct the rendering of accounts by the attorney and the production of records;
(c) give directions regarding the attorney's remuneration and expenses;
(d) require the attorney to furnish information or produce documents in his possession in the capacity of attorney;
(e) give any consent or authority which the attorney would have had to obtain from a mentally capable donor;
(f) authorise the attorney to benefit himself, or other persons, in some way beyond the general statutory authority.

---

18    Payable to "Public Trust Office". The fee is payable out of the estate of the donor but in cases of hardship may be postponed or even waived.

19    s.8. These may be exercised before registration if the court has reason to believe that the donor is becoming, or has become, mentally incapable.

These safeguards prevent the unscrupulous use of powers where the donor is not capable of understanding what is being done with his assets. However, the Court can only exercise its powers if doubts about the attorney's actions are brought to its notice.

*Directions*
The court has jurisdiction to supervise exercise of the attorney's powers, but not to exercise those powers. In one case involving a registered EPA[20] the applicant (who was not the attorney) argued that under section $8(2)(b)(i)$ of the 1985 Act the Court had unrestricted power in the disposal of the donor's property and could direct the attorney to dispose of it in her (the applicant's) favour in recognition of a moral obligation. It was held that this provision was only concerned with administrative matters such as management of the donor's property, rendering of accounts and remuneration of the attorney, and the Court did not have jurisdiction to grant provision out of the donor's estate when this was inconsistent with restrictions imposed in the EPA.

*Searches*
Anyone may apply to the Court for a search of the register and will be advised of the result. An office copy of any registered power may be requested at the same time using the same form.[21]

## Revocation

Once the EPA has been registered, it cannot be revoked by the donor without the confirmation of the Court. An attorney can give notice of disclaimer to the donor while the donor is still mentally capable or to the Court thereafter, and there is no prescribed form. The Court can cancel registration upon any ground upon which it could have refused the original registration and also on certain other grounds. In that event the power itself may be revoked and if so it must be delivered up to the Court for cancellation.

## The attorney

Anyone over 18 and not bankrupt or mentally incapable may be appointed as an attorney, and two or more people may be appointed to act jointly or jointly and severally. Different attorneys may be appointed for different purposes and a trust corporation (*e.g.* a bank) may be appointed. Solicitors and other professional persons can charge for their services, subject to any restrictions or conditions in the power.

*Standard of care and delegation*
An attorney must use such skill as he possesses and show such care as he would in conducting his own affairs. If being paid the attorney must exercise the care, skill and diligence of a reasonable man, and if acting in the course of a profession must exercise

---

20  *Re R. (enduring power of attorney)* [1990] 2 All ER 893, Vinelott J.
21  The application is on Form EP4 and a fee of £10 is payable.

proper professional competence. An attorney may not appoint a substitute or otherwise delegate his general authority, but may employ persons to do specific tasks.

*Conflict of interest*

An attorney must not allow a conflict of interest to arise between his duty to the donor and to someone else without disclosing this to the donor. If the EPA is registered such disclosure will not be possible, but directions can be sought from the Court and this may be of significance where self-interest arises, *e.g.* a parent attorney wishing to spend some of the donor's money on improvements to a home owned by the attorney in which the donor resides.

*Successors*

Where an EPA is registered for a person with a mental handicap, concern may be felt as to the implications of the death of the attorney (often a parent). If the donor's mental ability remains the same, there may be nothing to prevent another person being appointed under a new EPA at this time, and any changes in the law are more likely to be helpful than restrictive, but other courses are possible. A donor could simultaneously execute more than one power with only one coming into force initially and the other(s) so worded as to take effect at an appropriate later date (*e.g.* on the death of the previous attorney or on revocation of that power). The obligation to register each power only arises when it becomes effective.

*Protection*

Following registration of an EPA the court has jurisdiction to relieve the attorney of any liability incurred by reason of a breach of duty whether arising before or after the need for registration.[22] Further statutory protection is available for attorneys in specific circumstances.

## The donor

Anyone aged 18 or over may complete an EPA if they have the necessary mental capacity. Can persons who cannot cope with their own financial affairs execute a power? If so, an EPA could be invaluable for a person disabled as a result of an accident who received compensation, or a moderately handicapped person who held assets.

*Capacity of donor*

Until 1987 it was thought that an EPA would only be of use in a case of mental disability where this was caused by accident or injury and the EPA had fortuitously been executed beforehand. However, in an important appeal Mr Justice Hoffmann had to consider whether an EPA was valid if the donor understood the nature and effect of the power but was at the time of its execution incapable by reason of mental disorder of managing his property

---

[22]   s.8(2)(*f*).

and affairs. In his judgment he stated[23]: _

> "The Act does not specify the mental capacity needed to execute an enduring power of attorney and the answer must therefore be found in the common law. ...In principle ... an understanding of the nature and effect of the power was sufficient for its validity. At common law there is however the further rule that a power can no longer be validly exercised if the donor has lost the mental capacity to be a principal. ... mental incapacity revokes the power. ... the power ... would at common law have been revoked, at the latest, when (the donor) ceased to be able to manage and administer (his) property and affairs.
>
> ...There seems to me no logical reason why the validity of the power ... should be affected by considerations of whether it would have been exercisable. The court is not concerned with whether the power has been validly exercised but whether as a juristic act it should be registered with a view to its future exercise notwithstanding the donor's loss of mental capacity. The Act is intended to ensure that the power will continue to be exercisable notwithstanding mental incapacity. But ... I see no reason why the test for whether it was validly created should be the same as for whether it would have ceased to be exercisable. In principle they are clearly different.... In practice it is likely that many enduring powers will be executed when symptoms of mental incapacity have begun to manifest themselves. These symptoms may result in the donor being mentally incapable in the statutory sense that (he) is unable on a regular basis to manage (his) property and affairs. But ... (he) may execute the power with full understanding and with the intention of taking advantage of the Act to have (his) affairs managed by an attorney of (his) choice rather than having them put in the hands of the Court of protection. The exercise of the power is ... hedged about on all sides with statutory protection for the donor. In these circumstances it does not seem to me necessary to impose too high a standard of capacity for its valid execution.
>
> Finally I should say something about what is meant by understanding the nature and effect of the power. What degree of understanding is involved? Plainly one cannot expect that the donor should have been able to pass an examination on the provisions of the Act. At the other extreme, I do not think that it would be sufficient if he realised only that it gave (the attorney) power to look after his property. (Counsel) helpfully summarised the matters which the donor should have understood in order that he can be said to have understood the nature and effect of the power. First (if such be the terms of the power) that the attorney will be able to assume complete authority over the donor's affairs. Secondly, (if such be the terms of the power) that the attorney will in general be able to do anything with the donor's property which he himself could have done. Thirdly, that the authority will continue if the donor should be or become mentally incapable. Fourthly, that if he should be or become mentally incapable, the power will be irrevocable without confirmation by the court. ... I accept (counsel's) summary as a statement of the matters which should ordinarily be explained to the donor (whatever the precise language which may be used) and which the evidence should show he has understood."

### Medical report

In situations where doubt exists as to the capacity of the donor to execute the power, including cases where immediate registration may be appropriate, it is wise to obtain a medical report before execution. This may assist in the registration application, but in any event registration does not substantiate the validity of the power so the report is valuable for the protection of the attorney if the power is later questioned. In a contested case much depends

---

23 *Re K, Re F* [1988] 1 All ER 358.

upon the medical evidence, so the doctor should be well-briefed on the various tests of capacity. A suggested letter to the doctor is contained in Appendix V.

It has been suggested that it may be helpful to supply the doctor with a medical certificate for completion in the following terms[24]:

> "I ...... MD of .......... hereby certify that ..... of ............ who signed an Enduring Power of Attorney dated ...... in favour of ..... in my presence fully understood the nature and effect of the document he (she) was signing. In giving this certificate I offer no further opinion with regard to the mental capacity of the said ...."

The BMA recommends a fee of £27.50 for a doctor witnessing a power of attorney. Where there are differences of opinion within a family, medical practitioners may be reluctant to become involved and this can cause problems in obtaining a report or having the EPA witnessed by the doctor.

*Instructions*

It is not enough simply to have a medical report confirming that the donor has the necessary capacity; armed with this report where necessary, the solicitor will wish to satisfy himself that the donor has sufficient understanding of the information on the form and the four matters set out in the above judgment when the power is actually signed. In cases of difficulty it may be helpful to see the donor on two separate occasions, at least once on his own, to see if the instructions given on each occasion are the same,[25] and if capacity fluctuates it is prudent to have the donor's signature witnessed by a doctor.

## Implications for mental handicap

Although the above judgment related to an elderly person who had ceased to be capable of handling her own affairs, the principle has equal application to a mentally handicapped person who is not able to manage his property and affairs.

*Procedure*

Unless there is contention of some sort the statements of the attorney on the application for registration should be taken at their face value and the Court, which has basically an administrative function in regard to registration of an EPA, will have little reason or opportunity to interfere. However, the frequency of registration applications immediately following execution of powers, especially in the case of elderly persons, has made the Court doubtful as to the validity of some of these powers, so it is wise to have medical evidence available. If on first submission registration is refused, this administrative decision should be challenged and medical evidence produced.

---

24 Anthea Grainger, "Mental incapacity: the medical or legal view?" *Law Society's Gazette* , May 29, 1991.

25 If the solicitor knows the family and the circumstances well and is satisfied that the proposed power is in the donor's best interests, he may not wish to impose too rigid a test.

*Consequences*

We can now contemplate a situation where a moderately mentally handicapped adult executes an EPA appointing the parent as attorney which is promptly registered with the Court of Protection. Thereafter such parent may handle all the finances of his child simply by producing the EPA or a certified or office copy thereof. This will be appropriate where the child understands and approves of this course even though he is unable to sign.

# PART II - RECEIVERSHIP

## Preliminary

It is advisable or necessary to apply to the Court of Protection for the appointment of a Receiver when a person who is unable to execute a valid Enduring Power of Attorney has money or property and is incapable by reason of mental disorder of managing his own financial affairs. In the case of a person with a mental handicap this situation is likely to arise:

(a) where money has been left to that person by a Will (or through intestacy);
(b) where compensation is awarded to that person by a court;
(c) in any other case where that person becomes entitled to money and there are no trustees to administer this;
(d) where there are fears that the money of that person is being misused or misappropriated by another person;
(e) if the mental handicap becomes more significant with age.

Traditionally lawyers have advised that such application should be avoided whenever possible but this may no longer be the correct approach and it may be in the best interests of a handicapped person for a Receiver to be appointed. The Court can be helpful and provides a degree of supervision which can be valuable and may not exist with other forms of delegation, but the principle disincentive is still the formality, delay and cost involved.

*Information*

The Public Trust Office has produced an explanatory Handbook and anyone becoming involved with receivership matters should obtain a free copy. In cases of doubt as to whether an application is necessary a solicitor may consult the Enquiries and Applications Branch of the Court. Correspondence should be addressed to The Public Trust Office[26] and not to an individual by name, though the reference number must be quoted. A telephone call may be made to the case officer whose name appears on the correspondence, or an appointment made to discuss the matter.

*Solicitor's role*

A solicitor will usually be employed to deal with the initial receivership application and, where necessary, also at later stages.

---

[26]  Address in Appendix I.

Although he may receive instructions from the Receiver, it must be emphasised that his client is the patient, and when the solicitor perceives a conflict between the actions of the Receiver and the best interests of the patient he has a professional duty to refer the circumstances to the Court. It is the solicitor's duty to advise the Court on behalf of the patient and in co-operation with a Receiver to bring all relevant information to the notice of the Court.

## Legislation

The Mental Health Act 1983, Part VII contains the powers of the Court to make Orders and give Directions in regard to the financial affairs of patients. The Court of Protection Rules 1984 ("the Rules") which came into force on February 1, 1985, set out more detailed provisions.

## APPLICATIONS

Applications should be submitted in writing using forms provided by the Court in response to an initial enquiry by letter, but simple applications during the course of receivership may be by letter.

## Forms

The following is a list of the Forms available from the Court, some of which are automatically supplied to an applicant:

| | |
|---|---|
| CP1 | First application for appointment of a Receiver; |
| CP3 | Medical certificate; |
| CP5 | Certificate of family and property; |
| CP6 | Notification to patient of first application; |
| CP7 | Certificate of service of notification to patient; |
| CP9 | General form of application; |
| CP10A | Request for security by lodgment in Court; |
| CP10B | Bond to guarantee Receiver - guarantee company; |
| CP10D | Bond to guarantee Receiver - personal securities; |
| CP10E | Memorandum as to increased security; |
| CP12 | Receipt and undertaking; |
| CP13 | Certificate verifying claim for past maintenance; |
| CP14 | Special undertaking by trustees; |
| CP14A | Consent of proposed new trustee to act. |

## First application

The initial application will usually be for the appointment of a Receiver, but the Court may make other types of order instead.

*Who may apply*

Anyone who considers that the affairs and property of someone else may require the protection of the Court can ask for its help, but in practice referrals are usually by relatives, friends, medical authorities and solicitors. When social services departments assume more responsibility for funding persons with a mental handicap in the community it is likely that they will initiate more applications for their nominee to be appointed and this could result in conflict with the family. Where a problem has been brought to the notice of the Court it has power to direct that one of its officers should apply if there is no-one else who will do so.

## Who may be appointed

Usually the Receiver will be a relative or friend of the patient, but a solicitor, accountant or representative of a local authority may be appointed, and if there is no-one suitable the Public Trustee can be appointed as the last resort.[27] The Court decides who should be appointed and discourages appointment of joint receivers although there is nothing in the rules to prevent this. The person making application will often be appointed if willing but some other person may be appointed though no-one may be appointed without their consent. If the person proposed is not the patient's nearest relative the reason for this should be given. If a solicitor is appointed the Order makes provision for costs, subject to taxation.

## Procedure

There must be completed and submitted with the application:
- application form (Form CP1) - two copies;
- certificate of family and property (Form CP5);
- medical certificate (Form CP3);
- the commencement fee;
- copy of the patient's last Will (if available).

The applicant indicates whether he is seeking his own appointment as Receiver or that of someone else, and whether he is related to the patient. The certificate of family and property gives details of family, property, income, marital status, maintenance and other relevant information.

## References and security

The Court usually needs the name and address of someone willing to provide a reference as to the Receiver's fitness to act, though this will not be necessary in the case of a solicitor with a practising certificate. It is usual for the Court to require a fidelity guarantee bond or other suitable security to safeguard the patient's assets.[28] This may be obtained from an insurance company for an annual premium payable out of the patient's assets, and the amount will be set by the Court in proportion to the patient's annual income. Security may not be required if a solicitor is appointed especially if he has partners.

## Medical evidence

Medical evidence is required in support of an application because jurisdiction only arises if the Court is satisfied after considering such evidence that the person is not only suffering from a mental disorder but also incapable of managing his financial affairs. The patient's own medical practitioner will usually be asked to provide the report, but where the patient has moved to a different area

---

27   The Receiver may be the holder of a particular office rather than a named person, *e.g.* Director of Social Services.

28   R.55 and 56.

(*e.g.* on admission to a residential care or nursing home perhaps after a period in hospital) such practitioner will not be able to report on the present state of the patient's mind and the doctor with the most recent contact should then be approached or an appointment made with the intended new doctor.[29] If medical evidence cannot be obtained the facts should be reported to the Court with any evidence available and a direction may then be given for a medical visitor to visit the proposed patient and prepare a report, which will establish whether the Court has jurisdiction.[30]

*Notice to patient and relatives*
Before a Receiver is appointed the Court usually writes to the patient explaining why the application has been made, by whom, and what steps are proposed. This letter is treated as a formal notice and must be given to the patient in person unless there is medical evidence that this would cause harm or distress to the patient, but there is no provision that the notice must be read to a patient who is unable to read. The patient may respond by letter or telephone and may object to any of the proposals.[31]

If the applicant is related to the patient, notice of the application must be given to all relatives who are either equally related or more closely related, but if not a relative notice must be given to the patient's spouse, parents, brothers and sisters and children, if any of them exist, and failing this to any other known relatives.[32]

*Hearing*
Although a date will usually be notified for the hearing when a decision on the application will be made, it is seldom necessary to attend and the Court gives ample notice if attendance is required. Country solicitors may attend themselves or by London agent, and other persons need not attend unless requested by the Court.[33]

## Subsequent applications

Other applications may be made on Form CP9 or by letter if very straightforward, and are usually made by the Receiver who does not need to give notice to any other person, but if an application is not made by the Receiver he should be notified. Special provisions relate to applications for a new or replacement Receiver and for statutory Wills, settlements and gifts. All applications are heard in chambers and the Court determines who attends the hearings.[34]

---

29  It may be necessary to provide details of the individual's financial affairs because it is these that are relevant rather than financial affairs in general.

30  R.66(1)(*b*).

31  The letter is in Form CP6 and a certificate of service must be completed in Form CP7 and sent to the Court, rr.23 and 24.

32  Form CP5 asks for details of the persons who have been notified. There is no prescribed form for notification.

33  R.8, 18 and 36. The hearing is in chambers and will be at least 10 days after notification has been given to the patient.

34  R.36 and 37. A judge may direct a hearing in open court.

## Powers of the Court

The Court may with respect to property and affairs of a patient:

"do or secure the doing of all such things as appear necessary or expedient:
(a) for the maintenance or other benefit of the patient,
(b) for the maintenance or other benefit of members of the patient's family,
(c) for making provision for other persons or purposes for whom or which patient might be expected to provide if he were not mentally disordered; or
(d) otherwise for administering the patient's affairs."

In the exercise of these powers the Court must have regard first to the requirements of the patient, but shall also take into account the interests of creditors and the desirability of making provisions for obligations of the patient even if these are not legally enforceable. The Court has power to make such orders and give such directions and authorities as it thinks fit for these purposes, and there is a list of specific powers although these are not exhaustive. The powers to control and manage the patient's property are expressed to be exclusive, although in practice the Court usually exercises these through a Receiver.[35] Neither the Court nor Receiver has power to direct where the patient shall live, and jurisdiction is limited to the property and financial affairs of the patient and does not extend to the management or care of the patient's person.[36]

## The Lord Chancellor's Visitors

The Court can call upon the Lord Chancellor's Visitors to assist, where they visit patients and prepare confidential reports. There are several types of visitor:

*Medical visitors*
A small number of consultant psychiatrists who visit people with particular medical problems or advise on their capacity to manage. The Court has power to send one of these visitors to a patient's home with a view to a report being prepared, but only if a *prima facie* case of mental disorder has been shown.[37]

*Legal visitors*
Visitors with legal qualifications who visit patients in appropriate circumstances.

*General visitors*
Where a patient is in his own home or in a relative's home but there is no particular medical problem, the Court will arrange a visit from one of these experienced but unqualified people whose main job is acting as welfare officers within the Lord Chancellor's Department. They also visit patients in nursing or residential care homes in the private sector who are not being regularly visited by their relatives or by their Receiver.

---

35  1983 Act, ss.95 and 96.
36  *Re W* [1970] 2 All ER 502. It does not include deciding whether a mentally handicapped person should be sterilised; *T v. T* [1988] 1 All ER 613 and *Re F (a Minor)* [1989] 1 All ER 1155, CA.
37  R.66(1)(*b*).

*Receivership Division visitors*
This Division of the Public Trust Office has its own visitors who make an annual visit to every person for whom it is Receiver.

## ORDERS

Various types of Order may be made and a draft will usually be submitted for approval to the solicitor dealing with the application before the formal Order is issued and the solicitor will be asked to deal with any outstanding questions at that stage.

*Office copies*
When the formal Order is issued, office copies may be obtained for production to third parties. It is desirable for the Receiver or his solicitor to retain original Orders, as these are the authorities on the basis of which the Receiver acts.[38]

## Emergency

In cases of extreme urgency the Court can give directions or appoint an interim Receiver with limited powers before the necessary medical evidence is available, provided the Master has been given reason to believe the person concerned is incapable. This may arise where the assets of an incapable person are being misappropriated, but in all cases it is wise to telephone the Court first to confirm that an emergency application is appropriate.[39]

In other urgent cases, once the Court has received a medical report indicating that it has jurisdiction it may give directions by an Order or Certificate before the first hearing and appointment of a Receiver. The solicitor dealing with the application should include a letter setting out what is required (*e.g.* to pay nursing home fees) and the reasons for the urgency and asking for interim directions.

## Short Procedure Orders

If the patient's estate is simple and straightforward, or is less than about £5,000, it may not be necessary to appoint a Receiver, and instead the Court can issue an Order authorising the patient's assets to be used in a specified way for his benefit.[40] The person given the authority will usually be the person making the application. An example of such an Order dealing with the receipt by a mentally disabled person of compensation is set out in Appendix V, but this procedure is also appropriate where formal authority is required for such a person to take a tenancy or enter into a similar contract.

## Receivership

In any case which is not simple and straightforward or where

---

[38]  R.76.
[39]  1983 Act, s.98 and r.41(1).
[40]  Procedure derived from r.7 of the Court of Protection Rules 1984. With the advent of community care policies there has been a significant increase in applications of this nature which threaten the ability of the Court to cope.

more than £5,000 is involved, the Court will appoint a Receiver.

*First General Order*

Once the Court is satisfied that this step is necessary, the first Order is usually for the appointment of the Receiver who takes over control of the financial affairs of the patient subject to the directions and supervision of the Court. This Order specifies the powers of the Receiver at that stage and will include any special powers that are needed according to the terms of the application.

A Receiver may be given general power to spend income without further reference to the Court (subject to annual accounting) but must seek specific authority before spending capital though this may be given in general terms to the extent that the income is not sufficient for maintenance and resort to capital is necessary.[41] In suitable cases it may be helpful to provide that an appropriate sum is handed to the patient periodically for expenditure of choice, and the patient may be authorised to operate a personal bank or building society account if the Receiver so recommends.

*Effect and service*

On making a First General Order the patient ceases to have power over his own financial affairs, and the duties of the Receiver commence with the initial powers specified therein. The wording of the Order should be carefully checked and it should be returned immediately if any amendment is required. The Receiver is sent a personal copy which he should retain and is also supplied with as many office copies as are requested.[42] These may be produced to other parties as evidence of the Receiver's powers.

*Subsequent Orders*

Later Orders containing further directions and powers will be made as and when the need arises usually following an application to that intent. Specific authority is required to:
- make a loan or gift,
- buy or sell a house,
- grant or give up a lease or tenancy,
- change investments,
- borrow money, or
- become involved in proceedings.

*Discharge and termination*

Once a Receiver has been appointed it is unlikely that the Order will be discharged in the absence of medical evidence that the patient is able to deal with his financial affairs, and improvement is unlikely in the case of a person with a mental handicap. If the Receiver wishes to retire he should apply for the appointment of a replacement, but in other situations a new application may be made by another person. Receivership normally ends when:

---

41  This usually arises when the patient is in a residential care or nursing home and fees have to be paid.

42  These are photocopies which have been sealed by the Court.

- the Court is satisfied that the patient has recovered and is capable of handling his own affairs;
- it becomes necessary to appoint a new Receiver (*e.g.* on death or retirement);
- the patient dies (automatic discharge);   or
- all assets become exhausted.

A Receiver may need to be replaced if he has failed to carry out the directions of the Court, or if there is a family disagreement as a result of which the Court decides that it would be in the best interests of the patient for someone else to be appointed. There is a procedure laid down for dealing with this.

## Appeals

Where the Court makes a decision other than on a hearing, the applicant may seek to re-open this by making a formal application and a hearing will then be arranged for reconsideration of the matter. A person dissatisfied with a decision of the Court made on a hearing may appeal within eight days to a nominated judge.[43]

## RECEIVERS

A Receiver is an individual appointed by the Court to deal with the financial affairs of a patient, subject to supervision of the Court.

## Powers

The Receiver's powers are limited to dealing with the patient's financial affairs, are clearly defined in the Order and cannot extend to deciding where or with whom the patient shall live, or giving consent to medical treatment. An application to increase the powers may be made at any time by letter but should clearly indicate what is proposed with relevant background information.

### Signature

Any document should be signed by the Receiver (provided he has the necessary authority under the Orders then in force) in his own name adding: "as Receiver of (*patient*)".

### Bank account

A new bank account should be opened in the Receiver's name as receiver for the purpose of receiving all income due to the patient, discharging liabilities and providing such funding as the patient requires. Not all income need be dealt with through this account; in appropriate circumstances it may be possible to arrange for the patient to handle his own social security benefit order book, and income may be accumulated (*e.g.* in a building society account) if not needed. A deposit account may be used for surplus income, but if this is unlikely to be needed the Receiver notifies the Court that it is available for investment and puts forward proposals.

### Investments and property

The general powers are usually limited to dealing with the

---

43   R.54(5), 53 and 54(6).

patient's annual income and specific authority will be required to enter into any transaction involving capital (*e.g.* selling shares or investing money).

*Gifts and settlements*
Authority from the Court is needed before any gifts are made but this will be forthcoming in suitable cases *e.g.* gifts or settlements for the benefit of members of the patient's family or persons, or even for purposes or charities, for whom or for which the patient might be expected to provide.[44]

*Court proceedings*
Authority must be obtained from the Court before a Receiver may take legal proceedings in the name or on behalf of the patient, and the Receiver will then usually act as next friend or guardian *ad litem* unless there is a conflict of interest in which event someone else will be appointed.

*Costs and expenses*
A Receiver is not entitled to any remuneration for his duties unless he is a solicitor in which event he may charge and be paid costs on the basis approved by the Court. Other professional receivers, such as accountants, bank managers and the local authority, may be allowed remuneration for acting and ought to reach agreement with the Court at the time of the First General Order. Reasonable out-of-pocket expenses are re-imbursed, and fees for professional advice obtained will also be covered though approval to incurring such fees must be obtained in advance.

## Duties

A Receiver is generally responsible for collecting the patient's income, paying the bills and administering the patient's affairs in his best interests. The priority will be making provision for the maintenance and support of the patient, and this will include food, clothing, accommodation, recreation, extra comforts, pocket money, holidays and medical attention. The Receiver should try to be aware of the patient's wishes and use the patient's money for his benefit during his lifetime. He must comply with all Orders and Directions issued by the Court, and act within the powers and authorities given to him.

*Spending income and capital*
Authority will usually be given for the Receiver to spend as much as is necessary of the patient's income in maintaining the patient and providing him with clothing and extra comforts. Any surplus income each year is invested for the patient's benefit. Sometimes, especially if the patient is in a residential care home, the income may be insufficient to meet the fees, and in such cases authority may be given for the Receiver to resort to capital. The money is

---

44  1983 Act, s.96(1)(*d*). Guidance in a case of mental handicap is given by Hoffmann J. in *Re C (a patient)* [1991] 3 All ER 866. The court should be cautious about disposing of the estate whilst the patient is alive.

there to be used for the patient's benefit rather than preserved for those who would inherit on the patient's death. Whenever guidance is needed as to the accommodation, care and treatment of the patient, the Receiver should consult the patient's doctor and the social services department of the local authority for the area in which the patient resides.

### Registration
The Receiver should produce an office copy of the relevant Order to DSS and to all banks, building societies and other financial institutions holding money or assets in the name of the patient so as to take over control thereof. This work will usually be done by the solicitor employed by the Receiver, and arrangements should be made for all dividends and other income to be credited to a bank account opened in the name of the Receiver. Persons dealing with the patient[45] should be notified of the appointment of the Receiver so that they will not inadvertently seek to enter into transactions with the patient in person. This is especially important where the patient has any property of value and may be inclined to give it away to win favours.

### Care of property and possessions
It is the duty of the Receiver to see that any house or flat belonging to the patient is kept in a reasonable state of repair, and specific authority may be required from the Court to carry out other than minor repairs. Buildings should be adequately insured in the name of the patient, and any title deeds will usually be deposited at the receivership bank or with the solicitors instructed. So far as practicable a list of the patient's possessions should be prepared by the Receiver, and appropriate insurance should be arranged. The Court will agree to a sale only if this is necessary, and as an alternative to storage relatives may be allowed to use furniture and effects on an undertaking to hold them subject to the directions of the Court and to keep them insured.

### Disposal of property
Specific authority will be needed before the Receiver may dispose of any of the capital assets of the patient, but where necessary the Court authorises realisation and for the proceeds to be added to the income of the patient. This may be needed to cover the costs of residential or nursing home care, but the patient's doctor will be consulted as to future prospects for the patient before any steps are taken to sell a home.

### Tenancies
Where the patient is tenant of a house or flat the Receiver must consider whether this should continue. If the patient still resides in the property and the rent is reasonable in relation to the income available, arrangements should be made for payment of the rent on a regular basis, but if the patient ceases so to reside the Court

---

45    *e.g.* the staff at a residential care home, any social worker, etc.

should be consulted before it is decided to give up the tenancy.

*State benefits and tax*
The Receiver should ensure that the patient is receiving all social
security and local authority benefits to which he may be entitled,
and is responsible for dealing with the patient's tax affairs. This
will include completing the annual Tax Return, and prior approval
should be obtained before an accountant or solicitor is engaged at
the cost of the patient to handle these matters.

*Notifying the Court*
There are several matters concerning the patient which the
Receiver should promptly notify to the Court in case consequential
further Directions should be given, including the marriage (over
which the Receiver has no control) or death of the patient, or a
change of address of the patient or Receiver.

*Inheritance claims*
On the death of the patient's spouse, parents or anyone who has
treated the patient as a child of the family or has maintained the
patient up to the death, the Receiver (and the solicitor acting in the
receivership) should consider whether reasonable provision for
the patient's maintenance has been made by the Will or intestacy in
case a claim could be brought under the Inheritance (Provision for
Family and Dependants) Act 1975.[46] The circumstances should be
reported to the Court without delay in view of the strict time
limits that apply, but no application should be made other than
under the directions of the Court. This is an area where the
Receiver may find himself in conflict with the family, or himself
have a conflict of interest. A local authority providing residential
care or services for the patient may wish an inheritance claim to
be made for its own ultimate benefit and the Receiver may be
opposed to this for a variety of reasons. The authority may wish
its nominee to be appointed as Receiver in place of a member of
the patient's family and the Court has power to replace a Receiver
who will not carry out its directions. This type of conflict is more
likely to arise under the community care policies.

*Consultation*
For elderly patients the accommodation, care and treatment have
traditionally been decided upon by near relatives in consultation
with the doctor, but in the case of a younger mentally handicapped
patient it is essential for the Receiver to ascertain the views and
wishes of the patient wherever possible, sometimes through an
advocate, and to communicate these to the Court along with those
of the relatives and the Receiver himself. The Court should also be
made aware of the involvement of any social worker. In cases of
conflict over what is best for the patient, the Court provides a
useful independent forum, and whilst it has no power to make
personal decisions it may dictate how finances are to be used.

---

46    This topic is considered in greater detail in Chap.9, Part IV.

*Accounts*

The Receiver is usually required to submit yearly accounts to the Public Trust Office in regard to the patient's estate, on forms which will be provided for the purpose.[47] Bank statements and any passbooks for building society accounts should be produced, but vouchers for other investment income and receipts for items of expenditure need only be produced on request.

## Provision for the patient

The financial arrangements made will depend upon the needs of the patient and should be structured so as to be as supportive and provide as much freedom as circumstances permit. It should not be assumed that the Receiver will handle or authorise all expenses. Whilst the patient may be unable to handle his own affairs in an overall sense, there may be capacity to cope with small or day to day transactions and the payment of a regular allowance may be beneficial to the patient's welfare. This should always be considered, because the purpose of receivership is not to deprive the patient of all control over money.

*Residential care*

Where residential care is appropriate and the patient's income from all sources is insufficient to cover the fees, the Court may give the Receiver power to spend the capital on an annual basis. The principle in regard to elderly patients is that they should not be moved to a private nursing home where the costs would be likely to exhaust resources during lifetime unless financial assistance from some other source is assured, because continuity of care is desirable. This approach may not be appropriate in the case of a mentally handicapped patient whose capital is likely to be exhausted whilst there is still considerable life expectancy. It may be considered worthwhile to spend the capital in providing the best form of care initially in the hope that the local authority will then finance continuity of that care for the patient.

*Local authority care*

Where a local authority provides or sponsors residential care it is necessary to disclose the patient's assets so that an assessment may be made of ability to contribute towards the fees. Contributions out of capital as well as income are required. The Receiver should check assessments and arrange re-assessment at intervals as capital diminishes, and provide information to the Court so that Orders may be made enabling money to be found to pay the assessments.

## Investments

The Receiver will be responsible for looking after the savings and investments of the patient, and initially must ascertain those held and register his name and appointment in each case. Then he must consider whether the existing investments are the most suitable,

---

[47]   The provisions relating to accounts are contained in rr.60-65.

taking into account the needs of the patient, and seek directions from the Court as to any changes that should be made. Whilst the Receiver may make suggestions, professional advice will be required if stocks, shares or unit trusts are involved, and any decision is made by the Court.

*Advice*

In most cases only simple investments will be involved and it will not then be necessary to take advice, but where a large sum of money is available and the patient is young it will be necessary to consider a more sophisticated investment policy. If the patient has used a stockbroker prior to the receivership it will usually be appropriate to consult that firm. In other cases the Receiver (or the solicitors handling the receivership) may have a preference as to stockbrokers. Failing this, the Court will consult one of a panel of firms normally used by the Protection Division.

The following information should be given to stockbrokers when first consulted in regard to the patient's affairs, and amended as and when circumstances change[48]:

- investment policy (fixed by the Court when the first Order is made, but may subsequently be changed);
- patient's estimated income from all sources and anticipated expenditure, in each case on an annual basis;
- patient's capital assets (with acquisition date and cost where relevant for capital gains tax purposes);
- patient's age, state of health and life expectancy.

The stockbroker's report and recommendations should be sent to the Court for approval with the Receiver's observations, and a formal authority will then be issued in respect of the release of cash for specific investment. A copy should be sent to the brokers.

*Documents*

The Receiver will be responsible for receiving share certificates and documents in respect of investments, and may be required to deposit these with the bank or solicitor. Copies of contract notes should be sent to the Court and originals retained by the Receiver. Where investments are retained in the name of the patient with the receiver's name and address recorded, all company reports and notices (including rights issues, bonus shares, elections, etc.) will be sent to the Receiver. Those that require specific consideration and action (other than of a routine nature such as resolutions at an AGM) should be sent to the Court with the Receiver's proposals, if any, and Directions will be issued if appropriate. The Investment Division of the Public Trust Office can give advice.

*Common Investment Funds*

This is a special form of investment only available to courts which may be suitable in all but the larger cases. It comprises three unit trusts, each with a different objective, providing in a convenient

---

[48] The patient may initially live with family and require little income, but on moving to residential care it may be necessary to maximise income.

manner a spread of investments for funds held in court, namely:

*Capital Fund* - aims to provide capital growth;

*High Yield Fund* - aims to provide income with growth;

*Gross Income Fund* - tax free income for non-taxpayers.

The funds are managed by Henderson Fund Managers, and units are held in the name of the Accountant General of the Supreme Court to the credit of the patient, with arrangements being made through the Public Trust Office.

### Special Account

The Court Funds Office Division of the Public Trust Office also operates a deposit account which pays a competitive rate of interest twice a year without deduction of tax, although the interest is taxable. No notice of withdrawal is required and interest accrues on a day to day basis.

### Funds in or out of Court?

In all cases there is a choice between investing the monies in Court in the name of the Accountant General or authorising the Receiver to handle investments in the normal manner of an individual subject to all necessary authorities being obtained from the Court. The decision will be made by the Court, but the Receiver may indicate which course he would prefer or thinks more suitable. Various factors dictate which course is more appropriate, of which the following are merely examples:

- whether the patient held any investments;
- how much money is involved;
- whether the Receiver is a professional person;
- whether a solicitor is involved;
- the requirements of the patient.

### Investment Management - Funds in Court

The Receiver is largely insulated from investment problems when funds are held in Court, and in many cases this may be preferred. The Court is not restricted to using the Common Investment Funds and may invest directly on the stockmarket, but in that event will always instruct one of the panel of stockbrokers used by the Court.

### Investment management - Funds out of Court

There are three forms of investment management which the Court may authorise the Receiver to undertake on behalf of the patient, but normally these only apply in the larger cases:

*General powers authority* - general authority given to stockbrokers to manage the investments and deal directly with the Receiver;

*Investment powers authority* - stockbrokers further authorised to hold investments in their nominee company and distribute income quarterly;

*Investment management agreement* - management delegated to the trust branch of a bank.

In other cases where investment management is required this will be referred to one of the Court's panel of stockbrokers or to the patient's own stockbrokers where there is such a firm, with the Court overseeing the investment policy.

## FEES AND COSTS

One of the factors to take into account is the expense. We consider below the fees charged by the Court and the basis upon which solicitors (and other professional persons) may be authorised to recover their costs and expenses from the estate of the patient.

### Court fees

Unless the estate is small and yields income below a particular figure or the patient receives Income Support (in which event an application to the Court may not be necessary), fees are payable to the Protection Division at various stages in the receivership to cover the cost of applications to the Court and administration by the Public Trust Office.[49] Fees are on a scale fixed by Parliament and do not relate to the complexity of the patient's affairs. They usually come out of the patient's estate, but in cases of hardship to the patient or any dependents requests are considered to postpone or waive fees.[50]

Fees are calculated on *clear annual income* which is the income available to be paid to or for the benefit of the patient, but certain types of income are not included (*e.g.* non-taxable social security benefits). The fees as at January 1992 are[51]:

| | | |
|---|---|---|
| *Commencement fee* | - on appointment | £50. |
| *Administration fee* | - payable annually as per scale: | |
| | up to £1,000 | nil |
| | £1,000 - £2,000 | £75 |
| | £2,000 - £3,000 | £150 |
| | £3,000 - £5,000 | £225 |
| | £5,000 - £7,000 | £375 |
| | £7,000 - £10,000 | £600 |
| | £10,000 - £15,000 | £850 |
| | over £15,000 | £850 + 5% of excess |
| *Transaction fee* | - for special dealings *e.g.* sale of property | |
| | £50 or 0.25% of consideration if greater. | |

### Legal costs

Costs are supervised by the Supreme Court Taxing Office which has a branch to deal with taxations through taxing officers, although larger bills must be referred to a taxing master.[52] Costs are normally ordered to be paid from the patient's estate, but a Receiver may not employ a solicitor or other professional person

---

49  These fees are provided for in rr.77-83 and set out in an Appendix to the Rules. A leaflet on the fees is available from the Public Trust Office.

50  This power is not often exercised because of the requirement to cover running costs from fees.

51  A higher scale applies if the Public Trustee is Receiver, but no transaction fees are then payable and some solicitors' costs are unlikely to be incurred.

52  See rr.84-89.

at the expense of the estate, without prior authority from the Court, to do any work not usually requiring professional assistance.[53] A solicitor Receiver should ensure that the Order of appointment includes provision for remuneration by profit costs. There are four methods of claiming costs[54]:

1. *Fixed costs* - amounts specified for different classes of work[55] which the solicitor can claim by letter, though in a few cases a short statement may be required describing the work undertaken. VAT can be added in all cases, and categories II and III may be claimed together.

| | | |
|---|---|---|
| Category I | Work up to and including the date upon which First General Order is entered.[56] | £257 |
| Category II | (a) Preparation and lodgment of a receivership account. | £103 |
| | (b) ditto - if certified by a solicitor under Practice Notes.[57] | £118 |
| Category III | General management work in second and subsequent years | £301 |
| Category IV | Applications for appointment of a new trustee in order to make title to land.[58] | £218 |

2. *Agreed costs* - if costs do not exceed £750 (excluding VAT and disbursements) and there is no provision for fixed costs, the solicitor may submit a bill to the Court and suggest a figure which would be accepted.[59] If this appears reasonable the amount will be agreed, and failing this there is a discretion to direct taxation. A narrative bill should be lodged including a summary of the work done, hours spent and level of fee-earner together with counsel's fee notes and vouchers for any disbursements.

3. *Taxation* - if fixed or agreed costs are not sufficient the solicitor obtains an Order or Direction giving authority to

---

53   R.87(1).
54   *Notes for the Guidance of Solicitors on Costs in Court of Protection Matters* were issued in September 1990 and are likely to be updated at intervals. A copy may be obtained from Supreme Court Taxing Office (Court of Protection Branch).
55   The levels are reviewed each year and are stated as from November 1991.
56   Includes oath fees, but the commencement fee of £50 and fees for medical evidence and evidence of notification of the patient may be added. Receipts should be produced.
57   *I.e.* dated September 13, 1984, and March 5, 1985.
58   Trustee Act 1925, s.36(9), amended by Mental Health Acts 1959 and 1983.
59   Practice Direction dated March 17, 1992. Only in exceptional cases will the Court agree a bill for a fixed costs category of work higher than the fixed costs, and the normal alternative to fixed costs is taxation.

tax his costs, and prepares and lodges a bill for taxation.[60]
This bill may be prepared in one of two ways:

    *Summary bill*   - a summary narrative of work done,
giving time-costing information and indicating any special
factors[61]; may prove sufficient in small and uncomplicated
matters, but if in doubt contact the Taxing Office.

    *Itemised bill*    - for complicated matters it is usually
in the solicitors interests to prepare and lodge an itemised
bill for taxation in the form of a High Court bill, and the
taxing officer always has a discretion to ask for this. The
file of correspondence and relevant working papers should
be submitted with the bill in appropriate form and the
Order or Direction giving authority to tax (or a photocopy
certified by the solicitor) to the Supreme Court Taxing
Office.[62] The bill is provisionally taxed and returned by
post to the solicitor who may request an appointment
before the taxing officer to make representations. There is
also an appeal procedure. When taxation is finalised the
completed bill is returned to the Taxing Office with a
cheque payable to "H M Paymaster General" for the taxing
fee[63] and a Certificate of Taxation is prepared. Costs must
not be paid from any source until this is issued.

## Prior costs

A solicitor who has costs outstanding for work not connected with
the receivership for a period before the appointment may submit a
summary bill to the Court with a request that it be taxed as "prior
costs".[64] The taxing officer can ask for further information, and
will refer the bill to a taxing master if it exceeds a certain amount,
and an itemised bill can always be requested. Work done before
receivership was contemplated should be treated as prior costs but
work intended to lead to the appointment of a Receiver would be
costs relative to the application.

## Conveyancing

By a Practice Direction dated April 9, 1992 an additional category
of fixed costs has been introduced for conveyancing work, and this
comprises a fixed sum plus a value element which is generally
one-half per cent of the consideration. Alternatively the solicitor

---

60   RSC, Ord.62 applies. The guidance notes referred to above are especially
     helpful in this respect. Usually a separate bill is lodged for each Order or
     Direction, but if the costs relate to categories II and III the relevant items
     may all be included in the same bill. Under a general Direction costs of the
     First General Order may be taxed without specific authority provided that
     fixed costs have not already been paid.

61   Number of long and short letters sent, letters received and telephone calls,
     and time expended on attendances and otherwise by partners and other fee
     earners.

62   Address in Appendix I.

63   This is calculated from a scale on the amount of the bill as taxed.

64   This will include work not billed and also bills not paid. If a bill had already
     been sent to the patient that bill should be submitted.

can choose to have the costs taxed, but costs may not be agreed. The estate agents bill is not treated as a disbursement but is shown as an expense in the completion statement lodged with the Court, and approval should be obtained before payment unless the amount is within the limit set in the Order authorising sale. Charges not exceeding 2.5 per cent. of the sale price, to include commission, expenses, etc., are normally considered reasonable but the Receiver has a duty to act in the best interests of the patient so should negotiate any lower level of charges that applies in the locality.

*Legal aid*
Legal aid is not available for Court of Protection applications.

# PART III - OTHER DELEGATIONS

There are a number of procedures available in specific or limited circumstances which are now considered.

## STATE BENEFITS
Social security benefits may be paid to someone on behalf of a claimant under a disability.

## Agency
Claimants may nominate someone to collect the benefit for them from the post office. This is not provided for in the regulations but is a standard procedure, the form of authority usually being printed on the allowance order slip. Where this is to continue on a long term basis an *agency card* may be obtained to avoid the need for authorisation on each occasion, but the claimant must still sign each order. It assumes that the claimant is capable of claiming the pension or allowance and this is often not so for a person with a mental handicap. There is little supervision in practice.

*Powers of agent*
The agent is merely entitled to collect the money and is under an obligation to hand it over but in practice may handle the money on behalf of the claimant with actual or tacit authority. If the claimant becomes legally incapable of handling his own affairs the agency procedure should no longer be used because it relies upon an express delegation by the claimant.

*Alternative agency*
There is also a DSS system whereby residents in local authority accommodation can nominate an official of the authority (by office and not by name) to act as *signing agent* and collect pension payments or other allowances. This is subject to the same limitations as for general agency outlined above save that the claimant does not need to sign the order book each time.

## Appointee

The Secretary of State is empowered to appoint someone to exercise on behalf of a claimant any right that the claimant has under the Social Security Act, and to receive and deal with any sums payable.[65] Thus the appointee can collect, deal with and spend the benefit, but the claimant must be "unable to act for himself" and must not be under the supervision of the Court of Protection. Where a Receiver has been appointed or there is a registered EPA, there will be someone with power to act for the claimant so the appointee procedure is not appropriate. An appointee is described as[66]:

> "a person appointed by the Secretary of State to act on behalf of a claimant who is unable to manage his own affairs. The incapacity may be permanent, e g because of senility or mental deficiency, or temporary, e g following a serious accident. The appointee makes declarations, reports changes, receives and deals with any payments, and has a right of appeal as though he were himself the claimant."

Whilst this relatively informal procedure is helpful, appointment of a parent or carer could have the effect of trapping a claimant with the family through financial control when independence or freedom is desired.

### Procedure

The appointee must apply in writing to receive the money due to the claimant, and staff at the local DSS office are instructed to satisfy themselves as to the claimant's inability to manage his affairs and as to the suitability of the proposed appointee. This usually involves seeing the claimant or receiving medical evidence and interviewing the appointee but time pressures upon officers may result in only limited enquiries being made and the procedures are not adequate for dealing with conflicts of principle. Since April 1988 only one appointment is made for all benefits under the Social Security Act 1975, whereas before that date five separate appointments were possible.

### Powers

The appointee's powers do not extend beyond handling the social security benefit, so whilst this procedure may solve the financial problem if that is the only income available, it does not do so if there are other assets involved. All money collected by the appointee must be used for the benefit of the claimant.

### Eligibility

DSS policy is that a close relative who lives with or someone else who cares for the claimant is the most suitable person to act as appointee. The proprietor of a residential care home should be appointed as a last resort and not for administrative convenience, although in some cases this may be the only person available.

---

65  Social Security (Claims and Payments) Regulations 1987, reg.33.
66  *Supplementary Benefits: Procedure Manual*, DHSS, ss.9520-21, (known as the *S Manual*).

Where there is no-one to appoint the Director of Social Services should be proposed and for the sake of continuity it is then convenient to appoint the office holder rather than the individual. An appointee can use the agency procedure.

*Supervision*
The DSS are responsible for deciding whether an applicant is a suitable person to receive and administer the money in the best interests of the claimant. If doubts arise as to the conduct of an appointee the matter should be referred to the DSS who have power to and will take away the rights of an appointee who is not acting properly or in the best interests of the claimant.

## DSS powers

There are two additional powers which the DSS have and which may be of relevance to a claimant who lacks mental capacity.

*Payment to others*
The Secretary of State, acting through a senior local officer, may direct that benefit shall be paid, wholly or in part, to another person acting on behalf of the claimant if this appears necessary for protecting the interests of the claimant or a dependant.[67] This power is used sparingly.

*Direct payments*
Deductions may be made from benefit and direct payments made thereout to third parties on behalf of the claimant in accordance with detailed procedures.[68] This power is restricted to housing and accommodation costs and expenses for fuel and water services and there are limits on the amounts that can be deducted.

### TRUSTEES

Where it is desired to make financial provision for a person who is incapable of dealing with his own affairs it is possible to anticipate the problem by appointing trustees and leaving property to them on suitably worded trusts as described in Chapter 9.

## Procedure

The trustees hold and manage the trust property and make it available as best befits the circumstances of the beneficiary, so it is not necessary to delegate the financial powers of the beneficiary in regard to that property.

*Advantages*
The person making the provision is able to set up a system of financial control for the beneficiary, and this could be significant if assets such as a house are provided. In the absence of any legal custodial control effective financial control over the environment may be important. In many cases there may be no significant funds

---

67   Social Security (Claims and Payments) Regulations 1987, reg.34.
68   Reg. 35 and Sched.9.

available in the family to make trust provision, but if there are, great care must be taken as to the terms of any trust provision in view of the potential effect upon state funding.

*Disadvantages*
There is the danger that parents creating a trust may not be acting in the best long term interests of their child, by seeking to create too protective an environment and thereby denying the child an opportunity to live in the wider community. A more serious danger is that the trustees may themselves need supervision, yet this is unlikely to be provided. If they are members of the family who, or whose children, may benefit from the trust at a later date, they may fail to carry out the intention of treating the handicapped relative as the principal beneficiary under the trust. The existence of a trust, however well administered, does not necessarily prevent problems arising over the handling of the beneficiary's money or the need for a Receiver to be appointed, as the beneficiary may become entitled to money from other sources or the problems outlined below may arise.

## Problems

The powers of trustees are restricted to the trust funds, and they will have no legal power over the personal life, residence or behaviour of the beneficiary, although their control of the money may give them considerable influence.

*Income*
If and in so far as income is allocated to a handicapped beneficiary there could be an accumulation of unspent income in the hands of that beneficiary. Strictly this income ceases to be under the control of the trustees, even though in practice they may hang on to it. To minimise this problem where there is an entitlement to income the trustees may vary the investments so that they do not receive more income in each year than can be spent, and the problem may be avoided by giving the trustees discretionary powers over income.

*Taxation*
Any income paid to or expended on behalf of the handicapped beneficiary will have had income tax deducted which in most cases can be re-claimed because the beneficiary will not have utilised the personal allowance. If it is a discretionary trust the additional rate tax can be re-claimed. Difficulties may arise in submitting tax repayment claims on behalf of the beneficiary, but if this hurdle is overcome the tax recovered will be additional income which may accumulate if not spent.

## COURT AWARDS

It is not unusual for claims to be brought in the High Court or a County Court by or on behalf of a person under a disability, and special procedures must then apply.[69] In this Chapter we are only concerned with the manner in which damages are administered. The procedures for the appointment of a next friend or a guardian *ad litem* to represent such a person in the proceedings are dealt with in Chapter 2.

## Jurisdiction

The Court making an award of damages has jurisdiction to administer the damages on behalf of a person under a disability, which means a person who is a *minor* or a *patient*.[70] We are concerned with patients, for whom additional procedures are available in respect of the long term administration of damages. In the case of minors who are not also patients any damages are held under the supervision of the Court making the award until the minor attains legal majority. This jurisdiction is concurrent to that of the Court of Protection, but it is usually exercised by a District Judge who may have little experience of the problems involved in dealing with persons who lack mental capacity and be required to make decisions on a one-off basis with inadequate background information. Accordingly there are procedures to ensure that the Court of Protection is involved where this would be desirable. If a Receiver has already been appointed he will usually have brought the proceedings and will receive any damages in that capacity so these procedures need not apply.

### Approval of settlements

No settlement or compromise of any money claim brought by or on behalf of any person under a disability is valid without the approval of the Court,[71] and there is provision for any settlement of a claim before proceedings are commenced to be approved on an application made to the Court for that purpose. Any costs paid to the solicitors acting for such person must usually be taxed even if they are not paid out of the damages recovered, so as to ensure that they are not excessive in relation to the damages.

## High Court procedure

Money recovered by or on behalf of a person under a disability must only be dealt with in accordance with Directions given by the Court.[72]

### Restrictions

Unless a Receiver has been appointed who will take over control of the money[73] (and in appropriate cases the Court may direct that an application be made to the Court of Protection to such intent),

---

69   RSC, Ord.80;  CCR, Ord.10.
70   For definition see p.37. The term *mental patient* is used in the County Court Rules, which is an inappropriate term to use in the case of a person with a mental handicap.
71   RSC, Ord.80, r.10;  CCR, Ord.10, r.10.
72   RSC, Ord.80, r.12.
73   Subject to the supervision of the Court of Protection.

it must be paid into the High Court and invested or otherwise dealt with there. No payment may then be made out of court except in accordance with an Order of the Court, which may be specific or general in its terms.[74]

*Retention or transfer*

A decision has to be made as to whether to transfer damages to the Court of Protection and much depends upon the amount involved. Although the Rules make no distinction between minors and patients, and when approving settlements there is no difference in the court's functions and powers, in relation to the application and investment of funds there is an important distinction. Unlike the situation of minors,[75] the ultimate power and duty to protect *patients* is exercised by the Court of Protection which is not a division of the High Court or under its control, although the two courts are seldom in conflict. In consequence the High Court must be careful not to encroach upon the role of the Court of Protection which has far greater powers. The earlier practice of setting up trust funds should not be followed, because this type of activity is best left to the Court of Protection, if indeed it is necessary at all. In view of the additional cost of administration by the Court of Protection, smallish sums may be retained in and administered by the High Court. The practice is generally as follows:

over £50,000 the next friend is directed to apply to the Court of Protection for the appointment of a Receiver and the fund is then transferred;

below £5,000 retained in High Court and dealt with as if the patient were a child (*i.e.* applications may be made by a carer for sums to be available for the patient's benefit);

£5-50,000 consult the Court of Protection.

*Procedure on transfer*

Where a plaintiff who is a patient has been awarded damages in an action in the Queen's Bench Division, the transfer of the damages will be facilitated if the judgment includes a provision to the following effect[76]:

"... that the defendant do within ... days pay the said sum of £... into Court to be placed to and accumulated in a Special Account pending an application by the next friend to the Court of Protection for the appointment of a Receiver for the plaintiff and that upon such appointment being made the said sum of £... together with any interest thereon [subject to a first charge under the Legal Aid Act 1988] be transferred to the Court of Protection to the credit of the plaintiff to be dealt with as the Court of Protection in its discretion

---

[74] *I.e.* the Court may direct that a particular sum of money be expended on a specific item, or that the income earned be paid to a particular person for the benefit of the person under disability.

[75] Where an infant is also a patient, the Court of Protection will accept jurisdiction to administer damages if the patient is likely to survive to majority but unlikely to recover before then.

[76] Practice Note September 7, 1990, by Senior Master of the Queen's Bench Division and Master of the Court of Protection. [1991] 1 All ER 436.

shall think fit".

Similar provision should be included in an Order approving a compromise on behalf of a patient.

*Steps to be taken*

The next friend or carers will naturally be anxious to have access to the fund so certain steps can be taken to expedite this:

(a) apply for the appointment of a Receiver in anticipation of the award. The next friend is usually the person to make the application and may also be the most suitable person to act as Receiver, just as a Receiver already appointed would be the appropriate person to appoint as next friend (unless there was a conflict of interest);

(b) where the plaintiff is legally aided and the statutory charge applies, the solicitor should obtain and complete the appropriate undertaking and return this to the legal aid area office. A figure will be inserted which is sufficient to cover the full extent of the claim upon the legal aid fund including costs and disbursements incurred and to be incurred less any contribution paid and costs recovered. The area office inform the Court Funds Office by letter of the amount to be retained to cover the statutory charge, and the solicitor then obtains an Order from the court directing the release of that sum to the legal aid fund. The balance is then free for release to the Court of Protection.

(c) the procedure known as "Lodging the Part II Order" should then be followed. A payment schedule (Form 200) is prepared[77] and forwarded to the District Registry which made the award[78] with the request to forward the form to the Court Funds Office, Queen's Bench Division, 22 Kingsway, London WC2B 6LE.

When Form 200 reaches the Court Funds Office arrangements are made to transfer the balance of the money to the Court of Protection, leaving the sum reserved for costs in the Special Account at the Court Funds Office to earn interest until the legal aid area office confirms the extent to which it can be released to the legal aid fund or the Court of Protection .

## County Court procedure

The procedure in the county court is similar to that in the High Court save that the amount of money involved has been unlikely to exceed £5,000 so the Rules make no reference to the Court of Protection.[79] The increased jurisdiction of the county court and the tendency to transfer personal injury cases to that court for trial

---

[77] This will be found in the White Book and can be copied from the precedent.

[78] If the award is made in London and the patient is not also a minor Form 200 should be lodged in the Action Department of the Central Office at the Royal Courts of Justice; if also a minor, at the Masters' Secretary's Office.

[79] When a Receiver brings the action he will receive the money and it will not be retained in Court.

may now result in the rules being brought more into line with those of the High Court, though in the meanwhile these may need to be followed.

### Investment

Where money is to be held in court, an Order will be made stating the manner in which it is to be invested. This is more usual in the case of a minor where it is known that the money is only to be held until the minor attains legal majority. Direct investment in equities is not permitted, and the choices of investment are basically special account, government stock, Common Investment Funds or convertible stock.

### Conclusion

Where a mentally handicapped person recovers damages through court proceedings there is thus an additional procedure whereby the monies recovered can be administered by a court other than the Court of Protection. This may be cheaper and more convenient because the fees are less and applications may be dealt with in the area where the individual lives as it will usually be possible to transfer the court file to the local court. However, little expertise will be available and there may be no consistency of supervision.

### MISCELLANEOUS

There are other circumstances in which a person may have authority to receive money on behalf of someone lacking capacity.

### Government payments

Any pay, pensions or other periodical payments due from the government to a person who is, by reason of mental disorder, unable to manage his affairs may be paid to the person having care of the patient for his benefit.[80] This is more usual in respect of elderly people, and seldom will a person with a mental handicap become entitled to income of this nature.

### Tax Returns and repayments

Tax Returns must generally be signed by the taxpayer in person,[81] but there are circumstances in which it is impossible to comply with this requirement. The Inland Revenue will accept the signature of an attorney in cases of physical inability to sign and mental incapacity, but in the latter case it must be a registered Enduring Power of Attorney. The alternative is for the Return to be signed by a Receiver appointed by the Court of Protection. In March 1983, the Revenue agreed with the Court of Protection a basis upon which tax repayments might be made to the next of kin of a mentally incapacitated person in the absence of a Receiver. The financial limits have been increased at intervals, and in 1991

---

80 Mental Health Act 1983, s.142.
81 Taxes Management Act 1970, s.8.

became an annual tax repayment of £800 or less, or a repayment of £1,600 if the income for the year (other than from trusts, annuities, pensions and covenants) does not exceed £800.[82] There are also provisions under which a parent, guardian, spouse, son or daughter of a person suffering from mental disorder may register on the person's behalf for interest to be paid without deduction of tax.[83]

## Bank accounts

If money is held in a bank account in the name of the individual and it is not presently needed, it is merely necessary to retain the bank book in a safe place. Some banks will arrange limited facilities (*e.g.* payment of maintenance charges) for an account holder who is mentally incapable and some building societies allow withdrawals in certain circumstances. In some situations the National Savings Bank allow deposits and withdrawals on a patient's account.

*Joint accounts*
Another way of managing the money of a person who is incapable of doing so, or needs supervision, is to invest it in joint names with someone else. This may be suitable in a borderline case for an individual who needs support but is able to manage to a limited extent. Thus a mother may maintain an account jointly with her handicapped daughter and credit any money received by the daughter which will then be available for her benefit as and when required; the mother retains control or supervision whilst giving the daughter some status. Some parents adopt this procedure as a natural way of dealing with the problem. They do not wish to put the money in their own name because this might appear as if they were misappropriating the money, yet an account in the child's name may not be easy to manage and there is the risk that it might suddenly be frozen if doubts as to mental capacity were raised or a different policy was adopted.

The practical solution is often the best for small sums and day to day living, but if substantial sums are involved there are serious dangers in joint accounts not least being the difficulty of identifying just whose money it is. Tax complications can arise, and the death of or financial problems on the part of the joint owner leads to difficulties which may not be easy to resolve.

*Other solutions*
One alternative to a joint account is to open an account in the name of the parent as nominee for the handicapped child. The account is then conducted by the parent but the money in it is identified as

---

82   It should be borne in mind that income payments under a discretionary trust have suffered additional rate tax, so the potential tax repayment will be a bigger proportion thereof.

83   Income Tax (Deposit-takers) (Interest Payments) (Amendment) Regulations 1991 and Income Tax (Building Societies) (Dividends and Interest) (Amendment) Regulations 1992 (S.I.1992 No.11).

belonging to the child. Another solution in the case of a competent but vulnerable person is to open the account in the name of such person but to provide that a co-signatory is required for any withdrawals, or perhaps those over a set limit.

# PART IV - STATUTORY WILLS

A statutory Will is one made on behalf of a person who is mentally incapable of making a Will. It may be made for a person who has never made a Will and for whom the intestacy provisions would not be satisfactory, or alternatively to replace an existing Will which no longer represents what the wishes of the testator could reasonably be expected to be. It has been held that "the court must seek to make the Will which the actual patient, acting reasonably, would have made if notionally restored to full mental capacity, memory and foresight".[84]

## Jurisdiction

The Court of Protection has jurisdiction to make an Order or give directions or authority for the execution for the patient of a Will making any provision which could be made by a Will executed by the patient if he were not mentally disordered. The Court's powers are not exercisable at any time when the patient is a minor, and shall not be exercised unless the Court has reason to believe that the patient is incapable of making a valid Will for himself.[85]

## Procedure

Before authorising the making of a statutory Will the Court needs all relevant information, and a procedure note has been issued specifying what is required.[86] In general terms the Court needs:
- medical evidence on the patient's mental condition, so as to determine whether there is jurisdiction;
- a comprehensive statement of the patient's assets and liabilities, so as to appreciate the extent of the property to be disposed of by Will; and
- full particulars of patient's family and dependants, so as to comprehend claims to which patient should give effect.

All this information, together with a draft of the proposed Will, are usually contained in exhibits to the affidavit of the applicant filed in support of the application for the statutory Will. The Official Solicitor may be, and usually is, asked to represent the patient and a hearing will normally be arranged.[87]

---

84  Sir Robert Megarry V-C in *Re D(J)* [1982] All ER 37.
85  Mental Health Act 1983, s.96(1)(*e*) and (4).
86  Form PN9, *Applications for the execution of statutory wills and codicils and for gifts settlements and other similar dealings.*
87  On rare occasions, where the Official Solicitor has no observations on the application, a hearing may be dispensed with by the Court.

*Who may make the application?*

There are five categories of person entitled to apply for an order[88]

- (a) the Receiver for the patient;
- (b) any person who has made an application for appointment of a Receiver which has not yet been determined;
- (c) any person who, under any known Will of the patient or under his intestacy, may become entitled to any property of the patient or any interest therein;
- (d) any person for whom the patient might be expected to provide if he were not mentally disordered;
- (e) any other person whom the court may authorise.

Although an attorney under a registered EPA may be a suitable person to make the application, the attorney is not automatically entitled to do so and would need to be authorised by the Court under paragraph (e) above.[89] The test of testamentary capacity is different from that of capacity to manage or administer property and affairs, so medical evidence in each respect is required.[90]

*Medical evidence*

When obtaining medical evidence it must not be assumed that the doctor knows the test of testamentary capacity, and it should be explained that this involves the ability to understand:

- the nature of the act of making a Will and its effect;
- the extent of the property being disposed of; and
- the persons who might be considered to benefit and manner in which the property may be distributed.

## Contents

In making a Will in these circumstances the Court will consider the benefit of members of the patient's family and make provision for other persons or purposes for whom or which the patient might provide if he were not mentally disordered.[91] The following approach was laid down by Megarry J.[92]:

(i) the patient is treated as having a brief lucid interval at the time when the Will is made;

(ii) during this interval the patient is assumed to have a full knowledge of the past and to realise that he will shortly relapse into the previous mental state;

(iii) the actual patient must be considered, not a hypothetical one (though the Court should not give effect to any strong feelings which are beyond reason);

(iv) the Court seeks to make the Will which the patient would

---

88    Court of Protection Rules 1984, r.17. PN9A is a helpful procedure note.

89    The power to make a statutory will arises under the Mental Health Act 1983 and not under the Enduring Powers of Attorney Act 1985.

90    A medical certificate in Form CP3 is needed because statutory Wills are only available under the Mental Health Act to "patients" so it must be shown that the proposed testator is a "patient".

91    This may include charities, especially those which have helped the patient.

92    *Re D.(J)* [1982] 2 All ER 37.

make if acting reasonably and on competent legal advice;
(v) the Court uses a "broad brush" rather than an "accountant's pen".

*Formalities*

The patient need not be actually present when the statutory Will is executed on his behalf by an authorised person, usually the Receiver if one has been appointed. The Order should be retained with the Will.[93]

## Implications for mental handicap

The need for a statutory Will may arise when a person with a mental handicap who does not have testamentary capacity inherits money and either there are no close relatives who could be expected to inherit such money in their turn or there are relatives but they would wish others to inherit. One could contemplate a situation where the relatives were impressed with the care and support provided by a particular charity and felt it appropriate that such charity should inherit any remaining wealth on the death of the person who had been cared for. In making a Will the Court approaches the situation as the patient would and may have in mind the tax effectiveness of the provision made. Guidance is given in a recently reported case[94]:

> An elderly lady suffering from severe mental disability since birth but with assets of £1.6 million was being looked after in a mental hospital. It was held that the court, in exercising its power to make provision for other persons or purposes for whom or which the patient might be expected to provide if not mentally disordered, had jurisdiction to make *inter vivos* dispositions and direct the execution of a Will for the patient on the assumption that she would have been a normal decent person who would have acted in accordance with contemporary standards of morality. On that basis a person in the position of the patient would have felt a moral obligation to show recognition to the community and to her family since she had spent the whole of her life in the care of the community, as embodied in the national health service, the hospital and voluntary mental health charities, and had derived her fortune from being a child of a family. She might therefore be expected to have distributed her estate equally between her family and mental health charities. The court ordered immediate gifts accordingly and made a Will dividing the residuary estate between charity and the family in equal shares. The provision for the family was in accordance with the rules for intestacy, but a legacy was given to a person who had befriended the patient.

A statutory Will may also be of particular value where an individual who has some wealth but does not have testamentary capacity is able to enter into a valid marriage. In the event of a marriage which was thought to be financially motivated on the part of the other party, those concerned could seek to make an

---

93   s.97(1) contains the formalities for the signing and attesting of Wills made under these provisions. A precedent is set out in Appendix V.

94   *Re C (a patient)* [1991] 3 All ER 866, Hoffmann J. It is interesting that, in view of doubts as to future provision for the patient, the residuary charitable gift was not to specific charities but to those concerned with mental health as the executor may select (after consulting the family). This would enable those that actually helped the patient to be considered.

application for a statutory Will thereby over-riding the normal consequences of intestacy which will have been radically changed by the marriage.

*Testamentary capacity*

It should not be assumed that just because an individual is incapable of handling his property and affairs he is also incapable of making a valid Will. The legal tests are different in each case and a person whose affairs are being dealt with by a Receiver or an attorney under a registered EPA may nevertheless be able to make a Will. If a patient whose affairs are being administered under the jurisdiction of the Court wishes to make a Will or Codicil, prior approval should be obtained. The Court will want to be satisfied that the patient is of testamentary capacity and may call for medical evidence or request one of the Medical Visitors to visit and report. A consultant's opinion is suggested in respect of a patient who is in hospital. The final responsibility rests upon the solicitor who takes the instructions to satisfy himself both then and when the Will is signed that there is testamentary capacity, namely: an understanding of the nature of the document being executed, the property to be disposed of and the claims of those to be benefitted by or excluded from the Will. If the patient is in a hospital or nursing home it is advisable for the consultant who gave the opinion or the medical practitioner in charge of the patient's treatment to be one of the witnesses, and in other cases the medical attendant should be a witness if possible. When the Will has been executed a copy should be forwarded to the Court when directions will be given for safe custody of the original. Any previous Will should not be destroyed but retained in safe custody in an envelope endorsed with a note of the date of the new Will.

The safeguards in this procedure may also be applied to cases where the donor of a registered Enduring Power of Attorney wishes to make a Will, although reference to the Court of Protection will not then be necessary.

# PART V - CONCLUSION

## COMPARISONS

Where an individual with a mental handicap has money or assets there may be a choice between the execution and registration of an EPA, using a trust, or the appointment of a Receiver. When parents or others contemplate making provision for a handicapped person they have to choose between setting up a trust fund or leaving the money to the individual beneficially for administration by a Receiver or an Attorney. Comparison between these courses may be helpful, though none of them will usually be adopted unless necessitated by the existence of capital or income which cannot be dealt with in a more informal way.

## Attorney

*Advantages*
1. Can relate to all money held by individual;
2. Suitable for small sums of money;
3. Usually little restriction upon financial powers;
4. Cheap and easy to set up and operate (minimum formality and little or no delay, no annual fees payable);
5. Attorney is entitled and expected to use his discretion;
6. Extremely flexible;
7. Procedure for other persons to object;
8. No need to produce annual accounts.

*Disadvantages*
1. Only available where there is sufficient understanding;
2. Ceases to be available if the attorney dies or incapable[95];
3. No effective supervision but objections may be raised;
4. Attorney has no-one to turn to for approval;
5. Attorney's authority may be challenged;
6. No obligation to consult or visit the individual.

## Receiver

*Advantages*
1. Available in all cases where there is no capacity;
2. Relates to all money held by individual;
3. Change of Receiver is possible;
4. Supervision by the court;
5. Receiver can seek approval of the court.
6. Authority of Receiver cannot be questioned.

*Disadvantages*
1. May not be available for merely limited mental capacity;
2. Not suitable for small sums of money (though there are special procedures available);
3. Expensive to set up and operate (formality and delay, annual fees payable to the court);
4. Limited discretion (frequent reference to court required)[96];
5. Annual accounts must be produced;
6. No obligation to consult or visit the individual.

## Trust

*Advantages*
1. Trustees may be given wide discretionary powers;
2. Self perpetuating trustees;
3. No annual fees payable to the Court;
4. May be wide discretion over exercise of financial powers;
5. No need to produce annual accounts;
6. Financial authority of trustees cannot be questioned;

---

95  The donor may remain capable of appointing a new attorney, or an alternative attorney may initially be appointed;
96  Court may give wide authority to a Receiver with the necessary experience.

6.   May avoid means-testing for welfare and other benefits.

*Disadvantages*

1.   Only available when money is provided by other persons;
2.   Does not relate to individual's own money;
3.   Can be expensive to set up and operate;
4.   Inadequate supervision (with little control over charges of professional trustees);
5.   Trustees have no-one to turn to for approval;
6.   May lack desired flexibility once set up;
7.   No obligation to consult or visit the individual;
8.   Problems of unspent income and tax re-payments.

The chart at the end of this chapter may assist in comparing the courses available.

## Interaction

It is suggested that the barriers between Enduring Powers of Attorney, receivership and trusts are too tightly drawn and that more flexibility between these alternative forms of delegation could be introduced. For example, the Court of Protection should be able to appoint an attorney on behalf of the patient in simple cases, and where substantial sums are involved it could create trusts and ensure that suitable persons were appointed as trustees. Under existing law, if medical evidence is produced that the patient satisfies the test in *Re K., Re F.* the Court could discharge the Receiver and authorise an Enduring Power of Attorney to be executed by the patient[97] and registered, but the Court does not encourage this course. There must be many cases where a Receiver has been appointed on behalf of a person who is capable of appointing an attorney under the recently clarified test, yet this personal power is effectively denied to them.

### SUMMARY

There are thus a number of methods in which the financial affairs of a person with a mental handicap may be handled, ranging from the purely informal to court supervised. The circumstances of the particular case, as to the degree of handicap and communication and as to the amount of money involved, will dictate which method should be adopted. In some instances some choice may remain but in others there will be no choice. It should not be assumed that just because there is a choice of procedures they are adequate; in reality for the typical mentally handicapped person there is simply no adequate legal procedure for dealing with any personal monies.

---

97   The patient is deprived of this power as long as he is under the jurisdiction of the Court of Protection. Where there are competing applications for receivership and registration of an EPA the Court prefers the latter as far as possible; see article in the *Law Society's Gazette* (1987), p.1219.

## Options

When considering how to cope with financial matters, there are the following possibilities:

(1) if the handicap is mild the individual may be capable of dealing with financial matters with informal guidance from parents or carers and will have access to social security benefits. Much depends upon the nature and value of the assets involved and the motivation and strength of character of the individual,[98] but where there are only small personal savings steps can be taken to ensure that these are invested in ways that are readily available to the individual (e.g. an account at a local office of a building society which he is able to visit and whose staff are helpful). Larger sums may be invested in joint names or in the names of trustees (who will in effect be nominees);

(2) if there are few personal assets and there is an appointee for DSS benefits no further formality may be needed (this includes cases where family monies are dealt with by a trust);

(3) if there are or may be significant personal assets, or the individual is not capable of expressing his wishes in a normal way, but in either event is capable of understanding the nature and effect of an EPA, it would be wise for such a power to be executed and then registered if appropriate;

(4) if the individual is incapable of understanding the nature and effect of an EPA, then unless there are minimal assets and all state benefits can be received by the carers as appointees, an application should be made to the Court of Protection for the appointment of a Receiver;

(5) where provision is to be made for the individual it is usually thought appropriate to do so by way of a trust fund with the trustees being carefully chosen and having some (perhaps very wide) discretionary powers. The alternative of leaving money to the individual and relying upon the appointment of a Receiver should not be overlooked especially in view of the supervision that this provides, but in practice the desire to avoid means-testing usually dictates trust provision.

### Improvidence

Although some people with a mental handicap may be incapable of handling money at all, others may be capable yet incompetent and may spend foolishly or even give away any money or property that comes into their possession. The law does not permit anyone to exercise control over what another person does with their money provided that they have a basic level of understanding. It protects those who are incapable but not those who are simply incompetent or foolish. In these cases it is necessary for parents and others to make trust provision so as to ensure that capital and property intended for support does not come under the legal

---

98 The parents are not always the best people to decide just how much financial freedom should be allowed because they may be over-protective.

control of the improvident beneficiary.

## The decision maker

In all cases of delegation of financial powers the adviser should remember that the person making the decisions is deemed to be the disabled individual, even though in reality the decision is being made by someone with delegated powers (often the parent or carer). Conflicts of interest can arise in these circumstances and there is relatively little protection for the disabled individual. Difficulties of communication may disguise an ability to make decisions, and all too often views are expressed on behalf of a disabled person without taking the trouble to ascertain his views. The golden rule for lawyers is to remember who the client is, and this is not the person through whom instructions are received. A lawyer should refuse to act on instructions when he does not consider that these are in the best interests of the individual on whose behalf they are given, and in cases of clear abuse he should seek the intervention of the Court of Protection. Where there is an EPA, the court has supervisory powers which it may exercise when abuse is drawn to its attention, and in other cases the appointment of a Receiver may be appropriate. However, these powers may not be adequate to control trustees in the exercise of a discretion and this is a danger where trusts are relied upon by the family.

## LAW REFORM

It is unfortunate that the statutory procedures for delegation of the financial powers of persons who are incapable of making decisions should be found in legislation that deals principally with mental health,[99] especially when the majority of those who need these procedures are the elderly. Lawyers have traditionally regarded applications to the Court of Protection as the last resort, and old habits die hard. This view may not be justified, and there are circumstances where the appointment of a Receiver provides valuable safeguards for a vulnerable individual, but as long as the means-testing rules provide such a strong disincentive to parents who would otherwise leave money directly to their handicapped child the use of trusts will continue.

The alternative procedure of an Enduring Power of Attorney was brought in by statute as a result of the large number of elderly people who needed help in handling their own affairs and the limitations of ordinary powers. It was not expected that such procedure would apply to the mentally handicapped adult, but the interpretation of the legislation creates possibilities that have yet to be explored, though there is scope for abuse (or more likely, well meaning domination).

These two procedures have grown from different seeds and have

---

99  Of the 149 sections in the Mental Health Act 1983, only 20 deal with the Court of Protection's powers.

little in common. This is illogical when in most instances they do the same job, and the only fundamental difference at the inception is that the Receiver is appointed by the court whereas the attorney is appointed by the individual. There is a need for this area of law to be re-examined and comprehensive legislation introduced, independently of mental health law, dealing with decision making for people who lack capacity to make their own decisions.[100]

## Receivership

There is a great deal of ignorance about the work of the Court of Protection but efforts have been made by the Court during recent years to acquaint the public with its work, and changes in the Rules and policy have made the Court more user friendly.

### Remoteness and delay

The Court only operates in London and this makes it seem remote and impersonal. With the growth in the work undertaken by the Court, and taking into account the high cost of working in central London, a better service and image could probably be attained if the Court were to operate in regional centres where it could maintain closer contact with local firms of solicitors and social services departments, and be more accessible to the public.

Complaints are made about delays. Some delay is inevitable unless the Receiver is to be given total control over the financial affairs of the patient, and whilst this may be the situation under an EPA it may be undesirable in the case of a Receiver appointed by the Court (rather than by the patient).

### Fees and costs

The amount of the fees charged is another source of complaint, especially when the Court has not done any work itself on a particular case, but it is government policy that the Court must pay for itself without a subsidy. The present fee scales are based on the amount of money involved rather than the work done in the individual case and this can result in fees which appear excessive.

Although it is not essential to employ a solicitor, the complexity makes this desirable at some stages. Lawyers often find that fixed costs are not adequate and are discouraged from handling this type of work by the need to tax their bills in many cases and the fear (probably not justified) that they will not be adequately paid in any event. Few firms prepare their own bills for taxation, and employing outside costs draughtsmen results in a loss on the taxation process. The procedure for agreed costs introduced in 1990 may encourage more solicitors to undertake this type of work and the financial limit for this has since been increased, but it does not extend to fixed costs cases. Any hearing must take place in London, which proves expensive especially for provincial solicitors who are more likely to be instructed on behalf of mentally handicapped persons. In view of different hourly rates it

---

100  This topic is considered in greater detail in the introduction to Chap.2.

is not always cheaper to employ London agents, but in any event work of this nature tends to become personal and it is helpful for the solicitor having conduct of the matter to attend the hearing.

*Consultation*

The patient, although initially given notice of the application to appoint a Receiver and an opportunity to make representations, is not thereafter consulted by the Court. The patient's views, if any, are merely put to the Court, if at all, by the Receiver and the patient does not see the information on the basis of which decisions are made. As part of a procedure for consultation, the Receiver should be required to visit the patient at regular intervals and report as to his social and medical condition, needs and quality of life. When community care becomes a reality it would be desirable for an annual social report to be submitted by the patient's keyworker so that this could be compared with the picture painted by the Receiver and further enquiries made if appropriate, but this would increase the cost of the procedures and result in delays.

*Conflicts of interest*

The Receiver is often a member of the patient's family who may be affected by the way money is spent, or ultimately benefit if money is not spent, so conflicts of interest can arise.[101] Under the present procedure these may not always be recognised by the Court which will not receive an independent report directed at the options otherwise available to the patient and indicating what would be in the patient's best interests.

*Assessment*

The meaning of mental disorder is imprecise, and it is not clear how one assesses capacity to handle ones own affairs, yet only a single medical report is required and there is no provision for a social report. This is all the more significant in cases of mental handicap where the problem is not so much one of illness within the doctor's field of training and experience, but rather social competence linked to education, training and the inherent abilities of the individual (or lack of them). A doctor is unlikely, within the scope of an examination, to be able to make the necessary assessment and can do little more than diagnose the general condition and estimate the severity based upon the usual implications of that condition. The patient does not receive any information about the assessment notwithstanding that this is relied upon by the Court.

## Enduring Powers of Attorney

The scope for using Enduring Powers of Attorney in the case of people with a relatively mild mental handicap has not yet been fully recognised, but to the unscrupulous there is scope for abuse

---

101  It may be in the best interests of the donor for money to be spent so that he can live in the community, but the attorney may be a relative with whom the donor lives who would suffer financially from the move.

and even where the honesty of the attorney is beyond question there is a danger that the convenient delegation of financial powers will result in the freedom of the donor being unduly restricted. Conflicts of interest can arise as in the case of receivership, but for an attorney there is no outside supervision. Safeguards similar to those proposed for receivership may be appropriate, and the solicitor should always remember that his client is the donor in whose best interests he should act, not the attorney through whom he will usually receive instructions.

*Registration or validation*

A medical report seldom needs to be produced in connection with an EPA, yet is essential before a Receiver can be appointed. In consequence the registration of an EPA is an administrative task and neither validates the power nor deprives the donor of his personal powers. The result is that a registered power may be challenged and delays can and do arise when it is produced. There is an argument for a certification procedure rather than merely a registration procedure but then a medical opinion would be needed at the point of registration (and possibly also at the date of execution if the power was to be registered shortly thereafter).

*Professional attorney*

It has been suggested that there should be no need to register the power when the attorney is a professional person (*i.e.* a solicitor or an accountant). Although there is provision in the legislation for the Lord Chancellor by Order to exempt attorneys of particular descriptions from the requirements to give notice to relatives prior to registration, no such Order has yet been made and there does not appear to have been any pressure for this.

## Medical reports

Of particular concern in the case of persons with a mental handicap is whether a general medical practitioner is competent to provide a report upon the capacity of the individual. We have in Chapter 1 considered the difference between the medical, legal and social worker's approach, and from this it will be seen that whilst the doctor can diagnose the existence of mental handicap and perhaps identify its nature or cause, his training and experience may not equip him to comment upon the capacity of the individual to perform any particular range of tasks. Having diagnosed a particular condition the doctor may automatically confirm that certain tasks are beyond the competence of the individual, whereas those who work with the individual may believe that he has more potential. Without an imaginative approach there may be a lifelong denial of financial freedom leading to a lack of personal development. It is essential that procedures for financial management develop alongside the new thinking in personal skills development, and that those who are given financial control do not prove to be an additional handicap for the individual.

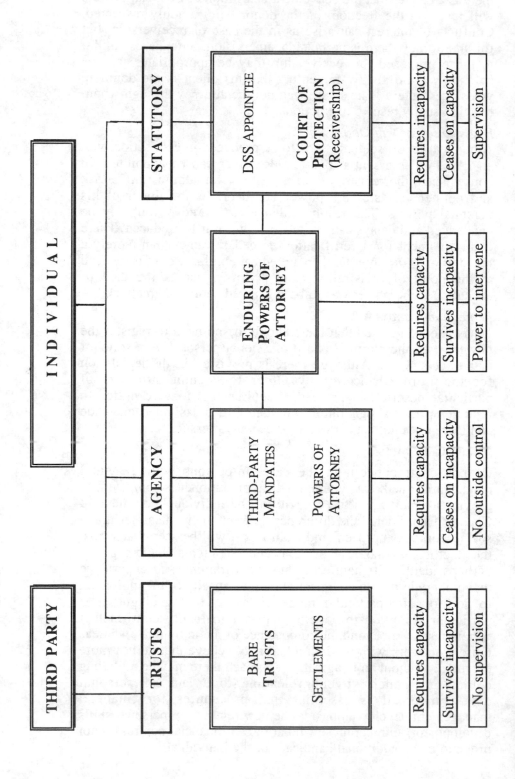

# CHAPTER 10B  DELEGATION OF FINANCIAL POWERS
## (SCOTLAND)

## GENERAL

### Capacity and incapacity

There is a presumption in favour of capacity. Proof of incapacity is required if a transaction is to be declared void, or if someone else is to be appointed to manage assets and affairs.

Incapacity in relation to a particular transaction is determined by reference to two elements, the capability of the person and the nature of the transaction. The answer will be clearcut: the transaction will be valid or void.[1]

Incapacity in relation to management is more complex. Decisions depend upon an assessment of what transactions are likely to be necessary in future, and of the person's capability in relation to them. In determining whether delegation of management powers is necessary and if so which method(s) would be appropriate, three principal elements have to be considered: the nature and extent of the person's assets and affairs; the management decisions which are likely to be necessary in relation to them; and the person's capacity. A fourth element which may be relevant to choice of method is whether the person resides in hospital. Examples of the interaction of the three principal elements are:

- A person with a mild mental handicap has substantial funds, and various commitments, but the funds are soundly and sensibly invested, with income mandated to a bank account from which commitments are paid by standing order, leaving the person to manage day-to-day expenditure, of which - with informal guidance which is available - he is capable. No delegation may be necessary.
- The same person has only modest assets, but there are problems and disputes which he cannot handle. An appointment may be required.
- A person with a severe handicap is quite incapable of any financial management but has no capital, and no income other than social security benefits. A DSS appointee is all that is required.

### Fundamental principles

Incapacity, however profound, does not disqualify a person from owning assets; the problem is one of management. No matter how profound the incapacity, neither parents nor anyone else retain automatic management powers once a person reaches the age of

---

1    See Chap.2, Part I "Rights and Capacity".

16. Except where the principle of *negotiorum gestio* applies, or informal arrangements are in operation, some specific procedure must be followed for management powers to be conferred.

While it may be helpful to a mentally handicapped person for someone to be appointed to manage financial matters, it is also a form of discrimination against the person, taking away the right which all adults otherwise have to manage their own affairs. The cardinal rule for advisers in selecting the appropriate management technique is to try to strike the right balance, providing such help as is necessary (upon an assessment of assets, management needs, and capacity) but not impinging unnecessarily upon persons' rights to manage their own affairs. A corollary is that in appropriate cases one should try to achieve arrangements which will in future encourage the person to exercise and develop capacity.

## Management techniques

Sadly, such considerations are often disregarded. The black and white world of capacity in relation to individual transactions, which are either valid or void, is carried over into questions of management, and it is frequently assumed that evidence of some incapacity will disqualify a person from managing anything. This misconception is often reinforced by legal texts which use in relation to all forms of incapacity meaningless but dangerous terms such as "insane" or "of unsound mind", which imply that evidence of any mental disability should cause complete loss of legal capacity. Moreover, this fallacy is embodied in the law itself: for example, appointment of a curator bonis results in complete loss of legal capacity to manage, so that if a curator is appointed because of matters of particular complexity, the person loses legal capacity in relation to management of simple matters of which he may in fact be capable.[2]

A further problem for the adviser is that the array of management techniques described below has evolved haphazardly, at common law and by diverse statutory and other provisions, and does not form a coherent and co-ordinated scheme. The adviser must pick his way through them, and select the arrangements which best suit the particular case. The techniques may be categorised as follows:

*Firstly*, where a particular legal procedure is followed to appoint someone to act as manager, sub-divided into:

- procedures of general application (appointment of curators bonis, or of tutors),
- a procedure applicable to people in a particular situation (hospital management),
- procedures applicable to particular assets (social security benefits, vaccine damage payments, court awards of damages, criminal injuries compensation payments, savings certificates, national savings bank accounts, government and

---

2   But a person with a curator bonis may be able to make a valid Will (see Chap.2, p.33) or to marry.

certain other pensions, and others).

*Secondly*, where informal arrangements without any formal appointment are operated (including *negotiorum gestio*, joint accounts, and bare trusts).

*Thirdly*, where a donor or testator pays and conveys to trustees under a formal trust, rather than to the mentally handicapped person.

*Fourthly*, where a manager is appointed by the person himself, at a time when he has capacity to make such appointment.

Techniques may also be classified in various other ways. The following characteristics are important:

- *The degree of formality to obtain appointment*; varying from a court petition supported by two medical certificates to appoint a curator bonis, to very simple procedures such as for a DSS appointee, and further to the self appointment of a negotiorum gestor.
- *The degree of accountability and supervision*; ranging from a high level in relation to curators, which can give rise to complaints of remoteness, rigidity and cumbersomeness, to little or none in relation to many other techniques, with risk of misapplication of funds and exploitation of the financial power of the manager. Available techniques tend to be at one extreme or the other.
- *As to whether the manager may be remunerated.* If so, professional standards of management are available, but significant management costs will be chargeable.
- *As to the manager's powers.* It cannot be stressed too often that a manager must be aware of the nature of his appointment, of what is within the scope and powers of his appointment, and what is not. Except in the case of curatories, which are closely supervised, ignorance is commonplace, and can be found even among professional patients affairs managers in hospitals.
- *As to the effect on capacity.* Curatories result in automatic loss of legal capacity to manage one's affairs. No other method of management in common use has that effect.
- *As to interrelationship with other techniques*; for example, several methods of management are superseded by appointment of a curator bonis, while others may co-exist.

In this chapter, the description of each management technique includes under "main characteristics" an analysis in relation to the above criteria.

## Management needs

The adviser requires to know the range of management techniques available, and the characteristics of each, and to apply this knowledge to an analysis of the management needs in each individual case. The solution may be to recommend a particular management technique, or a combination, or some other action not entailing imposition of any form of delegated management.

Categories into which needs may fall include the following:
- A need for delivery of services or provision of help, without any formal management arrangements. Examples are people needing informal guidance or help in matters such as budgeting, or needing help in overcoming communication difficulties.
- A need for a single act of management, such as executing a lease of a flat or a deed of family arrangement altering inappropriate provision in a relative's Will.
- A need for short-term management, such as dealing with particular problems or disputes, or simplifying complex financial arrangements.
- A need for long-term partial management, when a person can manage simple transactions, but not more complex matters.
- A need for long-term full management, where a person has no capacity to manage any of his financial affairs, and such incapacity is likely to be permanent.

Unacceptably prevalent is the bad practice of applying to the first four categories solutions appropriate only to the last.

## Professional responsibility

*Financial advisers*

Financial advisers have obligations[3] to "know the client" and give "best advice". These obligations apply fully when giving advice where someone involved, such as a relative, has a mental handicap. Financial advisers must accordingly understand the capacity and needs of that person, and apply to such understanding a knowledge of the techniques described in Chapters 8 and 9.

*Solicitors*

Solicitors must in addition consider the question of to whom they are professionally responsible. Frequently, they are consulted by relatives or others, rather than by the mentally handicapped person. Provisions for separate legal representation of such persons are a common feature of many legal systems with modern codes of provision regarding property management,[4] but such separate representation is relatively uncommon in this country. Accordingly, solicitors should consider whether there is any divergence between the course which those who have consulted them would wish to take, and the advice which they would give in the best interests of the mentally disabled person alone, taking account of the principles and considerations discussed above. Unless those consulting the solicitor are prepared to proceed on the basis of advice which the solicitor is satisfied is in the best interests of the mentally handicapped person, the solicitor may feel that it would be appropriate to proceed only if the person is

---

3    Financial Services Act 1986 and provisions in pursuance thereof.
4    In New Zealand separate legal representation is mandatory in applications for any personal or property order.

separately represented. There may be other situations where separate representation is appropriate, but this will not necessarily mean that the solicitor disagrees with those consulting him.

## Comparison with English law

As will be evident from the division of this topic into two separate chapters, the differences between the two legal systems are substantial. Scotland has no Court of Protection, or equivalent, and provisions regarding powers of attorney are quite different. There is no mechanism in Scots law for making a Will for a person lacking testamentary capacity. Some of the other delegations described in Part III of Chapter 10A are relevant to Scotland and are described more briefly here, with cross-references.

## CURATORY

The term "curator" has many applications in Scots law. Here it is used to mean a curator bonis appointed to manage the assets and affairs of a person over 16 lacking management capacity. The person to whom the curator is appointed is termed the "ward".

## Main characteristics

Curatory is a management technique of general application initiated by legal procedure, and is the only general technique in regular use.[5] A curator may be appointed to any mentally disabled person who has affairs which he is unable to manage, and in current practice manages all assets, whatever their nature. Appointment is by court petition, supported by two medical certificates. Curators are under the supervision of the Accountant of Court, to whom they must submit annual accounts for audit. They may be remunerated, and many are solicitors or accountants, though there has been a recent trend towards more appointments of lay curators. A curator's discretion as to investment and application of funds is strictly circumscribed. Appointment of a curator deprives the ward of all legal capacity, regardless of the level of actual capacity.[6] Upon appointment a curator automatically supersedes hospital management, DSS appointees and most other managers under specific statutory provisions. A curator is in turn superseded by service of a tutor-at-law (though there have been no recent appointments of a tutor-at-law).[7]

## Curator as judicial factor

Curators are one type of a larger class called judicial factors. This section describes curators, rather than judicial factors generally, because in relation to mentally disabled people curatory is by far

---

5   About 400 curators are appointed each year (Scottish Law Commission Discussion Paper No 94 *Mentally Disabled Adults*, para 4.2).

6   *Yule* v. *Alexander* (1891) 19R 167 *Mitchell and Baxter* v. *Cheyne* (1891) 19R 324

7   A petition for such appointment, opposed by an existing curator, is before the Court of Session at time of writing.

the predominant type of judicial factory. The major part of the law relating to curators, as described here, applies also to other relevant types of judicial factor, and when they are described later the differences are highlighted.

## Principal legislation, etc.

Judicial Factors Acts 1849, 1880 and 1889
Trusts (Scotland) Acts 1921 and 1961
Trustee Investments Act 1961
Law Reform (Miscellaneous Provisions) (Scotland) Acts 1980 and 1990
Mental Health (Scotland) Act 1984
Act of Sederunt (Rules of the Court of Session Amendment No.1) (Miscellaneous) 1990
Act of Sederunt (Rules of the Court of Session Amendment No.8) (Discharge of Judicial Factors) 1991
Act of Sederunt (Judicial Factors Rules) 1992.[8]

## Procedure prior to appointment

### Grounds of appointment

Curators are traditionally appointed upon evidence in the form of two medical certificates that a person is "of unsound mind" and incapable of managing his affairs or giving instructions for their management. Brief certificates to this effect are used in the great majority of cases despite judicial criticism,[9] and despite the developing use of more meaningful and informative certificates in tutor-dative procedure.[10] There must be property of a significant amount[11] or a claim of a significant amount which may be enforced.[12]

### Jurisdiction

Both the Court of Session and (without financial limits) the Sheriff Court have jurisdiction to appoint curators. Most commonly, the person resides within the jurisdiction of the court and has moveable property in Scotland, but there have been appointments where the person resides within the jurisdiction of the court but has moveable property outside Scotland, and where the person resides outside Scotland but has moveable property in Scotland.[13]

### Medical examination and certificates

Two doctors must examine the person, preferably separately, not more than thirty days before the petition is presented. If the person is resident in hospital, one doctor should be unconnected with the hospital. Each doctor issues a certificate. They are often

---

8    Applies to Sheriff Court curatories, in force from March 9, 1992.
9    *Fraser* v. *Paterson* 1987 SLT 562.
10   See Chap.3, "Tutors to Adults (Scotland)".
11   *Dunbar* (1848) 10D 866.
12   *Moodie* v. *Dempster* 1931 SC 553 at 555.
13   See Anton, *Private International Law* (2nd.ed.), pp.567- 570.

given on soul and conscience, but that is not essential.[14] Each
certificate gives the name, address and qualifications of the doctor,
the name and address of the person, and the date and place of the
examination, and confirms that the examination was carried out
apart from any other doctor. Each certifies at least the basic
requirement that the person is of unsound mind and unable to
manage his affairs or give instructions for their management. The
certificates may also cover matters relevant to special powers
sought in the petition: for example, if a house is to be sold, the
certificate will confirm that in the doctor's opinion the person will
never be able to live there again. If service of the petition on the
person would be detrimental to him, the certificate should say so,
but this will rarely apply to people with a mental handicap. The
certificate should be dated, preferably on the same date as the
examination, and should be either holograph or adopted as
holograph. Petitions have been allowed when owing to opposition
it has been possible to obtain only one certificate, or none.[15]

*Petitioner*
The petition may be brought by anyone with an interest in the
person's welfare or estate. The majority of petitioners are
relatives, but petitions may also be brought by a friend, solicitor
or banker, a responsible person from an institution where the
handicapped person resides, or someone already managing some
or all of the person's affairs, such as a negotiorum gestor. The
local authority has a duty to petition if satisfied that a curatory is
competent and necessary, and no-one else is taking steps to have a
curator appointed; and the Mental Welfare Commission may
petition in similar circumstances.[16] The Accountant of Court must
report to the court, if no-one else does, where a curator dies
undischarged or ceases to perform his duties.[17] A petitioner may
seek appointment of himself as curator.

*The petition*
The application takes the normal form of a petition (Court of
Session) or a summary application (Sheriff Court). The crave
usually seeks appointment as curator of a named person or such
other person as the court shall think proper, and seeks a finding
that the costs of the petition be paid from the person's estate or by
anyone opposing the petition. The petition gives the usual details
of the petitioner and the handicapped person; gives details of
family and any others interested in the person's estate; avers

---

14  Practice Note, June 6, 1968.
15  *Davies* v. *Davies* 1928 SLT 142, *Greig* 1923 SLT 434, *Leslie* (1895) 3
    SLT 128.
16  Mental Health (Scotland) Act 1984, ss.92 and 93.
17  Judicial Factors (Scotland) Act 1889, s.10. The report states the
    circumstances and names a person willing to act as curator. Medical
    certificates are not required and service is not usually ordered. The
    procedure has also been used where there are insufficient funds for the costs
    of a new appointment.

incapacity by reference to the medical evidence; gives details of the estate (the amount being relevant to the level of caution); and avers that appointment of a curator is necessary. The two medical certificates are lodged with the petition.

The petition may also seek dispensation with service upon the handicapped person, special powers, or an interim appointment; in each case supported by appropriate averments. It is served upon the handicapped person (unless the court dispenses with such service) and upon relatives and other persons who have an interest in his estate (if not themselves petitioners). The court may order service upon others.[18] The mental health officer has no role in curatory procedure, and petitions do not require to be intimated to the social work authority or to the Mental Welfare Commission.

## Who may be appointed curator

A curator must be an individual, and neither a partnership nor a limited company may be appointed.[19] The appointee must have no interest adverse to that of the handicapped person, must be of full legal capacity, and may not be a bankrupt. Although some texts indicate otherwise, persons resident outside Scotland may be appointed,[20] and there is generally no difficulty over appointing a person resident in England as curator, if otherwise suitable and appropriate.[21] A strong trend over many years towards appointment only of people with suitable professional qualifications, such as solicitors and accountants, has recently been reversed with appointments, in suitable cases, of lay curators, even on occasion when the estate has been quite large. The Accountant of Court's office often provides helpful assistance to lay curators, but does not favour situations where a lay curator is in practice reliant upon the assistance of someone else, such as a solicitor, who is not directly under the supervision of the Accountant.

## Procedure upon appointment

### Notification

Notification of the appointment must be given within 28 days in the following circumstances. When the petition has been brought by a local authority or the Mental Welfare Commission in respect of a hospital patient the managers of the hospital must be notified. In the case of persons under guardianship, the local authority (if petitioner) must notify the guardian, and the Mental Welfare Commission (if petitioner) must notify the local authority.[22]

---

18 See also r.6 of 1992 Act of Sederunt (Sheriff Court) regarding intimation to the Accountant of Court and display of a copy on the walls of court.

19 *McFarlane* v. *Donaldson* (1835) 13S 725; *Brogan, Petr* 1986 SLT 420.

20 In Court of Session procedure the appointee requires to lodge a Bond of Prorogation.

21 In *Jordan*, 1987 (unreported) a barrister resident in England was appointed curator to his sister, resident in Scotland.

22 But not, for some reason, the guardian. Mental Health (Scotland) Act 1984, ss.92 and 93.

*Caution*

Upon appointment, a curator must find caution[23] before commencing to administer the ward's estate, and must normally do so within one month of appointment. Emergency steps to protect the estate may be taken in the meantime. The amount of caution is set by the Accountant of Court and the bond of caution is lodged with the Accountant, who may subsequently vary the amount.

*Ingathering and inventory*

As soon as the curator has found caution and obtained a certified copy interlocutor of his appointment, he must ingather the estate. The extract appointment effectively transfers to the curator all moveable property of the ward in the British dominions,[24] but heritable property remains in the ward's name, unless special powers are obtained to do otherwise. The curator then prepares an inventory of the estate as it stood at the date of appointment, and lodges it with the Accountant of Court as soon as possible after obtaining caution (and in any event within six months of receipt by the Accountant of the Bond of Caution). The Accountant must be advised if further property is subsequently discovered.

*Guidance*

Guidance and advice may be sought from the Accountant of Court, who issues to each curator "Instructions for Completion of Factorial Inventory", and "Notes for the Guidance of Judicial Factors" with a style of annual account appended.

## Duties of curator

Described above are the initial duties to find caution, ingather the estate, and prepare and lodge an inventory. The duty to ingather includes a duty to enforce any entitlements or claims known to exist at the outset of the curatory, or which subsequently arise or come to light.[25] The curator must enter into the administration of the estate, and must exercise care, diligence and skill. Though not technically a trustee, a curator is in a position of trust with consequent fiduciary duties. He must make no personal profit other than the commission allowed by the Accountant of Court, and must seek discharge if a conflict of interest arises. He must lodge annual accounts with the Accountant of Court. He is personally responsible for due performance of his duties and must not delegate his responsibilities,[26] but may (and sometimes must)

---

23  Security for the due administration of the ward's estate, in the form of an individual policy from an insurance or guarantee company, block policies not being acceptable. Pronounced "káyshun".

24  Judicial Factors (Scotland) Act 1889, s.13.

25  The curator must claim all social security benefits to which the ward is entitled and must claim legal rights when there is no testamentary provision in favour of the ward; but see discussion in Chap.9, Part.IVB.

26  The duties to ingather and not to delegate mean that, so far as he can competently do so, the curator must bring to an end other subsisting management appointments or arrangements not automatically terminated by his appointment.

take professional advice. The curator has a duty to invest funds without delay; his powers of investment are dealt with in the next section.

*Breach of duty*

The Accountant of Court supervises curators and is responsible for ensuring that they perform their duties. He may make requisitions on curators, and report breach of duty to the court. Penalties which may be imposed for breach of duty include fines, payment of expenses, forfeiture of commission, and suspension or removal.[27] The curator can be held liable in reparation to make good loss to the estate through breach of duty.

## Investment and management

*Investment*

A curator is under a duty to invest, and has the same powers of investment as a trustee under the Trustee Investments Act 1961, as amended. He may obtain special powers to make or retain an investment outwith the scope of statutory trustee investments.[28] Schedule 1 to the 1961 Act (as amended by various Orders) lists permissible investments in three categories, namely narrower-range investments not requiring advice, narrower-range investments requiring advice, and wider range investments.

The first two categories are self-explanatory. The curator may without obtaining approval or professional advice invest funds in narrower-range investments not requiring advice, and may likewise vary investments within that category. Examples of that category are defence bonds, national savings certificates, British savings bonds, various types of national savings bonds, and bank deposits.

The curator may invest in narrower-range investments requiring advice provided that he acts in accordance with "proper advice", that is to say written advice from a stockbroker or other person suitably qualified to advise. Examples are gilt-edged and certain other fixed-income securities, debentures, local authority and similar loans, building society deposits, loans on heritable security,[29] feuduties and ground annuals, certificates of tax deposit, certain fixed-interest securities issued by international organisations, and variable interest government securities.

If the curator wishes to take advantage of the wider range, he must have the entire estate (other than special range estate - see below) professionally valued, and divide it into two parts equal in value at time of division. One part becomes the narrower range fund, which may be invested in narrower range investments, and the other becomes the wider range fund, which may be invested in

---

27    Judicial Factors Act 1849, s.6.
28    In *Fraser* v. *Paterson (No 2)* 1988 SLT 124 the court authorised retention of a shareholding in a family private limited company.
29    But the Accountant of Court does not generally regard heritable loans as suitable for curatories.

narrower or wider range investments. The two funds must be kept separate, notwithstanding variations in their relative values, except that exchanges of equal value may be made between the two funds. Additional estate must be split equally between the two funds, unless arising upon property in one of them, in which case it is paid into that fund. Surplus revenue is treated as additional estate. "Proper advice" is required, and prior approval of the Accountant of Court should be obtained, for wider range investments, which include quoted shares in United Kingdom companies, building society shares and authorised unit trusts.[30] When at inception of the curatory the estate includes investments within the wider range category, the curator must either reinvest in the narrower range, or comply with the procedure described in this paragraph.

As well as complying with the foregoing requirements, curators must have regard to the need for diversification, and to the suitability of investments to the purposes and aims of the particular curatory. Curators are also subject to a general common law obligation to invest prudently.

*Special range*
Special range estate comprises heritable property, household furniture, life policies, annuities, pensions and benefits, investments which are not trustee investments but cannot be realised, and any other estate outwith the scope of the narrower and wider ranges.

*Cash balances*
A consequence of the duty to invest is that a curator must not hold more than £500 for more than 10 days in cash or current account.[31] Sums in excess must be banked in an interest-bearing account in the curator's name as curator. Contravention incurs a charge to penal interest upon the curator, subject to discretion of the Accountant of Court to modify or remit. Serious malfeasance in this respect can result in loss of the curatorship and of all commission due, without compensation.

*Usual and special powers*
"Usual powers" are automatically conferred upon the curator by appointment. Accordingly, the curator may exercise usual powers without seeking the specific authority of the court. The usual powers enable the curator to ingather and realise the estate, to invest it within the scope of the investment powers described above, to pay debts, to apply revenue for the benefit of the ward, to give up tenancy of a house,[32] and to sell furniture.

---

30  The curator must consider whether the advantages of access to the wider range justify the additional administrative work. It is understood that the Accountant of Court would not normally consider this worthwhile for estates under £20,000.

31  Judicial Factors Act 1849, s.5 (as amended).

32  But tenancies to which right-to-buy provisions attach may have to be treated as contingent assets.

Anything outwith the curator's usual powers requires special powers, which may be divided into those obtainable from the Accountant of Court and those obtainable from the court.

*Powers obtainable from the Accountant of Court*

Prior approval must be obtained from the Accountant of Court to sell or borrow on the security of heritable or moveable estate,[33] grant feus or leases, remove tenants, excamb (exchange) any heritable estate, or acquire residential accommodation for the ward. The Accountant's approval protects the curator from challenge that he has acted at variance with the purposes of the curatory.[34] The Accountant may sanction allowances to persons whom the ward has a legal obligation to support, and payment of travelling expenses to relatives (and perhaps others) to visit the ward.

The Accountant may in certain circumstances approve encroachment on capital where the income of the estate is insufficient to maintain the ward. The curator applies by letter to the Accountant, providing such information as the Accountant may require. The Accountant may direct the curator either to apply to the court, or alternatively to intimate the application (and details of the right to object within 28 days) to the curator's cautioner, whoever petitioned for the curator's appointment, everyone (including the ward) upon whom the petition was served, and everyone else with an interest in the estate whose names and whereabouts are known. Details of service are reported to the Accountant, who may consent to the encroachment if there are no timeous objections. If there are any objections, the curator must apply to the court for special powers.[35]

The Accountant has discretion in special circumstances to give subsequent approval, if the curator has acted outwith his powers but demonstrably in the ward's best interests (or if the act was necessary and there was no time to obtain special powers).

*Special powers from the court*

To obtain special powers from the court the curator must prepare a report stating the circumstances, the curator's own views and the exact powers sought. The curator first submits his report to the Accountant of Court, who also prepares a report. Both reports are then submitted to the court, with a note seeking the court's sanction. In granting or refusing special powers the court may disagree with the Accountant.[36]

Special powers are required from the court, *inter alia*, to sell the

---

33   But special powers from the court must be obtained to sell the ward's former home.

34   Trusts (Scotland) Act 1921, s.4(1) and Trusts (Scotland) Act 1961, s.2(1).

35   Rule of Court 200B, introduced by 1990 Act of Sederunt (Court of Session) and 1992 Act of Sederunt, r.15 (Sheriff Court).

36   Special powers may be obtained from the court in the petition for appointment, or by application under the Judicial Factors Act 1849, s.7, or by petition under the Trusts (Scotland) Act 1921, s.5.

ward's former home, carry on a business, invest in an annuity, concur in the sale of property liferented by the ward, encroach on capital (unless the Accountant approves encroachment under the procedure described above), or claim legal rights in preference to a testamentary provision in favour of the ward.[37] While the Accountant may sanction payments to third parties where there is a legal obligation to support them, and may sanction travelling expenses to visit the ward (see above), special powers from the court are likely to be required for any other payments to third parties.

## Succession

Exercise of the curator's powers does not affect succession unless the act was necessary in the ward's interests or by operation of law. Thus, unless the exception applies, proceeds of sale of heritage by the curator remain heritable in succession.

## Preservation or best interests?

Originally judicial factors were appointed to preserve estate in an emergency, and in such cases "usual powers" were limited to those necessary to conserve the estate.[38] However, for each type of judicial factory the usual powers are those essential to carry out the purposes of the appointment, and use of judicial factory has diversified to include situations where conservation is not the prime purpose, and even situations where the purpose is to distribute rather than to conserve the estate.[39] However, both in texts and in practice over-emphasis of the aspect of preservation of the estate has persisted, due to the historical background and to application to judicial factories generally of dicta appropriate to those where preservation is the principle purpose. A notable example of such dicta is the description of a factor as "a conservator merely" by Lord Justice-Clerk Inglis in *Neilson and others*.[40]

Erroneous emphasis upon preservation is prevalent in relation to curatories for mentally disabled people, and this tends to be particularly inappropriate in relation to wards who have a mental handicap. Again, the causes are largely historical. Much of the law of curatories evolved at a time when all mental disabilities were perceived in terms of serious mental illness, and wards were labelled as "incapax" or "insane" and consigned to a category almost of non-persons, with no perceived needs other than costs of basic maintenance in an asylum. It was assumed that incapacity would be either total but temporary, in which case the ward would one day recover complete capacity, or total and permanent, in

---

[37] See Chap.9, Part IVB.

[38] N.M.L. Walker, *Judicial Factors*, p.75.

[39] Such as a judicial factor to wind up a partnership (*Cooper & Sons' Judicial Factor* 1931 SLT 26) or administer a trust estate at point of distribution (*Wharrie's Judicial Factor* 1916, 1 SLT 345).

[40] (1865) 3M 559 at 560. See comment by Walker, *op. cit*, p.76.

which case the only interests to consider were the interests of those who would inherit when the ward died. Such perceptions have always been completely irrelevant to the overwhelming majority of people with a mental handicap, and disappeared long ago in relation to all forms of mental disability. Nevertheless, ancient legal texts and cases are still on occasion referred to in a manner which appears not to acknowledge the changes in circumstances and perceptions which have occurred since their time.

Emphasis upon preservation appears to be based upon an assumption in the case law that situations of conflict between the ward's best interest and conservation will be rare. That assumption has rendered the case law progressively less relevant to modern conditions, but probably explains the unresolved incompatibility between the proposition that in such circumstances of conflict the ward's best interest should prevail, and assertions that the primary duty of a curator is to conserve the estate even when this might appear to be against the ward's best interest.[41]

Any principle that conservation is an objective in its own right is based on assumptions not relevant to the majority of mentally handicapped wards, and such a principle itself must therefore be regarded as probably irrelevant in their cases. It is submitted that the two guiding principles should be the duty of the curator to act in the best interests of the ward[42] and the principle that the curator should act as the ward would have done if capable.[43] The proposition that these are the guiding principles in relation to curatories for people with mental handicaps or other mental disabilities is certainly borne out by good modern practice in the conduct of such curatories. For example, the Accountant of Court has in recent years approved the following:

- substantial structural alterations to a house to cope with the ward's needs;
- purchase and alteration of a new house in a suitable environment;
- acquisition at a cost of £15,000 of a Snoezelen environment for a resident at the Royal Scottish National Hospital (with the approval of the court);
- where the estate comprised an unexpected legacy from a grandfather and had caused Income Support payments to cease, expenditure of the estate on a computer, a horse and other items to improve the ward's quality of life, and on provision for the mother's visiting costs;

---

41     See *Stair Memorial Encyclopaedia*, vol.24, para.247, where in relation to judicial factors generally these two principles are stated, without comment or resolution, in the same paragraph.

42     *Encyclopaedia*, passage cited, where this is acknowledged as being the overriding principle.

43     See *Gordon's Curator Bonis* (1902) 4F 577 and comment thereon in Walker, *op. cit*, p.110. These are of course the "best interests" and "substituted judgement" principles to which we refer on p.6, where we argue that they should be applied together.

- the cost of a trip abroad to see relatives for the last time; and
- the periodic purchase of photographic equipment (including three camcorders) for a ward who had a particular interest in photography.

The inappropriateness of an approach giving priority to conservation is emphasised by the example of cases where the estate consists primarily of an award of compensation for costs and losses arising from permanent incapacity. The award will have been calculated on the basis that it will be used up during the period of loss or incapacity, not on the basis that income alone will provide adequate compensation, leaving the capital intact to be inherited by the beneficiaries in the ward's estate.

*Personal powers*
A curator has no powers of custody or control, or other powers of personal guardianship, except in very rare cases where such powers are specifically conferred. In one old case a curator was authorised to have the ward transferred to an asylum.[44] The better modern practice is for a curator requiring personal powers to have himself appointed tutor-dative with the requisite personal powers.[45]

## Accounts and commission

*Annual accounts*
The Accountant of Court intimates to the curator the date up to which annual accounts must be made, and each year's account must be submitted to the Accountant within one month of that date. The account takes the form of an account of charge and discharge.[46] The first account commences with the estate as shown in the factorial inventory, and each subsequent account commences with the estate at close of the last account. Narrower, wider and special range estate is shown separately. Vouchers are submitted with the account and numbered in order, the numbers being marked against the relevant entries in the account. The accounts are audited by the Accountant, who prepares a report on them.

*Final account*
A similar account is prepared from the date of the last annual account to the date of termination of the curatory.

*Commission*
The only remuneration permitted to the curator is the commission fixed by the Accountant of Court on the basis of the intromissions in the approved accounts. The Accountant sets the commission in his own discretion at an amount which, in his experience, he considers to be fair and reasonable, but in practice he usually bases

---

44  *Christie's Curator* (1869) 7M 1130.
45  An example is *Usher's Curator, Petr,* 1989 (unreported) where a curator was appointed tutor-dative to consent to a major operation.
46  A style is annexed to the "Notes for the Guidance of Judicial Factors" issued by the Accountant of Court.

his figure on formulae which he has evolved giving from 20 per cent. to 3.5 per cent. on revenue received and from 1.5 per cent. to 0.25 per cent. on capital intromissions. In large estates there is added a responsibility allowance of 0.25 per cent. of the amount of caution. Where the curator is a solicitor he (or his firm) may not charge for legal work, but may submit a note of work done which the Accountant will take into account when fixing commission.

## Termination and discharge

### Circumstances

Circumstances in which a curatory for a person with a mental handicap may terminate include death of the ward, exhaustion of the estate, and cases where it is shown by medical evidence that the ward has gained sufficient capacity to manage his affairs, though in relation to mentally handicapped wards most such cases of "recovery" truly entail either (a) cases where the original appointment was inappropriate (which are not unknown), or (b) cases of partial incapacity where capacity has remained substantially the same but management requirements have become simpler, and within the ward's capacity. Cases occur, usually as a hybrid of (a) and (b), where informal help and guidance not previously available render continuation of the curatory unnecessary, though these also tend to be presented as "recovery". It might also be appropriate to seek termination of a curatory where it becomes possible for management needs to be met satisfactorily by a simpler method of management (such as hospital management); and to do so when the ward is to leave Scotland and all estate is to be transferred out of Scotland. The curatory continues where the curator demits office or dies, when the curator or his representatives require to lodge final accounts before seeking discharge.

### Judicial discharge

It is understood that it is now intended[47] that judicial discharge will only be sought where a certificate of discharge (see below) has been refused. Procedure is by court petition (Court of Session) or note (Sheriff Court). Evidence of the relevant event (such as death certificate or medical certificates) and a valuation of the estate at the relevant date are required. Where there is to be a new curator, medical evidence of continuing incapacity of the ward is required. The petition or note is served upon the cautioner and those on whom petitions for appointment are served, and in sheriff court procedure upon the Accountant of Court (in the Court of Session, an extra copy is transmitted to the Accountant). If there is no opposition, the matter is remitted to the Accountant of Court, the curator's final account is submitted, the Accountant issues a draft report for comment, and then reports to the court, which grants the discharge of the curator (and appoints the new one, if

---

[47] Under 1991 and 1992 rules.

such appointment be sought[48]).

A petition for recall may be presented when a curator is guilty of misfeasance, misdemeanour or neglect of duty. A petition for recall and appointment of a successor is also appropriate when a curator wishes to resign.

## Certificate of discharge[49]

Discharge of a curator by certificate of the Accountant of Court in certain circumstances was introduced with effect from November 18, 1991 (Court of Session) and March 9, 1992 (Sheriff Court). In relation to curatories for mentally handicapped people, the procedure is available in three situations:

- when the ward has died;
- when the estate has been exhausted;
- when the curatory has been recalled by reason of "recovery" of the ward.[50]

No court procedure is required to establish the first two grounds, but for the third recovery has to be established by the usual medical evidence and recall obtained from the court, before application for the certificate of discharge may be made. It is to be anticipated that in appropriate cases "recovery" will be interpreted as including the situations described under "Circumstances" above where it is shown to have become possible for the ward to manage his own affairs.

After final accounts have been prepared and audited by the Accountant, the curator applies in writing to the Accountant for a certificate of discharge.[51] The application is intimated to the cautioner and to any person with an interest in the ward's estate. The notice to them advises that the audited accounts of the curatory may be inspected in the office of the Accountant and that written representations about the application may be made to the Accountant within 21 days. The notice also explains the effect of the certificate of discharge.

On expiry of the 21 days, the Accountant considers the application and any representations, and intimates whether he has determined to issue a certificate. The intimation is sent to the curator, the clerk of court, and anyone who has made representations. Within 14 days the curator or anyone who has made representations may appeal to the court, where the appeal is determined. The judge may direct the Accountant to issue the certificate, or direct the

---

48 When the previous curator has died, the new curator's first account commences at his predecessor's date of death, not at his own appointment.

49 Judicial Factors Act 1849, s.34A (added by Law Reform (Miscellaneous Provisions) (Scotland) Act 1990) and Rules of Court 201Z–201FF (made by 1991 Act of Sederunt) (Court of Session); 1992 Act of Sederunt, rr.19 and 20 (Sheriff Court).

50 It is understood that it is intended that the procedure be available in all cases where the court recalls the appointment but has not been asked to discharge the curator.

51 If the curator has died, his representatives may apply.

curator to apply for judicial discharge, or make any other appropriate order. If there is no opposition, the Accountant issues a certificate of discharge after the 14 days have expired.[52]

## OTHER JUDICIAL FACTORS, AND TUTORS

### Judicial Factors

As already indicated,[53] curators bonis to mentally disabled adults are one type of judicial factor. There are several different specific types of judicial factor appointed for particular purposes, but judicial factory is not limited to these specific types.[54] A judicial factor may be appointed to administer a particular fund or asset, and there may be occasions when this will be preferable to appointing a curator bonis to administer the person's entire estate.

*Main characteristics*
The main characteristics of a judicial factor appointed in this way are the same as for a curator bonis, except that the appointment will be limited to the particular fund and the person entitled to the fund will not necessarily be deprived of all legal capacity.

*Procedure, powers and duties*
The limitations upon who may be appointed, procedure upon appointment (other than ingathering the entire estate), duties and powers regarding investment and management, accounts and commission, and termination in respect of judicial factors generally are substantially the same as described above for curators.

### Tutors-dative

Tutors-dative as personal guardians are described in Chapter 3, Part II. Tutors-dative are however both personal guardians and financial managers, unless the appointment is limited to personal powers.[55] Where both a guardian and a manager are required, there is a choice of either seeking appointment of both a tutor-dative as personal guardian and a curator as manager, or alternatively of a tutor-dative as both personal guardian and manager. While the same person may be both tutor-dative and curator,[56] normally it would seem to be more logical to avoid duplication of procedures and seek appointment of a tutor-dative with both roles. A tutor-dative as financial manager is under the same regime as a curator bonis.

---

52 The nature of the explanation is not specified, but the following wording has proved to be acceptable: "If a certificate of discharge is issued in my favour, the effect will be to discharge me from further responsibility and liability in respect of the curatory, and shall be sufficient authority for me to uplift my Bond of Caution."
53 See Curatory, curator as judicial factor, p.589.
54 *Leslie's Judicial Factor* 1925 SC 464 at 469.
55 *Dick* v. *Douglas* 1924 SC 787, 1924 SLT 576.
56 *Usher's Curator, Petr,* 1989 (unreported).

A tutor-dative may be appointed with management powers only, and as with guardianship powers the appointment may be limited to particular management powers, including a single act of management.[57]

*Main characteristics*

Tutors-dative may be appointed with either general or limited management powers, including powers limited to a single act of management. Any suitable person may be appointed using the procedure described in Chapter 3, Part II. It is thought that the appointment of a tutor-dative with full management powers will deprive the person of capacity, as is the case with curatories. The effect of a partial appointment upon capacity has not been tested, but where the appointment is limited in recognition of partial capacity, logic would indicate that such appointment would not remove such partial capacity. Except as regards mode of appointment and caution, tutors-dative as managers are under the same regime as curators and other judicial factors.[58] Accordingly, and subject to any limitation on the appointment, there apply to tutors-dative as managers the provisions described above for curatories in respect of factorial inventory, duties, investment and management, and accounts and commission.

## Tutors-at-law

The continuing competence of appointment of tutors-at-law has been questioned, but there seems to be no reason why the procedure should not still be competent. A petition is at present before the court, opposed by an existing curator bonis.

*Main characteristics*

A tutor-at-law, if served (appointed), becomes both personal guardian and general financial manager without any limitation of powers. Only the nearest male agnate (male relative on the father's side) may be appointed. There is some doubt as to the degree of incapacity warranting appointment.[59] Appointment is by court petition, supported by two medical certificates. Tutors-at-law are not judicial factors but were recently for the first time made subject to the supervision of the Accountant of Court, and the accounting requirements and investment restrictions applicable to

---

57   In a recent case a tutor-dative was appointed with no guardianship powers, and with management powers limited to the sole purpose of executing a deed of family arrangement - *Queen* (1992), unreported.

58   Judicial Factors Act 1849, s.25(1) (but it is understood that tutors-dative as managers must nevertheless find caution, though this was not required in *Queen* above).

59   Prior to the Court of Session Act 1868 a tutor-at-law could only be served if a person was "fatuous" or "furious" (indicating severe handicap or illness). The 1868 Act widened the definition to "insanity", including not only fatuity and furiosity but also unsoundness of mind rendering the person incapable of managing his affairs. However this provision was repealed by the Court of Session Act 1988 (on the assumption, apparently, that it was obsolete), creating doubt as to what is now to be the definition.

curators.[60] Tutors-at-law supersede all other managers, including curators bonis.

## HOSPITAL MANAGEMENT

### Main characteristics

Hospital management is a statutory procedure applicable only to hospital patients who are liable to be detained under the Mental Health (Scotland) Act 1984, or who are receiving treatment for mental disorder. Procedure is very simple.[61] Accountability and supervision are limited to internal controls established by hospital authorities, and some degree of supervision by the Mental Welfare Commission in some cases. The managers of the hospital may not be remunerated from patients' funds for providing this service. Powers are rather vaguely defined, and are limited to receiving and holding money and valuables, and expending them for the patient's benefit. The procedure is initiated by a medical opinion that the patient is incapable of managing and administering his property and affairs, but has no automatic effect on legal capacity. Hospital management is superseded by appointment of a curator bonis, but has no effect on (and may co-exist with) other methods of management.

*Legislation and guidance*
    Mental Health (Scotland) Act 1984, section 94.
    Report of the Working Party on Incapax Patients' Funds
        (the *Crosby Report*), HMSO 1985.
    *The Management of Patients' Monies at Ward Level*, SHHD.

### Procedure

*Medical opinion*
All that is required is a statement of opinion by the medical officer in charge of treating a patient who is liable to be detained in the hospital, or who is receiving treatment there for mental disorder (which includes mental handicap). The medical officer states that in his opinion the person is incapable of managing and administering his property and affairs, by reason of his mental disorder. The 1984 Act does not require the statement of opinion to be in writing, but it is clearly advisable that a written certificate should be provided and preserved: the *Crosby Report* provides a recommended style.

*Effect of opinion*
The medical opinion permits the managers of the hospital to exercise the powers described in the next section. There is no requirement to notify anyone.

---

60    Judicial Factors Act 1849, s.25(1) did not include tutors-at-law to adults until amended by the Age of Legal Capacity (Scotland) Act 1991, Sched.2.

61    The procedure is possibly in breach of Article 6(1) of the European Convention on Human Rights in that there is no determination by an independent and impartial tribunal established by law.

*Mental Welfare Commission consent*

The Secretary of State from time to time sets a limit to the amount of money and valuables which may be held and administered for any one patient without consent. The current limit (set in August 1989) is £3,000. The managers of the hospital must obtain the permission of the Mental Welfare Commission to exceed the limit in any individual case. Normally, the Commission will either set a higher limit for that case, or advise that a curator bonis should be appointed. In July 1989 the Commission indicated that it would normally consider appointment of a curator to be appropriate at a level of £50,000, in the absence of circumstances justifying the setting up of a curatory at a lower level. This figure has been criticised as possibly being higher than parliament intended for this method of management,[62] and it is understood that a revised level of £20,000 is under consideration.

## Powers

Subject to the limits described above, the managers of the hospital may receive and hold money and valuables, for which they can give a valid receipt or discharge. They can expend the money for the patient's benefit. They can also dispose of valuables for the patient's benefit, but must have regard to any sentimental value which they may have for the patient (or sentimental value which they would have had, but for the mental disorder).

*Refund of insurance premiums*

The managers of the hospital have a particular power to use insurance proceeds which they receive to reimburse anyone who has paid insurance premiums on behalf of the patient.

*Special death certificates*

The managers also have a particular power to apply for special death certificates under the Industrial Assurance and Friendly Societies Act 1948, Sched.1 and the Friendly Societies Act 1974, Sched.5 (which permit such societies to pay out sums due on the deaths of certain relatives).

*Competence of other procedures*

The 1984 Act is silent as to whether managers of hospitals may operate other management techniques in parallel with, or as alternatives to, hospital management. There would appear to be no reason why, provided that they comply with hospital management provisions, they should not operate additional techniques such as having themselves appointed to receive DSS benefits.

However, some hospitals operate as DSS appointees only, or even as negotiorum gestors.[63] This in practice often leads to confusion

---

62  Scottish Law Commission, *op. cit.*, para.4.161.
63  Styles of curatory petition provided at a Law Society of Scotland PQLE course in 1988 proceeded on the basis that hospitals had been managing as negotiorum gestors.

as to powers and procedures, and may be legally incompetent.[64] It is recommended that in all cases hospitals should comply with section 94 of the 1984 Act.

## Termination

*Appointment of curator, etc.*
Hospital management is terminated by appointment of a curator bonis, and the managers of the hospital are required to account for their intromissions to the curator bonis. The same provisions apply upon appointment of a tutor[65] or judicial factor, or appointment (in England, Wales or Northern Ireland) of a receiver or controller, or person with similar powers.

*No other termination procedure*
Except that the Mental Welfare Commission might withdraw permission to hold funds above the limit at which their consent is required, the 1984 Act contains no procedures for termination of hospital management, even in situations where this would clearly be required, such as where the patient regains capacity, or the patient or someone else challenges the medical opinion of incapacity, or where there are shown to have been serious deficiencies in management. In such circumstances it would probably be appropriate to apply for a declarator, or for judicial review.[66]

## MANAGEMENT OF PARTICULAR ASSETS

### Main characteristics

All of the management techniques described in this section apply to particular assets, which may be lump sums or ongoing payments from a particular source. None of these techniques may be used to impose management in respect of funds which have already reached the hands of the mentally handicapped person. In the case of lump sums, they may be applied no later than time of payment. In the case of ongoing payments, they apply only to payments subsequent to appointment.

Procedures are generally informal, and accounting and supervision are generally limited or non-existent. Managers may not be remunerated from the funds under their control. Their powers and responsibilities are generally defined vaguely, or not at all. Where the effect of appointment of a curator is specified,

---

64  In *B.* v. *Forsey* 1988 SLT 572 it was held that, as statutory detention procedures are available to hospital authorities, common law powers of detention are not. The principles followed by the House of Lords in this case would appear to be equally applicable in matters of management. If so, it is incompetent for hospitals to act (for example) as negotiorum gestors, rather than under the management scheme envisaged by s.94.

65  It must be assumed, though the Act is silent on the point, that this applies only where the tutor has management powers, and not where the tutor's powers are limited to personal guardianship.

66  See Chap.3, Part III, Court proceedings, Judicial review, p.156.

the curator supersedes, and (except, perhaps, where trusts are established) a curator's duty to ingather will probably extend to all funds managed by these various techniques, and his duty not to delegate will require him to have other management appointments terminated.

## State Benefits[67]

The Social Security (Claims and Benefits) Regulations 1987

*Appointees*
Reg.33 authorises the appointment of someone to apply for, receive and deal with benefits on behalf of a person unable for the time being to manage his own affairs. There are no financial limits, and any person over 18 may apply by completing the appropriate form and submitting it to the local Benefits Agency where staff are responsible for verifying the claimant's incapacity, usually by interview or medical certificate, and for ascertaining that the proposed appointee is suitable. The appointee may give one month's notice of termination to the DSS, who may revoke the appointment at any time. The appointment is superseded by appointment of a curator bonis (and similar appointments).

It is important that promptly upon appointment an appointee checks that all benefits to which the person may be entitled have been claimed. Otherwise, entitlement to backdating may be lost, because although mental incapacity is "good cause" for a late claim, once an appointee has been appointed it is for him (rather than the incapacitated person) to show "good cause" for delay.

The affairs of many mentally handicapped people are managed solely by this method. The procedure is at the opposite end of the spectrum from curatories in that it is simple and informal, and inadequately monitored. Some mentally handicapped people appear to be trapped within the power of financial control exercised by the appointee.

*Payments to third parties*
Reg.34 permits a benefit to be paid, wholly or in part, to another person acting for the claimant if that appears to be necessary to protect the interests of the claimant or dependents.

*Direct payments*
Under Reg.35 (and Sched.9) costs of housing, accommodation, fuel and water may be deducted from benefits and paid direct.

## Vaccine damage payments

If the requirements of the Vaccine Damage Payment Act 1979 are met, a single lump sum payment (currently £30,000) is made to those who become severely disabled as a result of a routine NHS vaccination against various specified diseases, or vaccination of the person's mother before birth, or infection from a vaccinated

---

67 See also Chap.10A, Part III, State benefits, p.564; and Chap.8, Part I, Procedure, p.411.

person. There are detailed rules regarding place and date of vaccination, and age.[68] If the disabled person is unable to manage his own affairs, payment may be made to trustees appointed by the DSS. Upon death, the payment falls into the estate of the disabled person.

## Miscellaneous statutory methods

Many statutes contain provisions for the management of particular types of assets on behalf of people lacking management capacity. Such provisions generally confer a discretion upon the payer to make payment to someone who is caring for the mentally handicapped person, or will apply the payment for the person's benefit. Common examples are:
- Savings Certificates Regulations 1991, under which the Director of Savings has discretion to make repayment to a recipient who has satisfied the Director that he will apply the payment for the maintenance, or otherwise for the benefit, of a mentally disabled person;
- National Savings Bank Regulations 1972, reg.7(4);
- Industrial and Provident Societies Act 1965, s.22;
- Mental Health Act 1983, s.142, which applies to Scotland, and which relates to any pay or pension from moneys provided by Parliament or the Consolidated Fund or under the control or supervision of any government department.

There are also provisions providing simplified methods for single acts of management.[69]

## Sheriff Court

Damages payable to "a person under legal disability" in a Sheriff Court action for personal injuries, or death of some other person, must be paid into court, unless the court directs otherwise. The sum is invested, applied or otherwise dealt with and administered by the court for the benefit of the person.[70] The equivalent Court of Session Rules apply only to pupils and minors, not to mentally disabled adults, but the Court of Session or any other court may request a Sheriff Court to administer a damages payment for a mentally disabled adult resident in the jurisdiction of that Sheriff Court.[71] In the past, a mentally handicapped party to such proceedings would normally have had a curator bonis appointed to conduct them, but where there is no other reason for a continuing curatory and proceedings have already commenced, consideration

---

68  For a description of vaccine damage payments, see Chap.8, Part I, p.401.
69  *e.g.* the Income Tax (Deposit-takers) (Interest Payments) (Amendment) Regulations 1991 and Income Tax (Building Societies) (Dividends and Interest) (Amendment) Regulations 1991, under which a parent, guardian, spouse, son or daughter of a mentally incapacitated person may register on the person's behalf for interest to be paid without deduction of tax.
70  Ordinary Court Rule 128.
71  Rules of Court 131-134, Ordinary Court Rule 128(2). An alternative would be to appoint a judicial factor (see "Other judicial factors and tutors" above).

should instead be given to whether it would be in the interests of that party for the proceedings to be conducted by a curator *ad litem* (if the court were prepared to make such appointment) and any damages payment administered by the Sheriff Court.

## Criminal injuries compensation

Under paragraph 9 of the Criminal Injuries Compensation Scheme the Criminal Injuries Compensation Board may establish a trust on such terms as the Board thinks fit to administer a compensation award. The Board also has general discretion to make "special arrangements" for administration of an award, and it is understood that SSMH Trustee Service Limited (see Appendix I) has been appointed to administer such an award.[72]

## INFORMAL MANAGEMENT TECHNIQUES

### Main characteristics

The informality of the management techniques described in this section means that neither the group as a whole nor some of the individual techniques can be precisely circumscribed by definition. They are all techniques or arrangements which are simply implemented by one or more people without any formal appointment or other procedure. Accountability is limited to remedies which may be subsequently invoked in some circumstances, but rarely are; and there is no supervision. Managers may not be remunerated. Their powers are generally ill-defined. The use of these techniques has no effect upon capacity. They can, and often do, overlap and co-exist with each other or with other management techniques but (except, perhaps, where a trust has been established) are superseded by appointment of a curator bonis.

These techniques generally work best when employed for clearly defined purposes and for a limited duration, with the agreement and co-operation of all concerned. They frequently give rise to problems if the desired purpose has not been clearly thought through, or if they are entered upon for an indefinite period with no thought as to how they will operate in future circumstances (such as the death of someone primarily involved) or how they may be brought to an end.[73] They can be vulnerable to challenge by third parties who are unwilling to co-operate or who seek evidence of authority.

### Advice

Advisers are likely to be consulted when problems have been encountered with these techniques. Even when not consulted about problems, they should point out any potential difficulties whenever they become aware that one of these techniques is being employed.

---

72 The Board had previously tended to suggest that curators be appointed even for small awards where curatory is uneconomic and thus inappropriate.

73 See *Scots Law and the Mentally Handicapped*, pp.80-81.

Generally, the best procedure will be to try to ascertain the purpose of the arrangement, then (if necessary and if possible) re-structure it in a more suitable and durable form.

## Negotiorum gestio

A negotiorum gestor is someone who spontaneously undertakes the management of a person's affairs without the person's knowledge, because the person either is absent or lacks capacity, in circumstances where it is a reasonable presumption that the person would have given authority if aware of the circumstances and able to do so. The principle of *negotiorum gestio* can apply to long-term management on behalf of a mentally disabled person, where no curator or other manager has been formally appointed.[74]

### Duties, liabilities and reimbursement

The gestor must show the same degree of care as a prudent person acting in relation to his own affairs, and provided that he does so he incurs no personal liability for any loss to the person's estate resulting from his actings. The person's estate is liable for obligations and liabilities incurred by the gestor for the person's benefit. Third parties may seek payment from the person's funds, or the gestor may pay them and himself be reimbursed from the person's funds. The gestor may also be reimbursed for reasonable expenses, but is not entitled to remuneration.

### Supersession

The gestor is superseded by appointment of a curator bonis, or of a tutor with management powers. *Negotiorum gestio* may co-exist with other management techniques.

### Disadvantages

The main disadvantages of this technique are lack of any controls or supervision to prevent detriment or misuse, and lack of any evidence of authority. The gestor cannot insist that third parties recognise his authority or implement his instructions and directions.

## Informal voluntary arrangements

Many transactions relating to mentally handicapped people are conducted by agreement of those concerned without any identifiable legal basis. Such transactions are often the practical response to the absence of suitable management techniques which are sufficiently simple and accessible - or alternatively, they may be the result of ignorance of available techniques.

Informal voluntary arrangements arise most frequently when a signature is required, for example to operate a bank or similar account, to grant a receipt or discharge for insurance proceeds or other sums, to claim a tax repayment, and so forth. It often happens in practice that a signature of some other person, or a

---

74 See for example *Fernie* v. *Robertson* (1871) 9M 437 and *Dunbar* v. *Wilson and Dunlop's Trs* (1887) 15R 210.

signature or mark by the mentally handicapped person (though lacking capacity), is accepted. Such arrangements depend upon the continuing co-operation of all concerned, and cannot be insisted upon. They may operate satisfactorily for years, but remain precarious. For example, problems have arisen with operation of bank and building society accounts in this way upon appointment of a new manager.

## Joint accounts

Often bank and other accounts are opened in joint names of a mentally handicapped person and some other person. The non-handicapped person may operate the account provided that it is operable by either, rather than by both. On the death or incapacity of the non-handicapped party problems may arise as to future management. There is likely to be a presumption that the funds are owned equally by the two parties, but problems about entitlement may arise at any time. For example, they may arise in relation to means-testing, income tax liability, or entitlement and inheritance tax liability on death of either party.

## Bare trusts

A bare trust is established when title to a fund or asset is taken in name of someone "in trust for" the mentally handicapped person, with no document adequately setting out the terms and purposes of the trust. Common examples are where a relative or carer opens an account or takes an investment in this way. Problems may arise upon the death or incapacity of the trustee. There is also a risk that the fund may lie dormant, producing no significant benefit for the mentally handicapped person, then become an embarrassment in its interrelationship with the establishment of general arrangements for provision such as are described in Chapter 9.

## TRUSTS

The use of formal trusts has been described in Chapter 9. This section is limited to considering their place in relation to management techniques as a whole.

## Main characteristics

Under a formal trust, a donor or testator pays and conveys funds or assets to trustees acting under a trust deed. The trustees hold and administer the funds or assets for the purposes set out in that deed and in accordance with its provisions, subject to the general law of trusts. The deed will include purposes and provisions for the benefit of the mentally handicapped person. Appointment of trustees is usually by the truster[75] either within the trust deed, or by separate deed of appointment; or alternatively by deed of assumption by existing trustees of one or more new trustees. Trustees are accountable to beneficiaries, including those who may

---

75   *I.e.* the person establishing the trust.

be entitled to the trust fund upon termination of the trust, but not normally to any independent supervisor such as the Accountant of Court. They may be remunerated if the trust deed so specifies, but not otherwise. The powers of the trustees are limited to the trust funds and assets, and are as set forth in the trust deed (subject to the general law of trusts). The establishment of the trust has no effect upon the legal capacity of the mentally handicapped beneficiary. A formal trust may co-exist with any other management technique, and neither supersedes nor is superseded by any other technique.

## Trusts compared with curatories

### Advantages
The cumbersomeness and limitations of curatories need not apply to trusts. Trust deeds may confer wider powers than those enjoyed by curators. Ongoing management costs of trusts will generally be less. Capital held within the trust will not be taken into account in assessment for means-tested benefits.[76] The mentally handicapped beneficiary does not lose capacity, and on the beneficiary's death the destination of remaining trust funds will be determined by the trust deed, thus avoiding any inappropriate disposal under the rules of intestate succession. Only a single individual may be a curator, but a suitably chosen team may (and usually is) appointed as trustees under a continuing trust[77] and a suitable corporate trustee (such as the SSMH Trustee Service) may be appointed.

### Disadvantages
While a formal trust is often the favoured technique, there are some disadvantages in comparison with curatories, and one must be aware of them. There is a statutory limitation on the period (in effect, a maximum of 21 years) for which trust income may be accumulated with capital, and if the trustees have power to make discretionary payments of income and may also accumulate, an additional rate tax charge will apply (though the beneficiary is likely to be entitled to reclaim some or all tax deducted from income paid to him). Neither the limitation on period of accumulation nor the additional tax charge apply to curatories. Also, trustees are not automatically subject to supervision and to scrutiny of annual accounts by an independent person, such as are exercised by the Accountant of Court in relation to curatories. Lastly, trustees of course manage only funds within the trust, whereas curators manage any accretions or additions to the ward's estate.

---

[76]   Under the Income Support (General) Regulations 1987, reg 52(2), the capital of a discretionary trust is only taken into account if, and insofar as, actually advanced; but in assessing charges for Part IV accommodation "any sum which is held on a Discretionary Trust for the benefit of a person may be treated as included in his resources", though this may shortly be brought into line with the income support provisions (see *The Power to Act*, pp.117-118).

[77]   In Scotland there is no limit on the number of trustees.

# AGENTS AND ATTORNEYS

## Main characteristics

The unique characteristic of agents and attorneys as managers for mentally handicapped people is that they are appointed by the person for whom they act. For that reason they are perhaps of limited relevance, because the appointment is only valid if the appointer has sufficient capacity to make it. However there are cases where a mentally handicapped person does have capacity to make such an appointment, and finds it convenient to do so. In the case of attorneys the appointment remains valid even if the appointer's capacity subsequently deteriorates.[78]

Agents may be appointed informally or formally; attorneys (who are a particular type of agent) are appointed by formal power of attorney. One or more persons, or a corporation, may be appointed. Both agents and attorneys are accountable to the appointer (which is of limited value if capacity to exercise such rights is limited, or has deteriorated[79]) and also to any subsequently appointed curator bonis, and to the appointer's executors upon his death. There is no formal supervision. Agents and attorneys may be remunerated only if the appointer so provides. Powers are limited to those granted by the appointer. Such appointments have no effect upon the legal capacity of the appointer, and neither affect nor are affected by other management techniques, unless specifically superseded by them e.g. the appointment by the person of an agent to collect social security benefits will be superseded by a DSS appointee; and a curator bonis will be entitled to revoke appointment of an agent or attorney (and, in view of his obligation not to delegate, would generally be obliged to do so).

Detailed exposition of the law of agency and of powers of attorney is beyond the scope of this work.

## Agency

Agents may be appointed formally, informally or impliedly. They must act in good faith, within the scope of their authority, and not make a secret profit. A mentally handicapped person may employ or appoint an agent provided that he has sufficient capacity to do so. Use of informally appointed agents to collect state benefits is described in Chapter 10A, Part III. A mentally handicapped person may employ a professional person such as a solicitor to act as agent. Deterioration in the capacity of the person who appointed the agent may terminate the agency,[80] though bona fide actings by

---

[78] Law Reform (Miscellaneous Provisions) (Scotland) Act 1990, s.71.

[79] See McCusker *Continuing Powers of Attorney - Continuing Problems?*, Journal of the Law Society of Scotland, July 1991, pp.255-257.

[80] It has been held that "permanent insanity" of either party ends the relationship of principal and agent, *Wink* v. *Mortimer* (1849) 11D 995.

an agent ignorant of an event terminating the agency are good against the principal's estate.[81]

## Powers of attorney

Scots law has no equivalent to the detailed provisions and procedures which apply to Enduring Powers of Attorney in England, as described in Chapter 10A, Part I. Section 71(1) of the Law Reform (Miscellaneous Provisions) (Scotland) Act 1990 confirmed that a power of attorney granted on or after January 1, 1991 remains in force notwithstanding subsequent loss of capacity, unless the power of attorney specifies otherwise. No formalities are required upon such loss of capacity.

A person granting a power of attorney must however have capacity to do so at the time when it is executed. Powers of attorney are strictly construed and it is necessary to express specifically in the deed all of the powers which are to be exercised, as none will be implied.[82] It follows that the granter must have adequate understanding of all of the detailed powers to be granted, as expressed in the deed, but he may have sufficient understanding to grant the powers though lacking capacity fully and properly to exercise them himself. This is accordingly a useful management technique for some people with limited capacity, but the range of people for whom it might be appropriate may be more limited than in England.

Powers of attorney are normally formally executed, and usually registered in the Books of Council and Session for preservation. The terms of a power of attorney may be proved by a copy authenticated on each page and at the end by the granter, or by a solicitor or stockbroker.[83] The attorney must act with prudence, in good faith, and within the scope of his appointment, must not make a secret profit, and may receive remuneration only if that is authorised in the power of attorney. It is recommended that in major transactions, even though clearly within the powers conferred, the attorney should consult the granter, if available and able to be consulted.[84] The attorney's appointment is terminated *inter alia* by recall by the principal (or the principal's curator) and by the principal's death.

## LAW REFORM

Over the last decade there has been increasing criticism that existing provision in Scots law for the management of the affairs

---

[81]  In several cases this has been held to be so following death of the principal, and the same principle would presumably apply following deterioration in capacity.

[82]  *Goodall* v. *Bilsland* 1909 SC 1152, *Park* v. *Mood* 1919 1SLT 170; and see Halliday *Conveyancing Law and Practice in Scotland*, para 13-03.

[83]  Powers of Attorney Act 1971, s.3.

[84]  Halliday, *op. cit.*, para.13-10.

of people with mental disabilities is inadequate and unhelpful.[85] In particular there have been criticisms of the curatory regime,[86] hospital management[87] and use of powers of attorney following incapacity.[88] The need for comprehensive law reform has become urgent. In September 1991 the Scottish Law Commission issued Discussion Paper No 94 entitled *Mentally Disabled Adults - Legal Arrangements for Managing their Welfare and Finances.* Proposals for discussion include a new scheme of property orders and financial managers (to include "one-off" orders, partial management, and inexpensive management of small estates); public management; administrative trusts created by the court; possible modification and extension of hospital management; and simplified procedure to release funds from bank accounts and the like for necessary expenditure. The Discussion Paper points out that the provisions of the 1990 Act regarding powers of attorney were an interim measure pending consideration of the issues by the Commission, and the Discussion Paper contains proposals for continuing powers of attorney, both for financial matters and for personal welfare. Procedural matters are considered, including the options of procedure before the courts, or specialist tribunals, or lay hearings.

It is to be hoped that the process of law reform will result in an accessible, workable and co-ordinated scheme of financial management which meets the management needs in modern society of people with all types of mental disabilities.

---

85  Ward, *Scots Law and the Mentally Handicapped,* 1984, Chap.XIX; Scottish Action on Dementia *Dementia and the Law; The Challenge Ahead,* 1988; Ward, *The Power to Act,* 1990.

86  Ward, *The Power to Act,* Chap.X; SLC *Mentally Disabled Adults,* paras.4.7-4.14.

87  Ward, *The Power to Act,* pp.111-113; SLC *Mentally Disabled Adults,* paras.4.156-4.161.

88  McCusker, *Continuing Powers of Attorney - Continuing Problems?* (above); SLC *Mentally Disabled Adults,* para 5.9.

# CHAPTER 11  SOCIETIES AND CHARITIES

## INTRODUCTION

When people join together to carry out a mutual purpose other than for profit, an "unincorporated association" comes into being which may be called a club, an association or a society. There are many such organisations providing assistance or support to people with a mental handicap and their families,[1] but often they could be set up and administered in a more effective manner. Individuals often wish to make donations, assist in fund raising or become involved as officers or committee members. A society may evolve from an informal group to a more formalised body and the ultimate step will be incorporation as a limited company. Many societies in England and Wales are registered as charities, and in Scotland many will qualify for recognition,[2] and others could do so if the persons responsible knew how to take this step which may bring important advantages but also lead to greater formality and regulation. In this chapter we provide an introduction to these matters.

### Governing Instrument

The document setting out the aims of a society, how it will run and the rules which govern its activities is referred to as its "governing instrument". For a company this will be the Memorandum and Articles of Association, but in the case of an unincorporated association it may be called the Constitution or Rules, though a written document is not essential unless registration is required as a charity, and minutes of meetings may be sufficient to record the agreements reached between the members. An alternative for a charity without a large fluctuating body of members is for the founders to execute a Trust Deed under which trustees are appointed to administer funds in accordance with the objects and powers set out in that deed. This does not create an unincorporated association, although the outward appearance may be the same especially if registered or recognised as a charity.

### Name

The name of the society indicates its functions so should promote these both to the persons whom it wishes to assist and those on whom reliance is placed for support. It may also indicate both the scope and territory of the society in a manner which neither unduly restricts these nor raises expectations which cannot be met.

---

1   See Appendix I for a list of national organisations.
2   After July 27, 1992 when the main provisions of Part I of the Law Reform (Miscellaneous Provisions) (Scotland) Act 1990 are expected to take effect.

Conflict can exist between different marketing objectives, for example, the name *Lancashire Spastic Children's Society* identifies the area of operation, the type of handicap and the emphasis upon children. From a fund raising point of view it includes the emotive words *spastic* and *children* but if in fact the society caters without territorial limits for other mental or physical disabilities and for adults, it would be misleading and discourage those living outside Lancashire, and the parents of a mentally handicapped child or spastic adult, from seeking assistance or offering support. A more accurate name would be *North of England Spastic & Handicapped Society*. The length of the name may be overcome by the adoption of a "logo" or the use of the shortened version of the name.

# PART I - ASSOCIATIONS AND COMPANIES

## UNINCORPORATED ASSOCIATIONS

There is no statutory definition of an unincorporated association and such a body has no legal existence as such, but the members have duties and liabilities to each other and may collectively enter into legal relationships with outsiders. Most of the law involved is to be found in decisions of the courts, including the general law of contract and agency.

### Constitution

The usual governing instrument is a constitution formally adopted by all the members at the inaugural meeting to record certain fundamental matters. There may be separate rules or bye-laws governing routine matters which may be changed from time to time on a more informal basis.

*Objects*
The objects or purposes for which the society is formed will be recorded, and it is usual to set out the main objects first and then add the powers which may be exercised in furtherance of those objects.[3] If assets are used for purposes which are not authorised the members may be liable to a legal action for an injunction (in Scotland, an interdict) and damages, or those who purport to enter into a contract on behalf of the society may be personally liable without any indemnity from the funds.[4] Any question of interpretation is ultimately a matter for the courts.

*Membership*
The constitution lays down procedures for admission, resignation and expulsion which may include restrictions upon persons who

---

3    It is desirable not to have a single object in too restrictive a form in case this can no longer be achieved or it is suggested that any subsequent proposal to change this object is unlawful as being too fundamental.

4    This could happen to the whole governing body if they acted beyond their authority, or at least to all committee members who were present at and voted in favour of the action.

may become members. New members may be required to sign an acknowledgment that they have received a copy and accept its terms. Any provision dealing with refusal of membership or removal of a member should state that this is to be for good cause only and give an opportunity to be heard by the governing body.

### Regulation

General provision will be made as to regulation of the affairs of the society, including the calling and conduct of meetings, the appointment of officers and committee, voting rights and finance.[5] Although the members have the ultimate authority, it is usual to delegate the actual running of the society to smaller numbers or to individuals who will be accountable for their decisions and actions. Officers and members should be indemnified out of the assets against any liability which they may incur by acting for the society unless arising from negligence or fraud on their part.

### Officers

The day to day administration is usually dealt with by officers with designated areas of responsibility. The *chairman* is the senior officer who will preside at meetings, whilst the *secretary* is responsible for calling meetings, keeping minutes and ensuring that the affairs of the society are conducted in accordance with its constitution. The *treasurer* looks after the finances and should keep proper accounts, deal with money through a bank account and present annual Accounts to the members. Other officers may be appointed including a President who brings prestige but has no duties other than of a formal nature.

### Committee

The officers are normally accountable to and members of the committee which is elected by the members at an Annual General Meeting and responsible for the general management of the affairs of the society. It may be convenient to authorise the committee to appoint sub-committees to deal with particular matters, and to co-opt people so as to introduce additional expertise.

### Trustees

An unincorporated association must appoint trustees to hold any property or investments.[6] They should not allow the assets under their control to be used in a manner inconsistent with the constitution, but will comply with any directions given by the officers or committee in accordance with their powers. In order to avoid the need to appoint new trustees at intervals when one dies or wishes to retire a trust corporation can be appointed, but the cost may be prohibitive.

---

5 The constitution will specify whether the annual Accounts must be audited and how the auditor is to be appointed.

6 There should be more than one trustee but it is usual in England to limit the number to four. In Scotland there are sometimes more than four trustees, and occasionally so many as to be cumbersome.

*Alteration*
Unless the constitution makes provision for alteration, in which case the procedure must be strictly complied with, it may only be altered with the consent of all the members for the time being. This will clearly be inconvenient, especially where there is a large membership, so suitable provision for alteration should be made, but those founding a society for a particular purpose may regard this as fundamental and wish to ensure that it cannot be changed by those who happen to be members at a later date. Usually alteration is only permitted by passing a resolution, of which notice must be given to all members, by a specified majority in general meeting.[7]

*Dissolution*
The constitution should state what is to happen on the dissolution of the society and in particular to any remaining assets.[8] If funds have been received or raised for a specified purpose they must be applied for that purpose,[9] but subject thereto and to any provision in the constitution any monies remaining after all assets have been disposed of may be distributed among the members at the date of the dissolution.

**Funding and taxation**

Consideration must be given to the way in which the society is to be financed. Trading activities may be undertaken, monies may be borrowed or grants obtained. In the case of a club formed purely for the benefit of members any necessary funds may be collected as membership subscriptions. Conversely, a voluntary society that runs a residential care home may rely upon the weekly fees charged supplemented by voluntary donations and legacies, with merely a nominal annual subscription being paid by the members.
An unincorporated association may be liable for taxes, and its assets are required to meet its liabilities. Members' clubs and societies should be distinguished from proprietary clubs and partnerships, as both may have the same outward appearance or be described by similar types of name.

*Corporation tax*
An unincorporated association comes within the definition of a company for tax purposes so will be liable to corporation tax on any income or chargeable gains.[10] Subscriptions from members are not taxed, but bank interest, rents or trading profits will be. Many receipts (*e.g.* from social evenings) will not be regarded as

---

7    An alteration which is incompatible with the fundamental objects of the society could possibly be challenged in the courts by an aggrieved member.

8    Apart from this the society may be dissolved by the agreement of all the members, by simply ceasing to exist, or by court order.

9    There may be a resulting trust in favour of the donor, but this does not apply in the case of raffles and collecting boxes unless expressed to be for charitable purposes in which event a charitable trust will be superimposed.

10   Income and Corporation Taxes Act 1970, s.526(5); Capital Gains Taxes Act 1979, s.155. Friendly societies are subject to special rules.

taxable income if received only from members on the principle of mutuality, but this does not extend to income from non-members because the association is then trading. The Inland Revenue does not seek to tax the profits of jumble sales, car boot sales, garden parties, etc. unless these become substantial.[11]

*Value Added Tax*

As normal rules of VAT apply, registration should be considered if relevant turnover is likely to exceed the statutory limits, or if it would otherwise be beneficial. Failure to register when this is required can have serious consequences. Organisations with several branches which wish to avoid registration can sometimes do so by establishing each branch as a separate society.

## Claims

Claims cannot be made against a society as such, but will usually be against the persons who incurred the liability or were negligent.[12] Some aspects of the law are unclear but the position appears to be that officers who enter into contractual relationships on behalf of the society will generally be obliged to face the implications of their actions subject to being indemnified out of the assets of the society if they have acted within their authority.[13] The committee may be liable by reason of having expressly or impliedly authorised any act or dealing, and will be vicariously liable for any wrongful act of a servant for which an employer would normally be liable. Members will only be obliged to contribute towards any liability if the terms of their membership require them to do so, or they have expressly authorised the act giving rise to the liability, and trustees acting as property owners or tenants may incur personal liability in that capacity but will be indemnified out of the assets of the society if they have acted properly. Adequate insurances should therefore be maintained.

## Summary

The majority of societies exist as unincorporated associations and it may not be necessary to consider any alternative. There should be a governing instrument defining the purposes for which the society exists and regulating its affairs, and this should be reviewed at intervals. Points for and against are set out at the end of this Part.

## COMPANIES LIMITED BY GUARANTEE

Where there are concerns about lack of legal status or liability of the committee or members, it may be wise to adopt a more formal structure. There are several possibilities, including registration as

---

11   See the Inland Revenue booklet, *Clubs, Societies and Associations.*

12   In England, representative actions may be brought in certain circumstances - RSC, Ord.15, r.12.

13   There may be a distinction here between their position in relation to third parties, and the internal position between officers and their organisation.

a Friendly Society[14] or an Industrial and Provident Society,[15] but the course usually adopted is registration as a company under the Companies Acts. There are various types of company, the more common ones being limited by shares, but if it is the personal participation of members that is important rather than the raising of capital, a company limited by guarantee is more appropriate.[16] All statutory provisions apply to these companies unless specifically excluded, but in reality much of the law relating to companies has no application to companies limited by guarantee.[17] It is also possible for a company to be formed without limited liability on the part of the members, but this is seldom desired.[18]

## Legislation

Companies Acts 1985 and 1989
Companies (Tables A to F) Regulations 1985
Company and Business Names Regulations 1981

The 1985 Act consolidated previous legislation and is the principal statute, but has been amended mainly by the 1989 Act which inserted or substituted some new sections.[19] References are to the 1985 Act unless otherwise stated.
Statutory forms and guidance notes are available free of charge.[20] Some of the forms are referred to below by their official numbers and guidance notes are referred to as NG followed by the number.

### Companies Registries
The appropriate Companies Registration Office will depend upon the situation of the registered office of the company rather than the addresses of the officers and members, and the company should be formed in the country in which it is to operate.

## Registration procedure

Any two or more persons may join together to incorporate a

---

14  If the association has a benevolent purpose with at least seven members they may register under the Friendly Societies Act 1974.

15  Only available to an association formed for the carrying on of an industry, trade or business which is either a bona-fide co-operative society or intended to be conducted for the benefit of the community.

16  There are some older companies which are both limited by guarantee and have a share capital, but since 1980 it has not been possible to form or convert to such a company.

17  e.g. share capital and shareholders, maintenance of capital and dividends, public issues and insider dealing, forms of borrowing, minority and investor protection, subsidiary companies and corporate reorganisations.

18  Advantages include exemption from filing accounts, but disadvantages are the absence of limited liability and the fact that all the other formalities of a company apply. The word "limited" may be omitted from the company name even where there is limited liability - see below.

19  The European Community has an ever increasing influence on company law and the 1989 Act implements some of its directives in regard to accounts and auditors but also makes amendments in certain other areas, including registration of charges, the *ultra vires* doctrine, written resolutions, use of seal, annual returns and the use of modern technology.

20  Apply to Stationery Section at Companies House (addresses in Appendix I).

company for any lawful purpose, with or without limited liability, by complying with the statutory requirements. These *promoters* stand in a fiduciary position towards the company, so cannot make a secret profit and must be open and honest in their dealings. Company registration agents will supply documentation and deal with the formalities, or supply a ready-made company.[21]

*Documents to be filed*

The following must be delivered on an application to register a company limited by guarantee:

1. Memorandum of Association in appropriate form;
2. Articles of Association suitable for the company;
3. Statement in the prescribed form giving particulars of the first directors and secretary, and the situation of the registered office;
4. Statutory Declaration of compliance with the requirements of the Act, by a solicitor engaged in the formation or a person named as director or secretary;
5. the required fee (£50).

The Registrar examines these to ensure that they comply with the statutory requirements, the company is being formed for a lawful purpose and the proposed name is not a prohibited one.

*Certificate of Incorporation*

On registration a Certificate is issued to that effect and a notice is published in the London or Edinburgh Gazette, as appropriate. The Certificate, which states the registered number, is conclusive evidence that all requirements of the Act in respect of registration have been complied with and that the association is a company.

*Accounting reference date*

Every company has an "accounting reference date" which is relevant in regard to the preparation of accounts. New companies have nine months from incorporation to select the date by filing Form 224, and if none is selected it will be the last day of the month in which the anniversary of incorporation falls. The date may be changed by the filing of a Notice on Form 225(1) though there are restrictions on this which are explained in NG17.[22]

## Memorandum and Articles of Association

Model forms are set out in regulations and Table C is the model for a company limited by guarantee.[23]

The *Memorandum* is signed by two or more persons and states their desire to be formed into a company and its name, whether the registered office is situated in England, Scotland or Wales, and the objects. It must also state that the liability of the members is

---

21   The company should be formed to suit the particular society, rather than making the society conform to one of the standard companies as so often happens in the case of a tradesman who incorporates his business.

22   see ss.224 and 225.

23   Companies (Tables A to F) Regulations 1985.

limited and that each member undertakes to contribute to the assets of the company in the event of its being wound up while he is a member, or within one year after he ceases to be a member, for payment of its debts contracted before he ceases to be a member, and of the costs of winding up, such sum as may be required not exceeding a specified amount.[24] This amount cannot thereafter be increased or reduced.

The *Articles* regulate the internal arrangements and management of the company, and form a contract between the company and the members. For a company limited by guarantee they must be in the form set out in Table C or as near thereto as circumstances permit,[25] and deal with such matters as membership, meetings, officers, finances, auditors and winding up.

## Objects

The purpose of the *objects clause* was originally to protect the subscribers (who would know the purposes to which their money could be applied), and persons dealing with the company (who could discover the extent of the company's powers).[26] The courts then evolved the *ultra vires* rule to the effect that a company only had power to carry out its objects, together with anything incidental thereto, and anything outside the objects was treated as *ultra vires* and void. This proved inconvenient and legislative reforms during recent years have effectively abolished the rule.[27] An *objects clause* is still required, and as a result of the former rule these clauses are usually very long commencing with the main objects and then listing everything that the company may do in furtherance of its objects. If the company is to be registered or recognised as a charity the Memorandum needs to contain clearly separated objects and powers. A member of the company still has a personal right to insist upon the objects clause being complied with, and may apply to the court to prevent the commission of an act by the company which is outside the scope of its objects, although there is no right to an injunction (interdict) if the company is legally committed to this act and one is unlikely to be granted if the act could subsequently be ratified.[28]

## Alterations

On a proposal to alter the objects, the court has powers which are intended to provide some protection for an oppressed minority. In the case of a company registered as a charity in England the prior

---

24   s.2(4). The sum specified in Table C is £100, though a smaller sum is usually adopted. These guarantees are not assets of the company and cannot be mortgaged or charged by the company whilst it is a going concern.

25   ss.3 and 8. Provided that the Articles follow this general form, they may be added to, subtracted from or varied according to the needs of the company.

26   *Cotman* v. *Brougham* [1918-19] All ER 265, HL.

27   Culminating in Companies Act 1989, ss.108-112, which introduced new sections into the 1985 Act, in particular s.35.

28   Ratification will amount to an alteration of the objects clause so a special resolution is required. The directors may still incur some personal liability.

consent of the Charity Commissioners is required,[29] and where permission has been given to omit the word "limited" any alteration must not take the company outside the conditions for this exemption.

The Articles can be altered or added to by special resolution, of which a copy must be filed with the Registrar within 15 days together with a printed copy of the amended Articles.[30] Any alteration must be made bona fide for the benefit of the company as a whole, but this is generally for the members to decide.

*Rules and bye-laws*

The Articles of a company may provide for the making of rules or bye-laws governing the conduct of its affairs and the relationship between the members. These can be changed with less formality by either the members in general meeting or the committee.

**Name**

Every company has a name by which it is known but this may be changed. The name must be displayed outside every office or place of business and included on all business documents, cheques, order forms, invoices, receipts and other publications. Fines may be imposed upon the company and its officers for non-compliance, and an officer who signs a cheque or order on which the name is not stated may become personally liable thereon.[31] Some names are prohibited,[32] and the use of certain words in company names is restricted.[33] The availability of the proposed name should be checked before it is put forward, because a company will not be permitted to use a name that is already on the register. The Secretary of State may order a company to change its name in these circumstances and also if the name gives such a misleading impression of the activities that it is likely to harm the public.[34]

*Dispensing with "Limited"*

The last word of the name must be Limited or Ltd. unless the company is able to comply with the statutory criteria to dispense

---

[29] Charities Act 1960, s.30A introduced by Companies Act 1989, s.111. The Charities Act 1992 extends this to any alteration of any provision in the Memorandum or Articles restricting the use of charity property. In Scotland prior clearance of the proposed change will be required under s.14(2) of the Law Reform (Miscellaneous Provisions) (Scotland) Act 1990 when brought into force.

[30] s.9(1). They cannot be altered so as to conflict with the Memorandum.

[31] s.349(4). Authorising signature by another may also result in liability.

[32] s.26. *e.g.* a name which is offensive or which includes the word "limited" or "unlimited" (or an abbreviation thereof) otherwise than at the end of the name. Guidance is given in NG8 and NG9.

[33] Company and Business Names Regulations 1981 (and the 1982 amending regulations). There are 79 words or expressions which require consent before use, *e.g.* National, English, Royal, Trust, and names which imply a connection with the Government or a local authority.

[34] ss.28(2) and 32.

with this.[35] Dispensation may be granted to a company limited by guarantee which by its Memorandum or Articles:

(a) is to be formed for the promotion of commerce, art, science, education, religion, charity or any profession and anything incidental or conducive to any of those objects;
(b) must apply its income solely for the promotion of those objects;
(c) prohibits the payment of dividends to its members; and
(d) requires all its surplus assets on a winding up to be transferred to a similar body rather than to its members.

A statutory declaration by the solicitor engaged in the formation, or a director or secretary of the company, that the company is one to which this provision applies is all that is required.[36] A company which obtains the exemption need not publish its name or send lists of members to the Registrar, although the fact that it is a limited company must be stated on business letters and order forms.[37]

*Business names*

A company may wish to carry on business under a name other than its own, and the restriction on the use of certain names will also then apply. The corporate name and an address for service of documents must be displayed on any business premises and appear on all business documents. The company and its officers may be liable to fines in default, and restrictions may be imposed upon the company bringing any proceedings.[38]

## Registered Office

A company must always have a registered office to which notices may be sent and a Statement setting out the address must be filed with the relevant Registrar. This need not be where the company carries on business, and the address of a professional office is often used. The address must be stated on all business letters and order forms, and documents can be served upon the company by leaving them at, or sending them by post to, its registered office.

A company may change the address of its registered office by giving proper notice to the Registrar, who will publish in the relevant Gazette notice thereof.[39]

A company limited by guarantee must generally keep certain items (including the register of members, minute book of general meetings, and register of directors and secretaries) at its registered office, where they shall be available for inspection (in some cases on payment of a prescribed fee).

---

[35] s.25(1) and (2). The equivalents *Cyfyngedig (Cyf)* and *Cwmni Cyfyngedig Cyhoeddus (CCC)* may be used by a company whose registered office is in Wales, but the fact that it is a limited company must also then be stated in English - s.351(3). A public limited company will state *PLC*.

[36] s.30 - see NG6. There is a ban upon altering the Memorandum or Articles at a later date so as to breach these requirements, with fines in default.

[37] s.351.

[38] Business Names Act 1985. Guidance is given in NG2.

[39] s.287. The notice must be given within 14 days of the change. The registered office must be still within the country (England or Scotland) of incorporation.

## Directors

The persons who manage the day-to-day running of the business of a company are the directors, and they act collectively as a board though powers may be delegated to an individual director or committee of directors. In the case of a society incorporated as a guarantee company the persons who are directors may be referred to as committee members.[40] Their appointment, qualification (if any), disqualification and retirement and the number to be appointed at any time are matters to be provided for in the Articles, although there are some statutory restrictions.[41]

*Powers*

The Act leaves to the Articles the distribution of powers between the members in general meeting and the board of directors, and in most cases the directors are given wide powers to conduct the business of the company. They are thus agents through whom the company acts. Of course the ultimate power lies in the general meeting where it may be resolved by ordinary resolution on four weeks notice to dismiss a director, or resolved to ratify a decision of the directors which exceeded their powers.

*Duties*

Directors owe a fiduciary duty and a duty of care to the company. They may not make a secret profit and must disclose any transactions between themselves and the company, though where the company is a charity such transactions may be prohibited or strictly controlled. There are certain circumstances in which a director can be held personally responsible for a liability of the company, but a director is not generally responsible for the acts of co-directors unless he has himself taken part. Directors must display the care and diligence of a reasonable man in the circumstances. They are required to exercise only such skill as they possess, but if appointed because of particular expertise must display the skill of a reasonably competent member of the relevant profession. A director may reasonably rely on co-directors and officers of the company.

*Directors meetings*

Much of the business of the company is carried on by the directors who will themselves meet for that purpose and minutes should be kept. The proceedings of such meetings should be as stipulated in the Articles, and such meetings may be known as those of the Executive Committee. While it is not necessary for a director to attend every board meeting (unless the Articles so require), reasonable diligence includes giving a reasonable amount of

---

40   By s.741(1) the expression "director" includes any person occupying the position of director by whatever name called.

41   *e.g.* an undischarged bankrupt cannot be appointed without leave of the court, and persons may be disqualified by the court from being a director. See Chap.2 at p.30 for appointment of a mentally handicapped person.

attention to the company's affairs, and continuous non-attendance could amount to a breach of duty.

### Publication and disclosure

A company must keep a Register of its directors and secretary at its registered office. Their names do not have to appear on notepaper save that if the name of any director is stated as such on any business letter then the names of all directors must be stated.[42] There are statutory controls on service contracts entered into by directors, including provision for disclosure of the terms and the need to obtain the approval of the members in general meeting.[43]

## Officers and members

The Articles determine what officers will be appointed, though every private company must have at least one director and a company secretary. Officers of a society will often be treated as *ex officio* members of the committee, but if it be a company this will have to be dealt with formally by their appointment as directors.

### Secretary

A company secretary must be appointed to deal with the statutory functions of that office, but this need not necessarily be the general secretary of the society and it may be appropriate to engage a professional person. It is usually the duty of the company secretary to call and prepare agendas for meetings, keep the minutes, maintain the registers and ensure proper operation of the company and compliance with companies legislation.

### Auditors

The auditors are appointed by the members at the AGM, although the first auditors may be appointed by the directors before then.[44] They must be suitably qualified, which means that they must belong to a Recognised Supervisory Body.[45] An auditor can be removed by an ordinary resolution of which special notice has been given, but must be given notice and can make representations to the members.[46]

### Members

The members comprise the subscribers of the Memorandum, and all other persons who have agreed to become members and whose names are entered in the Register of members.[47] The Articles set out the procedure for admitting new members and the persons who may be eligible. A new member signs a standard form of guarantee, which is an undertaking to contribute the specified sum to the assets of the company in the event of it being wound up, and

---

42 s.305.
43 ss.318 and 319.
44 ss.384 and 385. An individual or a firm may be appointed.
45 Companies Act 1989, s.30(1). This effectively means a professionally qualified accountant.
46 s.390A for remuneration; ss.391 and 391A for removal.
47 s.22. Entry on the Register is a condition precedent to membership.

personal liability is limited to that amount. Members are not issued with share certificates, and usually have one vote each (rather than a vote for each share held), though other voting structures are possible. They will not have invested any money in the company so do not expect to receive dividends, but the company may be financially supported by subscriptions or fees paid by the members.

## General Meetings

These are meetings of the members, and there are two kinds:

*Annual General Meeting* - the company must hold an AGM, specified as such in the notice calling it, with an interval of not more than 15 months between such meetings.[48] The directors call the meeting and the usual business is consideration of the directors report, approval of annual accounts, election of directors and appointment and remuneration of auditors.

*Extraordinary General Meeting* - any other general meeting. The Articles usually make provision for the calling of such a meeting, but regardless of this a meeting may be requisitioned by members of a guarantee company having at least one-tenth of the voting rights, which normally means one-tenth of the members.[49]

*Notice*

An AGM requires at least 21 days notice, and an extraordinary general meeting 14 days unless a special resolution is to be proposed in which case the period is 21 days.[50] Articles usually provide that this be clear notice, which means excluding the day of service and the day for which the notice is given, but that the accidental omission to give notice to a member or non-receipt of a notice shall not invalidate the proceedings at the meeting. The notice should always state the purpose of the meeting and any resolutions to be proposed, and special or extraordinary resolutions should be described as such.[51]

*Proceedings, voting and resolutions*

The proceedings at general meetings are dealt with in the Articles, including how many members constitute a quorum, appointment of a chairman and his powers, adjournments and voting. Voting can be by show of hands with each member present having one

---

[48]   s.366. Private companies may by "elective resolution" dispense with the AGM but this will not be appropriate for a guarantee company.

[49]   s.368 amended by 1989 Act. The requisition is signed by all involved and states the object of the meeting; on receipt the directors must convene a meeting within 21 days for a date not more than 28 days thereafter.

[50]   ss.369 and 378. These periods cannot be reduced by the Articles, but all the members entitled to attend and vote may agree upon a shorter period. Notice of 28 days is required for an ordinary resolution to remove a director.

[51]   s.378. There are provisions to be found in s.376 that enable members to move a resolution or circulate to other members a statement relating to a proposed resolution or any business to be transacted at a general meeting.

vote, but proxies may be allowed where a poll is demanded.[52]

A resolution is a decision of the company taken by the members at a general meeting, but there are different types:

*Ordinary resolution* - passed by a simple majority and effective in all cases unless another form of resolution is specifically required by legislation or the Memorandum or Articles.

*Extraordinary resolution* - passed by at least a three-fourths majority at a general meeting of which notice specifying the intention to propose this as an extraordinary resolution has been given. Seldom required by a guarantee company.

*Special resolution* - similar to an extraordinary resolution save that at least 21 days clear notice is required stating the intention to propose the special resolution. Required for important matters, such as alteration of Articles or objects clause.

*Elective resolution* - a special form of resolution introduced by the 1989 Act, but unlikely to be used by a society.

An amendment to a resolution must be voted upon first, but it must be relevant to the subject matter of the original resolution and cannot go beyond the notice convening the meeting.[53]

## Records

There are certain records that every company must keep and these must usually be available for inspection at the registered office or some other designated place, sometimes on payment of a fee.

### Registers

A register of members must contain their names and addresses and the dates of becoming and ceasing to be members. A register of the directors and secretary must state their names (and any former name), address and nationality, business occupation, date of birth and any other directorships. Registers must be kept of shares and debentures and of mortgages or charges, but only the latter will be appropriate to a guarantee company. The court has a discretion to rectify a register in certain cases.[54]

### Minutes

Minutes must be kept of general meetings, and these are usually approved by the next meeting and then signed by the chairman. They are evidence of the proceedings, and Articles may provide that they shall be conclusive evidence in which event they will be, as between the members, unless there is evidence of fraud. If minutes have been duly made there is a presumption that all the proceedings were in order and all appointments are valid.[55]

---

[52] s.372 now gives a statutory right to appoint a proxy who need not be a member of the company.

[53] It follows that special and extraordinary resolutions can seldom be amended as the exact wording of the resolution will have been set out in the notice.

[54] See generally ss.352, 289, and 356-360.

[55] ss.382(4) and 383. The Minute book may be bound or loose-leaf, and it is now permitted to keep the minutes on a computer - ss.722 and 723.

*Accounts*

A company must ensure that adequate accounting records are kept[56] and prepare Accounts for its "accounting reference period" which starts on the day of incorporation or the day following the end of the previous accounting period and ends on the accounting reference date.[57] The records must be open for inspection by the officers at all times, and must normally be kept for a minimum of three years though it would be wise to keep them longer than this.

The annual Accounts comprise a Balance Sheet and a Profit and Loss Account,[58] and these must give a true and fair view of the company's financial position and indicate the profit or loss for the period. They must be approved by the directors and then laid before the members in general meeting each year together with the directors' and auditor's reports.

## Filing documents

Certain documents must be filed with the appropriate Registrar either annually or on changes being made. There are financial penalties for late filing, and on conviction a person may be fined and disqualified from being a director or taking part in the management of a company for a period of years.[59] Anyone may inspect documents filed at the Registry and have a copy or extract from them on payment of the prescribed fee.

*Annual Return and Accounts*

Every company must file an annual return on Form 363 made up to a date not later than the company's return date, which is fixed initially at one year from the date of incorporation and subsequently becomes one year from the date when the last annual return was made. The annual return must be delivered with the prescribed fee within 28 days after the return date, signed by a director or the company secretary.[60]

Independently of the annual return, a company must file a copy of its annual Accounts (as described above), as approved by the directors and audited (though not necessarily laid before the members), and this must be signed by a director. The time allowed for filing and for presenting the accounts to the members is ten months from the end of the relevant accounting period.

*Directors' and Auditors' Reports*

Certain matters must appear in the directors' report but some of these do not apply if the company is without a share capital, does

---

56  s.221. The records must be sufficient to show and explain its transactions, and disclose at any time the financial position of the company.

57  Or a date up to seven days either side thereof. The period covered must not exceed 18 months, but the first accounts must cover at least six months.

58  This will be an Income and Expenditure Account where the company does not trade for a profit.

59  This is dealt with in NG28, *Late Filing Penalties.*

60  s.364. See NG25, *Notes for Completion of Annual Return.*

not trade for profit or does not have employees.[61] The report must be approved by the board and a copy delivered to the Registrar signed by a director or the secretary. The auditor, who has a duty to consider whether the report is consistent with the financial statements, will usually be able to give guidance on the report.

The auditors will carry out a full audit of the accounting records and may be employed to prepare the accounts in a suitable form. They must then make a signed report stating whether in their opinion the financial statements comply with the Companies Act and give a true and fair view of the state of the company's affairs at the date thereof and for the year in question.[62]

*Changes*

A printed copy of any special or extraordinary resolution must be filed within 15 days after being passed. Appointments, resignations and changes in particulars of the directors and company secretary must be notified on Form 288 within 14 days. Any change in the registered office must be notified on Form 287 and then takes effect, but for 14 days documents may continue to be served at the previous address.

*Charges*

If a company creates a charge over its property particulars must be submitted to the Registrar in the appropriate form within 21 days and a failure to do so will render the security void unless the court in its discretion gives leave to extend the period.[63]

## Disclosure

All business letters, order forms and invoices must include the name, number, registered office and country of registration of the company. If more than one address is shown, the registered office must be described as such, and if a business name is used, the company name must also be stated. On the company notepaper either all directors' names must be stated or none at all, unless a director is only mentioned in the text or as a signatory. Other information to be shown depends upon the nature of the company. A limited liability company exempt from the use of the word "limited" must state that it is a limited company, and if it is a charity this must also be stated. A company must also exhibit its name on the outside of any premises it occupies, and if this is a business name and customers have access to any part of the premises a notice must be exhibited in that part stating the full name and registered office of the company.[64]

A company must disclose its charitable status in order to protect persons with whom it has financial dealings, but it is sufficient if

---

61  s.234 and Sched.7.
62  This is covered in ss.235-237.
63  1985 Act, Part XII, Chap.1 (England/Wales), Chap.2 (Scotland).
64  See ss.348-351 and Business Names Act 1985, s.4.

the name includes the word "charity".[65] This applies to business letters, notices and official publications, cheques, invoices, orders for goods and all documents dealing with interests in land. Failure to comply could lead to fines and signing officers being held personally liable to the holder of a cheque or other order if the charity cannot meet its obligations.

## Contracts

A company has legal status and can hold property and sue in its own name, so it is not necessary for trustees to be appointed. It may enter into contracts either by affixing its common seal to a document, or under the general principles of agency. English companies may now elect whether or not to have a seal and Scottish companies no longer require a seal.[66] Formal documents are validly executed by the signatures of two directors, or one director and the secretary, or two persons authorised to subscribe the document on behalf of the company.

*Agency*

The alternative is to operate through an authorised agent. A director may have actual or implied authority, and a company may be bound by the act of an agent within his apparent authority. The Articles may restrict the authority of a company's agents to act on its behalf and persons dealing with the company would have notice of this, but the 1989 Act provides[67]:

> "In favour of a person dealing with a company in good faith, the power of the board of directors to bind the company, or authorise others to do so, shall be deemed to be free of any limitation under the company's constitution".

This provision only applies in favour of a person dealing with a charitable company if that person either gives full consideration in money or money's worth and does not know that the transaction is contrary to the constitution, or is unaware at the time that it is a charitable company,[68] but bona fide purchasers who subsequently acquire property without actual notice of such defect in the original transaction are protected. Whilst an ordinary company may subsequently ratify an act which is contrary to its objects clause, or a transaction by a director with the company, in the case of an English charitable company any such ratification will be ineffective unless first authorised by the Charity Commissioners.

## Liability

A registered company is a legal person separate from its members,

---

65 Companies Act 1989, s.111 with effect from February 1991.
66 ss.36A and 350 (as amended by the 1989 Act); s.36B as substituted by Law Reform (Miscellaneous Provisions) (Scotland) Act 1990.
67 In England by substituting a new s.35A(1) in the 1985 Act.
68 Charities Act 1960, s.30B introduced by s.111 of the 1989 Act. In Scotland, s.112 of the 1989 Act. Charitable companies are required to state their status on all correspondence and other business documents, so it is unlikely that anyone dealing with the company will not know it is a charity.

and in general the law will not go behind this.[69]

## Liability of directors

It should not be assumed that merely by operating as a company the persons concerned will be excused from all liability for their actions, though they may be able to seek indemnity from the company. There are situations in which the "veil of incorporation" may be lifted, either by statute or judicial interpretation, though mostly in commercial situations.[70] Trading in the knowledge that the company is insolvent results in personal liability for the directors, and there are circumstances where they may be disqualified from being a company director for a period.

## Liability of members

The members are only liable to the extent of their guarantees unless they have in some way allowed themselves to become personally responsible for some activity of the company.

## SUMMARY

Whether a society is established as an unincorporated association or is incorporated as a company limited by guarantee depends upon many factors.

## Incorporation

### Advantages

    (a) it exists in law independent of the members;
    (b) debts and contracts are those of the company, not the members;
    (c) it may hold property in its corporate name without the need to provide for continuing trustees;
    (d) it does not die from natural causes, though in certain circumstances it may be wound up or struck off;
    (e) it affords limited liability to the members and officers;[71]
    (f) the formalities are a useful discipline for those managing the company;
    (g) a charitable company normally has power to alter its objects (whilst remaining charitable);
    (h) it is subject to public scrutiny so can enhance its image if it is well run;
    (i) it can have all the powers and functions of an ordinary company, yet is easier to manage and has some privileges.

### Disadvantages

    (a) setting up and running expenses are greater than for an unincorporated association;
    (b) the requirements of the Companies Acts must be complied

---

69  *Salomon* v. *Salomon & Co. Ltd.* [1897] AC 22, HL.
70  Guidance on *Directors Responsibilities* is contained in NG27.
71  As we shall see, directors of a charitable company are the "charity trustees" and personally liable as such just as if they were committee members of an unincorporated association or trustees of a charitable trust.

with in regard to matters such as the submission of annual
returns, keeping of minutes, passing of resolutions;
(c) a qualified auditor must be appointed;
(d) further professional assistance may be needed;
(e) the formality may frighten off potential officers;
(f) although it may be possible to dispense with "limited" there
are restrictions upon the name that can be adopted;
(g) its accounts and certain other documents are open for
public inspection.

## Non-Incorporation

*Advantages*
(a) may be more acceptable to the members and officers;
(b) setting up and running costs are less than for a company;
(c) documentation is relatively simple, especially if a model
deed is followed;
(d) the procedure for altering the governing instrument or for
dissolution may be relatively simple;
(e) a qualified auditor is not essential, though desirable;
(f) professional assistance may not be needed;
(g) there is more freedom as to the name that can be adopted.

*Disadvantages*
(a) it does not exist in law independent of the members;
(b) it cannot hold property so must provide for continuing
trustees;
(c) the committee or trustees may become personally liable in
contract, or tort or delict;
(d) there is no external discipline imposed upon those
managing the association, so formalities may be neglected;
(e) third parties may be more willing to deal with companies
than unincorporated associations;
(f) treated in same way as a company for tax purposes.

# PART IIA - CHARITIES (England)

## Preliminary

A society, whether or not a company, may wish to obtain
charitable status by registering with the Charity Commissioners.
There are various benefits to be gained, mainly of a fiscal nature,
but because of the risk of abuse this also brings some degree of
regulation. We consider those provisions of relevance to a charity
whose objects are to further the welfare of or make provision for
persons with a mental handicap and their families.

*Legislation*
Charities Acts 1960,1985 and 1992
Recreational Charities Act 1958
The 1960 Act consolidated the existing law of charities in England
and Wales and extended its scope, whilst the 1985 Act gave further

powers to the Commissioners. The 1992 Act further strengthens their role as a regulatory body and increases the personal accountability of charity trustees.[72]

## The Charity Commission

Commissioners are appointed under the Charities Act 1960 who are immune from government control and make an annual report to the Secretary of State which is laid before parliament. Their function is to promote the effective use of charitable resources by encouraging the development of better administration, giving charity trustees information or advice, and investigating and checking abuses.[73] They regard themselves as friends and advisers of charity trustees and their services are free, but they cannot act in the administration of a charity or interfere with the trustees' discretion if this is being exercised properly.[74] Those running charities are encouraged to approach the Commissioners on an informal basis for advice whenever necessary, and helpful explanatory booklets are available on a variety of topics. The Commissioners may, on written application from trustees, give their opinion on any matter affecting the performance of their duties and, provided they have been given full information, their advice affords protection for trustees acting in good faith against allegations of breach of trust.

*Powers*
The Commissioners are responsible for registration of charities including deciding whether or not a body should be treated as a charity. They can authorise certain actions which trustees would not otherwise have power to take, unless such action is expressly prohibited by the trusts of the charity or would have the effect of extending or altering the purposes of the charity.[75] They have power to enquire into the affairs of a charity, or appoint someone to do so and report to them, and in so doing they may obtain information and evidence. They obtain and examine accounts of charities as far as their resources permit and seek to ensure that there is no excessive accumulation of funds or expenditure on administration, and that funds are used in accordance with the purposes for which the charity exists. They may remove or suspend a trustee and take steps to prevent the property of a charity from being misused, but informal procedures are usually successful in resolving any problems.

*Official Custodian for Charities*
This is a permanent corporate office held by a senior member of

---

72  The 1992 Act was not in force at May, 1, 1992 and its provisions are likely to be brought into effect piecemeal by the Secretary of State.

73  1960 Act, s.1. The 1992 Act gives them wider powers to intervene in the administration of charities and in particular to institute enquiries, obtain information and documents, and act for the protection of charities.

74  Act 1960 Act, s.24.

75  s.23.

the Commissioners' staff. The Official Custodian holds property in trust for charities thus avoiding the need for changes of ownership on a change of trustee. He acts only as a custodian trustee and has no power of management but retains in safe-keeping the securities transferred into his name and remits income to the charity trustees without deduction of tax. His powers derive from the Charities Act 1960 and no charge is made for the services provided.[76]

### *Charities Investment Fund*
This Fund was established by the Commissioners under the powers in the 1960 Act, to help small charities unable to take advantage of the wider powers of investment under the Trustee Investments Act 1961. It is a unit trust with a wide spread of investments limited to registered charities and managed by trustees appointed by the Commissioners.[77]

## Register of charities

The Commissioners maintain a register of charities which is open to public inspection. This provides conclusive evidence that the institutions included therein are charities thereby facilitating tax and other benefits. Local authorities are supplied with information relating to charities operating in their area, and may keep local indexes which are open to inspection. Not only may such public registers provide useful publicity to charities but it enables them to learn about other charities operating in the same field.

## CHARITY LAW

There are several forms that a charity can take, but the over-riding requirement is that the purposes or objects must be exclusively charitable.

## Charitable objects

There is no single statutory definition of charitable objects. The legal concept of charity is to be found in case law derived from the list of specific charitable purposes included in the preamble to the Charitable Uses Act 1601 (the Statute of Elizabeth I) and since then the courts have developed the meaning of charity by analogy to meet changing social circumstances. It is usually said that the law recognises four general classes of objects which are charitable, namely[78]:
- relief of poverty;
- advancement of religion;
- advancement of education;   and

---

76   The 1992 Act, s.29 provides for the Official Custodian to divest himself of all assets held on trust by June 1997.
77   The 1992 Act, s.16 provides for the court or the Commissioners to establish a Common Deposit Fund.
78   The judgment of Lord MacNaughton in *Income Tax Special Purposes Commissioners* v. *Pemsel* [1891] AC 531 is usually referred to as being the authority for this classification.

- other purposes beneficial to the community not falling under
  any of the other heads.

This classification is not exhaustive but the courts look to it for
guidance as to the kinds of purpose which should be regarded as
charitable and tend to ask whether the purpose is "within the spirit
and intendment" of the 1601 statute.[79] The first class is generally
acknowledged as including not only the relief of poverty but also
of sickness, the aged and the impotent (which covers disabled
people[80]). In order to be within the first class, the persons
receiving relief do not need to be "poor",[81] so a residential care
home which charges fees may be charitable.[82]

### Public benefit

There is in all cases the requirement that the purpose must be for
the public benefit. This means for the benefit of the public as a
whole or a sufficient section of the public, and the benefit of
specific individuals would not be sufficient except for the relief of
poverty which may be for a very small class of beneficiaries.[83]
With this exception, the potential beneficiaries may not be selected
on the basis of relationship to a donor or because they are
members of a particular non-charitable society. There is no
specific test of what amounts to public benefit and each case must
be considered on its own merits.

### Recreation or leisure

Additional categories are permitted under Recreational Charities
Act 1958 which include the provision of facilities for recreation
or other leisure-time occupations in the interests of social welfare
where the aim is to improve the conditions of life for people for
whom the facilities are mainly intended. Such facilities may be
targetted for people with a mental handicap or disability.

### Political activities

A political purpose cannot be charitable, but political activity may
be acceptable if undertaken in furtherance of charitable purposes.

---

79  A more restrictive approach, which provides less scope for charity law to
    reflect changing social requirements, is to ascertain whether the purpose
    bears sufficient resemblance to the original classes or earlier decided cases.
    The Charities Bill 1991 originally proposed that regard should be had to the
    manner and circumstances in which the organisation pursued its purposes,
    and not simply to what these purposes were stated to be.

80  Books on charity law tend to refer to the physically disabled and to treat
    mental disorders as being within relief of the sick. It is suggested that, in
    view of the distinction between mental illness and mental handicap, only the
    former should come within sickness and the latter should be the impotent.

81  The expression in the 1601 statute "relief of aged, impotent and poore
    people" must be read disjunctively -Re Glyn's Will Trusts [1950] 2 All ER
    1150. Affirmed (despite authorities to the contrary) in Joseph Rowntree
    Memorial Trust Housing Association Limited v. A-G [1983] 1 All ER 288.

82  Cf. Re Resch's Will Trusts [1969] AC 514 - a hospital for the relief of the
    sick charging fees which the poor could not afford.

83  It is not clear whether this extends to sickness, the aged and the impotent (as
    mentioned above) or only to poverty pure and simple.

The difference is that between a purpose and a power, and the Charity Commissioners have issued guidelines.[84] Political activity goes well beyond party politics and any charity considering any form of lobbying should consult the Commissioners first.

*Implications to mental handicap*
Charities within the scope of this book are likely to fall within the first or fourth classes, although there is some scope for educational charities. Helping categories of people within the community through the relief of the mentally or physically handicapped is recognised as being a charitable purpose and it is hoped that, in view of the potential for the voluntary sector to contribute towards the implementation of community care, interpretations will not be unduly restrictive in the future.

## Charity trustees

The term *charity trustees* has a special meaning distinct from that of ordinary trustees. It is defined as "the persons having the general control and management of the administration of a charity" and thus may refer to the trustees of a charitable trust, the committee of an unincorporated association, or the directors of a company.[85] Any form of charity must be managed by individuals who are treated as charity trustees, these being the persons legally responsible for the proper management of the charity and for ensuring that funds are expended only for authorised purposes. In some cases a committee is appointed whose powers are such that they will be the charity trustees, and *custodian trustees* are also appointed to hold property and in certain circumstances they may be required to take over as charity trustees.

*Appointment*
The governing instrument of a charity or general law will usually make provision for the appointment and retirement of the persons who are charity trustees but the Commissioners can at the request of the charity appoint a new trustee, or discharge an existing trustee from office. If the governing instrument does not specify the term a trustee will usually be appointed for life or until terminated by resignation, bankruptcy or other legally disabling circumstance. A trustee may only resign in accordance with a specific provision in the governing instrument or by the appointment of a new trustee in his place. The statutory power of appointing a new trustee of a Trust Deed in place of a trustee who is dead, absent from the country for more than 12 months, desires to be discharged, refuses to act or is incapable of acting, applies to a charitable trust.[86]

---

84  Commissioners' Annual Report 1981, paras. 54/55. Guidance is now set out in leaflet CC9 - *Political Activities by Charities*.
85  1960 Act, s.46.
86  Trustee Act 1925, ss.36-40. The 1992 Act, s.8 gives the Commissioners power to appoint, suspend or remove a charity trustee, and to appoint additional trustees even if not asked, or to appoint a receiver and manager.

Any person who is an adult may be a trustee, and an office-holder for the time being may be appointed.[87] A corporation may also be appointed if its constitution authorises this, although there may be a problem with the fees.[88] There is no limit to the number of persons who may be appointed trustees of a charity, but the Commissioners usually insist upon at least three.

### Delegation

The general rule is that trustees must act in person and decisions concerning the charity must be taken by trustees acting together. A Trust Deed may specifically authorise delegation, the constitution of an unincorporated association may allow a committee member to appoint a substitute and the Articles of Association of a company may provide for alternate directors, but in the absence of such provision a person cannot usually appoint someone to act in his place. In the case of a Trust Fund, an individual trustee may delegate his powers to another person by a Power of Attorney for a period not exceeding 12 months subject to notice being given to the other trustees (and any person having power to appoint new trustees) before or within seven days of the execution of the power.[89] A late amendment to the Enduring Powers of Attorney Act 1985 appears to allow a trustee to delegate without any such limitation.[90] Because of the duty of charity trustees to act personally the Commissioners do not favour a provision for alternate directors, and any delegation by the trustees must be subject to their close supervision, *e.g.* a sub-committee must report back promptly to its main committee.

### Duties

Charity trustees are responsible for the proper administration of the charity and manage the charity for the benefit of others. They may employ staff or obtain professional help paid for by the charity, but remain legally responsible and must supervise the work of the officers. They must act reasonably with a high standard of care and ensure that the property of the charity is used for the purposes for which it was given. They must not allow themselves to be in a position where there is a conflict between their own interests and those of the charity, and should not let their personal prejudices affect their conduct as trustees.

Duties may include fundraising, managing and investing funds, acquiring and maintaining property, ensuring that proper accounts are kept and deciding how the benefits are to be provided.

---

87 The 1992 Act, s.45 specifies categories of people who may not be appointed, *e.g.* undischarged bankrupts and those convicted of an offence involving dishonesty or disqualified from being company directors.

88 *e.g* a bank trust company, but not a commercial bank.

89 Trustee Act 1925, s.25 as amended by Powers of Attorney Act 1971, s.9. This power is useful if a trustee is going abroad for a period, and prior to 1971 it was restricted to such circumstances.

90 s.3(3). This provision has caused much controversy and is being examined by the Law Commission; see Consultation Paper No.118, March 1991.

Trustees have the general duty of protecting the charity's property and are accountable for the solvency and continuing effectiveness of the charity. They should ensure that property which is part of the permanent endowment is preserved and invested so as to produce a good income whilst safeguarding the capital, and that any land is not encroached upon. Bank accounts should be maintained under the control of at least two trustees, all income due should be received, and any tax and rating relief claimed.[91]

## Powers of Trustees

Duties are what trustees are required to do whereas powers are what they are permitted to do in carrying out their duties. Failure to exercise a power may result in failure to discharge a duty. The powers arise expressly under the governing instrument and under statute, and may also be implied.

### Investment

Unless the governing instrument extends the powers of investment these will be those found in the Trustee Investments Act 1961, but the trustees must decide what forms of investment will be most suitable to the needs of their charity and should obtain professional advice for this purpose.[92] Trustees may invest in land if they have an express power or obtain an order from the Commissioners.

### Buying land and buildings

There is usually power to buy land if it is needed to carry out the purposes of the charity and even where there is no express power this may generally be implied. Trustees should obtain appropriate professional advice and take all reasonable steps to ensure that any property is suitable for its intended use, and that the price is fair and the charity can afford it. The terms of any lease should be fair and reasonable. If trustees are buying with the help of a loan, they must be satisfied that it is on the best terms reasonably obtainable and can be financed out of income.

### Selling land and buildings

Before selling land trustees need to consider whether they have power to do so, and whether the sale is in the best interests of the charity (they should not be influenced by other factors). An order of the Commissioners is usually required before they can sell land which forms part of the permanent endowment, or which has been occupied for the purposes of the charity, and no commitment should be entered into until this is available.[93] Trustees must take

---

[91]  The 1992 Act, s.3 requires all charities (not only companies) to disclose their charitable status on all documents (including cheques) and failure to comply may involve the trustees in penalties and personal liability *cf.* Companies Act 1989, s.111.

[92]  A fund established to meet the needs of charities is mentioned above. The 1992 Act, ss.38 and 39 give the Secretary of State powers to relax some of the requirements of the 1961 Act.

[93]  There is a standard procedure. The 1992 Act, s.32 will simplify dealings with charity land, but a disposal must not be to a "connected person".

all reasonable steps to secure the most advantageous terms and this normally means obtaining (and acting upon) advice from a qualified surveyor acting solely in the interests of the charity, fully marketing the land and giving all interested purchasers an opportunity to increase their offers until the highest price has been reached.[94]

## Insurance

Trustees can and should, at the expense of the charity, insure charity property for its full value against loss or damage, and also against other usual risks.

## Legal action

Trustees have power to take legal action to protect the property of the charity, and may settle legal claims against the charity. Clearly in doing so they should act on competent professional advice.

## Remuneration

The general principle is that a trustee should not benefit from his trust, or put himself in a position where his personal interest may conflict with his duties as trustee. Any provision in the governing instrument which allows funds to be applied for non-charitable purposes such as remuneration of trustees may be open to question and result in registration being refused, but a charity trustee may have out-of-pocket expenses reimbursed and a professional person may in appropriate circumstances be allowed to charge for his services notwithstanding that he is a trustee.[95] It is hoped that charities will attract suitably qualified persons to provide the management expertise necessary such as solicitors, accountants and bank managers. Retired professional persons are often recruited so it is not a good idea to specify a retiring age for trustees.

# Liability of trustees

## Liability to Trust

Charity trustees who cause a loss of funds through a breach of trust, lack of care or dishonesty may be required to repay the loss. If only one of the trustees involved in a breach of trust is sued he may be entitled to a contribution from his co-trustees, but where a breach of trust has been committed in reliance on the advice of a solicitor trustee then such trustee may have to indemnify his co-trustees.[96] A new trustee will not be liable for breaches of trust prior to his appointment but he should not ignore them thereafter.

## Liability to third parties

A trustee is personally responsible in respect of all transactions which he enters into on behalf of the charity, even if the other party knows that he is a trustee, but is entitled to be indemnified

---

94 Trustees may even have to act dishonourably by "gazumping".
95 The 1992 Act, ss.40-42 provide, inter alia, that in the case of a company consent of the Commissioners must be obtained for certain payments to or contracts with directors.
96 See also Civil Liability Contribution Act 1978.

provided that he is acting within his authority. A trustee may also be liable in the usual way as an employer, or for any tort committed, but will be indemnified if he has acted reasonably and with due care. To guard against such risks all usual insurance policies should be taken out especially as the indemnity will be worthless if the funds of the charity are inadequate. The liability of a trustee for acts committed or omissions whilst a trustee may even continue after retirement (*e.g.* liability under a lease that the trustee entered into as a tenant) but in that event the retired trustee will join the present trustees in the action and seek indemnity from them and the assets.

*Company directors*
We have already seen that a company may be registered as a charity, and in that event the charity trustees will be the directors. It may be appropriate to form the charity as a company when the trustees are worried about personal liability, and indeed they will not in that event be liable for any trading losses or debts incurred in carrying on the charity. However, personal guarantees may be required in respect of any borrowings, and also a director may be personally liable for breach of fiduciary duty, acting without authority, being negligent or failing to comply with the Companies Acts. Directors of a charitable company have the same fiduciary duties as trustees of a non-incorporated charity, and if there is a breach of trust in regard to charitable funds they will be personally liable. Lay directors often think that it is proper to be a paid employee of a charitable company and also an unpaid director, but this is not so.

*Protection*
Where charity trustees are not certain whether a particular course is permitted they may apply to the court for directions, or to the Charity Commissioners for advice, in which event if they act in accordance with such advice they will be protected against any claim for breach of trust as long as they have disclosed all material facts. The court may relieve a trustee who has acted honestly and reasonably, and ought fairly to be excused from a breach of trust. Protection is also afforded to a trustee where loss has been caused solely by the fraud or default of a co-trustee provided that he has not contributed to the loss. A trustee must exercise proper supervision over an agent, but will generally be protected from liability for the default of an agent employed in good faith.[97]

## Custodian trustees

The role of a custodian trustee is to hold the trust assets. He plays no part in the administration of the charity which is in the hands of managing trustees and he must deal with the trust assets in accordance with their directions unless this constitutes a breach of

---

[97]   Trustee Act 1925, ss.61, 30 and 23. There is no power to authorise transactions which would have the effect of altering the trusts of the charity.

trust. He is entitled to be reimbursed for his expenses. Having a custodian trustee is useful where a large number of people are involved in running a charity and there are frequent changes in the managing trustees. It avoids the need for assets to be transferred to new trustees on every appointment and for a number of signatures to be obtained each time assets are disposed of. It also prevents problems arising in establishing title when there has been a failure to transfer trust assets into the names of new trustees.

## Permanent endowment

The permanent endowment of a charity is property which cannot under its trusts or constitution be expended for the purposes of the charity as if it were income. This may consist of land or buildings, investments or cash, and is generally regarded as the *capital* of the charity. Unless authorised by statute, or the governing instrument trustees can only spend such capital if and to the extent that they are authorised by the Commissioners and no part of the permanent endowment may be mortgaged or charged as security for money borrowed without the consent of the Commissioners or of the court. It is necessary to prevent capital from being spent or the charity may cease to exist through lack of funds contrary to the intentions of the founder thereby depriving the community of help and facilities intended to be provided indefinitely. When a charity wishes to spend part of its permanent endowment an application form should be obtained from the Commissioners and all appropriate information supplied. Such authority may be given (*e.g.* for essential work on buildings) on the understanding that the amount is recouped out of future income.

## Registration

Since 1960 almost all charities in England and Wales have had to be registered and to file copies of the governing instrument and accounts. These are open to public inspection, and basic particulars of charities are distributed to local authorities for their areas. Before accepting a new registration the Commissioners must satisfy themselves that the governing instrument constitutes a charity in law, but once registered the body is presumed to be a charity for all purposes (although the register may subsequently be rectified). The body must not only satisfy the Commissioners that its objects are exclusively charitable, but also that the powers and duties of the trustees are compatible with charitable status.[98] The procedure on registration is dealt with below.

### Exempt and excepted charities

Charities registered under the Industrial and Provident Societies Act 1974 or the Friendly Societies Act 1974 are exempt from registration with the Commissioners because they are regulated by

---

98   *e.g.* it should not be possible to alter the objects to non-charitable purposes. The 1992 Act, s.4 includes powers to limit the choice of a charity's name in manner similar to that for companies.

another system. They have hitherto been permitted to register, but the 1992 Act changes this, and those which are currently registered will be removed from the register.[99]

Charities with no permanent endowment, no use of land and an annual income from investments or property of less than £15, do not need to register, and if they do not do so many provisions (*e.g.* relating to accounts, audit and annual reports) will not fully apply to them. The 1992 Act raises this to £1,000.[100]

### Charities for disabled persons

Special rules apply to this type of charity which is defined as[101]:

> "any fund, institution, association or undertaking, having for its sole or principal object or among its principal objects the promotion of the welfare of persons who are blind, deaf or dumb, and other persons who are substantially and permanently handicapped by illness, injury, or congenital deformity".

It is unlawful to raise or attempt to raise funds from the public for any charity for disabled persons unless it has been registered by the registration authority in whose area its administrative centre is situated, or is exempted therefrom.[102] The registration authority must keep a register of such charities in its area and may refuse to register a charity on certain grounds but there is a right of appeal to the Charity Commissioners. The charity must comply with certain conditions as to the manner in which it is conducted, and must submit a copy of its accounts each year to the authority. It is unlawful for anyone selling goods to represent that a disabled person has been employed in producing or packaging the goods or will otherwise benefit from the business unless it is carried on by a charity registered as aforesaid.[103]

## Alteration of trusts

Where it is necessary to alter the purposes of a charity and the provisions of the 1985 Act are not available,[104] the Commissioners can make a *cy pres* Scheme whereby they authorise a change. The new purposes must be as near as possible to the original purposes consonant with the effective use of the charity's property. A Scheme can only be made if the original purposes are obsolete or impracticable or no longer express the original spirit of the gift, or if the charity can be better operated in conjunction with another

---

99 If concerned about this loss of registration they may alter their status so as to be no longer exempt, or describe themselves as "an exempt charity under the Charities Act 1960, Second Schedule".

100 1960 Act, s.4(4) and 1992 Act, s.2. Registration is thus voluntary, but if a charity decides to register it must conform to all the requirements.

101 War Charities Act 1940 as extended by National Assistance Act 1948, s.41.

102 This means County Councils, Metropolitan District Councils, London Borough Councils and the Common Council of the City of London.

103 Trading Representations (Disabled Persons) Act 1972.

104 These only apply to local charities for the relief of poverty, and certain very small charities.

similar charity.[105] In these circumstances trustees may have a duty to consider a Scheme but one can not be made unless they apply.

## SETTING UP A CHARITY

In some cases a charity is to be set up initially, but in other cases a society already exists and desires to achieve charitable status. Advice on specific matters is available from The National Council for Voluntary Organisations.[106] The following questions may arise when it is proposed to form a new charity:

1. What is the purpose or object of the charity to be?
   - what activities will be carried out to achieve this?
   - is there an existing charity, voluntary organisation or statutory body in the area already doing similar work?
   - if so, is there need for a new charity?
   - if a new charity is needed, has co-operation with existing bodies been discussed so that efforts are not duplicated?
2. Will benefits be restricted to people living in a particular area or place?
3. How will the funds to run the charity be obtained?
   - will grants from central or local government or other charities be needed and will they be made available?
   - will funds be raised directly from the public?
   - will enough funds be available to pay for planned activities?
4. Where will the charity operate from?
   - will there be the need to rent or buy premises?
   - will suitable premises be available?
   - what type of structure will be appropriate?
   - has all appropriate expert advice been obtained?
5. How many trustees will be needed?
   - do the proposed trustees have the skills needed?
   - what staff will it be necessary to employ?
6. Will the charity have a membership and if so, who will be eligible?

## Structure

There are several legal forms that a charity can take.

### Trust Fund

An individual may set up a charitable trust fund by Will or deed (sometimes called a Settlement) or a number of people may join together to create such a trust. Additional funds may be introduced at a later date either by the person who created the trust or others, and there is no time limit for the duration of such a trust provided it is for exclusively charitable purposes. Power is retained by the trustees who may be a self perpetuating body, so this structure

---

[105] Charities Act 1960, s.13. The 1992 Act provides for this process to be formalised by a Statutory Instrument.

[106] Address in Appendix I.

may be unsuitable for a large group which wants to participate in decision making. The trust document should set out the purposes and include provisions for achieving these and for managing the trust fund, and as to winding up if the purposes can no longer be carried out. Provision should be made for the retirement and appointment of trustees.

Where organisations wish to join together to achieve a purpose of a charitable nature but each wishes to play a part in management, they may adopt a *Constitution* which will have the same purpose as a trust deed. This differs from an unincorporated association in that instead of a fluctuating body of members, there are nominees from each constituent organisation on a committee of management which manages the trust, though trustees will be appointed to hold property and take over responsibility should the committee cease to function.[107]

### Unincorporated association

A society with an ever changing body of members who wish to co-operate to achieve mutually accepted and well defined objects may wish to operate as a charity. Its governing instrument must be in terms capable of being approved by the Commissioners, and if it wishes to hold property or investments it will need to appoint trustees for the purpose. There should be provision for changing the objects, subject to the written approval of the Charity Commissioners, in case it becomes impossible to achieve them.

### Company

A company is capable of being registered as a charity if its documentation is in appropriate terms.

### Public appeal

A new charity can be created if there is an appeal for funds for purposes other than the general purposes of an existing charity. If there is no formal governing document, the appeal literature may form the document governing the charity so great care should be taken as to the wording.

### Friendly Society

If a society has a benevolent purpose with at least seven members it may wish to consider registration under the Friendly Societies Act 1974.[108]

Advantages include the fact that any disputes arising in the society can go to arbitration through the Chief Registrar, and the society's property is held by trustees and passes automatically on a change of trustees. If the society has charitable objects it is exempt from registration with the Charity Commissioners.

Disadvantages are that a copy of the rules must be sent to the Chief Registrar with a fee on registration, and thereafter an Annual

---

[107] See precedent for Mental Handicap Trust in Appendix IV.
[108] See Registry of Friendly Societies *Guide to the Law Relating to Friendly Societies and Industrial Assurance* (2nd ed.) and annual Reports of the Chief Registrar of Friendly Societies.

Return with accounts must be filed. A friendly society is subject to the general control of the Chief Registrar who may appoint an Inspector to investigate its affairs.

## Constitution

All charities have a governing instrument which sets out the objects of the charity and the rules under which it is administered. This may be a trust deed (including a Will), the constitution or rules of an unincorporated association, or the Memorandum and Articles of Association of a company.

### Objects clause

Great care must be taken with the wording of the objects clause in the governing instrument of a charity. A decision will be needed as to whether this is to be specific, and thereby restrictive, or more general in its terms allowing flexibility which may extend beyond the expectations of those who set up or support the charity. Thus if the trust is for the benefit of mentally disabled persons its activities may be devoted to the needs of persons with a mental illness notwithstanding that the founders had in mind mental handicap. If the intention is the provision of residential care, education, leisure facilities, or the promotion of research, then this should be clearly stated as a principal object (if necessary, to the exclusion of anything else). The golden rule is that the purposes must be exclusively charitable, and must not be too vague or ambiguous, or illegal or impossible.

### Dissolution

The founders of the charity should consider what is to happen to the assets and funds if for some reason the charity ceases to exist. Whilst the law deals in general terms with this eventuality it is far better to provide in the governing instrument that the funds will be handed over to another specific charity or, in the discretion of the trustees (or the members) to charities of a particular type. In this way the fundamental purposes may continue to be fulfilled "as nearly as may be".

## Registration

The requirement of registration with the Charity Commissioners has been explained above, and we now deal with the procedure. A questionnaire is submitted with the draft governing instrument and certain other documents.[109] The Commissioners may request amendments and consult the Inland Revenue in any case of doubt because of the considerable tax privileges that registration affords. Once all is in order the promoters will be invited to apply for registration on the form provided and the governing instrument should be formally completed. When the charity is entered on the Register the promoters are notified of the registration number, the

---

109 It is desirable to refer the documents in draft form for informal approval in this way so that any amendments can be made with a minimum of formality, especially in the case of a proposed company.

details of the charity recorded in the index to the Register and any further requirements. There is a procedure for persons who may be affected by the registration to object and appeals may be made to the High Court against any decision concerning registration.

The Commissioners through their staff can be extremely helpful in providing advice and assistance based upon their experience of registering and supervising charities. The founders are not simply setting up their own business, but are creating an independent body intended to continue after their deaths. The Commissioners are concerned to establish not only that the documentation is satisfactory, but also that the proposed activities of the charity will comply with its objects, so it is helpful to submit copies of any minutes of meetings discussing the formation, fundraising letters and newspaper publicity.

### Local registration

Steps should be taken to inform the local authorities for districts in which the charity is to operate of the services to be provided, because such authorities have a statutory duty to inform disabled persons of the provision of such services.[110]

## Charitable status

Is it worthwhile for a voluntary organisation to achieve charitable status and do the benefits outweigh the burdens? This question will inevitably be asked and the answer depends upon the circumstances of the particular case.

### Advantages

These fall within four heads:

*Freedoms:* Purpose trusts are generally void, but not if for charitable purposes. Uncertainty in objects can be overlooked in view of overall charitable intent, and if there is a failure of the trusts the funds may be used for similar charitable purposes under the *cy-pres* doctrine. The trust can continue indefinitely.

*Incentives:* Specific tax exemptions, rating reliefs and other financial incentives available to a charity; greater freedom to raise funds and access to grants.

*Advice:* A charity may receive advice from the Charity Commissioners on all aspects of its affairs.

*Respect:* A body which is registered as a charity will have greater public credibility which is valuable when support or financial contributions are needed.

### Disadvantages

There are three heads, though these may be seen as advantages depending upon one's point of view:

*Restrictions:* More regulation, restriction on purposes which must be exclusively charitable (no political activity

---

110 Disabled Persons (Services, Consultation and Representation) Act 1986, s.9.

and some limit on trading) and no personal benefit for the persons involved in the management .

*Restraints:* Investments must be in the best interests of the charity, suit its requirements and be diverse.

*Supervision:* Audited accounts may need to be submitted to the Commissioners who have power to investigate and to intervene in the affairs of the charity.

## Attributes of charitable trust

A charitable trust differs as follows from a private trust:

*Beneficiaries* - charitable trusts are formed to benefit society rather than individuals or specific groups;

*Taxation* - charitable trusts enjoy exemption from most taxes, whereas private trusts are liable to ordinary taxation and in some cases additional tax liabilities;

*Objects* - vague objects will cause a private trust to fail but a charitable trust will not fail simply for this reason (though registration will be refused if the objects are not sufficiently certain to be enforced by the court);

*Cy pres* - the facility to prepare Schemes for variation of the trusts only applies to charitable trusts;

*Registration* - most charities are registered with the Charity Commissioners but private trusts are not registered at all;

*Enforcement* - charitable trusts are enforced by the Attorney General whereas private trusts are enforced by the beneficiaries;

*Duration* - charitable trusts can continue indefinitely whereas private trusts are subject to the perpetuity period.

# PART IIB - CHARITIES (Scotland)

**Note:** Scottish charities law has been substantially amended by Part I of the Law Reform (Miscellaneous Provisions) (Scotland) Act 1990, referred to in this section as "the 1990 Act". These provisions have not yet been brought into force, but (except where otherwise indicated) the law is described as it will be once they are in force. Regulations under the 1990 Act are awaited. At time of writing it is anticipated that the main provisions described below regarding recognition, supervision, accounting and related matters will be brought into force on July 27, 1992.

## Preliminary

Scotland has no Charity Commission and no statutory register of charities. Prior to the 1990 Act, the only form of recognition which could be obtained by charities other than disabled charities[111] was to obtain confirmation from the Inland Revenue

---

111 War Charities Act 1940 as extended by National Assistance Act 1948, s.41,

that they qualified for relief from income and corporation tax. Under the 1990 Act a body is a "recognised body" if it has received from the Revenue intimation, which has not subsequently been withdrawn, that it qualifies for such relief; and only a recognised body (or an English charity[112]) may represent itself or hold itself out as a charity in Scotland.

Scots law has various definitions of charity. Historically, it is correct to say that there is a general common law definition, which is somewhat narrower than the English definition described in Part IIA, together with various statutory definitions for particular purposes (such as the wider definition for the purpose of regulating street collections[113]). However, one of the statutory definitions now overshadows all others in importance: under the 1990 Act only a recognised body may call itself a Scottish charity, and the definition for tax purposes which enables it to become a recognised body is the English definition of a charity. Thus for most practical purposes, the Scottish and English definitions of what is a charity are now the same, but the legal regimes governing charities in the two countries are very different.

## BODIES AND DEFINITIONS

### Bodies which may be charities

Many types of entity may be or become charities. Common formats are unincorporated associations, trusts, guarantee companies, industrial and provident societies,[114] and friendly societies.[115] Charity law, and definitions of charities, are relevant to such organisations in two ways:

(i) They may seek the advantages of recognition, or of tax and similar benefits, or both. Prior to the 1990 Act, recognition was a problem in Scotland. Many major UK charities, registered with the Charity Commissioners in England, are well-known in Scotland, and there was a public expectation that any reputable charity would in some way be registered. Many charities obtained intimation from the Revenue that they qualified for tax relief, and thereafter quoted the relevant Revenue reference on their letterheadings, but never required actually to claim tax relief. Others sought registration as disabled charities from similar motives of recognition. Tax, rating and similar advantages are less nebulous; exemption from tax and relief from rates depend upon meeting the tax definition of a charity.

---

but repealed by the 1990 Act.

112  *I.e.* a charity registered as such under Charities Act 1960, s.4 or exempt or excepted from registration - see p.643.

113  Under the Civic Government (Scotland) Act 1982, see Part III below.

114  Registered under the Industrial and Provident Societies Act 1965, a popular format for housing associations.

115  Registered under the Friendly Societies Act 1974.

(ii) A charity falling within a particular definition may be subject to particular requirements and controls, such as those governing disabled charities or street collections. Under the 1990 Act, to call itself a "charity" at all a body must meet the requirements of that Act.

The new regime under the 1990 Act provides both recognition and a regulatory regime.

*Projects and funds which are not charities*

The general public tend to describe as charitable a fund-raising effort to send a disabled child for special treatment or training, or an appeal on behalf of the victims of a particular disaster. The first example is not a charity, and the second is unlikely to be (except perhaps under the definition of a disabled charity).

**Trusts**

In Scots law trusts may be divided into *private* and *public* trusts. All charitable trusts are public trusts, but not all public trusts are charitable. A private trust benefits identified (or at least identifiable) individuals, and it is those individuals who have an interest to enforce the provisions of the trust and to call the trustees to account. A public trust benefits a section of the public. Where the beneficiaries are a clearly specified class of people, any of them may have an interest to enforce performance, but the public generally cannot enforce, and where the trust deed expresses general ends or purposes, potential beneficiaries have no interest to enforce. The Lord Advocate may seek to enforce in the public interest. For a public trust to qualify as a charity for any purpose, it requires to come within the relevant definition of a charity. A "body" under the 1990 Act includes a sole trustee of a trust.[116] The term "foundation" does not denote a separate category in law: foundations are usually public trusts.

More significant than the difference between private and public trusts are the similarities: both are governed by the same trust legislation. The law described in Chapter 9, including for example the investment powers of trustees, applies equally to public trusts.[117]

**Charity at common law**

At common law "charitable" has been held to include the relief of poverty, provision of hospitals, provision of a free school, upbringing of destitute children, and the social or ethical amelioration of the people of a defined locality.[118] The common law definition is now substantially overshadowed by the tax

---

[116] 1990 Act, s.15(1).

[117] But although most of the provisions of the Charities Act 1992 apply only to England, the provisions of ss.38 and 39 enabling regulations to be made widening the investment powers of charity trustees apply also to Scotland.

[118] For authorities and further examples see Walker, *Principles of Scottish Private Law*, vol.IV, p.85

definition, but may still be relevant in interpreting "charity" or "charitable purposes" in a Will or trust deed, and in determining whether a trust is charitable so that the *cy pres* principle may be used, if necessary, to find some other charitable purpose.[119] Following the 1990 Act, it is possible that the common law definition may in future be extended effectively to coincide with the tax definition.

### Disabled charities

A disabled charity is[120]:

> "any fund, institution, association or undertaking, having for its sole or principal object or among its principal objects the promotion of the welfare of persons who are blind, deaf or dumb, and other persons who are substantially and permanently handicapped by illness, injury, or congenital deformity".

It might be argued that all mental handicaps do not come within this definition, but charities for the mentally handicapped have generally registered as a disabled charity to be safe, and to secure recognition. Registration is with the regional or islands council, and it is unlawful to raise (or attempt to raise) funds from the public for such a charity unless it has been registered. Various regulations apply to such charities.[121] These provisions will cease to apply in Scotland once Part I of the 1990 Act comes into force.

### The tax definition

The tax definition of a charity qualifies the charity for tax exemption,[122] and also rating relief.[123] Under the 1990 Act the tax definition is the key to becoming a recognised body. It is the English definition of a charity, described in Part IIA above, and comprises the four classes of the relief of poverty; advancement of religion; advancement of education; and other purposes beneficial to the community not falling under any of the previous heads. By statute, provision of facilities for recreation or other leisure-time occupation in the interests of social welfare is included.[124]

## FORMATION AND REGULATION

### Choice of format

The advantages and disadvantages of *unincorporated associations* are summarised at the end of Part I. The lack of limited liability may be decisive, but if it is not, economy and simplicity of management may point to selection of this form.

---

[119] See under "Re-organisation" below.

[120] War Charities Act 1940 as extended by National Assistance Act 1948, s.41.

[121] S.I. 1940 No.1431, S.I. 1948 No.1497.

[122] See Income and Corporation Taxes Act 1988, ss.505 and 506 and Sched.20, and "Charity Administration, Taxation" p.663 below.

[123] Under Local Government (Financial Provisions etc) (Scotland) Act 1962 (as amended) - see Part III below.

[124] Recreational Charities Act 1958.

A *trust* is not normally subject to the democratic control of a body of members, but the trustees may be appointed by and accountable to one or more bodies which are in turn democratically governed. A charitable trust may be established by an individual, or a trust may be selected as the appropriate format for raising, holding, or disbursing funds, or holding and managing property.

A *guarantee company* is often the favoured format, particularly for organisations or projects of sufficient size for the advantages of limited liability and the discipline of company management to outweigh the costs and formalities. It is a flexible form which can be adapted to many purposes. It can be useful, for example, as the vehicle for a partnership between public and private sectors, joint ventures between voluntary organisations, or the separate operation of a particular function established by an existing charitable body. A guarantee company should be run with the same care and discipline as a well-run commercial company, and all directors (whatever they may be termed) should be fully aware of their responsibilities as such. This is important when an unincorporated association graduates to company status, or when anyone without previous experience of company directorship joins the board. This may well apply to apparently very experienced people such as local councillors, who may be accustomed to the significant but different responsibilities of elected members of councils.

*Industrial and provident societies* confer limited liability, and the regime governing them is somewhat less rigorous and exacting than for guarantee companies, but the complexity of initial formation and registration usually outweighs that advantage unless a standard format and rules such as those for housing associations are available.

New *friendly societies* are rarely formed nowadays. They lack limited liability, but require to register rules and file annual returns and accounts. They are supervised by the Chief Registrar who can arbitrate on disputes. Property is held by trustees, and passes automatically on change of trustees. At least seven members are required for industrial and provident societies and for friendly societies.

## Recognition

### Clearance with Inland Revenue

Under the 1990 Act charities will certainly wish to obtain intimation from the Inland Revenue that they qualify for tax relief. Whatever form of organisation is selected, it is sensible to send the draft documents constituting the organisation to the Inland Revenue, Claims Branch, for comment. The Revenue normally respond promptly and helpfully. This should be done before the organisation is formally incorporated or constituted, to avoid the risk of having to make formal amendments.

When an existing organisation proposes to become a charity, it should likewise submit to the Revenue its existing constitution and any proposed amendments.

### Certification

If satisfied, the Revenue have hitherto issued a letter to the organisation stating that it is considered to be established as a charity, and will obtain tax relief if it applies its income to charitable purposes only. Under the 1990 Act such intimation (unless and until withdrawn) qualifies the organisation as a recognised body,[125] and the Revenue issues a certificate to that effect. A recognised body may call itself a "Scottish charity". The Revenue is concerned only to be satisfied that the organisation is established exclusively for charitable purposes and applies its income accordingly, and exercises no general supervisory role (but would of course be concerned about mismanagement with tax implications, and under the 1990 Act may notify the Lord Advocate if a charity appears to be acting inconsistently with its charitable status).

### Registration and transitional arrangements

The 1990 Act does not provide for establishment of a register of charities, though the Revenue are permitted to release certain information to enquirers (see below). It has been proposed that the Scottish Council of Voluntary Organisations maintain a voluntary register of charities. When the Act is brought into force the Revenue intend to write to all existing recognised bodies with their new numbers, and information about the new arrangements.

### Appeal and withdrawal of recognition

If the Revenue refuse to recognise an organisation as charitable, the only appeal is through the tax system. The organisation would require to appeal to the Special Commissioners against the refusal of tax relief, with further appeal to the courts.

Recognition will only be withdrawn if the organisation alters its constitution so as no longer to qualify, or possibly if a court decision were to cause the Revenue to revise its previous view of the definition of a charity. If a recognised body applies funds for non-charitable purposes, then that will be an *ultra vires* act which will result in loss of tax relief, and perhaps action by the Lord Advocate (to whom the Revenue may report it), but not to loss of charitable status.

## Information

### From Inland Revenue

The Revenue are permitted to release the name and address of a recognised body to an enquirer,[126] and it is understood that the full list of names of Scottish charities, with contact addresses, will be available for inspection. The Lord Advocate may direct the Revenue to note certain acts of non-compliance with the provisions

---

125  Provided that it is established under Scots law and managed or controlled wholly or mainly in or from Scotland - 1990 Act, s.1(7).

126  s.1(1)(b).

of the 1990 Act, and the Revenue must include any such notes when giving particulars of a charity to an enquirer.

*From recognised body*

A recognised body must within one month provide to anyone who requests them a copy of its constitution or equivalent document describing the nature of the body and its charitable purposes, a copy of its most recent annual accounts, and a note of its accounting reference date.[127] A reasonable charge for copying and postage may be made. Anyone who does not receive the relevant information in accordance with these requirements may complain to the Lord Advocate, who may have the contravention noted by the Revenue and may also apply for an order stopping specified activities of the charity until the relevant information has been provided.[128]

## Accounting and annual report

Where a recognised body is a company, the Companies Acts requirements apply.[129] The next three sections apply to charities which are not companies, except that the Lord Advocate's powers to obtain annual accounts applies also to companies.

*Accounting records*

A recognised body must keep accounting records which show and explain the body's transactions and give a reasonably accurate and up-to-date picture of the body's financial position. The records must be sufficient to enable proper annual accounts to be prepared, and must in particular record assets and liabilities, and show on a day-to-day basis all receipts and payments, with an adequate narrative. Accounting records must be kept for at least six years.[130]

*Annual accounts and report*

A recognised body must prepare annual accounts, comprising balance sheet, income and expenditure account and a report of the activities of the body (having regard to its charitable purposes). The accounts must give a true and fair view of the state of affairs of the body at the year end, and the surplus or deficit for the year. The Lord Advocate may require the body to give him, without charge, a copy of its annual accounts. If a recognised body fails to have annual accounts prepared within ten months of the financial year end (or within such longer period as the Lord Advocate may allow) the Lord Advocate may have this noted by the Revenue and may also set a deadline for preparation of the accounts. If they are still not prepared within the deadline, the Lord Advocate may appoint a suitably qualified person to prepare the balance sheet and income and expenditure account, and that person has the necessary

---

[127] ss.1(4) and (9), 5(7)(*a*) and (*b*).
[128] ss.1(5) and (6), 5(12) and (13).
[129] s.5(14). See Part I of this chapter.
[130] s.4(1)-(3).

powers of entry and access to information. He makes a report as to the affairs and accounting records of the body, and sends it to the Lord Advocate and to those who appear to him to be concerned in the management and control of the body; and those people are personally responsible for his costs.[131]

### Regulations
Regulations have yet to be promulgated concerning accounting records, annual accounts, and exemptions or simplified requirements for particular classes of bodies.[132]

## Supervision

The supervisory powers described here apply to recognised bodies, charities registered (or exempt from registration) in England which operate in Scotland, and non-registered bodies which represent or hold out themselves as charities.

### Investigation by the Lord Advocate
The Lord Advocate may make enquiry into any charity or class of charities. He may suspend any person concerned in their management or control for up to 28 days, and make consequential provision during such suspension. He may nominate an officer to make enquiries who has extensive powers of access, and to obtain information, backed up by criminal sanctions.[133]

### Powers of the Court of Session
The Court of Session has various powers[134] in cases of misconduct or mismanagement, or where action is necessary or desirable to protect property or secure proper application of property for the charity's purposes. The powers also apply where a charity is not a recognised body (and not registered or exempt from registration in England) regardless of whether there is misconduct, mismanagement or risk to property. Only the Lord Advocate may apply for exercise of the court's powers.

The court may grant interim or final interdict against the body (including interdict from representing or holding out itself as a charity), appoint a judicial factor (including an interim judicial factor) or trustee, freeze assets, stop or restrict transactions, and suspend or remove persons concerned in management or control.[135] It may also approve (with or without modification) a scheme presented by the Lord Advocate to transfer the assets of the body to another charity. Expenses of such proceedings may be awarded against persons concerned in management or control of the body. The Lord Advocate may have any exercise of these powers noted by the Revenue. Acting on information received

---

[131] s.5(1)(2)(4)(6)(8)-(11) and (13).
[132] ss.4(4), 5(3) and 5(5). At time of writing regulations are in course of preparation, and are expected to be introduced in September 1992.
[133] s.6.
[134] s.7.
[135] s.7(4).

from the Charity Commissioners, the Lord Advocate may apply to the court to freeze moveable assets in Scotland of an English charity; and the court may subsequently transfer those assets to another charity.[136]

## Disqualification

Certain persons are disqualified from being concerned with the management or control of a recognised body.[137] Contravention of the disqualification is an offence punishable by up to two years imprisonment, or a fine, or both. Disqualification applies to anyone convicted of an offence involving dishonesty,[138] an undischarged bankrupt, a person removed under the provisions described in the previous section, and a person disqualified from being a company director, but the Lord Advocate may waive the disqualification.[139] Disqualification does not by itself invalidate acts of management or control.

## Accountability and liability

Persons managing charitable organisations have the duties and liabilities under the general law relevant to the particular type of organisation.[140]

### Trustees
The duties and liabilities of trustees apply both when the charity is constituted as a trust, and also when persons hold and administer assets as trustees for any other type of organisation, such as a voluntary body. Trustees must show the same standard of care and diligence as that of a person of ordinary prudence in the management of his own affairs. Failure to attain that standard is a breach of trust, as are embezzlement, deriving personal benefit (unless authorised), *ultra vires* investment, failure to account, and failure to carry out the provisions of the trust. Trustees are only liable for their own acts and intromissions,[141] but where several are in breach of trust together they are jointly and severally liable. It is a defence that what was done was directed or permitted by the trust deed, and such deed may contain an immunity clause, but that is not effective in cases of gross negligence or actions in bad faith. The court may wholly or partly relieve from personal liability a trustee who has acted honestly and in good faith.[142]

Where trustees hold and administer assets for an organisation, breach of trust may be pursued by the organisation, or members of it. Members of a clearly specified class of beneficiary under a

---

136 s.7(6)-(8).
137 s.8.
138 Unless the offence is spent under the Rehabilitation of Offenders Act 1974.
139 But not so as to prejudice the operation of the Company Directors Disqualification Act 1986.
140 The duties and liabilities of company directors are described in Part I.
141 Trusts (Scotland) Act 1921, s.3(*d*).
142 Trusts (Scotland) Act 1921, s.32(1).

public trust have a right to enforce, and the Lord Advocate may enforce in the public interest. When trustees contract with third parties, even though they do so in their capacity as trustees, they are personally liable unless there is an express or implied agreement that the trust estate alone is held bound. In litigation, trustees are personally liable for expenses found due to an opponent unless the court directs otherwise.

## REORGANISATION

A change in direction or a new project will not necessarily require constitutional change. Something which an organisation has never done before may nevertheless be within its objects. It is wise to check carefully, and if necessary to take advice, before embarking on change. If change is necessary then before instituting formal procedure the proposed change should be submitted informally to the Claims Branch, Inland Revenue, to ensure that charitable status will not be prejudiced.[143]

### Voluntary bodies and companies

The constitutions of voluntary bodies normally specify procedure for amendment. Company law governs the alteration of the Memorandum or Articles of a company, and a special resolution (needing 21 days notice and a three-fourths majority) is required.

### Trusts

Except for appointment of additional trustees (which applies only to charities), the procedures described here apply to all public trusts, including charitable trusts. They do not apply to private trusts. Cy pres procedure is part of the common law, and applicable to public trusts of any size, though the costs can be prohibitive for smaller trusts. The 1990 Act establishes a new parallel procedure for reorganisation of any public trust, and two new procedures for smaller trusts.

#### The cy pres principle

Cy pres procedure is appropriate when the general purposes of a trust cannot be achieved in accordance with the specific provisions of the trust deed. If the trust is charitable, the court will not allow it to fail, but will allow the funds to be applied as nearly as may be possible to the intended purpose. However it is not sufficient to demonstrate that a change is desirable, or that administration under the existing trust deed is difficult, though the court may take a benign view where difficulty verges upon impossibility and there are very strong grounds for variation.

Procedure is by petition by the trustees to the Inner House of the Court of Session under the nobile officium. A draft scheme is submitted to the court, which will normally appoint a reporter to

---

143 Under the 1990 Act such clearance is mandatory for reorganisation of small trusts by resolution - s.10(6),(9) and (11); and for alteration of the purposes of a charitable company - s.14(2).

ascertain the facts and report on the suitability of the proposed scheme. The court can amend the proposed scheme.

### Reorganisation by the court [144]

Procedure is by application to the Court of Session, but jurisdiction may be extended to the Sheriff Courts. The application is intimated to the Lord Advocate, who may enter the proceedings, but there may be no award of expenses to or against him. The court may approve a scheme of variation or reorganisation of the trust purposes, or transfer of assets to another public trust, or amalgamation, if that will allow the trust's resources to be applied to better effect consistently with the spirit of the trust deed, having regard to changes in social and economic conditions since the trust was set up. Application is competent where:

- some or all of the trust purposes have been fulfilled so far as is possible, or can no longer be given effect to;
- the purposes of the trust provide use for only some of the trust property;
- the trust purposes refer to an area which ceases to have effect for the relevant purpose, or a class of persons or area no longer suitable or appropriate, or no longer administratively practicable;  or
- the trust purposes are now adequately provided for by other means, or would no longer enable the trust to become a recognised body, or (having regard to the spirit of the trust deed) cease in any other way to provide a suitable and effective method of using trust property.

### Reorganisation by resolution [145]

Trusts with an income not exceeding £5,000 per annum[146] may reorganise by resolution by a majority of the trustees, rather than by court application. The circumstances in which the procedure is competent are the same as for reorganisation by the court (see preceding paragraph). In order to apply trust resources to better effect consistently with the spirit of the trust deed, the trustees may modify the trust purposes (and amend the trust deed accordingly), transfer the whole assets to another public trust (and wind up the trust), or amalgamate with one or more other public trusts. In any such reorganisation, they must not depart unreasonably from the spirit of the trust deed, and must have regard to the circumstances of any locality to which the trust purposes relate. Before changing the trust purposes, they must consider whether it might be better to achieve economy by amalgamation. If the trust is a recognised body, they must ensure that that status will continue in relation to the trust, or any transferee or amalgamated trust.

Regulations will provide for advertisement, and the reorganisation must not take place until two months after the advertisement is first published. The regulations will also deal with objections and provide for notification to the Lord Advocate, who may direct that the reorganisation should not proceed.

---

144  s.9 of the 1990 Act, introducing criteria for reorganisation similar to those in England under the Charities Act 1960, s.14.

145  s.10.

146  The Secretary of State may amend the figure by order - s.10(15).

*Expenditure of capital* [147]

When a trust's annual income does not exceed £1,000 (The Secretary of State may amend the figure by order) the trustees may resolve to expend trust capital. A unanimous resolution of the trustees is required. The procedure is competent if the trustees unanimously resolve that the income is too small to achieve the trust purposes, and are satisfied either that there are no reasonable prospects of transferring the trust assets to another trust (see preceding section) or that expenditure of capital is more likely to achieve the purposes of the trust. The trustees must advertise and advise the Lord Advocate at least two months before proceeding to expend capital. The Lord Advocate may apply to the Court of Session to prohibit expenditure of capital, if there are insufficient grounds for expending it.

*Appointment of trustees*

The trustees of a trust which is a recognised body may appoint additional trustees to ensure that at no time does the number of trustees fall below three, regardless of any provisions of the trust deed.[148] If the number of trustees is less than three, and it appears to the Lord Advocate that the trustees will not or cannot exercise this power, he may exercise it.[149] He may do so when the trust has lapsed *i.e.* when there are no trustees at all.

## WINDING-UP

The constitutions of voluntary bodies normally specify procedure for winding up, and application of any remaining funds or assets upon winding-up. A trust may be wound up in accordance with the trust deed, or in consequence of a cy pres scheme or statutory reorganisation. Winding-up of companies, industrial and provident societies, and friendly societies is governed by relevant legislation, and an additional provision in relation to charitable companies is that the Lord Advocate may petition for winding-up.[150]

## Dormant charities

A new procedure under the 1990 Act[151] applies where a bank, building society or other prescribed institution holds an account for a recognised body on which there has been no transaction for the preceding ten years, and the relevant institution has no knowledge of the persons concerned in its management or control. The procedure is to be administered by the Scottish Charities Nominee, who must take action when advised of such an account by the relevant institution,[152] unless there are circumstances which

---

[147] s.11.

[148] s.13(1).

[149] s.13(2).

[150] s.14(3).

[151] s.12.

[152] Relevant institutions are relieved from the normal duty of confidentiality to enable them to notify the Nominee - s.12(11) and (12).

appear to him to render it inappropriate to do so. Where the balance does not exceed £5,000 (the Secretary of State may amend the figure by regulation) the Nominee is required to transfer it to such other recognised body as he may determine. For balances above that figure, the Nominee notifies the Lord Advocate, who may appoint new trustees, or apply to the Court of Session to appoint a judicial factor, or refer the matter back to the Nominee to transfer the balance to another recognised body. The Nominee's powers cease if the account ceases to be dormant or the person with management or control becomes known.

# PART III - CHARITY ADMINISTRATION

We outline in this Part some of the more significant implications of operating as a charity.

## "Bargain Bounty" Rule

If a charity repeatedly or on a substantial scale contracts in return for gifts to provide that which it would normally provide as part of its charitable activities, it is in danger of losing its charitable status. In other words, a charity cannot legally bind itself to provide a service for a particular person in return for a gift. That seems to be the general effect of the "bargain bounty rule".[153]

*Conditional gifts*
This became important in the context of mental handicap because of the desire of parents to give their homes or money to a charity on condition that the charity accommodates their handicapped child for life. In some cases a compromise has been reached whereby without entering into any legal obligation the charity indicates that it will take into account the needs of the child, along with other children, and the parents make their gift in the hope and expectation that the charity will indeed be able to provide a lifetime of care for their child.[154] The rule may have saved many charities from entering into legal arrangements which might have seemed attractive at the time but which, with inflation and changing care needs, they could prove unable to fulfil.

*Interpretation*
There are indications that the Charity Commissioners are now interpreting the rule in a more relaxed manner, and much may depend upon the scale of the bargains in relation to the general activities of the charity. A few moderate gifts to a national charity

---

153 The rule is derived from the judgment of Rowlatt J. in *IRC* v. *The Society for the Relief of the Widows and Orphans of Medical Men* 42 TLR 612, 11 TC 1 which was confirmed but distinguished in *Joseph Rowntree Memorial Trust Housing Association Limited* v. *A-G* [1983] 1 All ER 288. Both cases related to charities under the first of the four heads.

154 The Care Fund of the MENCAP City Foundation invites donors to complete a questionnaire expressing their wishes for the future of a handicapped child or other person, though no specific undertaking is given to benefit a particular person.

tied to binding obligations to look after certain handicapped persons would be unlikely to affect charitable status, provided that such persons were capable of being beneficiaries of the charity in any event. On the other hand, if the main activity of a body was to look after a small number of individuals in respect of most of whom conditional gifts had been made, charitable status would not be appropriate because this would in effect be a mutual benefit society. The Commissioners will give advice in particular cases.

*Tax treatment*

Another problem with these conditional gifts is the tax treatment. It is possible that the Revenue may not recognise such gifts as being charitable, in which event the tax exemptions or reliefs may not be available.

## Ex gratia payments (England)

Where an individual claims that a charity is not entitled to money and a dispute arises, the Commissioners have power to authorise a compromise which is expedient in the interests of the charity and in some cases this will be adequate.[155] Situations also arise in which, although a charity is legally entitled to a sum of money, there is a moral obligation to pay all or part of this sum to an individual. It has been held that the court and the Attorney-General have a discretionary power to authorise charity trustees to make *ex gratia* payments out of funds held on charitable trusts[156]:

> "It is ... a power which is not to be exercised lightly or on slender grounds but only in cases where it can be fairly said that if the charity were an individual it would be morally wrong of him to refuse to make payment. ... there may well be a considerable difference between cases ... where it appears that the testator never intended the charity to receive so large a gift as it did receive, and cases where the testator intended the charity to receive what it has received but the testator's relatives consider that he was not morally justified in leaving his money to a charity rather than to them. ... I think that cases in which an ex gratia payment would be justified would be rarer in the second category than in the first."

Where money has been left to a charity which wishes to make an *ex gratia* payment, the charity should apply to the Commissioners who look into the facts and make a report to the Attorney General. If money has been left on trust for general charitable purposes, the person who makes a claim of moral entitlement should apply to the Treasury Solicitor who will verify the facts and report to the Attorney General. In either case the Attorney General decides whether or not to authorise a payment and if so how much, and then notifies the Commissioners or the Treasury Solicitor. If in doubt he applies *ex parte* to the court for guidance.[157]

---

[155] Charities Act 1960, s.23. The 1992 Act, s.17 authorises the Commissioners to permit charity trustees to make *ex gratia* payments or waive entitlements where they feel a moral obligation to do so.

[156] *Re Snowden (decd), Henderson* v. *A-G* [1969] 3 All ER 208, Cross J.

[157] Guidance note issued by the Commissioners in March 1972. In the case of an educational charity, the Department of Education and Science will be involved instead of the Charity Commission.

## Taxation

If a charity is to benefit from tax relief it must spend its money only for charitable purposes, and in particular those for which it is set up, and nothing else. This can include the cost of its activities, buying assets used therein, grants to other charities, administration and fundraising costs and the cost of financing such items.

*Income and corporation tax*

Charities are exempt from tax on the following kinds of receipts, provided that they can be used only for charitable purposes and have actually been spent or saved up for such purposes[158]:

Rents from land and property;

Interest and dividends;

Covenanted donations;

Single gifts by companies paid after tax has ben deducted.

Other gifts from members of the public are not treated as income so are not liable to tax. Fund raising activities which amount to a trade may be taxable, and these are dealt with below. Where a charity receives all or part of the residue of the estate of a deceased person the final payment will include income received during the administration period which will have been taxed at the basic rate in the hands of the executors, so to the extent that it is not used for administration expenses and is allocated to the charity a tax deduction certificate (Form R185E) should be prepared by the executors and handed over within a reasonable period and the tax can then be reclaimed.[159]

A charity may be asked to produce its accounts to Inland Revenue and provide further information, and in England such information may be disclosed to the Charity Commissioners.[160] If a charity spends money for non-charitable purposes, or invests or lends money other than for the benefit of the charity, its tax exemption may be restricted. Special rules apply to larger charities.[161]

*Capital gains tax and Inheritance tax*

A gain is not a chargeable gain (and therefore not liable to CGT) if it accrues to a charity and is applicable and applied for charitable purposes.[162]

Gifts to charities are wholly exempt from inheritance tax, whether these be lifetime gifts or under a Will.[163] If the whole estate of a deceased person is left to a charity there will be no liability to the tax, but if part of an estate is given to a charity there will be no

---

[158] Income and Corporation Taxes Act 1988, ss.9, 505 and 506; Sched.20. There are various restrictions which are designed to prevent tax avoidance.

[159] To the extent that administration expenses can be paid out of capital there will be increased income and thus more tax for the charity to reclaim.

[160] Finance Act 1986, s.33.

[161] *I.e.* whose taxable income and chargeable gains exceed £10,000 per annum. Finance Act 1986, s.31, and Sched.7.

[162] Capital Gains Tax Act 1979, s.145.

[163] Inheritance Tax Act 1984, s.23.

tax on that part. The tax exemption must accrue for the benefit of the charity rather than other beneficiaries under the Will, so if part only of the residue is left to charity any tax liability that does arise should be deducted from the other part.[164]

*Value added tax*

Charities are not exempt from VAT but there are some benefits available especially through the zero-rating of a range of goods and equipment used by handicapped people.[165] Non-classified advertising in newspapers and magazines for educational and fund-raising purposes is also zero-rated. From April 1991 a number of extensions were made to the reliefs for charities and other eligible bodies mainly affecting goods donated for sale and fund-raising events held by charities' trading subsidiaries. VAT is now charged on non-domestic fuel usage (*e.g.* quarterly gas and electricity accounts for business premises) following a ruling by the European Court, but fuel supplied to charities for their non-business use is zero-rated. Donations, bequests and the proceeds of collections are not liable to VAT, and admission charges and ticket sales for one-off functions will be exempt. However, sales by charity shops and also subscriptions to a charity are liable to the standard rate (though if a subscription includes payment for a magazine an apportioned part may be zero-rated).

A society which has no business activities cannot register so may not reclaim any VAT on expenditure; if it has business activities and is registered, VAT will only be recoverable on expenditure relating to the making of taxable supplies in that business activity and not otherwise. It may be difficult to identify such expenditure in the case of a society which has both business and non-business activities, and apportionment of input tax on a fair and reasonable basis will usually be allowed though this may still be prejudicial to the society.[166] This is another reason why a separate trading company is often set up, but sometimes organisations with several branches avoid the need to register by establishing each branch as a separate society.

Supplies of certain welfare services and related goods by charities are exempt provided they are supplied otherwise than for profit. This may include provision of care, treatment or instruction to disabled people, but the supply of accommodation or catering is exempt only if it is ancillary to the provision of these services.[167] Thus although welfare services are regarded as being business activities they are treated as exempt supplies and charities are not

---

164 Inheritance Tax Act 1984, s.41.
165 Since May 1990 medical equipment, etc., bought with donated funds has been zero-rated. Zero-rating also applies to certain leases for charities and sales of non-domestic buildings.
166 Customs & Excise increasingly attempt to treat activities such as business sponsorship as advertising rather than donations, thus being a taxable supply by the charity.
167 The provision of residential care in a registered home will be exempt.

able to recover any input tax in respect thereof. VAT is a heavy burden upon charities running residential care homes, as they will not be registered but the tax is charged on most things that they buy and also on the building of extensions.[168]

*Stamp duty*
Stamp duty is not normally payable in respect of gifts to and purchases of property by charities although in some cases the document involved should be submitted for stamping with a stamp denoting that it is not chargeable with any duty.[169]

*Rating relief*
Premises occupied by charities and used wholly or mainly for charitable purposes (including property used for the sale of goods donated to a charity)[170] qualify for 80 per cent. non-domestic rating relief from the local authority (but not water and sewerage rates). The rating authority also have a discretion to provide further relief up to the full amount and this would usually be appropriate.[171] If property has been acquired with the intention of using it for the purposes of the charity such relief may be available even if it remains empty for up to two years.

## Trading

Some fund raising activities by charities count as a trade for tax purposes and profits will then be liable to tax. There are two situations where the profits of a trade are exempt from tax, though it follows that tax relief will not be available for any losses. These are where the trade is:

(i) exercised in the carrying out of the primary purpose of the charity, *e.g.* charges by a residential care home for its services to mentally handicapped residents[172];

(ii) mainly carried out by the "beneficiaries of the charity", *e.g.* sale of items made by handicapped people themselves (but not re-sale of items bought in for the purpose).

The disposal of donated goods is not a trade. Other activities such as jumble sales, bazaars, car boot sales, and carnivals by voluntary organisations to raise funds for charity may incur tax liability, but in practice the revenue make a special concession where the following conditions are satisfied:

(a) the organisation is not trading regularly;

---

168 The *Charities Tax Reform Group* of 9 Old Queen Street, London SW1H 9JA is campaigning for changes in the refund mechanism.

169 Finance Act 1982, s.129.

170 The Local Government Finance Act 1988 states that a hereditament is to be treated as being for charitable purposes if it is "wholly or mainly used for the sale of goods donated to a charity and the proceeds of sale of the goods (after the deduction of any expenses) are applied for the purposes of a charity". The operative word is donated, so charity shops may not qualify.

171 In Scotland, see Local Government (Financial Provisions, etc.) (Scotland) Act 1962 (as amended).

172 If the home was also providing "bed & breakfast" on a commercial basis to other persons the tax exemption would not apply.

(b) the trading is not in competition with other traders;
(c) the activities are supported substantially because the public
are aware that profits are devoted to charity;
(d) the profits are actually applied for charitable purposes.

*Implications*

There may be situations in which the trading activities of a charity
will not be exempt from tax. Having a power to trade otherwise
than in carrying out the primary purpose is not necessarily
inconsistent with being a charity, but if such trade assumes too
great an importance in regard to the other activities, the charitable
status may itself be brought into question. The Charity
Commissioners take a strong line on the question of charities and
trading, and unless the activity clearly falls within the Inland
Revenue concessions advice should be sought from the
Commissioners and the Inland Revenue.

*Practical steps*

If a charity intends to carry on commercial activities unconnected
with its purposes in order to raise money, it is usually necessary to
form a separate non-charitable trading company.[173] The profits
may then be transferred to the charity either by a covenant
relating to all such profits on an annual basis or by paying such
profits as dividends to the charity as shareholder. In either event
the charity may re-claim the tax deducted from the payment or
any tax credit. The new procedure called *Gift Aid* described below
may become the method adopted in future.

Care should be taken to ensure that the investment powers of the
charity are adequate to permit the holding of shares in such
trading company, and even then difficulties may arise in funding
the promotion expenses as charities should not engage in any
speculative investment. Often supporters of the charity will put up
the costs of setting up the trading company, at least until such time
as these can be met from the proceeds of the trading activities. The
financial structures of the charity and the trading company should
be kept distinct, and the separate identities made clear in publicity
material and dealings with suppliers. If all profits of the trading
company will be transferred to the charity, the company may need
more capital for expansion. Normally loans will be obtained from
commercial sources, and whilst it may be tempting for the charity
to lend the money, this is only permitted if the charity has
sufficiently wide powers of investment, the loan is a sound
investment, it is secured and a  market rate of interest is paid.[174]

---

[173] The Law Society memorandum *Revenue law reform 1991/92* concludes that
this type of arrangement is unsatisfactory and recommends that all income
received by a charitable body is exempt from tax to the extent that it is
applied for charitable purposes.

[174] The use of commercial companies limited by shares as a method of raising
capital or as a non-charitable trading arm is well known and is dealt with
(together with other aspects of trading) in Charity Commission leaflet CC20
- *Fund Raising and Charities.*

## Accounts (England)[175]

Charity trustees are under a duty to keep proper books of accounts and prepare consecutive statements of account consisting of an income and expenditure account relating to a period of not more than 15 months and a balance sheet relating to that period.[176] They must preserve records for at least seven years, and ensure that accounts are audited as required in the governing instrument, although there is no statutory requirement for audit. Trustees of charities with a permanent endowment must send copies of the accounts to the Commissioners each year, and trustees of other charities may do so (or be required to do so).[177]

## FUND RAISING

A charity is far more likely to attract funds for its activities than a non-charitable association. Grants and privileged loans may be available and there are Trust Funds which make gifts to charities whose purposes are consistent with their objects.[178]

### Tax saving schemes

Some methods of funding involve tax incentives for donors and benefits to the charity in certain circumstances.[179] In view of independent taxation for husband and wife, care should be taken as to who makes charitable gifts to ensure that tax relief is available.

### *Covenants*

A covenant to pay a fixed sum of money regularly for a specified period of time is a way of transferring income from one person or body to another. If in favour of a charity and capable of lasting for more than three years, the covenantor deducts and retains basic rate tax from the agreed payment and the charity claims this tax back.[180] Annual tax deduction certificates (Form R185(AP)) are signed by the covenantor and handed to the charity for submission to its tax office with a repayment form. A covenantor who has not paid (or had deducted from other income) an

---

175 For Scotland, see p.657.

176 Charities Act 1960, s.32. The 1992 Act, ss.19-27 impose more stringent requirements in England for maintaining and filing Accounts and for audit, and also for the filing of annual reports and returns.

177 s.8. These must contain information prescribed by Charities (Statements of Account) Regulations 1960. Specimen forms may be obtained free of charge from the Commissioners.

178 An example is the Special Projects Fund of Mencap City Foundation which is itself a registered charity. Applications for grants will be considered from registered charities working for mentally handicapped people and their families, and from projects being run in conjunction with such a charity.

179 Inland Revenue publish a series of helpful Notes: IR 64, 65, 74 and 75. Precedents will be found in Appendix V.

180 There must be no power to cancel but it may cease on death of covenantor. The covenant does not now need to be repeated after the end of the four year period, but payments can continue to be made with tax relief. In practice the sum is often stated to be an amount after the deduction of tax.

equivalent amount of tax will receive a bill for the difference between the tax deducted and that paid in the year, but those who pay tax at higher rates may recover the extra tax on the gross covenant payments.[181]

*Deposit covenant*

This enables a charity to obtain tax repayment in respect of a lump sum gift by converting that sum into four annual payments under a covenant. The donor allows the charity to deposit the lump sum in its name in effect as nominee and authorises the transfer of four equal amounts at annual intervals in payment of a covenant which the donor also signs, and repayment of any balance held on the donor's prior death is waived.

*Pay-roll giving*

Some employers operate a scheme[182] whereby people on PAYE may have donations of up to £50 per month deducted from their pay before tax, so if the basic rate of tax is 25 per cent. a gift of £50 will only result in £37·50 being deducted from the pay. Those paying tax at higher rates will benefit from greater tax relief. The employee can choose the charities to benefit from the gift and is not obliged to disclose this to the employer. Subject to restrictions imposed by the employer, the amount and the destination may be changed at any time. There are various agency charities which will administer the scheme.

*Gift Aid*

A new method for tax efficient giving to charities was introduced in 1990.[183] A single gift of at least £400[184] by an individual is regarded as having been paid net of tax and the charity can recover the tax "deducted" whilst the donor can obtain relief in respect of any higher rate tax on the grossed-up amount of the payment. Thus a gift of £750 is treated as a gross payment of £1,000 and the charity can reclaim tax of £250 whilst the donor is relieved of any higher rate tax liability thus making the net cost of the gift £600. In the case of a company similar rules apply so an effective gift of £800 would cost the company £600 this being the minimum amount that will qualify.[185]

In order to qualify the gift must be cash and made outright free of any conditions or benefits accruing to the donor or his family.[186]

---

181 Income and Corporation Taxes Act 1970, s.434(1A).
182 Under the Finance Act 1986.
183 Finance Act 1990, s.25 (for individuals) and s.26 (for companies). See leaflet IR113, *Gift Aid: a Guide for Donors and Charities*, available from Inland Revenue, Claims Branch (Trusts and Charities), St. John's House, Merton Road, Bootle, Merseyside L69 4EJ or Trinity Park House, South Trinity Road, Edinburgh EH5 3SD.
184 The minimum amount was reduced from £600 by the Finance Act 1992 with effect from May 7, 1992.
185 In these examples we have assumed a standard rate of 25 per cent., higher rate of 40 per cent. and corporation tax at 25 per cent.
186 s.25(2)(e) is quite explicit that "neither the donor, nor any person connected

There are schemes whereby a single gift may be divided among a number of charities. The revenue issue guidance notes on Gift Aid which should be studied by anyone considering using this method. In the case of a gift by parents to a charity operating a residential care home which looked after their son it is to be hoped that the revenue will allow Gift Aid to apply unless the gift is specifically intended to provide some extra care or facility for the child. A gift to enable a charity to purchase a property from the donor will not qualify. The donor must sign a certificate R190(SD)[187] in which he states that all the conditions are satisfied and that tax equal to the basic rate tax on the gift will be paid in the relevant tax year. Thus gifts cannot effectively be made out of capital because if the donor's taxable income[188] is less than the gross amount of the gift tax will have to be paid on the shortfall. Charities make an annual repayment claim on form R68 showing each gift and the certificates must then be produced.

The artificiality of the *deposit covenant* mentioned above will thus no longer be necessary for single gifts unless they are under £400 or exceed the donor's taxable income in the year of the gift. A charity may now receive a gift and invite the donor to sign form R190(SD) so as to enjoy immediate tax benefits. Charities with a trading subsidiary will no longer need to receive the profits under a covenant but may instead claim back the tax under Gift Aid.

*Company giving*

The procedure with covenants is different for companies, which must show the gross payments and tax deducted for a period on Form CT61(Z) and pay the tax. The gross amount is then allowed as a deduction from the profits on which corporation tax is assessed. This procedure is similar to that for interest payments. Covenants need not be a fixed amount each year but may be linked to profits, and this is the basis used by companies set up by charities for trading purposes whereby the annual profit is transferred back to the charity.

In addition to covenants and *Gift Aid*, companies (other than close companies) can get tax relief on donations in any year up to a limit of three per cent. of their annual dividend on ordinary shares for the year. The company deducts basic rate tax from the payment, pays this over to the Inland Revenue and sends the net amount to the charity with a tax deduction certificate (Form R185) thereby enabling the charity to claim back the tax. The Form CT61(Z) procedure outlined above then applies.

---

with him receives a benefit" exceeding £250 or 2.5 per cent. of the amount of the gift (whichever is the lesser). A "connected person" would include spouse, parents, children, grandchildren, brothers, sisters and their spouses, and all benefits received by any such persons are aggregated for the entire tax year.

187 Form R240(SD) for a company.

188 *I.e.* after deduction of all allowances, covenants and other gifts for the year.

*Business giving*

The proprietors of a business may adopt the above methods for making gifts to charities. In addition, companies or individuals carrying on a trade can get tax relief for payments to charities which are made wholly and exclusively for business purposes and are not of a capital nature. Sponsorship of charitable events may be tax deductible under this category, and firms may be willing to give their staff time and expertise to charities.

*Gifts of assets*

Gifts of assets to charities, including transfers at an undervalue, are not liable to CGT, but if property is sold to a charity the seller may be liable to tax on the basis of the price actually realised.[189] A donor who intends to make a gift to charity may thus consider giving property which has substantially increased in value in his hands, and should not sell such property in order to give cash. Gifts to charities are also not liable to inheritance tax and need not be included on tax returns.[190]

*Legacies*

Many charities, particularly the larger national ones, receive substantial sums under Wills in the form of legacies, specific assets or a share of residue. Testators may have a particular affinity with the area in which they live, yet seldom think of leaving legacies to local charities and usually choose the popular national charities. The inheritance tax exemption upon the value of outright testamentary gifts to charities is worth emphasising to testators, because this may have the effect of increasing the net estate.

If an asset is bequeathed to a charity which has substantially increased in value since the death it should not be sold by the executors during the administration of the estate, but should be transfered *in specie* even if it is immediately to be sold, because the charity will then be exempt from tax on the gain. Alternatively the executors should declare themselves to hold the asset for the charity absolutely before effecting the sale.

*Deeds of variation*

Even if there are no gifts to charity in a Will, it may be possible to obtain the inheritance tax exemption subsequent to the death if the beneficiaries complete a Deed of Variation within two years which in effect re-writes the Will so as to include a gift to charity. An election must be made in writing to adopt the variation for inheritance tax purposes, and a separate election may be made for CGT purposes.[191] There can be no backdating of the effect of the variation for Income Tax purposes, but this creates interesting possibilities for Gift Aid. If the testator makes a pecuniary legacy

---

189  Capital Gains Tax Act 1979, ss.145 and 146.
190  Inheritance Tax Act 1984, s.23 as amended by Finance Act 1986.
191  Doubts have recently been expressed as to whether exemption is truly available in these circumstances.

to an individual "with the wish that the legacy is given to charity", and the individual then within two years gives the money to a charity and makes an election any Inheritance Tax on the amount of the legacy will be repaid to the estate but it is thought that the charity may also claim the Income Tax repayment on the same money under the Gift Aid scheme. A similar result may possibly be achieved through a post-death Deed of Variation.

## Charities Aid Foundation (CAF)

This charitable organisation[192] was set up specifically to help and co-ordinate the raising and distribution of funds to other charities through its financial services. It also seeks, through its information services and its publication departments, to improve the mutual knowledge and awareness of donors and beneficiaries.

### Give As You Earn
This is a version of the Pay-roll giving scheme which is operated by CAF. A simple form is completed by the donor and returned to CAF which arranges for the specified periodic sum to be deducted by the employer and given to a nominated charity, and the donor will not be taxed on this sum. If the gift is £10 or more per month the donor can open a Charity Account as mentioned below.

### Charity Account
This is an effective means of giving to charity which combines the advantages of tax relief on gifts with a minimum of paperwork whilst retaining personal links with charities. The donor opens a Charity Account with CAF and pays money into this under a Deed of Covenant or Gift Aid. Tax is then recovered and added to the Account. The donor uses a personalised (or anonymous) book of vouchers or "cheques" to make gifts to charities of choice as and when desired, and the charities send these vouchers to CAF which then credits their bank accounts. There is no obligation to spend the money from the account within any specific period, and if the account-holder dies the balance is available for giving to charities usually in accordance with prior instructions or failing this according to the preferences of the executors.

The trustees have the same power of investment in respect of such funds as they have in respect of CAF's own property, and any income or gain is retained by CAF. They may refuse to pay funds to any institution which does not make its accounts available for inspection by the public, and make contributions to their founder, the National Council for Voluntary Organisations[193] for its charitable purposes, of three per cent. of the annual income of each covenant or one per cent. of each Gift Aid payment.

### Personal Charitable Trust
Setting up a charitable trust can be costly and time consuming, and there are many pitfalls for the unwary, but it may be seen as a

---

192  Addresses in Appendix I.
193  In Scotland it is to the Scottish Council for Voluntary Organisations.

necessary step where there is a mentally handicapped member of the family. CAF offer a viable alternative but this may not provide the flexibility of the private trust in regard to matters such as making interest free loans to charities. An individual can open a Trust Account with CAF either for his lifetime, or for a specific period. The account may be given a name of choice, or be anonymous, and gifts can be made to charity either from the capital in the account or the income that it generates. It is possible to provide that the trust shall only support a particular class of charities. An account may be funded and operated by more than one person, with up to three signatories, but there is no need to worry about continuity of trustees or (in England) submission of accounts to the Charity Commissioners. CAF manages the trust and deals with all tax repayments, and normally charges one per cent. per annum of the capital value as a contribution to its overheads.[194]

### Covenant Management Centre

CAF offers charities a comprehensive management service which extends to deposited covenants, membership subscriptions and other donations. The service includes recording all covenants and sending out annual requests for payment, obtaining tax certificates and regularly claiming refund of tax, and remitting monies to the charity weekly by bank transfer. An inclusive charge is made for each deed registered, which is deducted at source from the first payment.

## Public support

Charity trustees should consider all implications before adopting fund raising activities.

### Credit cards

Some credit cards are issued on the basis that a donation will be made to charity when the card is issued or first used, and later donations may be made depending upon the amount spent.[195] These do not cost more to use than their non-charitable equivalent although the cost of borrowing may be more than for other cards.

### Charity shops

There is a gift element in the shops run by charities. In many cases people give clothes and other items for sale in the shops, and in more sophisticated schemes the sale proceeds are shared with the donor. Jumble sales are a one-off version of the charity shop and a variation of this is the car boot sale.

### Public charitable collections (England)

House to house collections are controlled by statute and regulations made thereunder,[196] and must not be made without either a licence

---

[194] The use of such trusts by parents is considered in Chap.9.

[195] *e.g.* £5 initially plus 25p for each £100 spent. The card issued by Leeds Permanent Building Society includes MENCAP and SSMH.

[196] House to House Collections Act 1939; House to House Collections

or exemption from the requirement to obtain a licence. The police may grant exemption for a local collection of short duration, but otherwise a licence must be obtained from the district council or its equivalent. Collections of money or sales of goods in streets or public places are subject to regulations made by the local council.[197] These vary from one authority to another, but cover the places where and conditions under which the activity may take place, and matters such as obstruction and hindrance to traffic.

*Public charitable collections (Scotland)*
In Scotland, the same provisions cover both house-to-house collections and street collections.[198] Permission must be obtained from the district or islands council for any collections for any charitable, benevolent or philanthropic purpose. Written application must be made at least a month beforehand. The council may impose conditions, and may refuse permission on various statutory grounds. There is a right of appeal to the sheriff against conditions or refusal, but note the short time limit of 14 days.[199]
Permission is not required for collections at public meetings or by unmanned fixed public receptacles. Organisations which pursue charitable purposes throughout the whole or a substantial part of Scotland may be exempted by the Secretary of State from having to obtain permission so officials of larger organisations should check whether they are exempted, before seeking permission.
Scottish collections are all governed by the same regulations, made by the Secretary of State. Organisers should familiarise themselves with the regulations, which cover matters such as recording and supervision of collectors; provision of collectors' certificates and wearing of badges; not annoying people by importuning, nor remaining at house doors when asked to leave; and specifications for marking of envelopes and collecting boxes, and provisions about sealing and opening them. There are accounting requirements, different for exempt or non-exempt organisations. Holding a collection without permission or exemption, and contravention of some of the regulations, are offences.

*Lotteries, etc*
The conduct of all lotteries is regulated by statute.[200] There are three different authorised types:
*Small lotteries* incidental to other entertainments provided that the value of the prizes does not exceed £50, the net proceeds of the lottery and entertainment are devoted to purposes other than private gain, no cash prizes are given, and the whole lottery is

---

Regulations 1947 (as amended). These do not apply to collection boxes left in public houses and shops for which there are no statutory controls.
197 Police, Factories etc. (Miscellaneous Provisions) Act 1916. Further controls are introduced by the Charities Act 1992, Part II.
198 Civic Government (Scotland) Act 1982, s.119, Public Charitable Collections (Scotland) Regulations 1984, (S.I.1984 No.565).
199 1982 Act, s.119(6) and (9).
200 Lotteries and Amusements Act 1976.

carried out at and during the entertainment. These are the raffles held at functions.

*Private lotteries* where the ticket sales are restricted to persons in the same society or working or living together, and the net proceeds are devoted to the society or the provision of prizes.

*Society lotteries* organised by clubs and other such organisations, which are public, restricted to 52 in each year at not less than seven day intervals and must be registered with the district council (or its equivalent). If the value of tickets sold exceeds £10,000 or the largest prize exceeds £2,000 in value registration with the Gaming Board is also necessary.

Competitions such as bingo are regulated by the Gaming Act 1968, but activities such as whist drives and bingo on a small scale at entertainments held on unlicensed premises are permitted if promoted for purposes other than private gain.[201] Amusements with prizes (*e.g.* tombolas) incidental to non-commercial entertainment (*i.e.* fetes, bazaars, etc.) are also permitted.[202]

## Appeals for funds

An appeal to the public for funds may be an effective way of raising substantial funds, but will not result in any tax relief on the gifts unless linked with one of the procedures outlined above. Such appeals are more appropriate for disasters or specific projects which have public appeal.

## Professional fund-raisers

Persons whose business it is to raise funds for charities have a valuable role to play. It is important at the outset to establish the service to be given, the persons who will be involved, the methods to be used, the cost or basis of charging and the duration of the arrangement or how terminated. A written agreement should then be prepared and completed dealing with these points. Whilst it would be preferable for a fixed charge to be made for a given service, there can be attractions in making a payment on the basis of the amount raised, though in such cases the rate of commission should be disclosed to all potential donors. It is preferable for all money collected to be paid directly into a special account in the charity's name and under its control. The charity may then pay the agreed fee and expenses or commission to the fundraiser, rather than allowing such items to be deducted before the money is passed over to the charity. When accounts are produced and made available to the public in respect of the appeal, these should show the full situation and not just the net amount recovered.[203]

---

201  Gaming Act 1968, s.41.
202  Gaming Act 1968, s.33;  Lotteries and Amusements Act 1976, s.15.
203  Charities Act 1992, Part II, ss.59 and 60 define "professional fund raisers" and impose controls over their activities. There must be an agreement satisfying prescribed requirements and the basis of remuneration must be disclosed. Various new criminal offences are created.

# PART IV - CONCLUSION

## Role of Voluntary Organisations

Voluntary activity in the interests of disabled persons is to be encouraged, and the government is committed to backing the growth of the voluntary sector. As mental handicap is still not properly understood in society and as provision is seldom adequate, voluntary organisations have much to offer, and many now supplement state provision with pre-school playgroups, youth clubs, respite care, hostels, residential care, holidays or welfare services. Parents and carers are often involved and able to offer advice, support and information to newer parents.

This increased role means that the voluntary sector must become more professional in its approach to the provision of services, because people who receive services from charities are seeking quality services rather than charity. If there is to be a true working partnership with the state, more professional people must be recruited so that their knowledge and experience may be available. The starting point is the basis on which the organisation is set up, and whether this be as an unincorporated association or a registered company a sound governing instrument is essential.[204]

## Mental Handicap Trusts

A recent development linked with the need to make provision in the community for individuals moving out of mental hospitals is the use of mental handicap Trusts involving a partnership between the public and private sectors. Such a Trust would usually be registered as a charity. The objects might be:

> to advance the education and promote the relief of people with learning disability in (*a particular geographical area*) who, by reason of their mental handicap, need assistance by the provision of a suitable home environment and skilled training and supervision to enable them to develop their mental physical and spiritual capacities.

Constituent bodies may be the health authority, local authority (through its social services department), a housing association and a voluntary society comprising parents and others. For an effective working partnership these bodies must have equal status in the Trust, but there should be power to co-opt outsiders so as to introduce further knowledge and expertise. Property development and management services are provided by the housing association. The Trust can establish homes in the community and if these are registered as residential care homes substantial state funding is presently available through Income Support residential care

---

204 The Griffiths Report identified the potential contribution of the voluntary sector and commented on the following roles: self-help support group, information source/source of expertise, befriending agency, advocate for individuals, constructive critic of service providers, public educator, pilot of new approaches to services and campaigner.

allowances for which residents are eligible. These state allowances, which may be supplemented by deficit grants from the health authority, are not available if the local authority itself runs the home. Capital funding can come from grants and the re-settlement monies paid by the health authority, but the intention is that accommodation will also be provided for persons already in the community and once homes have been set up they will be available for future generations thereby making an important contribution to care in the community. Each Trust needs to decide whether it will merely concentrate upon the provision of housing or go further and actually employ care staff to look after the residents either on a visiting basis for those better able to cope or on a residential basis for the more profoundly handicapped. A middle course is for the Trust to purchase care staff from the social services department, and daytime activities may be provided by that department at an adult training centre.

Whilst the Trust provides a valuable opportunity for the health authority and social services department to work in partnership,[205] it also offers a facility for parents to contribute financially. Once parents are satisfied that the Trust is an independent charitable body solely concerned with the delivery of care to persons with a mental handicap they may be minded to assist in its work, and the charitable trusts set up by Will may be used to provide financial support in a tax effective way. A precedent for such a Mental Handicap Trust will be found in Appendix IV.

## Housing Consortium

A Housing Consortium with the status of a registered Friendly Society is another way of forming a partnership between statutory and voluntary organisations working with people who have a mental handicap to expand existing services.[206] It comprises a powerful combination of individuals and agencies with skills, experience and expertise, and with a strong commitment to the service. The objects may be to provide housing for such people, ensure that there is the necessary staff support to meet their needs and set comprehensive standards for the services provided.

## LAW REFORM

### England

The reform of charity law in England is under consideration in view of some of the abuses that take place under the present law. A basic question is which organisations should be granted charitable status, but reforms are more likely to concentrate upon the controls on the administration and supervision of charities.

---

205 In areas where boundaries do not overlap there is the opportunity for more than one of such authorities to combine energies through the Trust.
206 An example is the West Berkshire Housing Consortium of 120 Oxford Road, Reading, Berkshire RG1 7NL.

*Woodfield Report* [207]

This Report made many recommendations as to the administration of charities and the organisation of the Charity Commission. The majority of these relate to the financial affairs of charities and the arrangements for monitoring and investigating their affairs, and on the whole a tighter regime of control is proposed. Of particular interest to charities concerned with mental handicap are the following:

(a) charities with a small investment income but a large turnover of money should be brought under supervision;

(b) annual returns should be required, including a narrative report and particulars of trustees;

(c) all local charities should be required to send a copy of their accounts to the local authority, and to members of the public on payment of a fee;

(d) powers for Commissioners to de-register for failing to submit accounts, appoint a receiver and manager, and wind up a charity and transfer its property to another charity;

(e) restrictions on persons who may be trustees, and power to require minimum number;

(f) better review of local charities;

(g) model governing instruments to be available for wider general use;

(h) trustees to have power to purchase land as investment;

(i) reduced use of the Official Custodian;

(j) charges for new registrations and for giving consents;

(k) restrictions on deduction of remuneration before payment of donations to a charity;

(l) injunctions to be available to prevent use of a charity's name by other persons or organisations;

*Charities: a Framework for the Future*

This White Paper, published in May 1989 in response to the Woodfield Report, made proposals for legislation of which the most significant are:

(a) no change in the current definitions of charitable status;

(b) computerisation of the Register of Charities;

(c) charities with a yearly income of over £1,000 from any source to be required to register;

(d) tighter controls over the filing of annual accounts, with accounting requirements being related to a charity's size;

(e) specific requirements for trustees' reports which must set out means employed to promote the objects, and include a review of activities and achievements, and an explanation of financial information;

(f) wide powers for the Commissioners to intervene in the affairs of a charity (on the lines of the Woodfield Report);

(g) remove need for consent to land transactions;

(h) abolish the Official Custodian;

(i) introduce registration and filing fees;

(j) clarify the law on street and house-to-house collections, and prevent deduction of fees or expenses by fundraisers.

Some but not all of these changes have been enacted (though not yet brought into effect) by the Charities Act 1992 and where appropriate these have been referred to. Proposals to limit the liability of charity trustees were not included in that Act, but assurances were given that the whole topic of their liability would

---

[207] *Efficiency Scrutiny of the Supervision of Charities* (HMSO, 1987).

be given further consideration. The Government is also exploring the possibility of establishing a new form of incorporation which would limit the liability of trustees without bringing the whole organisation under company law. The new form would be under the jurisdiction of the Charity Commission, thereby avoiding the present problem of charitable companies being regulated by both company and charity law.

## Scotland

Charity law in Scotland has been substantially reformed by Part I of the Law Reform (Miscellaneous Provisions) (Scotland) Act 1990.[208] Once regulations have been made and the new regime brought into force, experience will tell whether further reform (such as institution of a statutory register of Scottish charities) will be required.

---

[208]   Not yet in force - see note at the beginning of Part IIB.

# APPENDIX I ORGANISATIONS AND ADDRESSES

## ADVICE AGENCIES

**Child Poverty Action Group**

1-5 Bath Street, London EC1V 9PY
071-253-3406

**Children's Legal Centre Ltd**

20 Compton Terrace, London N1 2UN
071-359-9392 Also advice line (2-5 pm) 071-359-6251

**The Disability Alliance**

1st Floor East, Universal House,
88-94 Wentworth Street, LONDON E1 7SA
071-247-8776 Advice line 071-247-8763

**Disability Law**
(formerly Network for the Handicapped)

16 Princeton Street, London WC1R 4BB
071-831-8031/7740

**Legal Services Agency**

58 Fox Street, Glasgow G1 4AU
041-204-2575

**National Citizens Advice Bureaux**

Bureaux services are available in most towns.

**Scottish Child Law Centre**

Lion Chambers, 170 Hope Street, Glasgow G2 2TU
041-333-9305

**Voluntary Council for the Handicapped Child**

8 Wakley Street, London EC1V 7QE

**Education**

*Association of Educational Psychologists*
3 Sunderland Road, Durham DH1 2LH

*Independent Panel of Special Education Experts*
12 Marsh Road, Tillingham, Essex CM0 7SZ.

*Advisory Centre for Education* (ACE)
18 Victoria Park Square, London E2 9PB.
071-354-8321

*Education Law Association* (ELAS)
Unit 1B, Aberdeen Studios, 22-24 Highbury Grove,
London N5 2EA. 071-354-8318

## Employment

*The Employment Service*
  Rockingham House, 123 West Street, Sheffield S1 4ER
  0742-739190

*Pathway Employment Service*
  MENCAP, Pathway Head Office, 169a City Road,
  Cardiff  CF2 3JB.

### FINANCIAL HELP

## Disablement Income Group (DIG) Scotland

5 Quayside Street, Edinburgh EH6 6EJ
031-555-2811

## Family Fund

Joseph Rowntree Memorial Trust, PO Box 50,
York YO1 1UY            0904-621115

## Independent Living Fund

PO Box 183, Nottingham, NG8 3RD

### SOCIETIES

## Barnardo's

Tanner's Lane, Barkingside, Ilford, Essex  IG6 1QG
081-550-8822

## Disability Scotland

Princes House, 5 Shandwick House, Edinburgh EH2 4RG
031-229-8632

## Down's Syndrome Association

153/5 Mitcham Road, London  SW17 9PG
081-682-4001

## National Centre for Down's Syndrome

Birmingham Polytechnic, Westbourne Road, Edgbaston,
Birmingham  B15 5TH

## Hyper-Active Children's Support Group

71 Whyke Lane, Chichester, Sussex  PO19 2LD
0903-725182

## National Association for Mental Health (MIND)

22 Harley Street, London  W1N 2ED
071-637-0741

## National Autistic Society

276 Willesden Lane, London  NW2 5RB
081-451-1114

**Scottish Association for Mental Health (SAMH)**

> 38 Gardner's Crescent, Edinburgh EH3 8QD
> 031-229-9687

**Scottish Council for Spastics**

> "Rhuemore", 22 Corstorphine Road, Edinburgh EH12 6HP
> 031-337-9876/9879

**Scottish Down's Syndrome Association**

> 158/160 Balgreen Road, Edinburgh EH11 3RU
> 031-313-4225

**Scottish Society for the Mentally Handicapped (SSMH)**
**SSMH Trustee Service Ltd.**

> 13 Elmbank Street, Glasgow G2 4QA        041-226-4541

**Sense Scotland**

> 8 Elliot Place, Glasgow        041-221-7577

**Spastics Society**

> 12 Park Crescent, London  W1N 4EQ        071-636-5020

**The Royal Society for Mentally Handicapped Children and Adults (MENCAP)**

*Legal Services Department; Mencap Visitors Service; National Trustees for the Mentally Handicapped Limited; ADCARE Foundation; Homes Foundation; National Federation of Gateway Clubs; Pathway*

> 123 Golden Lane, London, EC1Y 0RT        071-454-0454

**The Rathbone Society**

> 1st Floor, Princess House, 105/107 Princess Street,
> Manchester, M1 6DD        061-236-5358

## RESIDENTIAL CARE
*(In addition to some of the above Societies).*

**Ark Housing**

> 8 Balcarres Street, Edinburgh EH10 5JB    041-332-6672

**Camphill Village Trust**

> Delrow House, Hilfield Lane, Aldenham,
> Watford, Herts  WD2 8DJ        0923-856006

**CARE for Mentally Handicapped People**

> Cottage and Rural Enterprises Limited, 9 Weir Road,
> Kibworth, Leicestershire  LE8 0LQ        0533-793225

**A Cause for Concern**

> 118b Oxford Road, Reading, Berkshire  RG1 7NG
> 0734-508781

**Home Farm Trust Ltd**

> Merchants House, Wapping Road, Bristol  BS1 4RW
> 0272-273746

**Key Housing**

> Savoy Tower, 77 Renfrew Street, Glasgow G2 3BZ
> 041-332-6672

**Leonard Cheshire Foundation**

> 26-29 Maunsel Street, London  SW1P 2QN
> 071-828-1822

**Macintyre Westoning**

> Macintyre Central, 602 South Seventh Street,
> Central Milton Keynes MK9 2JA                0908-230100

**Ravenswood Foundation**

> 17 Highfield Road, London NW11 9DZ        081-905-5557

**The Shaftesbury Society**

> 18-20 Kingston Road, London SW19 1JZ    081-542-5550

**SSMH Homes**

> Prospect House, New Park Street, Hamilton ML3 0BN
> 0698-284728

## OTHER ORGANISATIONS

**Association of Parents of Vaccine Damaged Children**

> 2 Church Street, Shipston on Stour, Warwick  CV36 4AP
> 0608-61595

**The Association to Aid the Sexual and Personal Relationships of People with a Disability    (SPOD)**

> 286 Camden Road, London  N7 0BJ
> 071-607-8851 / 2

**British Institute of Learning Disabilities**
(formerly British Institute of Mental Handicap - BIMH)

> Wolverhampton Road, Kidderminster, Worcs. DY10 3PP
> 0562-850251

**Caresearch** (A Project of United Response)

> 162 Upper Richmond Road, Putney, London  SW15 2SL
> 081-780-9596

**Carers National Association**

> 29 Chilworth Mews, London W2 3RG        071-724-7776

**Community Living Development Team**

> King's Fund Centre, 126 Albert Street, London NW1 7NF
> 071-267-6111

**Contact-a-Family**

   16 Strutton Ground, London  SW1P 2HP    071-222-2695

**Crossroads Care**

   10 Regent Place, Rugby CV21 2PN          0788-573653

**Crossroads Scotland**

   24 George Square, Glasgow G2 1EG          041-226-3793

**Independent Development Council**

   c/o Values in Action (see below)

**National Citizen Advocacy**
(formerly Advocacy Alliance)

   Unit 2K, Leroy House, 436 Essex Road, London  N1 3QP
   071-359-8289

**National Council for Voluntary Organisations**

   Regent's Wharf, 8 All Saint's Street, London N1 9RL
   071-713-6161

**Scottish Council for Voluntary Organisations**

   18/19 Claremont Crescent, Edinburgh EH7 4QD
   031-556-3882

**Values into Action (VIA)**
(formerly Campaign for People with Mental Handicap)

   Oxford House,  Derbyshire Street, London
   071-729-5436

## OFFICIAL ADDRESSES

**Accountant of Court**

   Strategy House, 3 Cables Wynd, Leith,
   Edinburgh EH6 6DT.

**Charity Commissioners**

| St Alban's House | Graeme House | Woodfield House |
|---|---|---|
| 57-60 Haymarket | Derby Square | Tangier |
| LONDON | LIVERPOOL | TAUNTON |
| SW1Y 4QX | L2 7SB | TA1 4BL |

**Charities Aid Foundation**

*Charity Account*
   CAF, 48 Pembury Road, Tonbridge, Kent TN9 2JD.
   0732-771333.

*Trust Department and Covenant Management Centre*
   CAF, Foundation House, Coach & Horses Passage,
   The Pantiles, Tunbridge Wells, Kent TN2 5TZ.
   0892-512244.

## Commissions for Local Administration

*England*
21 Queen Anne's Gate               29 Castlegate,
London  SW1H 9BU.                   York YO1 1RN.

*Wales*
Derwen House, Court Road, Bridgend,
Mid Glamorgan   CF31 1BN.

*Scotland*
5 Shandwick Place, Edinburgh    EH2 4RG.

*Northern Ireland*
Office of the Northern Ireland Commissioner for
Complaints, 33 Wellington Place, Belfast  BT1 6HN.

## Companies Registries

*England and Wales*
Companies House, Crown Way,    Maindy,
Cardiff  CF4 3UZ    tel: 0222-380801
Companies House, 55-71 City Road,
London EC1Y 1BB   tel: 071-253-9393

There are satellite offices at Manchester, Birmingham, Leeds and Glasgow.

*Scotland*
Companies House, Exchequer Chambers,
100-102 George Street, Edinburgh  EH2 3DJ
tel: 031-225-5774

## Court of Protection

Enquiries and Acceptance Branch,
The Public Trust Office  (Protection Division)
Stewart House, 24 Kingsway, LONDON  WC2B 6JX
(071-269)   7358, 7157, 7446, 7126 or 7074

Supreme Court Taxing Office (Court of Protection Branch),
Royal Courts of Justice, Strand, LONDON      WC2A 2LL
071-936-6469

## Criminal Injuries Compensation Board

Whittington House, 19 Alfred Place, London  WC1E 7LG.

## European Commission of Human Rights

Secretary to the European Commission of Human Rights,
Conseil De L'Europe, Boite postale 431 R6,
67006 Strasbourg Cedex, France
010 33 88 41 2000

## Health Service Commissioners

*England*
Church House, Great Smith Street, LONDON   SW1P 3BW

*Wales*
Pearl Assurance House, Greyfriars Road CARDIFF  CF1 3AG.

*Scotland*
Second Floor, 11 Melville Crescent, EDINBURGH EH3 7LU.

**Law Commission**

Conquest House, 37-38 John Street, Theobalds Road,
London WC1N 2BQ          071-242-0861

**Mental Health Act Commission**

*Southern Region*
Floors 1 & 2, Hepburn House, Marsham Street,
London, SW1P 4HW          01-211 8061.

*North-West Region*
Cressington House, 249 St. Mary's Road, Garston,
Liverpool, Ll9 ONF          051-427 2061

*North-East Region*
Spur A, Block 5, Government Buildings, Chalfont Drive,
 Western Boulevard, Nottingham, NG8 3RZ
0602 293409

**The Mental Welfare Commission for Scotland**

25 Drumsheugh Gardens, Edinburgh, EH3 7RB
031-225 7034

**Parliamentary Commissioner**

*England, Wales and Scotland*
Office of the Parliamentary Commissioner for
    Administration, Church House, Great Smith Street,
London   SW1P 3BW.

*Northern Ireland*
Commissioner for Northern Ireland,
33 Wellington Place, Belfast  BT1 6HN

**Scottish Law Commission**

140 Causewayside, Edinburgh EH9 1PR

**Scottish Office Education Department**

Division 1, Room 420, New St Andrew's House,
Edinburgh  EH1 3SY

**Social Services Inspectorate**

Wellington House, 133-155 Waterloo Road, London SE1 8UG
071-972-2000

**Social Work Services Group**
**Social Work Services Inspectorate**

43 Jeffrey Street, Edinburgh EH1 3DG

# Appendix II  Further Reading

*Grouping into chapters is for general guidance only. Books relating to more than one chapter appear in the most relevant*

## Chapters 2 and 3

Chiswick et al., *Prosecution of the Mentally Disturbed* (Aberdeen University Press)
Cretney, *Elements of Family Law* (Sweet & Maxwell)
Hoggett, *Parents & Children: The Law of Parental Responsibility* (Sweet & Maxwell)
Masson & Morris, *The Children Act Manual* (Sweet & Maxwell)
Ward, *Scots Law and the Mentally Handicapped* (SSMH)
Ward, *The Power to Act* (SSMH)
White, Carr & Lowe, *A Guide to the Children Act 1989* (Butterworths)

## Chapter 4

Anderson-Ford & Halsey, *Mental Health Law and Practice for Social Workers* (Butterworths)
Blackie and Patrick, *Mental Health  - A Guide to the Law in Scotland* (Butterworths)
Gostin, *Mental Health Services - Law and Practice* (Shaw & Sons)
Gostin, *A Practical Guide to Mental Health Law* (MIND Publications)
Gostin & Fennell, *Mental Health: Tribunal Procedure* (Longman)
Hoggett, *Mental Health Law* (Sweet & Maxwell)
Jones, *Mental Health Act Manual* (Sweet & Maxwell)
Kennedy and Grubb, *Medical Law - Text and Materials* (Butterworths)
Mason & McCall Smith, *Law and Medical Ethics* (Butterworths)
Sinclair, *Proper Channels: A Guide to Complaining about Medical Treatment* (MIND)
Whitehead, *Mental Illness and the Law* (Basil Blackwell)
Williams, *The Law of Mental Health* (Fourmat Publishing)

## Chapter 5

Cooper, *The Legal Rights Manual* (Gower)
Cross & Bailey, *Cross on Local Government* (Sweet & Maxwell)
Harrison, *Access to Information in Local Government* (Sweet & Maxwell)
Jones, *Encyclopaedia of Social Services Law and  Practice* (Sweet & Maxwell)
Williams, *Social Services Law* (Fourmat Publishing)

## Chapter 6

Chasty & Friel, *Children with Special Needs. Assessment, Law
        and Practice - Caught in the Act* (Jessica Kingsley)
Poole, *Education Law* (Sweet & Maxwell)
Advisory Centre for Education,*ACE Special Education Handbook*
Scottish Consumer Council, *In special need: a handbook for
        parents and young people in Scotland with special
        educational needs* (HMSO)
Scottish Consumer Council,*The law of the school: a parent's guide
        to education law in Scotland* (HMSO)
The Scottish Office, *A Parent's Guide to Special Educational
        Needs*

## Chapter 7

Jones, *Registered Homes Act Manual* (Sweet & Maxwell)
Freedman & Lyon, *The Law of Residential Homes & Day Care
        Establishments* (Sweet & Maxwell)
*Care Home Management* (Croner Publications)

## Chapter 8

Annual publications by Child Poverty Action Group
    *CPAG's Housing Benefit and Community Charge Benefit
        Legislation*
    *Rights Guide to Non-Means-Tested Benefits*
    *National Welfare Benefits Handbook*
    *A Guide to Housing Benefit & Community Charge Benefit*
    Available from CPAG Ltd
    *Disability Rights Handbook* (Disability Alliance ERA)
Annual publications by Sweet & Maxwell
    Bonner, Hooker & White, *Non-Means-Tested Benefits: The
        Legislation*
    Mesher, *CPAG's Income-Related Benefits: The Legislation*
    Rowland, *Medical and Disability Appeal Tribunals: The
        Legislation*
Ogus & Barendt, *The Law of Social Security* (Butterworths)

## Chapter 9

Various (including Ashton),*Wills, Probate and Administration
        Service* (Butterworths)
Pearce, *A Guide to Inheritance Claims* (Fourmat Publishing)

## Chapter 10

Aldridge, *Powers of Attorney* (Longman)
Cretney, *Enduring Powers of Attorney - A Practitioner's Guide*
    (Family Law)
Letts, *Managing Other People's Money* (Age Concern)
Whitehorn, *Heywood & Massey: Court of Protection Practice*
    (Sweet & Maxwell)
Whitehorn, *Court of Protection Handbook* (Longman)


## Chapter 11

Warburton, *Unincorporated Associations: Law and Practice*
    (Sweet & Maxwell)
*Management of Voluntary Organisations* (Croner Publications)
Morse, *Charlesworth & Morse: Company Law* (Sweet &
    Maxwell)
Cairns, *Charities: Law and Practice* (Sweet & Maxwell)
Maurice & Parker, *Tudor on Charities* (Sweet & Maxwell)
Venables & Kessler, *Tax Planning and Fund Raising for Charities*
    (Key Haven Pubs Ltd)

# Appendix IIIa    Wills and Settlements
## (England)

**NOTE:**    We refer to Precedents here, and to Styles in Appendix IIIB, to reflect the customary terminology of England and Scotland respectively, and to differentiate between them.

It can be dangerous to provide precedents for fear that these are used without a sufficient understanding of the pitfalls thereby proving inappropriate. In order to offer practical guidance and illustrate ways in which the strategies set out in Chapter 9 may be adopted, there are set out a selection of Wills prepared for specific family circumstances. These are followed by a Settlement which sets out the trusts during lifetime and enables the Wills of parents and other persons to be kept short by leaving monies to the settlement trustees upon the trusts thereof. The first precedent is the most comprehensive and is used as the framework for the following precedents. Each of these precedents may be modified to cover a testator who has more than one mentally handicapped child and the permutations are then increased.

## PRECEDENT I

The first precedent is the most comprehensive and is used as the framework for the following precedents. Modifications may be made to cover a testator who has more than one mentally handicapped child and the permutations are then increased.

*Parents of two daughters (Jane and Jill) and a seriously mentally handicapped son (John) who have not attained their legal majority, but it is not anticipated that there will be further children. John stays at a home run by a local charity for periods of respite care but long term arrangements have not yet been made. The parents, who have a fairly substantial estate, contemplate that he will ultimately live in residential accommodation and do not wish their daughters to take on the burden of looking after him.*
*Although the "wait and see" provision has been included this may be omitted by deleting references to "my Trust Fund" and moving directly into "the Family Fund" and "the Charitable Fund". The duration of the trust is the lifetime of the handicapped child because in practice most testators prefer this.*

**THIS IS THE LAST WILL** of me
of

1. **I HEREBY REVOKE** all former testamentary dispositions made by me

2. **IN THE EVENT** of my wife [*name* ] being my lawful wife at my death and surviving me by one calendar month **I GIVE** all the real and personal

property whatsoever and wheresoever to which I may be entitled or over which I have any disposing power at the time of my death after payment of my just debts funeral and testamentary expenses and any legacies given by this my Will or any Codicil thereto (hereinafter called "my Estate") to my said wife absolutely and **I APPOINT** her to be the sole executrix of my Will

3. **IN THE EVENT** of my said wife not inheriting under the preceding provision **I WILL AND DECLARE** as follows:

(a)  **I APPOINT** [*name/address* and *name/address* ] (hereinafter called "my Trustees" which expression includes the trustees or trustee for the time being hereof) to be the executors and trustees of this my Will but if either of them die in my lifetime or are unable or unwilling to act then **I APPOINT** [*name/address*] in his or her place [and **I GIVE** to each of my Trustees the sum of £      free of tax if they shall prove my Will]

(b)  **I APPOINT** [*name/address or relationship and .... jointly* ] to be guardian(s) of any of my children who may be minors AND ALSO of *my son John* when an adult to the extent permitted by law

(c)  **I GIVE** the following specific *and/or* pecuniary legacies free of tax [provided that these gifts shall not take effect to the extent that similar gifts have been made from my said husband's estate - *wife's Will only*]

(i)  to [*name/address or relationship* ] my ...
(ii)  to [*name/address or relationship* ] the sum of £

(d)  **I GIVE** all my remaining furnishings personal and household effects to my [daughters *if of age otherwise* Trustees] beneficially free of tax with the wish (but without imposing any binding obligation) that they transfer or make available to my [children *or* son John ] any items that *they/he* may reasonably require [and that they disclaim any items not so required so that they fall into the remainder of my Estate]

(e)  **I GIVE** the remainder of my Estate to my Trustees **UPON TRUST** to sell call in and convert into money all such parts thereof as do not consist of money at my death with power to postpone such sale calling in and conversion for so long as they in their absolute discretion think fit without being liable for loss and **TO HOLD** the net proceeds of such sale calling in and conversion and all unsold property and my ready money **UPON TRUST** to divide the same into [*three*] equal shares and hold these:

**AS TO** [*one*] share(s) for *my daughter Jane* [if and when she attains her legal majority]

**AS TO** [*one*] such share(s) for *my daughter Jill* [if and when she attains her legal majority]

**AND AS TO** the remaining [*one*] share(s) if *my son John* survives me upon trust to invest the same at their discretion in their joint names in any investments hereby authorised with power to vary such investments from time to time and stand possessed thereof upon the trusts hereinafter declared concerning [my Trust Fund *or* the Family Fund and the Charitable Fund *in equal shares*]

(f)  **IF** either of *my said daughters* dies before attaining a vested interest in my Estate (whether or not in my lifetime) leaving a child or children living at my death or born thereafter who attain their legal majority such child or children shall take and if more than one equally between them the shares that such deceased daughter would have taken had she survived

(g)  **IF** *my son John* dies before me leaving a child or children living at my death or born thereafter who attain their legal majority such child or children shall take and if more than one equally between them the shares that would have been retained on trust if *my son John* had survived me

(h)  **IF** the trusts of any of these shares fail such shares (and any shares which may accrue thereto under this provision) shall accrue equally to and be held upon the trusts of the remaining shares which have not failed

(i)  **IF** the trusts of all these shares fail my Trustees shall hold my Estate [upon the trusts declared concerning the Charitable Fund - *or as appropriate* ]

[*If required*
4.  (i)  **MY TRUST FUND** shall be held by my Trustees **UPON TRUST** to accumulate the income thereof by investing the same and its resulting income

in any investments hereby authorised and to hold such accumulations as an addition to the capital of my Trust Fund with power to pay any such income in their absolute discretion and from time to time to any of my said children

(ii) **WITHIN** twenty-three months of my death my Trustees being at least two in number may by Deed appoint my Trust Fund between the Family Fund and the Charitable Fund in such proportions as they in their absolute discretion think fit [PROVIDED THAT they shall appoint at least [*one-half*] to the Family Fund] and **IN DEFAULT** of such appointment my Trust Fund shall at the expiration of such period be deemed to have been appointed to the Family Fund and the Charitable Fund equally]

5. (i) **THE FAMILY FUND** shall be held by my Trustees **UPON TRUST** during the lifetime of *my son John* to pay or apply the income thereof to or for or towards the personal support maintenance and education or otherwise for the benefit of the family beneficiaries defined below [and to the charitable beneficiaries defined below] or such one or more to the exclusion of the others or other of them in such manner and if more than one in such shares as my Trustees being at least two in number from time to time in their absolute discretion think fit **WITH POWER** during the period of twenty-one years immediately following my death in their absolute discretion to accumulate the income or any part thereof by investing the same and its resulting income in any investments hereby authorised as an addition to the capital of the Fund but also thereafter during that period to apply the whole or any part of the accumulated income as if it were income arising in the then current year **AND I REQUEST** my Trustees in exercising their discretion to have regard to the needs (if any) of *my son John*

(ii) **AFTER** the death of *my son John* my Trustees shall hold the income and capital of the Family Fund or the remainder thereof **UPON TRUST** to pay such funeral expenses (including the cost of a memorial) as they consider appropriate for *my son John* and [in their discretion to waive repayment of any loan that they may have made to any of the charitable beneficiaries and] subject thereto **UPON TRUST** for [such of my son John's children or remoter issue as are then living [and attain their legal majority] and if more than one in equal shares per stirpes so that no such issue shall take whose parent is alive and so capable of taking] WHOM FAILING such of my children or remoter issue as are then living [and attain their legal majority] and if more than one in equal shares per stirpes so that no such issue shall take whose parent is alive and so capable of taking WHOM FAILING upon the trusts of the Charitable Fund [*or as appropriate*]

(iii) **FAMILY BENEFICIARIES** means my children and remoter issue [and my nephews and nieces] [and *named persons*] [and the spouses widows or widowers (whether or not remarried) of any such persons] - *or as appropriate* AND it is my wish (without imposing any binding obligation) that my Trustees in exercising their discretion between such beneficiaries have in mind any services or benefits given by them to *my son John* during his lifetime

6. (i) **THE CHARITABLE FUND** shall be held by my Trustees **UPON TRUST** as to both the income and capital thereof for such one or more of the charitable beneficiaries defined below at such time or times and in such shares as my Trustees being at least two in number may at any time or times in writing appoint

(ii) **UNTIL** and subject to such appointments my Trustees shall pay or apply the income of the Charitable Fund to or for the benefit of such one or more of the charitable beneficiaries as they being at least two in number may in their absolute discretion think fit WITH POWER during the period of twenty-one years immediately following my death in their absolute discretion to accumulate such income or any part of it by way of compound interest by investing the same and its resulting income in any investments hereby authorised and to hold such accumulations as part of the capital of the Charitable Fund but also thereafter during that period to apply the whole or any part of the accumulated income as if it were income arising in the then current year

(iii) **CHARITABLE BENEFICIARIES** means any charitable society or organisation whether local or national whose objects or principal objects appear to my Trustees to be to promote the accommodation care welfare treatment education employment or advancement or to be otherwise for the benefit of mentally [*and/or physically* ] disabled persons AND it is my wish (without imposing any binding obligation) that my Trustees in exercising their discretion between such charitable beneficiaries have in mind any services or benefits given by them to *my son John* during his lifetime

(iv)  **MY TRUSTEES** being at least two in number may make a loan to any charitable beneficiary on such terms as they think fit (which may include free of interest)

7.  **MY TRUSTEES** being at least two in number have the following powers in addition to those under the general law in regard to the administration of my Estate and each of the said Funds

(a)  to invest any money in or upon the acquisition or security of any property of whatsoever nature and wheresoever situate (including any house or flat or chattel as a residence for or for the use of any beneficiary thereof) to the intent that they have the same full and unrestricted power of investment in all respects as if they were absolutely entitled thereto beneficially

(b)  [to raise any part or parts out of the contingent or expectant share therein of any of my children or remoter issue and pay or apply the same as my Trustees in their absolute discretion think fit for the advancement or benefit of such child or issue] - *if required*

(c)  in any case where they have an obligation or discretion to pay income or capital to or for the benefit of an infant to discharge that obligation or exercise that discretion if they so desire by paying the same to any parent or guardian of the infant or to the infant if of the age of 16 years and their respective receipts shall be a good and sufficient discharge to my Trustees who shall not be obliged to see to the application of the monies so paid

(d)  to exercise the power of appropriation conferred by the Administration of Estates Act 1925 without obtaining any of the consents required by that Act and even though one of my Trustees may be beneficially interested in the appropriation

(e)  to decide in their absolute discretion what sums are capital and what sums are income and what payments shall be charged against capital and what against income without being bound to apply in the preparation of their accounts or otherwise any of the technical rules of administration Provided that they shall exercise their discretion so as to act reasonably between the beneficiaries therein

(f)  to treat the receipt of anyone who appears to be the Treasurer or other authorised officer for the time being of any charity to whom they pay any money whether comprising income or capital as a sufficient discharge

8.  **MY TRUSTEES** being at least two in number have the following further powers exercisable in their absolute discretion at any time and from time to time in the administration of my Trust Fund and the Family Fund

(a)  to apply all or any part of the capital or income thereof as they in their absolute discretion think fit in or towards any Scheme or Plan which in their opinion may provide a sufficient degree of security and protection for *my son John* during the whole or some part of *his* life notwithstanding that such capital may thereby be exhausted AND in exercising this power to transfer to any other body society or person any part or the whole of such Fund as may in their opinion be necessary or desirable for the fulfilment of any such Scheme or Plan

(b)  to invest the whole or any part thereof in the purchase or improvement of any dwellinghouse or flat (whether freehold or leasehold) and to permit the same to be used as a residence for *my son John* whether alone or jointly with any other person or persons without being required to insist upon the payment by any other person whether or not a joint occupier thereof of any but my Trustees have a complete discretion as to the terms on which they permit such dwellinghouse or flat to be occupied

(c)  to exercise their powers of investment without seeking to balance the interests of beneficiaries entitled to capital and income respectively

(d)  to invest in chattels notwithstanding that the value of the Fund may become depleted and to permit any child of mine [any one or more beneficiaries] to have the use and enjoyment of any chattel forming part of such Fund in such manner and subject to such conditions (if any) as my Trustees may consider reasonable and without being liable to account for any consequential loss

(e)   to raise capital out of such Fund and lend it on such terms as to interest security and repayment and otherwise as they think fit to any person to whom or any charitable or other body to which they consider that it would be in the interests of *my son John* to make a loan without being liable for any consequent loss of capital

(f)   to borrow monies whether or not on the security of the said Fund on such terms as they think fit and treat such monies in like manner in all respects as if they formed part of the said Fund

(g)   to apply any part of the capital or income of such Fund in or towards the payment of the premiums on any policies of assurance to be included in or forming part of the said Fund and to effect any such policies on any lives in which any beneficiary hereunder has an insurable interest

(h)   to insure any trust property for such amount and against such risks as they think fit and pay the premiums out of the income or capital of the Fund to which such property belongs

(i)   to apply any part or parts of the capital or income of such Fund in or towards meeting the cost of:

(i) altering or adapting any residential accommodation in the ownership of any person or body for the more convenient occupation thereof by *my son John* as a home;

(ii) purchasing domestic appliances or procuring domestic assistance for *my son John* or the person or persons with whom *he* from time to time resides;

(iii) purchasing caravans or motor cars appropriate to the needs of *my son John* and the person or persons with whom *he* from time to time resides;

(iv) holidays for *my son John* or the expenses incurred by any person or persons to enable them to accompany *him* on holiday or the provision of holidays unaccompanied by *him* for any person who bears the daily burden of caring for *him*

(j)   to accept the receipt of any person caring or having financial responsibility for *my son John* as a full and sufficient discharge for any money intended to be paid to *him* or for *his* benefit

(k)   by deed or deeds (and so as to bind their successors) wholly or partially to release or restrict the future exercise of any power or discretion conferred upon them either permanently or for any specified period

(l)   to reimburse out of the income thereof any costs and expenses incurred by them in ascertaining the circumstances and needs (if any) of *my son John* and in making arrangements that they deem necessary or expedient for *his* care

9.  **MY TRUSTEES** may benefit from the following further provisions:

(a)   Any executor or trustee being a solicitor or engaged in any other profession or business may charge and be paid all usual professional or other charges for business transacted time expended and acts done by him or his firm in connection with the administration of my estate and the execution of the trusts hereof including acts which a trustee not being engaged in such profession or business could have done personally

(b)   No Trustee shall be liable for any loss or damage which may happen to my Estate or any of the said Funds or any part thereof or the income therefrom at any time or from any cause unless such loss or damage is caused by his or her own actual fraud

(c)   My Trustees may exercise any power given by this Will or by law notwithstanding that one or more of my Trustees may have a direct or personal interest in the way the power is exercised and may benefit thereby [Provided that there is at least one other trustee with no such interest]

(d)   My Trustees may accept additional monies investments and property which may be paid or transferred to them upon the trusts of any of the said Funds by any person either as a lifetime gift or under a testamentary disposition

(e)   My Trustees may appoint a trust corporation to be sole trustee or one of the trustees of this my Will upon such terms and conditions in all respects as may be acceptable to the corporation so appointed

(f)   A trust corporation which is a sole trustee may alone exercise any power expressed to be exercisable by my Trustees "being at least two in number"

10. **IT IS MY WISH**  that my body may be cremated and my ashes scattered in the Garden of Remembrance - *or as appropriate*

**AS WITNESS**  my hand this         day of         One thousand nine hundred and ninety-

**SIGNED**  by the said [*name* ] in our presence and then by us in his [hers]

## VARIATION 1

*Parents of a young seriously mentally handicapped child (James) who have prospects of other children. This situation poses every possible uncertainty because the future of the son and the existence of other children to benefit cannot be known. It may be desired to include a wider class of relatives as potential beneficiaries in the Family Fund, as well as charities.*

3. (e)  *as before* ... **UPON TRUST** (subject to the provisions of (f) below) for such of my children as survive me and attain their legal majority and if more than one in equal shares **PROVIDED** that if any of my said children dies before attaining a vested interest (whether or not in my lifetime) leaving a child or children living at my death or born thereafter who attain their legal majority such child or children shall take and if more than one equally between them the shares that such deceased child of mine would have taken had he or she survived

(f)  **IF** *my son James* survives me the share of my Estate in which (but for this provision) *he* would have acquired an absolute interest (whether vested or contingent) under (e) above shall instead be held by my Trustees on the trusts declared in this Will concerning [my Trust Fund *or* the Family Fund and the Charitable Fund *in equal shares*]

(g)  IF the trusts of my Estate should fail my Trustees shall hold it [upon the trusts declared concerning the Charitable Fund - *or as appropriate*]
*Omit other provisions of clause 3 and continue with consequential amendments*

## VARIATION 2

*Where there will be no surviving spouse*

2.  *as clause 3(a)*
3.  *as clause 3(b)*
4.  *as clause 3(c)*
5.  *as clause 3(d)*
6.  **I GIVE**  all the real and personal property whatsoever and wheresoever to which I may be entitled or over which I have any disposing power at the time of my death after payment of my just debts funeral and testamentary expenses and any legacies given by this my Will or any Codicil thereto (hereinafter called "my Estate") to my Trustees **UPON TRUST** to sell call in and convert into money all such parts thereof as shall not consist of money at my death with power to postpone such sale calling in and conversion for so long as they shall in their absolute discretion think fit without being liable for loss and **TO HOLD** the net proceeds of such sale calling in and conversion and all unsold property and my ready money **UPON TRUST** to divide the same into [      ] equal shares and hold the same:
*Continue as precedent I clause 3(e) with consequential amendments.*

## VARIATION 3

*If the testator has an estate that is below the threshold for inheritance tax, and in particular if it is too small to justify creating two separate trust funds, the following simpler precedent may be more appropriate.*

1. *as precedent I*
2. *as precedent I*
3. *as precedent I - changing "my Trust Fund" to "the Family Fund"*

4. (i)   *as clause 5(i) of precedent I*
   (ii)  *as clause 5(ii) of precedent I - concluding*
WHOM FAILING as to both the income and capital thereof for such one or more of the charitable beneficiaries defined below in such shares as my Trustees being at least two in number may in writing appoint - *or as desired*
   (iii) *as clause 5(iii) of precedent I including the charitable beneficiaries*
   (iii) *as clause 6(iii) of precedent I*

*Continue as precedent I from clause 7 with consequential amendments, and omitting some of the powers so as to shorten the Will.*

## VARIATION 4

### MENCAP Visitors Service

*Where the testator wishes to take advantage of the MENCAP Trustee Visitor Service a legacy in the following form will be appropriate in respect of each child involved:*

**I GIVE** to the MENCAP Visitors Service of the Royal Society for Mentally Handicapped Children and Adults of 123 Golden Lane London EC1Y 0RT the sum of Four thousand two hundred and fifty pounds (£4,250) OR such sum as shall at the date of my death equal the amount that shall at that time be currently required by the Society from any person wishing to make a cash donation to join the Service, whichever sum shall be the higher.

*It is not sufficient simply to leave the legacy, as the Service wishes to register the child in advance. A form is supplied for completion and return when the Will is executed. This states:*

**Please note** that I/We . . . . . . . . . . . . . . . . . of . . . . . . . . . . . . . . . . . have by a Will/Wills dated . . . . . . . . . . 19 . . bequeathed to the MENCAP Visitors Service of the Royal Society for Mentally Handicapped Children and Adults of 123 Golden Lane London EC1Y 0RT the sum of Four thousand two hundred and fifty pounds OR such sum as shall at the date of my/our death(s) equal the amount that shall at that time be currently required by the Society from any person wishing to make a cash donation to join the Service, whichever sum shall be the higher.
The Executors of my/our Will(s) are . . . . . . . . of . . . . . . . . . . . . and
. . . . . . . . . . . . . . . .of . . . . . . . . . . . . . . . . . . . . . . and they have been instructed to notify you in the event of my/our demise.

**Please send this form to:**  The Administrative Secretary
                MENCAP Visitors Service, MENCAP National Centre
                123 Golden Lane, LONDON EC1Y 0RT

VARIATION 5

*If the convenience of the Charities Aid Foundation is preferred to
the setting up of a private charitable trust the following clause may
be substituted. It is still necessary to define "charitable
beneficiaries" if the expression is used elsewhere.*

6. (i) **THE CHARITABLE FUND** shall not be invested but shall be paid
by my Trustees to the Charities Aid Foundation to be held by the Trustees of the
Foundation upon trust under the name of the . . . . . MENTAL HANDICAP
TRUST to the intent that the Fund shall be distributed for charitable purposes on
the terms of my Letter of Intent dated the . . . . day of . . . . 19 . .

(ii) **CHARITABLE BENEFICIARIES** as used in this Will means any
charitable society or organisation whether local or national whose objects or
principal objects appear to my Trustees to be to promote the accommodation care
welfare treatment education employment or advancement or to be otherwise for
the benefit of mentally [*and/or physically* ] disabled persons AND it is my wish
(without imposing any binding obligation) that my Trustees in exercising their
discretion between such charitable beneficiaries have in mind any services or
benefits given by them to *my son John* during his lifetime

## PRECEDENT II

The above precedents all assume that the handicapped beneficiary
is likely to be dependent upon substantial means-tested benefits or
funding AND that the testator is prepared to contemplate financial
provision which is entirely dependent upon the trustees exercising
their discretionary powers. If either of these conditions does not
apply it may be appropriate to leave the beneficiary a protected
life interest instead of (or as well as) the discretionary trust - the
Personal Fund. The charitable trust is still an option, so for a large
estate there could be three separate trust funds, namely the
Personal Fund, the Family Fund and the Charitable Fund.
Any of the above precedents may be adapted in this way by
substituting the Personal Fund for one or more of the other Funds
as in the following example. If the power to accumulate income is
included it may prevent this being an interest in possession trust,
and that is a disadvantage that may not be desired.

*Parents with a married daughter (Clare) and mildly mentally
handicapped adult son (Paul) living with them. The daughter will
ultimately take over responsibility for the son who, if provided
with a home near to her, will be able to live independently though
never be able to handle his own financial affairs. The Income
Support top-up to non-means-tested benefit will be small so a
private income from a Trust Fund would be more beneficial to
Paul and give him a greater degree of independence, especially if
the fund were also able to provide a home. A protected life
interest is appropriate and a charitable trust is unlikely to be
favoured, though the parents may decide to leave a greater share
to their daughter in the expectation that she will put this to good
use in supporting her handicapped brother.*

1. *as precedent I*
2. *as precedent I*

3. **IN THE EVENT** of my said wife not inheriting under the preceding provision **I WILL AND DECLARE** as follows:

(a) **I APPOINT** *my daughter Clare* and - *continue as precedent 1*

(b) **I APPOINT** *my daughter Clare* to be guardian of *my son Paul* to the extent permitted by law

(c) *as precedent I*

(d) **I GIVE** all my remaining furnishings personal and household effects to *my daughter Clare* beneficially free of tax with the wish (but without imposing any binding obligation) that *she* transfer or make available to *my son Paul* any items that *he* may reasonably require

(e) *as precedent I*

**AS TO** [*one*] such share(s) for *my daughter Clare* absolutely

**AND AS TO** the remaining [*one*] such share(s) if *my son Paul* survives me upon trust to invest the same at their discretion in their joint names in any investments hereby authorised with power to vary such investments from time to time and stand possessed thereof upon the trusts hereinafter declared concerning the Personal Fund

(f) **IF** *my daughter Clare* dies before attaining a vested interest in my Estate (whether or not in my lifetime) leaving a child or children living at my death or born thereafter who attain their legal majority such child or children shall take and if more than one equally between them the share(s) that *she* would have taken had *she* survived me

(g) **IF** *my son Paul* dies before me leaving a child or children living at my death who attain their legal majority such child or children shall take and if more than one equally between them the share(s) that would have been retained on trust if *my son Paul* had survived me

(h) **IF** the trusts of either [any] of these shares fail such share(s) shall accrue [equally] to and be held upon the trusts of the remaining share(s) the trusts whereof shall not have failed

(i) **IF** the trusts of both [all] these shares fail my Trustees shall hold my Estate - *as desired*

4. (i) **THE PERSONAL FUND** shall be held by my Trustees **UPON TRUST** to pay the income thereof to *my son Paul* during *his* life unless or until some act or event shall have happened or shall happen whereby the said income or any part thereof if belonging absolutely to *him* would become vested in or charged in favour of some other person and **IN THE EVENT** of the failure or determination during *his* life of such trust my Trustees shall during the remainder of *his* life pay or apply the income thereof to or for or towards the personal support maintenance and education or otherwise for the benefit of the family beneficiaries defined below or such one or more to the exclusion of the others or other of them in such manner and if more than one in such shares as my Trustees being at least two in number from time to time in their absolute discretion think fit WITH POWER - *continue as clause 5(i) of precedent 1*

(ii) *as clause 5(ii) of precedent 1*

(iii) *as clause 5(iii) of precedent 1 but omitting "charitable beneficiaries"*

*continue as precedent 1 from clause 7 with consequential amendments and in particular amending all references to "my Trust Fund" and "the Family Fund" to "the Personal Fund" and deleting all references to charitable beneficiaries and the powers relating to charities.*

# PRECEDENT III

*We now move up a generation and consider the situation of an elderly widow with moderate estate and 2 married sons (one of whom appears in Precedent I) each with 3 children. She wishes to leave her estate to her issue in the usual manner but a settlement has not been created for her handicapped grandchild so she must create her own trust funds on somewhat similar lines to that of her son in case he dies before her.*

1.  *as precedent I*

2.  **I APPOINT** my sons [*names* ] (hereinafter called "my Trustees" which expression includes the trustees or trustee for the time being hereof) to be the executors and trustees of this my Will but if either of them die in my lifetime or are unable or unwilling to act then **I APPOINT** [*name/address* ] in his place

3.  *as clause 3(c) of precedent I - deal with furnishings etc. in this provision*

4.  **I GIVE** all the real and personal property whatsoever and wheresoever to which I may be entitled or over which I have any disposing power at the time of my death after payment of my just debts funeral and testamentary expenses and any legacies given by this my Will or any Codicil thereto to my Trustees **UPON TRUST** to sell call in and convert into money all such parts thereof as shall not consist of money at my death with power to postpone such sale calling in and conversion for so long as they shall in their absolute discretion think fit without being liable for loss and **TO HOLD** the net proceeds of such sale calling in and conversion and all unsold property and my ready money for my said son [*name* ] and my said son [*name* ] in equal shares absolutely **PROVIDED THAT** if either of my said sons die before me leaving a child or children living at my death or born thereafter who attain their legal majority such child or children shall take and if more than one equally between them the share that such deceased son of mine would have taken had he survived

5.  **I DECLARE THAT** any monies due to my grand*son John* shall not be paid to him but shall be held by my Trustees **UPON TRUST** to divide the same into [two equal shares - *or as appropriate*] and to invest the same at their discretion in their joint names in any investments hereby authorised with power to vary such investments from time to time and stand possessed of [*one*] such share(s) upon the trusts declared below concerning the Family Fund *or the Personal Fund* and [*the other such share*] upon the trusts declared below concerning the Charitable Fund - *or relying solely on the Family Fund or the Personal Fund*

> *continue as precedent I from clause 5 with consequential amendments and in particular referring to grandson instead of son.*

## PRECEDENT IV

Where it is desired to create a lifetime Settlement for the benefit of a mentally handicapped child along the lines of the trusts outlined in the above Will precedents the following precedent may be useful. Variations similar to those suggested for Wills may be considered, and for maximum flexibility charities may be included in the potential beneficiaries. A separate charitable Settlement would be created if desired, or the facilities provided by the Charities Aid Foundation may be appropriate.

**THIS SETTLEMENT** is made the          day of          199  **BETWEEN** *David Smith* of                    (hereinafter called "the Settlor") of the one part and          of          and          of          (hereinafter called "the Trustees" which expression shall include the trustees or trustee for the time being hereof) of the other part

**WHEREAS** the Settlor desires to provide for *his* family and in particular *his* son *John Smith* (hereinafter referred to as *John*) and to that intent has paid to the Trustees the sum of One pound and contemplates paying or transferring to them further monies or assets to be held upon the trusts set out in this Deed

**NOW THIS DEED WITNESSETH** as follows:

1.  **IN THIS DEED** the following expressions have these meanings:
    (a)  **"the Trust Fund"** means the said sum of One hundred pounds and all further sums of money investments and property which may be paid or transferred to the Trustees to be held upon the trusts of this deed and any accumulations of income
    (b)  **"the Trust Period"** means the lifetime of John
    (c)  **"Family Beneficiaries"** means the children and remoter issue of the Settlor [and *named persons*] [and the spouses widows or widowers (whether or not remarried) of any such persons] - *or as appropriate*
    (d)  **"Charitable Beneficiaries"** means any charitable society or organisation whether local or national whose objects or principal objects appear to the Trustees to be to promote the accommodation care welfare treatment education employment or advancement or to be otherwise for the benefit of mentally [*and/or physically* ] disabled persons
    (e)  **"the Beneficiaries"** includes both Family Beneficiaries and Charitable Beneficiaries

2.  **THE TRUSTEES** shall invest the Trust Fund at their discretion in their joint names in any investments hereby authorised with power to vary such investments from time to time and hold the same upon the following trusts

3.  (i)  **THE TRUST FUND** shall be held by the Trustees UPON TRUST during the Trust Period to pay or apply the income thereof to or for or towards the benefit of any one or more to the exclusion of the others of the Beneficiaries in such manner and if more than one in such shares as the Trustees being at least two in number from time to time in their absolute discretion think fit
    (ii)  **DURING** the period of twenty-one years from the death of the Settlor the Trustees may in their absolute discretion accumulate all or any part of the income by investing it and its resulting income in any authorised investments as an addition to the capital of the Trust Fund but also thereafter during that period may apply the whole or any part of the accumulated income as if it were income arising in the then current year
    (iii)  **AT** the end of the Trust Period the Trustees shall hold the income and capital of the Trust Fund or the remainder thereof UPON TRUST to pay such funeral expenses (including the cost of a memorial) as they consider appropriate for *John* and [in their discretion to waive repayment of any loan that they may have made to any of the Charitable Beneficiaries and] subject thereto UPON TRUST for such of the children or remoter issue of the Settlor as are then living and if more than one in equal shares per stirpes so that no such issue shall take whose parent is alive and so capable of taking [*or as appropriate*] WHOM FAILING for such one or more Charitable Beneficiaries and in such shares as the Trustees being at least two in number in writing appoint
    (iv)  **IN** exercising their discretion between the Beneficiaries the Trustees may (but are not under any binding obligation to) have regard to the needs (if any) of *John* from time to time and any services or benefits given to him during his lifetime

4.  **THE TRUSTEES** being at least two in number have the following powers in regard to the Trust Fund in addition to those under the general law
    (a)  to invest the same in or upon the acquisition or security of any property of whatsoever nature and wheresoever situate (including any house or flat or chattel as a residence for or for the use of any of the Beneficiaries) to the intent that they have the same full and unrestricted power of investment in all respects as if they were absolutely entitled thereto beneficially and may exercise their powers of investment without seeking to balance the interests of beneficiaries

entitled to capital and income respectively
    (b)   *as clause 8(b) of precedent I with modifications*
    (c)   to invest in chattels for the use of any one or more of the Beneficiaries notwithstanding that the value of the Trust Fund may thereby become depleted and to permit any of the Beneficiaries to have the use and enjoyment of any chattel forming part of the Trust Fund in such manner and subject to such conditions (if any) as the Trustees consider reasonable and without being liable to account for any consequential loss
    (d)   *as clause 8(a) of precedent I with modifications*
    (e)   *as clause 8(e) etc.*
    (f)   *as clause 8(f) etc.*
    (g)   *as clause 8(g) etc.*
    (h)   *as clause 8(h) etc.*
    (i)   *as clause 8(i) etc.*

5.  **THE TRUSTEES** may benefit from the following further provisions:
    (a)   *as clause 9(a) of precedent I with modifications*
    (b)   *as clause 7(c) etc.*
    (k)   *as clause 8(k) etc*
    (c)   *as clause 7(f) etc.*
    (d)   *as clause 9(b) etc.*
    (e)   *as clause 9(c) etc.*
    (f)   *as clause 8(l) etc.*
    (g)   *as clause 9(d) etc.*
    (h)   *as clause 9(e) etc.*
    (i)   *as clause 9(f) etc*
    (j)   *as clause 8(m) etc.*
    (k)   The power of appointing new trustees of this settlement shall be vested in the Settlor during *his* lifetime and after *his* death in his wife Provided that neither the Settlor nor his wife may be appointed a trustee

6.  **IT IS HEREBY CERTIFIED** that this instrument falls within Category L in the Schedule to the Stamp Duty (Exempt Instruments) Regulations 1987

7.  **THIS SETTLEMENT** is irrevocable and none of the powers or discretions hereby or by law conferred upon the Trustees shall at any time be exercisable in any manner which might benefit the Settlor or any wife for the time being of the Settlor and no part of the capital or income of the Trust Fund shall at any time be lent or paid to or applied for the benefit of the Settlor or any wife for the time being of the Settlor.
**IN WITNESS** *etc* .

## PRECEDENT VI - LETTERS

*Suitable for both England and Scotland*

### Dependent beneficiary

Letter to be signed by a parent in the case of trusts by Will for the benefit of a dependent mentally handicapped child. This may be adapted in the case of a lifetime Settlement, or for separate family and charitable trust funds.

*Address*
*Date*

To the Trustees of my Will dated .....

In my Will I have created a discretionary [and charitable] Trust in respect of the share of my estate that I might otherwise have left to *my son* ..... . This is because *my son* will never be able to look after money and property *himself* and because of the implications of means-testing upon any financial entitlement *he* has. I am conscious that by reason of *his* limited mental abilities [and physical disabilities] he will throughout *his* life be dependent upon state benefits and local authority provision, and may also be supported or assisted by some charitable organisations. I do not have the means to enable *him* to be independent for the rest of *his* life, but am anxious to make the best long-term provision that I can for *him* .

It is my wish (but without imposing any binding obligation upon you) that you use your discretionary powers in regard to the Trust to promote the support that *my son* needs from time to time and to supplement the provision that is otherwise available to him. In so far as other persons provide personal care for *my son* I would wish them to receive practical support from the Trust so far as possible, and I hope that you will also be able to give financial assistance to any charitable organisations that provide services for *him*. You may also be able to improve *his* environment and the standards of amenity that he enjoys.

For these reasons I have made the Trust as flexible as I can and in seeking to fulfil my objectives I encourage you to be imaginative in the use of your powers. Subject to these primary objectives you may benefit [my wider family]. After the death of *my son* any monies remaining are to pass to my wider family as stipulated [*or if appropriate* I shall be content for any remaining money to be paid to charities concerned with the needs of persons such as my *son*, and especially those which have helped *him*.]

*Signature of Testator*

## Self-reliant beneficiary

Letter to be signed by a parent in the case of trusts by Will for the benefit of a potentially self-reliant mentally handicapped child.

*Address*
*Date*

To the Trustees under my Will dated .....

In my Will I have left the share of my estate that I might otherwise have left to *my son* .... [upon protective trusts for his benefit] [in a trust under which he is to enjoy an alimentary liferent] because *he* is limited in *his* ability to look after money and property and may become dependent at some stage in his life upon means-tested state benefits or local authority provision. I wish *him* to be financially independent for as much of *his* life as proves possible, and am anxious to make the best long-term provision that I can for *him* , but believe this can only be achieved by denying him access to capital or assets.

It is my wish (but without imposing any binding obligation upon you) that you use your discretionary powers in regard to the Trust Fund to promote the welfare and independence of *my son* and to supplement the provision that is otherwise available to him. In so far as other persons provide personal care for *my son* I would wish them to receive practical support from the Trust so far as possible [and I hope that you will also be able to give financial assistance to any charitable organisations that provide services for *him*.] You may also be able to improve *his* environment and the standards of amenity that he enjoys.

For these reasons I have given you certain powers and in seeking to fulfil my objectives I encourage you to be imaginative in the use of these powers. Subject to these primary objectives you may benefit [my wider family]. After the death of *my son* any monies remaining are to pass to my family as stipulated [*or if appropriate* I shall be content for any remaining money to be paid to charities concerned with the needs of persons such as my *son*, and especially those which have helped *him*.]

*Signature of Testator*

## CAF  Special  Deposit  Trust

Dear Sir,
                    SPECIAL DEPOSIT TRUST

We wish to set on record our intentions about the cheque for £1,000 enclosed herewith as a gift to Charities Aid Foundation, together with any further funds which we or other persons may from time to time transfer on the same terms. These funds, together with the income arising thereon, are to be held by the Trustees of the Foundation upon trust under the name of the . . . . . . MENTAL HANDICAP TRUST to the intent that they shall be distributed for charitable purposes in such proportions as may from time to time be determined by ourselves jointly or the survivor of us during our respective lifetimes, and thereafter our son . . . . . and our daughter . . . . . jointly or the survivor of them, and following the death of such survivor such persons as he or she may appoint, or failing such determination, as the Trustees for the time being of the Foundation may decide.

We may from time to time add to this Deposit Trust and it will terminate when all funds have been distributed, or when our [*handicapped son* ....] dies after which any funds remaining undistributed shall be distributed to such charities as may be decided by the persons nominated above or failing that to the Foundation Fund of the Charities Aid Foundation. It is our wish that any sums distributed shall only be distributed to charities concerned with the care or welfare of persons with a mental handicap, and it is our intention that any capital sums deposited will remain undistributed for not less than 12 months.

We wish the capital of this trust to be invested in CAF Common Investment Funds, in a high income fund or in such other investments as the Trustees may select. However, we contemplate that interest free loans may be made to suitable charities at the request of the person or persons nominated above. We understand that each year a sum equivalent to 1% of the capital value of the fund (minimum £100) may be donated to the Foundation and that this sum should cover any obligations of the Foundation to contribute to its Founder, the National Council for Voluntary Organisations (NCVO). The donation to the Foundation may be deducted at the discretion of the Trustees at such times and in such manner as they deem appropriate.

Your usual conditions (as set out in page 18 of your booklet "Personal Charitable Trusts" 1988 edition) shall apply, except Appendix I condition 1 and Appendix III, as regards payments to the NCVO.

We shall be grateful if you will sign the duplicate copy of this letter and return it to us in acknowledgement of your acceptance of this Trust.

Yours faithfully,

# APPENDIX IIIB    WILLS AND SETTLEMENTS (Scotland)

**NOTE:** We refer to Styles here, and to Precedents in Appendix IIIA, to reflect the customary terminology of Scotland and England respectively, and to differentiate between them.

## STYLE I

*See the warning at the beginning of Appendix IIIA. Advisers must carefully assess the circumstances, needs and wishes of each family, and to meet them must select and adapt when referring to styles. It is essential to read these styles in conjunction with Chapter 9. The Will below makes similar provision for the same family as Precedent I (England), except that:*

*(a) the family is now in Scotland,*

*(b) the testator wishes to appoint separate executors and trustees (which may be appropriate, for example, if a corporate trustee service is to be one of the trustees; see Style II for a style where executors and trustees are to be the same persons), and*

*(c) for simplicity, Jane and Jill are assumed to be adults, but if they are not then appropriate accumulation and maintenance provisions may be inserted for them. (see e.g. Halliday "Conveyancing Law and Practice in Scotland" para 47.80).*

*This style seeks to protect state funding rather than achieve Inheritance Tax or Capital Gains Tax advantages, and to protect state funding affords relatively weaker protection against a possible legal rights claim (see Style IV (Scotland)); provides for both a Family Fund and a Charitable Fund; and opts for a "wait and see" provision (which can be omitted by deleting references to "my Trust Fund" and moving directly into the "Family Fund" and the "Charitable Fund").*

I        , residing at                for the settlement of the succession to my means and estate on my death hereby provide as follows:

1. **(In the First Place)** In the event of my wife        surviving the period of thirty days from the date of my death, I leave and bequeath to her the whole means and estate, heritable and moveable, real and personal, of whatever kind and wherever situate that may belong to me at my death or over which I may then have power of appointment or disposal; And I nominate and appoint my said wife to be my sole executrix;

2. **(In the Second Place)** In the event of my said wife predeceasing me or failing to survive me by thirty days as aforesaid, I provide as follows:

2.1 **(FIRST)** *[specific bequests]*

2.2 **(SECOND)** *[pecuniary legacies]*

2.3 **(THIRD)** I direct my executors to divide the residue of my said whole means and estate into three equal shares and to pay and convey said shares as follows, namely

2.3.1 (One) one such share to *my daughter Jane*, whom failing leaving issue who survive me to such issue equally between or among them per stirpes if more than one, or whom failing without issue to my other residuary beneficiaries (including my Trust Fund) in proportion to their interests in residue,

2.3.2 (Two) one such share to *my daughter Jill*, whom failing leaving issue who survive me to such issue equally between or among them per stirpes if more than one, or whom failing without issue to my other residuary beneficiaries (including my Trust Fund) in proportion to their interests in residue, and

2.3.3 (Three) if *my son John* survives me, the remaining such share (hereinafter called **"my Trust Fund"**) to the Trustees nominated in terms of the provisions In the Third Place hereof to be held and administered by them in accordance with said provisions, or if *my son John* predeceases me leaving issue who survive me said remaining share to such issue equally between or among them per stirpes if more than one, or if *my son John* predeceases me without leaving issue who survive me to my other residuary beneficiaries in proportion to their interests in residue;

2.4 **(FOURTH)** Should I be survived neither by children nor by issue of children I direct my executors to pay and convey the entire residue of my said whole means and estate to the Trustees nominated in terms of the provisions In the Third Place hereof to be held and administered by them entirely in accordance with the provisions thereof in respect of the Charitable Fund as set forth in provision In the Third Place FOURTH - *or as appropriate*; and

2.5 **(FIFTH)** I nominate and appoint *[names and designations]* and the acceptors and acceptor, survivors and survivor of them to be my sole executors and executor;

3. **(In the Third Place)** I direct my executors to pay and assign my Trust Fund to [*names and designations of trustees*] and to such other person or persons, body or bodies, as may hereafter be appointed or assumed and to the survivors and survivor of them as my trustees for the purposes aftermentioned (the major number from time to time resident in the United Kingdom being a quorum and the power to act of any Trustee who is an individual being suspended during absence from the United Kingdom) and to the assignees of my Trustees, but these provisions In the Third Place hereof are granted in trust for the following purposes, namely,

3.1 **(FIRST)** For payment of the expenses of this Trust [including without prejudice to that generality the current customary remuneration from time to time charged by [said ..... Trustee Service Limited or] any [other similar] [trustee] service employed by my Trustees];

3.2 **(SECOND)** Within twenty-three months from the date of my death my Trustees may by formal Deed of Appointment appoint my Trust Fund between the Family Fund and the Charitable Fund hereinafter provided for in such proportions as my Trustees in their absolute discretion may think fit [provided that they shall appoint at least *[one-half]* to the Family Fund], and in default of such appointment my Trust Fund shall at the expiration of such period be deemed to have been appointed to the Family Fund and the Charitable Fund equally;

3.3 **(THIRD)**

3.3.1 (One) I direct my Trustees during the lifetime of *my son John* to pay or apply the income of the Family Fund to or for or towards the personal support, maintenance and education or otherwise for the benefit of the family beneficiaries defined below or such one or more of them to the exclusion of the others or other in such manner and, if more than one, in such shares as my Trustees shall from time to time in their absolute discretion think fit, with power to my Trustees during the period of twenty one years immediately following my death in their absolute discretion to accumulate with capital the whole or any part of said income but also thereafter during that period to apply the whole or any part of the accumulated income as if it were income arising in the then current year AND I REQUEST my Trustees in exercising their discretion to have regard to the needs (if any) of *my son John*;

3.3.2 (Two) Upon the death of *my son John* or the failure or termination for any other cause whatever of the foregoing provision THIRD (One) hereof, I direct my Trustees (a) if and to the extent that they deem it appropriate to do so, to meet

from the Family Fund the funeral expenses (including the cost of a memorial) of
and for *my son John* and such other costs, expenses, outlays, gratuities and
others in any way arising from his death as my Trustees may in their absolute
discretion consider appropriate, and (b) to apply, pay or convey the balance of
the Family Fund (with any accumulated income in accordance with the foregoing
provisions) to any issue of *my son John* then surviving, equally between or
among them per stirpes if more than one, WHOM FAILING to *my daughter
Jane* and *my daughter Jill* equally between them, provided that they then survive,
or to the survivor of them, declaring however that if either or both of them shall
be then deceased leaving issue who survive, such issue shall take, equally
between or among them per stirpes if more than one, the share to which each
such daughter would have been entitled had she then survived WHOM
FAILING to the Charitable Fund;

3.3.3 (Three) "Family beneficiaries" means my children and remoter issue [and
my nieces and nephews] [and *named persons*] [and the spouses, widows or
widowers (whether or not remarried) of any such persons] [and the charitable
beneficiaries defined below] [*or as appropriate*] AND I record (without imposing
any obligation upon my Trustees) that it is my wish that my Trustees in
exercising their discretion among and between the family beneficiaries shall have
in mind any services or benefits given by them to *my son John* at any time;

3.4 **(FOURTH)**

3.4.1 (One) I direct my Trustees to apply, pay or convey the income of the
Charitable Fund or such proportion or proportions thereof or such part or parts
of the capital thereof as my Trustees shall from time to time in their sole
discretion determine by any means (including the making of loans with or
without security and with or without interest) to such one or more of the
charitable beneficiaries defined below as my Trustees may from time to time
determine;

3.4.2 (Two) I authorise my Trustees in their own absolute discretion to
accumulate with the capital of the Charitable Fund during the period of twenty
one years immediately following my death the whole or any part or parts of the
income of the Charitable Fund;

3.4.3 (Three) "Charitable beneficiaries" means any charitable society or
organisation whether local or national whose objects or principal objects appear
to my Trustees to be to promote the accommodation, care, welfare, treatment,
education, employment or advancement or to be otherwise for the benefit of
mentally [*and/or physically*] disabled persons AND I record (without imposing
any obligation upon my Trustees) that it is my wish that my Trustees in
exercising their discretion among and between the charitable beneficiaries shall
have in mind any services or benefits given by them to *my son John* during his
lifetime;

3.5 **(FIFTH)** My Trustees shall have the following further powers exercisable
in their absolute discretion at any time and from time to time in the administration
of my Trust Fund and the Family Fund

[*Take in all, or such as may be appropriate, of the provisions of provision 8. of
Precedent I (England), adapting as follows:*]

    (b)  whether freehold or leasehold - whether owned or leased

    (d)  chattels - moveable items of any kind whatsoever

[*See also **Further provisions** in Style IV*]

3.6 **(SIXTH)** [*Standard investment powers, power to professional trustees to
charge for services, provisions as to non-liability of trustees for losses, power to
act in matters in which they have an interest, entitlement of trustees to fullest
privileges and immunities of gratuitous trustees (including power to resign
office) etc; and include the following*]

    to accept, hold and apply as part of my Trust Fund or the Family Fund or
the Charitable Fund such additional monies, investments, property or other
estate as may be paid, conveyed or transferred into each or any such Fund by
any person either by lifetime gift or by testamentary disposition;  And

4.  **(In the Fourth Place)** [*Funeral directions, revocation of previous Wills,
etc*] : **IN WITNESS WHEREOF**

# VARIATION 1

*The same circumstances as Variation I (England) (p.694).*

*as before until*
2.3 **(THIRD)** I direct my executors to divide the residue of my said whole means and estate into as many shares as I have children who survive me and have predeceased leaving issue who survive me and to pay and convey said shares as follows, namely
2.3.1 (One) one such share to each of my children who survive me other than *my son James,*
2.3.2 (Two) if *my son James* survives me, one such share (hereinafter called **"my Trust Fund"**) to the Trustees nominated in terms of the provisions In the Third Place hereof to be held and administered by them in accordance with said provisions, and
2.3.3 (Three) one such share to the issue of any of my children who may have predeceased me, equally between or among them per stirpes if more than one;
2.4 *et seq.*

*continue as before with consequential amendments*

# VARIATION 2

*Where there will be no surviving spouse.*

I              , residing at                    for the settlement of the succession to my means and estate on my death hereby provide as follows:

**(In the First Place)**
**(FIRST)** *as 2.1*
**(SECOND)** *as 2.2*
**(THIRD)** I direct my executors to divide the residue of the whole means and estate, heritable and moveable, real and personal, of whatever kind and wherever situate that may belong to me at my death or over which I may then have power of appointment or disposal into three equal shares and to pay and convey said shares as follows, namely

*thereafter as remainder of Style I from 2.3.1, but amend references to "In the Third Place" to "In the Second Place", and amend references to "In the Fourth Place" to "In the Third Place".*

# VARIATION 3

*The same circumstances as Precedent I Variation 3 (England) (p.695)*

1. *as Style I*
2. *as Style I, changing "my Trust Fund" to "the Family Fund" and omitting reference to "the Charitable Fund" in 2.4*
3. *as Style I, except*
*omit 3.2*
**(SECOND)** *as 3.3, omitting references to "the Charitable Fund" and the charitable beneficiaries*
*omit 3.4*
**(THIRD)** *as 3.5 omitting references to "my Trust Fund"*
**(FOURTH)** *as 3.6*
4. *as Style I*

# STYLE II

*See note at beginning of Precedent II (England), reading "alimentary liferent" for "protected life interest". This style makes similar provision for the same family as in that Precedent, and appoints the same persons to be both executors and trustees.*

1    *as in Style I*

2    **(In the Second Place)** In the event of my said wife predeceasing me or failing to survive me by thirty days as aforesaid, I hereby assign and dispone to [*names and designations of trustees*] and to such other person or persons as may hereafter be appointed or assumed and to the survivors and survivor of them as my Trustees for the purposes aftermentioned (the major number from time to time resident in the United Kingdom being a quorum and the power to act of any trustee being suspended during absence from the United Kingdom) and to the assignees of my Trustees my said whole means and estate; and I nominate and appoint my Trustees and their quorum foresaid to be my executors; but these provisions In the Second Place hereof are granted in trust for the following purposes, namely:
2.1  **(FIRST)** For payment of my debts, sickbed and funeral
       expenses and the expenses of this Trust;
2.2  **(SECOND)** [*specific bequests*]
2.3  **(THIRD)** [*pecuniary legacies*]
2.4  **(FOURTH)** I direct my Trustees to divide the residue of my said whole means and estate into two equal shares and to apply said shares as follows, namely
2.4.1 (One) to pay and convey one such share to *my daughter Clare*, whom failing leaving issue who survive me to such issue equally between or among them per stirpes if more than one, or whom failing without issue to be applied in the same manner as the other one-half share in terms of provision Two next following, and
2.4.2 (Two) if *my son Paul* survives me, to hold, administer and apply the other such share as **"the Personal Fund"** in accordance with the provisions of purpose Sixth below, or if *my son Paul* predeceases me leaving issue who survive me to pay and apply said other share to such issue equally between or among them per stirpes if more than one, or whom failing to be applied in the same manner as the other one- half share in terms of provision One immediately preceding;
2.5  **(FIFTH)** Should I be survived neither by children nor by issue of children - *as desired*
2.6  **(SIXTH)** I direct my Trustees to pay or apply the annual income of the Personal Fund for behoof of *my son Paul* for so long as he shall survive, and that as a strictly alimentary provision not capable of anticipation nor affectable by his debts or deeds [*insert usual provisions for alimentary liferent, taking in powers referred to in para. 3.5 of Style I as appropriate*]
2.7  **(SEVENTH)** Upon the failure or termination for any cause whatever of the foregoing liferent provision in favour of my said son I direct my Trustees - *as desired*

*further standard provisions as per 3.6 and 4 of Style I*

# STYLE III

*This style is designed to apply to the same circumstances as Precedent III (England). Grandmother leaves the residue of her estate to her sons, whom failing to their issue, but in the provision in favour of issue of her sons include*

subject to the terms of provision xxx hereof in respect of any share of residue payable to *my grandson John*
*and as regards John proceed as follows*
**(XXX)** I declare that any share of residue due to *my grandson John* in accordance with the foregoing provisions shall not be paid to him, but that my Trustees shall divide the same into [two equal shares - *or as appropriate*] to be held, administered and applied by my Trustees as the Family Fund [*or the Personal Fund*] in accordance with the provisions of purpose yyy hereof and as

the Charitable Fund in accordance with the provisions of purpose zzz hereof [*or as desired*]

*continue as from 3.3 of Style I, or substitute Personal Fund provisions of Style II, as desired.*

# STYLE IV

*The following trust purpose assumes that most of John's needs will be met from State or other funding, and that only limited additional provision is likely to be required for his comfort and benefit. It provides for a relatively modest trust fund, but with an emphasis on ensuring that the desired scheme is unlikely to be disrupted by a legal rights claim. This entails a closer identification of the trust fund with John. The protection against means-testing is correspondingly weaker, but should prove to be sufficient in relation to current means-testing regimes.*

[*Bequest of whole estate to wife if she survives by thirty days; alternative conveyance to trustees with standard trust provisions*]
　　(-----) I direct my Trustees to set aside a fund, hereinafter called *"John's Fund"*, of an amount determined as follows, namely (One) if I shall have survived my said wife by more than thirty days, the amount set aside to establish and initially to comprise *John's Fund* shall be the greater of (i) an amount equal to the legal rights entitlement of *my son John* in my estate, together with an amount equal to his legal rights entitlement (insofar as not paid) in the estate of my said wife and together with (in respect of both said entitlements) an amount equal to the interest which would have been payable thereon had such entitlements been paid out on the date of establishment of *John's Fund* or (ii) the sum of [*insert amount*] pounds, or (Two) if my said wife and I should die within thirty days of each other, the amount set aside to establish and initially to comprise *John's Fund* shall be the larger of (i) an amount equal to the legal rights entitlement of *my said son* in my estate with the interest which would have been payable thereon had such entitlement been paid out on the date of establishment of *John's Fund* or (ii) the sum of [*one-half of amount inserted above*] pounds; And I provide with regard to *John's Fund* as follows:
　　**(One)** Subject to the following provisions as to accumulation or allocation of surplus income, I direct my Trustees to pay or apply the annual income of *John's Fund* for behoof of *my said son*, subject always to the declaration that the prior and principal purpose of this provision in favour of *my said son* shall be to make additional provision for his comfort, needs and benefit over and above such provision as may otherwise be made for him (whether by way of state, local authority or other benefits or facilities, or otherwise), it being specifically declared for the avoidance of doubt that none of said income shall be available or applied in such manner as might reduce any such other benefits or facilities, and I specifically direct and authorise my Trustees that their investment policy shall from time to time be determined with reasonable regard to *my said son's* likely needs, with a view to avoiding undue over provision or under provision of income, and I declare that the following provisions of this purpose [-----] shall be without prejudice to the generality of this provision One;
　　**(Two)** *insert appropriate powers as in 3.5 of Style I*

*Further provisions: the following may be included or adapted as appropriate. Provision Six has been found to be useful in practice, despite doubts as to enforceability in many cases.*

　　**(Three)** Any income not paid or applied for behoof of *my said son* (herein called "surplus income") shall be accumulated with capital during the maximum period for which such accumulation is permitted by law;
　　**(Four)** During the remaining period of *my son's* lifetime after income may no longer be accumulated as aforesaid my Trustees shall have power in their own absolute discretion to pay any surplus income to [*specify beneficiaries*] [subject to the limitation that *my said son* shall be entitled to not less than one-

half of the income arising from *John's Fund*];

(**Five**) I provide that my Trustees shall not be obliged to apportion any income received or accrued according to the period to which it relates, but may treat as income all income actually received during the currency of said provision in favour of *my son John*, but I further provide that if upon the death of *my said son* any income shall remain in the hands of my Trustees, having been received by them but not paid or applied as aforesaid, the amount thereof shall (notwithstanding the foregoing provisions) then be treated as capital and dealt with in accordance with the provisions of purpose [-----] hereof, declaring however that this provision regarding income held by my Trustees at termination of said provision in favour of *my son John* shall not apply to the extent that such application would constitute a contravention of any prohibition against accumulations, and I declare that the decision of my Trustees as to what constitutes income or capital shall be binding on all concerned;

(**Six**) The foregoing provision in favour of *my said son* is granted subject to the condition that *my said son* shall be deemed to have authorised the persons who may from time to time be my Trustees (as a separate function from the performance of their duties as Trustees) to perform the following functions for *him* and on *his* behalf, namely, (i) to claim, receive, hold and administer any repayment of tax deducted at source or by my said Trustees in respect of income of or arising from this Trust and (ii) to administer on *his* behalf any income belonging to *him* in terms of the foregoing provisions and not expended by my Trustees for *his* behoof, and *he* shall be held bound to execute such mandates, authorities or other documents as may be required to give effect to the foregoing provisions;

**AND** I provide and declare that the provisions hereof in favour of *my said son* are intended and designed to make appropriate provision for *him* and to achieve optimum benefit for *him* from that provision, and said provisions hereof in favour of *my said son* are made in lieu and full satisfaction of *his* claim to legal rights, and in the event of legal rights being claimed by or on behalf of *my said son he* shall forfeit all right, interest and benefit under these presents, all of which forfeited rights, interests and benefits shall thereupon form part of the residue of my estate;

[-----] Upon the failure or termination for any cause whatever of the foregoing provision in favour of *my said son* I direct my Trustees to apply, pay or convey *John's Fund* (with any accumulated interest in accordance with the foregoing provisions) to [*insert beneficiaries*];
[*It is suggested that the trustees' investment powers include the following*]

With power to invest the trust estate in any investments of any kind whatever, including without prejudice to the generality of the foregoing (a) in Capital Bonds or other investments providing only or mainly capital appreciation at the expense of income, to the extent that my Trustees may from time to time deem it appropriate to do so in order to fulfil the requirement of purpose [-----] hereof to avoid undue overprovision of income, and (b) in acquiring in their own name articles or things in accordance with the powers conferred in said purpose [-----], and that without my Trustees being liable for any loss to the trust estate from depreciation or otherwise arising through their making or continuing to hold such investments.

# STYLE V

*This Deed of Trust is designed to create an inter vivos trust broadly similar in effect to the foregoing styles of Wills. Variations similar to the foregoing for Wills may be considered. In this style charities are included for maximum flexibility, but may be omitted if desired, or a separate charitable trust may be created. This style differs from Precedent IV (England) in that it envisages two grantors, who may not be parents (for example they may be grandparents), and also is drawn to permit future contributions to the trust fund by the original grantors or by others (see Style VA for a testamentary bequest to the trust).*

We and residing at having resolved to establish a trust for the purposes hereinafter set forth, do hereby pay and make over the sum of *One thousand* pounds to the following trustees, namely
and to such other person or persons as may hereafter be appointed or assumed and to the survivors and survivor of them as Trustees for the purposes aftermentioned (the major number from time to time resident in the United Kingdom being a quorum and the power of any Trustee to act being suspended during absence from the United Kingdom) and to the assignees of said Trustees; And we direct said Trustees to hold, administer and apply the said sum of *One thousand* pounds and all other sums of money, assets, investments, securities or other property, heritable or moveable, real or personal, of whatever kind and wherever situate which may hereafter be paid, conveyed or transferred to or collected or accepted by said Trustees, and that whether provided by us or either of us or any other person, for the purposes of the Trust hereby constituted (declaring that said Trust is hereinafter referred to as **"the Trust"** and shall otherwise henceforth be known as and referred to as **"the xxx Family Trust"**, and that said sum of *One thousand* pounds and all other sums of money, assets, investments, securities or other property hereinbefore referred to are hereinafter referred to as **"the Trust Fund"**) as follows, namely

**(FIRST)** In this deed
**"the Trust Period"** means the lifetime of [*John*]
**"Family Beneficiaries"** means the children and remoter issue of [us the grantors hereof] [and the spouses, widows or widowers (whether or not re-married) of any such persons] - *or as appropriate*
**"Charitable Beneficiaries"** means any charitable society or organisation whether local or national whose objects or principal objects appear to the Trustees to be to promote the accommodation, care, welfare, treatment, education, employment of advancement or to be otherwise for the benefit of mentally [*and/or physically*] disabled persons
**"the Beneficiaries"** includes both Family Beneficiaries and Charitable Beneficiaries;

**(SECOND)** The expenses of administration of the Trust shall be met from the Trust Fund;

**(THIRD)**
**(One)** During the Trust Period the Trustees shall pay or apply the income of the Trust Fund (except insofar as it may be accumulated with capital as hereinafter provided) to or for or towards the benefit of any one or more to the exclusion of the others of the Beneficiaries in such manner and if more than one in such shares as the Trustees from time to time in their absolute discretion think fit;
**(Two)** If and to the extent that they may from time to time deem it appropriate, advantageous or convenient to do so, the Trustees may (a) allocate to separate funds within the Trust Fund parts thereof received at different times and/or from different donors, and (b) accumulate with capital any income upon the Trust Fund or any separate fund comprised therein during the maximum period for which such accumulation is permitted by law in respect of the Trust Fund or the relevant separate fund comprised therein;
**(Three)** At the end of the Trust Period the Trustees (a) if and to the extent that they deem it appropriate to do so shall meet from the Trust Fund the funeral expenses (including the cost of a memorial) of and for [*John*] and such other costs, expenses, outlays, gratuities and others in any way arising from his death as the Trustees may in their absolute discretion consider appropriate [and] (b) [in their discretion may waive repayment of any loan that they may have made to any of the Charitable Beneficiaries, and (c)] shall apply, pay or convey the balance of the Trust Fund (with any accumulated income in accordance with the foregoing provisions) to [*specify ultimate beneficiaries*]; and
**(Four)** In exercising their discretion between the Beneficiaries the Trustees may (but are not under any binding obligation to) have regard to the needs (if any) of [*John*] from time to time and any services or benefits given to him during his lifetime;

**(FOURTH)** The Trustees shall have the following powers in regard to the Trust Fund in addition to those under the general law
  *[take in all, or such as may be appropriate, of the following]*

(a) To invest the same in or upon the acquisition or security of any property of whatsoever nature and wheresoever situate (including any dwelling as a residence for or for the use of any of the Beneficiaries) to the intent that they have the same full and unrestricted power of investment in all respects as if they were absolutely entitled thereto beneficially and may exercise their powers of investment without seeking to balance the interests of beneficiaries entitled to capital and income respectively
(b) *as clause 8(b) of Precedent I (England) with modifications, including altering* whether freehold or leasehold *to* whether owned or leased
(c) To invest in moveable items for the use of any one or more of the Beneficiaries notwithstanding that the value of the Trust Fund may thereby become depleted and to permit any of the Beneficiaries to have the use and enjoyment of any moveable item forming part of the Trust Fund in such manner and subject to such conditions (if any) as the Trustees consider reasonable and without being liable to account for any consequential loss
(d) *as clause 8(a) of Precedent I (England) with modifications*
(e) *as clause 8(e) etc.*
(f) To accept, hold and apply as part of the Trust Fund such additional monies, investments, property or other estate as may be paid, conveyed or transferred into the Trust Fund by any person either by lifetime gift or by testamentary disposition
(g) *as clause 8(f) of Precedent I (England) with modifications*
(h) *as clause 8(g) etc.*
(i) *as clause 8(h) etc.*
(j) *as clause 8(i) etc.*

**(FIFTH)** *[Standard investment powers, power to professional trustees to charge for services, provisions as to non-liability of trustees for losses, power to act in matters in which they have an interest, entitlement to fullest privileges and immunities of gratuitous trustees (including powers to resign office) etc; see also 7(c) and (f), 8(j), (k) and (l) and 9(c) of Precedent I (England)].*

**(SIXTH)** We hereby certify that this instrument falls within Category ... in the Schedule to the Stamp Duty (Exempt Instruments) Regulations 1987; and

**(SEVENTH)** This Deed is irrevocable and none of the powers or discretions hereby or by law conferred upon the Trustees shall at any time be exercisable in any manner which might benefit us the grantors hereof or either of us or any person who may hereafter have contributed any addition to the Trust Fund or any spouse of the foregoing and no part of the capital or income of the Trust Fund shall at any time be lent or paid to or applied for the benefit of us or either of us or any person who may hereafter have contributed as aforesaid or any spouse of any of the foregoing:  **IN WITNESS WHEREOF**

## STYLE VA

*A testamentary bequest in favour of the Trust established under Style V.*

I direct my Trustees to pay and transfer *[specify bequest]* to **"the xxx Family Trust"** established by Deed of Trust by *[names and designations of grantors of Deed of Trust]* dated *[specify]*, to be held, administered and applied in accordance with the provisions and purposes of said xxx Family Trust.

## STYLES OF LETTERS

*See "Precedent Letters" in Appendix IIIA, Precedent VI.*

# APPENDIX IV CHARITABLE TRUSTS

**Note:** We give only English versions of the Precedents in Appendix IV, but they may be readily translated for Scotland.

## CHARITABLE SUPPORT TRUST

*Parents of an adult child being cared for at a home or in a community run by a charitable organisation often wish to provide financial support for that charity in the long term interests of their child, and this is an attractive alternative to supporting the child directly in view of means-testing and the inability of the child to handle money. They will be concerned lest for some reason the child ceases to be looked after by the charity, and this inhibits them from making substantial gifts in their lifetime or by Will.*

*The charity will be anxious to receive support from the families of persons cared for (and may even have been set up by such families) so one option is an independent Charitable Support Trust which will support the charity but also has the flexibility to provide support for any former resident of the particular care home or community wherever he or she may be. Although there can be no legally binding arrangement, parents assume that the Trustees will in particular (but not exclusively) endeavour to support the children of those who contribute to the Trust either directly or in the manner in which they support the charity.*

*A wider version of this strategy, illustrated in the following Precedent (though this may be adapted to cover the former situation), is where a group of parents in a particular locality, perhaps through membership of a local Society, wish to join together to make flexible financial provision by a charitable Trust for all persons with a mental handicap within the locality. This will include their own children, and the Trustees will be expected to take into account donations to the Trust when exercising their discretionary powers but will not be bound to support only the children of donors (and would be unwise to do so).*

**THIS DECLARATION OF TRUST** made the          day of          One thousand nine hundred and ninety-two

BY                                                    of

                                                       of

and                                                    of                                    ("the Trustees" of whom the first two are nominees of Cumbria Society as provided for in this deed)

**WITNESSES** as follows:

### 1. Definitions and Interpretation

Expressions used in this deed have the following meaning:

1.1    **"the Charity"** means the charity established by clause 3

1.2    **"the Trustees"** means and includes the trustees or trustee for the time being of this deed and "Trustee" means any one of the Trustees

1.3    **"the Trust Fund"** means the sum referred to in clause 2 and any other money or property paid or transferred to the Trustees at any time to be held by them on the charitable trusts declared by this deed and the investments from time to time representing the same

1.4 **"Cumbria Society"** means Cumbria Society for Mental Handicap a company limited by guarantee (registered number 9999999) and being a registered charity (number 888888)

1.5 **"Cumbria"** means the administrative County of Cumbria at the date hereof

1.6 Unless the context otherwise requires the singular includes the plural and the masculine includes the feminine and vice versa

1.7 Clause headings are for reference only and shall not influence their interpretation

## 2. Recital

The Trustees have collected from concerned persons the sum of £100 (One hundred pounds) to be held by them on the charitable trusts declared by this deed and it is contemplated that further money and property will be paid or transferred to the Trustees to be held on the same trusts

## 3. Name of Charity

The charity established by this deed shall be called "The Cumbria Mental Handicap Support Trust"

## 4. Trust Fund

The Trustees shall hold the Trust Fund on trust either to retain or sell the same or any part of it and to invest the proceeds in or on any investments authorised by this deed (with power from time to time to vary such investments) and to pay or apply the net income and any part of the capital at their absolute discretion in furtherance of the objects of the Charity declared in Clause 5

## 5. Objects of the Charity

The objects of the Charity are to enable persons with a mental handicap who are or have at any time been resident in Cumbria to enjoy higher standards of care and amenity than might otherwise be available to them by making financial grants or loans (including the loan of chattels or property) on such terms as the Trustees think fit to:

5.1 such persons, either collectively or individually

5.2 Cumbria Society or any other charitable organisation providing care or support for any such person

5.3 any other person or body providing care or support for any such person

## 6. Powers of Trustees

In furtherance of these objects but not further or otherwise the Trustees shall have the following powers:

*Appointment of Clerk*

6.1 To appoint any suitable person as clerk at such reasonable salary and on such terms as to notice and otherwise as the Trustees think fit provided that one of the Trustees may only be appointed without remuneration

*Employment of Staff*

6.2 To employ such persons (other than a Trustee) to perform such duties as the Trustees consider necessary for the proper administration of the Charity at such reasonable salaries and on such terms as to notice and otherwise as the Trustees think fit and to provide for the payment of such pensions and superannuation for such persons as may be reasonable and necessary

*Delegation of Powers*

6.3 To delegate to a committee consisting of not less than two of their number any of the Trustees' powers of management provided that all proceedings of such a committee are reported in due course to the Trustees

*Borrowing*
6.4    Subject to such consents as are required by law to borrow money whether or not on the security of the Trust Fund or any part of it with power to charge any part of the capital or income with the repayment of the money so borrowed

*Fund Raising*
6.5    To raise funds by appealing for and inviting contributions (whether periodical or otherwise) from any person by way of donation covenant grant loan legacy or subscription and to accept donations on any special trusts in connection with the Charity provided that the Trustees shall not undertake any permanent trading activity

*Acquisition of property*
6.6    To purchase take on lease or in exchange hire or otherwise acquire any property or chattels for use for the purposes of the Charity

*Disposal of property*
6.7    Subject to such consents as may be required by law to sell mortgage let or exchange any property or funds of the Charity

*Investment*
6.8    To invest the Trust Fund in the purchase of or at interest on the security of such stocks funds shares securities or other investments or property of whatever nature and wherever situated as the Trustees in their absolute discretion think fit to the intent that the Trustees shall have the same full and unrestricted powers of investing and transposing investments as if they were beneficially entitled to the Trust Fund

## 7.    Accounts

The Trustees shall keep a minute book and proper books of account and shall prepare consecutive statements of account consisting of an income and expenditure account relating to a period of not more than 15 months and of a balance sheet relating to the end of such period

## 8.    Banking

The Trustees shall maintain such bank and building society accounts for the Charity as they consider convenient and every sum received on account thereof shall be paid to the credit of such accounts. All cheques and orders for the payment of money from any such account shall be signed by two Trustees save that the Trustees may from time to time resolve that the signature of more than two Trustees shall be required for specific sums

## 9.    Trustee's interest in the Trust Fund

No Trustee shall take or hold any interest in any part of the Trust Fund otherwise than as Trustee for the purpose of the Charity and no Trustee shall receive remuneration at the expense of the Charity save that:

*Trustee expenses*
9.1    A Trustee may be reimbursed any reasonable and proper expenses incurred by him in carrying out his duties including travelling expenses

*Professional Charges*
9.2    Any Trustee (other than a parent sibling uncle or aunt of a potential beneficiary) being a solicitor accountant or other person engaged in any profession shall be entitled to charge and be paid all usual professional or other charges for work done by him or his firm in connection with the Charity to the extent authorised by the Trustees
9.3    There shall at all times be a majority of Trustees who act without remuneration and a Trustee shall not attend any part of a meeting of Trustees at which his proposed charges are discussed

## 10.    Number of Trustees

There shall be not less than four nor more than six Trustees save that fewer than four Trustees may appoint an additional Trustee

## 11. Appointment of Trustees

The following provisions relate to the appointment of Trustees:
11.1   The statutory powers of appointing new Trustees apply
11.2   Without prejudice to any other power a new Trustee may be appointed by a resolution of a meeting of the Trustees and whenever a Trustee is appointed a memorandum of such appointment shall be prepared and signed by the persons present at the meeting
11.3   Cumbria Society may nominate two persons to be Trustees at any time and the Trustees shall give effect to the appointment of such nominees
11.4   Every new Trustee shall before acting as such sign in the minute book for which provision is made a declaration of acceptance and of willingness to act in the trusts declared in this deed

## 12. Regulations

The following regulations govern the procedure of the Trustees:
12.1   The Trustees shall hold meetings at least twice in every calendar year and at such other times and in such places as they shall from time to time decide and any Trustee may at any time convene a special meeting of the Trustees upon at least fourteen days' notice being given to the other Trustees of the matters to be discussed
12.2   There shall be a quorum when three Trustees are present at any meeting
12.3   The Trustees shall at each of their meetings appoint one of their number to be chairman and as such he shall have a second or casting vote
12.4   Every matter shall be determined by the majority of votes of the Trustees present and voting on the question
12.5   Any resolution of the Trustees may be rescinded or varied from time to time by the Trustees
12.6   The Trustees shall provide and keep a minute book in which shall be entered the proceedings of the Trustees and which shall be signed by the chairman at the conclusion of each meeting or at some future meeting if the minutes shall have been duly confirmed
12.7   The Trustees shall provide books of account in which shall be kept proper accounts of all money received and paid by or on behalf of the Trustees
12.8   The Trustees shall arrange for the accounts to be audited yearly by a chartered or certified accountant.
12.9   The Trustee may amend these Regulations or make new Regulations from time to time as they shall at their discretion so decide
12.10 The Trustees may invite persons having an interest in the object of the charity to form advisory committees who shall recommend to the Trustees those persons who shall receive grants or loans from the Charity (such advice shall be precatory only and shall not detract from the overall discretion of the Trustees)

## 13. Trustees indemnity

In the execution of the trusts and powers of this deed no Trustee shall be liable for any loss to the Charity arising by reason of any improper investment made in good faith (so long as he shall have sought professional advice before making such investment) or any mistake or omission made in good faith by him or any other Trustee or any other matter other than wilful and individual fraud wrongdoing or wrongful omission on the part of the Trustee who is sought to be made liable

## 14. Amendment

The Trustees may amend any of the provisions of this deed (except those in clauses 5 and 14 and in this clause) by any deed or deeds supplemental to this deed provided that no amendment shall be made which will cause the Charity to cease to be a charity at law

## 15. Failure of trusts

In the event of the failure of the trusts of this deed any assets remaining after satisfaction of the debts and liabilities of the Charity shall not be paid to or

distributed among the Trustees but shall be given to such other charitable institution or institutions having objects similar to those of the Charity as the Trustees shall decide and in default to Cumbria Society
**IN WITNESS** etc.


## MENTAL HANDICAP TRUST

*Name*
1. The name of the Charity is "*(Name)* **Trust for Mental Handicap**" (hereinafter called "the Trust").

*Objects*
2. The objects of the Trust are to advance the education and promote the relief of people with learning difficulty in *(Area)* who by reason of their mental handicap need assistance by the provision of a suitable home environment and skilled training and supervision to enable them to develop their mental, physical and spiritual capacity.

*Powers*
3. In furtherance of the said objects but not otherwise the Trust may also:-

    (1) Employ any person to supervise, organise and carry on the work of the Trust and to provide for the payment of pensions and superannuation to and on behalf of them and their dependants;

    (2) Promote conferences and cooperation between voluntary organisations, central and local government, statutory authorities and members of the public;

    (3) Promote, carry out and assist in research surveys and investigations;

    (4) Arrange, provide and assist in providing exhibitions, meetings, lectures, classes, seminars and courses;

    (5) Collect and disseminate information and exchange information with other bodies having similar objects;

    (6) Undertake, execute, manage or assist any charitable trusts so far as may be lawful;

    (7) Procure to be written and print, publish, issue and circulate gratuitously or otherwise any reports or periodicals, books, pamphlets, leaflets or other documents, or films or recorded tapes;

    (8) Purchase, take on lease or in exchange, hire or otherwise acquire any property rights and privileges and construct maintain or alter any buildings necessary for the work of the Trust;

    (9) Make regulations for any property so acquired;

    (10) Subject to such consents as may be required by law, sell, let, mortgage or dispose of or turn to account all or any property or assets of the Trust;

    (11) Subject to such consents as may be required by law, accept gifts, or borrow or raise money on such terms and on such security as shall be thought fit;

    (12) Solicit, obtain, collect and receive money and funds by way of contributions, donations, affiliation fees, subscriptions, legacies, grants, interest free loans and any other lawful method, and accept and receive gifts of any description (whether subject to any special trusts or not) provided that the Trust shall not undertake permanent trading activities in raising funds for the said objects;

    (13) Invest the monies of the Trust in or upon such investments, securities or properties as may be thought fit subject nevertheless to such conditions (if any) as may for the time being be imposed or required by law;

    (14) Affiliate or become affiliated to any charity with charitable purposes consistent with the objects of the Trust;

    (15) Do all such other lawful things as are necessary for the attainment of the said objects.

*Area*
4. The area of benefit of the Trust shall be *(Area)* which comprises the Districts of ...... Provided that nothing in this clause shall prevent the Trust from

assisting persons from outside the area of benefit to take advantage of facilities within the area.

*Constituent Organisations*

5. The constituent organisations of the Trust will be the following organisations:-

    *(Name)* Health Authority

    *(Name)* County Council

    *(Name)* Society for Mental Handicap

    *(Name)* Housing Association Limited

(together called "the founding members") and such other organisations within the area of benefit as shall be approved by the founding members.

*Trustees*

6. (1) The property and assets of the Trust shall be held by Trustees.

(2) One Trustee shall be nominated from time to time by each constituent organisation of the Trust. It shall be for the constituent organisation to decide whether such appointment shall be ex-officio or for a term of years.

(3) No Trustee shall also be a member of the Committee of Management.

(4) The Trustees shall concur in and perform all acts necessary to enable the Committee of Management to carry out the objects and general management of the Trust unless the matter in which they are requested to concur is in breach of trust or involves a personal liability upon them.

(5) In the execution of the trusts hereof no Trustee shall be liable for any loss to the property of the Association arising by reason of any improper investment made in good faith (so long as he shall have sought professional advice before making such investment) or for the negligence, fraud, wrongdoing or wrongful omission of any agent employed by him or by any other Trustee hereof (provided reasonable supervision shall have been exercised) although the employment of such agent was strictly not necessary or expedient or by reason of any mistake or omission made in good faith by any Trustee hereof of by reason of any other matter or thing other than wilful and individual fraud wrongdoing or wrongful omission on the part of the Trustee who is sought to be made liable.

(6) The Trustees shall at all times be kept indemnified by the Committee of Management against all liability in respect of any act or default on the part of the said Committee for which the Trustees are not to be liable in the terms of this clause.

(7) The Trustees shall determine such questions as the Committee of Management may refer to them from time to time.

(8) The Trustees shall have power at their discretion temporarily to assume the general management of the Trust of the Committee of Management until such time as the management of the Trust could be put on a regular footing.

(9) The Trustees shall meet at least once in every financial year with the Committee of Management to approve the audited accounts of the Trust and to conduct such other business as may be proper.

(10) The Trustees shall receive notice of all meetings of the Committee of Management and may attend such meetings if they wish.

(11) At any meeting of the Trustees they shall elect one of their number as Chairman of the meeting. All questions arising shall be decided by a simple majority of Trustees present and voting, provided that in case of equality of votes the Chairman of the meeting shall have a second or casting vote.

*Committee of Management*

7. (1) The objects and general management of the Trust shall be carried out by a Committee of Management (hereinafter called "the Committee")

(2) Two members of the Committee shall be nominated from time to time by each of the constituent organisations and each member shall hold office for three years or otherwise as the constituent organisation shall decide.

(3) A nominated member of the Committee shall have power to appoint a deputy in his or her place who shall have all the powers of the nominated member so long as such appointment lasts.

(4) The Committee may co-opt up to four additional members who shall serve for such period (being not more than three years) as the said Committee

may determine provided that any such member may be co-opted for a further period or periods.

(5) The quorum at a meeting of the Committee shall be one-third of the members for the time being.

(6) The Committee shall elect a Chairman from among their numbers who shall serve for a year but shall be re-eligible and at any meeting at which the Chairman is absent the Committee shall elect a Deputy Chairman for that meeting.

(7) The Committee shall meet not less than ten times in each calendar year.

(8) The Committee shall elect a Treasurer and Secretary and such other officers as they may deem necessary.

(9) Proper Minute books shall be kept by the Committee.

(10) All questions arising at a meeting of the Committee shall be decided by a simple majority of members present and voting, provided that (a) no co-opted member shall vote on the co-opting of additional members and (b) in case of equality of votes the Chairman of the meeting shall have a second or casting vote.

(11) The Committee shall report at least annually on the activities of the Trust to the constituent organisations.

(12) The proceedings of the Committee shall not be invalidated by any failure or any defect in the co-option or qualification of any member prior to the time when such failure or defect is pointed out.

(13) The Committee may appoint such sub-committees with such terms of reference, powers and memberships as it may from time to time think fit and such sub-committees shall report as soon as possible on all acts and proceedings to the Committee Provided that each sub-committee shall include a nominated member from each constituent organisation unless such organisation waives its right to representation on that sub-committee.

*Finance*

8. (1) All monies received by the Trust shall be applied towards the objects of the Association and no part shall be paid or transferred directly or indirectly by way of dividend bonus or otherwise by way of profit to any member of the Committee but nothing herein shall prevent the payment in good faith of reasonable and proper remuneration to any officer or employee not being members of the Committee or the repayment of reasonable out-of-pocket expenses.

(2) The Committee shall keep proper accounts of the finances of the Trust.

(3) The financial year shall run initially from 1st April in one year to 31st March in the next but may be varied by the Committee

(4) The accounts shall be audited at least once a year by an auditor appointed by the Trustees.

(5) Audited accounts shall be approved annually at a joint meeting of the Trustees and the Committee and submitted annually to the constituent organisations of the Trust.

(6) A bank account shall be maintained in the name of the Trust at such bank as the Committee shall from time to time decide and cheques on behalf of the Trust may be signed by any two of three persons nominated by the Committee.

*Alterations to the Constitution*

9. (1) If the Committee desires to recommend any alteration to this Constitution it shall call a joint meeting of the Trustees and the Committee, of which meeting not less than 21 days' notice (stating the terms of the proposed alteration) shall be given.

(2) A decision to alter this Constitution shall require the assent of not less than two-thirds of the Trustees and of the members of the Committee (voting separately) for the time being present and voting at such joint meeting.

(3) No alteration shall be made to clause 2 (objects), clause 10 (dissolution) or this clause until the approval in writing of the Charity Commissioners or other authority having charitable jurisdiction shall have been obtained and no alteration shall be made which would have the effect of causing the Trust to cease to be a charity in law.

*Dissolution*

10 (1) If the Committee by a simple majority decide at any time that on the ground of expense or otherwise it is necessary or advisable to dissolve the Trust it shall call a joint meeting of the Trustees and the Committee, of which meeting not less than 21 days' notice (stating the terms of the Resolution to be proposed thereat) shall be given.

(2) If such decision shall be confirmed by a simple majority of the Trustees and of the members of the Committee (voting separately) for the time being present and voting at such joint meeting the Committee shall have power to authorise the disposal of any assets held by or on behalf of the Trust.

(3) Any assets remaining after the satisfaction of any proper debts and liabilities shall be given or transferred to such other charitable institution or institutions having objects similar to the objects of the Trust as the Committee may determine and if and in so far as effect cannot be given to this provision then to some other charitable purpose for the benefit of persons with a mental handicap.

**This Constitution** was formally adopted at a joint meeting of the Trustees and the Committee of Management held on the                     day of                     1990 at                     in the County of *(Name)*.

.................. CHAIRMAN
.................. SECRETARY
.................. TRUSTEE                     .................. TRUSTEE
.................. TRUSTEE                     .................. TRUSTEE

**NOTES**

This Trust Deed is based upon a precedent provided by *John M. Todd Esq. solicitor of Messrs. Brockbank Tyson & Company, Whitehaven* for the South Cumbria Trust. Similar drafts have been used for three other Trusts in Cumbria.

The aim of this Trust is to harness the efforts of the Social Services Department and the Health Authority in providing homes for persons with a mental handicap by jointly linking with a Housing Association. A local society is an equal member so as to involve the parents and families of persons with a mental handicap in the area.

Under this type of Trust homes would be provided not only for those being resettled from long stay hospitals but also for people already living in the community with their families. The housing association would have capital funds to buy houses and surplus housing from the social services department would also be used. The local society would make a valuable contribution in its fund raising capacity, and the health authority would provide revenue funding for the patients transferred back into the community. Social services would be required to staff the houses to the extent needed by the residents which in appropriate cases would be 24 hours a day.

One of the main advantages in establishing such a Trust and thereby bringing together the relevant organisations is that through this medium they can jointly attract revenue and capital from a variety of sources. This may possibly include the financial provision that parents make by Will following their death, as a transfer of capital to this charity in circumstances where the trust

was providing accommodation for the child may make it
inappropriate for the local authority to initiate a claim under the
Inheritance (Provision for Family and Dependants) Act 1975.

This Trust represents one of the early attempts at partnership
between the public and private sectors in the provision of
community care as proposed in the Griffiths Report. It may be
modified or amended to suit the particular circumstances, but may
nevertheless be a useful basis on which to draft a constitution for a
charitable trust fund. A further feature of this draft is the
provision of a Committee of Management responsible for the day
to day running of the Trust, working alongside Trustees who are
intended to be 'elder statesmen', less closely involved but available
to give advice on points of difficulty and with powers to act in
times of crisis.

As the Trust may actually be responsible for running residential
care homes in the community, and may also directly employ
people, it is now thought by the writer that it would be preferable
to form a company limited by guarantee in which the balance of
power could be similar though there would be no need to appoint
trustees. This topic generally is considered in Chapter 9.

# APPENDIX V SUNDRY PRECEDENTS

**Note:** Scottish adaptations in square brackets.

## AGREEMENT ON ADMISSION OF A RESIDENT

DATE                               199

PARTIES:

(1)                     of
   (*the Resident* who will sign this Agreement or make a mark if capable)
(2)                     of
   (*the Appointee* acting on behalf of the Resident - *where appropriate*)
(3)                     of
   (*the Advocate* representing the Resident - *where appropriate*)
   [*If the Resident should have a tutor-dative, substitute* (**the Tutor-Dative** to the Resident) *and amend references to the Advocate accordingly*]
(4)                     of
   (*the Authority* being the social services department [social work department] of the Local Authority which is sponsoring the Resident - *where appropriate*) and
(5)  . . . . . SOCIETY of . . . . . a company limited by guarantee registered in England [Scotland] (no.999999) and registered charity (no.88888) [a Scottish charity/recognised charity (no.77777)]
   (*the Society*)

INTRODUCTION:

(a) The Society runs a registered residential care home known as "the Home" at .... .
(b) The Resident is in need of accommodation and personal care and has applied to the Society for a place at the Home
(c) The Society has agreed to provide accommodation and personal care for the Resident on the terms of this Agreement
(d) The Appointee is the appointee for the purpose of receiving all weekly state benefits to which the Resident is entitled with power to spend such monies for the benefit of the Resident and has agreed to pay a contribution towards the fees
(e) The Authority supports the Resident's application and has agreed to pay the balance of fees over and above the monies available from state benefits
(f) The Advocate is recognised by the Society as being the personal advocate of the Resident and is satisfied with this arrangement on behalf of the Resident

TERMS AGREED:

### 1. Accommodation and care

Subject to payment of the weekly fees mentioned below, the Society will provide to the Resident at the Home:
   1.1 A single room with all usual furnishings for personal occupation
   1.2 Food, light, heat, laundry and all necessary personal care as normally required by a resident of a residential care home
The aim will be to increase choices and opportunities for and the responsibilities and independence of the Resident. The level of support provided will be determined according to the needs of the Resident

## 2. Fees and personal expenses

The weekly fees are £          and these include the provision by the Society of the accommodation and care stated above. The Appointee and the Authority (*where appropriate*) will use their best endeavours to ensure that the fees are paid promptly. The following further provisions apply:

2.1  The fees may only be increased by the Society giving to the Resident and the Appointee and the Authority (*where appropriate*) at least eight weeks notice in writing save that any increase in the level of Income Support residential care allowance for the Resident shall apply to the fees immediately. The fees will be reviewed from time to time but any increase will be on account of inflation, for the provision of extra care or as a result of the need to comply with regulations coming into force after this Agreement

2.2  If the Resident is admitted to hospital for longer than seven days the Society will retain his/her room on request for up to six weeks at a weekly charge of 80% of the normal fee and special arrangements may be made for longer periods

2.3  If the Resident leaves the Home without giving the required notice fees will be charged at the normal rate for the unexpired notice period

2.4  In the event of the death of the Resident fees will be charged to the date of death but not thereafter

2.5  It is intended that the Resident shall retain for personal expenditure out of the entitlement to state benefits the sum of £          per week but the Society may make additional sums available from time to time

2.6  If the Resident is absent from the Home by prior arrangement for a period in excess of 4 days (*e.g.* for a holiday or to visit family) the Society may increase the money available to him/her for personal expenditure but such absences should not normally exceed four weeks in any calendar year

## 3. Resident's obligations

The Resident also agrees (with the support of the Appointee, the Advocate and the Authority *where appropriate*):

3.1  To provide for medical requisites, hairdressing, clothing, toilet requirements and items of a luxury or personal nature from his/her own resources

3.2  To allow the Society to take charge of and dispense all the Resident's prescribed medications, though the Resident will be encouraged to administer his/her own medication if capable

3.3  To permit the Society to inspect and ensure the safety of any electrical items brought into the Home by the Resident

3.4  That the Society is not responsible for the safety of the Resident if he/she leaves the Home other than under the direct supervision of the Society or a member of the staff of the Home

3.5  To participate in an assessment of his/her needs and the development of a personal plan

[*If the Resident should have a tutor-dative, the first two lines of clause 3 will read* The Resident also agrees (with the support of the Appointee and the Authority *where appropriate*) and as regards clauses 3.2, 3.3 and 3.4 the Tutor-Dative agrees:]

## 4. Society's obligations

The Society also agrees:

4.1  To maintain at the Home at all times the standard of care required by the registration authority

4.2  To allow the Resident as much personal freedom and autonomy as his/her abilities permit and only to restrict the movements of the Resident for his/her personal safety or the safety of others or to the extent agreed in advance with the Resident or the Advocate or the Authority (*as appropriate*)

4.3  To allow the Resident at the discretion of the Society to introduce items of personal furniture into his/her room subject to eventual removal being the responsibility of the Resident

4.4 On request to provide safekeeping for personal effects required to be brought into the Home up to such limit of value as the Society may from time to time impose

4.5 To maintain a complaints procedure and apply this fairly in the event of a complaint being made by the Resident. If the complaint cannot be resolved between the Resident (through the Advocate or the Appointee) and the Society it may be referred to the registration officer whose address is . . . . . . . .

## 5. Insurance

Insurance cover is provided by the Home up to a maximum value of £    for the personal effects (excluding cash) left in the Resident's room subject to all such items being declared for insurance purposes upon admission

## 6. Termination

5.1 The first four weeks of admission shall be regarded as a trial period for the benefit of all parties and if not then terminated this Agreement shall continue in force until terminated by the death of the Resident or by four weeks notice in writing being given of the desire to terminate this arrangement

5.2 The Society shall give any such notice to the Resident, the Appointee, the Advocate and the Authority (*as appropriate*) but any of those parties may give notice to the Society though a copy shall be given to the other such parties and it is intended that there shall be co-operation between all such parties in regard to any decision affecting the Resident

5.3 The Society will normally only give notice to terminate if:

5.3:1 the fees are not promptly paid,     or

5.3:2 having consulted the Resident and taken advice from appropriate health care professionals concerning his/her present and likely future needs, the Society is no longer able to meet those needs,  or

5.3:3 the Society considers the circumstances or behaviour of the Resident to be seriously detrimental to the Home or welfare of other residents

S I G N E D  by or on behalf of the parties

---

# CARE EMPLOYMENT CONTRACT

[Applicable to both England and Scotland. In Scotland, if AB has a tutor-dative, the tutor-dative should also be a party, and the adaptations in square brackets should apply]

**AN AGREEMENT** dated             1992

## B E T W E E N :

| | |
|---|---|
| (1) | ("the Appointee") |
| (2) | ("the Trustees") and |
| (3) | ("the Carers") [and] |
| [(4) | ("the Tutor-Dative")] |

## W H E R E A S :

(a) *Deceased* late of *address* ("the Home") died on     leaving her daughter *full name* ("*AB*") surviving her and having by her Will dated    1990 created a Trust Fund *inter alia* for the benefit of *AB*

(b) The Trustees are trustees of that Trust Fund and have power to expend the same for the benefit of *AB* and have retained the Home as a trust asset

(c) *AB* is 00 years of age but has a serious mental handicap and requires constant care and supervision

(d) The Appointee is the appointee for the purpose of receiving all weekly state benefits to which *AB* is entitled and has the power to expend these for her benefit

(e) It is desired that *AB* shall continue to reside at the Home and be cared for there and to that intent the Appointee and the Trustees have agreed to employ the Carers on the terms set out in this Agreement

## IT IS NOW AGREED:

### 1. Job title and commencement

The Appointee and the Trustees (together referred to as "the Employers") shall jointly employ the Carers as resident housekeepers at the Home and as personal carers of *AB* and of such other persons (if any) as the Employers may from time to time designate commencing on          1992 and subject to termination as provided below

### 2. Occupation of the Home

The Carers are required to reside together at the Home in order properly to perform their duties and shall do so on the following basis:

*Personal licence only*
2.1 They occupy the Home as licensees only free of rent and nothing contained in this agreement shall be construed to create a tenancy and the parties acknowledge that they have no intention of creating any tenancy

2.2 The licence given to the Carers to reside at the Home is personal to them and is not assignable and terminates automatically without notice as soon as they cease to be employed by the Employers or to reside at the Home

2.3 The management and control of the Home remains vested in the Employers who have a right of entry at all times for the purpose of exercising such management and control

*Duty to take care*
2.4 The Carers shall take reasonable care of the interior of the Home including all fixtures, fittings and furnishings and shall keep the same clean and tidy but not otherwise be required to carry out repairs or decorations to the Home

*Restrictions upon use*
2.5 The Carers shall not use the Home for any purpose whatsoever save as residential accommodation for themselves and *AB* and such other persons (if any) as the Employers may from time to time designate

2.6 The Carers shall not:
2.6:1 do or permit or suffer anything which may cause nuisance or annoyance to the Employers or to the occupiers of other nearby premises
2.6:2 purport to let any part of the Home or take in any lodger or paying guest
2.6:3 keep in the Home any animals or birds not approved by the Employers
2.6:4 make any alterations or additions to the Home

### 3. Duties and caring role

Subject to such directions as the Carers may from time to time receive from [the Tutor-Dative in relation to para.3.2 (the Tutor-Dative's authority being paramount in matters within the scope of his/her appointment) and otherwise from] the Employers and from *AB*'s medical practitioner (with which they will faithfully comply) the Carers shall:
3.1 have the day-to-day control and management of the Home including

responsibility for catering services and domestic arrangements

3.2 be responsible for the personal care and welfare of *AB* including any nursing attention that may be required

3.3 order on behalf and at the expense of the Employers from suitable suppliers all food, provisions, utensils, cleaning materials and other things required for the day-to-day running of the Home. In case of doubt they shall refer to the Employers for directions and no payment for such items shall normally be made by the Carers personally

3.4 be responsible on a daily basis for the general supervision and discipline of any additional staff that may be employed

## 4. Additional staff

Any further staff employed at the Home shall be engaged and dismissed by the Employers who shall give reasonable consideration to the advice or wishes of the Carers in that regard and as to staffing requirements and matters generally

## 5. Outgoings

The Employers are responsible for all payments in respect of the maintenance and upkeep of the Home including water gas and electricity charges, maintenance and repairs, insurances, television licence, telephone charges, food, provisions, utensils, cleaning materials and other things required for the day-to-day running of the Home

## 6. Remuneration

The Employers shall pay to the Carers remuneration at the rate of £0,000.00 per annum or such other sum as may from time to time be agreed to be divided equally between the Carers and paid weekly. The Carers shall enjoy the following further benefits and facilities during the course of their employment but no pension scheme shall be applicable to them:

6.1 all normal meals and daily refreshments whilst they or either of them are residing in the Home and caring for *AB* (which shall not include alcohol)

6.2 use of normal laundry facilities within the Home for their personal requirements

6.3 reasonable use of the telephone for personal local calls

## 7. Hours of employment

There shall be no normal working hours and the Carers are required between them to work at such times and for such periods as are necessary for the proper discharge of their duties and responsibilities which may be reviewed at intervals with the Employers

## 8. Holidays

8.1 The Carers are entitled to three weeks holiday in each calendar year (inclusive of public holidays) and proportionately for any part thereof.

8.2 Holidays must be taken at such times as may be convenient to and agreed in advance with the Employers and no more than two weeks may be taken at any one time

8.3 Holiday entitlement unused at the end of the calendar year cannot be carried over into the next year

8.4 Normal basic remuneration will be paid during each authorised holiday and the Carers will be entitled to payment in lieu of holidays accrued due but untaken on termination of employment

## 9. Sickness and incapacity

If at any time either of the Carers shall by reason of sickness or incapacity be wholly prevented from carrying out his or her duties the Employers must be informed as soon as practicable and the following provisions then apply:

9.1 Medical certificates shall be produced to the Employers in respect of any absence of more than seven days and continuing thereafter

9.2 Normal basic remuneration shall be paid for the first four weeks and one-half thereof for the next four weeks and thereafter any remuneration shall be in the discretion of the Employers

9.3  In each case the amount of any statutory sick pay or social security sickness benefit to which the Carer is entitled may be deducted from the remuneration

9.4  If the illness or incapacity of either of the Carers continues for more than eight weeks the Employers shall be entitled to terminate the employment of both of the Carers at any time thereafter on giving to them two weeks notice in writing

## 10.  Termination

The employment of the Carers may be terminated:

10.1  by the Carers on giving the Employers not less than four weeks notice in writing

10.2  by the Employers on giving the Carers notice in writing as follows:

10.2:1  during the first four years of continuous employment not less than four weeks notice

10.2:2  during the fifth to twelfth years not less than one weeks notice for each year of continuous employment

10.2:3  thereafter not less than twelve weeks notice

10.3  by the Employers without notice or payment in lieu of notice in the event of serious or persistent misconduct by the Carers or either of them including failing to carry out the reasonable directions of the Employers and neglecting to provide for the needs and secure the welfare of *AB*

## 11.  Disciplinary and grievance procedure

*As desired.*

## 12.  Vacation of the Home

11.1  Immediately upon the Carers ceasing to be employed by the Employers for whatever reason they shall vacate the Home and remove from it all items belonging to them

11.2  If either of the Carers remains at the Home after termination of this employment he or she shall do so only as a licensee at will

## [13.  Tutor-Dative

The Tutor-Dative is not one of the Employers and has no rights or obligations as such, but :

13.1  shall have the authority conferred in clause 3 hereof, and

13.2  so far as it is within the scope of his/her authority to do so, and without limiting future proper exercise of his/her authority, consents to this Agreement]

**SIGNED** by the parties

## LETTER TO DOCTOR (England)

The following letter may be sent to a doctor when a medical opinion is requested prior to completion of an Enduring Power of Attorney:

Dear Dr. *X.*,

Our client and your patient: *AB*

We have been consulted by *AB* and need to decide whether he is mentally capable of signing an Enduring Power of Attorney. If not, it will be necessary for an application to be made to the Court of Protection for the appointment of a Receiver. We understand that *AB* has been your patient for some years and shall be obliged if you will now arrange to examine him on the next convenient occasion specifically for the purpose of giving us a report as to his mental capacity.

The relevant test for the purpose of executing a Power of Attorney is not whether he is capable of managing his own property and affairs, but whether he knows that there are financial affairs that will in the future need to be dealt with and understands that it is desirable to arrange for some trusted person to have authority to handle those affairs and is capable of choosing such person. *AB* 's father has been helping with financial matters on an informal basis for some years and it seems likely that he will be chosen.

In the event that *AB* satisfies the above test but would not be capable of handling his own affairs, it would be necessary for any Enduring Power of Attorney to be registered with the Court of Protection before it could be used, so appropriate safeguards then apply. The parents have found from experience that he is not capable of handling his financial affairs, but your views on this would also be appreciated.

Please telephone us if you need any further guidance and we look forward to receiving your report along with a note of your fee.

Yours *etc*

## STATUTORY WILL (England)

A statutory Will may take the following form:

**This is the last Will** of me *A B* of ........... acting by *C D* the person authorised in that behalf by an Order dated the ... day of ... 1990 made under the Mental Health Act 1983

\* \* \* \* \* \* \*

**IN WITNESS** whereof this Will is signed by me *A B* acting by *C D* pursuant to the said Order this ... day of ... 1990

*'A B' by 'C D'*

**SIGNED** by the said *A B* by the said *C D* and by the said C D with his own name pursuant to the said Order in our presence and attested by us in the presence of the said *C D*

**SEALED** with the Official Seal of the Court of Protection this ... day of ... 1990

WE ... solicitors of .......... **HEREBY CERTIFY** that this Will is an exact copy of the draft thereof as approved by the Court.

### SHORT PROCEDURE ORDER (England)

The following is an example of a short procedure order made by the Court of Protection when it is not necessary to appoint a Receiver in view of the small amount of money involved:

COURT OF PROTECTION                                               999999

    Certificate under Rule 41                  1st January 1991

    IN THE MATTER OF (*name* )

    (hereinafter referred to as the Patient)

(*Parent* ) of (*address* ) the Applicant in this matter is authorised in the name and on behalf of the Patient to receive the sum of £500 in respect of the interim award from the Criminal Injuries Compensation Board and due to the Patient.

The said (*parent* ) is directed to apply the sum of £500 or so much thereof as may be necessary in or towards the maintenance or other necessary requirements of the Patient and he is to account to the Court for the said sum ay such time and in such manner as the Court may direct.


Requested by:-    Messrs LAW & CO
                Solicitors
                (*address* )

# INDEX

ABWOR. *See* ASSISTANCE BY WAY OF
    REPRESENTATION
AIDS
  testing for, 182, 186
ABNORMALITIES
  genetic, 10
  non-specific, 10
ABNORMALITY OF MIND
  meaning, 76
ABORTION
  damages claims, 128
  ethical issues, 127–128
  legislation, 127
  medical treatment of adult, consent to,
    186
  parents, status of, 127–128
ABUSE
  protection from, negative role of law, 2
  sexual, 109
ACCESS TO INFORMATION
  civil rights relating to, 52–53
  individual, by, 52
  others, by, 52–53
ACCOMMODATION
  England, generally, 245–246
  local authority, role of, 245–247
  residential,
    charges, 426–430
    contributions, 426–430
    generally, 426
    sponsorship, 430–431
  Scotland, generally, 246–247
ACCOUNTS
  charities,
    England, 667
    Scotland, 655–656
  curator, of, 599
ADDRESSES, 679–685
ADMINISTRATION
  charities. *See* CHARITIES
  grant of, capacity relating to, 35
  social security system, 389–390
  trust. *See* TRUST
ADMISSION
  court proceedings, 57–58
ADMISSION TO HOSPITAL
  compulsory, 193–194
  Mental Health Act 1983, under, 193–194,
    195

ADULT
  child, 151–152
  continuing education, 311
  control of,
    financial control, 134
    foster parents, 134
    restraint, 133–134
    statutory guardianship, 132–133
  day centres, 311–313
  further education, 309–311, 325–326
  guardianship,
    England, 132
    law reform, 118
    statutory, 132–133
  homes, 335–336
  medical treatment, consent to, 184–187,
    188–189
  placement schemes, 335–336, 459–460
  respite care, funding of,
    family based care, 464
    generally, 464
    private dwellings, 465
    top-up, 464
  training centres, 308–309, 311
  tutor to,
    background, 136
    Scotland, generally, 136–141
    tutor-at-law, 140–141, 603–604
    tutor-dative,
      comment, 140
      delegation of financial powers, 602–
        603
      duration, 138–139
      effect of appointment, 140
      legal aid, 139–140
      person to whom appointed, 136–137
      person who may be appointed, 138
      powers of, 137–138
      procedure, 139
      review, 138–139
  weekly funding, 441–442
ADVOCACY
  background, 7
  citizen-advocacy, 7
  law reform, 117–118
  self-advocacy, 7
AFTER-CARE
  England, 244–245
  local authority, role of, 244–245
  Scotland, 245